ROMAN PUBLIC LIFE

BY

A. H. J. GREENIDGE, M.A.

LECTURER AND LATE FELLOW OF HERTFORD COLLEGE, AND
LECTURER IN ANCIENT HISTORY AT BRASENOSE COLLEGE, OXFORD

THE LAWBOOK EXCHANGE, LTD.
Clark, New Jersey

ISBN 978-1-58477-242-2

Lawbook Exchange edition 2003, 2019

The quality of this reprint is equivalent to the quality of the original work.

THE LAWBOOK EXCHANGE, LTD.
33 Terminal Avenue
Clark, New Jersey 07066-1321

*Please see our website for a selection of our other publications
and fine facsimile reprints of classic works of legal history:*
www.lawbookexchange.com

Library of Congress Cataloging-in-Publication Data

Greenidge, A. H. J. (Abel Hendy Jones), 1865-1906.
    Roman public life / by A.H.J. Greenidge.
        p. cm.
    Originally published: London: Macmillan and Co., Limited, 1901.
    Includes bibliographical references and index.
    ISBN 1-58477-242-5 (cloth: alk. paper)
        1. Constitutional history—Rome. 2. Rome—Politics and government. I. Title.

    DG81 .G81 2002
    937'.6—dc21   2002024321

Printed in the United States of America on acid-free paper

ROMAN PUBLIC LIFE

BY

A. H. J. GREENIDGE, M.A.

LECTURER AND LATE FELLOW OF HERTFORD COLLEGE, AND
LECTURER IN ANCIENT HISTORY AT BRASENOSE COLLEGE, OXFORD

London

MACMILLAN AND CO., Limited

NEW YORK: THE MACMILLAN COMPANY

1901

To

𝕸. 𝕷. 𝕻.

𝕵. 𝕿. 𝖂. 𝕲.

AND

𝕵. 𝕰. 𝕲. 𝕳.

PREFACE

THE object of this work is to trace the growth of the Roman constitution, and to explain its working during the two phases of its maturity, the developed Republic and the Principate. The title selected perhaps expresses more succinctly than any other could do the nature of the plan which I wished to undertake. My desire was to touch, however briefly, on all the important aspects of public life, central, municipal, and provincial; and, thus, to exhibit the political genius of the Roman in connexion with all the chief problems of administration which it attempted to solve. This design, like many other comprehensive plans which have to be adapted to the limits of a single volume, was necessarily subjected to modifications in detail; and, since one of these modifications has affected the whole scope of the book, it requires some mention in a preface.

I had intended to carry the treatment of my subject beyond the confines of the Principate, and to describe the political organisation of the later Empire as elaborated by Diocletian and his successors. I found, however, that a discussion of this period would cause my work to exceed the reasonable limits which can be conceded to a handbook, and I was forced to abandon the enterprise much against my will. I was somewhat comforted in this surrender by the suggestion that the constitution of the later Empire was perhaps not strictly "Roman." This is a verdict with which I agree in part. The organisation which had Constantinople as its centre was certainly the organisation of an Empire which was permeated with the social ideals of later Rome, which had adopted a Latin code, and which employed an administrative system whose origin was to be found in Italy ; but in the forms of rule which the monarchy presented the break with the past was remarkable. The absolutism was no new thing, but the guise assumed by this absolutism was startlingly novel. It is not only that classic traditions were forgotten, that, as Gibbon says, "the purity of the Latin language was debased by adopting, in the intercourse of pride and flattery, a profusion of epithets, which Tully would have scarcely understood, and which Augustus would have rejected with indignation," but that, even where the continuity in public institutions can be traced, it is one of names rather than of ideas. In the Principate we see a perverted Republic ; in the monarchy a *Res publica* only in the narrowest etymological sense of those words. Perhaps the accession of Diocletian does, after all, mark the close of a true "Roman" public life.

The task, even as thus limited, has been a long one, and would have been still longer had it not been for the kindly assistance rendered me by a former pupil, Miss Muriel Clay, of Lady Margaret Hall. The help which she has given in the reading of the proofs, and in the verification of the references to original authorities, has not only facilitated the production of the book, but has materially improved it by the removal of errors and obscurities. I have also to thank her for the Index of subjects and the Index of Latin words which accompany the volume.

A. H. J. G.

Oxford, *April* 1901.

CONTENTS

(The references are to the pages)

CHAPTER II

THE GROWTH OF THE REPUBLICAN CONSTITUTION

CHAPTER III

THE CLASSES OF THE POPULATION AND THE THEORY OF THE
CONSTITUTION IN THE DEVELOPED REPUBLIC

The Classes of the Population

The Theory of the Constitution

CHAPTER XI

ITALY AND THE PROVINCES UNDER THE PRINCIPATE

The Organisation of Italy

The Organisation of the Provinces

The Worship of the Emperor

APPENDIX I

APPENDIX II

INDEX

SELECT BIBLIOGRAPHY

1. THE POLITICAL INSTITUTIONS OF ROME

HERZOG, E.—*Geschichte und System der römischen Staatsverfassung.* Leipzig, 1884-91.

KARLOWA, O.—*Römische Rechtsgeschichte*, Bd. I. ("Staatsrecht und Rechtsquellen"). Leipzig, 1885.

LANGE, L.—*Römische Alterthümer.* Berlin, 1856-71.

MADVIG, J.—*Die Verfassung und Verwaltung des römischen Staates.* Leipzig, 1881-82.

MISPOULET, J.—*Les institutions politiques des Romains.* Paris, 1882-83.

MOMMSEN, TH.—*Römisches Staatsrecht.* Bd. I. ("die Magistratur"), II. Abt. i. ("die einzelen Magistraturen"), II. Abt. ii. ("der Principat"), III. ("Bürgerschaft und Senat"). Leipzig, 1887-88.

MOMMSEN, TH.—*Abriss des römischen Staatsrechts.* Leipzig, 1893.

RUBINO, J.—*Untersuchungen über römische Verfassung und Geschichte.* Cassel, 1839.

SCHILLER, H.—"Staats- und Rechtsaltertümer" (*Handbuch der klassischen Altertums-Wissenschaft*, herausg. von Dr. Iwan von Müller, Bd. IV. Abt. ii.). München, 1893.

WILLEMS, P.—*Le droit public Romain.* Louvain, Paris, 1888.

ZOELLER, M.—*Römische Staats- und Rechtsaltertümer.* Breslau, 1895.

2. THE CITY OF ROME, THE MONARCHY AND THE EARLY HISTORY OF ROME

BERNHOEFT, F.—*Staat und Recht der römischen Königszeit im Verhältniss zu verwandten Rechten.* Stuttgart, 1882.

DYER, T.—*The History of the Kings of Rome.* With a prefatory dissertation on its sources and evidence. London, 1868.

GILBERT, O.—*Geschichte und Topographie der Stadt Rom.* Leipzig, 1883.

IHNE, W.—"Early Rome, from the foundation of the city to its destruction by the Gauls" (*Epochs of Ancient History*). London, 1876.

LANCIANI, R.—*Ancient Rome in the light of recent discoveries.* London, 1888.

LANCIANI, R.—*The ruins and excavations of ancient Rome.* London, 1897.

Lewis, G. — *An inquiry into the credibility of the early Roman history.* London, 1855.

Middleton, J. — *The remains of ancient Rome.* London and Edinburgh, 1892.

Pais, E. — *Storia di Roma.* Turin, 1898-99.

Poehlmann, R. — *Die Anfänge Roms.* Erlangen, 1881.

Richter, O. — Art. "Rom" (Baumeister, A. — *Denkmäler des klassischen Altertums*). München, Leipzig, 1889.

Rubino, J. — *Untersuchungen* (Abschn. ii. "von dem Königthume"). Cassel, 1839.

Schwegler, A. — *Römische Geschichte im Zeitalter des Kampfs der Stände.* Tübingen, 1853-58.

3. THE SENATE

Mommsen, Th. — *Römische Forschungen*, Bd. I. Berlin, 1879.

Rubino, J. — *Untersuchungen* (Abschn. iii. "von dem Senate und dem Patriciate"). Cassel, 1839.

Willems, P. — *Le Sénat de la République Romaine.* Louvain, 1883-85.

4. THE EQUITES

Bélot, E. — *Histoire des chevaliers Romains considérée dans ses rapports ave les différentes constitutions de Rome.* Paris, 1869-73.

Marquardt, J. — *Historiae equitum Romanorum libri quattuor.* Berlin 1840.

5. THE POPULAR ASSEMBLIES

Borgeaud, C. — *Le plébiscite dans l'antiquité. Grèce et Rome.* Geneva, 1886.

Huschke, P. — *Die Verfassung des Königs Servius Tullius als Grundlage zu einer römischen Verfassungsgeschichte.* Heidelberg, 1838.

Mommsen, Th. — *Römische Forschungen*, Bd. I. Berlin, 1879.

Rubino, J. — *Untersuchungen* (Abschn. iv. "von den Volksversammlungen") Cassel, 1839.

Soltau, W. — *Entstehung und Zusammensetzung der altrömischen Volksversarmlungen.* Berlin, 1880.

Soltau, W. — *Die Gültigkeit der Plebiscite.* Berlin, 1884.

6. THE STATE DIVISIONS

Beloch, J. — *Der italische Bund unter Roms Hegemonie.* Leipzig, 1880.

Huschke, P. — *Die Verfassung des Königs Servius Tullius.* Heidelberg, 1838.

Kubitschek, J. — *De Romanarum tribuum origine et propagatione.* Vienna, 1882.

Kubitschek, J. — *Imperium Romanum tributim discriptum.* Vienna, 1889.

Mommsen, Th. — *Die römische Tribus in administrativer Beziehung.* Altona, 1844.

7. ADMINISTRATION UNDER THE PRINCIPATE

CUQ, E.—" Le conseil des empereurs d'Auguste à Dioclétien " (*Mémoires presentés à l'Académie des inscriptions*). Paris, 1884.

HIRSCHFELD, O.—*Untersuchungen auf dem Gebiete der römischen Verwaltungsgeschichte.* Berlin, 1877.

LIEBENAM, W.—*Forschungen zur Verwaltungsgeschichte des römischen Kaiserreichs.* Leipzig, 1888.

LIEBENAM, W.—*Die Laufbahn der Procuratoren bis auf die Zeit Diocletians.* Jena, 1886.

8. THE CIVIL AND CRIMINAL COURTS

BETHMANN-HOLLWEG, M. A. VON.—" Der römische Civilprozess " (*Der Civilprozess des gemeinen Rechts*, Bde. I. II.). Bonn, 1864.

GEIB, G.—*Geschichte des römischen Criminalprocesses bis zum Tode Justinians.* Leipzig, 1842.

GREENIDGE, A.—*The legal procedure of Cicero's time.* Oxford, 1901.

KELLER, F. L. VON.—*Der römische Civilprozess und die Actionen.* 5te Ausg. bearbeitet von Adolf Wach. Leipzig, 1876.

MOMMSEN, TH.—*Römisches Strafrecht.* Leipzig, 1899.

PUNTSCHART, V.—*Die Entwicklung des grundgesetzlichen Civilrechts der Römer.* Erlangen, 1872.

RUDORFF, A.—*Römische Rechtsgeschichte*, Bd. II. Leipzig, 1859.

WLASSAK, M.—*Römische Processgesetze. Ein Beitrag zur Geschichte des Formularverfahrens.* Leipzig, 1888-91.

WLASSAK, M.—*Edict und Klageform.* Jena, 1882.

ZUMPT, A.—*Das Criminalrecht der römischen Republik.* Berlin, 1865-69.

9. PRIVATE AND CRIMINAL LAW

CUQ, E.—*Les institutions juridiques des Romains.* Paris, 1891.

CZYHLARZ, C. VON.—*Lehrbuch der Institutionen des römischen Rechts.* Prague, Vienna, Leipzig. 1895.

GIRAUD, C.—*Histoire du droit Romain ou introduction historique à l'étude de cette législation.* Paris, 1847.

GOODWIN, F.—*The Twelve Tables.* London, 1886.

IHERING, R. VON.—*Geist des römischen Rechts auf den verschiedenen Stufe seiner Entwicklung.* Leipzig, 1877-83.

KARLOWA, O.—*Römische Rechtsgeschichte.* Leipzig, 1885.

LABOULAYE, E.—*Essai sur les lois criminelles des Romains concernant la responsibilité des magistrats.* Paris, Leipzig, 1845.

MITTEIS, L.—*Reichsrecht und Volksrecht in dem östlichen Provinzen des römischen Kaiserreichs.* Leipzig, 1891.

MOMMSEN, TH.—*Römisches Strafrecht.* Leipzig, 1899.

MUIRHEAD, J.—*Historical introduction to the private law of Rome.* Second edition revised and edited by H. Goudy. London, 1899.

ORTOLAN, E.—*Histoire de la législation Romaine.* 1884.

ORTOLAN, E.—*Explication historique des instituts de l'empereur Justinien.* Paris, 1851.

REIN, W.—*Das Criminalrecht der Römer von Romulus bis auf Justinianus.* Leipzig, 1844.

ROBY, H.—*An introduction to the study of Justinian's Digest.* Cambridge, 1886.

RUDORFF, A.—*Römische Rechtsgeschichte.* Leipzig, 1857-59.

SOHM, R.—*The institutes of Roman law.* Translated by J. C. Ledlie, with an introductory essay by E. Grueber. Oxford, 1892.

VOIGT, M.—*Die zwölf Tafeln. Geschichte und System des Civil- und Criminal-Rechtes, wie Processes der XII. Tafeln nebst deren Fragmenten.* Leipzig, 1883.

VOIGT, M.—*Römische Rechtsgeschichte.* Leipzig, 1892.

ZUMPT, A.—*Das Criminalrecht der römischen Republik.* Berlin, 1865-69.

10. PUBLIC ECONOMY

CUNNINGHAM, W.—"An essay on Western civilisation in its economic aspects" (*Ancient Times*, Book III.). Cambridge, 1898.

DUREAU DE LA MALLE, A.—*Economie politique des Romains.* Paris, 1840.

MARQUARDT, J.—*Römische Staatsverwaltung*, Bd. II. 2te Aufl., besorgt von H. Dessau und A. von Domaszewski. Leipzig, 1884.

11. SOCIAL CONDITIONS

FRIEDLÄNDER, L.—*Darstellungen aus der Sittengeschichte Roms in der Zeit von August bis zum Ausgang der Antonine.* Leipzig, 1862-71.

INGRAM, J.—*A history of slavery and serfdom* (ch. iii.). London, 1895.

MARQUARDT, J.—*Das Privatleben der Römer.* 2te. Aufl., besorgt von A. Mau. Leipzig, 1886.

VOIGT, M.—"Privataltertümer und Kulturgeschichte" (*Handbuch der klassischen Altertums-Wissenschaft*, herausg. von Dr. Iwan von Müller, Bd. IV. Abt. ii.). München, 1893.

WALLON, H.—*Histoire de l'esclavage dans l'antiquité.* Paris, 1879.

12. THE GUILDS

COHN, M.—*Zum römischen Vereinsrecht.* Berlin, 1873.

LIEBENAM, W.—*Zur Geschichte und Organisation des römischen Vereinswesens, drei Untersuchungen.* Leipzig, 1890.

MOMMSEN, TH.—*De collegiis et sodaliciis Romanorum.* Kiel, 1843.

WALTZING, J.—*Etude historique sur les corporations professionelles chez les Romains depuis les origines jusqu'à la chute de l'Empire d'Occident.* Louvain, 1895-99.

13. RELIGIOUS ORGANISATION IN ITS POLITICAL ASPECT

BEURLIER, E.—*Essai sur le culte rendu aux Empereurs Romains.* Paris, 1890.
BOISSIER, G.—*La religion Romaine d'Auguste aux Antonins.* Paris, 1874.
BOUCHÉ-LECLERCQ, A.—*Les pontifes de l'ancienne Rome.* Paris, 1871.
GUIRAUD, P.—*Les assemblées provinciales dans l'Empire Romain.* Paris, 1887.
MARQUARDT, J.—" De provinciarum Romanarum conciliis et sacerdotibus " (*Ephemeris Epigraphica*, vol. i. pp. 200-14).
MOURLOT, F.—*Essai sur l'histoire de l'Augustalité dans l'empire Romain.* Paris, 1895.

14. THE MUNICIPAL TOWNS

KUHN, E.—*Die städtische und bürgerliche Verfassung des römischen Reichs bis auf die Zeiten Justinians.* Leipzig, 1864-65.
LIEBENAM, W.—*Städteverwaltung im römischen Kaiserreiche.* Leipzig, 1900.
MOMMSEN, TH.—" Die Stadtrechte der latinischen Gemeinden Salpensa und Malaca in der Provinz Baetica" (*Abhandlungen der philologisch-historischen Classe der königlich sächsischen Gesellschaft der Wissenschaften*, Bd. II.). Leipzig, 1857.

15. THE PROVINCES

ARNOLD, W.—*The Roman system of provincial administration to the accession of Constantine the Great.* London, 1879.
MARQUARDT, J.—*Römische Staatsverwaltung*, Bd. I. Leipzig, 1881.
MOMMSEN, TH.—*The provinces of the Roman Empire from Caesar to Diocletian.* Translated by William P. Dickson. London, 1886.

16. SOURCES AND DOCUMENTS

BRUNS, C.—*Fontes juris Romani antiqui.* Freiburg, 1893.
KIPP, TH.—*Quellenkunde des römischen Rechts.* Leipzig, 1896.

17. INSCRIPTIONS

Corpus Inscriptionum Latinarum. Berlin.
Inscriptiones Regni Neapolitani, ed. Mommsen. Leipzig, 1852.
MOMMSEN, TH.—*Res gestae divi Augusti ex monumentis Ancyrano et Apolloniensi.* Berlin, 1883.
ORELLI-HENZEN.—*Inscriptionum Latinarum selectarum collectio.* Zürich, 1828-56.
PELTIER, C.—*Res gestae divi Augusti.* Paris, 1886.
WILMANNS, G.—*Exempla inscriptionum Latinarum.* Berlin, 1873.

18. DICTIONARIES OF ANTIQUITIES CONTAINING ARTICLES ON ROMAN CONSTITUTIONAL LAW

DAREMBERG-SAGLIO.—*Dictionnaire des antiquités Grecques et Romaines* (A to Lib). 1875, etc.

PAULY.—*Real-Encyclopädie der classischen Alterthumswissenschaft.* 6 Bde. Stuttgart, 1839.

PAULY-WISSOWA.—*Real-Encyclopädie,* etc. (a new edition of the above, A to Corn). 1893, etc.

SMITH.—*Dictionary of Greek and Roman antiquities.* Third edition, edited by W. Smith, W. Wayte, and G. E. Marindin. London, 1890.

19. HISTORIES OF ROME

DURUY, V.—*History of Rome and of the Roman people, from its origin to the establishment of the Christian Empire.* Translated by W. J. Clarke. Edited by J. P. Mahaffy. London, 1883-86.

GARDTHAUSEN, V.—*Augustus und seine Zeit.* Leipzig, 1891-96.

GIBBON, E. — *The history of the decline and fall of the Roman Empire.* Edited by J. B. Bury. London, 1896-1900.

HERTZBERG, G. — *Geschichte des römischen Kaiserreichs* (Oncken, W.— *Allgemeine Geschichte,* Hauptabth. 2, Thl. 1). Berlin, 1880.

HOW (W.) and LEIGH (H.).—*A history of Rome to the death of Caesar.* London, 1896.

IHNE, W.—*Römische Geschichte.* Leipzig, 1868-90.

LONG, G.—*The decline of the Roman Republic.* London, 1864-74.

MERIVALE, C.--*History of the Romans under the Empire.* London, 1875-76.

MOMMSEN, TH. — *The history of Rome.* Translated by W. P. Dickson. London, 1894.

NIEBUHR, B.—*Römische Geschichte.* Neue Ausgabe von M. Isler. Berlin, 1873-74.

NIEBUHR, B.—*History of Rome.* Translated by Walter (F.), Smith (W.), and Schmitz (L.). London, 1827-44.

PELHAM, H.—*Outlines of Roman History.* London, 1893.

PETER, C.—*Geschichte Roms.* Halle, 1881.

RANKE, L. VON.—*Weltgeschichte.* Thl. II. ("die römische Republik und ihre Weltherrschaft"). Thl. III. ("das altrömische Kaiserthum"). Leipzig, 1883.

SCHILLER, H.—*Geschichte der römischen Kaiserzeit.* Gotha, 1883-87.

CHAPTER I

THE EARLIEST CONSTITUTION OF ROME

§ 1. *The Growth of the City*

IN the developed political life of Italy there is a survival of
a form of association known as the *pagus*[1]—an ethnic or, at
least, a tribal unit, which is itself composed of a number of
hamlets (*vici*, οἶκοι). This district with its group of villages
perhaps represents the most primitive organisation of the Italian
peoples engaged in agriculture and pastoral pursuits.[2] The
pagus seems to resemble the tribe (*tribus*) of the fully formed
city-state,[3] while the *vicus* may often have represented, or
professed to represent, a simple clan (*gens*). In the centre of
the district lay a stronghold (*arx*, *castellum*), in which the people
took shelter in time of danger.

There are, indeed, traditions of isolated units still smaller
than the *pagus*. The clan is sometimes pictured as wandering
alone with its crowd of dependants.[4] But migration itself would
have tended to destroy the self-existence of the family; the
horde is wider than the clan, and the germ of the later *civitas*
must have appeared first, perhaps, in the *pagus*, later in the
populus which united many *pagi*. The union may have been

---

[1] *Pagus* (connected etymologically with πήγνυμι, *pago*, *pango*) implies the
idea of "foundation" or "settlement."

[2] Cf. Liv. ii. 62 "Incendiis deinde non villarum modo, sed etiam vicorum,
quibus frequenter habitabatur, Sabini exciti."

[3] So Servius Tullius is said, according to one account, to have divided the
territory of Rome into twenty-six *pagi*. *Pagus* is δῆμος in Greek (Festus p. 72), but
this proves little as to its origin ; it is the *pagus* as part of a state that is thus
translated. The δῆμος or δᾶμος in Greece had often been (as in Elis) a self-
existent community.

[4] Liv. ii. 16. Yet even here the *Claudia gens* is represented as expelled from
a *civitas*.

25   B

slight at first, and may often have been based merely on the possession of some common shrine. Much of the civil and criminal law was administered within the family in the form of a domestic jurisdiction which survived in historical Rome; but a common market would involve disputes, and these would have to be settled by an appeal to an arbitrator (*arbiter*) even before the idea of a magistracy was evolved. Lastly come military necessities whether of defence or aggression. It is these that create a power which more than any other makes the state. The mild kingship of the high-priest of the common cult gives way to the organised rule of an *imperium*, and the king, *praetor* or *dictator*, is the result, the coherence of infant organisation being dependent on the strength of the executive power.

In the earliest city of Rome, to which we are carried back by tradition or archaeological research, this development has already been attained. The square city (*Roma quadrata*) was the enclosure of the Palatine, the "grazing-land" of the early Roman shepherd;[1] the bounds of the oldest *pomerium* were known in later times to have been the limits of this site,[2] and traces of the tufa ring-wall may yet be seen. From this centre the city spread in irregular concentric circles.[3] Traces of ritual have preserved a memory of a city of the seven hills (*Septimontium*)—not those of the Servian Rome, but five smaller elevations, three (Palatium, Cermalus, Velia) on the older city of the Palatine, and two (Oppius, Cispius) on the newly-included Esquiline; while two valleys on the latter (Fagutal and Subura) also bear the name *montes*,[4] and are, with the sites that really deserve the name, inhabited by the *montani*, who are distinguished from the *pagani*, the inhabitants of the lower-lying land beneath. It is not impossible that these seven "hills" were once the sites of independent or loosely connected villages (*vici*, or perhaps even *pagi*) which were gradually amalgamated under a central power, and, as the walls of the state could never have been coterminous with its territory, each successive enclosure must show the

---

[1] The ancients derived Palatine from the *balare* or *palare* of cattle (Festus p. 220) or from the shepherd's god Pales (Solinus i. 15). It is perhaps derived from the root *pa* (*pasco*), See O. Gilbert *Geschichte u. Topographie der Stadt Rom in Altertum* i. p. 17.

[2] Tac. *Ann.* xii. 24.

[3] This tendency is best exhibited in Richter's map showing the extension of Rome (Baumeister *Denkmäler* art. "Rom" Karte v.).

[4] Festus pp. 340, 341. See Gilbert *Topographie* i. pp. 38, 162.

incorporation, voluntary or enforced, of a far greater number of smaller political units than those which the fortifications directly absorbed. Modern inquirers, following up a further hint supplied by the survival of a ritual, have held that there was another advance before the epoch of the Servian Rome was reached, and that what is known as "the Rome of the four regions" survives in the sites associated with the chapels of the Argei,[1] and is preserved in the administrative subdivisions of the city to the close of the Republic.[2] To form these regions the Caelian, the Quirinal, and the Viminal hills were added, while the Capitol with its two peaks now became, not indeed a part of the town, but, as the "head" of the state, its chief stronghold and the site of its greatest temples. The final step in the city's growth was the enclosure associated with the name of Servius Tullius, a fortification extending beyond the limits of the true *pomerium*, which added to the city the whole of the Esquiline to the north-east, the Aventine to the south-west, stretched to the west to the bank of the Tiber where the Pons Sublicius crosses the river, and formed the enceinte of Republican Rome.

It is possible that an amalgamation of slightly different ethnic elements may be associated with this extension of the city. That a difference of race lay at the basis of the division of the primitive people into their three original tribes was believed in the ancient, and has often been held in the modern world. The Tities (or Titienses) were supposed to be Sabine,[3] the Ramnes (or Ramnenses) Roman ; the Luceres were held by some to be also Latin, by others to be Etruscan. There is, however, a rival tradition of the artificial creation of these tribes by the first Roman king,[4] and, when we remember the arbitrary application in the Greek world of tribe-names that had once been significant,[5] we may hold it possible that the great συνοικισμός

---

[1] Varro *L.L.* v. 45 ff.

[2] i.e. in the four city tribes—*Palatina* (Palatine, Cermalus, Velia), *Esquilina* (Oppius, Cispius, Fagutal), *Suburana* or *Sucusana* (Coelius, Subura), *Collina* (Quirinalis, Viminalis—a region outside the old Septimontium). See Belot *Histoire des Chevaliers Romains* i. p. 401.

[3] The Sabine origin of the Tities rested perhaps on the Sabine *sacra* of the *sodales Titii* (Tac. *Ann.* i. 54). Cf. the Thracian origin ascribed to the Eumolpidae at Athens on account of the character of their cult.

[4] Cic. *de Rep.* ii. 8, 14 "populumque et suo et Tatii nomine et Lucumonis, qui Romuli socius in Sabino proelio occiderat, in tribus tris . . . discripserat."

[5] e.g. the manner in which the Ionic tribe-names were imposed at Athens after their primitive signification had been lost.

typified by the name of Romulus was not accompanied by any large alien intermixture with the primitive Latin population. The existence of Sabine gods like Sancus, or Sabine ritual as typified in Numa Pompilius, is no more evidence of Sabine intermixture than the early reception of Hellenic deities is of Greek ;[1] and though it is possible that a Sabine tribe once settled on the Quirinal, and it is almost certain that at the close of the monarchical period an Etruscan dynasty ruled in Rome, yet the language, religion, and political structure of the early state were of a genuinely Latin type. There was, indeed, contact with peoples more developed in material civilisation or more gifted in their spiritual life, and to this contact the debt of Rome was great. Rome adopts the Chalcidian alphabet ; she receives early Greek divinities such as Hercules, Castor, and Pollux ; she models her statue of Diana on the Aventine on that of Artemis at Massilia ; she imitates the Greek tactical organisation in her early phalanx. But it is very doubtful whether the obligation extended to the reception of the political ideas of Hellas. Parallels between Roman and Hellenic organisation may be observed in certain institutions such as the *equites* and the *census ;* but these are military rather than purely political, and in all the fundamental conceptions of public law—the rights of the citizens individually and collectively, the power of the magistrate and the divine character even of secular rule—Rome differed widely from the developed Greek communities with which she was brought into contact, and seems in her political evolution to have worked out her own salvation. The more developed civilisation of Etruria doubtless filled up certain gaps in her political and religious organisation both by contact and by rule. The strength of the religious guilds (*collegia*) of Rome may be due in part to an imitation of the Etruscan hierarchy ; the refinements of the science of augury may also be Tuscan ; and tradition, as we shall see, derives from the same source the *insignia* of the Roman king.

§ 2. *The Elements of the Population—Patricians, Plebeians, Clients*

The free population of Rome as a developed city-state was composed of the two elements of Patricians and Plebeians. The ultimate source of this distinction, which is undoubtedly

[1] Cf. Niese *Grundriss der röm. Gesch.* pp. 20 sq.

anterior to the foundation of the city, can only be a matter of conjecture; but the origin of the Patriciate may probably be explained as the result partly of earlier settlement, partly of superior military prowess. The warriors within the pale receive the new settlers, but only on certain conditions; these conditions are perpetuated and become a permanent badge of inferiority. The happiest guess of the many made by Roman antiquarians as to the origin of the Patricians was that they were originally the "free-born" men (*ingenui*), the men who could point to fathers (*patres*) and in their turn become full heads of families[1] —the men in short who, at a time when the family with its juristic head, and not the mere individual, was the true unit of life, were the only full citizens of Rome. Such men alone could be partners in the true ownership of property, or sue and be sued in their own right,[2] and such an exclusive right to a full personality in private law they claimed in virtue of their public services or privileges—the duty of taking the field on horseback or in heavy armour, the right of uplifting their voices in the assembly when they acclaimed a king or ratified a law.

The whole free community, other than the *patres* or Patricians, is regarded as the "complement" of the latter, "the multitude" (*plebs, plebeii*) which, with the fully privileged class, makes up the state.[3] It is possible that, in a very primitive stage of Roman history, these Plebeians may all have been in the half-servile condition of clientship; but, even when the earliest records of Rome are revealed to us, this has ceased to be the case. Not only has the son of the original client evolved a freedom of his own, but a man may *become* a plebeian member of Rome without subjecting himself to the degradation of *clientela*. No less than five ways are described or can be imagined in which the non-citizen could become a citizen, and at least one of these reveals the possibility of the perfectly free Plebeian. In the old life of the *pagus* and the *gens*, the weaker sought protection of the

[1] Cincius ap. Festum p. 241 "Patricios Cincius ait in libro de comitiis eos appellari solitos, qui nunc ingenui vocentur." Cf. Liv. x. 8 (300 B.C.; from the speech of Decius Mus) § 9 "Semper ista audita sunt eadem, penes vos auspicia esse, vos solos gentem habere, vos solos justum imperium et auspicium domi militiaeque"; § 10 "en unquam fando audistis, patricios primo esse factos non de coelo demissos sed qui patrem ciere possent, id est nihil ultra quam ingenuos?"
[2] Mr. Strachan-Davidson remarks (Smith *Dict. of Antiq.* ii. p. 354) that, on the evolution of the rights of the plebeians, these too should have been *patricii*, but that the word *patricius* survived as a "token of an arrested development."
[3] *Plebs* is connected with the root which appears in *compleo, impleo,* πλῆθος.

stronger by a willing vassalage, which ripened, when the state
was formed, into the Plebeiate which had its origin in clientship.
A similar position was ultimately gained by the descendant of
the manumitted slave. The stranger (*hostis*) from a city which
had no treaty relations with Rome, or no relations which
guaranteed a mutual interchange of citizenship, must, if he
wandered to this new home, also make application to a patron
and become his client. It is less certain what was the fate of
the inhabitants of a conquered city who were violently deported
to Rome. The annalists, indeed, represent such men as being
received into the citizen body, and as becoming members of
the tribe and the *curia;* [1] but it is probable that in the prehistoric period they became clients, immediately of the king to
whom they had made their subjection, ultimately perhaps of
patrician houses to which he chose to attach them as dependants.[2]
In all these cases clientship may have been the original lot of
the Plebeian ; but this could hardly have been the fate of the
immigrant who moved to Rome from a city which already
possessed the *jus commercii* with that state, and by the exercise
of the right of voluntary exile from his native land (*jus exulandi*)
claimed the Roman *civitas*. The existence of such relations
between Rome and cities of the Latin league is attested for a
very early period, and they may even have been extended to
cities outside the league.[3] As the *jus commercii* implies the right
of suing and being sued in one's own person before Roman
courts, there seems no reason why such an immigrant should
make application to a Roman patron ; [4] but, if he did not, he
was in the chief aspects of private law a perfectly free man, and

---

[1] Liv. i. 28 "populum omnem Albanum Romam traducere in animo est,
civitatem dare plebi, primores in patres legere." Dionysius (ii. 35) represents
the people of Caenina and Antemnae as being, after their subjection, enrolled
εἰs φυλὰs καὶ φράτραs.

[2] Cf. Dionysius' account of Romulus' institution of clientship (ii. 9 παρακατα-
θήκαs δὲ ἔδωκε τοῖs πατρικίοιs τοὺs δημοτικούs, ἐπίτρεψαs ἑκάστῳ . . . ὃν αὐτὸs
ἐβούλετο νέμειν προστάτην . . . πατρωνείαν ὀνομάσαs τὴν προστασίαν).

[3] The *jus commercii* has been read into the relations of Rome with Carthage as
depicted in Polybius' second treaty [Polyb. iii. 24, 12 ἐν Σικελίᾳ, ἧs Καρχηδόνιοι
ἐπάρχουσι, καὶ ἐν Καρχηδόνι πάντα καὶ ποιείτω καὶ πωλείτω (the Roman) ὅσα
καὶ τῷ πολίτῃ (the Carthaginian) ἔξεστιν]. But jurisdiction here may have been
the work of some international court, and the *jus commercii*, without the *jus
exulandi*, would hardly have made a foreign immigrant a citizen of Rome.

[4] Cicero shows that there was a controversy whether *applicatio* was consistent
with *exilium* (*de Orat.* i. 39, 177), "Quid ? quod item in centumvirali judicio
certatum esse accepimus, qui Romam in exilium venisset, cui Romae exulare jus

illustrated a status to which the quondam-client must from an early period have tended to approximate. Where the right of intermarriage (*jus conubii*), as well as the right of trade, was guaranteed in a treaty between Rome and some other town, it is questionable whether this gift ever implied the possibility of matrimonial union with members of the Patriciate. It is at least certain that, at the time of the Twelve Tables (451 B.C.), and therefore probably from a very early period, a disability common to all the Plebeians was that they might not inter- marry with members of patrician clans. Yet, although there was this great gulf parting the two orders, it was possible for either class to be transferred to the status of the other. We shall see that tradition represents a vote of the Patricians in their assembly as a means sufficient to recruit their order by the addition of a new family; while, after the Plebs had evolved an assembly of its own, a *transitio ad plebem* might be effected by an act of that body.[1] Adoption from a patrician into a plebeian family produced the same result.

That the clientship of which we have spoken was not peculiar to Rome, but was an old established Italian institution, is a truth reflected in the legend of the *gens Claudia* which moved from Regillum to Rome with a vast multitude of dependants.[2] It is separated by but a thin line from slavery. While the latter was based on conquest in war, the former was probably the result of voluntarily-sought protection in the turmoil of a migratory life, or perhaps at times the consequence of the suzerainty of a powerful village being extended over its weaker neighbours. In the developed state the principal object of this relation is legal representation by the *patronus*, for the client possesses no legal personality of his own. For the condition of the client we can but appeal to that of the slave and the son

esset, si se ad aliquem quasi patronum applicavisset intestatoque esset mortuus, nonne in ea causa jus applicationis, obscurum sane et ignotum, patefactum in judicio atque illustratum est a patrono?"
[1] Zonaras vii. 15. P. Clodius first tried this method; when it was opposed he resorted to the artifice of adoption. Courtly writers imagined a *transitio* for the plebeian Octavii, Suet. *Aug.* 2 "Ea gens a Tarquinio Prisco rege inter minores gentes adlecta . . . mox a Servio Tullio in patricias transducta, pro- cedente tempore ad plebem se contulit."
[2] Liv. ii. 16 (504 B.C.) "Attus Clausus (driven out from Regillum) magna clientium comitatus manu Romam transfugit. His civitas data agerque trans Anienem . . . Appius inter patres (i.e. the Senate) lectus haud ita multo post in principum dignationem pervenit." Cf. Suet. *Tib.* 1.

of the family. Such property as he possessed may have been merely a *peculium*, the small accumulation of cattle and means of husbandry which his master allowed him to form; had the client wronged a citizen, we may assume that his body might be surrendered in reparation of the damage (*noxae deditio*); the origin of Roman occupation of land on sufferance (*precario*) may perhaps be traced to the permission by the patron to till a little plot of land which might be resumed at will;[1] in default of direct heirs (*sui heredes*) such personal belongings as the client possessed may have fallen to the members of the protecting clan (*gentiles*), for it was to the clan rather than to the family that he was attached.

The description which we possess of the mutual obligations of patrons and clients,[2] although it contains many primitive elements, obviously refers to a time when the client was allowed to possess property of his own and was often a man of considerable wealth, but when, in spite of this power, he does not seem to have appeared in person in the public courts. It was the duty of the Patricians to interpret the law to their clients, to accept their defence in suits, and to represent them when they were plaintiffs.[3] The client, on the other hand, was bound to help to dower the daughter of the patron if the latter was poor; to pay the ransom if he or his son were captured by enemies; and, if his lord was worsted in a private action or incurred a public fine, to defray the expense from his own property. If any of these duties were violated by the client, he was held guilty of treason (*perduellio*), and as the secular arm suspended him from the unlucky tree, so the religious power devoted to the infernal gods the patron who had woven a net of fraud for his dependant.[4] Even after the effective infliction of religious sanctions had disappeared, the duty to the client ranked only second to that which was owed by a guardian to his ward.[5] The earliest

---

[1] Savigny *Recht des Besitzes* (7th ed.) p. 202. On the general condition of the client see Ihering *Geist des röm. Rechts* i. p. 237.

[2] Dionys. ii. 9, 10.

[3] ἐξηγεῖσθαι τὰ δίκαια . . . δίκας λαγχάνειν . . . τοῖς ἐγκαλοῦσιν ὑπέχειν (Dionys. ii. 10). If representation in the civil courts is meant, it must have resembled that of the *paterfamilias*, who sues in his own right, for procuratory was unknown in early Roman procedure (Just. *Inst.* iv. 10 "cum olim in usu fuisset alterius nomine agere non posse ").

[4] Verg. *Aen.* vi. 609 "fraus innexa clienti." Cf. Servius ad loc.

[5] Gell. v. 13 "Conveniebat . . . ex moribus populi Romani primum juxta parentes locum tenere pupillos debere, fidei tutelaeque nostrae creditos; secundum

clientship was strictly hereditary; but the bond must have become weaker with successive generations, after the evolution of plebeian rights, and at a time when *clientes* themselves possessed votes in the *comitia curiata*.[1] Nay, the Plebeian at this period may himself be a patron, and his attainment of full citizenship in private law must have been held to qualify him for this duty of protection. Yet the client body still continues to be recruited by new members; for the antique form of *applicatio* still exists, and the manumitted slave owes duties to his patron. We know too that in the fourth and third centuries the patronal rights over the freedman extended to the second generation.[2]

A faint trace of hereditary clientship, based on a purely moral sanction, and accompanied perhaps by the performance of some of the duties of the old relationship, still exists in the second century. The family of Marius, we are told, had been clients of the plebeian Herennii, and some of the rights of the relationship were held to extend to him. But we are also told that at this period a principle was recognised that this bond was for ever broken by the client's attainment of curule office,[3] that is, by the ennoblement of him and his family.

§ 3. *Roman Family Organisation* — *The Gens, the Familia, the Bondsman and the Slave* — *The Disposition of Property* — *The Conception of "Caput"*

The clan (*gens*) was an aggregate of individuals supposed to be sprung from a common source, a social union, with common rights in private law, which had as its theoretical basis the notion of descent from a single ancestor. According to the juristic theory of the clan, all its individual members would, if their descent could be traced through every degree, have sprung from two individuals who were within the power of this ultimate

eos proximum locum clientes habere, qui sese itidem in fidem patrociniumque nostrum dediderunt." The third place was filled by *hospites*, the fourth by *cognati* and *adfines*.

[1] Liv. ii. 56.

[2] Suet. *Claud.* 24 "(Claudius) Appium Caecum censorem (312 B.C.) . . . libertinorum filios in senatum allegisse docuit; ignarus temporibus Appii (312-280 B.C.) et deinceps aliquamdiu 'libertinos' dictos, non ipsos qui manu emitterentur, sed ingenuos ex his procreatos."

[3] Plut. *Mar.* 5.

ancestor, a sign of this original *potestas* being the common gentile name.[1]

The members of a clan are to one another either *agnati* or *gentiles*. In many cases the difference of nomenclature was based merely on the degree of certainty in the relationship. They were *agnati* when the common descent could be traced through all its stages; they were *gentiles* when the common descent was only an imagined fact, based on the possession of a common name. As a rule *agnati* are also *gentiles;* but there might be groups of agnates who could never be *gentiles*—groups, that is, of proved relationship through the male line, who could not, for reasons which we shall soon specify, form a *gens.*

If we believe that the Roman Patriciate represented those who alone possessed the legal status of heads of families (*patres*)[2] —since, the *familia* being the unit of the clan, the rights of a clan-member (*gentilis*) imply the position of a *paterfamilias*—it follows that the Roman *gentes* were, as they are represented by tradition, originally exclusively patrician, and that the terms *gentilis, gentilitas* implied a perfect equality of status among the only true members of the state.

The words became restricted to a certain section of the community in consequence of the evolution of plebeian rights, i.e. in consequence of the Plebeians becoming in strict law *patres familias.* The logical consequence of this should have been, where groups of such families bore a common name and were believed to have a common descent, that these groups should form *gentes.* But history is illogical, and this conclusion was not reached.

No such group could possibly form a *gens* of its own, if it could be regarded as having been originally in dependence on a patrician clan. Although in course of time legally independent and freed from all trammels of clientship, it was yet disqualified from clan-brotherhood by this original connexion; it remained an offshoot (*stirps*), a mere dependent branch, and could never be a self-existent *gens.* This disqualification is exhibited in the definition of *gentilitas* given by the jurist Scaevola (consul 133 B.C.), which gives as two of its conditions free birth in the second degree, and the absence of servile blood in one's ultimate ancestry.[3]

---

[1] Festus p. 94 "gentilis dicitur ex eodem genere ortus et (?) is qui simili nomine appellatur."   [2] p. 5.

[3] Cic. *Top.* 6, 29 "Gentiles sunt inter se, qui eodem nomine sunt; qui ab ingenuis oriundi sunt; quorum majorum nemo servitutem servivit; qui capite non sunt deminuti."

This definition excludes from membership of a *gens* all those Plebeians who had sprung originally from emancipated slaves. No one who could be proved to have the taint of servile blood could ever be a *gentilis*. But there is every reason to believe that *servitus* was interpreted in a further sense, that clientship was regarded as a quasi-servile position, and debarred a group of families, whose ancestor could be proved to be a client, for ever from being a clan.

As a rule it would have been difficult, if not impossible, to furnish this proof; but there was one legal sign of it—the bearing by a plebeian *stirps* of the same name as a patrician clan. The presumption of the law, in the case of the coexistence of a plebeian group of families with a patrician group of the same name, was apparently that the former had once been clients of the latter, and could never, therefore, form a *gens* of their own.[1]

But, if there were plebeian families that had no origin in clientship, there was nothing to prevent these from being *gentes*. It is true that Patricians sometimes made the claim that all the plebeian families had originated from clientship.[2] But this is, as we saw,[3] probably not true of the origin of many of the plebeian families, and there is abundant evidence that the theory was not recognised by law. We know, for instance, that gentile inheritances were shared by the plebeian Minucii, and gentile sepulchres by the plebeian Popilii.[4]

The foregoing description shows that the *gens* rests on a natural basis, that it professedly represents the widest limits of blood-relationship; hence it would seem to follow that it could not be artificially created or its members redistributed; that the numbers of the clans could not be regulated numerically,

---

[1] The test is illustrated by a controversy between the patrician Claudii and the plebeian Claudii Marcelli, Cic. *de Orat.* i. 39, 176 "Quid ? qua de re inter Marcellos et Claudios patricios centumviri judicarunt, cum Marcelli ab liberti filio stirpe, Claudii patricii ejusdem hominis hereditatem gente ad se rediisse dicerent, nonne in ea causa fuit oratoribus de toto stirpis et gentilitatis jure dicendum." Suetonius (*Tib.* 1) says of the clan of the Claudii Marcelli, as compared with their patrician namesakes, "nec potentia minor nec dignitate."

[2] Liv. x. 8, quoted p. 5.

[3] p. 5.

[4] Cic. *in Verr.* i. 45, 115 "Minucius quidam mortuus est ante istum (Verrem) praetorem ; ejus testamentum erat nullum. Lege hereditas ad gentem Minuciam veniebat"; *de Leg.* ii. 22, 55 "Jam tanta religio est sepulchrorum, ut extra sacra et gentem inferri fas negent esse ; idque apud majores nostros A. Torquatus in gente Popilia judicavit."

except conceivably by the addition to the existing number of
a precise number of added clans—a most improbable procedure;
and that, as being a natural and not an artificial creation, it was
a union which was not likely to be of primary importance
politically, and the rights of whose members were in all
probability those of private rather than of public law. These
expectations are verified, but the attempts to point out certain
purely political characteristics of these associations deserve
examination.[1]

(i.) It has been held that the clans were the unit of voting
in the original popular assembly at Rome, the *comitia curiata*.[2]
But the passage on which this conclusion is based only implies
that, originally, membership of this *comitia* depended on possession of a *gens;* eventually, at a time when the *curia* included
Plebeians, on possession of a *familia*, and therefore presumably
of a *stirps* or *genus*.

(ii.) A distinction is presented by ancient authorities between
the *gentes majores* and *minores*—a distinction within the patrician
gentes that survived into the Republic. Of the *gentes minores* we
know but one name, that of the patrician Papirii;[3] a list of some
of the *gentes majores* has been reconstructed with some plausibility
from those clans which furnished *principes senatus;* they are the
Aemilii, Claudii, Cornelii, Fabii, Manlii, and Valerii.[4] Tradition
is inclined to represent this distinction as having originated
politically,[5] but it is a tradition working on the impossible
hypothesis that the Patriciate derived its origin from membership of the Senate. This political distinction doubtless existed
within the Senate; but it was probably derived merely from
the respective antiquity, and therefore dignity, of the *gentes*

[1] The theory of the artificial origin of the *gens* is based on the symmetrical figures
given by tradition. The full numbers of the early *gentes* are given as 300 ; these
are symmetrically divided, ten into each of the thirty *curiae*, as the *curiae* are
divided into the three original tribes. Hence Niebuhr (*Hist. Rome* i. p. 319) says,
"The numerical scale of the *gentes* is an irrefragable proof that they were not
more ancient than the constitution, but corporations formed by a legislator in
harmony with the rest of his scheme."

[2] Niebuhr op. cit. p. 333 ; from Laelius Felix (ap. Gell. xv. 27) "Cum ex
generibus hominum suffragium feratur, curiata comitia esse " (*genus* because
the assembly came to include Plebeians, some of whom had no *gentes*).

[3] Cic. *ad Fam.* ix. 21, 2.   [4] Momms. *Staatsr.* iii. p. 31.

[5] Cic. *de Rep.* ii. 20, 35 "(L. Tarquinius) duplicavit illum pristinum patrum
numerum ; et antiquos patres majorum gentium appellavit, quos priores sententiam
rogabat ; a se ascitos minorum"; Liv. i. 35 "(Tarquinius) centum in patres
legit ; qui deinde minorum gentium sunt appellati."

from which its members were drawn.   And this association with
the Senate leads us naturally to the third question connected
with the political character of the *gentes*, i.e. their relation
to the primitive council of the state.   The theory of an
ultimate connexion between the two originates with the
correspondence of the number of the *gentes* and of the Senate.
Both are given by tradition as 300.   The Roman community
is said to have originated with the amalgamation of three
domains (*tribus*) into one.[1]   The rise of the Senate from 100,
its original number as constituted by Romulus, to 300 as its
final number, is accounted for by the gradual amalgamation of
these three tribes with their 100 *gentes* each.[2]   A parallel
to the original centumviral constitution of the Senate is found
in the *centumviri* of the Italian towns, and is supposed to be
derived from the same invariable division of a *tribus* into
100 *gentes*.[3]

The chief objections to this view are the symmetrical number
into which it divides the *gentes*, and the fact that the Senate is,
according to the best tradition, a body of nominees selected
by the chief magistrate.   But yet there is an element of truth
in the theory.   The Senate did rise from 100 to 300 in consequence of the incorporation of fresh elements into the community, and therefore in consequence of an increase of the *gentes*.
The kings and early consuls would doubtless, in the exercise
of their powers of selection, wish to see each of the patrician
clans represented in their council.   Hence the addition of
new clans would add new members to that body, and hence
the inferior place occupied in the Senate by the *gentes minores*,
the younger branch of the Patriciate.

Although the clan itself was inexpansive, the number of
the clans, even in the old patrician community, was not.   It
was possible for new *gentes* to be added to the community, and
even for old *gentes* to quit it.   Tradition speaks of the reception
of six clans that had once belonged to the parent state of Alba
—the Cloelii, Curiatii, Geganii, Julii, Quinctilii (or Quinctii), and
Servilii ;[4] and Sabine races as well, such as the Valerii,[5] are also
said to have been admitted.   The reception of new *gentes* was

[1] p. 3.
[2] The *gentes minores* are sometimes identified with the *gentes* of the last
admitted of these tribes, the *Luceres* (Ortolan *Hist. of Roman Law* i. § 33).
[3] Momms. *Hist. of Rome* bk. i. ch. v.
[4] Liv. i. 30 ; Dionys. iii. 29.   [5] Dionys. ii. 46.

effected by the Patricians and, as we should expect, by the assembly which represents the whole patrician body, the *comitia curiata*, under the presidency of the king.   They were coopted by their peers,[1] and it is improbable that the patrician order could have been recruited by the act of the king alone.[2]   He might conceivably have chosen Plebeians as members of his advising body, the Senate, as the first consuls are said to have done,[3] although such a selection is extremely improbable ; but even this act would not have raised such Plebeians to the Patriciate.   The admission of new *gentes* implies that foreigners, or even a portion of the plebeian body, might be coopted into the Patriciate ; in the former case it might be the reception, in the latter the creation, of a *gens*.   This possibility of recruiting the patrician order—whether by the creation or reception of *gentes*—ceased during the Republic, because the assembly of the Curies came eventually to admit Plebeians, and there was no political assembly composed exclusively of members who fulfilled all the conditions of being *gentiles*.   The only instance of the expulsion of a *gens* preserved by legend is that of the Tarquinii ; and the decree that this whole clan had forfeited its right to be a member of the Roman state is said to have been passed by the Populus.[4]

The account of *gentes* being received into the Roman community is accompanied by a tradition of their keeping together in their new settlement.   Thus the Claudii, on the reception of the *civitas*, are said to have received a special tract of territory across the Anio for themselves and their clients.[5] Such a tradition at once suggests a close connexion between the *gens* and the soil, which there is no reason to doubt.   But the further questions have been raised, whether the *gens* as a whole was the owner of the land on which it settled, and whether this

---

[1] Liv. iv. 4 "nobilitatem vestram per cooptationem in patres habetis" ; Suet. *Tib.* 1 "gens Claudia in patricios cooptata."   So Servius and Numa are said to have been transferred by the Populus from the ranks of the δῆμος to those of the πατρίκιοι.

· [2] As is implied in Suet. *Aug.* 2 (quoted p. 7).   [3] Dionys. v. 13.

[4] Liv. ii. 2 "Brutus ad populum tulit ut omnes Tarquiniae gentis exsules essent" ; Varro ap. Non. p. 222 "omnes Tarquinios ejicerent, ne quam reditionis per gentilitatem spem haberent."

[5] Suet. *Tib.* 1 " Patricia gens Claudia... orta est ex Regillis, oppido Sabinorum ... post reges exactos sexto fere anno, in patricias cooptata.   Agrum insuper trans Anienem clientibus, locumque sibi ad sepulturam sub Capitolio, publice accepit."   Cf. Liv. ii. 16 (cited p. 7).

was the form of common possession recognised in early Rome.
It must be admitted that tradition knows nothing of such a tenure.
Dionysius represents the territory given to the Claudii as destined
to be divided up amongst the various *familiae* of the *gens ;*[1] while
in other accounts of land-assignments we hear of such being
made to the *curia* (φράτρα)[2] or to individuals (*viritim*),[3] but
never to the clan. Yet a plausible theory of common possession
has been based on the survivals both of legal terms and of clan
rights.[4] Amongst the terms describing early territorial possession
we have, apart from *ager publicus*, the *heredium* and the *ager
privatus*. The private possession of the *heredium* is attributed to
Romulus,[5] and is thus regarded as a modification of some form
of common tenure; and the *heredium* consisted of only two
jugera,[6] an amount obviously insufficient for the maintenance of
a family. Hence there must have been *ager privatus* as well,
owned by some larger unit, and this unit would naturally have
been the *gens*. It has also been thought that the terms
descriptive of individual ownership—*manus, mancipium*—referred
originally to movables,[7] as though immovables belonged to a
common stock. Lastly, we find connected with the clan the
survival of a corporate right to property and collective duties
connected with it. According to the rules of regular intestate
succession, in default of the *suus heres*, property lapses to the
proximus agnatus and then to the *gentiles ;*[8] and it was in connexion with this right, which lasted down to the end of the
Republic,[9] that the definition of a *gentilis* was of such legal
importance.[10] This inheritance is by the *gentiles* as a whole, for
there is no *proximus gentilis*, and in historic times it must have
been an inheritance by individuals, the property being divided
amongst those who could prove their claim ; but it may be the
relic of an earlier inheritance by the *gens* as a corporation.

But the *gentiles* have rights in a *corporate* capacity as well.

[1] Dionys. v. 40.   [2] ib. ii. 7.
[3] Cic. *de Rep.* ii. 14, 26.   [4] Momms. *Staatsr.* iii. p. 23.
[5] Varro *R.R.* i. 10, 2 ; cf. Plin. *H.N.* xix. 4.
[6] Festus p. 53 " Centuriatus ager in ducena jugera definitus, quia Romulus
centenis civibus ducena jugera tribuit."
[7] It is possible, however, that *manus* in such expressions is merely the symbol
of power.
[8] " Si adgnatus nec escit gentiles familiam habento."
[9] Suet. *Caes.* 1, of Caesar's refusal to divorce Cornelia ; as a consequence he was
" uxoris dote, et gentiliciis haereditatibus multatus."
[10] p. 10.

By the Twelve Tables they have the guardianship of the insane [1]
and a reversionary right of guardianship over women and
children.[2] Guardianship (*tutela*) must have given them all the
rights of a person in Roman law, to exercise which they must
have had a personal representative. But this devolution itself
shows the *gens* acting as a corporation.

Of corporate action in their own interests, or with a view to
the interests of the state, there is little evidence, although there
are traces of common activity for the purpose of keeping up the
dignity of the family. The patrician Claudii repudiate by common agreement the *praenomen* "Lucius," because two of its bearers
had been respectively convicted of highway robbery and murder,[3]
and the patrician Manlii renounce the *praenomen* "Marcus" in
consequence of a crime committed by a clansman of that name ; [4]
but such an agreement could hardly in historical times have had
other support than the will of individual members to observe it.
Perhaps the closest of the later ties of the *gens* were its common
worship and sacrifices. They never, as in Greece, rose to the
rank of great public worships, but excessive care was taken by
the state to maintain them ; chiefly from the view that, if the
worship of a race died out, the community would lose the
favour of the divinity to which it had belonged. Hence the
close connexion of gentile *sacra* with property and inheritance.[5]
Property, in the last resort, passed to the *gentiles ;* and the *sacra*,
that they might be maintained, were a necessary burden associated
with it. For the *sacra* to pass out of the family was of little
importance ; had they passed out of the *gens*, there was no
security for their continuance. In cases of transition from a
family of one clan to a family of another, it was the duty of the
pontifices to inquire how the continuity of the sacred rites might
be maintained,[6] and hence one of the forms observed in the case
of a change of *gens* by adrogation was the *sacrorum detestatio*, a

---

[1] "Si furiosus escit, ast ei custos nec escit, adgnatum gentiliumque in eo
pecuniaque ejus potestas esto."
[2] Cic. *pro Domo* 13, 35.   [3] Suet. *Tib.* 1.
[4] Cic. *Phil.* i. 13, 32.   [5] Maine *Ancient Law* pp. 6, 27.
[6] Cic. *pro Domo* 13, 35 "Quas adoptiones (i.e. legal ones) . . . hereditates
nominis, pecuniae, sacrorum secutae sunt. Tu . . . neque amissis sacris paternis
in haec adoptiva venisti. Ita perturbatis sacris, contaminatis gentibus, et quam
deseruisti et quam polluisti, etc."; *de Leg.* ii. 19, 48 "haec jura pontificum
auctoritate consecuta sunt, ut ne morte patris familias sacrorum memoria occideret,
iis essent ea adjuncta, ad quos ejusdem morte pecunia venerit." The transmission
was thus a part of *jus pontificium*, not of *jus civile*. Cf. Serv. in *Aen.* ii. 156.

public declaration that the individual who sought this change had ceased to claim any participation in the *sacra* of his race. The care for the continuity of the *sacra* of the clan was long one of the professed, and perhaps real, bars to marriage between Patricians and Plebeians.[1]

This question of the *sacra* is an index to the fact that membership of a *gens* might be either natural or artificial. The natural mode of entrance was by birth; and in the case of the patrician clans, before the right of intermarriage was extended to the Plebs, marriage with a patrician mother and by the ceremony of the *confarreatio* was necessary to constitute *gentilitas* for the child. Later any form of marriage sufficed, as it had doubtless always done in the case of the plebeian clans. The child, in accordance with the patriarchal principle, belonged to the clan of his father.

The form of religious marriage peculiar to the Patricians necessitated a change of *gens* on the part of the wife; for a woman married by the ceremony of *confarreatio* became a partner in the property and *sacra* of her husband,[2] and there is even some trace of her having originally changed her gentile name as well.[3] The ordinary plebeian form of marriage by mere agreement (*consensus*), which ultimately became almost universal, did not lead to a woman's falling into the *potestas* of her husband, unless this power were assumed, originally by prescriptive right (*usus*), later by the ceremony of fictitious purchase (*coemptio*). In such a case she became a member of her husband's family, but it is questionable whether the logical conclusion was pressed and she also became a member of his *gens*. The anomaly, if it existed, may perhaps be explained by the fact that the Plebeians, who evolved these forms of marriage, had, as a rule, no *gentes*.

The clan might also be changed by adoption. *Adrogatio*— perhaps the only form known to the old patrician community— was the method by which the head of a family voluntarily submitted himself to the *potestas* of another. *Adoptio*, on the other hand, was the change from one *potestas* to another. If there was

---

[1] Cf. the story of Verginia in Liv. x. 23 (296 B.C.) "Verginiam Auli filiam patriciam plebeio nuptam L. Volumnio consuli matronae, quod e patribus enupsisset, sacris arcuerant." She then founds an altar to "Pudicitia plebeia," in imitation of that to "Pudicitia patricia."

[2] ἀνδρὶ κοινωνὸν ἁπάντων χρημάτων τε καὶ ἱερῶν (Dionys. ii. 25).

[3] Plut. *Qu. Rom.* 30 Διὰ τί τὴν νύμφην εἰσάγοντες λέγειν κελεύουσιν· "Ὅπου σὺ Γάιος, ἐγὼ Γάια;

a form of true adoption by patrician law,[1] it has been lost to us, and the earliest that we hear of is the plebeian form by threefold sale recognised in the Twelve Tables.   At a later period it might also be effected by a written testament.

The family (*familia*)[2] in its original and proper meaning is the aggregate of members of a household under a common head; this head was the *paterfamilias*—the *only* member of the household who possesses legal rights.

The two ideas underlying the Roman conception of the family are those of unity and power, and both are singularly perfect. The former is attained, and the latter exercised, by the head. It is through him alone that the family is a person; and the authority he wields over the members subordinated to his will is called *potestas*.[3]   The power over the children is described as *patria potestas*, as over the slave it is *dominica*.   The two do not differ legally; there is only a difference of ethical signification. Under this *potestas* fall, firstly, the children, both sons and daughters; secondly, the descendants of these children; thirdly, the wife united to her lord by a form of marriage which makes her a member of the family; fourthly, the wives of the sons and grandsons who have entered the *familia* by a similar binding form of marriage.   There is a complete absence of independent rights amongst these members of the household.   As to the wife, any property that she might be possessed of, or which she acquired, passed absolutely into the power of her husband.   He was responsible for her conduct and possessed the right of moderate chastisement.   Severer punishment for wrongs to the household required the support of the family council.   No legal action might be brought by the woman against her lord, for they were not two personalities, but one.   He might divorce her on good grounds,[4] but if she were married under a form which subjected her to his power, she had no legal means of freeing herself from his tyrannous rule.   Her position is that of a daughter and she inherits equally with her children.   The decision as to whether the

---

[1] e.g. a testamentary adoption by a public act in the *comitia calata*.

[2] *Familia* is etymologically a "household."   Cf. Sanskr. *dhâ* "to settle," *dhâman* "settlement."

[3] The original term was, perhaps, *manus* signifying "power" (see p. 32), but this word came in course of time to be restricted to the control over the wife who had become a member of the *familia*.

[4] Plutarch (*Rom.* 22) quotes a law of Romulus allowing the divorce of the wife ἐπὶ φαρμακείᾳ τέκνων ἢ κλειδῶν ὑποβόλῃ καὶ μοιχευθεῖσαν.

child of the marriage was to be reared (*liberi susceptio*) belonged to the father, but was, in the interest of the state, subjected at an early period to certain modifications. The "laws of Romulus" —that is, the early pontifical law—enjoined the rearing of every male child and of the first-born of the females; the exposure of offspring was to receive the assent of five neighbours,[1] and disobedience of these canons was to be visited with severe penalties on the parent who neglected the welfare of the state. The children and their descendants are never released from the absolute rule of the father as long as he lives. They cannot own property; for all that they acquire belongs to the common stock and is at the disposal of the head of the family. At best the father might permit the son, as he might permit the slave, to employ his own earnings for his own use. This is the *peculium*. Yet the grant is a mere concession, and one which may be withdrawn at any moment. If the son dies it lapses to the father; if the father dies it falls to the heir.

The child, as having no property, cannot give satisfaction for wrongs which he has committed. He is regarded as irresponsible, and responsibility for his conduct devolved on the father, who might either give compensation to the injured man, or surrender the delinquent for him to visit with his vengeance, or to use as a means of working out the damage (*noxae deditio*);[2] in the latter case the child becomes for ever the property of another. The father might sell him; if beyond the limits of the country, the son becomes a slave; if within the limits, he is one in private though not in public law (*in causa mancipii*), and exchanges servitude to the father for that to the purchaser. In an age which recognised no free contract of labour, the sale of the son was a means of putting him out to business.[3] The injunction of the Twelve Tables (perhaps the recognition of a custom far earlier than this law) that the thrice-repeated sale of a son involved loss of the *patria potestas*,[4] was an attempt to put an

[1] Dionys. ii. 15.

[2] This *jus noxae dationis* first disappears finally in the law of Justinian (*Inst.* iv. 8, 7; *Dig.* 43, 29, 3, 4). Before its abolition a modification had been introduced by the rule that, when the child had acquired an equivalent for the damage he had caused (*quantum damni dedit*), the owner should be forced to manumit him.

[3] Even by Constantine the sale of new-born children (*sanguinolenti*) was permitted, but only *propter nimiam paupertatem* (*Cod.* 4, 43, 2).

[4] "Pater si filium ter venum duuit, filius a patre liber esto." It has been thought, however, that by the time of the Twelve Tables the sale had become merely fictitious.

end to an inhuman traffic. The child as a thing might be stolen or detained, and as such be the object of recovery., In this case the father "vindicates" him as he would a chattel or a beast that had strayed from the nomestead.[1]

The father might scourge or imprison his child,[2] even put him to death. The formula employed in adrogation (the procedure by which a man puts himself into the paternal power of another) shows that the *jus vitae necisque* was the most distinctive aspect of the *patria potestas*.[3] It was a power never questioned throughout the whole of Republican history, and which received no legal limitations until the time of the Middle Empire.[4] Sometimes it was employed as a means of saving the honour of the family, and there are instances of the son guilty of theft, the daughter of unchastity, being thus put to death;[5] sometimes it was enforced in the interest of the state to punish a public crime.[6]

Although law is in a sense an outline of life, it would be very misleading to fill up the content of Roman private life by analogy with this harsh outline. Like most of the theory of Roman law it had little correspondence with the facts; and this non-correspondence of fact and theory is the source of the strength and the beauty of Roman family life. If legal obligations do not exist between husband and wife, father and child, their place, in a civilised community, must be taken by moral obligations; and the very absence of legal sanctions will make these moral bonds peculiarly strong. It was so with the Roman family. It was an isolated, self-existent unit. The members clung closely to one another and to their head. The power of the father—the source of the unity of the household —fostered the devotion to the hearth, the love of home, which

---

[1] This *vindicatio filii* was in later Roman law replaced by a writ issued by the praetor (*interdictum de liberis exhibendis*), the effects of which were like that of Habeas Corpus.   [2] Dionys. ii. 26, 27.   [3] Gell. v. 19, 9.

[4] Hadrian punished the killing of a son with deportation (*Dig.* 48, 8, 5); Constantine declared it *parricidium*.

[5] Instances are given in Voigt (*Zwölf Tafeln* ii. 94). M. Fabius Buteo (223-218 B.C.) put his son to death as a punishment for theft (Oros. iv. 13), and a certain Pontius Aufidianus his daughter for immorality (Val. Max. vi. 1, 3); there are also instances of banishment inflicted by the father, presumably under the threat of inflicting the death penalty if the children returned.

[6] We may cite two instances lying at the very extremes of Republican history, the semi-mythical one of L. Junius Brutus in 509 (Plut. *Popl.* 6, 7), and the historical one of A. Fulvius Nobilior, who in 63 B.C. put his son to death for partnership in the Catilinarian conspiracy (Sall. *Cat.* 39).

is such a distinctive attribute of the Roman. It created the belief that the members of the household, owing allegiance to a common chief, should act loyally by one another in all the relations of life, and loyalty to a living head begat loyalty to his predecessors; traditions of this union as persisting under the rule of a long line of deceased ancestors, account for the hereditary policy of Roman houses — the championship of principles advocated for centuries by such clans as the Valerii, the Porcii, and the Claudii.

The moral influence on the *pater* was also great. He defends, not his own selfish rights, but the rights of a corporation dependent on him; "self-help" is the essence of the principles of early Roman law. In private matters the authority of the state is weak, that of the individual strong. The rule of the Roman father was the benevolent despotism that embraces many within the sphere of its despotic interests, that forces others to observe its rights because its interests are *not* personal, that produces a deep sense of moral and religious responsibility towards the weak, a stern unyielding attitude towards the man who would infringe upon their rights. The only "individual" known to Roman law is the *pater-familias*, but his was a glorified individuality, which, through its rule over the family, gathered strength to rule the world.

If it be thought that the loss of character must have been proportionally great in the case of the dependent members of the household, it must be remembered that the *patria potestas* is, for the individual, a transitory condition of things. Each subject member is preparing himself to be a *pater* in his own right. With the death of the existing head, *all* the hitherto dependent members are freed from the *potestas ;* each forms a *familia* of his own ; even his grandchildren by predeceased sons become heads of houses ; the daughters are also freed from power, although, out of deference to the weakness of the sex, they are still under guardianship (*tutela*).[1] The family splits up into a number of *familiae*, and none of these is of more importance than the

---

[1] Modern writers are inclined to reject the appeal made to the *sexus fragilitas* by the Roman jurists, and to believe that the original motive lay in the desire to keep the property of the family together (cf. Czyhlarz *Inst.* p. 275) ; but, as this motive did not operate in the case of sons, it is difficult to see why it should have done so in the case of the wife or daughters, apart from a belief in the incapability of women to defend their own claims. For the motive underlying the *tutela mulierum* see p. 31.

other. For the evils of primogeniture were unknown to Roman law. No hereditary caste based on the accident of birth was ever formed; and when we find an aristocracy of birth arising, it is the fittest son who can succeed his father in political office; for the bulk of the property, on which political influence was based, has not passed into the hands of some incapable elder brother.

But, apart from the moral checks on the authority of the father, which the absence of legal restraints made peculiarly strong, the civil law, public opinion, and the positive morality which found expression through certain religious or semi-religious organs, did impose certain restraints on a possible abuse of power. If the father is a lunatic (*furiosus*) he is, with his property, put under the care of his next of kin;[1] if he is wasteful (*prodigus*) and is squandering the property, of which (though legally it is his own) he is regarded only as the trustee, he is debarred from all commercial relations (*commercium*),[2] and prohibited from disposing of goods of which he is an unworthy administrator.

A very real customary control, one not actually enjoined by the civil law, but enforced by the powerful sovereign, which the Romans called the custom of their ancestors (*mos majorum*), was the obligation incumbent on the father of consulting a council of relatives (*consilium domesticum*) before taking any extreme step with respect to the members of his family. This was never limited to the agnatic circle; it admitted blood relations and relatives by marriage, while personal friends outside the family might be summoned as well.[3] Any severe punishment of a child and the divorce of a wife had to be submitted to the judgment of this assembly. How strong the sentiment in favour of this procedure was may be judged from the fact that in later times we find the censor (in Republican times the personal exponent of the moral sense of the community) degrading a senator who had divorced his wife

---

[1] p. 16.

[2] Ulp. *Reg.* 12, 2 " Lex xii. Tab. prodigum, cui bonis interdictum est, in curatione jubet esse agnatorum"; cf. Ulp. in *Dig.* 27, 10, 1 "Lege xii. Tab. prodigo interdicitur bonorum suorum administratio." There can be no doubt of the antiquity of this interdiction of the "prodigus," proceeding as it does from the theory that the property belongs to the family rather than to its head; but from what authority it proceeded in the earliest period of Roman history is uncertain.

[3] See the account in Val. Max. v. 8, 2 (p. 23) "adhibito propinquorum et amicorum consilio."

without taking advice of the family council.[1] The sentiment was but one expression of the principle which runs through the whole of Roman life, that no man should act in an important matter without taking counsel of those best qualified to give it.

Certain extreme abuses of the paternal power were prohibited by religious law (*fas*), which in such cases enjoins *capital* penalties. By a supposed law of Romulus, a man who sells his wife is to be sacrificed to the infernal gods; if he divorces her without due cause, half of his property is to be confiscated to his wife and half to the goddess Ceres.[2] With the secularisation of Roman law such penalties disappeared, and it is questionable whether they often required enforcement,[3] for such religious bans are mainly the expression of a strong moral sentiment.

Lastly, there was the principle that the paternal power cannot interfere with the *jus publicum*. It is a principle that applies both to persons and to property. In its first application it means that the son can exercise his vote independently of the paternal control; that he can fill a magistracy which subjects his father to his command; that, at least in later times, even the function of guardianship (*tutela*) can be exercised without the father's will; for this, too, is a public duty.[4] With respect to property, public law, though not infringing on the theory that all goods belong to the *paterfamilias*, yet does not regard them as the object of purely individual ownership. The father is rather a trustee than an owner, and even under the Servian constitution, that is, according to tradition, before the close of the monarchy, the value of a freehold is taken to qualify the members of the *familia*, not merely its head, for service to the state, and ultimately for the exercise of political rights.[5]

[1] Val. Max. ii. 9, 2 "M. Val. Maximus et C. Junius Brutus Bubulcus censores . . . L. Annium senatu moverunt, quod, quam virginem in matrimonium duxerat, repudiasset, nullo amicorum in consilio adhibito." See Greenidge *Infamia in Roman Law* p. 65.   [2] Dionys. ii. 26, 27.

[3] For the alleged lateness of divorce at Rome, even after the Twelve Tables had freely permitted it, see Gell. iv. 3 (*Infamia in Roman Law* p. 65).

[4] *Dig.* i. 6, 9 (Pomponius) "filius familias in publicis causis loco patris familias habetur, veluti ut magistratum gerat, ut tutor detur." Compare the story in Liv. xxiv. 44 (213 B.C.) "Pater filio legatus ad Suessulam in castra venit"—the consul went to meet him; and the old man on horseback passed eleven lictors—"ut consul animadvertere proximum lictorem jussit et is, ut descenderet ex equo, inclamavit, tum demum desiliens, 'Experiri,' inquit, 'volui, fili, satin' scires consulem te esse." Cf. Gell. ii. 2.

[5] Festus s.v. *Duicensus* (p. 66) "dicebatur cum altero, id est cum filio census."

An instance of the triumph of the state in its conflict with
private property is furnished by the position of the bondsman
(*nexus*). It may be appropriately discussed here ; for the *nexus*
is in private law practically in the position of the son under
power. He was a man who had contracted a debt on the
security of his person,[1] and who, on non-fulfilment of that
obligation, had had his body and his services attached by the
creditor. In private law he is a slave ; in public law he is a
free-born Roman citizen, and may be summoned for service in
the legions when the state needs his help.

It would be an anachronism to enter on a full treatment of
Roman slavery in connexion with the beginnings of Roman
history. Almost all that we know of the legal relations of
slaves to their masters, of their capacities and their disabilities,
their hopes of freedom, their position in the home, and their
influence on the public life of the city, refers to a far later
period. Yet the class doubtless existed from the earliest times,
and as Roman legal conceptions became modified but never
completely altered by the course of time, it is possible to give
a faint outline of the conditions of slavery in the Regal and
early Republican periods.

Slavery may at all periods of the history of Rome be defined
as an absence of personality. The slave was a thing (*res*) and
belonged to that more valuable class of chattels which the
Romans called *res mancipi*, and which included land and beasts
of burden. He was, therefore, a part of the homestead (*familia*),[2]
the transfer of any portion of which required the most solemn
forms of Roman law. As a thing, the master is said to exercise
dominium over him ; he might deal with him as he pleased, and
had over him the power of life and death. The slave, on the
other hand, has not only no rights against his master, but cannot
conclude legal relations with others. He has no legal relatives,
no legal wife ; he may be permitted to retain the fruits of his

---

[1] Probably by a *mancipatio fiduciae causa*, one, i. e., by which he had formally
transferred (*mancipavit*) his body on the condition that it was not to be seized
for a certain time, and that the transfer should be dissolved (*solutio nexi*) if the
debt were paid within this time.

[2] Ulpian *Reg.* 19, 1 ; Gaius ii. 15. *Res mancipi* at a later period included
lands in Italy (with their servitudes), slaves and *quadrupedes quae dorso collove
domantur*. In the expression *familia pecuniaque*, "familia" probably denotes
the slaves. Pierron (*Du sens des mots familia pecuniaque*) has shown the theory
of Ihering and Cuq, that the former denotes *res mancipi*, the latter *res nec mancipi*,
to be untenable.

own labour, but even his master's will cannot make it his
property. How far this " thing " possessed a potential personality
we do not know—how far, that is, the personality inherent in
him could be realised by subsequent emancipation. Liberation
could at best have raised the slave to the condition of the client
at this early period—a slight ascent in the scale of actual
rights, but one that might have been valued for the greater
personal freedom and the surer guarantee of religious protection
which it gave. But the fact that the slave is a part of the
homestead, and at the same time an intelligent being, makes him
in the truest sense a member of the family. The owner is said to
have power (*potestas*) over him, a word which is used only of rule
over reasonable beings ; and this *dominica potestas* does not differ
essentially from the *patria potestas* which is exercised over the
son. The treatment of the two was doubtless different, for the
one would some day be a lord, the other would remain a slave,
but their legal relation to the *dominus* was the same.

But the legal status of the slave is no true index of his
condition. This will depend on two factors, his origin and
his *social* relations to his master; and on both these grounds
the early slavery of Rome must have compared favourably with
that of later times. The slave trade was probably unknown,
and the condition must have been mainly the result of capture
in war from neighbouring states. Slavery is not altogether
degrading when it is wholly the consequence of the laws of
war. The slave was an Italian, perhaps of as noble birth as his
master, and this, though it may have aggravated the bitterness
of the lot, must have rendered possible an intimate social intercourse which would not have been possible with the barbarian,
and must have forced on the master's mind the conviction that a
sudden turn in fortune's wheel might place *him* in the same
position in the city of his serf. Again, the servitude was domestic;
whether employed in the home, or on the common lands of the
clan, or on the petty plot of ground that the master called
his own, the slave was never severed from his master or his
master's kindred. We hear in early times of his sitting at
his master's table,[1] and of his being the tutor and playmate of
his lord's children.[2] He may in some cases have been better off
than the client or the unattached Plebeian engaged in some petty
trade. Certainly the opportunities for the primitive culture

[1] Plut. *Cato maj.* 3.   [2] Plut. *Cor.* 24.

afforded by the Roman household were more open to him than to the other orders excluded from the Patriciate. In the case of domestic slavery extending over a small area, public opinion is generally a powerful restraint on the master's caprice. We do not know whether this opinion found a religious expression in such principles as those which protected the client's rights; but the fact that the censor of the later Republic, who perpetuates the obligations of religious law, punishes acts of cruelty committed by the *dominus*,[1] may show that the slave was not wholly without the pale of divine protection.

If, as we have seen, the Roman's chief mode of livelihood, the land, was not his own property but that of the clan, no individual disposition of it during lifetime or after death was possible, although there may have been some right of bequest over the movables classed as *res nec mancipi*. When the theory of common possession was modified by the recognition of a heritable allotment, bequest may have become possible; but doubtless intestate inheritance still continued to be the rule. A law of inheritance is first known to us from the Twelve Tables, which allowed the utmost freedom of bequest and legacy; but there was a survival both of theories and practices which show that testamentary disposition was originally regarded as the exception and not the rule.

First, we may notice that even in later times the immediate heirs of a man were regarded as having a claim to property, a kind of potential ownership, during the lifetime of the *pater*, and that inheritance is regarded merely as a continuation of ownership (*dominium*);[2] and in accordance with this view we find the practice of holding an inheritance in joint ownership, the co-heirs bearing the name of *consortes*.[3]

Secondly, the earliest testaments of which we have knowledge were public acts performed before the *comitia* of the people. The most ancient was the patrician form of testament—the *testamentum comitiis calatis*—effected at the *comitia curiata* which

---

[1] See the section on the censor.

[2] Paulus in *Dig.* 28, 2, 11 "in suis heredibus evidentius apparet continuationem dominii eo rem perducere, ut nulla videatur hereditas fuisse, quasi olim hi domini essent, qui etiam vivo patre quodammodo domini existimantur." What the *filius familias* acquires by the death of his father is merely *libera bonorum administratio*.

[3] Gell. i. 9 "Tamquam illud fuit anticum consortium, quod jure atque verbo Romano appellabatur 'ercto non cito'"; Serv. in *Aen.* viii. 642 "'citae' divisae, ut est in jure 'ercto non cito,' id est patrimonis vel hereditate non divisa."

were summoned (*calata*) twice a year for this purpose.[1] The
original purpose of this public testament is obscure. It is possible
that originally it took place when there was no direct heir (*suus
heres*) to receive the inheritance, and that it was accompanied
by some form of adoption of a successor. The person adopted
might have been the son belonging to another family ; although
of such a procedure there is no further trace in Roman law.[2]

The publicity of the act and the infrequency of its occurrence
show how exceptional a will must have been, and that the
normal mode of succession was that by intestacy. But we have
no warrant for saying that this testament at the *comitia calata*
was an act of private legislation and was permitted by the
assembled burgesses. The gathering was perhaps merely a form,
and the persons assembled may have acted only as witnesses ;[3]
but the very publicity would have made it almost impossible to
pass over a son of the family, unless there were expressed grounds
for his disinheritance.

The second kind of public will was the military testament
(*in procinctu*),[4] but our authorities leave us in doubt as to whether
this testament could be made in any gathering of the soldiers
prepared to meet the enemy and in any place, or whether it was
a formal act possible only in the great gathering of the *exercitus*
in the Campus Martius—that gathering which was finally
organised as a legislative assembly, existed by the side of the
assembly of the Curies, and came to be known as the *comitia
centuriata*.

---

[1] Gell. xv. 27 "Isdem comitiis, quae 'calata' appellari diximus, et sacrorum
detestatio et testamenta fieri solebant. Tria enim genera testamentorum fuisse
accepimus ; unum, quod calatis comitiis in populi contione fieret, alterum in procinctu, cum viri ad proelium faciendum in aciem vocabantur, tertium per familiae
emancipationem, cui aes et libra adhiberetur" ; Gaius ii. 101 "aut calatis
comitiis faciebant, quae comitia bis in anno testamentis faciendis destinata erant ;
aut in procinctu, id est, cum belli causa arma sumebant." Cf. Ulpian (*Reg.* 20,
2) on the *testamentorum genera tria*.

[2] This testament is never associated with adrogation, although this took place
before the same assembly.

[3] In Gell. (cited n. 1) it is associated with the *sacrorum detestatio* (see p. 16),
and perhaps this was its main object. The pontiffs and people had to be satisfied
that the *sacra* would be continued and the family not become extinct.

[4] See the passages of Gellius, Gaius, and Ulpian, cited n. 1, and compare
Festus p. 225 "procincta classis dicebatur, cum exercitus cinctus erat Gabino
cinctu confestim pugnaturus." In the second century B.C. we find some kind of
military testament, called by this name, made by Roman soldiers in Spain
(Velleius ii. 5 "facientibus . . . omnibus in procinctu testamenta, velut ad
certam mortem eundum foret ").

In the first case it may have been an old patrician form of testament, an informal will permitted in an emergency, perhaps to enable a childless soldier to transmit his inheritance. We do not know whether it had absolute validity, or only a validity dependent on circumstances, such as the absence of direct heirs, or the satisfaction of religious conditions approved by subsequent pontifical scrutiny; on this hypothesis the comrades of the testator could hardly have acted other than as witnesses to the will.

On the second hypothesis it would have a closer analogy to the testament made in the *comitia calata*, and may have been introduced only when Plebeians were admitted to political rights in this assembly. It is true that this is not a necessary conclusion, for the *patres* gathered armed for war in the Campus long before the enrolment of the Plebs for military duties or their admission to political rights; but we may at least say that, when this enrolment and admission were effected, this form of testament could be used by the Plebeians. If we accept the traditional date for the Servian constitution, it was common to the two orders before the close of the monarchy.

But there was a third type of will, one purely plebeian, which from the comparative simplicity of its form and the readiness with which it could be employed (since it did not depend either on chance or formal gatherings of the people) gradually came, in its subsequent developments, to replace all others, and became the prevailing Roman form of testament-making. This was the testament *per aes et libram*, one use of the *mancipatio* or solemn transference of property " by the copper and the scales." In the form in which it is known to us, it is a late development, for the sale of the property has entirely ceased to be a real, and has become a fictitious sale; the mancipation in fact has become a mere formality, and its employment is said to have been dependent on the condition that the testator "subita morte urguebatur"[1]—a condition which implies that the comitial testament could in ordinary cases be resorted to. But as the Plebs had originally no access to this form of will, the testament *per aes et libram* must have been in use among them long before its recognition as a form valid for the whole community. It was then regarded as a mere formal application of the mancipation

---

[1] Gaius ii. 102 "Qui neque calatis comitiis, neque in procinctu testamentum fecerat, is, si subita morte urguebatur, amico familiam suam, id est, patrimonium suum mancipio dabat, eumque rogabat, quod cuique post mortem suam dari vellet."

to a special emergency, and as supplementary to the comitial testament; until its superior utility came to be recognised, the sentiment in favour of a free disposition of property grew to be strong, and the Twelve Tables, which effected the triumph of plebeian over patrician forms of procedure, recognised it as the normal mode of testate disposition.

By this act the testator, in the presence of five witnesses and the *libripens*, transferred the whole of his patrimony (*familia*) into the custody and guardianship of a person called "the purchaser of the family" (*familiae emptor*). In order to make a legal disposition of his property the vendor makes a formal announcement of the purport of the sale, and the buyer, as he pays the single copper coin for the patrimony, repeats the same form of words, "Let my custody and guardianship of your patrimony be purchased by this coin, to the effect that you may make a legal testament in accordance with public law."[1] The words, which may not represent the most ancient formula, show that the *familiae emptor* is a mere trustee. Although the transference does not appear to have been conditioned by any express stipulation on the part of the vendor,[2] it was understood that it should only take effect on the death of the testator. On this the *familiae emptor* becomes guardian of the patrimony. He is not an heir but an executor, who distributes the property in accordance with the instructions of the testator from whom he has purchased.

The second stage is reached by the added importance given to the form of instruction (*nuncupatio*) uttered by the vendor. The Twelve Tables gave absolute validity to such instructions,[3] and the mere expression of the will of the testator came to be considered the essential part of the testament. In this announcement a true heir (*heres*) could be mentioned, and the *familiae emptor* sinks into the background. It is true that his presence is still necessary to the ceremony; he still professes to take the patrimony into his guardianship; but, like the man who holds the scales and the five witnesses, he is merely a formal assistant.

---

[1] Gaius ii. 104 "Familiam pecuniamque tuam endo mandatela tutela custo-delaque mea, quo tu jure testamentum facere possis secundum legem publicam, hoc aere esto mihi empta." For *familia pecuniaque* see p. 24.

[2] The stipulation that it was a trust would still have taken the patrimony wholly from the testator during the remainder of his life. We hear nothing about the formal reservation of a life interest.

[3] "Cum nexum faciet mancipiumque, uti lingua nuncupassit ita jus esto."

The testament has ceased to be a contract; it is a one-sided expression of will and an arbitrary disposition of property. It may be either verbal or written; the last stage in the history of the civil testament is reached when the testator is allowed to exhibit a document to the witnesses of the mancipation with these words, "These waxen tablets contain my will and bequest; I ask you, Quirites, for your testimony."[1]

Thus at a very early stage of Roman history, perhaps as early as the middle of the fifth century B.C., a man could exercise the most absolute power over the disposal of his goods. The only limitation was that the direct heirs (*sui heredes*) must be formally disinherited if they were to lose their rights. A mere passing over of a *filius familias* without formal disinheritance (*exheredatio*) rendered the will invalid; and in this case the *sui* succeeded to the vacant estate.

The social and political effects of such a dangerous liberty as the right of arbitrary testamentary disposition depend upon its use, and its use depends on the character of the people. The Roman character was, at all periods of history, devoted to the hereditary theory. It is one that was so strongly believed in that it asserted itself in spheres where it was never contemplated —during the later Republic in succession to office, in the early Empire in the succession to the Principate—and as applied to property it was an essential condition of the permanence of the Roman family. For the maintenance of a house a rigid system of intestate inheritance is bad; it may not produce great wealth, but it often produces great poverty. The only satisfactory system is a minute examination of each particular case by the state or by individuals. Such a control by the state was utterly alien to the *laisser faire* principles of the Roman, and history shows that the Decemvirs were right when they entrusted this discretionary power wholly to the *pater*. His functions as trustee were but extended to a period beyond his lifetime, and freedom of bequest was used as a means of equitable adjustment of property to the circumstances of the members of the family. The son who had made a rich marriage need not receive so much; the one destined to carry on the family traditions of office might receive more than the others. To him the *heredium* might be given, while the younger sons were drafted into colonies. We do not

[1] Gaius ii. 104 "Haec ita, ut in his tabulis cerisque scripta sunt, ita do, ita lego, ita testor, itaque vos, quirites, testimonium mihi perhibetote."

know the principles; but that the principles tended to the preservation of the family is proved by the long traditions of the noble Roman houses.

A legal view of the Roman family would be incomplete without consideration of the rights or infringement of rights dependent on it.

The full legal status of a Roman citizen was designated by the word *caput*. It denoted all the rights that he possessed, but primarily it is a conception of public law, for the possession of private was originally regarded as an annexe to the possession of public rights. Thus *caput* is retained even though the exercise of private rights is hindered for a time, as it is in the case of a son under power; the *filius familias* possesses a *caput*, although it is modified by his subjection to his father. This theory of the dependence of private on public rights, common to Greek and Roman law, probably accounts for the perpetual tutelage of women. The *materfamilias* holds an honourable position in the household; she is its queen, as her husband is its king, but yet she is subjected by marriage to the legal position of her own daughter, and, on her husband's death, is in the custody of her sons; for a primitive society cannot be brought to believe that a being who cannot fight, and may not fill offices of state or exercise a vote, is capable of looking after its own interests. Appearance before a court of law at Rome, whether for the purpose of defending one's own or another's rights, was regarded as a public act; and Roman sentiment so strongly disapproved a woman's taking part in public life that, when one was found bold enough to plead her cause in the Forum, the Senate in alarm made an official inquiry of the gods what the portent signified.[1] It is possible that in the earliest stage of Roman law women were not regarded as having any rights to defend; later they are regarded as having rights, and therefore a *caput*, but as incapable of defending them. When, in the latest stage, the disabilities of sex disappear partly through enactment,[2] but chiefly through a series of legal fictions, the capacity of women to defend their own interests first emerges.[3]

---

[1] Plut. *Comp. Lyc. c. Num.* 4 λέγεται γοῦν ποτε γυναικὸς εἰπούσης δίκην ἰδίαν ἐν ἀγορᾷ πέμψαι τὴν σύγκλητον εἰς θεοῦ, πυνθανομένην, τίνος ἄρα τῇ πόλει σημεῖον εἴη τὸ γεγενημένον.

[2] Such as the *lex Claudia*, which abolished the *legitima tutela agnatorum* (Gaius i. 171).

[3] A trace of the old disability survives in the prohibition of advocacy to

The limitation by which a series of civil rights is destroyed is spoken of as a "lessening of *caput*" (*capitis deminutio*). It is in every case an infringement of rights already possessed by the individual. Now the loss of public rights could only follow on a loss of citizenship; but this is not the diminution but the annihilation of *caput*, and could not therefore in the earliest stage of Roman law (when there was no status recognised but that of citizenship) be called a *capitis deminutio*. The term must have been wholly confined to a loss of private rights, i.e. to the loss of the rights conveyed by the control of a *familia*.[1] Thus the *adrogatus* suffers a lessening of *caput* by passing into the power of another. But a change from a higher to a lower status (even when the higher did not imply active rights) may at an early period have been regarded as an infringement of *caput*. We know, for instance, that the *datio in mancipium* of a son of a family was thought (at what period is uncertain) to involve it, because the child passes from a better to a worse station, although in his former condition he had no active rights of his own. It is stranger still that, certainly at an early period, the fact of a woman's passing into her husband's power (*conventio in manum*) was held to have this consequence. It is one that is scarcely intelligible in the case of a *filia familias* who passes from one *potestas* to another; but in the case of a woman only under the burden, lighter and ever tending to be more relaxed, of the *tutela* of her relatives, it is a natural though not strictly legal conception.[2] Some other applications of the system are still more artificial, and are perhaps creations of late Roman jurists who came to consider that the essence of a loss of *caput* was a change of status (*status commutatio*).[3] Thus adoption, which is the change

women ; the praetors declined to grant them a formula on behalf of others. A certain Carfania (Gaia Afrania) "inverecunde postulans et magistratum inquietans" is said to have been the occasion of this rule (Ulp. in *Dig.* 3, 11, 5).

[1] This usage was preserved in the praetor's edict ; he spoke of "qui quaeve . . . capite deminuti deminutaeve esse dicentur" (*Dig.* 4, 5, 2, 1), meaning what the later jurists call *cap. dem. minima*, i.e. loss of *familia*.

[2] See Eisele "Zur Natur u. Geschichte der capitis deminutio" in *Beiträge zur Römischen Rechtsgeschichte* p. 160. He combats the counter view that *capitis dem.* meant an annihilation of personality. Mommsen (*Staatsr.* iii. 8) takes this latter view—a natural result of juristic refinement, but a conception that would have been quite unintelligible to a primitive community.

[3] Gaius i. 162 "Minima capitis deminutio est, cum et civitas et libertas retinetur, sed status hominis commutatur ; quod accidit in his qui adoptantur, item in his quae coemptionem faciunt, et in his qui mancipio dantur, quique ex mancipatione manumittuntur."

from one *potestas* to another, and even manumission, which is the freedom from power, were supposed to involve it. These applications contain some historical truth only in so far as both these changes involve a temporary mancipation.

The original *capitis deminutio* is thus a purely private law conception and implies the distinction between persons *sui juris* and *alieni juris*. To the first category belong those who are free from the power of another, to the latter those who are under the *potestas, manus,* and *mancipium;* amongst citizens, therefore, the son, the wife, and any one mancipated to another. The person *alieni juris* is not altogether devoid of private rights, but they are singularly incomplete in their effects. Thus the son under power has the right of marriage (*conubium*), but the children of the marriage are not in his power but in his father's; he has (if not in the earliest period, yet throughout the greater part of Roman history) the right of taking part in the legal business of trade (*commercium*), yet all that he acquires by this business belongs to his father. In his case, however, the condition is transitory, while in the case of the slave and the *mancipatus* (apart from the possibility of emancipation) it is permanent.

Conversely, the fact of being *sui juris* does not always imply freedom of action; this might be limited through consideration of age or sex. Minors and women may be free from *potestas,* but the former were subject to a temporary, the latter originally to a perpetual *tutela.*

§ 4. *The Citizens and the Political Subdivisions of the State*

The whole collection of Roman citizens forms the *populus Romanus quiritium,*[1] or *populus Romanus quirites.*[2] Of the terms thus placed in apposition, *populus Romanus* is the more general descriptive name, and *quirites* the official title by which the citizens are addressed in the assembly. Yet both words appear to have the same signification; *populus* is the armed host,[3] and the *quirites* are the "bearers of the lance."[4] If the latter etymology is

---

[1] Liv. i. 32. [2] Gell. i. 12, 14 ; x. 24, 3.
[3] Mommsen (*Staatsr.* iii. 3, n. 2) connects the word with *populari.* The *magister populi* (i.e. the dictator) is master of the infantry host.
[4] Varro ap. Dionys. ii. 48. Other views derived it from the Sabine town Cures (Varro *L.L.* v. 51 ; Strabo v. 3, 1) or connected it with *Curia* (Lange *Röm. Alt.* i. p. 89 ; Belot *Hist. d. Chev. Rom.* i. p. 312).

correct, the word *quirites* came, by a course of development which
finds many parallels in Roman history, to mean exactly the
opposite of its original signification. At the end of the Republic
it signifies the citizens in their purely civil capacity, wearing the
toga, the garb of peace, and exercising political functions within
the city; Caesar once quelled a mutiny of his legions by
addressing them as *quirites*, showing by this address that they
were disbanded and were no longer soldiers.[1]

A more real historical difficulty with respect to the original
connotation of these words, is to determine whether they denoted
the whole people, Plebeians as well as Patricians. Roman
records do not use *populus* as equivalent to the patrician community alone; but these records all refer to a time after the
Plebeians had won political rights, at least the rights of serving
in the legions and of voting. If *populus* and *quirites* denoted
the aggregate of fighting, and therefore privileged, men, they
must have originally referred exclusively to the patrician community. After the Servian constitution the words denote the
whole people (*universus populus*). *Populus* and *plebs* are henceforth only distinguished as the whole to the part—the distinction being necessary, since the Plebs continued to form a
corporation apart, and this corporation excluded the patrician
families.[2] So, in a later official formula, *senatus populusque
Romanus* denotes two corporations, the latter composed of all
the members of the state, but in this the individual members of
the smaller corporation are included.

Civis, a word of uncertain origin, signifies less definitely than
quirites the possession of active political rights. Hence its
application to women and to the partially-privileged members of
the state—to those who were, at certain periods of Roman
history, given rights in private law, while debarred from the
exercise of the suffrage or the attainment of office. It is possible
that the distinction between the full citizen (*civis optimo jure*)
and the partial citizen (*civis non optimo jure*), although probably
not a primitive,[3] may yet be an ancient conception of Roman

---

[1] Suet. *Jul.* 70.

[2] Capito ap. Gell. x. 20 "Plebes . . . in qua gentes civium patriciae non
insunt: plebiscitum . . . est . . . lex, quam plebes, non populus, accipit."
Cf. Festus p. 233.

[3] According to the primitive conception private are dependent on public rights ;
see p. 31. But the growth of the Plebs, and alliances with other states, had
effected many modifications in this conception.

law. Those Plebeians who had never been, or who had ceased to be, entirely dependent on a *patronus* for the exercise of their legal rights, would practically have belonged to this latter class. Before the reform of Servius, which gave them political privileges, they might have been called *cives ;* it is only after this reform that they could have been called *quirites.* It was, perhaps, in consequence of this change in the constitution that *cives* replaced *quirites* as the designation of the full citizens with reference to all their rights.

If we ask what the original rights of the citizen of Rome were, it is impossible to frame a simple category applicable to all the *cives.* Taking our stand at a period just before the Servian reforms, we find that private rights were possessed in varying degrees by all the members of the community. These rights are generally summed up as those of trade and of marriage (*commercii et conubii*). The first is the legal capacity to acquire full rights in every kind of property, to effect its acquisition, and to transfer it by the most binding forms, and to defend the acquired right in one's own person by Roman process of law (*legis actio*). This *commercium* was possessed equally by the Patricians and the free Plebeians. It was no infringement of the right of commerce that the right of occupying domain-land wrested from the enemy may for a long time have been possessed only by the dominant order ;[1] for such land was not acquired, but only held on a precarious tenure from the state, and the privilege was, perhaps, one of fact rather than of law. The *jus conubii* is the right to conclude a marriage which is regarded as fully valid by the state (*matrimonium legitimum* or *jure civili*), and which, therefore, gives rise to the *patria potestas.* This right was possessed by the Patricians and by at least the free Plebeians, but by each class only within itself. There was no right of intermarriage between the orders, and the member of each effected his position as a father by a different ceremony.[2] The rights consequent on membership of a clan—those of inheritance and of religious communion—were, as we saw, probably shared with the Patricians by those Plebeians at least whose ancestors had never been in a condition of clientship.

Public rights—those of voting, of serving as a fully-equipped soldier in the legions, and probably of holding office as a delegate

[1] Nonius, s.v. *plebitas,* p. 101 "Hemina in annalibus, 'Quicumque propter plebitatem agro publico ejecti sunt.'" Cf. Liv. iv. 48.   [2] p. 17.

of the king—were possessed exclusively by the Patricians ; and
to these privileges we must add the right of holding the fullest
communion with the gods (*jus auspiciorum*).

Auspicium, or the divination by birds, came eventually to be
applied to any circumstance that might be interpreted as an
expression of the will of the gods. The capacities of human
beings with reference to these signs are partly a right of invoking,
partly a power of interpreting them. Both the right and the
power rest on the assumption that there is a medium of intercourse between the national gods and the citizens of the state,[1]
and the peculiarities of the conception which the Romans formed
of this divine patronage are shown by their views both of the
nature of the revelation and of the qualifications requisite for
the "medium."

(i.) The revelation is not an answer to a question about future
events, for true divination is not an attempt to pry into the
hidden counsels of the gods ; this profession of the Chaldaeans
was never looked on with favour at Rome, and no science of the
future was encouraged by the state. The Roman consultation of
the gods is only employed as the test of the rightness of an already
formed human resolution.[2] It tells men only whether they are
to carry out a course of action already purposed ; it may confirm
them in it or warn them from it ; and it is the duty of men to
seek a sign either of encouragement or of warning. It is of the
highest importance to remember this view of the guidance of the
gods, for it is the chief sign of the way in which the Romans, in
spite of their genuinely religious spirit (nay, as an outcome of it),
subordinated the theocratic to the lay element. The chief effect
of this subordination is the unfettered use of human reason ;
religion is employed as a test, rather than as a guide, of rightness
of action. This is a thoroughly lay view of the function of
religion in life, very unlike that of the Jewish prophet who
questions God in detail, but only for interpretation of a law

---

[1] Cic. *de Leg.* ii. 13, 32 (on the question whether auspices were merely directed
to the *utilitas* of the state, or formed a true method of divination) "si enim
deos esse concedimus . . . et eosdem hominum consulere generi, et posse nobis
signa rerum futurarum ostendere ; non video cur esse divinationem negem."

[2] Cic. *de Div.* ii. 33, 70 (the difficulty of answering for results may appeal
to a *Marsus augur* but not to a Roman) "non enim sumus ii nos augures, qui
avium reliquorumve signorum observatione futura dicamus." Cf. i. 58, 132
"Non habeo . . . nauci Marsum augurem, non vicanos haruspices, non de circo
astrologos, non Isiacos conjectores, non interpretes somniorum. Non enim sunt
ii aut scientia aut arte divini."

which is the product of His, not of the human will. The belief
that the gods do not give instruction, but merely advice, gave an
" inward freedom " to the Roman, which made him at times resent
the divine interference, and we shall find many instances of his
forcing an interpretation to suit his wishes. The omen that is
not seen need not be attended to, and precautions are taken that
it shall not be seen. In undertaking acts of state, the magistrates are bound to ask for signs ; but all the efforts of human
ingenuity are directed to secure that the signs shall be favourable.[1]

(ii.) It is plain that, on this theory of religious intervention,
no priestly medium is required between the gods and their worshippers. Divination as the science of the future is an elaborate
art, which cannot be possessed by the ordinary man. It requires
the knowledge of ritual to compel the divine utterance ; it
assumes that the gods have special confidence in the select
participators of an inner cultus, to whom they reveal what is
hidden from the many ; it requires the devotion of a lifetime,
and often special rules of asceticism and purity, to interpret the
hidden signs ; it leads, in short, to the belief in oracular power,
in · the prophetic gift, in the claims of a priesthood specially
set apart.[2] There was none of this at Rome. The right of
invoking auspices is not a priestly gift ; it is one that is possessed,
in a higher degree by the magistrate, in a lower degree by all
the full citizens of the primitive Roman community. It is true
that there is a class of wise men, the augurs, whose chief function
is the interpretation of signs, but their function is limited to
interpretation ; they have no more power than any private individual, and less power than the magistrate, of eliciting such a
revelation. Yet, if the assistance of the augur was called in,
and his interpretation given, this verdict was final. We are told
that disobedience to it, at least by the magistrate in taking the
public auspices, was in early times visited with a capital penalty ;[3]
a statement which probably means that the heads of the Roman
religion, the pontiffs, reckoned such an impiety as one for which

[1] See the treatment of the auspices in the section on the magistracy (p. 163).
[2] Strangely enough the Greek belief in oracular or prophetic power did not
lead to the conception of a priesthood set apart from the people. But the Greek
science of divination, though associated with oracles and prophecy, did not aim
much higher than the Roman. Its object was generally to win approval for a
contemplated course of action.
[3] Cic. de Leg. ii. 8, 21 " Quaeque augur injusta, nefasta, vitiosa, dira defixerit,
inrita infectaque sunto ; quique non paruerit, capital esto."

the gods would accept no expiation, and for which, therefore, the penalty of excommunication (*sacer esto*) was pronounced.

The right of taking the auspices is said to have been a gift peculiar to the Patricians; but the extent of this gift can be estimated only with reference to a fourfold division of the auspices, which, from its nature, must have been primitive and not a creation of the later *disciplina* of the augurs.

The auspices were divided into *impetrativa* (or *impetrita*) and *oblativa*.[1] The *auspicia impetrativa* were those which were sought and asked for, and such signs might be taken from observation of the sky or from the flight or sounds of birds. The *oblativa* were those which were forced on the attention, and which, since they were not sought, were generally regarded as an impediment to action, and, therefore, as unfavourable. They were gathered from a heterogeneous collection of signs of ill-omen (*dirae*). It is plain that the right to take or, as it is expressed, to have auspices (*habere auspicia*) can refer only to the first of these two categories; it was this right that was assumed to be peculiar to the Patricians; it was the members of the original clans alone, the primitive *patres*, who had the right of asking signs of the gods, and it was held that every important act of their lives, whether public or private, should be pervaded by this divine intercourse. It was believed that it was through auspices that the city had been raised, political development attained, and former victories won.[2] The existence of the patrician order is from this point of view a necessary condition of the existence of the state itself, for without it the right of eliciting the divine will would be wholly lost.[3] But no human power could prevent the Plebeians from following the religious scruples of their betters in giving heed to those warnings which were thrust upon their notice. The *auspicia oblativa*, whether the gods destined them for others besides the patrician body or not, must from the earliest times have been respected by the Plebeians, and have guided their political conduct when they became a corporation within the state.

[1] Serv. ad *Aen.* vi. 190 "auguria aut oblativa sunt, quae non poscuntur, aut impetrativa, quae optata veniunt." For the categories of these two kinds of auspices see the discussion of the auspices in the section on the magistracy (p. 162).

[2] Liv. vi. 41 "Auspiciis hanc urbem conditam esse, auspiciis bello ac pace, domi militiaeque omnia geri, quis est qui ignoret?"

[3] This view is most fully expressed in the formalities of the *interregnum*. See the section which treats of this institution (p. 147).

The right of *taking* auspices was neither a priestly nor even
a magisterial function, but was possessed by every Patrician.
But the man in a private capacity could exercise it only in his
private concerns; the auspices destined to guide public action
are vested in the person of the patrician magistrate.   Hence the
distinction between *auspicia publica* and *privata*.   There was a
time when no important act of business or domestic life was
undertaken without an appeal for divine guidance.[1]   Marriage
especially demanded the taking of the auspices; and even when
the custom of such private divination had become wholly
discarded, a survival of the custom is found in the presence of
auspices, friends of the bridegroom who superintend the due
performance of the rites.[2]   The *confarreatio* was older than the
traditional institution of the augural college, and it is not
probable that official intervention was brought to bear on
marriage, still less on such concerns as were more strictly private.
Hence it is difficult to see how the Plebeians could have been
prevented from taking the *auspicia privata*, although their use
of them was probably scoffed at by their patrician rulers.   On
the one hand, we find that the incapacity of the Plebeians to
share in the auspices was one of the arguments used against
the permission of *conubium* between the orders;[3] on the other,
that the *auspex* continues to be an integral part of a ceremony
which was founded on plebeian marriage law.

It was different with the auspices taken on behalf of the
state (*auspicia publica*).   It is the Patricians alone who have
these auspices, and only a magistrate belonging to the order can
exercise the right of looking for them (*spectio*).[4]   This remains
not only a purely magisterial, but a purely patrician privilege,

[1] Cic. *de Div.* i. 16, 28 "Nihil fere quondam majoris rei, nisi auspicato, ne
privatim quidem, gerebatur: quod etiam nunc nuptiarum auspices declarant,
qui, re omissa, nomen tantum tenent." In i. 17, 31 we have the story of Attus
Navius taking auspices by *aves* in a private matter. Cf. Liv. vi. 41.

[2] Cic. *de Div.* i. 16, 28 (see last note); Suet. *Claud.* 26; Tac. *Ann.* xi. 27.

[3] Liv. iv. 2 "Quas quantasque res C. Canuleium adgressum? Conluvionem
gentium, perturbationem auspiciorum publicorum privatorumque adferre." Yet
this passage has only an indirect reference to the matrimonial *auspicia*. The
argument is that intermarriage would cause the pure Patriciate to disappear, and
with it the general right of taking *auspicia impetrativa*.

[4] Cic. *de Div.* ii. 36, 76 "a populo auspicia accepta habemus." The relation
of *auspicia habere* to the *spectio* is that the former denotes the abstract right of
questioning the gods, the latter its exercise in a particular case (Momms. *Staatsr.*
i. 89 n. 3). The specification by the magistrate of the signs which he wished
to see was known as *legum dictio* (Serv. ad *Aen.* iii. 89; cf. p. 43 n. 2).

and the so-called plebeian magistrates of later times, great as their power was, had not the gift. It is quite true that, after the Plebs had forced its way into the consulship, this right could not be denied to the plebeian holders of the supreme office. But the admission was based on the legal fiction that the holder of an office once reserved to the *patres* was, for religious purposes, a patrician magistrate.[1]

The enjoyment of full political rights in ancient Rome was conditioned only by membership of a patrician *gens ;* full citizenship here, as in most ancient states, being dependent on birth, and the membership of a purely private association satisfying all the demands that the state made as a condition of the attainment of its rights. But there were other forms of association of a definitely political character, amongst which the citizens were distributed, and as members of which they exercised active political rights or were subject to personal burdens. These were the three patrician tribes of Ramnes, Tities, and Luceres, and the thirty *curiae.* With reference to the question whether these were primary and natural associations of an ethnic character or artificial creations made by a supreme authority after the founding of Rome, we have already seen [2] that the *tribus* are probably an ethnic survival artificially employed ; in the case of the *curiae*, it must remain far less certain whether they were of spontaneous growth or purely artificial creations, or (what is perhaps more probable) in the main natural associations, artificially regulated in number and grouping to suit a political purpose.

The tribe, which was a division not merely of the citizen body but of the land, was the basis for taxation and the military levy.[3] We know nothing of the first burden, but it is probable that no detailed scheme of direct taxation existed in the early Roman state. The revenues from the king's domains probably rendered him self-sufficing, while the patrician burgesses served in the army at their own cost, and were doubtless expected to

---

[1] A similar confusion was at an earlier period introduced with reference to the givers of the auspices. They are said to be given by the people (Cic. *de Div.* ii. 36, 76 ; p. 39), but the great bulk of the people (i.e. the Plebs) did not possess them. [2] p. 3.

[3] Dionys. iv. 14 (Servius Tullius) τὰς καταγραφὰς τῶν στρατιωτῶν καὶ τὰς εἰσπράξεις τῶν χρημάτων . . . οὐκέτι κατὰ τὰς τρεῖς φυλὰς τὰς γενικάς, ὡς πρότερον, κ.τ.λ.   Varro *L.L.* v. 181 "Tributum dictum a tribubus, quod ea pecunia, quae populo imperata erat, tributim a singulis pro portione census exigebatur."

defray the expenses of their retainers. It is probable that in cases of emergency a tax in kind was levied from the landholders of the tribes.

Of the military burdens tradition has preserved some plausible details. The army was known as the *legio* or "gathering,"[1] and was composed of three "thousands" (*milites*),[2] one from each of the three tribes. These foot-soldiers were commanded by three or nine tribal officers, the *tribuni militum*.[3] The cavalry consisted of three hundred *celeres*, one from each of the three tribes, each commanded by three *tribuni celerum*. When the Patriciate was enlarged by the addition of the *gentes minores*,[4] these three hundreds (*centuriae*) were increased to six.[5]

Besides the heavy infantry and the cavalry, there may have been a corps of light-armed troops (*velites* and *arquites*), and these would doubtless have been composed mainly of clients. We do not know whether the free Plebeians were forced to serve; but, if they did, it would only have been in this inferior capacity, which required no time for training and no cost of maintaining a panoply. It is evident that the whole burden of the regular levy, and of such war-taxation as then existed, fell upon the Patricians, and before the close of the monarchy an effort was made to remedy this unequal distribution of burdens—an effort which had as its result the abolition of the patrician tribes as the leading divisions of the state and a serious infringement of patrician rights.

The thirty *curiae*, originally local units, as is proved by their names,[6] were divided, ten into each of the three tribes. The members of the clans belonging to the same *curia* were called *curiales*. But, although the *curiae* had local centres, membership of these bodies did not depend on residence in a given locality. It was hereditary; and if the members of a *gens* migrated from its *curia*, the *gentiles* were still members of that state-division. The *curiae* were religious as well as political associations, which

[1] From *legere*, Varro *L.L.* v. 87.
[2] Varro *L.L.* v. 89 "milites quod trium milium primo legio fiebat, ac singulae tribus Titiensium, Ramnium, Lucerum milia singula militum mittebant."
[3] ib. 81 "tribuni militum quod terni tribus tribubus Ramnium, Lucerum, Titium olim ad exercitum mittebantur." On the other hand, Servius (in *Aen.* v. 560) says that the *tribuni* were so called because they presided over one-third of the whole force.   [4] p. 12.   [5] Liv. i. 36.
[6] e.g. Calabra, Foriensis, Veliensis. Other names (such as Titia) may be eponymous.

had from the first, or finally developed, a close corporate life. Each had its peculiar *sacra*[1] and a place of worship, containing an altar and chapel, which itself bore the name *curia*;[2] and the religious affairs of each were conducted by a priest called *curio*, assisted by a *flamen curialis*.[3]   The thirty *curiones* formed a college, of which the *curio maximus* was the president.[4]

It is difficult to say how far the religious organisation of the *curiae* was a natural or artificial development.   But artifice was certainly at work in determining their important political character.   The primitive popular assembly at Rome is the *comitia curiata*, composed wholly of Patricians.   Here each member of a patrician clan above the legal age—probably the age of eighteen, at which military service commenced—had the right of giving a single vote ; a majority of the *curiales* decided the vote of the particular *curia*, and the decision of the assembly was determined by the majority of the groups.

They also had, in a secondary degree, an importance of a military kind ; for the supply of knights to the corps of *celeres* is said to have been effected through the *curiae*.[5]

§ 5.   *The Monarchical Constitution*

It is generally agreed that the monarchical constitution of early Rome rested on a limited sovereignty of the people, a power restricted by the extraordinary authority of their sole magistrate. This popular sovereignty was asserted in jurisdiction, in legislation, and in the ratification of magisterial power.   The attribution of the right of appeal in criminal cases (*provocatio*)[6] to the people shows that with them rests either the sovereign attribute of pardon or some right of trying criminal cases in the last resort. Tradition makes the Roman people the sole source of law,[7] that is, of standing ordinances of a general kind which are to bind the community,[8] although the initiative in legislation can come only

---

[1] Festus p. 62 "curionia sacra, quae in curiis fiebant"; p. 64 "curiales flamines curiarum sacerdotes."

[2] ib. p. 49 (s.v. *curia*) "locus est, ubi publicas curas gerebant."

[3] See note 1.   [4] Festus p. 126 ; Liv. xxvii. 8.

[5] Festus p. 55 "Celeres antiqui dixerunt, quos nunc equites dicimus . . . qui primitus electi fuerunt ex singulis curiis deni, ideoque omnino trecenti fuere."

[6] Liv. i. 26 ; Cic. *de Rep.* ii. 31, 54.   [7] Dionys. ii. 14.

[8] " Generale jussum " (Capito ap. Gell. x. 20).

from the king; and apart from the rulings of the pontifical
college, which did not require the sanction of the people, this
theory of primitive legislation seems to be correct; for the very
early laws passed by the *comitia* on the downfall of the monarchy
do not appear to mark any violent break in the theory of the
constitution.   We do not know whether the king employed the
formula afterwards used by the Republican magistrates, which
elicited the " will and command " of the burgesses (*velitis,
jubeatis, quirites*); but law (*lex*) is from the first something
"laid down" by a competent authority, and binding, therefore,
in virtue of the power that ordains it.[1]   After its ordinance it
may or must create a contractual relation between individuals,[2]
but there is no hint of its being the result of a contract or
co-operation between independent authorities.   The source of
law is, therefore, simple; it is the people's will; but, through
the bar to utterance created by the magistracy, this will is
very limited in its capacity for expression.   The people are also
affirmed to have been in a certain sense the source of honour,
and typical illustrations of this power are presented by the
traditional beliefs that the regal *insignia* of Etruria, adopted by
the kings of Rome, were only assumed by them with the consent
of Senate and people,[3] and that the appointment of officers for
special purposes, although these may have been in theory merely
delegates of the king, had to be ratified by laws of the *curiae*.
The quaestors, the earliest prototypes of the later magistrates
at Rome, are said to have been so appointed.[4]

The people, therefore, possessed certain sovereign rights, but
each right was limited by the vast authority of their personal
representative, who wielded the whole of the executive, and so
much of the legislative power as is implied in the sole right of
initiative.   We cannot even speak of the people as *vesting* this
power in their king; for their right of election was, as we shall
see, probably as limited as their power of legislation.

---

[1] *Lex* is probably connected etymologically with the German *legen* (Gothic
lagjan) as θεσμός with τίθημι.

[2] In business we have *leges locationis, venditionis*, in the structure of corporations a *lex collegii*.   On the other hand, in the *legum dictio* of augury, which is
the statement of the mode of the answer of the gods to a request, in the *lex data*
given to individuals by a magistrate (e.g. the *leges censoriae*) or granted by Rome
as a charter to a subject state, there seems to be the idea of a purely one-sided
ordinance.

[3] Dionys. iii. 62 ; Cic. *de Rep.* ii. 17, 31.

[4] Tac. *Ann.* xi. 22 ; Ulp. in *Dig.* i. 13.

This personal head possessed a variety of titles which marked the various aspects of his rule—titles which survived into the Republic, and, on the differentiation of the functions which he united, were applied to various magistrates. As supreme judge he was *judex*, as leader and commander in war *praetor*,[1] *dictator*, and *magister populi*.[2] The most general title which marked him out as universal head of the state, in religious as in civil matters, was that of *rex*, the "regulator" of all things human and divine —a title which survived in the *rex sacrorum*, the heir of the king in sacrifice and in ritual. The powers on which this position was based were summed up in the word *imperium*.[3]

The severance of the king from the state, over which he ruled, was also expressed in certain outward signs (*insignia*), which distinguished him from the rest of the burgesses. He was preceded by twelve "summoners" (*lictores*),[4] each carrying a bundle of rods (*fasces*), and the axe-head gleamed from these bundles even within the walls, for the king's military jurisdiction could be exercised within the city. His robe was of "purple," or rather of scarlet—the colour in which most nations have seen an emblem of sovereignty—but his dress probably varied with the ritual which he was performing, and the three kinds of striped garment (*trabea*) which survived in the Republic —that of purple for the priestly office, of purple and saffron for augury, of purple striped with white for the *rex*[5]—were probably all vestments of the king. Tradition also assigns him the eagle-headed sceptre, the golden crown, the throne (*solium*),[6] and the chariot within the walls, from which the curule chair (*sella curulis*) was believed to be derived.[7] The statement that

[1] Varro *L.L.* v. 80 "Praetor dictus, qui praeiret jure et exercitu." But the title is, perhaps, a purely military one (*prae-itor*, "the man who goes before the army").
[2] Festus p. 198 "in magistro populi faciendo, qui vulgo Dictator appellatur."
[3] Cic. *de Rep.* i. 26, 42. *Regnum* denotes the position of the king as head of the state (ib. ii. 27), but not the regal power.
[4] *Lictor* is probably derived from *licere*. For other attempts at derivation see Gell. xii. 3. They summon, not only to the assembly, but also to the courts, and are thus the chief mark of jurisdiction and coercive power (*coercitio*). The individual *curiae* were probably summoned by the thirty *lictores curiatii*, who survive into the later Republic. See Momms. *Staatsr.* i. p. 392. For the number of lictors that accompanied the king see Cic. *de Rep.* ii. 17, 31 ; Liv. i. 8 ; Dionys. ii. 29 ; iii. 61, 62.
[5] Serv. in *Aen.* vii. 188, 612 ; xi. 334 ; Ov. *Fast.* ii. 503.
[6] Cic. *de Fin.* ii. 21, 69 ; Dionys. iii. 61.
[7] Festus p. 49 "currules magistratus appellati sunt, quia curru vehebantur."

THE MONARCHICAL CONSTITUTION

the triumphal *insignia* of the Roman magistrate were but the revival of the ordinary adornments of the king[1] is extremely probable ; for the crown, the *toga picta* (a development of the purple robe),[2] and the chariot reappear in the Roman triumph.

Other royal prerogatives were connected with the primitive conception of a patriarchal monarchy. The king, although he lacks the absolutism of the *paterfamilias*, occupies much the same position in the state as the father does in the family. In a sense he is owner of the whole community, and as such capable of commanding the *munera* of the burgesses.[3] But a large portion of the public domain was more peculiarly set apart for his own private use.[4] This crown-land must have been worked mainly by the king's own clients, who held it *precario* from him ;[5] for there seems no reason to doubt the belief that a large proportion of the half-free Plebeians were in the immediate *clientela* of the king, connected with the community chiefly through him, its representative. These may have been captives who had submitted to the *fides* of the state, and whom their conqueror had not attached as dependants to other leading families of the community.

The theory of a kingship is best expressed in the mode in which the monarch ascends the throne. The alternative principles that have usually been recognised are the hereditary, the elective, or that of divine right.

Of the hereditary principle there is no trace at Rome. It is contradicted by the facts of the traditional history, which believed that, when the hereditary principle was first realised in the last king, the monarchy came to an end ; and it is expressly denied by later authors who reflected on the character of the early monarchy.[6] There is rather more to be said for the theory of divine right. Romulus is the son of a god and awaits the verdict of heaven before he assumes his rule. Numa, his successor, insists that the same verdict shall be appealed to.[7] But, if the taking of the auspices be the sign of a divine origin,

[1] Dionys. iv. 74.
[2] Festus p. 209 "Picta quae nunc toga dicitur purpurea ante vocitata est eaque erat sine pictura." It was already *picta* (διάχρυσος) in Polybius' time (Polyb. vi. 53).　　　　[3] Liv. i. 56.
[4] "Arvi et arbusta et pascui lati atque uberes" (Cic. *de Rep.* v. 2, 3). Cf. Liv. ii. 5.　　　　[5] p. 8.
[6] Cic. *de Rep.* ii. 12, 24 "Nostri illi etiam tum agrestes viderunt virtutem et sapientiam regalem, non progeniem quaeri oportere." Cf. App. *B.C.* i. 98.
[7] Liv. i. 7 and 18.

then everything in Rome proceeds almost equally from the gods. Probably in earlier as in later Rome religion played a most important subsidiary part in public life, but we have no warrant for believing that it was ever the sole guiding power. As we shall see, in discussing the question of the inauguration of the king, this theory raises into a primary and material what was merely a secondary and formal element in the transmission of the monarchy, although this formal element was one of the utmost necessity and importance.

The Roman thinkers were thus thrown back on the theory of election. Tradition is unanimous in representing the monarchy as elective—depending, i.e., on free popular election, or on such election guided by the Senate.[1] On the death of a king there is no immediate successor with a title to rule ; an interim-king (*interrex*) is appointed for a few days, and on his proposal a king is elected by the patrician burgesses at the *comitia curiata*, subject to the sanction of the patrician Senate (*auctoritas patrum*).[2]

In the expression of these views the Roman thinkers were attempting to reconstruct the monarchy from a knowledge of their own magistracy ; for they rightly believed that this magistracy was a very slight modification of the original kingship. The elective principle of the Republic was not regarded as a novelty in the theory of the magistracy, and there were two reasons for this view. The first was that there was a real continuity, for the elective process was always subsidiary to another, that of nomination by the magistrate who guided the elections. The latter became an almost formal process in the Republic, but the question was not asked whether at one time it may not have been the material element. Secondly, there was really an elective element in the monarchy, which survived as a form into the Republic, a form which the hypothesis of monarchical election adopted by Roman antiquarians could not explain. It is strange that, in seeking for their theory of regal appointment, they should not have appealed to the clearest survival of the monarchy, the dictatorship, on which so much of the rest of their reconstruction of the monarchical power was based.

---

[1] Liv. i. 17 ; Cic. *de Rep.* ii. 17, 31.

[2] The *interregnum*, though only an occasional office in the Republic, is represented as an invariable part of the procedure in the transmission of the kingly power (Liv. i. 47).

In the two definite survivals of the Roman monarchy election
was not recognised; the dictator was nominated by the consul,
not by his predecessor, for it was only an occasional office; and
the *rex sacrorum* was nominated by the *pontifex maximus*,[1]
no longer by the preceding *rex;* for this office simply continued the priestly functions of the king, the religious headship
being vested in the *pontifex.* This oldest principle of appointment survived in Republican Rome as an integral part of the
elective process, to reappear again in the Principate, in cases
where election had become a mere form, as the living principle.[2]
It is, in fact, the one principle that has a continuous history;
election is the Republican interlude.

If, therefore, we are led to consider the monarchy as not
purely an elective office, and substitute for election the principle
of nomination, we must consider that it was the right, and
probably the duty, of the king of Rome to nominate his
successor. If there had been no due nomination during his
lifetime, and consequently no distinctly marked out successor
to the monarchy, the duty of providing such a successor lapsed
to the Senate, from which body the *interrex* was appointed.
The *interregnum* is said by tradition to have dated from the first
vacancy in the regal office, after the death of Romulus.[3]   When
such a vacancy had occurred, the auspices, under which the
state had been founded, and which were the mark of divine
acceptance of the kingly rule, "returned to the *patres*,"[4] and
we are told that this was from the first interpreted to mean,
not to the *comitia curiata*, but to the patrician Senate.   The
earliest *interregnum* is represented as an exercise of collective
rule by the Senate; but, on the analogy of the sole magistracy,
it took the form of a creation of a succession of *interreges.*
The first step was the division of the Senate into *decuriae;*[5] each
decury had fifty days of government allotted to it; within this
period each individual member of the *decuria* exercised rule for
five days, and, according to one account, the succession of the
decuries was determined by lot (*sortitio*).[6]   The rule is represented
as collegiate, the whole decury possessing the *imperium*, while

---

[1] Dionys. v. 1; Liv. xl. 42.
[2] Tac. *Ann.* i. 14 and 81; Dio Cass. liii. 21, 7; lviii. 20, 3.
[3] Cic. *de Rep.* ii. 12, 23; Liv. i. 17; Dionys. ii. 57.
[4] [Cic.] *ad Brut.* i. 5, 4.
[5] Cf. Serv. in *Aen.* vi. 808 "Romulo mortuo cum . . . Senatus . . . regnasset per decurias."   [6] Dionys. ii. 57 διακληρωσάμενοι.

the individual who ruled for five days had the *fasces* and the external emblems of the royal power.[1]   In later times we shall see that, though the *interregnum* was retained, the whole procedure was simplified by the abandonment of the collegiate principle.   If it ever existed, we must suppose that, as soon as ever the resolution of the Senate was taken, the collective rule could be interrupted by any *interrex*, except the first, nominating the king.[2]   The *interregnum*, although represented by our authorities as an invariable part of the procedure in the appointment of a king, was probably from the first a makeshift, only resorted to when the ordinary procedure had been interrupted through unforeseen causes, and there was no definitely designated successor.[3]

Yet, though the monarchy was not strictly elective, certain quasi-elective processes were connected by tradition with the appointment of the king, on the part both of Senate and people.

The authority of the Senate (*auctoritas patrum*) is mentioned in connexion with all the transmissions of the supreme office.[4]   It is an authority, however, which did not spring from any theory of the Senate's possessing elective powers, but was simply a result of the universal principle that no man in authority should act without taking advice of his *consilium*, and was merely an outcome of the constitutional necessity which the king was under of consulting the Senate on all great measures affecting the popular welfare.   The greatest of these would be the appointment of a successor.

Secondly, we are told of a formal ratification of the king's power by the people assembled in the *comitia curiata*, one which continued into the Republic under the title of the *lex curiata*, a formal   sanction   always   required   for   the   ratification   of   an

---

[1] Dionys. ii. 57 τοῖς λαχοῦσι δέκα πρώτοις ἀπέδωκαν ἄρχειν τῆς πόλεως τὴν αὐτόκρατορ' ἀρχήν : Liv. i. 17 "decem imperitabant, unus cum insignibus imperii et lictoribus erat."

[2] In the accounts of this procedure an important element is probably omitted, i.e. that each individual *interrex* nominated his successor. The first could not nominate the king, as he had not received the auspices in due form.

[3] Mommsen (*Staatsr.* i. pp. 213, 214) takes a different view, arguing that the king was in every case nominated, not by the *rex*, but by the *interrex*, on the legal ground that the appointment of a successor would have been one of those "actus legitimi qui non recipiunt diem vel condicionem" (such as *hereditatis aditio*, *tutoris datio*), and which "in totum vitiantur per temporis vel condicionis adjectionem" (Papin. in *Dig.* 50, 17, 77). But, even in the regal period, there may have been one condition which did not vitiate such acts, i.e. death (see p. 29).

[4] Liv. i. 17, 22, 32, 41, 47.

imperium already assumed.[1] It is said to have had this
character even in the time of the monarchy, and this was thought
to be shown by the fact that the king himself proposed the
lex curiata which was to give the sanction for the exercise of
his own power.[2] Such procedure was, indeed, necessary, since
no one but the king had the right of putting the question to
the people; consequently we must accept the view that the *lex
curiata* was not absolutely necessary for the exercise of power, and
might be legally, though not perhaps constitutionally, withheld,
as it was by King Servius during the early part of his reign.[3]
   The Roman jurists, who believed that the king was elected,
credited the people with two distinct acts in the creation of a
king—first, his election, and then the formal ratification of this
election.[4] A parallel for this seemed to be furnished by
Republican usage, where the *lex* was taken by magistrates already
elected as a necessary preliminary to the exercise of the *imperium*.
But at this period the magistrates were not elected by the
comitia curiata, and the *lex* of this assembly is a mere survival,
a reminiscence of the formal sovereignty which continued to
be vested in the *curiae*. The *lex curiata* is much more
comprehensible in origin if the king was first nominated
independently of the people and then challenged their allegiance.
It was probably little more than an acclamation on the first
summons of the *curiae* by the king. The preceding king
must have already made known to the people his choice of a
successor, and the popular sentiment would have been already
expressed; thus there was little chance of adverse shouts when
the new king challenged the allegiance of his burgesses. If
there was a chance of the challenge not being accepted, it might,
as we saw, be withheld. But an exercise of the regal *imperium*
which was not sanctioned by these two acts of Senate and
people—the expressed will of the one and the declared allegiance of the other—was regarded by later authorities as
unconstitutional.[5]

[1] Cic. *de Leg. Agr.* ii. 10, 26 ; ii. 11, 28 ; *ad Fam.* i. 9, 25.
[2] Cic. *de Rep.* ii. 13, 25 "Numam ... qui ... quamquam populus curiatis
eum comitiis regem esse jusserat, tamen ipse de suo imperio curiatam legem tulit."
[3] Liv. i. 41 "Servius, praesidio firmo munitus, primus injussu populi,
voluntate patrum regnavit."
[4] Cic. *de Rep.* ii. 17, 31 "Tullum Hostilium populus regem, interrege rogante,
comitiis curiatis creavit, isque de imperio suo ... populum consuluit curiatim."
[5] The last *injustus dominus* of Rome ruled "neque populi jussu neque
auctoribus patribus" (Cic. *de Rep.* ii. 24, 45 ; Liv. i. 49).

E

There was also a religious aspect of the king's appointment. His assumption of power was regarded as incomplete until it had been shown that the gods sanctioned the rule which he had assumed. This was done by the first taking of the auspices [1]—a ceremony observed by magistrates of the Republic before entering on the exercise of their office. This was the final test for the right to exercise secular power; but the king's position as high - priest of the community was supposed to require another initiatory act.

This was the inauguration, which differed from the taking of the auspices. In the ordinary form of the *auspicia* the individual entering on office has himself the right of *spectio*; [2] in the Republic it belonged to magistrates as such, and was never regarded as a merely priestly function. In the special inauguration, on the contrary, the *spectio* is taken by some other than the person inaugurated. The priest-king Numa is naturally associated with this ceremony by tradition; by him an appointed augur is employed to watch for signs, [3] and this ceremony of inauguration by one of the priesthood, other than the person so inaugurated, is represented as being from this time onwards a standing part of the procedure requisite for entrance on the regal office. But this legend of Numa is rendered somewhat incredible by the fact that the augurs have no right of *spectio*, and that of all the priests of the Republic it is only the semi-magisterial *pontifex maximus*, the head of the state religion, who has the right of taking auspices. The fact that the *rex sacrorum* in the Republic had a special inauguration [4] might lend support to the legend, were it not that this *rex* had become wholly a priest and thus lost his right of intercourse with the gods through the *spectio*. The question of the inauguration of the king, unimportant in itself, runs up into two wider questions; the first is whether there was a separation in idea between the king's magisterial and his priestly functions; the second, whether the king was himself *pontifex maximus* and thus the supreme head of the Roman religion.

For an answer to the first question it is not safe to appeal to later examples, for the priesthood and the magistracy may have

---

[1] Thus Romulus takes his own auspices on the Palatine (Liv. i. 6).
[2] p. 39.
[3] Liv. i. 18 "de se . . . deos consuli jussit."
[4] Labeo ap. Gell. xv. 27, 1 ; Liv. xl. 42, 8.

been first sundered during the Republic. But tradition[1]
and survivals represent the king as the *first priest* in the
community. His successor, the *rex sacrorum*, ranks, as a
priest, above the three great *flamines* and the *pontifex maximus*
in the order of the priesthood (*ordo sacerdotum*);[2] the religious
duties of this *rex* point to the fact that the king's functions
were a regular *cultus*, not the occasional religious duties of a
Roman magistrate,[3] while his wife, the *regina sacrorum*, had her
own simultaneous sacrifices.[4]

But the position of first priest did not in the Republic imply
the headship of the Roman religion; the chief pontiff, who is
its head, comes, as we saw, low in the order of the priesthood.
The importance of *cultus* and of religious authority springing from
higher knowledge are not the same. The pontiffs are only
secondarily a priestly, primarily they are a religious order, whose
position is based on the knowledge of religious law (*fas*). The
separation between the true priesthood and the presidency of
religion may, indeed, have been a Republican development, due
to the secularisation of the magistracy; the priestly functions of
the magistrate being continued in the *rex sacrorum*, and the
religious presidency being also separated from the civil power, but
vested in another official, the chief pontiff. But it is possible
that the separation may have been primitive, and that *cultus* and
the knowledge of religious law did not go together. It is
evident that great uncertainty prevailed as to the king's relation
to the pontifical college. While one account speaks of Numa
selecting Numa Marcius as "*the* pontiff,"[5] another describes the
same king as instituting five pontiffs,[6] and we are further told
that, before the *lex Ogulnia* (300 B.C.), the college consisted of four
members.[7] The discrepancy between the two last accounts has

[1] Dionys. ii. 14 ; iv. 74 ; Plut. *Ti. Gracch.* 15.
[2] Festus p. 185 ; Labeo ap. Gell. xv. 27 ; Ov. *Fasti* ii. 21.
[3] This is shown by his sacrifices on the Kalends and on the Nones (*sacra nonalia*) and his offering of a ram to Janus in the *regia* on the *Agonalia* (Jan 9) (Festus p. 10 ; Varro *L.L.* vi. 12 ; Ov. *Fasti* i. 317).
[4] Festus p. 113 ; Macrob. i. 15, 19.
[5] Liv. i. 20 "Numa Pontificem . . . Numam Marcium M. f. ex patribus legit, eique sacra omnia exscripta exsignataque attribuit, quibus hostiis, quibus diebus, ad quae templa sacra fierent, atque unde in eos sumptus pecunia erogaretur. Cetera quoque omnia publica privataque sacra Pontificis scitis subjecit, ut esset, quo consultum plebes veniret : ne quid divini juris, negligendo patrios ritus, peregrinos que adsciscendo, turbaretur, etc." But afterwards (in 449 B.C.) Livy (iii. 54) implies the existence of a college, without mentioning its institution. Cf. iv. 44.
[6] Cic. *de Rep.* ii. 14, 26.
[7] Liv. x. 6.

been reconciled by supposing that the king himself was reckoned as a member of the college, and that the expulsion of the king reduced the number from five to four.[1] It is possible that the king did not bear the title *pontifex maximus* and was yet head of the college ; it is even possible that, as one account which we have quoted seems to indicate,[2] there was a chief pontiff as his delegate. We can hardly refuse him a place at this board in face of the evidences which point to his universal headship of religion. The creation of the augurate and the priesthoods is his work. Romulus appoints the augurs ;[3] Numa institutes the three great Flamines, the Salii, and the Pontifex, although most of the important ceremonies of religion are performed by himself personally.[4] Consequently we may conclude that the appointment of special individuals to these priesthoods must have been a part of the king's office.[5] It has even been held (chiefly as an inference from the fact that the Vestals and Flamens were in the *potestas* of the *pontifex maximus* of the Republic) that the former were the king's unmarried daughters who attended to the sacred fire of the state in the king's house, the latter his sons whose duty it was to kindle the fire for the sacrificial worship of particular deities, Jupiter, Mars, and Quirinus. This pleasing picture may have represented the primitive state of the patriarchal kingship ; but this had been long outgrown before the close of the monarchy. There we find a fully developed hierarchy and the existence of religious guilds, such as those of pontiffs and augurs, who cultivate the science, not the mere ritual of religion, and who have no possible connexion with the king's household arrangements.

At the head of this imposing organisation stands the *rex*, and, in virtue of this position, he is the chief expounder of the rules of divine law (*fas*). It is a law which has hardly any limits, running parallel with civil justice (*jus*) but far beyond its bounds. Three methods of its operation may conveniently be distinguished.

---

[1] Bouché-Leclerq *Les Pontifes de l'ancienne Rome* p. 9. That the king was pontiff is stated by Plutarch (*Numa* 9), Servius (ad *Aen.* iii. 81), and Zosimus (iv. 36), but the evidence may be vitiated by the position of the Princeps as *pontifex maximus.*

[2] Liv. i. 20 (p. 51 n. 5) ; cf. Ambrosch *Studien* p. 22.

[3] Cic. *de Rep.* ii. 9, 16 ; *de Div.* i. 2, 3.

[4] Liv. i. 20 "Tum sacerdotibus creandis animum adjecit, quamquam ipse plurima sacra obibat, ea maxime quae nunc ad Dialem flaminem pertinent."

[5] As, e.g., the nomination of Flamines belonged to the Latin dictator (Ascon. in *Milon.* p. 32).

One is purely religious and ritualistic and is expressed in the control of priesthoods, religious colleges, and cults. The second asserts itself in a control over the life of the ordinary citizen in matters criminal and civil. The third is that which connects the Roman state with other independent communities and forms the international law of the period.

(i.) The control over priesthood and *cultus* belongs to the history of religion rather than to that of constitutional law, and it chiefly presents a legal aspect in connexion with the question of religious jurisdiction. The difficult questions that arose in Republican times from the clashing of the religious and the civil power could hardly have been heard of as yet, for the supreme control of both was vested in the same man. But the very nature of this disciplinary juris- diction over priests has been a matter of some dispute. The favourite hypothesis of a family jurisdiction has been applied to the case, and the hypothesis may conceivably be correct so far as the Flamens and the Vestals are concerned, although even in this sphere it is doubtful by what paternal right the head of religion could do the Vestal's paramour to death. Other phases of the power are still more inexplicable on this ground. A right of punishing augurs for a breach of ritualistic rules survived into the Republic, and seems to be a jurisdiction exercised over them as members of a religious body. There is, however, no trace of the priesthood holding a privileged position, and in all secular matters its members are subject to the ordinary law. Such privileges as they possess rest on religious scruples. When the Flamen was caught (*captus*) for the god, he became free from the paternal power,[1] and the civil authority could not compel him to take an oath.[2] The persons of the Vestals were in- violable ;[3] the sanctity of both Flamens and Vestals also invested them with the right of *asylum*. The bonds were struck off the prisoner who took refuge in the Flamen's house ; and, if the criminal on the way to punishment met him or the Vestal, he could not be scourged or executed on that day. But it is only in these two cases that the severance from the world is strongly marked ; we have no reason for believing that, in the earliest period of Rome's history, the members of the religious orders

---

[1] Gaius i. 130. The same was the case with the Vestal (Gell. i. 12).
[2] For the Flamen see Liv. xxxi. 50 ; Festus p. 104. For the Vestal, Gell. x. 15.
[3] Plut. *Numa* 10.

were isolated from the mass of the people with privileges and a jurisdiction all their own.

The control of the *cultus*, and the maintenance of its purity, are marked as one of the earliest duties of the *pontifex maximus*, and must have belonged to the king. It is he that sees that no ancestral right is neglected, no foreign one acquired.[1] Here we have a religious power that governs more than the priesthood ; the maintenance of the *sacra privata* are as important in its eyes as that of the *sacra publica*, and its supervision must have extended beyond the limits of the Patriciate ; for it is impossible to believe that religion cared only for the *sacra* of the patrician clans, and aimed only at preventing them from corrupting their ancestral worship. The Plebeian and the client were under the protection of the gods, and might bring down a curse on the community by reckless innovation or neglect.

(ii.) The control exercised by *fas* over the citizens' life in matters not immediately connected with ritual and worship may be first illustrated by its penal sanctions. We cannot, indeed, say that there was a time when the Roman law regarded every crime as a sin, for from the very first we are confronted with a dualism, and religious and secular sanctions exist side by side. But religion has left a deeper impress here than elsewhere—in the name given to punishment,[2] in the form of its infliction, in the still stranger fact that, by the disappearance of religious sanctions, breaches of obligation that the modern world regards as crimes remained unpunished by the secular arm.

The punishment for sin must be some form of expiation. This is the *piaculum* adjudged in the monarchy as in Republican times by the head of religion ; and not adjudged arbitrarily, for even by the close of the monarchical period classes of offences had doubtless been drawn up by the pontiffs with the equivalent expiation, which was directed to avert the anger of the gods from the whole community. Apart from the regularly recurring lustrations at the census—the consequence of the sense of universal sinfulness in the community—individual misdeeds could be expiated in this way. Such was a murder that was unin-

---

[1] Liv. i. 20 (cited p. 51).

[2] *Supplicium*, from *sub-placo*, death as a sin-offering (Festus p. 308 "supplicia . . . sacrificia a supplicando ") ; *castigatio* ("castum agere") purification through atonement. On the other hand *poena*, *multa*, *talio* bear witness to a theory of compensation and private vengeance. See Rein *Criminalrecht* p. 39.

tentional or in which mitigating circumstances were present,[1] and
such was the violation of the chastity of Juno's person through
the touching of her altar by a *paelex*.[2] In graver cases expiation
could only be accepted where there was no intent,[3] as in the
wrong done to a god by swearing falsely in his name.[4] There
was also a class of deadly sins for which the gods would accept
no atonement but the life and the goods of the sinner himself.
Amongst the acts which called forth this *consecratio capitis* were
the violation of the relations of client and patron,[5] the ill-treat-
ment of elders by their children,[6] the pulling up or alteration of
boundary stones,[7] the destruction of a neighbour's corn by night.[8]
The god thus appeased was often the deity who was held to be
specially offended by the act; but sometimes the head and the
goods were not dedicated to the same divinities. The person
was adjudged to Jupiter, the dispenser of life; the landed
property to the gods who nourish the human race, Ceres and
Liber.[9] This custom of consecration gradually ceased to have
its literal fulfilment. A man might still be declared *sacer*, but
excommunication had taken the place of immolation. Such a
man was cut off from all divine and, therefore, from all human
help, and his slayer was blood-guiltless.[10] This theory, of a man
being cut off from the community while his life was spared,
became of great importance in the history of Roman criminal
law. It survived in the "interdiction of fire and water" (*aquae
et ignis interdictio*), and familiarised the Romans with the idea
that the severest penalty did not require the sacrifice of life.

In matters of private law we have already witnessed the
presence of religion in marriage, adoption, testament, and the
transmission of the *sacra*. Its authority may be further illustrated
by the formularies of civil procedure. Here the form of words

[1] Liv. i. 26 ; Dionys. iii. 22 ; Festus pp. 297 and 307.
[2] Festus p. 222 ; Gell. iv. 3.
[3] Macrob. i. 16, 10 "prudentem expiare non posse."
[4] Cic. *de Leg.* ii. 9, 22.
[5] Dionys. ii. 10 ; Serv. ad *Aen.* vi. 609.
[6] Festus p. 230.
[7] Dionys. ii. 74 ; Festus p. 368.
[8] Plin. *H.N.* xviii. 3, 12.
[9] Bouché-Leclerq *Les Pontifes* p. 196. In the *lex sacrata* which protected
the tribunes we meet with this distinction (Liv. iii. 55).
[10] Festus p. 318 "At homo sacer is est, quem populus judicavit ob male-
ficium ; neque fas est eum immolari, sed qui occidit, parricidi non damnatur."
This is the meaning of *sacer* as employed in the *leges sacratae* of the early
Republic (Liv. ii. 8 ; iii. 55).

was all-important, and in the early Republic all binding *formulae*, whether for oaths that were to be effectual, for vows or for consecration, were known only to the pontiffs. The solemn forms of law (*legis actiones*) issued from the same authority, and in one of their most frequent manifestations, the *sacramentum*, the procedure was distinctly religious.[1] But who could say whether the king, when he gave the prescribed form of words for an action, acted as a religious or a civil head, as the representative of *fas* or *jus* ? Here we are on the borderland between the two.

(iii.) Nations know no common *jus*, and *fas* is the sole support of international law. Each people is protected by its own divine guardians ; hence a war of two nations is a contest between their gods, and a treaty between two peoples a compact between their respective divinities. But each nation is to some extent under the protection of the other's gods. Jupiter of Rome is powerless if the war commenced by Rome is unjust, and will punish his own people if they have stained his honour by violating a treaty. Even though there is no belief in community of guardianship, the rights of other peoples are still conceived to be under the protection of the Roman gods.

These beliefs necessitated elaborate religious preliminaries to the declaration of a war in order that it might be just and holy (*justum piumque*),[2] as well as ceremonies for the conclusion of a peace that was to bind the public conscience (*fides publica*).[3] Such a ritual may have been performed, originally, by the king himself ; but tradition states that, at a very early period, a special guild of priests, the Fetiales or public orators, were appointed for this purpose.[4] Their chief functions were the

[1] The *sacramentum* (literally " oath ") in the *actio sacramento* is best explained as an atonement (*piaculum*) in the form of a money payment for the expiable, because involuntary, perjury of the litigant who has maintained a false claim. When the process was secularised, the *sacramentum* came to be considered a simple wager. See Danz *Der sacrale Schutz* pp. 151 ff.

[2] Cic. *de Rep.* ii. 17, 31 "constituitque jus, quo bella indicerentur ; quod per se justissime inventum sanxit fetiali religione, ut omne bellum, quod denuntiatum indictumque non esset, id injustum esse atque impium judicaretur."

[3] Varro *L.L.* v. 86 " Fetiales . . . fidei publicae inter populos praeerant ; nam per hos fiebat ut justum conciperetur bellum et inde desitum, ut foedere fides pacis constitueretur. Ex his mittebantur, antequam conciperetur, qui res repeterent, etc."

[4] Cic. *de Leg.* ii. 9, 21 "Foederum, pacis, belli, indutiarum ratorum fetiales judices nuntii sunto ; bella disceptanto." The word *fetialis* is probably connected with *fateri* (and Oscan *fatium*). Thus the "Fetiales" are speakers (*oratores*), cf. Festus p. 182. Dionysius (ii. 72) ascribes the creation of the Fetiales to Numa ; Livy (i. 32) speaks as if they were due to Ancus Martius, but in another

declaration of war and the conclusion of peace, but the ritual observed in both of these acts may be more appropriately described when we are dealing with the international relations of Rome. There were other religious preliminaries to a war which, though not necessitated by divine law, it was highly expedient to observe, in order to increase the chances of victory. Vows (*vota*) were offered to the native gods, and for these to be valid they must be couched in a form prescribed by the pontifical college.[1] And sometimes the king, before a battle or a siege, chants an incantation (*carmen*), the purport of which is to weaken the loyalty of the enemies' gods to their worshippers, and to bring them over to the side of Rome. He bribes them with temples, offerings, and the honours of a special cult.[2] If the bribery is effective and the city falls, he must carry out his pledge. The conquered gods are received at Rome ; and their worship is guaranteed by the distribution of their cults over the patrician clans.[3] The instances preserved of this *devotio* and *evocatio* naturally date from the time of the Republic.[4] During this period the forms are prescribed by the pontiffs. But the antiquity of the procedure is beyond question. The results of evocation on the part of the king, who was his own pontiff, are manifested in the local worships of the conquered towns of Latium, which found an early home at Rome.

If we turn from the religious to the civil powers of the king, it is easier to estimate their extent than to determine the precise modes of their exercise. Later belief credited him with the sole executive power of the state. The Roman kings possessed πᾶσα ἀρχή, and exercised the *imperium* at their own

passage (i. 24) implies their earlier existence. Cicero attributes them to Tullus Hostilius (Cic. *de Rep.* ii. 17, 31). The ceremonies of the college are described in Dionys. ii. 72 and Liv. i. 32.

[1] Sometimes, the better to secure divine assistance, the enemy, his cities, and his lands were all devoted to the gods. For the incantation see Macrob. iii. 9, 10 "Dis pater Vejovis Manes, sive quo alio nomine fas est nominare. . . uti vos eas urbes agrosque capita aetatesque eorum devotas consecratasque habeatis ollis legibus, quibus quandoque sunt maxime hostes devoti ; eosque ego . . . do devoveo." The site of such cities was cursed, as in Republican times that of Fregellae, Carthage, and Corinth.

[2] Macrob. iii. 9, 7 "Si deus, si dea est, cui populus civitasque . . . est in tutela, teque maxime, ille qui urbis hujus populique tutelam recepisti . . . a vobis peto ut vos populum civitatemque . . . deseratis . . . proditique Romam ad me meosque veniatis, nostraque vobis loca templa sacra urbs acceptior probatiorque sit."

[3] Cincius ap. Arnob. iii. 38 "solere Romanos religiones urbium superataruɯ partim privatim per familias spargere, partim publice consecrare."

[4] e.g. the *evocatio* at the siege of Veii, the *devotio* on the fall of Carthage.

discretion.[1] Such statements are not surprising if we remember what is implied in the *imperium*, and that there appear to have been no legal limitations to its exercise during the monarchy. *Imperium* implied the combination of the highest military and civil authority ; it united jurisdiction with command in war, and it included the further right of intercourse with the people (*jus rogandi*) ; while the later restrictions on this power, the limitation of office by time or by colleagueship, had not yet been created. The king held office for life, and he had no colleague ; for the other officials in the state must have been mere delegates whom, in the strict theory of the constitution, he permitted to exist.

But if the king's power was legally free from restraint, and we do not believe that there was any large body of *leges* binding his authority, it could not have been free from the limitations imposed by custom and constitutional usage. Customary law securing rights for the people is said to have been raised to the level of positive law by Servius Tullius.[2] But even the earlier usages must have formed a kind of code—such a code as that which contained the pontifical ordinances known as the *leges regiae*.[3] It was the belief in the existence qf this early customary law which led to the later description of the king's power as an *imperium legitimum*.[4] Amongst his constitutional obligations was that of consulting the Senate in any important matter.

There can be little doubt that the original council of elders (*senatus*) was a body of nominees selected by the king as his permanent advising body (*consilium publicum*).[5] In consequence

---

[1] Plut. *Ti. Gracch.* 15 ; Tac. *Ann.* iii. 26. See next citation.

[2] Tac. *Ann.* iii. 26 "nobis Romulus, ut libitum, imperitaverat : dein Numa religionibus et divino jure populum devinxit, repertaque quaedam a Tullo et Anco. Sed praecipuus Servius Tullius sanctor legum fuit, quis etiam reges obtemperarent."

[3] Pomponius in *Dig.* 1, 2, 2 "et ita leges quasdam et ipse (Romulus) curiatas ad populum tulit ; tulerunt et sequentes reges. Quae omnes conscriptae extant in libro Sexti Papirii, qui fuit illis temporibus, quibus Superbus Demarati Corinthii filius, ex principalibus viris. Is liber, ut diximus, appellatur jus civile Papirianum, non quia Papirius de suo quicquam ibi adjecit, sed quod leges sine ordine latas in unum composuit." This code was commented on by Granius Flaccus (Paul. in *Dig.* 50, 16, 144), a contemporary of Julius Caesar. C. Papirius is said to have been *pontifex maximus* (Dionys. iii. 36), and Mommsen (*Staatsr.* ii. p. 41) thinks that the *leges regiae* were simply pontifical ordinances, specifying amongst other things such offences as we have mentioned as coming under *fas* (p. 54).

[4] Sall. *Cat.* 6 "imperium legitimum, nomen imperii regium habebant."

[5] "Regium consilium" (Cic. *de Rep.* ii. 8, 14). The function of the Senate was περὶ παντὸς ὅτου ἂν εἰσηγῆται βασιλεὺς διαγινώσκειν (Dionys. ii. 14).

the position of senator could not have been a life-office; there could neither have been any definite mode of attaining the dignity, nor any claim on the part of an individual to retain it. A new king might decline to summon some of his predecessor's councillors; he might even, perhaps, change the *personnel* of his advisers during the course of his reign. It was in later times believed that the freedom of selection was so great that no stigma attached to members who were " passed over " (*praeteriti*) by the king.[1]

Yet tradition attributes a definiteness to the Senate which is not consistent with the idea of a purely arbitrary selection. Its numbers at any given time are fixed, and it is to some extent made representative of the whole patrician community—for an increase in the number of full burgesses involved a corresponding increase in the numbers of this body.[2] The number, originally 100,[3] was raised by successive steps to 300 before the close of the monarchy.[4] The two obvious units of representation were the *curiae* and the clans; but the latter, from their larger numbers, formed a better basis for reflecting the opinion of the whole community, and tradition does seem to have imposed a kind of constitutional necessity on the king of distributing his councillors as evenly as possible amongst the patrician *gentes*.[5] It was thus that the distinction between the older and the newer clans was perpetuated in the procedure of the Senate;[6] but the clan-influence left its strongest mark by giving a name to the members of the body itself. It was the leading heads of families (*patres familias seniores*) that the king summoned; and, in asking their advice, he addressed them as "heads of houses" (*patres*).

The primitive Senate is credited with two standing powers— the *patrum auctoritas* and the initiation of an *interregnum.* Neither of these prerogatives was directly contemplated by the constitution, and the Senate never becomes a corporation possessing powers in its own right until the time of the Empire.

---

[1] Festus p. 246 "Praeteriti senatores quondam in opprobrio non erant, quod, ut reges sibi legebant sublegebantque, quos in consilio publico haberent, ita post exactos eos consules quoque et tribuni militum consulari potestate conjunctissimos sibi quosque patriciorum et deinde plebeiorum legebant."
[2] p. 13.   [3] Liv. i. 8.
[4] ib. 17 and 35; ii. 1.   On the nature of this increase see Willems *Le Sénat* p. 21.
[5] p. 13.   [6] p. 12.

Tradition mentions the "authority of the fathers" as being necessary for the appointment of a new king; it leaves it to be inferred that it was required for the validity of laws as well, an inference probably not true of the period of the monarchy. As we have already explained, it was a legal right only in so far as it was an extreme instance of the necessity the magistrate was under of taking advice. Perhaps towards the close of the monarchy, with reference to the choice of a successor to the throne, custom had made it a standing prerogative. The *interregnum* rests on a somewhat different basis; it was a power which religion enjoined should be in the hands of the whole patrician community—usage had delegated the power to the patrician Senate; so here again we have a prerogative which rested wholly on custom.

A privilege only less constant than these was probably the control of foreign policy. The formula of the Fetiales, which is said to have dated from their institution during the monarchy, contains the clause: "But on these matters we will consult the elders at home, how we may obtain our rights."[1] It was thus the duty of the king to consult the Senate in all matters affecting the international relations of the state. For a declaration of war, perhaps, even this was not sufficient. Tradition believed that, in this matter, reference must be made to the people assembled in the *comitia curiata*.[2]

On the other hand, the right of making treaties (*foedera*) with states could not have been limited in this way. For the treaty made in time of peace the Senate, and perhaps the people, were consulted; but this could hardly have been the case with the treaty which closed a war and which was made on the field of battle. In the Republic there survives a shadowy and disputed right of the *imperator* in the field to make a treaty which shall bind the people. The right was denied, but only on the ground that the general could not take an oath binding on the public conscience. But the king was at once general and high-priest; he could doubtless take this oath even without the assistance of his servants, the Fetiales.

There were other manifestations of the king's power as general over which the people would have no control. The

[1] Liv. i. 32.
[2] Dionys. ii. 14. One of the privileges of the people was περὶ πολέμου διαγινώσκειν ὅταν ὁ βασιλεύς ἐφῇ.

disposal of the booty taken in war and of the conquered lands was one of these,[1] and the statements which record this right find support in Republican survivals. The control of the spoils of war (at least of the movable portions) belongs to the Republican general, subject to the advice of his council of war and sometimes to subsequent ratification by the Senate. The first condition may have been necessary in the time of the monarchy, but hardly the second.

The council of war was a type of the smaller special *consilia*, which the king doubtless employed to advise him in different branches of the administration ; and such special councils must have been chosen from the great *consilium publicum*, the Senate. One of the most important of these was that which furnished his assessors in jurisdiction. That it became the custom, in the more important cases judged by the king in person, to employ a *consilium* of some sort, is stated in the charge brought by tradition against Tarquinius Superbus that he neglected this essential guarantee of even justice.[2] In the secular criminal jurisdiction of the king such a council would doubtless have been taken from the Senate. In the religious jurisdiction, which we have considered, the pontiffs would have been the advising board.

Senators also must have been chiefly chosen as delegates of the king, except, perhaps, those appointed for subordinate command in war ;[3] there military fitness would be chiefly looked to.

The chief of these delegates was the prefect of the city (*praefectus urbi*), an *alter ego* left behind in the capital by the king when he himself was absent in the field.[4] To him must have been delegated the whole of the executive power, and with it the right and duty of consulting the Senate. It is not probable that the right of questioning the people was or could be delegated.[5] In criminal jurisdiction a distinction was believed

---

[1] Cic. *de Rep.* ii. 9, 15 "Cum ipse (Romulus) nihil ex praeda domum suam reportaret, locupletare cives non destitit " ; ii. 14, 26 " ac primum agros, quos bello Romulus ceperat, divisit viritim civibus." Cf. Dionys. ii. 28 and 62.

[2] Liv. i. 49 "cognitiones capitalium rerum sine consiliis per se solus exercebat."

[3] ib. 59 ; see p. 41.

[4] Tac. *Ann.* vi. 11 "namque antea, profectis domo regibus ac mox magistratibus, ne urbs sine imperio foret, in tempus deligebatur qui jus redderet ac subitis mederetur . . . duratque simulacrum, quotiens ob ferias Latinas praeficitur qui consulare munus usurpet." Cf. Liv. i. 59 ; Dionys. ii. 12.

[5] Yet Livy and Dionysius represent the *tribunus celerum* as summoning the assembly (Liv. i. 59 ; Dionys. iv. 71).

to have been made in the cases brought before the king; the more important were tried by himself in person, the less important transmitted to judges chosen from the Senate.[1] This may be the germ of a distinction which is said to have been perfected by Servius Tullius. Crimes affecting the public welfare he tried himself; wrongs done to private individuals he entrusted to others.[2]

This principle of delegation is mentioned only in connexion with criminal jurisdiction. But, whatever its extent, it necessitated the grant by the magistrate to his delegate of a *formula* or *lex*, which was the expression of *jus*. This *jus*, "that which is right or fitting," expressed the order of society, as realised through human agency, not directly through the divine will.[3] It is possible that even in early Rome it was treated as a right, a faculty of action (*facultas agendi*) or liberty enjoyed by one man against another, by individuals against corporations or by corporations against individuals. The differentiation between the rights of the state and the rights of the individual, always marked in procedure long before it is formulated in theory, finds expression in the change which tradition attributes to Servius.[4] But there was never any clear line of demarcation between the two spheres. Much of what we call criminal law was at Rome a matter for civil actions dependent on private initiative, and such actions could in early times be brought only by the head of the family. But in so far as the early Romans had a criminal law, in so far, that is, as an offence against the individual could be regarded as a wrong done to society, this law was a part of the *jus publicum*.

The king was the sole exponent of this sense of violated right, and the sole interpreter of the *jus* fixed by custom or by law. Over the penalty he probably had little control. It was enjoined in his ruling and carried out by his lictors; but, in its various

---

[1] Dionys. ii. 14 (amongst the powers of the king were) τῶν τε ἀδικημάτων τὰ μέγιστα μὲν αὐτὸν δικάζειν, τὰ δ' ἐλάττονα τοῖς βουλευταῖς ἐπιτρέπειν. It is difficult, however, to determine whether the reference is to civil wrongs or to crimes.

[2] ib. iv. 25 ἐκεῖνος (Servius Tullius) διελὼν ἀπὸ τῶν ἰδιωτικῶν (ἐγκλημάτων) τὰ δημόσια, τῶν μὲν εἰς τὸ κοινὸν φερόντων ἀδικημάτων αὐτὸς ἐποιεῖτο τὰς διαγνώσεις, τῶν δὲ ἰδιωτικῶν ἰδιώτας ἔταξεν εἶναι δικαστάς, ὅρους καὶ κανόνας αὐτοῖς τάξας, οὓς αὐτὸς ἔγραψε νόμους. The principle here described perhaps refers to delegation rather than to the distinction between *jus* and *judicium* in civil process.

[3] For derivations of *jus* see Clark *Pract. Jurisprudence* pp. 16-20 ; Bréal "Sur l'origine des mots designant le droit en Latin" in *Nouvelle Revue Historique de droit* vol. vii. (1883) pp. 607 sq.

[4] Dionys. l.c.

forms—death by the *arbor infelix* or from the Tarpeian rock—it was fixed by the *mos majorum*. The trial was a personal investigation (*quaestio*) undertaken by the king, with the assistance of a chosen body of advisers ; and he might give judgment himself. But sometimes his judgment was conditioned. He specified the crime under which the accused was to be tried, and the penalty to be inflicted, but left the finding on the facts to his delegates.[1] Two such classes of delegates are attributed to the regal period, the *duumviri perduellionis* and the *quaestores parricidii*.[2]

There may have been an appeal from the delegates to the king, but tradition does not credit the king with any power of pardon. Whether the power of pardon resided anywhere depends on our interpretation of the trial of Horatius,[3] which was believed to furnish the archetype of the *provocatio*. From this story appears the belief, which is often stated by other authorities,[4] that the appeal to the people existed in the regal period, but one modified by the view that the citizens had no standing right of appeal against the king such as that secured against the Republican magistrate by the *lex Valeria*. The king, Tullus Hostilius, *allows* the appeal.[5] The early dictatorship was similarly exempt from the necessity of permitting it, and on one occasion the precedent of Horatius was appealed to for the purpose of showing that, as the king had allowed, so the dictator should allow, the appeal.[6] But the dictatorship is a revival of the *military* side of the monarchy with the military jurisdiction which the king exercises over Horatius. It is quite possible that before the close of the monarchy custom had established different spheres of criminal jurisdiction for the people and the king respectively ;[7] in some the people might have had a right to be judges in the

---

[1] Liv. i. 26.

[2] Zonaras vii. 13 (who attributes their institution to Publicola) identifies the *quaestores* with the *quaestores parricidii*, οἳ πρῶτον μὲν τὰς θανασίμους δίκας ἐδίκαζον, ὅθεν καὶ τὴν προσηγορίαν ταύτην διὰ τὰς ἀνακρίσεις ἐσχήκασι καὶ διὰ τὴν τῆς ἀληθείας ἐκ τῶν ἀνακρίσεων ζήτησιν. Cf. Varro *L.L.* v. 81. Mommsen (*Staatsr.* ii. pp. 523 sq.) thinks the financial quaestors as standing officials originated with the Republic ; but he believes (p. 539) that they had their origin in the criminal *quaestores* (a word which bears the same relation to *quaesitores* as *sartor* to *sarcitor* or *quaero* to *quaesivi*, p. 537). Cf. Tac. *Ann.* xi. 22 (p. 81) ; Ulpian in *Dig.* i. 13.   [3] Liv. l.c.

[4] Cic. *pro Mil.* 3, 7 ; *de Rep.* ii. 31, 54 ; Festus p. 297.

[5] Liv. i. 26 "Si a duumviris provocarit provocatione certato . . . auctore Tullo, . . . 'provoco' inquit."

[6] ib. viii. 33.

[7] Cf. Ihering *Geist des röm. Rechts* i. pp. 257 ff.

last resort, and it is the idea of calling away a case to another court that is suggested by the word *provocatio*, not the modern idea of pardon.[1] In other spheres the king could judge alone ; the *provocatio* here is an act of grace. If, however, we consider the extent of the military and religious jurisdiction of the king, the competence of the people must have been small ;[2] and the *provocatio* itself may be a growth of the later monarchical period, the result of custom, and of a custom based chiefly on the permit of the king.

Civil jurisdiction is said to have been based on the king's judgment.[3] How far this royal jurisdiction was personal we cannot say, but under all circumstances the king was the chief source of the *jus privatum*, in so far as he and his pontiffs alone knew the formularies of action,[4] the most precise verbal accuracy in which was necessary for the successful conduct of a suit. It is probable that in many cases the king gave merely the formulary of action, that is, the ruling in law, and then sent the case before a private judge or arbitrator (*judex privatus, arbiter*), thus illustrating (although not, perhaps, on the scale recognised during the Republic) the fundamental division of judicial procedure into *jus* and *judicium*. This division of jurisdiction is probably primitive and not, as has sometimes been thought, a modification introduced by the later monarchy.[5] Even in Republican times the *judex* was chosen by consent of the parties.[6] He was an arbitrator between the litigants agreed to by a mutual compact,[7] and an outcome of the notion of self-help so prominent in early Greek and Roman law. But one who knows the forms of action has to stand by and see that the words of these forms

[1] *Provocatio* seems to mean a challenge, i.e. a challenge by an accused to a magistrate to appear before another tribunal, on the ground that he is not acting within his own right ; cf. Gaius iv. 93 (of the *actio per sponsionem*) " Provocamus adversarium tali sponsione."

[2] " In this conflict of competence the position of the king was far more favourable than that of the people, since the people could only be summoned by the king. Hence the share of the people in criminal jurisdiction was reduced to a minimum " (Ihering *Geist des röm. Rechts* i. p. 258).

[3] " Judiciis regiis " (Cic. *de Rep.* v. 2, 3).   [4] p. 56.

[5] Savigny *System* vi. p. 287 ; Bernhöft *Staat und Recht der Königszeit* p. 230. The idea of its being an innovation has sometimes been associated with Dionysius's description (iv. 25, see p. 62) of a change in jurisdiction introduced by Servius Tullius.

[6] Cic. *pro Cluent.* 43, 120 " Neminem voluerunt majores nostri non modo de existimatione cujusquam, sed ne pecuniaria quidem de re minima esse judicem, nisi qui inter adversarios convenisset."

[7] Ihering *Geist des röm. Rechts* i. p. 169.

are correctly repeated. This depositary of *jus* is the king or one of his pontiffs. Hence eventually the public official comes to assist at the appointment of the judge. From this it is but a slight step to give the formula of action which settles the law of the case, and to leave it to the *judex* to decide the question of fact.

§ 6. *The Servian Constitution*

At some period before the close of the monarchy the absurdity of the existing constitutional arrangements began to be felt. In matters of private law there was not a single important difference between a free Plebeian and a Patrician ; and large numbers of that portion of the Plebs which had sprung from clientship were virtually in a condition of independence. Although their tenure of the soil might be precarious, their right of acting for themselves in the law courts questionable, it must have been practically impossible to avoid the appearance of full ownership where the lord had not asserted his right for generations, or to prohibit the personal enforcement of claims where the original patronage had been long forgotten or had lapsed through the extinction of the patrician family on which the original client had been dependent. It was, in fact, impossible to say where the class of free Plebeians ended and that of protected Plebeians began. It was better, for the purposes contemplated by the impending reform which bears the name of Servius Tullius, that they should be regarded as on an equality, and that both classes should make up a single order. The essence of this reform is, in fact, the recognition of *equality of rights in landed property.* Ownership of Roman land *ex jure quiritium* was guaranteed to the whole plebeian order— probably even to those dependants and emancipated slaves whose clientship, and therefore whose precarious tenure of the soil, was patent ;[1] and with respect to the rights of *commercium* the order was put on a level with the Patriciate.

So far the object of the reform seems to be to confer privileges on certain classes of the Plebeians. Its real meaning was wholly different. The intention of the reformer—one which explains

---

[1] Dionys. iv. 22 ὁ δὲ Τύλλιος καὶ τοῖς ἐλευθερουμένοις τῶν θεραπόντων . . . μετέχειν τῆς ἰσοπολιτείας ἐπέτρεψε . . . καὶ πάντων ἀπέδωκε τῶν κοινῶν αὐτοῖς μετέχειν, ὧν τοῖς ἄλλοις δημοτικοῖς.

F

the readiness with which the change seems to have been accepted by the Patricians[1]—was to impose burdens on the whole plebeian community. A recognition of the rights of property was a necessary preliminary to the imposition of taxation and of the full quota of military service. The *patres*, who welcomed this distribution of burdens, did not foresee that from these obligations would flow a fresh series of rights which would impair their monopoly of political power.

The Plebeians were being recognised for the first time as, in a sense, members of the state. The first problem was the choice of a medium through which they should be incorporated in it; for simple membership of a state which was not based on membership of some lower unit was inconceivable to the Graeco-Roman world. Many of the Plebeians had no clans; they could not, therefore, be made members of the three primitive tribes,[2] and when the change was first mooted, it was, probably for the same reason, thought impossible to make them members of the *curiae*.[3] New tribes must be invented which should include the whole community. The chief burden of taxation, now imposed equally on all classes, was to lie on land. What more natural than that the tribes should be territorial divisions, so defined as to include all the territory held in ownership by the Roman people? It is established that the tribes, which are specially described as local,[4] contained only that land which was subject to quiritarian ownership,[5] and from this fact the deduction has been drawn that all land subject to quiritarian ownership was included in the tribes. As the Servian tribes were believed only to have comprised the city itself, as enclosed by the Servian walls,[6] this view leads to the startling conclusion

---

[1] The change, however, was not supposed (except perhaps by Tacitus *Ann.* iii. 26, see p. 58) to rest on a *rogatio*. Mommsen (*Staatsr.* iii. p. 161) explains this tradition by noting that the alteration was a mere administrative act, which would fall within the competence of the king.

[2] It is possible that these three tribes would have been to some extent local; but locality was an accident. Membership of them was transmitted by birth.

[3] Dionysius (iv. 22) makes them at a later time members of the *curiae*.

[4] Dionys. iv. 14 ; Gell. xv. 27.

[5] Cic. *pro Flacco* 32, 80 "sintne ista praedia censui censendo, habeant jus civile, sint necne sint mancipi ? . . . in qua tribu denique ista praedia censuisti ?" The *ager publicus* was not included in the tribes, nor were the Capitol and Aventine, because they were not private, but public property (Liv. vi. 20 ; Dionys. x. 31 and 32).

[6] Liv. i. 43 " Quadrifariam urbe divisa, regionibusque et collibus, qui habitabantur, partes eas tribus appellavit " ; Dionys. iv. 14 ὁ Τύλλιος, ἐπειδὴ τοὺς ἑπτὰ

that no land was held in private ownership outside the city, as its limits were fixed by Servius—that the land outside, so far as it was not *ager publicus*, was held by some larger corporation such as the *gens*.[1] But such a conclusion is most improbable; it was the evolution of private ownership which had created the rich Plebeian, who had often no clan and could not hold in common with others, and such a holder was the least likely man in the world to have land in or near the city, even as its limits were fixed by Servius.

Consequently if, as seems to have been the case, the tribes did include all land-owners, they must have extended far beyond the bounds of the city. Our authorities knew them at a time when their names indeed survived, but when they had become strictly divisions of the city, by the complete separation of the country from the urban tribes. If we believe in the urban character of the four original *tribus*, we must accept the clearly expressed but generally discredited belief preserved by Dionysius that besides these four tribes, which comprehended only the city, Servius established twenty-six others which took in the country districts.[2]

The view that the four tribes[3] comprised the country districts is preferable, and is not incompatible with the fact that they certainly designated parts of the city, nor even with the possibility of their having been engrafted in some way on the older divisions of the *Ramnes, Tities,* and *Luceres*.[4] Local creations of an artificial character, independent of juxtaposition, are not

λόφους ἐνὶ τείχει περιέλαβεν, εἰς τέτταρας μοίρας διελὼν τὴν πόλιν . . . τετράφυλον ἐποίησε τὴν πόλιν εἶναι, τρίφυλον οὖσαν τέως. So Festus p. 368 "urbanas tribus appellabant, in quas urbs erat dispertita a Ser. Tullio rege." Cf. Varro *L.L.* v. 56. Mommsen (*Staatsr.* iii. p. 163) now holds that the tribes were "parts of the state-town limited by the *pomerium*." Ostia, once thought to belong to Palatina, has been shown to belong to Voturia. But the reason for this may be the subsequent loss of the *territorium* of the city. See p. 68.

[1] Momms. *Staatsr.* iii. p. 168. Rome was at this time a great commercial state (cf. treaty with Carthage, 509 B.C.). That such a primitive institution as gentile tenure could have existed at this time is inconceivable.

[2] Dionys. iv. 15 διεῖλε δὲ καὶ τὴν χώραν ἅπασαν, ὡς μὲν Φάβιός φησιν, εἰς μοίρας ἕξ τε καὶ εἴκοσιν, ἃς καὶ αὐτὰς καλεῖ φυλάς. Mommsen (*Staatsr.* iii. p. 169) seems to lean to the view that those country districts, comprising land not in quiritarian ownership, were *pagi*.

[3] *Sucusana* (or *Suburana*), *Palatina, Esquilina,* and *Collina*. See p. 3.

[4] Cf. Momms. *Staatsr.* iii. p. 125 "The four tribes are probably nothing more than the three Romulian increased through the *territorium* of the town on the Quirinal"; p. 164 "Servian Rome, probably a double town composed of the old city, Palatine and Esquiline, and the new town of the Colline."

unknown in early legislations; they are found in the almost contemporary work of Cleisthenes of Athens. But even this hypothesis is unnecessary; each tribe may have stretched continuously with fairly definite boundaries beyond the city walls. The country portions of these tribes were for a moment wholly lost by the disastrous wars which followed the expulsion of the kings, and when the *ager Romanus* was again regained, a new organisation was adopted. The territory outside the walls was parcelled out into country tribes,[1] and these grew in number as Rome's conquests spread. The four Servian tribe-names were kept as designations only of regions within the city.

Although the tribes were divisions of the land, and individuals were registered in that tribe in which their land-allotment lay,[2] there is no good reason for accepting the current belief that the landless citizen was not enrolled in a tribe.[3] It has generally been assumed that the only object of the Servian tribes was to furnish a system of registration for taxation and the military levy. If this was the case, and we believe that these burdens were imposed only on landed property, it follows as a consequence that only holders of land were *tribules*. But there is no evidence that their scope was so limited. They appear to be divisions of the *populus Romanus*, and the disinherited or ruined Patrician who has lost his land is still a member of that *populus*. The tribe to which a landless man belonged would depend upon his domicile; it is a man's local position in a tribe, not the land he holds in it, which is given as a criterion of his membership and of the political rights which it subsequently conferred.[4]

The system of registration, which was the central idea of the Servian reforms, was essentially military. It recognised only those persons who were qualified for service by wealth, regarded them as forming an army (*exercitus*), and divided this army into its two branches of infantry and cavalry. This military organisation recognised one primary and two secondary principles as the basis of classification; the first was wealth, the second age,

[1] Districts like Ostia, which must have belonged to the Servian tribes, now formed parts of the new creations (see p. 67).
[2] Servius is said for this reason to have prohibited transference of domicile or allotment. Dionys. iv. 14 (Servius) τοὺς ἀνθρώπους ἔταξε τοὺς ἐν ἑκάστῃ μοίρᾳ τῶν τεττάρων οἰκοῦντας, ὥσπερ κωμήτας, μήτε μεταλαμβάνειν ἑτέραν οἴκησιν μήτ᾽ ἄλλοθί που συντελεῖν. [3] Momms. *Staatsr.* iii. pp. 182, 184.
[4] Laelius Felix ap. Gell. xv. 27 "Cum ex generibus hominum suffragium feratur, 'curiata' comitia esse, cum ex censu et aetate 'centuriata,' cum ex regionibus et locis, 'tributa.'"

the third took the form of a subdivision for strategic purposes, the military unit employed being the " hundred " (*centuria*).

For the moment we may overlook the cavalry and fix our attention on the bulk of the citizens who form the infantry. These are split up into five divisions, which were at a later period called *classes*. The basis of division was wealth, and the crucial question is " what kind of wealth ? " It is almost certain that it could not have been wealth reckoned in money. Although Rome was a seaport and a trading state, it is doubtful whether even the old libral *as*, which was used as a medium of exchange by weight, was in current use at this time;[1] and therefore the detailed accounts given of the money valuations by which the classes were fixed must refer to a later period in the history of this organisation. The alternative that has been suggested is land.[2] There would be no difficulty in accepting this substitute, paralleled as it is by the similar organisation of Solon, were it not that the hypothesis ignores sources of wealth which the earliest Roman law seems to have classed with land, i.e. slaves and domesticated beasts. These *res mancipi* are as much the object of quiritarian ownership as land, and they may exist without it. A man might own no land and yet be rich in cattle and sheep which he drove on the *ager publicus*, or in slaves engaged in productive handicrafts,[3] and the state was interested in all that was duly owned and was properly the subject of assessment (*res censui censendo*) ;[4] the Servian census must have been based on *res mancipi*, and to a certain degree it was a census based on currency, for cattle (*pecus*) were recognised as a medium of exchange (*pecunia*).

On the basis of such a census five classes were distinguished ; the census of each, in terms of the later assessment, which was probably expressed in *asses sextantarii*, being respectively 100,000, 75,000, 50,000, 25,000, 11,000 asses.

---

[1] Servius himself is credited with the introduction of *aes signatum*—carefully adjusted copper weights stamped by authority. Plin. *H.N.* xviii. 3 "Servius rex ovum boumque effigie primus aes signavit." Mommsen (*Römisches Münzwesen*) thinks that the stamp was a guarantee not of the weight but of the purity of the metal. In this case the metal must have been used as a medium of exchange ; as a medium of barter the weight would be sufficient. Mommsen's opinion is (op. cit. p. 175) that a regular copper coinage was not introduced at Rome until about the period of the *decemviri* (450-430 B.C.), and more recent numismatists pronounce even this date to be too early. [2] Momms. *Staatsr.* iii. p. 247.
[3] The existence of the guilds in regal times (Plut. *Num.* 17) rather proves than disproves the competing manufacture by slaves.
[4] Cic. *pro Flacco* 32, 80. See p. 66.

Each of these divisions was subdivided into two with reference to age, the *juniores* (from eighteen to forty-five) being the effective fighting force, the *seniores* (forty-five to sixty) the home defence. The final division is into the military unit, the century (*centuria*), consisting nominally of a hundred men. This was the minimum strength of the lowest unit, but the census list did not represent the effective fighting force of the legion organised for battle, but the numbers qualified for service; consequently the centuries of a particular class were raised to the quota required to include all the members of that class. The numerical proportion of the centuries of the different classes to one another is very striking. The centuries of the first class (eighty in number) are almost equal to those of the four other classes put together (collectively ninety in number). If this table exhibits the real proportion of social classes to one another, it would show a wonderfully equal distribution of land in the state, one so equal as to cause most of the landholders to be placed in the same class, for the list would mainly represent holders of land (the other *res mancipi* not being usually divorced from its possession). But the proportions of the classes may only show that the centuries of richer citizens were still regarded as forming the more permanent force, the other divisions, not much more numerous though drawn from a larger population, being merely supplementary. We know that members of the first class were more perfectly equipped,[1] and the fact of their being the main strength of the army would be proved if it were true that this class alone was originally *classis* ("the line") and that all the others were *infra classem*.[2]

---

[1] For this difference of armour see Liv. i. 43 ; Dionys. iv. 16, 17. It survived into Polybius' time (Polyb. vi. 23 οἱ δὲ ὑπὲρ τὰς μυρίας τιμώμενοι δραχμὰς ἀντὶ τοῦ καρδιοφύλακος σὺν τοῖς ἄλλοις ἁλυσιδωτοὺς περιτίθενται θώρακας).

[2] Gellius vi. (vii.) 13 " 'Classici' dicebantur non omnes, qui in quinque classibus erant, sed primae tantum classis homines, qui centum et viginti quinque milia aeris ampliusve censi erant. 'Infra classem' autem appellabantur secundae classis ceterarumque omnium classium, qui minore summa aeris, quod supra dixi, censebantur " ; Festus p. 113 "infra classem significantur qui minore summa quam centum et viginti milium aeris censi sunt."

Belot (*Hist. d. Chev. Rom.* i. 204, 205) thinks that the 125,000 asses mentioned here was the figure of the lowest census—the fifth class—at the time of the *lex Voconia* (169 B.C.), mentioned in this connexion by Festus. The designation in asses was still kept, but the *as* must now be multiplied by 10 (12,500 × 10 = 125,000 asses). Belot starts from his hypothesis that the *as* of the census is the old libral *as*. See the tables on the next page. Mommsen (*Staatsr.* iii. p. 249 n. 4), on the other hand, supposes that the law referred to the census of the first class, and that it was through an interpretation meant to limit its operation, when

As will be seen from the accompanying table of the census, the mass of citizens whose property fell below that of the lowest class was not wholly unprovided for. They were organised, according to Livy, into six, according to Dionysius into five, centuries. Some of these were composed of professional persons, whose services were indispensable to an army, and who were, perhaps, members of the trade guilds (*collegia*) which are said to have existed in the regal period.[1] Such were the carpenters (*fabri*) who formed two centuries, and the horn-blowers and trumpeters (*cornicines* and *tibicines*) who formed one each.

THE SERVIAN CLASSIFICATION

THE CAVALRY

18 centuries, with no fixed property qualification.

THE INFANTRY

1st Classis—100,000 asses (Livy and Dionysius),[2] 120,000 asses (Pliny and Festus).[3]
     Seniores, 40 cent. ⎱ 80.
     Juniores, 40 cent. ⎰

2nd Classis—75,000 asses (Liv. and Dionys.).
     Seniores, 10 cent. ⎱ 20.
     Juniores, 10 cent. ⎰

3rd Classis—50,000 asses (Liv. and Dionys.).
     Seniores, 10 cent. ⎱ 20.
     Juniores, 10 cent. ⎰

4th Classis—25,000 asses.
     Seniores, 10 cent. ⎱ 20.
     Juniores, 10 cent. ⎰

5th Classis—11,000 asses (Liv.), 12,500 (Dionys. 12½ minae).
     Seniores, 15 cent. ⎱ 30.
     Juniores, 15 cent. ⎰

     Fabri—2 cent. (voting with 1st class, Liv.; with 2nd class, Dionys.)
     Accensi, cornicines, tibicines, 3 cent. (Liv.), 2 cent. (Dionys.) (voting with 4th class, Dionys.).
                      6 cent. (Liv.). 5 cent. (Dionys.).
     Capite censi, 1 cent.

Total, 193 centuries (Dionys.), 194 (Liv.).

---

the value of money had altered, expressed in terms of the *centum milia aeris* of libral asses. That it was so interpreted is shown by the fact that the *centum milia aeris* of the Voconian law (Gaius ii. 274) became *centum milia sestertium* (Schol. to Cic. *Verr.* ii. 1, 41, 104, p. 188 Orell.), i.e. 25,000 denarii (Dio Cass. lvi. 10).

[1] Plut. (*Num.* 17) mentions τέκτονες and χαλκεῖς amongst the *collegia* (Momms. *Staatsr.* iii. p. 287 n. 1).   [2] So too Polybius (vi. 23, cited p. 70).

[3] Plin. *H.N.* xxxiii. 3 " Maximus census CXX assium fuit illo (Servio) rege, et ideo haec prima classis." Festus p. 113 (cited p. 70).

THE CENSUS

As interpreted by Mommsen,[1] who holds that the figures are given in *asses sextantarii* [i.e. *asses* of two ounces weight—⅓ of the libral *as* (the later *sestertius*)].

As interpreted by Belot,[2] who holds that the figures are given in *asses librales* (the later *sestertii*).

		The older *as* (⅓ denarius).	Later (*circa* 269 B.C.) equivalent to ₁₀ denarius.	
1*st*	*Classis*	40,000	100,000	100,000
2*nd*	,,	30,000	75,000	75,000
3*rd*	,,	20,000	50,000	50,000
4*th*	,,	10,000	25,000	25,000
5*th*	,,	4,400	11,000	12,500

Another century was formed by the *accensi* or *velati*. These were men with no heavy armour, who might be enrolled as occasion required (*adscripticii*), or who marched to battle as light-armed troops ready at any moment to take the armour and places of the fallen legionaries.[3] No property qualification was required for these three groups, the reason being that their place in the army did not demand it. But to these Livy and Dionysius add another unpropertied class, the century of *proletarii*, which included the whole mass of the people not registered in the *classes*.[4] If, however, we believe in the originally military character of the organisation, there seems no place for this

---

[1] *Staatsrecht* iii. pp. 249, 250.   Böckh (*Metrologische Untersuchungen* p. 444) also takes the view of the asses being *sextantarii*. He makes the qualifications in terms of the libral *as* and the *as* of two ounces respectively : 20,000 = 100,000, 15,000 = 75,000, 10,000 = 50,000, 5000 = 25,000, 2000 = 10,000.

[2] *Histoire des Chevaliers Romains* (Table at commencement of vol. i.).

[3] Festus p. 18 "accensi dicebantur qui in locum mortuorum militum subito subrogabantur, dicti ita, quia ad censum adiciebantur"; p. 369 "velati appellabantur vestiti et inermes qui exercitum sequebantur, quique in mortuorum militum loco substituebantur." Cf. p. 14 "adscripticii veluti quidam scripti dicebantur, qui supplendis legionibus adscribebantur. Hos et accensos dicebant, quod ad legionum censum essent adscripti. Quidam velatos, quia vestiti inermes sequerentur exercitum."

[4] Liv. i. 43 "hoc minor census reliquam multitudinem habuit ; inde una centuria facta est immunis militia" ; Dionys. iv. 18 (the remaining citizens with a qualification under 12½ minae Servius placed in one λόχος) στρατείας τε ἀπέλυσε καὶ πάσης εἰσφορᾶς ἐποίησεν ἀτελεῖς.   Cf. vii. 59 οὗτοι στρατειῶν τε ἦσαν ἐλεύθεροι τῶν ἐκ καταλόγου καὶ εἰσφορῶν τῶν κατὰ τιμήματα γενομένων ἀτελεῖς καὶ δι' ἀμφω ταῦτ' ἐν ταῖς ψηφοφορίαις ἀτιμότατοι.   Cf. Cic. *de Rep.* ii. 22, 40 "in quo etiam verbis ac nominibus ipsis fuit diligens ; qui, cum locupletes assiduos appellasset ab asse dando, eos, qui aut non plus mille quingentos aeris aut omnino nihil in suum censum praeter caput attulissent, proletarios nominavit ; ut ex iis quasi proles, id est quasi progenies civitatis, exspectari videretur. Illarum autem sex et nonaginta centuriarum in una centuria tum quidem plures censebantur, quam paene in prima classe tota."

class which is not already filled by the *accensi* and *velati*. At a
later period the *accensi* became a more definite body, acting as
assistants to the magistrates and forming a corporation with
certain immunities,[1] and at this period the *proletarii* may have
been recognised as the class liable to taxation, which fell below
the minimum census. But they probably do not belong to the
original Servian organisation.

The citizens included in the census list were collectively
described as *classici*, and were spoken of as *locupletes* and *assidui*,
the latter word probably meaning people "settled on land,"
"landholders," as most of those originally enrolled in the
classes were.[2] The others were the children-begetting citizens
(*proletarii cives*). The use of the census for purposes of taxation
gave other names to this class. In contrast to the *assidui*,
who were registered on their property, they were called *capite
censi* as being registered on their *caput* or mere headship of
a family; and further, when the incidence of taxation extended
below the minimum census, they were spoken of as *aerarii*,
because their participation in the burdens of the state was
shown only by the payment of taxes (*aes*). The word *aerarii*
seems always to have denoted those outside the census list.[3]

The cavalry was an adaptation of the old patrician corps of
equites[4] to the new conditions. The six original centuries were
preserved and consisted as before of Patricians;[5] they still bore
the names of the ancient tribes, and were called respectively
Titienses, Ramnes, Luceres, priores and *posteriores*.[6] They continued

---

[1] Ulpian in *Fragm. Vat.* 138 "ii qui in centuria accensorum velatorum
sunt, habent immunitatem a tutelis et curis."

[2] The word is not technical enough to be used as an argument that the *classes*
included only landholders. The favourite ancient derivation was from *ab asse
dando* (Cic. *de Rep.* ii. 22, 40, see p. 72), whether for the payment of taxation
or for the furnishing of military equipment.

[3] *Capite censi*, if we trust Cicero (*de Rep.* ii. 22, 40, see p. 72), came to
mean those below 1500 asses (the subsequent limit to the incidence of taxation).
The limit of census for military service was also reduced to 4000 asses (Polyb. vi.
19), and finally to 375 (Gell. xvi. 10, 10), and those below this census continued
to be called *capite censi* (Gell. l.c. ; Sall. *Jug.* 86). *Aerarius*, on the other hand,
seems to have preserved its old meaning of those excluded from the centuries
—Ps. Asc. in *Divin.* p. 103 "(Censores) prorsus cives sic notabant . . . ut, qui
plebeius (esset) . . . aerarius fieret, ac per hoc non esset in albo centuriae suae,
sed ad hoc [non] esset civis, tantummodo ut pro capite suo tributi nomine aera
praeberet."   [4] p. 41.

[5] It is not known when they ceased to be patrician ; Mommsen (*Staatsr.* iii.
p. 254) thinks on the reform of the Servian constitution, *circa* 220 B.C.

[6] Liv. i. 36.

to be known as the *sex centuriae*, or (after the centuries acquired voting power) the *sex suffragia*.[1]

To these were added twelve new centuries (*centuriae equitum*), composed, like the *classes*, of Patricians and Plebeians. But, unlike the *classes*, they were not enrolled on a property qualification. This is explained by the fact that they are not a list of men qualified for service but actually in service, a standing corps selected by the king and whose expenses were largely defrayed by the state. In later times, each knight was on his entrance into the corps given the means wherewith to furnish himself with a pair of horses[2] (*aes equestre*), and also a regular sum of money for their support (*aes hordearium*), the latter money being defrayed by unmarried women and orphans, who were possessed of property but could not by the nature of the case be rated in the census.[3]

Each of these centuries formed a troop of one hundred men under a *centurio*,[4] and these eighteen centuries of Roman knights with public horses (*equites Romani equo publico*) continued unaltered in numbers and (with the exception that the *sex suffragia* ceased to be chosen from the Patricians) in character to the end of the Republic. Although no definite census was required for the class, it was probably chosen from the first from the richest and most distinguished citizens; for its permanent existence implies leisure. The class was not divided by age into *seniores* and *juniores*, for an obvious military reason. They were all *juniores*, and probably young men, whose release from the centuries was granted as soon as age had impaired their efficiency for service.

This centuriate organisation seems to have little or no connexion with the four Servian tribes,[5] beyond the accidental

---

[1] Cic. *de Rep.* ii. 22, 39.

[2] Festus p. 221 "paribus equis, id est duobus, Romani utebantur in proelio, ut sudante altero transirent in siccum. Pararium aes appellabatur id, quod equitibus duplex pro binis equis dabatur."

[3] Liv. i. 43 "ita pedestri exercitu ornato distributoque equitum ex primoribus civitatis duodecim scripsit centurias. Sex item alias centurias . . . sub isdem, quibus inauguratae erant, nominibus fecit : ad equos emendos dena millia aeris ex publico data [i.e., as Livy understands it, 10,000 *asses sextantarii* = 1000 denarii], et, quibus equos alerent, viduae adtributae, quae bina milia aeris in annos singulos penderent" [2000 asses = 200 denarii]. Cf. Gaius iv. 27.

[4] The number of the century was here fixed, and not, as in the case of the *classici*, expansive.

[5] Cf. Liv. i. 43 "neque eae tribus ad centuriarum distributionem numerumque quicquam pertinuere." There is no evidence, e.g., that each tribe furnished a certain number of centuries.

one that the basis of qualification was mainly land, and that all land which was private property was registered in the tribes. Its primary meaning was the assembly and registration of those liable for military service. It acquired a secondary meaning when (at what period we do not know but perhaps from its first organisation) it was used as a scheme for the collection of taxes on the registered wealth of the citizens in the *classes*. The act of registration (*census*) was a solemn religious function conducted by the king. He numbered his fighting force, saw that each warrior was in his due rank, excluded from these ranks men who were stained with sin, and then concluded the examination with a ceremony of purification (*lustrum*). It is only with reference to the collection of taxes imposed at this levy that the tribe would be of importance. The century was a military unit, dissolved as soon as the army was disbanded; the tribe was permanent, hence the war-tax (*tributum*) was perhaps collected from the first by the presidents of the tribes.[1]

A transference of political rights from the patrician body to this new assembly was so far from being the motive of the change that it was probably never contemplated. But such a transference was from the nature of things inevitable. Apart from the general fact that a citizen army must gain the preponderance in political power, there were certain public acts which were inevitably performed from the first by the assembly of the centuries, or were very soon found to be more rapidly, easily, and appropriately performed by that assembly than by the *comitia* of the *curiae*.

Firstly, it may have been the custom for the oath of allegiance to the king, first expressed in the *lex curiata*,[2] to have been renewed at every taking of the census. This expression of allegiance, asked for by the magistrate, was now a *lex centuriata*.[3]

Secondly, most of the popular utterances or *leges* of early Rome must have referred to military matters, and convenience, if not a sense of consistency, must soon have dictated that they

---

[1] *Tributum*, however, cannot be derived from *tribus* (as by Varro quoted p. 40). The parallel words *attribuere, contribuere, ultro tributa*, etc., seem to show that it means something added to, conferred on, or collected for another.   [2] p. 48.

[3] As such it was in the Republic given for the censors. Cic. *de Leg. Agr.* ii. 11, 26 "majores de singulis magistratibus bis vos sententiam ferre voluerunt ; nam cum centuriata lex censoribus ferebatur, cum curiata ceteris patriciis magistratibus, tum iterum de eisdem judicabatur."

should be pronounced by the army. The choice of officers rested
with the king, but if the appointment of the higher delegates
required the ratification of the people,[1] this must soon have been
given by the centuries. The regal jurisdiction which the people
challenge by the *provocatio* is essentially military jurisdiction;[2]
and consequently the exercise of this jurisdiction, when the
king allowed the appeal, must soon have been felt to belong to
the army. It was to this assembly that the announcement of a
proposal to declare war[3] would most appropriately be made; it
was above all by this assembly, which represented the tax-
payers, that the war-tax (*tributum*) would most appropriately
be assessed.

We cannot trace the successive steps in the acquisition of
power by the centuries or its growth from an army into a
comitia. They must have been the chief political changes which
filled the closing years of the monarchy and the early days of
the Republic; for even the abolition of monarchy itself, revolutionary as it was, was less of an alteration in the structure of
the constitution than this transference of the attributes of
sovereignty from one assembly to another, from a single to a
mixed order. The *comitia curiata* was not suddenly stripped
of its powers; but the organising genius of a single supreme
magistrate had prepared the way for a change, which was a
prototype of the gradual insensible revolutions through which
Rome was to pass.

The change which closes the history of this period, although
not so radical, was far more sudden and violent. The monarchy
itself was overthrown. History has tried to invest this revolution
with all the legal grounds and legal forms which it could summon
to its assistance. Servius had had it in his mind to complete his
democratic work by laying down the full *imperium;*[4] and Tarquin
the Proud, the last of the great Etruscan line, had broken through
the constitutional usages of the monarchy[5] and had ruled without
challenging the allegiance of the people.[6] That there was some
fearful abuse of the kingly power, typified in the associations that
gathered round the words *rex* and *regnum* and in the oath which

---

[1] p. 43.   [2] p. 63.   [3] p. 60.
[4] Liv. i. 48 "id ipsum tam mite ac tam moderatum imperium tamen, quia
unius esset, deponere eum in animo habuisse quidam auctores sunt, ni scelus
intestinum liberandae patriae consilia agitanti intervenisset."
[5] ib. 49.   [6] Cic. *de Rep.* ii. 22, 44.

made any one who aspired to monarchy an outlaw,[1] we may without hesitation allow; for Rome, as shown by the power she continued to entrust to her magistrates, had not outgrown the idea of royalty. But there was no constitutional mode of deposing a king. The auspices had returned to the fathers in unhallowed fashion, and the war waged by Tarquin and Etruria is a war for the maintenance of the principle of divine right. But yet Rome held that the divinity of the magistracy still remained; the auspices again left the fathers' hands and were conferred on two citizens chosen from the *patres*.[2]

[1] Cic. *de Rep.* ii. 30, 52 ; Liv. ii. 1 ; App. *B.C.* ii. 119. It is sometimes represented as a law which made any one who aimed at royalty *sacer* (Liv. ii. 8). For the dual sanction of the oath and the law compare the means by which the *sacrosanctitas* of the tribunes was secured (p. 100).

[2] It is strange that the *interregnum*, which would have secured a continuity, is not mentioned in this case. The election of the first consuls was supposed to have been conducted by the *praefectus urbi*, who almost certainly had not the *ius rogandi* (p. 61). Liv. i. 60 "duo consules inde comitiis centuriatis a praefecto urbis ex commentariis Servii Tullii creati sunt, L. Junius Brutus et L. Tarquinius Collatinus."

CHAPTER II

THE GROWTH OF THE REPUBLICAN CONSTITUTION

THE two new magistrates, who were appointed to the headship of the state, were, like the king, armed with the *imperium* and its united powers of military leadership and jurisdiction. Hence they bore the old titles of *praetores* and .*judices*,[1] while those designations which denoted a single supremacy in the state, such as *dictator* or *magister populi*, were necessarily discarded. The new magistrates were to hold office for a year and then to trans- mit their power to two successors. But their right of nomination was not final. They were, indeed, free to name as their successors whom they pleased, but this nomination had to be ratified immediately by the people assembled in their centuries ; and perhaps they were already expected to submit to this *comitia* the names of all candidates who offered themselves for this post, although they could certainly decline to receive such names,[2] and nomination, or, as it was sometimes called, *creatio*, was an essential part of the early consular elections. A new practice, that of direct election, was thus introduced into the Roman constitution, but it was merely an advance on the previous practice of ratifying a nomination.[3] A far newer idea—one which distinguished the consulship from the monarchy, and continued to differentiate

---

[1] For the title *praetores* see Cic. *de Leg.* iii. 3, 8 " regio imperio duo sunto iique a praeeundo judicando consulendo praetores judices consules appellamino "; for that of *judices*, Varro *L.L.* vi. 88, who quotes from the *commentarii consulares* the formula used in, summoning the *comitia centuriata*, " qui exercitum impera- turus erit, accenso dicito : ' C. Calpurni, voca in licium omnes Quirites huc ad me.' Accensus dicito sic ' Omnes Quirites in licium visite huc ad judices.' ' C. Calpurni,' consul dicito, voca ad conventionem omnes Quirites huc ad me.' Accensus dicito sic ' Omnes Quirites ite ad conventionem huc ad judices.' "

[2] See the section on the magistracy (p. 187).

[3] This ratification indeed remained. Even though elections were conducted before the centuries, a *lex* was still passed by the *curiae* ratifying this election (p. 49) ; and the *patrum auctoritas* was still required to sanction each fresh appointment.

it from the dictatorship subsequently created—was that of *colleagueship*,[1] of two officials exercising exactly the same sphere of competence, with the inevitable effect of collision if agreement could not be secured. Perpetual collision was averted by the simple rule that the dissent of one magistrate rendered null and void the action of his colleague. But if such dissent was not expressed (or not capable of expression through the absence of the colleague) the command of a single magistrate had binding force on the community. His regal competence was not diminished, but only potentially checked, by the presence of a colleague. Colleagueship, considered as the safeguard against abuse of the *imperium*, grew to be so firmly impressed on popular imagination as the characteristic feature of the new office, that the earlier titles derived from the monarchy gave place to that of *consules*.[2]

But this limitation was not sufficient. The unrestricted military jurisdiction of the magistrate was felt not to be in harmony with the new *régime*. A law was passed by P. Valerius, the first of the consuls, allowing an appeal to the people in their centuries against every sentence of a magistrate which was pronounced against the life of a Roman citizen. This *lex Valeria* (509 B.C.) completed the popular jurisdiction which had been growing up during the monarchy,[3] and from this time no power but the people has the right to pronounce the final death sentence within the walls ;[4] outside this sphere the military jurisdiction of the consul can be asserted without appeal—hence the distinction between the *imperium* at home (*domi*) and abroad (*militiae*) ; the limit between the spheres being originally the *pomerium*, later the first mile-stone from the city.[5] Without this

---

[1] If it existed before it could have been only in the priestly colleges, but these seem rather advising bodies to the king.

[2] From *con-salio*, i.e. people who leap or dance together, "partners" (in a dance). Momms. *Staatsr.* ii. p. 77 n. 3 ; he compares *praesul* and *exul*.

[3] Liv. ii. 8 (509 B.C.) "Latae deinde leges . . . ante omnes de provocatione adversus magistratus ad populum "; Cic. *de Rep.* i. 40, 62 "Vides . . . Tarquinio exacto, mira quadam exsultare populum insolentia libertatis ; tum annui consules, tum demissi populo fasces, tum provocationes omnium rerum " (i.e. the *provocatio* became *universal* instead of being confined to certain *spheres*).

[4] By this time the direct capital jurisdiction of the pontiffs had probably become extinct.

[5] Liv. iii. 20 "neque provocationem esse longius ab urbe mille passuum, et tribunos si eo (lake Regillus) veniant, in alia turba Quiritium subjectos fore consulari imperio." But the question between the *pomerium* and the first mile-stone was in later times still a disputed one (Liv. xxiv. 9).

limit the axes are borne within the *fasces*, within it they are laid aside. Tradition adds that it was this final recognition of popular sovereignty which led to the custom of the consul lowering the *fasces* before the people when he addressed them.[1] It does not appear that this great change was forced on the higher organs of the state by any popular agitation. It is no part of a distinctively plebeian movement. Senate and People, Patricians and Plebeians must have equally accepted as inevitable the doom of a power which had been dwindling to a shadow during the monarchy.

The change from monarchy also witnessed the first attempt to weaken the unity of the executive power. The consuls were given two general assistants, the annually appointed *quaestores*. We have noticed the tradition which assigns these officials to the regal period,[2] but it is not wholly inconsistent with that which represents them as a part of the new constitution of 509. From being temporary delegates they now became permanent assistants of the consuls. Their sphere was as unlimited as that of the consuls themselves ; they were meant simply to obey his behests. But two departments in which they represented the supreme magistracy must have stood out prominently from the first. These were criminal jurisdiction and finance.[3] The "city quaestors" (*quaestores urbani*), as they were subsequently called to distinguish them from their provincial colleagues, were known as *quaestores parricidii*[4] and *quaestores aerarii*. In their first capacity they were delegates whom the magistrate employed in criminal jurisdiction, probably occupying with respect to procedure much the same place as the *duoviri* in the trial of Horatius.[5] The designation *parricidii* may, however, show that they were employed in such criminal cases as did not directly affect the welfare of the state,[6] and by their side the *duoviri*

---

[1] Cic. l.c.   [2] p. 63.

[3] The *quaestores parricidii* and *aerarii* are identified by Zonaras (vii. 13), following Dio. See p. 63. They were called *quaestores, οἵ πρῶτον μὲν τὰς θανασίμους δίκας ἐδίκαζον* (whence their title), *ὕστερον δὲ καὶ τὴν τῶν κοινῶν χρημάτων διοίκησιν ἔλαχον*. So Varro (*L.L.* v. 81), "quaestores a quaerendo, qui conquirerent publicas pecunias et maleficia." The identity of the two offices is denied by Pomponius in *Dig.* 1, 2, 2, 22 and 23.

[4] *Quaestores parricidii* were mentioned in the Twelve Tables (Pompon. in *Dig.* 1, 2, 2, 23).

[5] Liv. i. 26.

[6] They are mentioned in the trial of M. Volscius (459 B.C.) for an ordinary criminal offence (Liv. iii. 24), but also in the public trials of Sp. Cassius in 485 B.C.

II THE GROWTH OF THE REPUBLICAN CONSTITUTION 81

perduellionis reappear at intervals during the early Republic. Their financial functions are generally taken to imply the existence of a state treasury (*aerarium*). Tradition credits the first consul Valerius Publicola with its institution, and makes the quaestors the guardians of its wealth and probably of its archives.[1] The public chest of Rome must have been a primitive matter enough at a time when coined money was not in general use ; but it is not improbable that finance did at this time become a definite department. It could no longer be a purely domestic matter; the lands of the kings had become crown lands of the state; the series of wars into which Rome was plunged must have rendered a constant collection of the war-tax necessary ; none would more naturally have been entrusted with the control and disbursement of revenue than the perpetual delegates of the consuls ; and the formalism of Roman character would lead us to believe that the consuls had regular modes of acting through their quaestors, and that these officials so far limited the power of their masters. It is not improbable that the quaestors were originally nominated by the consuls without the direct intervention of the people ; but this does not exclude some popular ratification of the choice.[2] It was not until about the year 449 that their election was transferred to the newly-constituted *comitia* of the tribes.

And, as the consuls nominated their delegates, so the regal tradition was continued which gave them the nomination of their council of state, the Senate. In their choice of members

(Liv. ii. 41 ; Cic. *de Rep.* ii. 35, 60), and of Camillus in 396 B.C. (Plin. *H.N.* xxxiv. 3, 13) ; but various accounts are given of the procedure in these two trials.
    [1] Plut. *Public.* 12 ταμιεῖον μὲν ἀπέδειξε τὸν τοῦ Κρόνου ναόν . . . ταμίας δὲ τῷ δήμῳ δύο τῶν νέων ἔδωκεν ἀποδεῖξαι. The first quaestors appointed were Publius Veturius and Marcus Minucius. Pomponius (p. 80) puts the creation of the financial quaestors after the first secession of the Plebs ; Lydus (*de Mag.* i. 38) attributes them to the Licinian law of 367.
    [2] Tac. *Ann.* xi. 22 "Sed quaestores regibus etiam tum imperantibus instituti sunt, quod lex curiata ostendit ab L. Bruto repetita. Mansitque consulibus potestas deligendi, donec eum quoque honorem populus mandaret. Creatique primum Valerius Potitus et Aemilius Mamercus sexagesimo tertio anno post Tarquinios exactos, ut rem militarem comitarentur" (i.e. 447 B.C. ; hence Mommsen, *Staatsr.* ii. p. 529, thinks the change was due to the Valerio-Horatian laws of 449 B.C.). Plutarch (see note 1) thinks they were elected from the first. The meaning of the passage of Tacitus seems to be that the king nominated his quaestors after his own election, and their appointment was then ratified by the *lex curiata*. Another explanation is that the *lex* recited that the kings had appointed quaestors and empowered the consuls to do so. Cf. Ulpian in *Dig.* 1, 13.

G

they were legally as unfettered as the king had been, and could summon new members or omit to summon those already on the list.[1] So far as law went, the personnel of the Senate might now be changed annually. But custom must have been stronger than law. The body had gained a definiteness in its constitution, based on its representative character and probably on actual life-membership, which could not be easily destroyed, and the consul had a colleague at his side to check any attempt at capricious removal or selection. The short tenure of office must already have made a magistrate unwilling to exercise a power which might be so easily turned against himself in the near future. The discretionary power of the magistrate would have made the choice of Plebeians possible, now that they were possessed of all the essential rights of full citizenship ;[2] but it does not appear that this choice could have been often, if ever, exercised. The patrician clans had a close hereditary connexion with the Senate ; the *interregnum*, which was the transmission of auspices by the *patres*, had long been one of its privileges, and the prejudices of the patrician magistracy would hardly have allowed it to dip into the inferior order for councillors. If there be any truth in the story that, on the abolition of the monarchy, the thinned ranks of the *patres* were again raised to 300 by the inclusion of persons specially enrolled (*adlecti* or *conscripti*),[3] these added members were probably, like their predecessors, patrician. This large increase (placed by some at 164 members) gave rise to a transitory distinction between the older members and the new members, which—

[1] Festus p. 246, cited p. 59.

[2] Zonaras (vii. 9) makes Servius Tullius introduce Plebeians into the Senate.

[3] Liv. ii. 1 " Deinde, quo plus virium in senatu frequentia etiam ordinis faceret, caedibus regis diminutum patrum numerum primoribus equestris gradus lectis ad trecentorum summam explevit : traditumque inde fertur, ut in senatum vocarentur qui patres quique conscripti essent : conscriptos videlicet in novum senatum appellabant lectos "; Festus p. 254 " ' Qui patres, qui conscripti ' : vocati sunt in curiam, quo tempore regibus urbe expulsis P. Valerius consul propter inopiam patriciorum ex plebe adlegit in numerum senatorum C. et LX. et IIII. ut expleret numerum senatorum trecentorum " (for these numbers cf. Plut. *Public.* 11 τοὺς δ' ἐγγραφέντας ὑπ' αὐτοῦ λέγουσιν ἑκατὸν καὶ ἑξήκοντα τέσσαρας γενέσθαι). So *adlecti*, Festus p. 7 " *adlecti* dicebantur apud Romanos, qui propter inopiam ex equestri ordine in senatorum sunt numero adsumpti : nam patres dicuntur qui sunt patricii generis, conscripti qui in senatu sunt scriptis adnotati." Plutarch (*Qu. Rom.* 58, *Rom.* 13) makes the added members Plebeians. Tacitus (*Ann.* xi. 25) wrongly identifies these added members with the *minores gentes*. (Claudius creates Patricians A.D. 48—" paucis jam reliquis familiis, quas Romulus majorum et L. Brutus minorum gentium appellaverant.")

expressed in the formula of summons "qui patres, qui conscripti (estis)"—was finally merged in the general appellation of
"conscript fathers."[1]   The expression may have originated
with the abandonment or modification of some original principle
of selection; but, if *conscripti* be taken to apply wholly to
Plebeians, some date later than the commencement of the
Republic must be accepted for the origin of the term.[2]

The history, indeed, of the next hundred and fifty years
shows that the Senate is the stronghold of patrician prejudice.
The power from which the Plebeians try to shake themselves free, is the *patrum auctoritas*, and the magistracy must
soon have yielded to the demands of the new burgesses, had it
not been backed up by a patrician council.   Yet during the early
Republic the Senate was a power distinctly secondary to the
magistrates.   Its two undoubted prerogatives were the *interregnum*
and the *patrum auctoritas*.   The first was exercised, perhaps,
more occasionally even than it had been under the monarchy, for it
could not be resorted to if one of the two consuls existed to
nominate a successor.   The second power, on the other hand,
must have become far more formal than it had been in the time
of the monarchy.   Then it had been little more than the claim of
the council to be consulted on important business;[3] now it was put
forward as an integral part of the procedure of the state; it was
framed after the voting in the assembly had taken place, and no
law or election could be valid which had not, after it had passed
the people, received this formal consent of the *patres*.   We cannot
trace the widening of the other powers of the Senate; but we
must assume that it took up a more independent position in
face of the consuls than it had done in that of the king.   Perhaps
the establishment of a treasury and of financial quaestors, who
may have been selected from the council, led to its first connexion with finance.   The new importance that foreign affairs
assumed, in the constant wars in which Rome was engaged
with the nations of Italy, must certainly have strengthened its
control of this department.

---

[1] Willems (*Le Sénat* ii. 39 ff.) makes *patres conscripti* simply equivalent to
"assembled fathers."

[2] The first clear instance of a plebeian senator dates from the year 401.
Liv. v. 12. P. Licinius Calvus, created military tribune with consular power,
was "vir nullis ante honoribus usus, vetus tantum senator et aetate jam
gravis." Cf. Liv. iv. 15. Of Sp. Maelius (439 B.C.) it is asked "quem senatorem
concoquere civitas vix posset, regem ferret." [3] p. 60.

But, on the whole, the earliest period of the history of the Republic is the epoch of the power of the magistracy. The traditions of the monarchy were so little forgotten that eight years after the establishment of the Republic, kingship in a modified form was again restored.[1] In 501 B.C., during a war with the Latins, the consuls nominated an individual with the royal title and powers. It was understood that this *magister populi*, or, as he was afterwards called, *dictator*,[2] was to remain in power only so long as the danger lasted; as the danger was originally military, a single campaign of six months was held to be the maximum duration of the office. During this time he was to exercise the full regal *imperium*, within as well as without the city, and the accompanying military jurisdiction without appeal. He was originally understood to be a purely military official and the commander of the infantry force; the command of the cavalry he entrusted to a magistrate who, on the analogy of the magistracies of the monarchy, was a delegate of his own, and bore the title "master of the horse" (*magister equitum*).[3] The dictatorship was conceived of as a purely military office, and, though it was occasionally used for other purposes in the later constitution, never lost its primitive character. Although it impeded for a time some of the most characteristic functions of the consuls, it was not a suspension, but a part of, the constitution. A small, struggling, and essentially military society, such as that of early Rome, contemplated martial law as an occasional necessity; there were times when the peril of the state was so

[1] Liv. ii. 18 ; Festus p. 198 ; Pompon. in *Dig.* 1, 2, 2, 18.
[2] The title was, perhaps, originally *praetor*. This would naturally have been the case if Mommsen's theory is right that they were regarded as superior colleagues of the consuls (*Staatsr.* ii. p. 153). The earliest official title known to us is *magister populi*, and it was the technical title in the augural books. Cic. *de Leg.* iii. 3, 9 "isque ave sinistra dictus populi magister esto." Cf. *de Rep.* i. 40, 63 "Gravioribus vero bellis etiam sine collega omne imperium nostri penes singulos esse voluerunt, quorum ipsum nomen vim suae potestatis indicat. Nam dictator quidem ab eo appellatur quia dicitur ; sed in nostris libris vides eum, Laeli, magistrum populi appellari." The later title, *dictator*, was perhaps adopted in deference to Republican sentiment ; Mommsen (*Staatsr.* ii. p. 145) conjectures, in imitation of the Latin dictator, a constitutional survival of the monarchy. The meaning of the word is wholly uncertain. Ancient guesses say (i.) from *dicitur* (Cic. *de Rep.* l.c.) ; (ii.) from *dicto audiens* (Varro *L.L.* v. 8] "quoi dicto audientes omnes essent") ; (iii.) from *dictare* (Priscian viii. 14, 78), or (iv.) because they issued edicts (Dionys. v. 73).
[3] Pompon. in *Dig.* 1, 2, 2, 19 "Et his dictatoribus magistri equitum injungebantur sic, quo modo regibus tribuni celerum : quod officium fere tale erat, quale hodie praefectorum praetorio, magistratus tamen habebantur legitimi."

great that it was felt that the citizens' ordinary guarantees
of protection should sink into abeyance if they were thought
likely to interfere with the safety of the commonwealth. The
dictatorship had an internal as well as an external side to its
military character; it was even, perhaps, on its earliest institution, meant to control disobedient citizens as well as to oppose
the enemy,[1] and was thus to some extent a party weapon in the
hands of the Patricians against the refractory Plebs. We shall
find that this summary military jurisdiction within the city was
subsequently abolished, without much loss to the utility of the
institution. Its true merit was the unity of administration
which it created, the advantages of which were made more
apparent by the clashing powers of the magistrates at a later
stage of history. But the experience of the evils of divided
authority did not first point out the necessity of the office.
The dictatorship was an integral part of the original Republican
constitution; the law allowing it was forgotten—perhaps it was
the first *lex Valeria* which secured the appeal against the
ordinary magistrates; but the right of the consul to declare
martial law, as he did by appointing a dictator, was never
questioned as was the parallel right, usurped by the Senate in
later times, of arming the consul with military jurisdiction.
But, although the nomination of a dictator could not be regarded
as a violation of, or even as a break in, the constitution, it was
rightly held to be a powerful party weapon in the hands of the
patrician magistracy; and the attempts of the Plebs were
directed, however unsuccessfully, to limit this mighty power
which over-rode all privilege and law.

But the appointment of a dictator was supposed to be due
to exceptional circumstances. It is only when we look to the
peaceful life of the state, to the administration of law by the
magistrate or the expression of popular will in the *comitia*, that
we can estimate the strength of the position held by the
patrician families.

The criminal law, which was doubtless during this period
becoming more and more secularised and divorced from the
direct control of religion, was the monopoly of the official class.

---

[1] Cic. *de Leg.* iii. 3, 9 " Ast quando duellum gravius, discordiae civium
escunt, oenus, ne amplius sex menses, si senatus creverit, idem juris, quod duo
consules, teneto"; Imp. Claudius *Oratio* i. 28 "Quid nunc commemorem
dictaturae hoc ipso consulari imperium valentius repertum apud majores nostros
quo in asperioribus bellis aut in civili motu difficiliore uterentur?"

A criminal case was an inquiry undertaken solely on the initiative of the magistrate; no question could come before the people until he had investigated it, and was then only submitted in a *form prepared by him*. In the early popular courts at Rome there was no power of amendment; the people could answer only " Yes " or " No " to the question put before them. We are ignorant of the extent of popular jurisdiction ; it is possible that only sentences affecting the *caput* of a citizen were submitted to the assembly.[1] But there was no real guarantee that even such questions could be forced from the magistrate's court. The *lex Valeria* which admitted the *provocatio* imposed no penalty on the magistrate who violated its provisions ; the only hope lay in the veto of his colleague, and, if two consuls were in agreement, they might ride roughshod over the law. The consuls were ostensibly the only guardians of the criminal code ; as it is inconceivable that, in an age which made little use of writing, two men selected on very varied grounds could have been regarded as fit expounders of this form of *jus*, we must, even in the domain of criminal law, go behind them and seek its true source in that formidable body, the college of pontiffs. The learning and activity of this body is known to us, however, chiefly in connexion with the divine or family or, as it would have been called in later times, the civil law. The change from monarchy to aristocracy introduced, in Rome as in Greece, an epoch of religious tyranny. A king, who is the head of the religious as well as of the secular life of the state, may hold the balance between the classes. He is more likely to repress than to encourage his advisers ; he may find in popular rights a useful check to religious insolence. But remove the king and substitute an aristocracy like the Patriciate whose members hold supreme office in turn ; let there be no distinction between clergy and laity in this body, so that there can be no conflict between the secular and sacred power, which may enable a third power to gain a footing ; and let this body have a monopoly of the civil law—and we get unequalled

---

[1] Cicero (*de Rep*. ii. 31, 53) gives as the tenor of the first Valerian law " ne quis magistratus civem Romanum adversus provocationem necaret neve verberaret." Dionysius (v. 19) adds ζημιοῦν εἰς χρήματα to ἀποκτείνειν ἢ μαστιγοῦν, and Plutarch (*Publ*. 11) seems to give it the same wide scope. He also thinks that Valerius fixed the *multa suprema* (l.c.), i.e. the largest fine the magistrate could impose without appeal. These statements may, however, be deductions from the later *provocatio*.

possibilities of judicial tyranny. For two hundred years (509–304) the knowledge of the forms of procedure, the *legis actiones*, which formed the whole content of the civil law, was open to the patrician pontiffs alone.[1] We are told that, even after the outlined codification and publication of the law in the Twelve Tables, the formularies could only be repeated correctly under the guidance of the college, which for this purpose annually appointed one of its members to "preside over private suits." It is true that the theory of civil procedure was the same as it had been in the time of the monarchy ; the magistrate decided what special rule of process was applicable, and then the case was settled by an arbitrator chosen by the litigants.[2] But the magistrate must often have been unskilled, one of the college must always have stood by his side, and the pontiff so officiating was not merely an adviser to the parties but a witness to the performance. The pontiffs, however, were more than interpreters. They had, as the guardians of *fas*, their own sphere of law, relics of which survived into the late Republic, and within this sphere they were judges. They had a graduated scale of expiations for sins (*piacula*) ; they were the police who protected the sanctity of festal days (*feriae*), and inflicted spiritual penalties on the magistrate himself who dared to exercise jurisdiction on a day which they had declared holy ; they issued and enforced commands which protected sacred places (*loci sacri*) and burial-grounds.[3] Vows (*vota*), to be effective, must be prescribed by them, and peculiarly efficacious were those fixed forms of prayer (*certae precationes*) which they had dictated word for word (*de scripto praeire*).

Against this phalanx of patrician power what forces could the Plebeians boast ?

A certain amount of voting power in the *comitia* was all

---

[1] Pompon. in *Dig.* 1, 2, 2 (§ 3) "exactis deinde regibus . . . omnes leges hae exoleverunt iterumque coepit populus Romanus incerto magis jure et consuetudine aliqua uti quam per latam legem, idque prope quinquaginta (MSS. "viginti") annis passus est." After the Twelve Tables (§ 6) "ex his legibus . . . actiones compositae sunt, quibus inter se homines disceptarent : quas actiones ne populus prout vellet institueret, certas sollemnesque esse voluerunt . . . Omnium tamen harum et interpretandi scientia et actiones apud collegium pontificum erant, ex quibus constituebatur, quis quoquo anno praeesset privatis."   [2] p. 64.

[3] The later praetorian interdicts (*de locis sacris, de mortuo inferendo*) are really within the domain of *fas* and must at one time have been enforced by the pontiffs.

that they possessed. But this voting power, except on certain
established points—the declaration of war and, when the law
was observed, criminal jurisdiction—was very ineffective, for
the assembly was wholly dependent for its summons and
expression of opinion on the patrician consuls, and liable to
interruption from the pious scruples of patrician augurs ; and we
have already seen how even the choice of magistrates could be
hampered by the formalities which still conditioned the election.[1]
But, even had these adverse circumstances been avoided, the
voting power of the Plebeians was small. The *comitia centuriata*
contained chiefly the propertied—for the most part the landed—
class; and even in this assembly the two first classes and the
knights, which would have consisted mainly of Patricians, had
a majority of votes (118 out of 193). The small farmers and
the artisans commanded but 74 or 75 votes; the great mass of
the Proletariate was either wholly unrepresented or could dispose
of but a single vote. It is important to inquire whether these
classes excluded from the centuries were represented elsewhere,
or whether there was an assembly possessing any real power in
which Patricians and Plebeians were alike represented.

It has been proved beyond a doubt that at some period
during the first three centuries of the Republic Plebeians came
to be included in the *comitia curiata*.[2] The change was the
result of two circumstances; firstly, the perfect equality of
private rights between the members of the two orders—adrogation and adoption, both of which followed the possession of a
familia, and in many cases *gentilitas*, being common to both—
which rendered it impossible to draw distinctions amongst
the *curiales;* and secondly, the reactionary influence of the
centuriate assembly, which emphasised the idea that Patricians
and Plebeians together made up the Populus.

Such a change must have been gradual; but, when it had
occurred, the admission of the Plebeians made this assembly
thoroughly democratic in form, for a vote in this *comitia*
depended neither on land or wealth, but simply on personal
membership of a *curia*, which was common to all the citizens.
But it is the very comparison of such a body with the thoroughly
timocratic organisation of the *comitia centuriata* which leads us
to believe that, at the time when the Plebeians were admitted,
the *curiae* had ceased to be a power. The condition reached

---

[1] p. 78.   [2] Mommsen *Staatsr.* iii. p. 93.

by the *comitia curiata* in historical times will be described else-where.   Its most distinctive right—the *lex curiata*—had perhaps been a real power in the hands of the Patricians, as long as they were its sole members, although their preponderance in the *comitia centuriata* would have made a conflict between these two bodies unlikely; but there probably never was a time when the masses of the Plebs gathered *curiatim* upset the verdict of the Patricians and wealthy Plebeians assembled *centuriatim*.

When we consider this situation, it is not surprising that the leading features of the first period of development of the Roman constitution (494–287 B.C.) were an attempt to limit the power of the magistrates, and a struggle of the Plebs for equality with the Patriciate.   The two struggles do not run on parallel lines but are interwoven at every point, since the magistracy represented the Patriciate.   Nor do they represent merely an effort to weaken or to obtain political privilege; in their earlier stages the motive of the Plebs is not ambition, but defence. Their first efforts have the negative object of the protection of rights, not the positive design of an attempt to share in a political power which was closed to their order.

Tradition represents the earliest social struggles of the Plebs as centring round two questions—the possession of the public land, and the law of debtor and creditor.   They were no doubt closely connected, for assignment of land meant relief of debt, but the agitation that gathered round the public land was directed by individuals, was merely occasional, and led to no permanent results; it is less a part of constitutional than of political history, and its true nature is obscured by the fact that we cannot say how far the annalists have transferred to this early period the circumstances of the agrarian agitation of a later day.   But the early mode of assignment of the public land deserves consideration; for, as one of the undoubted grievances of the Plebs, it may have been one of the motives that led to the first great political reform.   Land conquered from the enemy was sometimes assigned to poorer citizens in small allotments by the state (*ager assignatus*); in later times it was sometimes sold by the state through its quaestors (*ager quaestorius*); and in both these cases it became private property. But, in the early Republic, the custom was growing up of leaving a great portion of conquered land—especially such as was fit only for pasturage or had been devastated in war—as state domain (*ager publicus*), and of allowing it to be held in usufruct (*occupatio*) by squatters who paid to the state for their privilege a proportion of the produce (*vectigal*), a tithe or a fifth. Large portions of such *ager publicus* had probably been originally a part of the king's domains, and had been held by his clients, who would, of course, have been members of the lower class of the Plebs. But under the new conditions of things it was all the property of the state ; and the theory was started, or confirmed, that in this case Patricians alone could be its occupants,[1] a privilege that had probably originated with the assumption that only the conquerors of the land could share in the spoils of war.[2] This privilege—comprehensible but legally absurd in that it involved the theory that clients of the state must belong to a particular order—could no longer be upheld on the same grounds, for Plebeians now marched to battle and could justly claim a share in the prizes of war. But the maintenance of this principle, even if justly carried out, could not have wholly solved the social problem. The Proletariate, who had no share in winning the prize, would have still been justly excluded ; but it would at least have benefited the small plebeian farmer, and perhaps it was he that had most need of benefit.

For the small independent landholder was in a hopeless plight—far more hopeless than that of the client or emancipated slave who could claim his lord's protection. His condition was due to the law of debtor and creditor—one, it seems, that was unknown to the old patrician community, and had originated within the plebeian order, but which the Patriciate, by adopting plebeian forms of law, could use with terrible force against its inventors. The original procedure was one of the manifold forms of *nexum*, or binding obligation created by the copper and the scales (*per aes et libram*). A man who borrowed was allowed to sell his perpetual services to his creditor conditionally—the condition being the non-repayment of the debt within a given time.[3] When the prescribed period had elapsed, the debtor and

---

[1] p. 35.

[2] The privilege could not have been based on quiritarian ownership, since this tenure was precarious.

[3] The contract of *nexum* was in fact a conditioned mancipation, like a testament, the *nuncupatio* being made by the vendor, who perhaps purchased with a single coin (*nummo uno*), as in the later *mancipationes fiduciae causa* (Bruns *Fontes*).

his whole *familia* passed into the power of his purchaser; he
became his bondsman (*nexus*) until the debt was paid by his
labour. As in such circumstances the debt was never likely
to be liquidated, the small farmer became a mere dependent
member of the household of the rich landowner, leaning on his
mercy and subject to his caprice. No judicial process was
necessary to create the condition. The simple proof (perhaps
given before a magistrate) of the witnesses to the contract was
all that was required. The enslavement of the citizen was, it
is true, forbidden by Roman public law,[1] and the *nexus* remained
a burgess.[2] But a very thin line separated such a condition
from one of actual slavery.

It is probable that in early times plebeian law recognised no
debt except that created by the nexal contract. But as Roman
commerce extended it was impossible to observe this limitation;
refinements of procedure extended this penalty to debts incurred
by the patrician form of mere verbal promise (*stipulatio, sponsio*).
The form of procedure in this case is known to us from the
Twelve Tables. If the debt was confessed or proved before a
court, an interval of thirty days was given to the debtor wherein
to pay; at the end of this period he was arrested by the creditor
(*manus injectio*) and brought before the consul, by whom, if no
champion (*vindex*) presented himself to contest the debt, he was
bound over (*addictus*) to the creditor. The latter could take him
home and put him in bonds, but must give him a pound of corn
a day. Another interval of sixty days followed, within which
the prisoner was presented to the magistrate on three court days
(*nundinae*). On the last his fate was sealed. He was no longer
in the condition even of the *nexus*. His creditor might put him
to death or sell him as a slave beyond the Tiber.[3] If there were

---

[1] Except as a penal measure ordained by the state. The *furem manifestum*
according to Gellius (xx. 1), "in servitutem tradit" (lex); he is more correctly
described as *addictus* by Gaius (iii. 189). The *incensus* might be sold as a slave
(Cic. *pro. Caecin.* 34, 99). Later a free man who collusively allowed himself to
be sold as a slave, in order to share the purchase money with the vendor, was
adjudged a slave as a punishment for his fraud (*Dig.* 40, 13, 3; *Inst.* 1, 3, 4;
Cod. 7, 18, 1).   [2] p. 24.

[3] Gell. xx. 1 "Aeris confessi rebusque jure judicatis triginta dies justi sunto.
Post deinde manus injectio esto, in jus ducito. Ni judicatum facit aut quis endo
eo in jure vindicit, secum ducito, vincito aut nervo aut compedibus. . . . Si volet
suo vivito. Ni suo vivit, qui eum vinctum habebit, libras farris endo dies dato.
Si volet plus dato." The *addictus* like the *nexus* did not become a slave, but
still retained his position in his census and in his tribe (Quinctil. *Decl.* 311).

more creditors than one,[1] they might divide the debtor's body
into equal portions; and the Twelve Tables gave immunity to
the creditor who took more than his fair share of the flesh.
This death-penalty was doubtless a humane alternative to
perpetual imprisonment. Even if it did not submit the penalty,
as a capital one, to appeal (*provocatio*), the danger, which could be
brought home to relatives and friends by gradual mutilation,
disfiguring but not fatal, must have roused their efforts to
effect a ransom. It was the application of this law of debt,
perhaps in even a harsher and more primitive form, that called
forth the first resistance from the Plebs. The perpetual struggle
for existence in which Rome was now engaged kept her armies
constantly in the field, and the small farmer on service, who had
no slaves, had to let his farm go to ruin in his absence and to
mortgage his body when he returned.[2] The most obvious remedy
was a general strike against the military levy; and this was
attempted. Already in 495 a riot had been raised in Rome,
which was only appeased by the promises of a popular consul,
Servilius, that the *nexi* should be released for service, and that no
one should seize goods or pledges from a soldier while he was in
the field. The liberated citizens scattered the Volsci and
Aurunci; their reward was a more rigorous enforcement of the
law of debt by the other consul Appius. Servilius was appealed
to, but would not use his right of veto against his colleague. It
was plain that no one could rely on a consul's *auxilium* being
used on behalf of the Plebs.[3] A fierce stand against the conscription was now made by the desperate Plebeians; the
patrician answer was the appointment of a dictator. Again the
army took the field against the Volscians and the Sabines; but,
when victory was assured, the legions were not disbanded, and
a pretext was found for another campaign. On the march
from Rome the plebeian contingents suddenly turned aside
to a hill in the territory of Crustumerium, which, from the oath
taken on its summit, was thenceforth called the "Mount of
Curses" (*sacer mons*).[4] A plan, carefully thought out in the

---

[1] In the case of a nexal contract there could not be more creditors than one.
A man could not, by the nature of the case, mancipate himself to several people
at once.
[2] Liv. ii. 23 "Fremebant se, foris pro libertate et imperio dimicantes, domi a
civibus captos et oppressos esse; tutioremque in bello quam in pace, et inter
hostes quam inter cives, libertatem plebis esse."
[3] ib. 27.   [4] Dionys. vi. 45.

coteries and gatherings that had preceded the campaign,[1] was now carried into effect. The Plebs had already gathered in informal meetings (*concilia*) to discuss their grievances. All that they lacked to become a corporation which might rival that of the Populus, was to have at their head magistrates with great and recognised powers. They were now met in battle array to carry out this resolve; and it was not unnatural that the two plebeian magistrates whom they chose to rival the power of the consuls should bear the military appellation of tribunes.[2] It was made a condition of reconciliation with the patrician state which they had quitted, that these officers should have the power of suspending the decree of the consuls when levelled against a member of the Plebs. But, since little confidence was to be reposed in the government, the Plebs bound themselves by an oath, similar to that taken on the expulsion of the king, to destroy any one who offered injury or insult to their magistrates. The recognition of these new magistrates, with the powers their appointment involved, was effected by a *lex centuriata* perhaps passed in the very year of the secession (494 B.C.). The office of the *tribuni plebis* or *plebei* was modelled as closely as possible on that of the consuls. They were originally two in number, and had, with reference to each other, the mutual power of veto which the collegiate principle implied. They were from the first magistrates of the Plebs, hence none but Plebeians were eligible,[3] and they must from the first have been elected by an assembly of the Plebs. This assembly, however, did not perpetuate its original military character, and the unit of voting naturally selected for the city-gatherings at which the tribunes were appointed was the *curia*, to which Plebeians had for some time belonged. This assembly of the Plebs was known as the *concilium plebis curiatim*.[4]

[1] Liv. ii. 28. The senators complain "nunc in mille curias contionesque (cum alia in Esquiliis, alia in Aventino fiant concilia) dispersam et dissipatam esse rem publicam."

[2] Varro *L.L.* v. 81 "tribuni plebei, quod ex tribunis militum primum tribuni plebei facti, qui plebem defenderent, in secessione Crustumerina."

[3] The principle of cooptation was said to have been recognised in the *carmen rogationis* of the tribunate, and in this case it was held that Patricians were eligible. Liv. iii. 65 (449 B.C.) "Novi tribuni plebis in cooptandis collegis patrum voluntatem foverunt. Duos etiam patricios consularesque, Sp. Tarpeium et A. Aternium, cooptavere." But, with the disuse of this principle, the plebeian qualification was observed.

[4] Cic. ap. Ascon. *in Cornel.* p. 76 "Tanta igitur in illis virtus fuit, ut anno

With respect to power the tribunate has, from its origin, a double character.   It possesses a negative control of the whole people (generally in the person of its magistrate) exercised in defence of the Plebs, and a positive authority within the plebeian community.   The first power asserts itself in the right of veto, the second is shown in the power of eliciting resolutions (*scita plebei* or *plebiscita*) from the plebeian *concilium*.   The first power, that of offering assistance (*auxilium*) to any Plebeian[1] who feels himself aggrieved by the decree of the magistrate, and suspending this decree by the exercise of the "veto," was the *raison d'être* of the tribunate.   The tribune was created to meet the consular imperium (*contra consulare imperium*),[2] and the fact that he could only exercise this power in person imposed on him certain obligations.   The tribune might not stay a night without the walls, and the doors of his house were open day and night.[3]   It was doubtless through the insufficiency of these presidents of the Plebs to cope with the demands for their assistance that their number was raised first to four (471 B.C.), and before the year 449 B.C. to ten[4]—changes which were ratified by the centuries and the Senate.

But a negative control over the magistrates of the state must be wholly ineffective unless there be some means of enforcing this control.   Had the tribunes possessed no coercive power, the consul, in carrying out the law of debt or in summoning Plebeians

xvi. post reges exactos propter nimiam dominationem potentium secederent, . . . duos tribunos crearent. . . . Itaque auspicato postero anno tr. pl. comitiis curiatis creati sunt."   (For the number two Ascon. *in loc.* quotes Tuditanus and Atticus.) Cicero apparently understands by this the mixed assembly of the *curiae;* and so does Livy (ii. 56, on the *lex Publilia* transferring the elections of the tribunes to the tribes), "quae patriciis omnem potestatem per clientium suffragia creandi, quos vellent, tribunos auferret."

[1] It must have been so restricted at first.   Later (as we shall see in dealing with the intercession) the *auxilium* was extended to the whole people.

[2] Cic. *de Rep.* ii. 33, 58 "contra consulare imperium tribuni plebis . . . constituti."

[3] Gell. xiii. 12 "(tribunis) jus abnoctandi ademptum, quoniam, ut vim fieri vetarent, adsiduitate eorum et praesentium oculis opus erat."   Cf. iii. 2.   Plut. *Qu. Rom.* 81 ὅθεν οὐδ' οἰκίας αὐτοῦ κλείεσθαι νενόμισται θύραν, ἀλλὰ καὶ νύκτωρ ἀνέῳγε καὶ μεθ' ἡμέραν, ὥσπερ λιμὴν καὶ καταφυγὴ τοῖς δεομένοις.

[4] For the increase to four see Diodor. xi. 68 (471 B.C. in connexion with the *lex Publilia*) ; other accounts represent the original number as five (Ascon. l.c. p. 93, and Livy ii. 33 ; two elected, three coopted ; cf. note on p. 93).   The increase to ten is assigned by Livy and Dionysius to 457 B.C. (Livy iii. 30 ; the tribunes allowed the levy "non sine pactione tamen ut . . . decem deinde tribuni plebis crearentur.   Expressit hoc necessitas patribus"; cf. Dionys. x. 30).

for the levy, would simply have set their veto aside.   We should have expected that such breaches of the law would have been guarded against by judicial prosecution before the courts of the community.   But this was not consistent with the Roman idea of magistracy.   Each magistrate had, to a greater or less degree, the power of enforcing his own decrees (*coercitio*), limited only by the right of appeal or the veto of his colleague ; and this power could not be denied to the tribune.   A logical consequence of his right of veto was that he could exercise this *coercitio* against the consuls themselves ; the sanctity of his person (guaranteed by the Plebs and accepted by the Populus) rendered resistance hopeless ; and all the weapons of the *coercitio*—arrest, imprison-ment, fines, stripes, and death—were at the disposal of the champion of the Plebs.

Coercitio implies summary jurisdiction ; and the infliction of fines beyond a certain limit, scourging, or death subjected a magistrate to the *provocatio*, and therefore made him a partner in a trial before a popular assembly.   Hence the judicial power of the tribune, also a necessary consequence of his power of veto. Undoubtedly when the office was created this consequence was not foreseen.   When it was found to be a necessary accompani-ment of the tribunician power, tradition tells us that it was questioned by the Patricians.   The historically worthless but typical trial of C. Marcius Coriolanus in 491 B.C. elicited a protest that the *jus* of the tribunes extended only to Plebeians.[1] The protest was idle, for the *jus auxilii* could not exist without the *jus poenae* against its violators.   The violation of plebeian rights which was thus met by tribunician coercion and jurisdic-tion, was always an infringement of the safety or dignity of the tribune himself.   Even the infliction of wrong on an individual through the violation of the tribune's decree was a wrong done to the Plebs through him ; it was not held to affect the rest of the community ; hence the not unnatural belief of our annalists that, when the tribune pronounced a sentence

[1] Liv. ii. 35 "contemptim primo Marcius audiebat minas tribunicias ; auxilii, non poenae, jus datum illi potestati ; plebisque, non patrum, tribunos esse." Coriolanus was probably impeached before the Plebs as a *hostis tribuniciae potestatis* in consequence of his advice that the tribunate should be abrogated (Liv. ii. 34). See Rein *Criminalrecht* p. 484.   Cf. Liv. ii. 56 (471 B.C. ; the tribune seizes some *nobiles* who would not yield to his *viator*) "Consul Appius negare jus esse tribuno in quemquam, nisi in plebeium ; non enim populi, sed plebis, eum magis-tratum esse."

against which there was an appeal, he brought the matter before the assembly of the Plebs.

This right of reference implies the power known as the *jus agendi cum plebe*. It was a power that could not have been contemplated on the establishment of the tribunate, but it proved a necessary consequence of the *auxilium*. Its acquirement meant a new infringement of the rights of patrician magistrates; for the summoning of the Plebs meant the calling away of a large portion of the Populus from the consuls. Two summonses of two assemblies containing the same individuals by different magistrates meant an inevitable conflict of authority, and the tribunician right of transacting business with the Plebs could not be secured but by a definite guarantee against consular interference. This guarantee was given, tradition says, by a resolution of the Plebs itself, passed in 492 B.C., two years after the institution of the tribunate, under the presidency of the tribune Sp. Icilius.[1] The date is probably too early, and the resolution must have been subsequently ratified by a *lex* of the centuries. It enacted that when the tribune addressed the Plebs no one should speak against or interrupt him; that the tribune should fine the offender and demand securities. If securities were not forthcoming, the offender should be punished with death and his property confiscated to the gods. If the fine were disputed the judgment should rest with the people. Whether by "people" here was meant Populus or Plebs, it was doubtless on this law that the plebeian assembly based its jurisdiction in the case of injury or insult being offered to its magistrate.

But the right of acting with the Plebs, which was thus guaranteed to the tribune, had another and more positive aspect. It might be used to elicit formal resolutions passed by the whole plebeian *concilium* in their own interests, and to give this body the character of a guild which, within certain limits, could pass rules binding on all its members. So long as the resolutions of this body were purely self-regarding, did not infringe on the

---

[1] Dionys. vii. 17 δημάρχου γνώμην ἀγορεύοντος ἐν δήμῳ μηδεὶς λεγέτω μηδὲν ἐναντίον μηδὲ μεσολαβείτω τὸν λόγον. ἐὰν δέ τις παρὰ ταῦτα ποιήσῃ, διδότω τοῖς δημάρχοις ἐγγυητὰς αἰτηθεὶς εἰς ἔκτισιν ἧς ἂν ἐπιθῶσιν αὐτῷ ζημίας. Any one who does not give securities (ἐγγυηταί) is to be punished with death καὶ τὰ χρήματ' αὐτοῦ ἱερὰ ἔστω. τῶν δ' ἀμφισβητούντων πρὸς ταύτας τὰς ζημίας αἱ κρίσεις ἔστωσαν ἐπὶ τοῦ δήμου. Cf. vi. 16, and Cic. *pro Sest.* 37, 79 "Fretus sanctitate tribunatus, cum se non modo contra vim et ferrum, sed etiam contra verba atque interfationem legibus sacratis esse armatum putaret."

public law, and were voluntarily accepted by all the members, they did not need formal ratification by any higher authority. But sometimes resolutions were passed which the Plebs was incapable of carrying into effect; in this case they were mere petitions to the only recognised legislative power, the consuls presiding over the *comitia centuriata*. We have an instance of this procedure, dated within forty years of the establishment of the tribunate, which shows how far-reaching the demands of this *concilium* might be. In 456 B.C. the tribune Icilius elicited from this assembly a resolution to the effect that the Aventine, until that time state property,[1] should be assigned to the Plebs. With this petition he approached the consuls and the Senate, and requested them to gain the consent of the *comitia centuriata* in due form of law.[2] The same procedure must be imagined for any *plebiscita*, which refer to matters affecting the whole community, down to the year 287, when, as we shall see, these resolutions of the Plebs were first raised to a level with the laws. In framing its resolutions the Plebs was as dependent on the tribune as the *comitia* was on the consuls; the *rogatio* of the magistrate could only be answered by the "Yes" or "No" of the burgesses. Its elective proceedings were similar to those of the whole people. The tribune, before he quitted office, nominated successors and submitted their names to the Plebs. The differences were that the voting was by *curiae* and not by *centuries*, that the *patrum auctoritas* had here no place, and that the formal taking of the auspices was not necessary to the validity of the proceedings, although doubtless the tribunes employed their right of taking private auspices[3] to give a sanctity to the act of the Plebs.

In one further and less important respect was this community of the Plebs modelled on the larger community of the Populus. In the year when the tribunate was established, the magistrates of the Plebs were given two assistants,[4] who bore the same

---

[1] p. 66 note 5.

[2] Dionys. x. 31, 32 ; see Mr. Strachan-Davidson in Smith *Dict. of Antiq.* s.v. *plebiscitum.*   [3] p. 39.

[4] Dionys. vi. 90 ἄνδρας ἐκ τῶν δημοτικῶν δύο καθ' ἕκαστον ἐνιαυτὸν ἀποδεικνύναι τοὺς ὑπηρετήσοντας τοῖς δημάρχοις ὅσων ἂν δέωνται καὶ δίκας, ἅς ἂν ἐπιτρέψωνται ἐκεῖνοι, κρινοῦντας ἱερῶν τε καὶ δημοσίων τόπων καὶ τῆς κατὰ τὴν ἀγορὰν εὐετηρίας ἐπιμελησομένους : Gell. xvii. 21 "tribunos et aediles tum primum per seditionem sibi plebes creavit"; Pompon. in *Dig.* 1, 2, 2, 21 "Itemque ut essent qui aedibus pracessent, in quibus omnia scita sua plebs deferebat, duos ex plebe constituerunt, qui etiam aediles appellati sunt."

H

relation to them as the two quaestors did to the consuls. Their functions were as undefined as those of the quaestors; but, when the powers of the tribunate were slightly better established, these delegates seem, like their prototypes, to have been concerned mainly with criminal jurisdiction and finance. They also kept the archives of the Plebs in the temple of Ceres, and it was thought that it was from this that their name *aediles* (possibly not their original title) was derived.[1] They served the tribunes in the exercise of their *coercitio*, seizing the offender or inflicting the death penalty. We find them performing this function in the trial of Coriolanus.[2] After the tribunes had gained criminal jurisdiction, they assisted them as delegates.[3] Their original financial functions are somewhat indefinable; but such functions are suggested by their office at the temple of Ceres and the archives which they guarded there—functions which find exact parallels in those of the quaestors at the temple of Saturn. It may have been one of their duties to exercise some supervision over the forced labour (*operae*) of the Plebeians, and this may have led to an early connexion with the repair of roads and buildings. Their police functions, their supervision of the market, above all their maintenance of the state religion amongst the masses, can hardly be referred to this early period.[4]

The aediles may originally have been nominated by their superiors; but election by the *concilium* of the Plebs, under the presidency of a tribune, is the only form of their appointment which is known to us. The office was legalised with the tribunate, and its holder possessed the same personal

---

[1] Dionysius (l.c.) suggests that they originally bore another title. Pomponius (l.c.) derives the name from their office in the temple of Ceres; Varro from their care of the repair of *aedes* both sacred and private (Varro *L.L.* v. 81 "aedilis, qui aedes sacras et privatas procuraret"), a derivation which Mommsen (*Staatsr.* ii. p. 480) favours. Their relation to the aediles of the Latin towns is wholly uncertain. Mommsen (ib. p. 474) holds strongly to the view that the Latin aedileship was borrowed from the Roman. For a different view cf. Ohnesseit *Ztschr. der Savigny-stiftung* 1883, pp. 200 sq.

[2] Plut. *Coriol.* 18 (the tribune Sicinnius) προσέταξε τοῖς ἀγορανόμοις ἀναγαγόντας αὐτὸν ἐπὶ τὴν ἄκραν εὐθὺς ὦσαι κατὰ τῆς ὑποκειμένης φάραγγος. So later in the trial of P. Scipio. Liv. xxix. 20; xxxviii. 52.

[3] Liv. iii. 31 (456 B.C.; the consuls sell booty taken from the Aequi) "itaque ergo, ut magistratu abiere . . . dies dicta est, Romilio ab C. Calvio Cicerone, tribuno plebis, Veturio ab L. Alieno, aedile plebis."

[4] Yet Livy attributes both to the fifth century; they perform police-duties in the year 463 (Liv. iii. 6), and are entrusted with the care of the state religion in 428 (Liv. iv. 30).

sanctity as the tribune, conferred first by oath and then by law.[1]

For the power of these plebeian magistrates rests wholly on a superstitious belief, consciously applied to fill up a gap in the public law. It might have been thought that magistrates elected by a large body of the citizens, whose powers were recognised by public law, would have been sufficiently protected by their position. But the Romans were slaves to legal formulae. The Plebs was not the community, nor even at first a legalised corporation within the city; the tribunes were, therefore, not magistrates of the state, and wore none of the insignia of office; they had not the *imperium* and the *auspicia*, and therefore could not be protected by the law of treason (*perduellio*), which avenged wrongs done to the state in the person of its magistrate. A substitute must be found in a religious sanction. Perhaps Rome is the only state that has definitely invested the demagogue or "champion of the people" with a halo of sanctity. This was first given him by the people whom he championed. The Plebs on the Mons Sacer had sworn an oath to destroy any one who destroyed their tribune—an oath which they perpetuated to their descendants. The sanctity of the tribunes, therefore, had originally no valid religious ground, for the Populus had not pronounced such an offender to be *sacer*, nor had the oath been taken by a magistrate on behalf of the whole community. It was simply a proclamation by a section of the people of the infringement of rights which they held would justify a revolution; and the declaration was accepted by the Roman state when it recognised the tribunate. But the inviolability of plebeian magistrates did not gain legal recognition until the reinstitution of the office in 449 B.C. Then the violator of the majesty of the tribune was made a *sacer homo*[2] in its later sense

---

[1] Livy, however (iii. 55, cited note 2), represents the *sacrosanctitas* of the aediles as being based only on law.

[2] Dionys. vi. 89. The *sacrosanctitas* of the tribune is guaranteed νόμῳ τε καὶ ὅρκῳ. Cf. App. *B. C.* ii. 108 ἡ τῶν δημάρχων ἀρχὴ ἱερὰ καὶ ἄσυλος ἦν ἐκ νόμου καὶ ὅρκου παλαιοῦ. For these two grounds of inviolability see Liv. iii. 55 (restoration of tribunate in 449) "et cum religione inviolatos eos, tum lege etiam fecerunt, sanciendo 'ut qui tribunis plebis, aedilibus, judicibus, decemviris nocuisset, ejus caput Jovi sacrum esset, familia ad aedem Cereris, Liberi Liberaeque venum iret.' Hac lege juris interpretes negant quemquam sacrosanctum esse ; sed eum, qui eorum cuiquam nocuerit, sacrum sanciri. Itaque aedilem prendi ducique a majoribus magistratibus : quod etsi non jure fiat (noceri enim ei, cui hac lege non liceat) tamen argumentum esse, non haberi pro sacro sanctoque

of "an outlaw" for the whole community, and the aediles and
the plebeian *decemviri* were protected by the same ban.   Yet the
Roman jurists held that this law did not give *sacrosanctitas*, at
least to the tribune ; that was given by the "ancient oath" of
the Plebs ; the law only announced a penalty which might be
carried out by any member of the community.   This view was
of importance, because it recognised the capital jurisdiction of
the Plebs in all cases where their magistrates had been injured ;
and, although subsequent practice was unfavourable to this
jurisdiction, its legality cannot be questioned.   The tribune was
himself the defender of his own personal inviolability and that
of his fellow-officers ; for it was he who summarily inflicted the
punishment or proposed the penalty to the *concilium.*   The
crime of infringing plebeian liberties could not originally have
borne a definite name ; in later times it was brought under the
vague conception of *majestas*, "the infringement of the greatness
of the state."   The penalty might be a capital one, while the
acts construed as infringement might be very slight indeed.
Physical compulsion, blows, an attempt at murder were all
obvious cases ; but forcible resistance to a tribune's will[1] came
under this head, and, after the law which guaranteed the right
of meeting to the Plebs, any act, whether of magistrates or
individuals, which interrupted a meeting of the Plebs summoned
by a tribune.[2]

In fact, during the earliest years of the struggles of the Plebs,
the rights of the corporation are represented only by the powers
of the tribune, through whom alone it claimed official recognition ;
and thus from 494 to the epoch of the decemviral legislation
(451) the tribunate is engaged in efforts to gain a better representation of the plebeian community, and to secure an equality
in the administration of the law, which should render the
clumsy negative system of the constant interposition of their
auxilium less necessary.

The first attempt seems to have been to some extent secured
by the *plebiscitum* passed by Publilius Volero in 471, which
enacted that the *concilium* of the Plebs, instead of meeting as

aedilem : tribunos vetere jurejurando plebis, cum primum eam potestatem
creavit, sacrosanctos esse " (cf. Liv. ii. 33 "sacratam legem latam" on the Mons
Sacer).

[1] Resistance to the will of a *magistratus populi* is not *perduellio* iu later
Roman law, but rather *vis*.   But resistance to the tribune is always *majestas.*

[2] Dionys. vii. 17.   See p. 96.

before by *curiae*, should now meet by tribes (*tributim*).[1] As this was a purely self-regarding ordinance, it probably did not require the consent of Senate and people,[2] and we are told that it was looked on with disfavour by the Patricians. The grounds of their objections are not easily fathomed, nor is the gain to the Plebs brought about by the change particularly clear.[3] The number of the tribes at this time is unknown, but it was probably twenty-one. This growth had been brought about by an abandonment of the Servian principle. After the Roman territory, lost in great part during the earliest years of the Republic, had been regained, a wholly new subdivision of the *ager Romanus* had been adopted. The four Servian tribes were confined to the ring-wall of the city, and the land without the walls was now separated into *tribus*, which were called the country (*rusticae*) as opposed to the city tribes (*tribus urbanae*). Sixteen of these country tribes bear the names of patrician *gentes;*[4] they must have been named from the clan settlements and were obviously the first created. It is affirmed by Dionysius[5] that, at the time of the trial of Coriolanus (491 B.C.), the number of the tribes was twenty-one ; but it has been conjectured with some plausibility that the twenty-first was added in this very year 471, when the tribe was first used for voting purposes, in order to create an inequality of votes, and that it bears its *local* name (Clustumina or Crustumina) in memory of the secession of the Plebs to the Sacred Mount.[6] The Plebs may have petitioned the consuls to add one more to the divisions of the state ; for it was they alone who could effect the change, the creation of a tribe being an administrative act which none but the magistrates of the community could carry out.

These tribes were, like the earlier ones, local, and although there is no evidence for the view that landholders alone were included in them, yet the seventeen country tribes would

---

[1] Liv. ii. 56 (Publilius Volero) "rogationem tulit ad populum, ut plebei magistratus tributis comitiis fierent" (followed by the words cited on p. 94).

[2] This is Livy's view (l.c.), "nec, quae una vis ad resistendum erat, ut intercederet aliquis ex collegio . . . adduci posset."

[3] The ground of objection given by Livy (ii. 56, cited p. 94) rests on the belief that the tribunes had been formerly elected by the *comitia curiata*.

[4] Aemilia, [Camilia], Claudia, Cornelia, Fabia, [Galeria], Horatia, [Lemonia], Menenia, Papiria, [Pollia], [Pupinia], Romulia or Romilia, Sergia, [Voltinia], Voturia or Veturia (from Momms. *Staatsr.* iii. p. 168 ; the names he encloses in brackets are those to which there are no extant patrician *gentes* to correspond).

[5] Dionys. vii. 64.   [6] Momms. *Staatsr.* iii. p. 153.

naturally consist for the most part of peasant proprietors, and would, therefore, be a better organ for plebeian sentiment than the *curiae*, throughout which the landless plebeian clients might still be the representatives of their patrician lords.

This change soon produced an unexpected consequence. At some period between the passing of the Publilian law and the enactment of the Twelve Tables, the new plebeian practice was adopted as a basis for gatherings of the whole people. The Populus began to meet by tribes, and to form a *comitia tributa*. The Twelve Tables prove that this body early gained judicial competence ;[1] but the history of the great change which placed a democratic assembly of the Populus by the side of the timocratic *comitia centuriata* is wholly unknown to us. It is probable that the original power of this new parliament was not extensive, and it may have been confined originally to the hearing of minor judicial appeals from the magistrates. About twenty years later it was found convenient to entrust the election of quaestors to the new assembly. Its attractiveness lay in the ease and rapidity with which the people might be summoned to meet by tribes within the walls, as compared with the stately formalities of the gathering of the army in the Campus.

The second great movement of the tribunate was an attempt to secure an equal administration of the law.

In the year 462 the tribune C. Terentilius Arsa made a proposal to the *concilium* of the Plebs that a commission of five should be appointed to clear up the forms of legal procedure, and by this means to fix limits to the judicial caprice of the consuls ;[2] and in the next year a resolution of the whole college of tribunes was framed to this effect. It was obviously a measure which demanded the sanction of the Populus, and this it was for many years impossible to obtain. Even apart from the fact that the tribunes apparently intended their commission to consist wholly of Plebeians, it was felt to be a proposal that was revolutionary in

[1] See Appendix.
[2] Livy (iii. 9) says, "ut vviri creentur legibus de imperio consulari scribendis." Even if this expression is due to a misunderstanding of the title of the decemvirs, "consulari imperio legibus scribendis" (Momms. *Staatsr.* ii. p. 702), it no doubt expresses a fact. For the nature and object of the decemvirate see Pompon. in *Dig.* 1, 2, 2, 4 (of the appointment of the decemvirs) "datumque est eis jus eo anno in civitate summum, uti leges et corrigerent, si opus esset, et interpretarentur neque provocatio ab eis sicut a reliquis magistratibus fieret"; ib. (of the publication of the laws) "quas in tabulas eboreas perscriptas pro rostris composuerunt, ut possint leges apertius percipi." Cf. Dionys. x. 1, 60.

the extreme ; for it was nothing less than the demand for a code, for a written system of rules which should replace the elastic principles of justice, which were one of the mainstays of patrician power, and which would vulgarise the awful sanctity of the consulate and the pontifical college. It must also have been felt that codification must mean a compromise—some recognition of plebeian claims which would weaken the position of the ruling caste. Hence a stout opposition on the part of magistrates and Senate, and the bill, if it passed the *concilium plebis* at all,[1] was not allowed to go a step further. But the Plebs persisted in its efforts, and its answer to patrician opposition was to return year after year the same tribunes, formulating the same demands. In 458 B.C. the college approached the consuls on the subject, and asked them to formulate their objections to the bill;[2] for the moment there was the hope of an agreement, but at the end of the year the consent required was again refused. Three years more of agitation followed, and then it was felt that the original proposal must be abandoned. The tribunes expressed their willingness for the initiative to be taken by the patrician magistrates, and for a joint commission to be appointed. Meanwhile the years of discussion had caused the original proposal to assume larger dimensions. Reform which should bear a wholly non-party character was suggested in place of a mere codification. Information of the Greek Codes was to be gathered by a commission of three—a suggestion which was valuable in many ways; it was useful for purposes of delay, it gave an appearance of learning and thoroughness to the work, and perhaps some such basis was felt to be absolutely necessary for framing rules on points which the very indefinite Roman procedure had never considered. The return of the envoys in 452, after an absence of three years, renewed the demands of the tribunes for the instant prosecution of the work. A controversy between the orders as to the constitution of the commission ended in a compromise. Plebeians might be admitted ; but, as a matter of fact, the patrician influence was so strong that the first board elected by the *comitia centuriata* appears to have consisted wholly of members of that order.[3] The appointment of the commission

---

[1] Livy (iii. 11, 25, and 29) seems to speak of the law not being allowed to pass the Plebs ; but then he does not recognise the two stages of legislation. See p. 97.

[2] Liv. iii. 31.   [3] ib. 33 ; cf. Momms. *Staatsr.* ii. p. 714.

was a complete abrogation of the constitution. The consulship was abolished; the Plebs gave up their tribunate, some have thought in perpetuity, misled by the hope that the publication of the law would render such a check on the consular power unnecessary, and as 'a part of the compromise with the Patricians, and stipulated only that certain privileges which they had already gained by law should not be abrogated.[1] The provisional government appointed for the year 451 took the form of a board of ten men with consular power but not subject to the law of appeal.[2] The work was done within the year, and the code posted up on ten tablets (*tabulae*) and published to the masses. The people were summoned and told that the commission had created equal rights for all,[3] and the whole body of law was passed as a *lex* by the *comitia centuriata*. But at the end of the year it was declared that the work was not quite complete. Again the constitution was suspended, and a new board of ten appointed, this time inclusive of Plebeians.[4] Two new sections were added, thus bringing up the number of the *tabulae* to twelve; these also were confirmed by the centuries, and after the government of the "wicked ten" had abused its power and fallen, were published with the rest of the code by the consuls of 448.[5]

Although the law of the Twelve Tables (*lex duodecim tabularum*) was for the most part a codification of existing rules, it marks a distinct advance in the recognition of plebeian rights, and thus was of the utmost political importance. In framing rules for the whole state the question before the commissioners was whether the customary law embodied in the code should be that which prevailed in the patrician, or that which held good in the plebeian community. In almost every important particular plebeian law was preferred. The reason was not any regard for plebeian rights (the decemvirs re-enacted the rule

[1] Liv. iii. 32 "postremo concessum patribus, modo ne lex Icilia de Aventino, aliaeque sacratae leges abrogarentur." As to the *sacratae leges*, the aedileship would have gone with the tribunate; and there was nothing more to be protected by the *leges sacratae*.

[2] Their title was *Decemviri consulari imperio legibus scribendis* (Capitoline Fasti). Cf. Liv. iii. 32 ("placet creari xviros sine provocatione, et ne quis eo anno alius magistratus esset") and Pompon. in *Dig.* (cited p. 102).

[3] Liv. iii. 34 "se . . . omnibus, summis infimisque jura aequasse."

[4] Dionys. x. 58; Liv. iii. 35.

[5] Liv. iii. 57. The accounts of the material of the "Tables" vary. Livy (l.c.) says "in aes incisas in publico proposuerunt"; Pomponius (in *Dig.*, cited p. 102) says "in tabulas eboreas perscriptas" (perhaps *roboreas* or *aereas*, Kipp, *Quellenkunde des R.R.* p. 8). It is possible that they were of wood.

forbidding marriage between the orders), but the simplicity and the capacity for universality of this law. The code is not a hap-hazard collection, but a scientific compilation ; the aim was a "levelling" of the law, an arbitrament between classes, such as had often formed the task of the Greek legislator ; and in effecting this object the commissioners showed more wisdom than any Greek legislator of whom we hear. The idea of legislating for a class, or the still more foolish idea of perfect logical adjustment, are strikingly absent. The code is thoroughly Roman in its caution and good sense, its respect for the past, which it disregards only when old custom violates the rules of common sense, and its judicious contempt for symmetry. Such a code as this might be changed in detail, but was never likely to be repealed. It remained the "fountain of all public and private law," and justly, for, according to Tacitus, it was the "consummation of equal right."[1] Its rhythmical sentences were learnt by heart by school-boys in Cicero's time.[2] Elaborate commentaries were written on it by the republican lawyer Aelius, and the imperial jurist Gaius, and by Labeo, who stands at the meeting-point between the two *régimes;* and in the sixth century A.D. Justinian, in the old age of the world, still respects many of the provisions which date from the infancy of Roman legislation.

The Twelve Tables contained the "whole body of Roman law" (*corpus omnis Romani juris*),[3] not in the sense that they were a complete and detailed system, but in the sense that they pronounced on all important or disputed points in all departments of law, private, criminal, and public.

The ordinances of private law embraced regulations as to marriage and family relations, testamentary disposition, inheritance, debt, and usury. The marriage recognised was the consensual contract of the Plebeians strengthened by *usus.* Emancipation was recognised as a consequence of the threefold sale of a son, and a form of adoption, probably already in use in the plebeian community, was thus made universal.[4] The law also facilitated the emancipation of slaves who had purchased their freedom and so helped to create the wealthy freedman class.[5] Perfect freedom

---

[1] Liv. iii. 34 "fons omnis publici privatique est juris"; Tac. *Ann.* iii. 27 "creatique decemviri et accitis quae usquam egregia compositae duodecim tabulae, finis aequi juris."

[2] Cic. *de Leg.* ii. 23, 59 "Discebamus enim pueri XII, ut carmen necessarium; quas jam nemo discit."

[3] Liv. iii. 34.   [4] p. 19.   [5] Ulpian *Reg.* ii. 4.

of testamentary disposition, in accordance with the plebeian form of testament *per aes et libram*, was recognised; while in intestate inheritance and in guardianship the rights of the *agnati*, common to the Plebeians, were recognised as prior to those of the *gentiles*, sometimes peculiar to the Patricians.[1] The freedom of contract, guaranteed by the Tables, implied the old harsh law of debt; but the penalty was defined, the procedure carefully described, and every loophole of escape offered to the debtor.[2] At the same time usury was severely punished; ten per cent (*unciarium fenus*) was recognised as the legal rate of interest, and the usurer who exceeded it was punished more severely than the thief and compelled to restore fourfold.[3] The rules of procedure for all civil actions were laid down, such as the summons of parties and witnesses and the length of the trial. But the law did not reveal the forms of action; these were still hidden with the pontiffs.

In criminal matters the Twelve Tables recognise the old principle of self-help; a limb was to be given for a limb; but for minor wrongs compensation was allowed, and twenty-five asses were full reparation for a common assault. But there are survivals of the old religious penalties; the man who destroyed standing corn was hanged as an offering to Ceres,[4] and the involuntary homicide could expiate his guilt with the *piaculum* of a ram. The law was heavy on the abuse of freedom of speech; for death was the penalty for incantations or libels against a citizen.[5] The same penalty was inflicted on the *judex* who had accepted bribes;[6] while for *perduellio* in the form of "rousing an enemy against the state or handing over a citizen to the enemy" the death penalty was also enjoined.[7] Reference must have been made to criminal procedure since the *quaestores parricidii* were mentioned in the law.[8]

The principle of the constitution which guaranteed a fair trial to the citizen was upheld; for we have the statement of Cicero that the Twelve Tables granted the *provocatio* "from every kind of court and punishment."[9] In two other particulars they limited

---

[1] p. 10.   [2] p. 91.   [3] Cato *R. R.* praef.
[4] Plin. *H. N.* xviii. 3, 12.   [5] Cic. *de Rep.* iv. 12.   [6] Gell. xx. 1.
[7] Marcian in *Dig.* 48, 4, 3 "Lex duodecim tabularum jubet eum, qui hostem concitaverit quive civem hosti tradiderit, capite puniri."
[8] Pompon. in *Dig.* 1, 2, 2, 23. See p. 80.
[9] Cic. *de Rep.* ii. 31, 54 "ab omni judicio poenaque provocari licere indicant XII Tabulae compluribus legibus."

the jurisdiction of the people. It was maintained that no law or criminal sentence (for this took the form of a *lex*) should be directed against a private individual (*privilegia ne inroganto*), and it was laid down that no capital sentence could be passed except "by the greatest of the *comitia*" (*nisi per maximum comitiatum*),[1] i.e. by the assembly of the centuries. Later interpretation held that this clause struck a blow at the capital jurisdiction of the *concilium plebis ;* it is, however, doubtful how far this extraordinary jurisdiction, resting on a religious sanction, could be affected by a law which, as we shall see, never treated the Plebs as a political corporation at all. Another important constitutional provision of this code was one which granted the right of free association. The Twelve Tables, while severely prohibiting secret gatherings (*coetus nocturni*)[2] which had presumably treasonable designs, permitted the free formation of guilds (*collegia* or *sodalicia*). Such colleges were to require no special charter ; the rules which they made for their own guidance should be valid, provided they were no infringement of the public law.[3] Lastly, the code guaranteed the sovereignty of the popular assembly by declaring that its last enactment should be final, without setting limits to the sphere of its legislative activity.[4] This was a token of the Roman conviction that there should be no finality in law. The Twelve Tables themselves were not guarded against repeal. It was a forecast of further development following the course of the old, of a constitution whose stages were marked by elasticity and growth, not by rigidity and revolution.

The new law does not appear to have made mention of the Plebs and its tribunes, for they were hardly a part of the constitution ; and yet, in the crisis that followed the fall of the decemvirate, the question that gathered round these ignored powers was great enough to obscure every other issue.

The Plebs might have been satisfied with the compromise, had it not been for the unfortunate attempt at despotism made by the second board of decemvirs. It is impossible to believe that

---

[1] Cic. *de Leg.* iii. 4, 11.   [2] *Decl. in Catil.* 19.
[3] This rule is said to have been taken from a law of Solon's (Gaius in *Dig.* 47, 22, 4). Other traces of Greek influence are perhaps to be found in the sumptuary regulations, especially those about funerals, and perhaps in the prohibition of interment within the city. Gaius finds also a Solonian parallel to the *actio finium regundorum* ordained by the law (*Dig.* 10, 1, 13).
[4] Liv. vii. 17 "in duodecim tabulis legem esse, ut quodcumque postremum populus jussisset, id jus ratumque esset."

this usurpation was really countenanced by the Patriciate, and
that they aimed at staving off indefinitely the inevitable assaults
of the Plebeians on the magistracy by indefinitely perpetuating
this rule of ten annual commissioners without appeal; but they
tolerated their rule, and backed up their excuses for not retiring,
until two acts of tyranny raised mutinies in both the Roman
camps. The plebeian soldiers cast off their allegiance to the
ruling board, and first, under military leaders of their own choosing, occupied the Aventine; they then, accompanied by the
majority of the unarmed Plebeians of Rome, wended their way
a second time to the Mons Sacer (449 B.C.). The Senate in
alarm sent two of its members, Valerius and Horatius, who were
of good repute among the Plebs, to ask their wishes. The
answer was: amnesty for the breach of military discipline
involved in the secession; the restoration of the *provocatio*
(which meant the dissolution of the decemvirate) and of the
tribunician power.[1] The demands had not increased since the
first secession; protection was all that the Plebeians yet
demanded.

Everything was granted; the *decemviri* were forced by the
Senate to an unwilling abdication; the tribunate was re-established, and, as no plebeian magistrate existed, the unusual step was
taken of having the election conducted by the *pontifex maximus*.[2]
A resolution was then elicited from the Plebs by the tribune
Duilius that consuls should be created subject to the right of
appeal. It was accepted by the Senate,[3] who appointed an
interrex. The *comitia* of the centuries returned Valerius and
Horatius. Under the guidance of the consuls the assembly
proceeded to pass a series of laws (the *leges Valeriae Horatiae*)
which more than satisfied the demands of the Plebs. One
guaranteed the perpetuity of the *provocatio* by the enactment
that "no one should in future create a magistrate from whom

---

[1] Liv. iii. 53.

[2] ib. 54 "'ibi extemplo, pontifice maximo comitia habente, tribunos plebis
creaverunt."

[3] ib. "Confestim de consulibus creandis cum provocatione M. Duilius
rogationem pertulit." Such a resolution would not need confirmation by the
people, as, after the fall of the decemvirs, an *interregnum* would naturally ensue ;
and this was a matter for the Senate. But Livy also represents the tribune as (in
accordance with a *senatus consultum*) passing the act of amnesty, iii. 54
"Tribunatu inito, L. Icilius extemplo plebem rogavit, et plebs scivit, ne cui fraudi
esset secessio ab decemviris facta." In later Roman law amnesty resides with the
Senate.

there was no appeal; any one who created such a magistrate should be protected by no law sacred or profane and might be slain with impunity."[1] The law was evidently called out by the unlimited power of the decemvirate which had just been abolished; it did more than merely affirm the first *lex Valeria*,[2] for it rendered the creation of an absolute judicial power by the *rogatio* of a magistrate a capital offence, even when this proposal had been accepted by the people. But the scope of the appeal was not extended; the "creation" of a magistrate referred to election sanctioned by the people, and did not, therefore, affect the right of the consul to nominate a dictator from whom there was no appeal; nor did it extend the limits of the appeal beyond the original boundaries—the *pomerium* or, at the utmost, the first milestone from the city.[3]

Two other laws aimed at giving a legal existence to the plebeian community. One gave a legal sanction to the *sacrosanctitas* of the plebeian magistrates by enacting that any one who injured them should be *sacer* to the whole community.[4] Another gave a more binding character to the formal resolutions passed at the *concilium* of the Plebs. Its import is obscure, but there can be no doubt that it marks an important stage in the validity of *plebiscita*. We are told that it was meant to settle the controverted question whether resolutions of the Plebs were binding on Patricians;[5] and that it did this by enacting that "whatsoever the Plebs commanded by its tribes should bind the people (*ut, quod tributim plebes jussisset, populum teneret*)." It is possible that our authority has misunderstood the purport of this law, but hardly likely that the misconception is so great as that imagined by some modern theorists. It is certain that there is no implication that *plebiscita* had from this time the force of *leges;* it was agreed that the resolutions of the Plebs did not gain the force of Acts of Parliament until more than 160 years later. Recent attempts to interpret the Valerio-Horatian law have been based on the supposition that it was concerned with some mode in which a *plebiscitum* might become a *lex*, that it facilitated the transformation of a resolution of the Plebs into a binding law of

---

[1] Liv. iii. 55 "ne quis ullum magistratum sine provocatione crearet, qui creasset, eum jus fasque esset occidi : neve ea caedes capitalis noxae haberetur."
[2] p. 79.   [3] p. 79.   [4] p. 99.
[5] Liv. iii. 55 "omnium primum, cum velut in controverso jure esset, tenerenturne patres plebiscitis, legem centuriatis comitiis tulere 'ut quod,'" etc. Cf. Dionys. xi. 45.

the Populus, through an intermediary channel, consuls or Senate.[1] The wording of the law (hardly so remote from its original as has been supposed) scarcely gives a warrant for this view ; it speaks only of giving a " binding character " to such resolutions. It must be remembered that at this time the plebeian community was not really bound by the resolutions of its own *concilium*, for this was not a legally recognised corporation. The Valerio-Horatian law may have made it such, a corporate body passing resolutions binding on all its members. But a law which is valid for a corporation is valid for those outside the corporation. The ordinances, it is true, which have this binding force must refer immediately only to the affairs of the community which dictates them. This was the case with *plebiscita* now. All self-regarding ordinances of the Plebs bound the Plebeians in the first degree, the Patricians, if it infringed existing rights, in the second degree. All *plebiscita* of a wider scope must still have been mere petitions to the consuls.[2] We can hardly conceive that the law discriminated accurately between what was possible to the Plebs and what was not ; it was sufficient to recognise the already established maxim that corporations could frame their own rules *dum ne quid ex publica lege corrumpant.*[3] From this time onwards, down to 287, whenever we find *plebiscita* affecting matters of national interest or creating changes in the constitution,[4] we must assume that they were brought by the magistrates before the people to be ratified as laws ; although doubtless the undefined limits of plebeian prerogative were often exceeded.

The first great utterance of the Plebs, which followed the Valerio-Horatian law, was one of this character, for it attached a criminal (and therefore a public) penalty to a derogation of duty to the Plebeians. On the proposal of M. Duilius, the tribune, the Plebs resolved that "any one who left the Plebs without tribunes or created a (plebeian) magistrate without appeal should be scourged and executed."[5]   It was a mode by which the Plebs

---

[1] Mr. Strachan-Davidson in Smith *Dict. of Antiq.* s.v. *plebiscitum*, and *English Historical Review* Nos. 2 and 19.

[2] p. 97.   [3] p. 107.

[4] Types of such laws between 449 and 287 B.C. are the *lex Terentilia* (462), *Canuleia* (445), *Licinia* (367), *Ogulnia* (300).

[5] Liv. iii. 55 " M. Duilius deinde tribunus plebis plebem rogavit, plebesque scivit : 'qui plebem sine tribunis reliquisset, quique magistratum sine provocatione creasset, tergo ac capite puniretur.' "

tried to guard itself from any possible surrender of its liberties
such as that which had created the decemvirate.

The Plebs, thus secured in its original privileges, recognised
as a corporate body, and feeling, as a result of the Twelve Tables,
that its law was in the main the law of the state, began to aim
at something more than protection.   From this time begins the
continuous struggle for the complete equalisation of the two
orders.   It was opened by the tribune Canuleius in the year
445.   He rightly held that social must precede political equality,
and proposed in the assembly of the Plebs that marriage should
be permitted between Patricians and Plebeians.[1]   The only
reasonable objection which the consuls, representing the feeling
of the Patriciate, could bring forward against the measure, was
the time-worn pretext that was said to have influenced the
decemvirs in inserting the prohibition in their code, viz. that the
Plebeians had no auspices, and that the disappearance of a pure
race would mean a break in the chain which connected the state
with heaven.[2]   But the pretext expressed the real fears of the
Patriciate.   Intermarriage between the orders would break
down the religious barrier which guarded the consulship; this
was the prize for which the Plebs was striving.   In fact a
suggestion, emanating from the tribunes at the beginning of the
year, had already assumed the form of a *rogatio* to the effect
that "the people should have power to choose consuls at its
pleasure either from the Plebs or from the *patres.*"[3]   Over the
marriage question the usual contest ensued, and with the usual
result.   The consuls led the opposition as long as they could;
at last the Senate was beaten, the magistrates were forced to
bring the question before the people, and marriage between the
orders was legalised.[4]   The tribunes followed up their victory

[1] Liv. iv. 1 "de conubio patrum et plebis C. Canuleius tribunus plebis
rogationem promulgavit."

[2] See p. 39 and cf. Liv. iv. 6 ; the consuls (in a *contio*) gave as the official
reason "quod nemo plebeius auspicia haberet ; ideoque decemviros conubium
diremisse, ne incerta prole auspicia turbarentur."

[3] Liv. iv. 1 "et mentio, primo sensin inlata a tribunis, ut alterum ex plebe
consulem liceret fieri, eo processit deinde, ut rogationem novem tribuni promul-
garent, 'ut populo potestas esset, seu de plebe, seu de patribus vellet, consules
faciendi.'"

[4] The situation at the beginning of the year thus is described by Livy (iv. 2),
"eodem tempore et consules senatum in tribunum, et tribunus populum in
consules incitabat."   At last (Liv. iv. 6) "victi tandem patres, ut de conubio
ferretur, consensere."

by pressing their measure for the opening of the consulship. It was felt that open resistance would be useless; and a device was resorted to which illustrates the Roman genius for adaptability, for dignified political chicanery, and for satisfying at the same time the demands of reason and prejudice. The immediate evil felt was the irruption of the Plebeians into supreme office; but there must have been for some time a growing sense that the executive machinery of the state was by no means equal to the demands made on it. The two consuls were at once military leaders, the sole administrators of the higher civil and criminal jurisdiction, and the sole officials entrusted with the duty of registering and distributing burdens over the citizens. Such a combination of functions could not continue to exist with the widening of Rome's political horizon, and the first attempt was now made at a division of the military, judicial, and registrative duties of the supreme magistrate.

To effect this object, and at the same time to make a concession to the Plebs, it was decided to replace the consulship by the office of military tribune with consular power (*tribunus militum consulari potestate*).[1] The change, permission for which may have been granted by a special *lex*,[2] consisted in raising some of the ordinary legionary delegates of the consul to a level with the commanding officer and suppressing the latter.[3] These extraordinary officials were elected at the *comitia centuriata* under the presidency of one of the chief magistrates, whether consul or consular tribune, for the time being. The normal number, six, was no doubt suggested by the six tribunes of the old *legio* or army. But this full number was not always appointed. The question how many military tribunes should be created for a given year depended on the exigencies of the state. Sometimes three were elected, sometimes four, at other times six, a number which seems never to have been exceeded.[4] It rested formally with the magistrate who guided the elections, practically perhaps with the Senate, to determine how many of these officers should

---

[1] Liv. iv. 6.   [2] ib. 35.

[3] Claudius in *Tab. Lugd.* "quid (commemorem) in pluris distributum consulaie imperium tribunosque militum consulari imperio appellatos, qui seni et saepe octoni crearentur."

[4] Livy sometimes speaks of eight (v. 1, vi. 27); cf. *Tab. Lugd.* cited note 3. It is probable that this number includes the six tribunes and the two censors (Momms. *Staatsr.* ii. p. 184); e.g. Livy gives eight for the year 403, the Fasti Capitol. for the same year (351 A.U.C. *C.I.L.* i. p. 428) six and two censors.

be appointed for any given year.   As military posts below the
supreme command had long been opened to the Plebs, it goes
without saying that Plebeians were eligible to the consular
tribunate ; their admission, in fact, had been one of the motives
of the change.[1]   Yet the patrician element was almost exclusively
present in the earlier years of this magistracy, and to the end of
the office it largely preponderated.   Even if we reject the
account that it was not until forty-five years after the institution
of the consular tribunate (400 B.C.) that a Plebeian was actually
elected to this post,[2] it is a significant fact that while purely
patrician colleges are found, there is no instance of one composed
exclusively of Plebeians.   This fact may be simply a demonstration of the aristocratic character of elective office, and shows that
the masses preferred the safety of the state to the advancement
of their own order ; for military skill and experience, and even
knowledge of law, were still chiefly to be sought in the ranks of
the *patres*.[3]   Gradually, however, the Plebs became familiarised
with power and displayed greater trust in the leaders of their
own order.   The year 400 does in any case mark a turning
point in the history of the office.   After it we find more
Plebeians elected ; in 399 and 396 they form a majority of the
college, and events were tending to the demand, which was soon
to be made, that a place in the supreme magistracy should be
reserved for candidates who represented a majority of the citizens.

The power exercised by the consular tribunes was, briefly,
that of the consuls ; they had the same *jus*, *imperium*, and
potestas,[4] and they enjoyed their insignia.[5]   They presided over
the elections for their successors, and took the auspices on these
occasions, the recognition of a Plebeian's right to consult the people
auspicato breaking down the last barriers of religious prejudice.[6]

---

[1] Pompon. in *Dig.* 1, 2, 2, 25 "cum . . . plebs contenderet cum patribus et
vellet ex suo quoque corpore consules creare, et patres recusarent, factum est ut
tribuni militum crearentur partim ex plebe, partim ex patribus consulari potestate."

[2] Liv. v. 12.   This is maintained to be an error by Mommsen, *Röm. Forsch.*
i. 66 ; *Staatsr.* ii. p. 188.   He holds that in 445 B.C. one L. Atilius Longus was
a Plebeian, and that in 400, 399, 396 the Plebeians had a majority.   Livy's
view is upheld by Willems *Le Sénat* i. 58-60.

[3] If it be taken to prove that the preponderance of voting power in the
comitia centuriata was still on the side of the Patricians, it would throw a valuable
side-light on the relative economic position of the two orders.

[4] *Imperium* (*Tab. Lugd.* quoted p. 112) ; *potestas* (Liv. iv. 6) ; *jus* (Tac.
Ann. i. 1).

[5] Liv. iv. 7 "et imperio et insignibus consularibus usos."

[6] ib. v. 13, 52.

If this magistracy was considered inferior in dignity to the consulship and only a "shadow" of that high office,[1] it must have been only because it was shared by more colleagues, and from a conviction of its occasional character. Yet it was noted as a curious fact that, from constitutional reasons unknown even to the early annalists, no consular tribune had ever enjoyed a triumph.[2]

It must not be supposed that the consulship was in any way abolished by this exceptional magistracy; it was simply kept in suspense during certain years. Each year it was decided afresh whether consuls or military tribunes should be appointed. Tradition represents the decision as resting with the Senate;[3] but whether it exercised this function by law,[4] or merely as the advising body of the magistrate who was to hold the election, is unknown. This discretionary power shows that the tribunate was regarded as an exceptional office; but its military and political convenience caused it practically to replace the consulship during the years when it was in vogue. The period of the military tribunate is one of seventy-seven years, extending from 444 to 367. These years show twenty-two consular *collegia*, and fifty-one of military tribunes.[5] The stop-gap lasted for half a century, and the compromise was maintained until in 367 a final settlement of the plebeian claim was reached.

Meanwhile the consulship had been modified in yet another way—one which was detrimental to the power of the office, but was meant to preserve influence to the Patriciate. In the institution of the censorship we find at work the same double motive which had influenced the government in creating the consular tribunate—the sense that two men could not manage all the business of a growing state, and the desire not to share with the Plebeians the unimpaired powers of the supreme office.

It had been the custom for the king, and subsequently for the consuls, to make an estimate, at certain intervals of time, of the effective military strength of the state. This was originally a registration of all the patrician burgesses; but, after the

---

[1] "Proconsularis imago" (Liv. v. 2).   [2] Zonar. vii. 19.
[3] Liv. iv. 55 "pervincunt, ut senatus consultum fiat de tribunis militum creandis"; iv. 12 "cum ... obtinuisset, ut consulerentur patres, consulum an tribunorum placeret comitia haberi." Dionysius (xi. 60) represents the people as being consulted too.
[4] i.e. in accordance with the law, if there was one, establishing the office.
[5] Momms. *Staatsr.* ii. p. 191.

Servian reforms, it became a numbering of all the citizens, for the purpose of discovering those liable to military service, the class in which they should be enrolled, and, in case of tribute being imposed, the liability of each household to the property-tax (*tributum*).   For these purposes it was sufficient for the heads of families (*patres familiarum*) to be summoned and questioned. Their answers formed the record, in accordance with which military and financial burdens were imposed, and political influence in the *comitia centuriata* was determined.   The recognition of citizenship itself was dependent on this enrolment, for it is probable that from the earliest times membership of a tribe was the symbol of the possession of civic rights; while now the fact that the tribe was the basis of the *concilium plebis* and the *comitia tributa* gave a vote to every one enrolled in one of the *tribus*.   The importance which the census had assumed was not compatible with the consular performance of its duties. The judicial and military functions of the annual magistrates interfered both with its regularity and its completeness, and the temporary suspension of the consulship offered a chance of vesting these duties in other magistrates.   In the year 443 B.C. two new officials, called *censores*, were created,[1] who were to be elected by the *comitia* of the centuries.   The office was to be confined to the Patriciate, possibly because it was felt that the solemn ceremony of purification (*lustratio*) which closed the census could not adequately be performed by plebeian hands. No one as yet dreamed of the future greatness of the office; its beginnings were small,[2] and the tribunes offered no opposition to the law which established an office which was to become the greatest of political prizes.

The censorship, though a standing, was in a certain sense an occasional office, for the tenure of power by the censors could never have been coterminous with the interval between each census—an interval usually of five years.   The original tenure is unknown; possibly the censor was supposed to continue in office until his duties were fulfilled.   It was not until the year 434 B.C. that the censorship was limited to a definite term of a year and a half by a *lex Aemilia*, proposed by the dictator

---

[1] Liv. iv. 8 "ortum autem initium est rei, quod in populo, per multos annos incenso, neque differri census poterat, neque consulibus, cum tot populorum bella imminerent, operae erat id negotium agere."   Cf. Dionys. xi. 63.
[2] Liv. l.c. "Idem hic annus censurae initium fuit, rei a parva origine ortae."

Mamercus Aemilius.[1]   The censors' duties were as wide as the ramifications of the census.   His primary function was that of registration, but one of the meanings of registration was the imposition of pecuniary burdens on individuals; hence the censor's first connexion with finance.   Another consequence of registration was of still greater import.   Qualifications of character must always have been considered a necessary condition for the performance of even the meanest public functions at Rome.   Admission to the centuries and to the tribes, and therefore the exercise of the active rights of voting and serving in the army, was possible only to one not stained by crime.   The secular ground, one quite sufficient for a self-respecting community, was perhaps assisted by the religious idea that no impure man should be present at the mystic ceremony of purification.   Such a testing of character could have been performed only in the most cursory way by the consuls.   But now that a magistracy had been appointed which had leisure for a rigorous scrutiny, it was inevitable that the rule of manners (*regimen morum*) should in time overshadow every other aspect of the censor's office, and that this dual papacy should become the most dignified and dreaded organ of the state.

Beyond the establishment of the consular tribunate, the censorship and the transference of the election of quaestors to the newly created *comitia tributa*,[2] the years 449 to 377 are not marked by any great constitutional changes.   They were years of compromise but not of settlement; the restlessness of the reforming party was stayed by the constant pressure of war.   It could not accuse the military policy of the governing class, which led its armies to victory and made all needful concessions to plebeian talent.   It was the epoch of wars with the Aequians, Volscians, and Etruscans, of the siege of Veii, in which Rome made her first great territorial conquest, and of the Celtic migrations, which laid Rome in ashes, but made her the bulwark of the central Italian nations against northern invasions, and gave her strength to remodel and reform the Latin coalition of which she was the immediate head.   Occasional discontent was at this, as at every other period, excited by the need of

[1] Liv. iv. 24. Mommsen indeed thinks (*Staatsr.* ii. p. 349) that this *lex Aemilia* first made the censorship an independent magistracy with a fixed tenure. It was probably an independent magistracy before, but with no fixed tenure. Hence the belief that the censors originally held office for five years, the period of the *lustrum* (Liv. l.c., cf. ix. 34).   [2] pp. 81, 102.

land distributions and the pressure of debt. Sp. Maelius fell
in 439 and M. Manlius in 384; but the government, though
it would not have its hand forced, was not wholly unwilling to
make concessions to poverty. The citizen troops on foreign
service were given pay in 406, and the land conquered from Veii
was some years later allotted amongst the Plebs. While the
discontent of the poor was thus kept in check, the government
could afford to make harmless and unavoidable concessions to
Plebeians of higher rank. In 421 the number of quaestors was
raised from two to four; for, owing to the prolonged absence of
armies, it was thought fit that a special quaestor should be
assigned to each consul in the field.[1] The tribunes demanded that
a fixed proportion of these places should be reserved for Plebeians.
This was refused, but the compromise was arrived at that any
of the four places might be filled from the Plebs, a concession
which was unavoidable, for the absurdity of admitting Plebeians
to the highest rank in the state and excluding them from this
subordinate duty must have been felt. The permission did
not, however, take effect until twelve years later (409 B.C.);
but then Plebeians were returned for three out of four vacancies
at the *comitia* of the tribes.[2] The first regular elective magistracy,
however limited its powers and dignity, had now been won for
the Plebeians.

Meanwhile the provisional government drifted on. It won
military successes; it was gradually building up a hegemony in
Italy. But the effect of war now, as at an earlier period, was
ruinous to those to whom this government had to look for support.
In spite of the palliative measures of pay for the army and occasional land distribution, a large portion of the yeoman farmers
were again in a pitiable state. We cannot now speak of the social
grievances of Plebeians as a whole; those members of the Plebs
who began to occupy the benches of the Senate,[3] and who aspired
to the military tribunate or quaestorship, were as wealthy as

---

[1] Liv. iv. 43 (discord between the Patres and the Plebs) "exorta est, coepta
ab duplicando quaestorum numero . . . praeter duos urbanos quaestores duo ut
consulibus ad ministeria belli praesto essent." The tribunes demanded "ut pars
quaestorum . . . ex plebe fieret." The compromise arrived at was that "quattuor
quaestores promiscue de plebe ac patribus libero suffragio populi fierent."

[2] ib. 54. The Plebs, indignant at the election of consuls in place of military
tribunes, "eum dolorem quaestoriis comitiis simul ostendit, et ulta est, tunc
primum plebeiis quaestoribus creatis: ita ut, in quattuor creandis, uni patricio K.
Fabio Ambusto relinqueretur locus." For the election at the *comitia tributa*
see p. 102.   [3] p. 83 note 2.

their patrician compeers. The race for office was keen between the members of the two orders. The Patrician had now to beg for his place on the curule chair. The first law against canvassing (*ambitus*) was passed in 432 ; it prohibited a candidate from whitening his toga with chalk before the elections [1]—a primitive measure, but one which shows that the plebeian electorate had at last become a power. But though isolated members of the Plebs were soaring into the upper regions, the mass of this body still consisted of bankrupt agriculturists. The situation which they regarded as desperate was, apart from the harsh law of debt, the normal condition of a modern proletariate. But the ideal of the ancient citizen was higher than our own ; they wished to be proprietors of freehold land or of land held on an undisturbed tenure from the state.

This discontent was the opportunity of the richer Plebeians,[2] who wished to secure perfect political equality between the orders. In 378 loud cries were raised against the capitalists ; a war with the Volsci gave the tribunes the chance of impeding the military levy, and some temporary concessions to debtors were unwillingly wrung from the government.[3] When the next year saw the burdens re-imposed, two ambitious Plebeians, L. Sextius and C. Licinius Stolo, came forward with the proposition that the only sure way of permanently remedying the evils of the lower class was by securing one of the places in the consulship to members of their own order. They formulated a programme which was an attractive jumble of social and political measures. The *plebiscitum* which they promulgated promised a temporary relief from debt, proposed a limit to the amount of public land which any individual might possess, and declared that the military tribunate should be abolished, the consulship should be restored, and that one of the two consuls *must* henceforth be a Plebeian. This comprehensive measure, which attacked land, capital, and office,[4] was easily met. The two tribunes

---

[1] Liv. iv. 25. The *principes plebis*, in despair at the choice of the military tribunate always falling on Patricians, came to the conclusion that it was "ambitione artibusque" of the Patricians. Hence a tribunician measure "ne cui album in vestimentum addere petitionis liceret causa." After great resistance "vicere tribuni ut legem perferrent."

[2] "Principes plebis" (Liv. l.c.).

[3] ib. vi. 31 "conditiones impositae patribus, ne quis, quoad bellatum esset, tributum daret, aut jus de pecunia credita diceret."

[4] ib. 35 "omnium igitur simul rerum, quarum immodica cupido inter mortales est, agri, pecuniae, honorum, discrimine proposito, conterriti patres, etc."

stood alone, and their eight colleagues were without difficulty
induced to put their veto on the revolutionary measure. But
it was soon shown that, if the veto might be used against the
interest of the Plebs, the negative powers of the tribunes might
be employed, with as much legality and as little justification,
to paralyse the life of the state. The two tribunes, in virtue
of the paramount authority which their *sacrosanctitas* had in the
course of years secured to them, forbade the election of any
magistrate of the people. For five years successively Licinius
and Sextius were re-elected tribunes; during the whole of this
period (375–371) the only magistrates appointed were the
plebeian aediles and tribunes, and the state was without a head.
A war with Velitrae led the tribunes to relax their anarchical
edict for the year 370. But the long stand had reduced the
number of vetoing tribunes to five. Another clause was now
added to the original proposals to the effect that the two
duumviri sacris faciundis, the keepers of the sacred books, the
storehouse which furnished political intrigue with its surest
weapons, should be raised to ten, and that half of these *decemviri*
should be Plebeians.[1] None of the tribunes of 368 seems to
have been prepared to offer any effectual resistance to any of
the provisions of the law,[2] and the Patricians, driven from their
first stronghold, took refuge in a dictator. It was a sign that
they had lost the game, for the dictatorship could not be
perpetuated. But it required the most strenuous exertions of
the leaders of the Plebs to keep their followers up to the level
of their original demands. The spiritless commons who had
failed to elect members of their own order, consular tribunes
and quaestors, when it had been in their power to do so, were
for dividing the proposals, passing the social measures at once
and leaving the question of the consulship for a future time.
But Licinius and Sextius were not prepared to be social leaders
without reward. The only division to which they subjected
the complicated measure was to carry in 368 the clause sharing
the new decemvirate with the Plebeians; the other clauses were
postponed. In the next year, 367 B.C., they were tribunes
for the tenth time. The opposition was worn out, and the

---

[1] Liv. vi. 37 "Novam rogationem promulgant, ut pro duumviris sacris
faciundis decemviri creentur ; ita ut pars ex plebe, pars ex patribus fiat."
[2] ib. 38. His statements are inconsistent. He speaks of the college as
being unanimous, and yet of *intercessio* being used at the meeting.

Licinio-Sextian laws were passed in their original form. The greatest of plebeian victories had been won; from this time the Plebs is really the dominant element in the state. It was of little consequence that it did not assert its omnipotence for some years yet; all that it desired further was bound to come. As the magistracy was far more powerful than the people at Rome, the body that exercised the whole of the highest prohibitive power through the tribunate, and monopolised half of the highest positive authority in the consulship, was bound to be supreme. Even the purely patrician privilege of the *patrum auctoritas* was no great disturbance to this power. It became more a matter of form, the more the plebeian element entered into the Senate.

The Licinian laws had the unexpected effect of adding two new magistracies to the state. These were known as the Praetorship and the Curule Aedileship. The institution of the former office was a constitutional change of the first magnitude, being nothing less than the addition of a third colleague to the consuls. It is represented as having been a part of the compromise between the orders, the Plebeians allowing a third purely patrician magistracy to be created in exchange for the confiscated consulship.[1] But, even if we assume that the praetorship was originally confined to the *patres*—a statement which has with some reason been doubted[2]—it was necessity rather than ambition which directed the creation of the office. The impossibility of the consul's paying adequate attention to duties of jurisdiction had been one of the motives which led to the establishment of the consular tribunate. Now that the consulship was permanently restored, provision had to be made for the permanent severance of civil jurisdiction from that office. As jurisdiction implied the *imperium*, and all the possessors of

[1] Liv. vi. 42 " concessum . . . a plebe nobilitati de praetore uno, qui jus in urbe diceret, ex patribus creando," probably by a clause introduced into the Licinian rogations when they were submitted by the consul to the Populus (see p. 97). The true motive is given by Pomponius in *Dig.* 1, 2, 2, 27, " Cum consules avocarentur bellis finitimis neque esset, qui in urbe jus reddere posset, factum est ut praetor quoque crearetur, qui urbanus appellatus est, quod in urbe jus redderet."

[2] Mommsen (*Staatsr.* ii. p. 204) doubts it, chiefly on the ground that no law is mentioned as opening the office to Plebeians thirty years later. Probably the same doubt hung over the praetorship as over the second place in the consulship, i.e. whether the Licinian law, by reserving one consulship to the Plebs, had left the other posts open to both orders or not.

this regal prerogative were necessarily colleagues, the praetor was a colleague of the consuls. He was created, as the phrase ran, "under the same auspices,"[1] and therefore by the same assembly and under the same formalities of election. He bore the early title of the consuls, which, in spite of its inappropriateness to his usual peaceful duties, came to cling to him exclusively. But, though he was needed chiefly for purposes of jurisdiction, one branch of the *imperium* could not be singled out to the exclusion of the others. The praetor possesses all the aspects of the supreme power, the capacity for command in war, for initiating legislation, for summoning and transacting business with the Senate. How these powers were harmonised with, and subordinated to, the similar powers of the consuls, will be described elsewhere. The main business of the original praetor did not clash with that of his colleagues, for, though in theory perhaps the consul never did lose his control of civil jurisdiction,[2] practice decided against his interference with it, and the praetor was for more than 120 years (366-242) the sole civil magistrate of Rome. At the close of this period a second praetor was appointed, whose duty it was to decide cases between foreigners (*peregrini*) and between Roman citizens and foreigners—an addition rendered necessary by the growth of Rome's territory and business, and which has no further political significance.

The praetorship, if it ever was a patrician preserve, did not long remain such. Thirty years after its institution (337 B.C.) a Plebeian, Q. Publilius Philo, successfully contested the post. The objections of the presiding magistrate, whether based on law or custom, were overruled and Plebeians declared eligible for the office.[3]

The appointment, simultaneously with the praetor, of two additional aediles, secured nothing for the Patricians, but a great deal for the state. The military duties which prevented the consul from administering justice and attending to registration, also hindered him from devoting himself to the *minutiae* of

---

[1] Liv. vii. 1 "collegam consulibus atque iisdem auspiciis creatum." Cf. Gell. xiii. 15.

[2] An instance of the exercise of a consular veto over a judicial decision of a praetor in 77 B.C. is preserved by Valerius Maximus (vii. 7, 6).

[3] Liv. viii. 15 "eodem anno Q. Publilius Philo praetor primus de plebe, adversante Sulpicio consule, qui negabat rationem ejus se habiturum, est factus ; senatu, cum in summis imperiis id non obtinuisset, minus in praetura intendente."

police and market regulations. It was an anomaly that these duties, so far as they fell to the lot of any special officials, should be in the hands of two plebeian assistants of the tribune.[1] It was from them that the two new magistrates borrowed their names, and the similarity of title and functions had the happy result of fusing into one corporation the plebeian officials and the new magistrates of the community. The latter were known in later times as *aediles curules*, from the curule chair which they had in common with the magistrates vested with the *imperium*. The Patriciate is said to have been the original condition of eligibility to the office;[2] but this was very soon abandoned in favour of the practice that the curule aediles should be chosen in alternate years from Patricians and Plebeians.[3] Later still— at what period is uncertain—the magistracy was annually accessible to members of both orders.

The accession of Plebeians to the consulship had been the key of the position; it had broken down the last pretended religious scruple, and a few years saw the patrician defences of every office overthrown. The year 356 witnessed the first plebeian dictator;[4] no law appears to have been required to secure the Plebs admission to this office, the qualification for the consulship being considered *ipso jure* to open a passage to the dictatorship. In 351 a Plebeian was first admitted to the censorship;[5] but mere admissibility was not enough, and in 339 one of the laws passed by the plebeian dictator, Q. Publilius Philo, *reserved* one of the two places in the censorship for members of his order.[6] How difficult it would have been for the Plebs to secure this office, apart from such a regulation, is shown by the fact that the first exclusively plebeian censorship dates only from the year 131 B.C.[7] With respect to the occupa-

[1] p. 98.
[2] Liv. vi. 42 "Factum senatus consultum, ut duo viros aediles ex patribus dictator populum rogaret."
[3] ib. vii. 1 (366 B.C.) "verecundia inde imposita est senatui ex patribus jubendi aediles curules creari. primo, ut alternis annis ex plebe fierent, convenerat; [this was the rule in 213 (Polyb. x. 4)]. postea promiscuum fuit" [Mommsen (*Staatsr.* ii. p. 482) thinks as late as the last century of the Republic].
[4] ib. 17 "dictator C. Marcius Rutilus primus de plebe dictus"; he appointed a plebeian master of the horse.
[5] ib. 22. The same C. Marcius Rutilus "professus censuram se petere" was elected.
[6] ib. viii. 12 "ut alter utique ex plebe . . . censor crearetur."
[7] ib. *Ep.* 59 "Q. Pompeius et Q. Metellus, tunc primum utrique ex plebe facti, censores lustrum condiderunt."

tion of both of the consular places by Plebeians, a doubt seems
to have existed of its legality, which was removed in 342 by a
plebiscitum passed into law which declared "uti liceret consules
ambos plebeios creari."[1]   We have already noticed their capture
of the praetorship in 337 B.C.

There was but one more fort, but that a strong one, which
the plebeian *principes* had to storm.   This was the circle of
the priestly colleges.   The two religious guilds of paramount
political importance, apart from the decemvirate (*sacris faciundis*)
to which Plebeians had been already admitted, were those of
the pontiffs and augurs.   The pontifical college, which in the
monarchy had consisted of five members, was now composed of
four, the place occupied by the expelled king having never
apparently been filled up.[2]   The augural college, which should
have consisted of six, was also at this time reduced by some
accident to four members.[3]   In the year 300 B.C. two tribunes,
Q. and Cn. Ogulnius, brought forward a bill for raising the
number of the augurs to nine, and that of the pontiffs to eight,
the added numbers in either case to be taken from the Plebs.[4]
The measure was understood to be primarily in the interest of
the noble Plebeians, already in possession of curule office and
triumphal ornaments, but it did to a large extent assist the
rights of the Plebs as a corporation ; for the religious veto
henceforth, though it might be used by the nobility against the
interests of the lower orders, could not be employed by the
Patricians to check plebeian measures.   The bill, which became
law, established the religious equality of the two orders, so far
as religion was a political force.   It is true that, as we shall
see, the Plebs were always excluded from certain non-political
priesthoods ; but, on the other hand, one of the religious
colleges of national importance established in later times—the

---

[1] Liv. vii. 42.   The law was proposed by the tribune L. Genucius.   It was
not, however, until the year 172 B.C. that both consuls were plebeian (Liv.
xlii. 9 ; Fast. Cap. *C.I.L.* i. 1 p. 25).   [2] p. 52.

[3] Livy (x. 6) marvels at the fact ; he thinks that it must have been accidental
("morte duorum"), since the augural college should have consisted of three or of a
multiple of three.   Cicero (*de Rep.* ii. 9, 16) says that Romulus coopted (*cooptavit*)
one from each of the three tribes ; they were therefore four ; that Numa added
two (ib. ii. 14, 26).   This makes six, which Livy (l.c.) thinks the normal number
at the time of the passing of the Ogulnian law.

[4] Liv. x. 6.   These numbers remained unaltered until the time of Sulla (81 B.C.),
who raised the colleges of pontiffs and augurs to fifteen (Liv. *Ep.* 89).   A six-
teenth was added to both colleges by Julius Caesar (Dio Cass. xlii. 51).

triumviri epulones, created in 196 B.C. for preparing the *epulum Jovis* and banquets given in honour of the other gods [1]—seems from its origin to have been composed wholly of Plebeians.[2] The change, however, though indirectly favourable to the Plebeians, was not of a democratic character; the priesthoods were kept within a few distinguished families through the principle of appointment. The method was that of cooptation, which we find existing in 453 B.C.[3] It was not until the last century of the Republic that the *lex Domitia* (104 B.C.) ventured to give the election, not indeed to the Populus, but to a special assembly composed of seventeen out ·of the thirty-five tribes chosen by lot, and even then the forms of nomination by the head of the college, and of cooptation by its members, were scrupulously observed.[4]

In sketching the invasion of office and honours by the plebeian nobles we have ventured to anticipate somewhat the chronological sequence of events. The commons, too, had during this period their share of political emancipation. Thirty-nine years before the Ogulnian law something had been done by legislation to increase the independence of the Plebs as a corporation, and to free the assemblies of the Populus from the legal control of the Patricians. In 339 B.C. a plebeian dictator, Q. Publilius Philo, carried a law making *plebiscita* binding on the people (*ut plebiscita omnes Quirites tenerent*).[5] The meaning of this law was clearly not understood by our authority. Its pretended wording is almost identical with that of the Valerio-Horatian measures;[6] but what was done on that occasion did not need repetition, and the object of the Publilian law must have been to secure more immediate legal validity to such measures passed by the Plebs as did not refer to that corporation alone—to make, in fact, the stages of transition from *plebiscitum* to *lex* a matter of formal and not of real importance.[7] Another law passed by the same

---

[1] Liv. xxxiii. 42. The number was afterwards increased to seven, from which time the college was known as that of the *VIIviri epulones*.

[2] Marquardt *Staatsverw.* iii. p. 333.

[3] Liv. iii. 32 "augur (mortuus est) C. Horatius Pulvillus; in cujus locum C. Veturium eo cupidius, quia damnatus a plebe erat, augures legere." The *pontifex maximus* was early an exception to this rule; see the *comitia sacerdotum* in the section dealing with the people.

[4] Cic. *de Leg. Agr.* ii. 7, 18; Vell. ii. 12.

[5] Liv. viii. 12.   [6] p. 109.

[7] Mr. Strachan-Davidson conjectures that the law of Publilius Philo "may have struck out the intervening consultation of the Senate, and may have required the

dictator had reference to the *patrum auctoritas.* We have seen what this power had become, probably from the dawn of the Republic.[1] It was a claim by the patrician members of the. Senate to accept or reject any measure of the Populus, when assembled by curies or by centuries. It never affected *plebiscita,* and we know too little of the *comitia tributa* to say whether the measures of that body were submitted to it or not;[2] the hampering of the *comitia curiata* was by this time of no importance, and the *lex Publilia* confined itself to the application of the *auctoritas* to the centuries. By this law it was enacted that the consent to laws passed by the *comitia centuriata* should be given before the voting commenced.[3] This provision was shortly afterwards (perhaps in 338 B.C.) extended by a *lex Maenia* to elections.[4] It is evident that neither of these provisions could have made the *auctoritas* nugatory, for it was not more difficult for a section of the Senate to decline to submit a question to the people than to reject it when passed. The provisions may, however, be a sign that the *auctoritas* was becoming a mere form; but its formal character was due to the rapidly increasing preponderance of Plebeians in the Senate.

But though the popular assemblies were thus free from patrician control, and the magistrates, subject only to the self-imposed limitation of taking advice from the Senate, could elicit any utterance they pleased from the *comitia,* there was one grave defect in the existing system of legislation which called for remedy. The plebeian magistracy, which circumstances had raised to a pre-eminence above all other powers, had not the freedom of the other magistrates. The *rogationes* of the tribunes, when accepted by the Plebs, still required some further sanction to become laws. This anomaly might have been remedied in one of two ways; either by giving the tribune the right of summoning and presiding over meetings

consul to bring the petition of the Plebs at once before the Populus" (Smith *Dict. of Antiq.* s.v. *plebiscitum,* ii. p. 439).   [1] p. 83.
[2] The only evidence that they were is furnished by Livy's account of a *lex Manlia* of 357 B.C. (Willems *Droit Public* p. 183). See Liv. vii. 16 (Manlius the consul) "legem, novo exemplo ad Sutrium in castris tributim de vicesima eorum, qui manumitterentur, tulit. Patres, quia ea lege haud parvum vectigal inopi aerario additum esset, auctores fuerunt."
[3] ib. viii. 12 "ut legum, quae comitiis centuriatis ferrentur, ante initum suffragium patres auctores fierent."
[4] Cic. *Brut.* 14, 55. Cf. Liv. i. 17 "hodie . . . in legibus magistratibusque rogandis usurpatur idem jus (the *patrum auctoritas*), vi adempta."

of the people, making him in fact a magistrate of the community, and thus abolishing all distinction between Populus and Plebs, or removing the impediments which still hampered tribunician legislation in the *concilium plebis*. The conservatism of the Roman character, and perhaps the class feeling reviving again at the beginning of the third century in consequence of a renewed outbreak of the Plebs, caused the latter course to be adopted. In the year 287 the commons, oppressed by debt, again seceded—this time to the Janiculum. The plebeian dictator appointed to effect a settlement met social grievances by a political concession. He passed a law which most of our authorities represent as verbally identical with the Valerio-Horatian and Publilian laws,[1] but which seems to have been of a very different and far more definite character. The lawyers[2] regard the *lex Hortensia* as the measure which gave decrees of the Plebs the full force of laws. Henceforth there is between *lex* and *plebiscitum* merely a difference of form and name ; their *potestas* is the same,[3] and even legal formulae use the words as practically identical.[4] A law could repeal a plebiscite and a plebiscite a law ;[5] in the case of a conflict between the two, the rule of the Twelve Tables held good that the later repealed the earlier ordinance. It is not, therefore, surprising to find that in the annalists, even those with pretensions to accuracy, Populus and Plebs are used indifferently,[6] and it is only at times by carefully noting who is the presiding magistrate on the particular occasion, that we can determine whether the ordinance he elicits

---

[1] Laelius Felix ap. Gell. 15, 27 "(plebi scitis) ante patricii non tenebantur, donec Q. Hortensius dictator legem tulit, ut eo jure quod plebs statuisset, omnes quirites tenerentur"; Plin. *H.N.* xvi. 10, 37 "ut quod ea (plebs) jussisset, omnes quirites teneret."

[2] Gaius i. 3 "olim patricii dicebant plebi scitis se non teneri, quia sine auctoritate eorum facta essent ; sed postea lex Hortensia lata est, qua cautum est, ut plebi scita universum populum tenerent, itaque eo modo legibus exaequata sunt"; Pompon. in *Dig.* 1, 2, 2, 8 "pro legibus placuit et ea (plebiscita) observari lege Hortensia : et ita factum est, ut inter plebis scita et legem species constituendi interesset, potestas autem eadem esset."

[3] Pompon. l.c.

[4] The *lex Agraria* of 111 B.C. (Bruns *Fontes*) thus refers to a *lex Sempronia* of 123 B.C., "[ex] lege plebeive scito, quod C. Sempronius Ti. f. tr. pl. rogavit." Cf. *lex Rubria* (ib.) " ex lege Rubria seive id pl. sc. est."

[5] Thus Cicero, exiled by a *plebiscitum*, was restored by a *lex centuriata*. See the section on the people.

[6] Of the many instances one of the most remarkable is to be found in Sall. *Jug.* 84, "Marius . . . cupientissima plebe consul factus, postquam ei provinciam Numidiam populus jussit." Here *plebs* should be *populus* and *populus*, *plebs*.

is a decree of the *comitia* or the *concilium*. The difference in the legislative powers of the two assemblies came in course of time to be little more than a difference in magisterial right;[1] while the *comitia* of the centuries and tribes were presided over by magistrates with the *imperium*, the *concilium* of the Plebs could be summoned and addressed only by plebeian magistrates. Yet the past history of the various assemblies was decisive as to their elective and judicial functions, and practice tended still further to fix the scope of the powers of each. But at the time of the *lex Hortensia* the difference between the two parliamentary sovereigns —the Populus and the Plebs—was even more marked; for the Patricians, excluded from the *concilium*, were still a considerable body, and the tribune had not yet become, like the magistrates with *imperium*, quite a servant of the Senate.[2] The Hortensian law had at the time a political significance which it afterwards lost; but it had a hidden import which was of vital consequence for the history of the state. By perpetuating the Plebs as a separate corporation it preserved the tribunate in all its primitive majesty, and thus maintained the power subsequently to be used as an instrument of senatorial and monarchical rule.

The tendencies of plebeian emancipation were almost all in favour of the upper classes; that it never was a democratic movement or one led by democratically-minded men is most strikingly evidenced by the utter indifference shown by the leaders to the economic evils under which the masses laboured, and which they used as instruments to further their ambition. Solon abolished slavery for debt at a single stroke; to the Roman it is a sacred thing, an expression of *Romana fides;* while the Greek προστάτης struggled for others, the Roman patron fought for himself. But continued pressure caused some tentative efforts to be made in the latter half of the fourth century to mitigate the curse of debt. A *lex Marcia* of 352 B.C. gave the debtor the right of summary arrest (*manus injectio*) of the usurer, to recover the fourfold penalty for the illegal interest;[3] while in 326 an attempt was made to give the future masters of the world the mastery over their bodies. In 313 a *lex Poetilia* was passed forbidding the imprisonment of *nexi* who could swear

---

[1] "Legislative" is here used in the modern sense. At Rome a judicial and elective act of the people was equally a *lex*.

[2] At least in 304 B.C. they had no right of *relatio* with the Senate (Liv. ix. 46).

[3] Gaius iv. 23.

that they had reasonable hopes of ultimately satisfying their creditors ;[1] it therefore abolished most contracts on the security of the person ; although the *addictio* and imprisonment of debtors by order of the court continued through the Republic and into the Empire. But if the harshness of the law was one evil, ignorance of its forms was another almost equally great. An accident supplied the remedy. The pontiff Appius Claudius had reduced the forms of action to writing ; but the book meant for the guidance of the pontiffs was immediately revealed to the profane eyes of the people by his clerk, one Cn. Flavius, a freedman's son. The fraudulent secretary also posted up a tablet containing a list of court days (*dies fasti*) on which the *legis actio* was possible.[2] The *penetralia* of the pontifical college had now become the property of the masses, and although the chief pontiffs still furnished for centuries the highest names to Roman law, they professed the science openly,[3] and secular teaching soon tore the veil from the hidden features of jurisprudence.

But, apart from these minor benefits, the mass of the Plebeians did not share to any very large extent in the triumph of their order. The true reason of the individual Roman being thus thrust into the background can only be given by a review of the causes, soon to be treated, which moulded both the theory and practice of the developed Roman constitution. It must suffice here to trace the painfully inadequate results which were secured by these centuries of agitation by a glance at the distribution of power in the Roman state, at the date of the war with Pyrrhus, or the outbreak of the struggle with Carthage.

The old nobility had relaxed its exclusive hold of office, but

---

[1] Varro *L.L.* viii. 105 "Hoc (the condition of *nexum*) C. Poetilio Libone Visolo dictatore (313 B.C.) sublatum ne fieret ; et omnes, qui bonam copiam jurarunt, ne essent nexi dissoluti." Livy (viii. 28), who attributes the measure to 326 B.C., makes it a universal release of *nexi*: "jussique consules ferre ad populum, ne quis, nisi qui noxam meruisset, donec poenam lueret, in compedibus aut in nervo teneretur : pecuniae creditae bona debitoris, non corpus obnoxium esset."

[2] Liv. ix. 46 "Cn. Flavius . . . patre libertino . . . civile jus, repositum in penetralibus pontificum, evulgavit, fastosque circa forum in albo proposuit, ut quando lege agi posset, sciretur"; Pompon. in *Dig.* 1, 2, 2, 7 "postea cum Appius Claudius composuisset (for "proposuisset") et ad formam redegisset has actiones, Cn. Flavius scriba ejus libertini filius subreptum librum populo tradidit . . . hic liber, qui actiones continet, appellatur jus civile Flavianum."

[3] Pompon. l.c. §§ 37, 38. Gaius Scipio Nasica was given a house for consultations. The first professor, Ti. Coruncanius ("qui primus profiteri coepit," circ. 280 B.C.), was also the first plebeian *pontifex maximus*.

only to give room for the still firmer grasp of a new. This was an aristocracy of mixed origin, composed indifferently of the leading patrician and plebeian families. The test of *nobilitas* was the capacity to point to ancestors who had held office which carried with it the right to sit on the curule chair. Its outward sign was the possession of the so-called *jus imaginum*. The *imagines* themselves were portrait-masks in wax, modelled from the face of the dead, and their primary use was for the purpose of funeral ceremonies. The original was moulded to be placed on the face of the deceased, and so to perpetuate his life in another world; but a copy was kept to give verisimilitude to his fictitious resurrection, which the burial of one of his descendants demanded. At such funerals actors were hired to represent the mighty dead; they wore their *imagines*, and were adorned with the insignia of the offices which these had filled in life, with the *toga praetexta* of the consul or praetor, the purple robe or the *toga picta* of the censor, and they sat on curule chairs round the Forum to listen to the orator who reminded them of their own great deeds.[1] As such a public funeral in the Forum was a concession of the state, the prospective right of having one's mask exhibited, which constituted the *jus imaginum*, was a strictly legal privilege. It was possessed by all those who had been in possession of the *toga praetexta* and the *sella curulis*[2] —the dictator, master of the horse, consul, censor, praetor, and curule aedile. But, even apart from the occasions of such solemn mummery, the *imago* was a sign of the rank of its possessor. When not funereally employed it was suspended on a bust in the wings of the central hall (*atrium*) of the noble's house. Beneath each portrait ran an inscription (*titulus* or *elogium*), which gave the names and deeds of the person represented. The portraits were joined by lines along the walls which showed the *stemma* or family tree. It is possible that this display in the *atrium* was looked on as a public exhibition, and it may originally have been limited by law; but in later times it seems best to conclude that the funerary exhibition alone was the subject of the specific *jus*.[3] But this outward token of nobility, which at Rome took the place of the modern title of honour, was of

[1] Polyb. vi. 53.
[2] Cic. *in Verr.* v. 14, 36 "togam praetextam, sellam curulem, jus imaginis ad memoriam posteritatemque prodendae."
[3] In other words, images of other than curule ancestors might be set up in the *atrium*.

K

importance as emphasising the distinction between the *nobiles* and
the *ignobiles*, in drawing the plebeian aristocracy closer to the
patrician, which before the date of the Licinian laws had been in
exclusive possession of this right, and in asserting the hereditary
claim to office which the Roman electorate was only too ready to
recognise.   The acceptance of the claim was less dangerous than
it is in most modern states, since primogeniture was not recog
nised in the transmission of honours,[1] and it was the capable
and not the elder son whom the vote of the *comitia* raised to
the curule chair.   The claim too might become dimmed by
disuse, and the Plebeian whose immediate ancestors had held
high rank showed a brighter scutcheon than the Patrician who
was connected with a noble *stemma* by ignoble links.[2]   But the
Patriciate itself conferred a kind of nobility, and one that, whatever its basis, might have been justified by office, for there could
have been few members of the order who could not point to curule
ancestors in the past.   Although the Plebeian who *first* secured
curule office, and thus ceased to be *ignobilis*, was called a *novus
homo*, the designation seems never to have been applied to the
member of a patrician *gens*.[3]   Nobility, if once secured, could never
be lost ; but the hereditary claim to the suffrage of the electors was
of little avail if unaccompanied by exceptional merit or by wealth.
The claims of the latter were in fact given a kind of legal recognition by the rule established about the time of the first Punic
war, that the cost of the public games should not be defrayed
exclusively by the treasury.[4]   The aedileship, whether curule or
plebeian, was, as we shall see, not an obligatory step in the
ascending scale of the magistracies ; but, as it was held before
the praetorship and the consulship, it is obvious that the brilliant
display given to the people by the occupant of this office would
often render fruitless the efforts of his less fortunate competitors,
and that this legitimised bribery would exclude from office both
the poorer *nobiles* and the struggling *novus homo*.[5]

The idea of a privileged nobility, which closed its ranks to
new men, had become fixed by the date of the second Punic

---

[1] p. 22.
[2] Sallust. *Jug*. 95 (of Sulla) "gentis patriciae nobilis fuit, familia prope jam
exstincta majorum ignavia."
[3] Cic. *pro Mur*. 7. 16 ; Ascon. *in Scaurian*. p. 22.
[4] Dionys. vii. 71.
[5] Cf. Cic. *de Off*. ii. 17, 58 "Vitanda tamen suspicio est avaritiae.   Mamerco,
homini divitissimo, praetermissio aedilitatis consulatus repulsam attulit."

war.[1] By the close of that war the old stock had reached its
maturity and had begun to decline; and, although men like Cato
or Cicero might force themselves to the front by pertinacity and
ability, or the belief in privilege might be rudely shaken by the
people's thrusting into the coterie a Varro · or a Marius, the
aristocrats came to look on the introduction of new blood as a
pollution to the order.[2]   Time, which purifies all things, had
made the slave-blood of the successful Plebeian as blue as that of
the descendant of kings by whom he sat.

But, in spite of this unholy alliance of the ancient foes, the
distinction between the orders never was abolished.   In Cicero's
time the separate rights of the Patricians could still be enumerated and defended by the orator.   Besides the shadowy and
ineffective powers of the *patrum auctoritas* and the *interregnum*,
they possessed half the places in the great priestly colleges,
which were shared between the orders, and certain priests—the
Rex Sacrorum, the three great Flamines and the Salii—were
chosen exclusively from their ranks.[3] The place of the Patriciate in the theory of the constitution—as illustrated by the
auctoritas and the *interregnum*—is, as we shall see, very great
indeed ; but this theoretical importance conferred very little
power, and the Plebeians, with their exclusive magistracies closed
to the *patres*, with one place reserved for them in the consulship
and censorship and the other accessible to their order, had won
in the long race for honours.

[1] Liv. xxii. 34 (of the election of Varro, 217 B.C.) "Patres summa ope
obstabant, ne se insectando sibi aequari adsuescerent homines."
[2] Sallust. *Jug.* 63 "consulatum nobilitas inter se per manus tradebat ; novus
nemo tam clarus neque tam egregiis factis erat, quin indignus illo honore, et
is quasi pollutus, haberetur."
[3] Cic. *pro Domo* 14, 38 "Ita populus Romanus brevi tempore, neque regem
sacrorum, neque flamines, neque salios habebit, nec ex parte dimidia reliquos
sacerdotes, neque auctores centuriatorum et curiatorum comitiorum : auspiciaque
populi Romani, si magistratus patricii creati non sint, intereant necesse est, cum
interrex nullus sit, quod et ipsum patricium esse et a patriciis prodi necesse est."
The passage is closely followed by Livy vi. 41, in the speech against the Licinio-
Sextian laws, with which he credits Appius Claudius. We meet with other archaic
survivals in connexion with the Senate—the distinction, e.g., between the "greater
and lesser *gentes*" (p. 12) was never lost, and the chief of the Senate, the first
member on the list, was always chosen from the *gentes majores* (see p. 12).

CHAPTER III

§ 1. *The Classes of the Population*

BY the date of the *lex Hortensia* (287 B.C.) the Republican constitution had, in all essential points (considered as the constitution of a city-state), completed its growth; but, before we
proceed to examine the theory and practice of the developed
polity, it is necessary to pause and inquire what changes these
centuries of Republican development had made in the status of
the citizen, and in that of the other classes of the city, who
shared partially in, or were excluded from, his rights, and what
modifications had been undergone by the few main legal rules
which mark the outline of their social environment.

The merging of Patricians and Plebeians into one community
created the necessity for a universal conception of citizenship
applicable to the whole body which possessed active political
rights, while the growing practice of granting partial civic rights
to the members of certain Italian communities led to the
distinction between the fully-privileged and the partially-
privileged citizen. The former is the *civis optimo jure*, the latter
the *civis non optimo jure*. It is only of the former that we shall
speak here; the consideration of the latter will be more
appropriately deferred to that portion of our work which treats
of the Italian confederation.

The normal mode of the acquisition of citizenship was
naturally birth, either from two citizens or from a citizen and a
foreigner. The question of the necessity of the marriage of the
parents for the full citizenship of the children we shall soon
consider; the primary question that presents itself to a nation is

that of the allegiance of the child who is the product of a citizen and a foreigner. In such a case the older principle of Roman law (an instance probably of a universal principle of Italian law) was that, where *conubium* existed between the parents, the children followed the status of the father; where *conubium* did not exist, nature dictated that they should follow the condition of the mother.[1]   But an arbitrary exception to this principle was made at an unknown date in Roman law by a *lex Minicia* which enacted that, in case of unions without *conubium* between a Roman and a foreigner, the children should follow the status of the less privileged parent; the child of a *civis Romana* by a *peregrinus* was, therefore, himself a *peregrinus*.

The exceptional modes by which citizens were created were (i.) state-conferment of the *civitas* on *peregrini* or of full *civitas* on *cives non optimo jure*, and (ii.) the manumission of slaves.

(i.) State-conferment of the *civitas* was only an exceptional measure in so far as it required a special legislative act.[2]   The extraordinary liberality of Rome in this respect, never equalled in the life of the ancient city-state—a liberality which spread the name of Roman citizen first over Italy and then over the greater part of the civilised globe—was not an outcome of any suddenly adopted policy, but persisted from the birth of the city[3] to the world-embracing edict of Caracalla (212 A.D.). A few figures are sufficient to represent the extent of the increase effected by this means.   The male citizens who appeared on the census rolls were, at the close of the first Punic war (240 B.C.), 260,000; in 124 they had risen to 394,726; in 85, after the incorporation of the greater part of Italy, to 963,000.[4]   Under Augustus (28 and 8 B.C. and 14 A.D.) the figures were 4,063,000, 4,233,000, and 4,937,000; and the census of Claudius (47 A.D.) gave a return of 5,984,072 *civium capita*.[5]

---

[1] Ulpian *Reg.* v. 8 "conubio interveniente liberi semper patrem sequuntur; non interveniente conubio matris conditioni accedunt, excepto eo qui ex peregrino et cive Romana peregrinus nascitur, quoniam lex Mensia ["Minicia" has been read in the Veronese palimpsest of the parallel passage of Gaius i. 78, ed. Krueger and Studemund] ex alterutro peregrino natum deterioris parentis conditionem sequi jubet."

[2] Or, in the Principate, an administrative act.   See the section on the powers of the Princeps.   [3] p. 6.

[4] Beloch *Der Italische Bund* pp. 101, 102.

[5] Tac. *Ann.* xi. 25 ; Beloch op. cit. p. 78.   According to Beloch (l.c.) a comparison between the ante-imperial and post-imperial census is vitiated by the fact that the *aerarii* were excluded from the former, included in the latter.   See the section on the censor.

This gift of citizenship was, in the Republic, conferred exclusively by a decree of the people (*jussu populi*). Such decrees might be either of a standing or a particular character ; they might confer the gift immediately on the recipients or through intermediary delegates. Standing rules are mainly such as governed the condition of the dependencies of Rome. We shall find that the rights of Latin colonies provided facilities for the attainment of citizenship ; the criminal laws sometimes gave a foreigner the gift of *civitas* as a reward for successful prosecution ;[1] and, after the fall of the Republic, the enlistment of legionaries from the provinces was one of the most fertile sources from which the citizen body was recruited. Particular conferments, if not made directly by the people, might be effected through the Senate acting as its delegate,[2] or through commissioners charged with the founding of colonies. These were generally the specially-appointed *IIIviri coloniae deducendae ;* and in all such cases of delegation the power was conferred by a *lex*.[3] In the last century of the Republic we find the custom growing up of permitting by special enactment such powers to generals in the field. Marius in the Cimbric war had the gift of citizenship in his hands, and a *lex Cornelia Gellia* granted a similar power to Pompeius during his Spanish campaigns.[4] This was the stepping stone to the right possessed by the sole commander-in-chief, the Princeps, to confer the citizenship at his pleasure.

(ii.) Any perfectly valid form of manumission conferred citizenship on slaves. Every form was undertaken at the initiative of the master, but for it to be perfectly sound (*manumissio justa*)[5] he must observe certain rules of law. The most usual form was the *manumissio vindicta*. It was one of the many fictitious forms of the old capture of property (*vindicatio*), the primitive Roman method of recovery. A man of straw, called the *adsertor in libertatem,* appeared before any magistrate, who could claim the conduct of the *legis actio,*[6] declared the slave to be free, and touched his head with a staff (*vindicta*).[7] The master yielded,

[1] *Lex Acilia Repetundarum* l. 76.
[2] Cic. *pro Balbo* 10, 25 "quod iis . . . liceat, si populus Romanus permiserit, ut ab senatu, ab imperatoribus nostris, civitate donentur."
[3] Cic. *Brut.* 20, 79 ; *pro Balbo* 21, 48.
[4] See the section dealing with the *comitia.*
[5] Suet. *Aug.* 40 ; Senec. *de Vit. Beat.* 24.
[6] It implied the *imperium.* At Rome these magistrates would be consul, praetor, dictator, or interrex ; in the provinces the governors.
[7] Gaius iv. 16.

and this cession of his rights (*in jure cessio*) was followed by the declaration of the magistrate that the slave was free.[1]

The second form was the enrolment on the register of citizens by the censor, when the census was in progress, at the request of the master (*manumissio censu*). It was the false declaration of the master that the man was free which gave validity to this form.[2]

The third and later form was manumission by testament (*manumissio testamento*), by which the master either commanded the freedom of the slave in his will, or left it as a trust to his heir.[3]

The comparative inconvenience of these forms had led to other simpler modes of manumission—by announcement of the freedom before friends (*inter amicos*), or through a letter to the slave bidding him live as a freeman (*per epistolam*), or even by inviting him to dine as a freeman at his master's table (*per mensam*).[4] Manumission effected in this informal way, though protected by the civil courts, did not confer the political rights of citizenship.

The citizen who was made such by manumission was a *libertinus ;* all others were, at the close of the Republic, free-born (*ingenui*). The distinction conferred by *ingenuitas* was, as we shall see, an important one, since this condition was a requisite for the army, the magistracy, and the higher orders (*ordines*) of the state. But the conception of "free birth," though a simple one at the end of the Republic, is one that has had a history, and *ingenuitas* did not at all times bear the same meaning. At the end of the fourth century B.C. an *ingenuus* was one who was sprung, not merely from free but from free-born ancestors, for the term *libertinus*—always its antithesis—was used to cover, not merely the manumitted slave, but his descendant in the first degree.[5]

---

[1] "Praetor addicit libertatem." See Cic. *ad Att.* vii. 2, 8.

[2] For the censor as such had no power to confer freedom (Mommsen *Staatsr.* ii. p. 374). Cicero (*de Orat.* i. 40, 183) mentions the juristic controversy whether the slave was free from the moment of the announcement or from the *lustrum*, which gave validity to the censorian ordinances. *Servi publici* were manumitted by the magistrates, but whether by the consul only or by any magistrate is unknown (Momms. *Staatsr.* i. p. 321). The greatest instance of state emancipation is that of the *Volones* in 214 B.C. (Liv. xxiv. 16).

[3] In the first case it is called *directa libertas* (*Dig.* 40, 4, 35), in the second *libertas fidei commissa* (*Dig.* 40, 4, 11).

[4] Theophilus (i. 5, 4) calls them φυσικοὶ τρόποι ἐλευθερίας.

[5] Suet. *Claud.* 24 (Claudius said that App. Caecus, censor in 312 B.C., had chosen the sons of *libertini* for the Senate) " ignarus, temporibus Appii et deinceps aliquamdiu, ' libertinos ' dictos, non ipsos, qui manu mitterentur, sed ingenuos ex his procreatos."

Before the close of the Republic the son of a freedman or of a freed-woman was *ingenuus*, the only condition being "birth in a state of freedom."[1] The status of the mother alone was taken into consideration, that of the father being neglected, and the condition of marriage, which could not be taken into account if one of the parents was unfree, was necessarily not required.

Legal marriage must in early times have been a condition of *ingenuitas* in the plebeian, as it certainly was in the ancient patrician community. But before the close of the Republic this condition too was disregarded, and illegitimate children (*spurii filii*) were placed on a level, as regards honours and offices, with those born from wedlock.[2] It was one of the many triumphs of the law of nature over the law of the state.

The rights (*jura*) of the citizen in the developed Republic were those which we have enumerated as belonging to the free Plebeian of the monarchy,[3] with most of the exclusively patrician privileges added. They included the rights of marriage and of commerce, with their consequences, the *patria potestas* and the right of making testaments, and in addition, the power of occupying domain land and the rights of suffrage and of office. The Patricians still possessed some minor privileges,[4] and the old theory was still upheld which reserved the *auspicia* for the *patres*. But, with Plebeians in possession of the *imperium*, this doctrine was maintained by the fiction which gave the occupant of a "popular" and, as it still continued to be called, "patrician" magistracy the patrician *auspicatio*.

The duties of the citizen are certain services which he owes to the state, which are paid either by his personal labour or by his property.

The name for these duties (*moenera, munera*, connected with *munire*, to "fortify") shows that they were connected with the military defence of the city. Originally most of such burdens

---

[1] Justin. *Inst.* i. 4 "qui statim ut natus est liber est"; Cic. *de Nat. Deor.* iii. 18, 45 "in jure civili, qui est matre libera, liber est." This is the sense in which Cincius (*ap. Fest.* p. 241) and Livy (x. 8) declare *patricius* to have been originally equivalent to *ingenuus*. See p. 5.

[2] The *s(ine) p(atre) filii* of Gaius (i. 64) and Plutarch (*Qu. Rom.* 103) was a conjecture of the jurists based on the abbreviated form of *sp(urii) filii* (Momms. *Staatsr.* iii. p. 72 n. 4). *Spurii filii* was the official designation, while *liberi naturales* denoted the natural relationship to the father (Meyer *Der römische Concubinat*).

[3] p. 35.   [4] p. 131.

were probably defrayed by the personal labour of the citizens.[1] Even the financial burdens which afterwards pressed on property (*munera patrimonii*) were largely defrayed by their enforced toil (*operae*).[2] In the municipal legislation of the close of the Republic we find the services of the citizens demanded for imposts such as the repair of roads and walls (*munitio*), which are in modern times covered by rates.[3]   But the *tributum*, at whatever time it was first imposed, came to satisfy most of the necessities formerly met by this enforced labour.   Other public needs were, in the Republic, met by contracts concluded by the censor, of which we shall speak in connexion with that office. A clear distinction could now be drawn between the great burden on property—the tribute—and the great burden on the person—military service.[4]

The tribute was, from the time of the Servian census, imposed on the property which formed the basis of the *classes*— originally, therefore, on *res mancipi ;*[5] later it was levied on all property and was paid by all registered citizens who were *sui juris*, the *aes hordearium* and *equestre* for the support of the knights being still paid by children and women who were also *sui juris*.[6]   The lowest property taxed was, as we have seen, one of 1500 asses.[7]   The taxation was not, however, like military service, graduated according to the *classes*, but was collected uniformly, usually at a rate of one *as* in the 1000 ($\frac{1}{10}$ per cent).   The tribute was an extraordinary tax and was imposed, like military service, only when the necessities of the state demanded it, practically when there was no reserve fund in the *aerarium*.   The state regarded it as a loan rather than as its due, and sometimes considered itself bound, when its finances were more flourishing, to return the money to the contributors.[8] The vast revenues accruing to the state as a result of the third

---

[1] p. 45.   [2] p. 98.

[3] *Lex Coloniae Genetivae* (a foundation of Caesar's in 44 B.C. at Osuna in Spain) c. 98 "Quamcumque munitionem decuriones hujusce coloniae decreverint . . . eam munitionem fieri liceto, dum ne amplius in annos singulos . . . operas quinas . . . decernant."

[4] The other chief personal burdens are guardianship (*tutela*) and serving on juries ; but the consideration of both belongs rather to civil and criminal than to public law.

[5] p. 69.   [6] p. 74.   [7] p. 73.

[8] Liv. xxxiii. 42 (196 B.C.) "Pecunia opus erat, quod ultimam pensionem pecuniae in bellum conlatae persolvi placuerat privatis."   Cf. v. 20 and Plin. *H.N.* xxxiv. 6.

Macedonian war in 167 B.C. caused the cessation of the tribute,[1] and no further direct tax was collected at Rome until at the end of the third century A.D. it was reimposed by Diocletian and Maximian. Tribute was, indeed, inconsistent with Rome's imperial position. It had been meant to defray the cost of the legions, but, with the creation of the empire, each province defrayed the expenses of its own military occupation.

Service in the legions (*militia*) was in theory a burden; exemptions from it were occasionally granted as though it were a troublesome duty,[2] and the citizen who did not present himself for the conscription was sold as a slave[3] across the Tiber.[4] But the treatment of the levy and the feeling of the citizens raised this burden (*munus*) into a privilege (*honor*); it was for this reason that free birth was always required as a qualification for a legionary, and that the ranks were never tainted by the admission of men of servile blood. The Servian census was still the scale by which military service was measured, both in the *legio* and in the select corps of citizen cavalry (*equites*). The legal duration of service throughout the greater part of the Republic was sixteen, or at the most twenty yearly campaigns (*stipendia*) for the foot soldier, and ten campaigns for the knight. The performance of the *munera* of tribute and military service required a third duty, which was the condition of both. This was the presence of the citizen who was *sui juris* at the census for the purpose of registration. All who neglected this duty (the *incensi*) could be sold as slaves across the Tiber.[5]

The concepts of the individual as the subject of rights, of their tenure and of their infringement, gave rise to a gradually developed theory of the *jura* with which the citizen was invested, and the mode in which they might be lost, which plays a large part in the speculations of the jurists. It attached itself to the primitive idea of a *capitis deminutio*, the lessening of status caused by the loss of family rights.[6] Gradually juris-

---

[1] Cic. *de Off.* ii. 22, 76 "Paulus tantum in aerarium pecuniae invexit, ut unius imperatoris praeda finem attulerit tributorum"; Plutarch, *Paul.* 38.

[2] *Lex Acilia Repetundarum* c. 79; amongst the rewards granted to a Latin who prosecuted successfully under this law are "militiae munerisque poplici in sua quojusque ceivitate vocatio immunitasque."

[3] Cic. *pro Caec.* 34.

[4] Cic. l.c.; *de Orat.* i. 40.

[5] Cic. *pro Caec.* 34; Dionys. iv. 15.   [6] p. 32.

prudence evolved the idea of a *caput* or personality possessed by every individual independent of citizenship, an idea running parallel with the conception of a law of the civilised world (*jus gentium*) independent of the *jus civile*. From this point of view loss of *citizenship* could be spoken of as a *capitis deminutio*. There was besides an infringement of personality greater even than the loss of citizenship of which the natural man might be the victim. This was the loss of freedom. These two great derogations of *caput* were spoken of as *magna capitis deminutio ;* [1] but finally a more precise classification gave the following three grades of loss of status : [2]—

(i.) *Capitis deminutio maxima* was the loss of *civitas* and *libertas*, consequent on a man's becoming a prisoner of the enemy. With the loss of freedom, political and therefore private rights[3] ceased *ipso jure* to exist. The obligations of international law might also produce this condition ; the Roman general who concluded a treaty with the enemy, which the people would not accept, was handed over as a scape-goat for the broken faith of the community [4] (*deditus*), and similar treatment was meted out to one who had violated the sanctity of envoys,[5] or to a general who had made war with a state in alliance with Rome.[6] This loss of status was also produced by the civil law, in so far as it enjoined slavery as a penal measure—e.g. in the case of the *incensi* or of those who shirked military service [7]—or permitted the sale of the debtor or of the child into a foreign land.[8]

(ii.) *Capitis deminutio media* (or *minor* [9]) was the loss of *civitas* alone.

This might be voluntarily incurred by the assumption of the citizenship of another town, for the principle of the older Roman law was that a man might not be a member of two independent communities.[10] The exile from Rome which

---

[1] Eisele *Beiträge zur römischen Rechtsgeschichte* p. 205.
[2] Gaius i. 159-162 ; Ulp. xi. 10-13.   [3] p. 31.
[4] For the form of *deditio* see Liv. ix. 10 ; App. *de Reb. Hisp.* 83. The references are to the two great historic instances at the Caudine Forks (321) and Numantia (137).
[5] Liv. xxxviii. 42 (188 B.C.) "eo anno L. Minucius Myrtilus et L. Manlius, quod legatos Carthaginienses pulsasse dicebantur, jussu M. Claudii praetoris urbani per fetiales traditi sunt legatis, et Carthaginem avecti."
[6] ib. v. 36 ; Suet. *Caes.* 24.   [7] p. 138.
[8] p. 91.   [9] Gaius i. 159.
[10] Cic. *pro Balbo* 11, 28 ; *pro Caec.* 34, 100.

followed condemnation for a criminal offence was of this type of rejection of citizenship, for the exile was always assumed to be a voluntary act. Enforced abstention from the Roman *civitas*, which necessitated a continuance in exile, was produced by the decree of outlawry (*aquae et ignis interdictio*)[1] often passed by the people against an individual who was in voluntary banishment for a crime.

(iii.) *Capitis deminutio minima*—originally a loss of family rights —was improperly construed by the later jurists as a change of family status.[2] Its applications have been already considered.[3]

There were means of recovering the status lost in either of these three modes. The loss of *familia* in its original sense[4] might be recovered by emancipation; the loss of *civitas*, if enforced by the state, by a special act repealing this disability (the *restitutio in integrum* of the criminal law). *Libertas* could be regained by the exercise of a right known as the *jus postliminii*. The return, unintentional or premeditated, of the captive within the limits of his own country destroyed the state of bondage, and restored the *ingenuitas* and the rights of the former prisoner. Although described as a legal fiction[5] it was a direct consequence of the simple principle that a Roman could not be enslaved on Roman soil.

The Roman family had been subjected to many modifications since we last considered it.[6] The *patria potestas*, indeed, existed in all its old rigour, and the power of life and death over the children still found occasional expression; but the unity of the family had been largely dissolved by the laxity of the marriage tie. A modification of the *usus* marriage had come into vogue, which recognised the consent of the parties, without the prescriptive tenure by which the *potestas* was asserted, as the only bond—one, therefore, dissoluble at any moment by rejection on the part of the husband or by mutual consent. The wife remained a member of her father's *familia*, and if she was *sui juris*, retained her own property; for the tutelage of women

---

[1] p. 55.
[2] Ulp. *Reg.* xi. 13 "per quam, et civitate et libertate salva, status dumtaxat hominis mutatur." Cf. Gaius i. 162.
[3] p. 32.   [4] i.e. by *adrogatio*, see p. 32.
[5] Justin. *Inst.* i. 12, 5 "postliminium fingit eum qui captus est semper in civitate fuisse"; Gaius i. 129 "hi qui ab hostibus capti sunt, si reversi fuerint, omnia pristina jura recipiunt."
[6] p. 18.

was out of accordance with the spirit of the age, and, though not abolished, was evaded by cunningly contrived legal fictions.[1] Never, perhaps, have women been freer from social trammels and legal bonds than they were in the last century and a half of the Republic, and one of the features of their independence was an indirect, but very powerful, influence on politics.

But the greatest change in Roman society was due to the growth of a slave population, which, in the city and that part of Italy which formed the Roman domain, reduced the free citizens to a minority.

The rules of the *jus gentium*—which in this instance, as in many others, is pure international law—permitted the captive to be enslaved until such time as he set foot again in his native land, if this country of his were an independent state.[2] This principle, applied to the victorious wars of Rome, had flooded Italy with specimens of various nationalities which were applied to various uses. These prisoners of war were, as a rule, immediately transferred from the ownership of the state to that of private individuals. They were sold by the quaestors,[3] often in the camp,[4] and the slave-dealer tracked the footsteps of a successful general.[5] War alone might have provided all that were needed for the most luxurious community, if we may judge from the result of the second conquest of Macedon, which swept 150,000 Epirot captives into Italy,[6] and from the consequences of the campaigns of Caesar and Lucullus. But it was supplemented by a brisk slave trade, which after the fall of Corinth and Carthage (146 B.C.) centred at Delos, and which at the close of the Republic had reached such dimensions that, during the reign of the Cilician pirates, 10,000 slaves are said to have been imported and sold there in the course of a single day.[7] It was chiefly from the latter source that the versatile natives of the East were brought, Phrygians, Mysians, Lydians, Lycians, Paphlagonians, the Hellenised members of the "nations born to slavery," who,

---

[1] Cic. *pro Mur.* 12, 27 "mulieres omnes propter infirmitatem consilii majores in tutorum potestate esse voluerunt ; hi invenerunt genera tutorum, quae potestate mulierum continerentur."

[2] By the *jus postliminii ;* see p. 140.

[3] Plaut. *Capt. Prol.* 34.

[4] Liv. x. 42, 46.   [5] Caesar *B.G.* iii. 16.

[6] Polyb. xxx. 15 (Paulus) πέντε δὲ καὶ δέκα μυριάδας ἀνθρώπων ἐξανδραποδίσασθαι.

[7] Strabo xiv. p. 668.

while professing to interpret, often guided and controlled, the wills of their slower Roman masters.

Their use was twofold ; they were either labourers in the workshop and the field, or domestic members of the villa or the palace, and their presence in either capacity was fraught with important political consequences for Rome.   Their cultivation of the mechanical arts and crafts made the Roman noble's household self-sufficient[1] and the competition of the free artisan almost a hopeless task.   In the country they were gradually replacing both the free labourer and the yeoman farmer.   The advantage of cheap labour, which could not be snatched from the master's hands by the needs of distant wars, was at an early period recognised by the nobles in the cultivation of their vast estates.[2] After the acquisition of the province of Sicily, which supplied cheap food to Rome, slave labour on the large estates became an economic necessity ; for it was the only condition on which corn could now be productively grown.   The lot of the plantation slave, unknown to his master and exposed to the mercies of the overseer, was a shameful parody of the earlier domestic servitude. Yet the state did nothing.   The slave possessed no rights, as in the time when he, perhaps, required none.   In the case of domestic slavery, the moral influence of an intellectually superior race was often an adequate substitute for the absence of rights, and a further *solatium* was found in the door of emancipation which was ever open to the favourite.   The Roman was not ungrateful, and he recognised that it was the slave who made him an individual power in the world.   The unequalled administrative capacity of men like C. Gracchus, Crassus, Caesar, and Pompeius, which has found no parallel in the modern world, was largely due to their absolute command of men of perhaps less originative power, but often of greater capacity for combination and detail than they.

Usefulness to the master was in fact the end to which the changes in the law relating to servitude were directed.   The slave might benefit his lord by a contract entered into with a third party, but could not make his condition worse.[3] The *dominus* could sue on the contract, although the slave having no legal

[1] Marquardt *Privatleben* pp. 135 sq.
[2] Appian *B.C.* i. 8.
[3] Gaius in *Dig.* 50, 17, 133 "melior condicio nostra per servos fieri potest, deterior fieri non potest."

personality could conclude only a natural obligation (*naturalis obligatio*), but he was not liable for the losses.   To protect third parties, however, and to give the necessary legal credit to this useful agency, the praetor gradually established a series of quasi-liabilities for the master, which were really in his interest ; for without them slave-agency would have become impossible. Thus, if the master had countenanced the slave's contract, he was liable (*actio quod jussu*) ; if the slave had embarked his *peculium* in trade with the master's knowledge, this property, though in strict law not his own, could be claimed by the creditors, after the slave's debts to the master had been deducted (*actio tributoria*). Finally, any liability incurred by the *peculium* could be recovered by creditors, the master's right of deducting his own claims against it being preserved (*actio de peculio*), and any material advantage derived by the master from the contract of a slave was taken into consideration and the property of the *dominus* made liable to that extent (*actio de in rem verso*).[1]   The slave, in fact, as having no personality of his own, is the best of agents, and the theory of agency, which the law of Rome has bequeathed to us, is one of the most perfect and permanent results of her system of slavery.

Apart from these relations to his master the slave was still ignored by law.   He could not give evidence in court except under torture.[2]   In case wrongs were done him, it was not he but his master that demanded reparation ;[3] while his lord himself was the judge of the delicts which he had committed against himself or the household.[4]   That for crimes against others the slave was tried by the ordinary process of criminal law was a concession to society rather than to the wrongdoer, and the sense of insecurity of the free population amidst their far more numerous dependants was expressed in the atrocious law that the murder of a Roman in his own house should be avenged by the death of the whole *familia* that were sleeping beneath the roof at the moment of the commission of the crime.[5]

---

[1] Gaius iv. 69-74 ; Justin. *nst.* iv. 7.
[2] Cic. *Part. Orat.* 34, 118 ; *pro Cluent.* 63, etc. As, however, the master's consent had to be obtained, the evidence and torture of slaves in the public courts were rare. In domestic jurisdiction the inquisition on slaves was held before a family *consilium*.
[3] Gaius iii. 210, 217, 222, 223.
[4] Cato *R.R.* 5 ; Dionys. vii. 69.
[5] Cic. *ad Fam.* iv. 12 ; Tac. *Ann.* xiv. 42.

The state itself owned slaves who were known as *servi publici*. Some were in the service of temples or of colleges of priests. Others were at the disposal of magistrates, such as the censors or aediles,[1] for the minor duties of attendance and police. Their agency in contracts was doubtless as useful to the state as that of private slaves was to individuals. Such an agent (*actor publicus*) was kept by the treasury for the acquisition of property,[2] which, as his *peculium*, fell under the *dominium* of the state.

We have seen that manumission in due form made a citizen of a slave. The *libertini*, therefore, are not a third class in the state, and only demand a separate treatment in so far as their grant of freedom was conditioned by the performance of certain duties to their former masters, and in so far as the lack of free birth (*ingenuitas*) entailed certain political disabilities.

The relation of the *libertus*[3] to his former master, who now became his *patronus*, was to some extent modelled on that of the ancient client to his lord. The freedman owed his manumitter reverence and obedience (*obsequium*);[4] he could not prosecute, or appear as a witness against him, in the criminal courts,[5] and he required the permission of the praetor to bring even a civil action against his former master or that master's near relatives.[6] The patron's right of succession to the freedman's estate if he died intestate and without heirs,[7] if it was not a family right, was justified by the fact that the capital with which the freedman started life must have been generally the gift of the master, whether it took the form of a *peculium* or not. This circumstance must have been also felt to justify manumission on the condition of continuing to perform certain services to the *dominus*. But the privilege of imposing such conditions was abused, and had to be limited by the edict of a praetor Rutilius,[8] which practically confined them to the performance of certain personal

---

[1] Liv. xliii. 16 ; Gell. xiii. 13. For *servi publici* in the municipal towns see *Lex Coloniae Genetivae* c. 62.

[2] *Actor publicus*, in Rome (Tac. *Ann.* ii. 30) ; in the municipal towns (Plin. *Ep.* vii, 18, 2).

[3] *Libertinus* describes the freedman's political position, *libertus* his relation to his master.

[4] Ulp. in *Dig.* 1, 16, 9, 3.   [5] Macer in *Dig.* 48, 2, 8 ; Paul. *Sent.* v. 15, 3.

[6] Ulp. in *Dig.* 2, 4, 4, 1 "Praetor ait 'parentem, patronum, patronam, liberos parentes patroni patronae in jus sine permissu meo ne quis vocet.'"

[7] Gaius iii. 40-44.

[8] Ulp. in *Dig.* 38, 2, 1, 1. Mommsen (*Staatsr.* iii. p. 433) thinks that the author of the change was the famous P. Rutilius Rufus, consul 105 B.C.

services (*operae*). The fact that the freedman was still regarded as an appendage of the *familia* was most clearly shown by the criminal jurisdiction—even extending to capital punishment—exercised over him by the head of the family even at the close of the Republic.[1]

The political position of the *libertini* was probably better at the beginning than at the end of the Republic. Under the Servian *régime* they were, with all other citizens, members of the tribes ; whether they were at first members of the centuries depends on the question whether free birth was always a requisite for military service, and this is a point on which evidence entirely fails us ;[2] but when the *comitia centuriata* had ceased to be a military and become a purely political institution, there is no reason to assume their exclusion. They would have been members of the *comitia tributa* and *concilium plebis* from the earliest institution of these two bodies. The freedmen (rarely landowners and usually mechanics) belonged in the main to the four old city tribes. This accident had become a legal prescription by the year 312 B.C. In that year the revolutionary census of App. Claudius, which we shall describe elsewhere,[3] spread them over all the tribes,[4] and probably, according to their census, over all the centuries. In 304 B.C. the old arrangement, which limited the freedman's vote, was reverted to.[5] The censors of 169 went further and restricted them all to a single tribe.[6] The conflict required the intervention of law, and it was probably the *lex Aemilia* (of M. Aemilius Scaurus, consul in 115 B.C.) which re-established the old principle of restriction to the urban tribes.[7] But the question of the freedman's vote

---

[1] Suet. *Caes.* 48 ; Val. Max. 6, 1, 4. Willems (*Droit Public* i. p. 125 n. 8) remarks that there is nothing to show that this power was exercised over *justi liberti*. The freedmen so punished may have been informally manumitted. For the relegation of a freedman by his *patronus* see Tac. *Ann.* xiii. 26.

[2] Cf. Plut. *Poplic.* 7. Plutarch, in this story of the imaginary freedman Vindicius, represents his class as having no voting rights at the beginning of the Republic. Appius Claudius (312 B.C.), he says, first gave them ἐξουσίαν ψήφου : but he does not state the assemblies in which this right was exercised.

[3] See the section on the censor (p. 223).

[4] Liv. ix. 46.

[5] ib. ; Val. Max. ii. 2, 9. Nothing is said about their division into *classes ;* according to the arrangement of the reformed *comitia centuriata* (see the section on the *comitia*), this restriction to four tribes would have given them the command of only forty centuries.   [6] Liv. xlv. 15.

[7] *Auct. de Vir. Ill.* 72 (M. Aemilius Scaurus) "consul legem de sumptibus et libertinorum suffragiis tulit " ; Willems *Droit Public Rom.* p. 123.

became a battle-cry in the last century of the Republic. In 88 B.C. the democratic tribune Sulpicius passed a law which gave the *libertinus* the tribe of his patron.[1] It was repealed by the optimates; but the second triumph of the democrats in 84 B.C. again restored the law,[2] until Sulla's ascendency finally established the limitation to the four city tribes.

The freedmen were excused the burden, because not thought worthy of the honour, of regular military service in the legions.[3] The same prejudice did not apply to the fleet, and for this service *libertini* were freely employed.[4] The lack of free birth was also a ground of exclusion from the magistracy, and therefore from the Senate, to which this was the stepping-stone.[5]

§ 2. *The Theory of the Constitution*

The Roman constitution had lost none of its complexity by growth. The accretions of ages had changed a curious but comparatively simple type of polity into a jumble of constitutional law and custom, through which even the keen eye of the Roman jurist could not pierce, and which even his capacity for fictitious interpretation and the invention of compromises could not reduce to a system. The lack of logic, which is the usual accompaniment of a conservatism not thorough-going enough to be consistent, produced a machine the results of which appeared for a time to be eminently satisfactory. It conquered the world, and succeeded for a time in governing it with some show of decency and a fair measure of success. Had the equilibrium been maintained in practice as in theory, mixed constitutions would have had the most assured claim to the respect and acceptance of the world. But as the knots which the jurist could not untie were cut by the sword, and the constitution reverted to a type far simpler even than that of its origin, we must assume a weakness in the mixed system, which might not have rendered it inadequate as the government of a city state or even of Italy, but certainly rendered it incapable of

[1] Dio Cass. xxxvi. 25.   [2] Liv. *Ep.* 84.
[3] Exceptions due to the stress of times are mentioned for the years 296 (Liv. x. 21) and 217 (Liv. xxii. 11). Even in the social war they formed cohorts separate from the legions.
[4] First mentioned in 217 B.C. (Liv. xxii. 11).
[5] See the section on the magistracy (p. 184).

III   THE THEORY OF THE CONSTITUTION   147

imperial rule. The test was a severe one, and the constitution
which could not answer the strain need not be wholly condemned. For empire is a mere excrescence on the life of a
state, a test neither of its goodness nor of its vitality. A
pure treatment of the Roman constitution will neglect, as
far as possible, this abnormal growth, and, although much of
its structure was the result of war,[1] will be able to show that
its essential peculiarities were not the effect of conquest.

The Roman state was still a limited sovereignty of the
people; so limited, indeed, that the people, i.e. the patricio-
plebeian *populus Romanus*, was dependent, not merely for the
expression of its will, but even for its *existence*, on the life of
its supreme magistrates. In the practice of the Republic down
to its closing days, the cessation of the consulate, by the non-
election or the death of its occupants, caused the suspension of
the life of the state. The people could not meet except under
the shadow of the higher *imperium* or *auspicia*—those of lesser
patrician magistrates were of no avail; for the praetor, though
technically a colleague of the consuls,[2] could not hold the
consular elections [3]—and the city was in a state of suspended
animation until the *auspicia* in all their purity should be restored,
were it but to a single man. The auspices, meanwhile, have
returned to the "fathers,"[4] and it is they only who can restore
them. The first fundamental element, therefore, in the theory
of the Roman constitution, however absurd it may seem, is that
ultimate sovereignty rests with the patrician members of the
Senate.[5] How this theory was put into practice, and what
modifications the practice had undergone since the time of the
monarchy, may be seen by examining the procedure consequent
on a Republican *interregnum*.

The conditions requisite for an *interregnum* were the non-
existence of consuls, or magistrates with consular power, or a
dictator. The retirement of all the other so-called patrician
magistrates, i.e. *magistratus populi*, was another necessary preliminary, for the auspices could not return to the *patres* so long
as they were held, whether as *majora* or *minora auspicia*,[6] by a

[1] e.g. the institution of the censor, praetor, curule aediles, and (although they
are not a part of the developed constitution), the consular tribunes.
[2] p. 121.
[3] Cic. *ad Att.* ix. 9, 3 "in libris (i.e. the augural books) habemus non
modo consules a praetore, sed ne praetores quidem creari jus esse."
[4] p. 47.   [5] p. 47.   [6] See the section on the magistracy (p. 165).

patrician magistrate.[1]   Hence, when a sudden occasion arose for
the appointment of an interrex, it was the duty of the Senate to
give notice to the patrician magistrates and to request them to
retire from office.[2]   The plebeian magistrates still remained in
the exercise of their functions.

It was, in the later Republic, the Senate which took all further
necessary action.   In the early Republic there was no possibility
of its being summoned, and the patrician senators met at
their own discretion to appoint the interrex.   But after the
tribune, who was still in office, had gained the right of transacting
business with the Senate, it was he who put the question, and
the Senate who suggested that the *patricii* should meet for the
purpose.   From this time onwards the electors felt no obligation
to meet except on the suggestion of the Senate.[3]

The collegiate principle of the regal *interregnum* and the use
of the lot[4] had both disappeared ; the agreement of the patrician
senators took the form of the election (*creatio*)[5] of a single interrex
(*prodere interregem*).   This magistrate nominated his successor, as
the consul nominated the dictator,[6] each succeeding interrex
holding office for five days.   There was no limit to the number
that might be created, the interreges varying from the minimum
of two to the known maximum of fourteen ;[7] but there must
be at least two, the first being incapable of holding the consular
election, probably because he was regarded as having received
the *auspicia* irregularly.   The qualifications for the interrex were,
that he should be a Patrician[8] and a senator, and the instances
seem to show that he was invariably chosen from the past

---

[1] Cic. *de Leg.* iii. 3, 9 "ast quando consules magisterve populi (i.e. dictator)
nec escunt, auspicia patrum sunto, ollique ex se produnto qui comitiatu creare
consules rite possint" ; *ad Brut.* i. 5, 4 "dum unus erit patricius magistratus,
auspicia ad patres redire non possunt."

[2] In 43 B.C., on the deaths of Hirtius and Pansa, this communication could
not be made in time.   Hence the extraordinary measure of appointing two
privati with *consularis potestas* to hold the election for the consulship (Dio Cass.
xlvi. 45).

[3] The *senatus consultum* containing this suggestion might be vetoed by one
of the tribunes.   Ascon. *in Milon.* p. 32 "dum . . . Pompeius . . . et T. Munatius
tr. pl. referri ad senatum de patriciis convocandis qui interregem proderent non
essent passi."   [4] p. 47.

[5] Liv. v. 31, 8 "interrex creatur M. Furius Camillus."

[6] The technical expression *prodere interregem* refers in Republican times, not
only to the appointment of the first interrex by election, but to the nomination
of each of the other *interreges* by his predecessor (Liv. vi. 41 ; v. 31).

[7] Liv. vi. 1 ; viii. 23.

[8] Cic. *pro Dom.* 14, 38, quoted p. 131.

holders of curule office.[1]   The first interrex was no doubt
guided by the wishes of the Senate, or of the *patres*, in the choice
of his nominee, and the whole list may have been prepared before
his appointment.   With the creation of the highest regular
patrician office, i.e. with the election of a single consul, the
interregnum necessarily came to an end and the interrex retired.

The reappointment of a chief magistrate called the people
into life again ; and, as a rule, it perpetuated itself by perpetuating the magistracy.   There was, indeed, one large section of
the people which had a continuity of existence as a corporation
—this was the *concilium* of the Plebs with its presidents, the
tribunes.   From the year 287 this *concilium* was an independent
legislative sovereign, and nothing more clearly marks the
theoretical dualism of popular sovereignty at Rome than the
fact that one parliament could continue to exist while the other,
the *comitia* in its various shapes, was dormant.   The division of
executive, judicial, even of deliberative power, is not uncommon
in governments of the mixed type ; the division of unlimited
legislative authority is rarer and nowhere so clearly marked as
in Rome ; for an act of parliament did not require the co-operation of the two assemblies—the separate *fiat* of each had the
force of law.[2]   It is true that in practice this fundamental
dualism was not acutely felt, for the individual elements of
the Populus and the Plebs were to all intents and purposes the
same.   We may emphasise the practical similarity and the
theoretical difference best by glancing at the two assemblies of
the tribes.   Except in elective matters they differed hardly at all in
the sphere of their competence—each was a legislative and judicial
assembly.   But they were under the presidency of magistrates of
different kinds, and this caused a slight difference in their
constitution.   When the tribunes of the Plebs summoned the
people by tribes, the members of the few patrician families did
not attend ; when the consul or praetor summoned the people
by tribes, the Patricians could be present.[3]   A fundamental
distinction in theory here produces little effect in practice.

While this dual sovereignty—harmless except for its in-
cidental effect of the preservation of the tribunate—was a result
of the course taken by the evolution of plebeian privileges, a
far more serious consequence was produced by what we noticed

---

[1] Willems *le Sénat* ii. pp. 14, 16.   [2] p. 126.
[3] See Appendix on the *comitia tributa*.

as the second leading idea in the Roman constitution's period of
growth,[1] the weakening of the magistracy.   This weakening—
partly the result of a struggle for freedom, partly of accidental
circumstances such as the distractions of war—from the first
assumed a form which prevented Rome from ever expanding into
a democracy. The early Greek states adopted the system of
weakening the sole magistracy, first by dividing its functions
amongst several holders, and then, when this was not sufficient,
by deliberately taking powers from them and giving them to
carefully organised popular bodies.   In Rome the principle of
division was not wholly unknown ; thus the censorship and
praetorship take over some of the functions of the consulate,
but the principle of wholesale transference was entirely absent ;
even the usurpation of capital jurisdiction by the people was
modified by the condition that they could meet only on the
summons of a magistrate.   The principle of weakening adopted
at Rome was that of the increase of the number of magistrates,
without any essential alteration of the character of the magistracy.
The increase was effected partly by a consistent application of
the principle of colleagueship, partly by the setting up of new
powers in conflict with the old.   The result was chaos.   In the
developed constitution there were twenty annual magistrates—
ten tribunes, two consuls, eight praetors—each armed with the
power of passing valid acts of parliament, and of vetoing the
resolutions of his colleagues and inferiors.   It is true that there
was a legal subordination amongst them ; the consul was inferior
to the tribune, the praetor to the consul; and the rigorous
application of law would have reduced the Roman constitution to
an oligarchy of ten.   As a matter of fact, the tribunate was too
early enlisted on the side of the nobility to think of pressing its
powers ; dissension reigned within the college, and the history
of the collective magistracy was one of perpetual conflict and
therefore of weakness.   In this weakness the people shared, for
they were wholly dependent on the magistracy.   In shaking
the authority of their representatives they had shaken their own ;
and certain radical defects in the popular organisation, which we
shall discuss when we consider the assemblies more in detail,
added to their incapacity to rule.   Since the guidance of magistrates and of people was equally impossible, and central government must reside somewhere, its fitting place was not unnaturally

[1] p. 89.

sought in the single experienced, permanent, and deliberative body in the state, the Senate.[1] The assumption of the reins of government by a power, which as an independent authority was not contemplated in the original constitution, necessarily gave rise to a body of constitutional custom by the side of the older constitutional law. The applications of this new code can only be estimated by a more detailed treatment of the three factors of government—the magistracy, the people, and the Senate.

[1] The power of this body was much increased by the long wars waged in West and East; but its ascendency was assured before these wars began. See the section on the Senate.

CHAPTER IV

§ 1. *General Characteristics of the Magistracy*

THE collective powers of the magistrate had, as we saw, been summed up in the word *imperium ;* they had, perhaps, also been expressed by the vaguer term *potestas.* When, in course of time, magistracies were created which did not possess the *imperium, potestas* was necessarily the only word which expressed the *generic* power of the magistracy ; *imperium* became a special *species* of this power. Thus one could speak of the *consulare imperium* or of the *consularis potestas*, but only of the *tribunicia potestas.*[1]

It is difficult to treat collectively of the special manifestations of this authority ; for the magistracies were graduated by differences of power. To avoid confusion and repetition it will be best, in this general sketch, to give a complete list of magisterial powers, and to point out in each case where they are accorded to, or withheld from, the particular occupants of office. Magisterial powers may be divided into (i.) administrative, (ii.) those exercised in connexion with the people, (iii.) those exercised in connexion with the Senate ; and (iv.) certain general powers which underlie all these spheres of activity—the right of interpreting the will of the gods through auspices, and the right of enforcing decrees.

(i.) *Administrative powers.*— The sphere of administrative activity had from the first days of the Republic been divided into the two departments of command at home (*domi*) and

---

[1] For an instance of its cumulative use see Cic. *in Verr.* act. i. 13, 37 "erit tunc consul Hortensius cum summo imperio et potestate"; for one of its disjunctive uses see *Dig.* 4, 6, 26, 2 "consulem praetorem ceterosque qui imperium potestatemve quam habent."

abroad (*militiae*), the dividing line between the two being sometimes the *pomerium*, sometimes the limit marked by the first
milestone outside the city.[1]

The home administration can be adequately considered
only when we deal with the separate magistracies. But the
common form in which it asserted itself may be considered
here. This was the right of issuing commands in the form of
edicts (*jus edicendi*), applicable to the special branches of administration under the control of the magistrates, from the
quaestor to the consul.[2] The edicts of all the magistrates cor-
responded to one another in their general form ; they contained
commands, prohibitions, and advice. They were all at an early
period issued in writing, and the difference between them was
simply that while some, such as those of the consuls and quaestors,
were occasional and, when the necessity for them had passed,
withdrawn, others, such as those of the censors, praetors, curule
aediles and provincial governors, were continuous (*perpetua*), as
being called forth by ever-present necessities, and were therefore transmitted by magistrates to their successors (*tralaticia*).
Prominent in their continuity were those of the censors and
praetors ; while the one created a code of Roman morality, the
other developed a system of legal procedure.

The administrative duties abroad belonged exclusively to the
magistrates with *imperium*, i.e. in the ordinary course of things to the
consuls and praetors, in exceptional circumstances to the dictator.[3]
The treatment of provincial administration may be deferred until
we deal with the provinces and the pro-magistracy which imperial
government created. Here we may appropriately notice the
exceptional powers which military command gave to the magistrate over the persons and services of the burgesses, and the
honours which it conferred on its possessor.

The first right conferred by military command (*imperium* in
the narrower sense [4]) was that of the formation of an army by

---

[1] p. 79.

[2] Mommsen (*Staatsr.* i. p. 203) denies the right of the quaestor to issue edicts ;
but the absence of distinct mention of quaestorian edicts is no ground for denying
him what appears to have been a common magisterial right.

[3] For the pro-magistrates see the sections on the consuls and the provinces.

[4] In the course of the Republic *imperium* came to denote *par excellence*
command abroad, as was natural, since here alone the power was unshackled.
Hence the phrase *cum imperio esse* descriptive of a magistrate who can assert this
latent power (Cic. *ad Fam.* viii. 8, 8 "qui praetores fuerunt neque in provincia

enforced conscription (*dilectus*). It was exercised, however, only
by the magistrate in supreme command, that is, by the consuls
or the dictator, not by the praetor. It was a purely magisterial
right, and in the levy of the regular consular army of four
legions the consuls were probably independent of any guidance.
Custom eventually dictated that, when exceptional forces were
needed, the permission for the raising of these should come from
the Senate.[1] Within this permission the consuls acted at their
own discretion. They summoned all the *juniores* to meet them,
formerly on the Capitol, later in the Campus Martius; and under
their inspection the military tribunes selected whom they would
and bound the conscripts to obedience by a military oath (*sacramentum*).[2] Although this oath was in form one of personal allegiance
to special commanders, was tendered to both colleagues[3] and had
to be renewed with every change of command,[4] its primary import
was to give the soldier the right of using weapons against enemies,
and to change what would have been acts of mere brigandage
(*latrocinium*) into those of legitimate service (*legitima militia*).[5]
A secondary association with the oath may in early times have
been that he who broke it was *sacer*, and that the vengeance of
the gods could be satisfied by summary execution inflicted by
the general on the offender.[6] The power of inflicting capital
punishment for military offences did not, however, need this
religious sanction; it was a consequence of the *coercitio* of the
imperator, when outside the sphere of the *provocatio*[7] and unchecked by the veto of a colleague.[8] A further right preliminary to the conduct of war was the nomination of the officers
of the army—the military tribunes, centurions, decurions, and
commanders of every branch. Appointment to all these posts,
from the highest to the lowest, was originally in the hands of
the consuls; but the tendency of the Republic was to remove
selection to the higher military commands from the discretion of

cum imperio fuerunt ") and the opposition between *magistratus* and *imperium.*
Lex Tab. Bant. l. 16 "quibus quisque eorum mag(istratum) imperiumve inierit ";
Lex Acilia Rep. l. 8 "dum mag(istratum) aut imperium habebunt."
[1] Liv. iii. 42 ; xxviii. 45.
[2] Polyb. vi. 19, 21. The tenor of the oath was (c. 21) ἦ μὴν πειθαρχήσειν καὶ
ποιήσειν τὸ προσταττόμενον ὑπὸ τῶν ἀρχόντων κατὰ δύναμιν.
[3] The soldier is said "jurare in verba consulum " (Liv. ii. 52).
[4] Liv. iii. 20.
[5] ib. viii. 34 " latrocinii modo caeca et fortuita pro sollenni et sacrata militia
sit."   [6] Dionys. xi. 43.
[7] p. 79.   [8] See the section on the *intercessio.*

the magistrate.   In 362 B.C. the creation of six of the military
tribunes of the standing army of four legions was transferred to
the people in the *comitia tributa ;* [1] by the year 207 all of the
twenty-four had been thus elected,[2] and the standing military
tribunate had become one of the regular minor magistracies of
the state.[3]   The tribunes for other legions that might be raised
were still nominated by the consuls,[4] and sometimes the people
gave up its right of election in their favour.[5]   In raising supplies
most magistrates were dependent on the Senate ; but the consul's
original control of the *aerarium* survived in the right he possessed
of ordering the quaestor to pay him any money he required for
military expenses.[6]

When the preparations for war were completed and the
consuls took the field, their discretionary authority in the
conduct of the campaign, in finance and in jurisdiction, was
almost absolute.   The first power was hampered only by the
condition that they could not wage war against a state which
stood in any degree of alliance with Rome without the consent
of the people ; the second received some slight limitation from
the appointment of military quaestors in 421 ;[7] the third was
theoretically unlimited throughout the whole history of the
Republic, but received some slight modification from the
growing sense of the sanctity of the life of a Roman citizen,
which made the generals during the last century of the Republic
more chary of pronouncing capital sentences upon their officers
and soldiers.[8]   It is important to remember that this absolute
jurisdiction *militiae* was not in the least confined to the army ;
every Roman citizen within the sphere of the general's administration, and every provincial, when these spheres had
developed into standing provinces, were equally subjected to
martial law.[9]   The provincial in fact was often in better case

---

[1] Liv. vii. 5.   [2] ib. xxvii. 36.   [3] *Lex Acilia* l. 2.
[4] They were called *Rufuli* (Liv. vii. 5 ; Festus p. 260).
[5] Liv. xlii. 31 (171 B.C., commencement of war with Perseus) "consules ex
senatus consulto ad populum tulerunt, ne tribuni militum eo anno suffragiis
crearentur, sed consulum praetorumque in iis faciendis judicium arbitriumque
esset." Cf. xliii. 12.   [6] Polyb. vi. 13.   [7] p. 117.
[8] See Greenidge, "The provocatio militiae and provincial jurisdiction" in
Classical Review x. p. 225.
[9] The fact that the delegates and sometimes the crimes were distinct in the
two cases does not make the military jurisdiction of the *imperator* differ from his
ordinary criminal jurisdiction, as Mommsen seems to think (*Staatsr.* i. p. 123).
For the proofs of unity in the conception of jurisdiction *militiae* see the article
cited in the last note.

than the Roman sojourning in the provinces. He could sometimes appeal to the liberties granted to his town by charter;
but the Roman found that his palladia—the *provocatio* and the
intercessio—had vanished in this sphere.[1]

A victory over the foe gave the general the right to claim
two further privileges—the one a titular designation, the other
a popular manifestation of success—which were strictly regulated
by constitutional law. Every holder of the *imperium* was
necessarily an *imperator*; but from a very early period of the
Republic it was considered improper for the possessor of the very
limited *imperium* within the walls to use this title. It was
reserved for the general in command of an army; *imperator* is
both the official and the familiar title by which he was addressed
by his soldiers. But, even under these circumstances, it was
not employed by the general himself as a part of his official
designation. For this a victory was requisite; the soldiers
after the battle proclaimed him conqueror by shouting the
familiar name; from this time he was supposed to have it
impressed on him in a peculiar manner and could bear it in
his list of titles.[2] Custom decreed that the honour should be
assumed only in consequence of a great and decisive victory;[3]
but the ambition and rivalry of provincial governors finally
caused the most trifling successes to be commemorated in this
way.

The salutation was the usual preliminary to a triumph—the
solemn procession of the general through the city to the Capitol
at the head of his victorious army. As the title *imperator* could
be conferred only on a commander-in-chief, and was inconsistent
with delegated authority, the triumph was necessarily confined
to the magistrates with the capacity for supreme command—the

[1] At the close of the Republic, however, custom dictated that the governor
should send capital cases in which Romans were involved to Rome. See the
section on the provinces.

[2] Tac. *Ann.* iii. 74 "Tiberius . . . Blaeso tribuit, ut imperator a legionibus
salutaretur, prisco ergo duces honore, qui bene gesta republica gaudio et impetu
victoris exercitus conclamabantur." The earliest instance recorded is that of the
elder Scipio Africanus (Liv. xxvii. 19). At the close of the Republic the title
might be conferred by the Senate. Cic. *Phil.* xiv. 4, 11 (to emphasise the fact
that Antonius was a public enemy Servilius had proposed *supplicationes*) "Sed
hoc primum faciam, ut imperatores appellem eos, quorum virtute . . . periculis
. . . liberati sumus." For who, he asks, has not been called *imperator* within the
last twenty years "aut minimis rebus gestis, aut plerumque nullis"? (cf. Cic.
ad Att. v. 20, 3).

[3] Dio Cass. xxxvii. 40.

dictator, consul and praetor,[1] and to the one of these who at the moment of victory was in highest authority.   Thus the dictator usually excluded the consul,[2] the consul the praetor ; and when two consuls were in command, the right resided with the one who had the *imperium* and the *auspicia* on the day of the victory.[3] The same rule held when the honour was granted to pro-magistrates ; here too independent command was the necessary condition of a triumph.

Other qualifications were fixed by custom.   The return of the victorious army was originally necessary—a rule which rendered the most deserving general, who had handed over his forces to a successor, incapable of triumphing,[4] and which, with the growth of standing armies, had to be abandoned for the rule that the province must be reduced to a state of peace (*provincia pacata*).[5]   The war must be a *justum bellum*, not the mere crushing a revolt of citizens or slaves ;[6] and finally, the custom was fixed that it must be a war, the magnitude of which was attested by the fall of 5000 foes.[7]

The right to triumph was one entirely at the discretion of the general ; and as long as he chose the Alban Mount as the scene of his military pageant, no power could hinder him.[8]   It was only when he wished to enter the city of Rome for the more imposing procession to the Capitol that he found difficulties in his way.   The triumph implied the display of the full military *imperium* within the city ;[9] and, though instances are not lacking of magistrates who on their own responsibility successfully asserted this right,[10] the custom became fixed that permission

---

[1] For the consular tribune see p. 114.

[2] An important exception is recorded in Liv. vii. 11 (360 B.C.).   Here the consul triumphs after the abdication of the dictator, and the honour is clearly a concession of the latter.

[3] Liv. xxviii. 9 (207 B.C.).

[4] In this case the lesser honour of an "ovation" was sometimes granted (Liv. xxvi. 21 ; xxviii. 9).   [5] Liv. xxxix. 29 (185 B.C.).

[6] Gell. v. 6 ; Val. Max. ii. 8, 7.   In this case, too, the ovation was sometimes granted, e.g. in the slave-wars of 99 and 71 B.C. (Cic. *de Orat.* ii. 47, 195 ; Gell. v. 6).   For this reason Caesar's triumph in 46 was over Gaul, Egypt, Pontus and Africa ; that of Augustus in 29 over Dalmatia and Egypt.   In neither case was it held over the citizens whom they had crushed.

[7] Val. Max. ii. 8, 1.   [8] Liv. xxxiii. 23 ; xlii. 21.

[9] Mommsen thinks the use of it as well (*Staatsr.* i. p. 132), e.g. that it was in consequence of the absence of the *provocatio* that the *cives Romani Campani* were executed in 271 (Val. Max. ii. 7, 15).

[10] e.g. L. Postumius Megellus in 294 B.C. (Liv. x. 37), App. Claudius in 143 B.C. (Suet. *Tib.* 2).

for this display should be accorded by the state. Originally it
may have been granted by the people,[1] but the permission for
the exercise of the full *imperium* for the single day soon required
the consent of the Senate, all the more necessary as its control
of finance enabled it to grant or refuse the morey which
paid the expenses of the triumph.[2]   The case was otherwise
with the pro-magistrate.   The proconsul had only the *imperium
militiae*, and none within the walls, and it was impossible, therefore, for the Senate to recognise the display of a power which
did not exist.   In this case a special dispensation from the laws
was necessary, which could originally be granted only by the
people.   The Senate took the initiative by asking the tribunes
to introduce a *plebiscitum* sanctioning the arrangement.[3]   The
continuity of the *imperium* from magistracy to pro-magistracy
was originally a condition of the triumph.   Thus it was refused
to the elder Scipio Africanus who had been elected proconsul
without having exercised any previous *imperium*.[4]   By the close
of the Republic both these scruples had been set aside.   The
triumph was decreed to proconsuls by the Senate, and without
regard to their having held any previous *imperium*.[5]

(ii.) *Powers exercised in connexion with the people.*—The dealings
which the magistrate had with the assembled people were
of two kinds; he might summon them for the purpose of
imparting information : in this case the meeting was called a
contio ;[6] or he might convene them for the purpose of passing
decrees binding on the community : such an assembly assumed
one of the various forms of the *comitia*.   The first power
(*contionem habere*) was often preliminary to the exercise of the
second (*cum populo agere*); for a *contio* or a series of *contiones*
generally preceded the formal meetings of the assemblies at

---

[1] "Senatus consulto jussuque populi" (Liv. iv. 20).
[2] Polyb. vi. 15 τοὺς . . . θριάμβους . . . οὐ δύνανται χειρίζειν ὡς πρέπει, ποτὲ δὲ
τὸ παράπαν οὐδὲ συντελεῖν, ἐὰν μὴ τὸ συνέδριον συγκατάθηται καὶ δῷ τὴν εἰς
ταῦτα δαπάνην.
[3] Liv. xxvi. 21. Cf. Liv. xlv. 35, where the Senate's request to the tribune is
made through a praetor. One cannot say in this case that the *imperium* is
conferred for the day, since the Plebs had no power to confer the *imperium*.
[4] ib. xxviii. 38 ; cf. xxxi. 20.
[5] e.g. the two triumphs of Pompeius in 80 and 71 B.C. See Cic. *pro Lege
Man.* 21, 62 "quid tam incredibile, quam ut iterum eques Romanus ex senatus
consulto triumpharet ? "
[6] A shortened form of *conventio*. Cf. *S. C. de Bacchanalibus* (Bruns *Fontes*)
l. 23 "haice uti in conventionid exdeicatis."

which laws or *plebiscita* were passed,[1] and was in fact an in-dispensable preliminary, since, in the case of legislation, it was the chief opportunity for recommendations or criticisms of a bill, and, in the case of popular jurisdiction, was the only means by which the people could form an estimate of the evidence. The magisterial *contio* was, in fact, the great vehicle for constitu-tional agitation and, as such, the most democratic institution in Rome.

But the use of the *contio* was not confined to the prelimi-naries of legislation. It was the form in which the people were summoned to witness any public act,[2] and to listen to the magistrate's commands when these were expressed in the form of verbal edicts.[3] The essential feature of such an assembly was that the people were invited to meet a magistrate and to listen to his views; the masses were mere auditors; and the fact that this was no chance gathering was further emphasised by the solemnity of the proceedings—the formal summons, the opening prayer,[4] and the elevation of the magistrate on the tribunal. We cannot say with certainty how far this right of holding a *contio* extended. It was certainly possessed by the consuls, praetors, censors, and tribunes, and probably by all the magistrates down to the quaestor.[5] The conflict of magisterial authority was felt here as in other departments, and the higher magistrate could summon to himself the *contio* convoked by an inferior.[6]

The Roman constitution recognised no right of public meet-ing; a gathering of the citizens by a citizen might be treated as a breach of the peace, or might be summarily visited by the *coercitio* of a magistrate. But the increase of the magistrates, and the corresponding divergence of their views, supplied a partial substitute for this popular self-repression. It was open

---

[1] Gell. xiii. 16 "cum populo agere est rogare quid populum, quod suffragiis suis aut jubeat aut vetet, contionem autem habere est verba facere ad populum sine ulla rogatione."

[2] It was, e.g., the mode in which the people were summoned to witness public executions outside the Pomerium (Cic. *pro Rab.* 4, 11 ; Tac. *Ann.* ii. 23).

[3] *S. C. de Bacch.* quoted p. 158.

[4] Liv. xxxix. 15 "contione advocata cum sollemne carmen precationis, quod praefari priusquam populum adloquantur magistratus solent, peregisset, consul ita coepit."

[5] Messala ap. Gell. xiii. 16 includes the *magistratus minores*. Mommsen, guided by the (in this case probably false) analogy of the *jus cum populo agendi*, would exclude the aediles and quaestors (*Staatsr.* i. p. 200).

[6] Gell. l.c.

to any magistrate to introduce a citizen to the *contio*, and give him a right to speak (*producere in contionem, dare contionem*);[1] it was equally open to a colleague or superior to veto this permission;[2] but custom must have made such a use of the *intercessio* very infrequent. The right of granting a *contio* gave a limited power of debate on legislative matters to distinguished private individuals; but this was not its only use. It was the sole means by which political leaders, who might happen to be in a private station—as Pompeius after his return from the East, or Cicero after his recall from exile—could express their views;[3] it was also a convenient mode in which a magistrate might justify a line of conduct. We find a foreign king and a public informer thus produced to influence the popular mind. The *jus contionis dandae* meant an increase in magisterial power, and was no true concession to democracy; the demagogue in opposition, who was not a magistrate or useful to a magistrate, had no opportunity of making his voice heard in Rome.

The right of eliciting binding resolutions from the people when assembled in their *comitia* (*jus cum populo agendi*) always remained an inherent attribute of the *imperium*; as such it belonged, under ordinary circumstances, to the consul and praetor; under exceptional conditions, to the dictator, interrex, and consular tribunes. It was also possessed by one at least of the occasional delegates of the highest magistrates, the master of the horse.[4] By these magistrates the *comitia* might be assembled in any form—by curies, by centuries, or by tribes. None of the lower magistrates possessed in their own right the power to summon and preside over the assembly; but the extension of the *provocatio* and the consequent growth of popular jurisdiction rendered it necessary that the lower magistrates with judicial powers should meet the people. Thus the curule aediles defended

[1] Cic. *ad Att.* iv. 1, 6 "habui contionem, omnes magistratus praeter unum praetorem et duos tribunos pl. dederunt"; i. 14, 1 "Pisonis consulis impulsu levissimus tribunus pl. Fufius in contionem producit Pompeium"; ii. 24, 3 "Caesar is qui olim, praetor cum esset, Q. Catulum ex inferiore loco jusserat dicere, Vettium in rostra produxit."

[2] Sall. *Jug.* 34 "ubi Memmius (a tribune) dicendi finem fecit et Jugurtha respondere jussus est, C. Baebius tribunus plebis . . . regem tacere jubet."

[3] See note 1.

[4] Cic. *de Leg.* iii. 4, 10 "cum populo patribusque agendi jus esto consuli praetori magistro populi equitumque eique quem patres produnt consulum rogandorum ergo." For the question whether the praefect of the city had this right see p. 61; an argument for his possession of it in the Republic is his right of consulting the Senate.

their sentences before the *comitia tributa ;*[1] the delegates of the consular criminal jurisdiction, the *quaestores parricidii*, and *duumviri perduellionis* brought their judgments before the *comitia* of the centuries.[2] No plebeian magistrate had the *jus agendi cum populo ;* hence when the tribune, in the exercise of his jurisdiction, wished to obey the command of the Twelve Tables, which confined the hearing of capital cases to the *comitia* of the centuries, he had to ask a patrician magistrate—in this case the praetor—to call a meeting for him by a given day (*diem a praetore petere*).[3] When the praetor had named a day (*diem dixit*) the tribune then appeared in the assembly as the accuser.[4]

The right of eliciting formal resolutions from the Plebs (*jus cum plebe agendi*) belonged exclusively to the plebeian magistrates. The tribunes alone had the presidency of the *concilium*, but here again the growth of popular jurisdiction rendered it necessary that the plebeian aediles should defend their sentences before the Plebs.[5]

(iii.) *Powers exercised in connexion with the Senate.*—The right of bringing matters before the Senate (*jus cum patribus agendi, consulendi senatus, referendi ad senatum*) is one that runs parallel to the right of transacting business with the Populus, and, as such, it is attributed by Cicero[6] to the same magistrates —to the consuls and praetors, the dictator, magister equitum, and interrex. It of necessity attached to the consular tribunes of early times, and was one of the attributes of the *praefectus urbi*.[7]

This right necessarily did not attach originally to the tribunes of the Plebs, for they were first the outcome of a

---

[1] For the curule aediles see Cic. *in Verr.* i. 12, 36 ; Val. Max. viii. 1, 7.

[2] Liv. iii. 24 ; Dionys. viii. 77.

[3] Liv. xliii. 16 (169 B.C., P. Rutilius tr. pl.) " C. Claudio diem dixit . . . et utrique censori perduellionem se judicare pronunciavit, diemque comitiis a C. Sulpicio praetore urbano petiit . . . absoluto Claudio, tribunus plebis negavit se Gracchum morari." Antias ap. Gell. vi. 9 "Licinius tribunus plebi perduellionem ei diem dixit et comitiis diem a M. Marcio praetore peposcit."

[4] Whether the tribune presided over this assembly is uncertain. When the tribune in Livy (l.c.) breaks up such an assembly the act may simply refer to his retirement as a prosecutor (see last note).

[5] Liv. x. 23 ; xxv. 2 ; xxxiii. 42 ; Gell. x. 6.

[6] *De Leg.* iii. 4, 10, cited p. 160.

[7] Gell. xiv. 7 "(Varro ponit) per quos more majorum senatus haberi soleret eosque nominat 'dictatorem, consules, praetores, tribunos plebi, interregem, praefectum urbi' . . . 'deinde extraordinario jure tribunos quoque militares qui pro consulibus fuissent . . . jus consulendi senatum habuisse.'"

M

---

162   ROMAN PUBLIC LIFE   CHAP.

revolution, and then for centuries the presidents of a corporation independent of the people. But, after the *lex Hortensia* had made the *concilium plebis* one of the legislative organs of the community, it would have been dangerous to senatorial government to deny the president of this assembly the right of consulting the Senate.[1] The admission of the tribunes into the circle of the magistrates with the *jus consulendi* was one of the conditions of the Senate's permanent control over initiative in legislation.

(iv.) *General powers: the auspicia and the coercitio.*—We have now to consider certain magisterial powers which cannot be regarded as forming a separate department, since they are coextensive with the whole sphere of official authority. The first that we shall treat, the taking of the auspices, was as much a duty as a right. The observance of the *auspicia publica* is not merely an act that the magistrate may perform, but one that he must perform if his powers are to be duly exercised. The *imperium* and the *auspicia* are indissolubly connected;[2] they are the divine and human side of the same power, and every important act of human activity should be prefaced by an appeal for divine assistance. We have already explained that the only auspices which are properly connected with the magistracy were those known as *impetrativa*, and that the looking for these—the gift of *spectio*—was always a peculiar attribute of the patrician magistracy,[3] and was, therefore, not possessed by the tribunes and aediles of the Plebs. With respect to the other category of auspices—the *oblativa*—not only are all magistrates on a level with one another, but they are all below the level of the meanest citizen. The citizen, if he is a devout man, may suspend the business he has in hand, if an evil sign appears. The magistrate is bound to do so, if the sign is by common consent evil, or has been pronounced such by the college of pontiffs or by the Sibylline books. Roman theology recognised five categories of auspices; four of these belong to the class *impetrativa*, one to the class *oblativa*.[4] The latter, as being the simpler and the one common to all the magistrates, may be considered first.

[1] This right of the tribunes originated later than 304 B.C.; see p. 127.
[2] Liv. xxii. 30; xl. 52. Cf. Wilmanns n. 27 "L. Mummi. L. F. Cos. duct(u) auspicio imperioque ejus Achaia capt(a) Corinto deleto Romam redieit triumphans."
[3] p. 39.
[4] Festus p. 261 "quinque genera signorum observant augures publici, ex coelo, ex avibus, ex tripudis, ex quadripedibus, ex diris."

(1) *Dirae.*—These were a heterogeneous collection of signs of ill omen. Anything that broke the silence (*silentium*)[1] when the auspices were being taken was of this character, such as the fall of anything in a temple (*caducum auspicium*),[2] or a sudden noise, such as the squeak of a mouse.[3] Such too was any sudden event that seemed to warn back from a course once taken—the flight of ravens towards the walker or round his head, and the stumbling of his foot on the threshold;[4] the struggle of birds in the air ending in the defeat of those that had flown from the direction of the general's camp;[5] the seizing of the boundary stones of a newly laid-out city by wolves,[6] and countless others. A peculiarly dreadful omen was a fit of epilepsy, called, from its power of suspending the assemblies, *morbus comitialis*. Such signs, to be effective hindrances, must have an obvious connexion in time and place with the act they impede, and must, besides, be noticed by the agent. Hence a flash of lightning was the most effective of *auspicia oblativa*. Less potent signs could be ignored by veiling the senses. The augur, who is asked by the officiating magistrate if there is silence, does not look round him, but straightway answers "yes";[7] in sacrifice flutes are blown to drown all other sounds,[8] and the general bent on fighting takes the precaution of travelling in a closed litter.[9] If another person forced the omen on the magistrate's notice, he was bound to attend to it. This announcement (*nuntiatio* or *obnuntiatio*) we shall speak of elsewhere; it belongs to the history of the conflict between the authorities of the different magistrates.

The four other classes of omens belong to the category of *auspicia impetrativa*. These were—

(2) Signs from the flight of birds (*signa ex avibus*), the oldest form of augural discipline, as the very words *augures* and *auspicium* prove, and one that in the early Republic was used in all

---

[1] *Silentium* is defined negatively; see Cic. *de Div.* ii. 34, 71 "id enim silentium dicimus in auspiciis, quod omni vitio caret." Cf. Festus p. 351.

[2] e.g. the fall of the cap from the head of the sacrificing priest (Val. Max. i. 1, 5). Cf. Festus p. 64.

[3] Val. Max. i. 1, 5 "occentusque soricis auditus Fabio Maximo dictaturam . . . deponendi causam praebuit."

[4] ib. 4, 2 (the omens that T. Gracchus encountered when seeking the tribunate).

[5] ib. 4, 7.   [6] Plut. *C. Gracch.* 11.

[7] Cic. *de Div.* ii. 34, 72 "Illi autem, qui in auspicium adhibetur, cum ita imperavit is, qui auspicatur 'Dicito, si silentium esse videbitur'; nec suspicit nec circumspicit: statim respondet, 'silentium esse videri.'"

[8] Plin. *H.N.* xxviii. 2, 11.   [9] Cic. *de Div.* ii. 55, 77.

solemn acts of state, such as the summons of the *comitia* or the appointment of a dictator.[1]

(3) Closely akin to this was the augury from the motions and sounds of four-footed beasts (*signa ex quadrupedibus*) ; but by the close of the Republic these forms of divination, which required study and research, had given place to the two remaining classes, which were more easily interpreted, or more readily manipulated for political purposes. These were the *coelestia auspicia* and the *auspicia ex tripudiis*.[2]

(4) Chief of the heavenly signs (*celestia auspicia*), and the surest expression of Jupiter's will, were thunder and lightning. Thunder seems sometimes to have been regarded as a wholly evil omen ;[3] but the course taken by the lightning determined its significance—if on the watcher's left, it was lucky ; if on the right, unlucky.[4]

(5) The *auspicia ex tripudiis* were signs given by the feeding of tame birds (*aves internuntii Jovis*)—generally domestic fowls. If, while they ate, something fell from their mouths (*tripudium solistimum*), still more if the falling object made a ringing noise (*sonivium*), the sign was taken as an assent of the gods to the business in hand. This mode of augury was convenient for two reasons. It was always available ; the birds could be taken about in cages under the custody of their keepers and interpreters of their acts, the *pullarii*. Hence it was the mode of augury specially favoured in the camp, and the sacred chickens were the invariable attendants of a Roman army. Again, the favourable sign might be so easily gained. The irate Roman admiral, who threw his chickens that would not eat into the sea, lacked the patience to wring the wished-for omen from them by protracted hunger, or by feeding them with porridge which they could not swallow with sufficient rapidity.[5]

[1] Liv. i. 36 ; Cic. *de Leg.* iii. 3, 9.
[2] Cic. *de Div.* ii. 33, 71 "haec certe quibus utimur, sive tripudio sive de coelo, simulacra sunt auspiciorum, auspicia nullo modo."
[3] Liv. xxiii. 31 (215 B.C., Marcellus) "cui ineunti consulatum cum tonuisset, vocati augures vitio creatum videri pronunciaverunt."
[4] Cic. *de Div.* ii. 35, 74 "Fulmen sinistrum auspicium optimum habemus ad omnes res, praeterquam ad comitia."
[5] ib. i. 15, 27 "nam nostri quidem magistratus auspiciis utuntur coactis. Necesse est enim, offa objecta, cadere frustum ex pulli ore, cum pascitur. (28) Quod autem scriptum habetis, tripudium fieri, si ex ea quid in solidum ceciderit : hoc quoque, quod dixi, coactum, tripudium solistimum dicitis." Cf. ii. 34, 72 ; 35, 73. For their use in camp see Cic. *de Div.* i. 35, 77 ; Val. Max. i. 4, 3.

The auspices were at first an accompaniment of the *imperium*; later, when they became an attribute of the whole patrician magistracy, their importance varied with the *potestas* of the magistrate. Officials with *imperium* were said to possess *maxima auspicia*, and the pro-magistrates were naturally included in this list, for the auspices were as necessary in war as in peace; those of the censors, on account of the importance of this office, were reckoned *maxima*, although the occasions on which they were taken were so unique that they were not brought into the same category as those of the consuls and praetors; those of the lower magistrates, aediles and quaestors, were called *minora*.[1] This was little more than a formal difference, had reference merely to the importance of the respective spheres of operation, for which observations were made, and did not determine the kinds of auspices that might be taken by each magistrate.

The occasions of the magistrate's auspication embraced every public act of any importance. In three cases above all was it regarded as essential; these were the nomination of a magistrate, the holding of the *comitia*, and the departure of a general for war. The chief rule of observance was that the auspices must be taken on the same day and in the same place in which the act was to be performed. The fact that the Roman civil day (*dies civilis*) began at midnight[2] was convenient for procuring the requisite *silentium*; and sometimes, to prevent any flaw (*vitium*), the act itself was performed before daybreak. Thus the consul, when he nominates a dictator, "rises in the stillness of the night"[3] to do so. The ceremonial for all public auspication[4] was as follows. A sacred enclosure (*templum*) was marked out on the required spot—within or without the *pomerium*, according to the purpose in view—within which the magistrate pitched his tent (*tabernaculum capere*),[5] which had one side open for observation. After midnight he rose, and, seated on the floor, performed the rite. Its validity depended on his personal observation

In the last passage the incident connected with P. Claudius Pulcher (249 B.C.) is described.

[1] Messala ap. Gell. xiii. 15 "Patriciorum auspicia in duas sunt divisa potestates. Maxima sunt consulum, praetorum censorum. . . . Reliquorum magistratuum minora sunt auspicia."   [2] Gell. iii. 2.

[3] "Oriens de nocte silentio" (Liv. viii. 23).

[4] That in the camp, by means of the sacred chickens, had naturally to be exempted from these formalities.

[5] Cic. *de Nat. Deor.* ii. 4, 11; these tents were called *minora templa* (Festus p. 157).

alone; but he might invite skilled assistants to his aid.[1] The consequence of inability to get a favourable omen was necessarily the non-performance of the contemplated act; the only course open was to wait for another day, and to seek the auspices over again (*repetere auspicia*).[2] If the act had been performed in spite of ill omens, or if subsequent reflection showed a flaw in the ceremonial, the act was said to be subject to a *vitium* which rendered it invalid; the law passed did not hold good, and the magistrate thus faultily elected (*vitio creatus*) had to resign his functions.[3] In the case of the election of the consuls being thus vitiated the consequences might be serious; for if the flaw was discovered after their entrance on office, a renewal of the auspices (*renovatio auspiciorum*)[4] could only be effected through an *interregnum*. It was in this connexion that the power of the augurs came into play, for they were the interpreters of the heaven-sent signs. It was no wonder that membership of the augural college was the highest ambition of the Roman statesman, when its decree could upset a law, stave off a capital charge, or force a consul to abdicate. It is true that the augurs could give their advice only on the request of a magistrate or of the Senate; but, as a measure or election not favoured by the government would readily be challenged in this way, the decision as to the future of the state often rested wholly with the college of augurs. Their power of interpretation extended to the far more frequent *auspicia oblativa*, and in reporting these even the initiative might, as we shall see, be taken by an augur.

Since the *auspicia publica* were personal signs vouchsafed to individuals, a collision between the auspices of colleagues engaged in the same business was not impossible. What the result of such a collision was in the case of magistrates engaged *domi* is unknown.[5] In the field the effective auspices were in

---

[1] The manipulation of auspices at the end of the Republic had caused the skilled assistant to be neglected (Cic. *de Div.* ii. 34, 71 "apud majores nostros adhibebatur peritus, nunc quilibet").

[2] Liv. ix. 39, etc.

[3] See the section dealing with the powers of the people. The *vitium* effected the elections even of tribunes of the Plebs—but purely as a result of *auspicia oblativa*. See Liv. x. 47 (293 B.C.) "exacto jam anno novi tribuni plebis magistratum inierant: hisque ipsis, quia vitio creati erant, quinque post dies alii subfecti."

[4] ib. v. 31, etc.

[5] Mommsen thinks that the auspices of the consuls might have alternated, like their fasces, from month to month (*Staatsr.* i. p. 95).

the hands of the consul whose turn for command had come,[1] or, in case of joint command, in those of the higher magistrate ; thus the auspices of the consul extinguished those of the praetor.[2] In the later Republic the difficulty scarcely existed, as joint command of two magistrates with *imperium* became very infrequent, and the proconsul or propraetor took the auspices alone.

The auspices were the mode in which the god's will was revealed to the magistrate. The other universal power—the *coercitio*—was the mode in which the magistrate's will was forced on man. It was the method in which he compelled obedience to his commands, or secured the performance of state obligations which it was his duty to enforce. It was, therefore, in touch with criminal jurisdiction, but differed from it in two ways. Firstly, *coercitio* was not directed to the enforcement of the permanent obligations of man to his fellow man, which is the object of the criminal law, but rather to the repression of exceptional acts directed against the state as a whole ; and secondly, the means of *coercitio* actually available could be employed by the magistrate on his own responsibility, while the power of jurisdiction he shared with the people. This second difference, however, was unknown to constitutional theory. The magistrate might avail himself of any means of coercion against a harmful or disobedient citizen — he might employ fines, bonds, and scourging ;[3] but the fine, beyond a certain limit, and the scourging gave rise to the *provocatio ;* in this case magisterial coercion led on to jurisdiction.

The objects of magisterial *coercitio* were by no means always private citizens. It could be directed against senators and *judices*, and could be exercised by any superior over any inferior magistrate, to compel his respect or to force him to a performance of his duties.

The severest mode of coercion—the infliction of the death penalty—was, as we saw, originally inherent in the *imperium*, but was rendered impossible by two Valerian laws of 509 and

---

[1] Thus before Cannae Varro takes the field in spite of the ill-omens which the observation of his colleague Paulus had revealed (Liv. xxii. 42).

[2] Val. Max. ii. 8, 2.

[3] Cic. *de Leg.* iii. 3, 6 "magistratus nec oboedientem et noxium civem multa, vinculis, verberibus coerceto, ni par majorve potestas populusve prohibessit, ad quos provocatio esto." A *lex Porcia* prohibited the scourging of a Roman citizen by a *gravis poena* (Liv. x. 9) ; but that technically it merely submitted the threat of such *coercitio* to appeal is shown by the fact that the law is classed amongst those regulating the *provocatio* (Cic. *de Rep.* ii. 31, 54).

449 B.C.[1]   A third *lex Valeria* of 300 B.C. prohibited the execution or scourging of one who had appealed; but the weakness of former enactments was repeated in this law; it declared the magistrate's contravention of it to be *improbe factum*.[2]   An effective sanction seems first to have been supplied by one of the three Porcian laws;[3] certainly at the end of the Republic a violation of the *provocatio* entailed a capital penalty on the magistrate.

With respect to the capital jurisdiction of the tribunes, we have seen how their tacit recognition of the appeal gave rise to this jurisdiction.[4]   But in theory the coercion of the tribune, when used in defence of the sanctity of his own person, was not subject to appeal.[5]   Here the old religious penalties remained in force, and a period as late as the year 131 B.C. witnessed the spectacle of a tribune dragging a censor, who had degraded him, to the Tarpeian rock with intent to hurl him down—a fate from which he was saved only by the veto of the tribune's colleagues.[6]

Scourging, which is found in the early Republic as a punishment employed in the military levy,[7] was practically abolished as a mode of *coercitio* by the third *lex Valeria* of 300 B.C.[8] and the *leges Porciae*, which submitted the threat of such punishment to appeal, the latter laws imposing a heavy penalty on the magistrate who inflicted it.

Imprisonment (*abductio in carcerem, in vincula*), although not recognised as a penalty in Roman law, plays a double part in the *coercitio*. It was one of the modes by which the magistrates defended their dignity and secured obedience, not merely from private citizens, but from lower magistrates and senators; and it was adopted as a precautionary measure to secure the appearance on trial of one whom they accused. The use of this severe measure against magistrates by any power but the tribunate is

---

[1] pp. 79, 109.

[2] Liv. x. 9 "cum eum qui provocasset virgis caedi securique necari vetuisset, si quis adversus ea fecisset, nihil ultra quam improbe factum adjecit." The meaning of this sanction has been much disputed: it may mean "incapable of making a will," on the analogy of "improbus (i.e. qui probare non potest) intestabilisque esto." Mommsen (*Strafrecht* p. 632) takes the expression to mean that the act of the magistrate would be regarded as "unjustified," i.e. as an ordinary criminal offence.   [3] Cic. *de Rep.* ii. 31, 54.

[4] p. 95.   [5] Dio Cass. liii. 17.

[6] Plin. *H.N.* vii. 44 ; Liv. *Ep.* 59.   [7] Liv. ii. 55 ; vii. 4.

[8] The *virgis caedi* in the third *lex Valeria* (note 2) probably refers to scourging as well as to death by the rod.

rare;[1] but it plays a great part in the tribunician annals, and the temporary imprisonment of a consul became a familiar feature of party strife during the closing years of the Republic.[2] It was a summary method of silencing the opposition of a too zealous optimate, and the veto of the tribune's colleague was the only means of releasing the head of the state.[3] Preventive imprisonment for the purpose of securing the appearance of an accused at trial was rare at Rome. The custom of giving sureties or bail (*vades, vadimonium*) was early recognised;[4] but it rested entirely with the magistrate whether he should accept such a security.[5]

The imposition of a fine (*multa*) was the most common mode of enforcing obedience, and was possessed by all the magistrates with the possible exception of the quaestor.[6] As early as 454 B.C. the power of fining (*jus multae dictionis*), which had hitherto belonged to the consuls alone, was conferred " on all magistrates "—including, therefore, the tribunes and plebeian aediles—by a *lex Aternia Tarpeia* passed in the assembly of the centuries.[7] The *lex Menenia Sextia* (452 B.C.) fixed the highest fine that could be imposed by a magistrate on his own authority (*multa suprema*) at two sheep or thirty oxen[8]—the former the limit for the poor man, the latter for the rich. After coined money, or at least metal by weight, had come into vogue during the decemviral period, a *lex Julia Papiria* (*de multarum aestimatione*) of 430 B.C. fixed 3000 libral asses as the extreme amount

---

[1] Capito ap. Gell. iv. 10 "Caesar consul viatorem vocavit eumque (Catonem), cum finem non faceret (of speaking in the Senate) prendi loquentem et in carcerem duci jussit." Cf. Suet. *Caes.* 17.

[2] The earliest recorded case is in Liv. *Ep.* xlviii. (Momms. *Staatsr.* i. p. 154). A typical instance belonging to the year 60 B.C. is described in Cic. *ad Att.* ii. 1, 8 ; Dio Cass. xxxvii. 50.

[3] It was thus that the imprisonment of M. Bibulus, consul in 59 (Cic. *in Vat.* 9, 21), and of M. Crassus, consul in 55 (Dio Cass. xxxix. 39), was prevented.

[4] The annals introduce bail as early as the trial of Kaeso Quinctius in 461 B.C. (Liv. iii. 13).

[5] Liv. xxv. 4 (212 B.C.)

[6] Mommsen (*Staatsr.* i. p. 143 n. 1) takes the view that the quaestor had no power of *coercitio* through *multa* and *pignus*. For an opposite opinion see Karlowa *Rechtsgesch.* i. p. 171 and Huschke *Multa* p. 36.

[7] Dionys. x. 50 ἐπὶ τῆς λοχίτιδος ἐκκλησίας νόμον ἐκύρωσαν (the consuls Sp. Tarpeius and A. Aternius) ἵνα ταῖς ἀρχαῖς ἐξῇ πάσαις τοὺς ἀκοσμοῦντας ἢ παρανομοῦντας εἰς τὴν ἑαυτῶν ἐξουσίαν ζημιοῦν · τέως γὰρ οὐχ ἅπασιν ἐξῆν ἀλλὰ τοῖς ὑπάτοις μόνοις. Cf. Cic. *de Rep.* ii. 35, 60.

[8] Dionys. l.c.; Gell. xi. 1. Dionysius (probably by an error of the copyist) represents the fine as being two oxen or thirty sheep.

that a magistrate might impose.[1] The infliction of a fine larger than this *multa suprema* subjected the official who pronounced it to an appeal to the people.[2] The *provocatio* against *multae* went before the *comitia* or the *concilium* of the tribes according as the fines were imposed by patrician or plebeian magistrates, and we shall see how this appeal brought the aediles into contact with these two assemblies.[3] Certain laws continued to fix an absolute limit even to fines submitted to the judgment of the people. They were generally limited to less than half of the property of the accused.[4]

But the tribunes' power of imposing money penalties extended far beyond the limits of that of the other magistrates. The power of confiscating all the goods of an individual by consecrating them to a god (*consecratio bonorum*), a relic, like the execution from the Tarpeian rock, of the old religious jurisdiction and as little subject to the appeal, had been occasionally put in force by them in extreme cases,[5] and like other vanished relics of antiquity was revived during the party struggles of the close of the Republic.

Another mode of coercion, specially used against magistrates and the official class, was the seizing of articles of their property as pledges (*pignoris capio*).[6] It was possessed by all the magistrates who had the *coercitio*, and was employed rather as a

---

[1] Cic. *de Rep.* ii. 35, 60 "levis aestimatio pecudum in multa lege C. Julii, P. Papirii consulum constituta est"; Liv. iv. 30 "legem de multarum aestimatione pergratam populo . . . ipsi (the consuls Julius and Papirius) praeoccupaverunt ferre"; Gell. xi. 1 "in oves singulas aeris deni, in boves aeris centeni . . . Suprema multa est ejus numeri, . . . ultra quem multam dicere in dies singulos jus non est." Gellius, however, attributes the pecuniary estimate to the *lex Aternia*.

[2] The view has been sometimes held that the *multa suprema* was one beyond which the magistrate could not under any circumstances go. In this case there is no known limit at which the appeal became possible. That there was one, however, is shown by the *provocatio ab omni judicio* allowed by the Twelve Tables (Cic. *de Rep.* ii. 31, 54. See p. 106).   [3] p. 246.

[4] *Lex Tab. Bant.* l. 12 "Sei quis mag(istratus) multam inrogare volet [*quei volet, dum minoris*] partus familias taxsat, liceto."

[5] e.g. in case of continued resistance to the veto. See Liv. xliii. 16 (169 B.C., P. Rutilius) "Ti. Gracchi primum bona consecravit, quod in multa pignoribusque ejus, qui tribunum adpellasset, intercessioni non parendo, se in ordinem coegisset"; or for a supposed stigma inflicted by a censor on a tribune (Plin. *H.N.* vii. 44). Cicero, *pro Domo* 47, 123, mentions the consecration of the goods of L. Metellus by C. Atinius (131 B.C., Plin. l.c.) as an instance of "furor tribuni plebis, ductus ex nonnullis perveterum temporum exemplis." P. Clodius (58 B.C.) consecrated the goods of Cicero and the consul (ib. § 124).

[6] *Lex Quinctia de aquaeductibus* (Bruns *Fontes*) l. 20 "tum is praetor . . . multa pignoribus cogito coerceto."

punishment than as a security for good behaviour. Hence the pledges were often destroyed,[1] and we find a consul seeking satisfaction for his outraged dignity in breaking up the curule chair of the praetor who would not rise to greet him as he passed by.[2]

Although, after the *provocatio* had limited the right of inflicting death and scourging, the means of *coercitio* were much the same for every magistrate, a formal difference in its mode of exercise existed between the higher and lower magistrates, and between the magistrates with *imperium* and the tribunes. The consuls and other magistrates with *imperium* had the right of summoning delinquents before their tribunal (*vocatio*) as well as of summarily arresting them in person (*prensio*).[3] The quaestors and lower officials had neither of these rights; and the theory of the tribune's being an exceptional magistrate who should render assistance in person[4] was so far preserved that he had only the right of arrest.[5] We sometimes meet with tribunes who carried out their mandates with their own hands, but their presence alone was sufficient for the *prensio* to be effective; in early times they used their aediles for the act of violence, in later times their *viatores*.[6] By the close of the Republic the distinction was obliterated, and the tribunes, without formal right, summoned individuals before them.[7]

A mere enumeration of the powers of the Roman magistracy throws little light on the working of the civic constitution. The question which we shall now consider—the conflict of powers—is from this point of view more instructive if only because it shows why Rome could not be governed by her magistrates.

---

[1] Cic *de Orat.* iii. 1, 4, "pignora caedere" or "concidere"; the destruction was performed as an example "in conspectu populi Romani."

[2] *Auct. de Vir. Illustr.* 72, 6. Cf. the procedure of the consul Servilius against the revolutionary praetor Caelius Rufus in 48 B.C. Dio Cass. xlii. 23 τόν τε δίφρον αὐτοῦ συνέτριψεν.

[3] Varro ap. Gell. xiii. 12 "vocationem (habent), ut consules et caeteri, qui habent imperium; prensionem, ut tribuni plebis et alii, qui habent viatorem; neque vocationem neque prensionem, ut quaestores et ceteri, qui neque lictorem habent neque viatorem. Qui vocationem habent, idem prendere, tenere, abducere possunt."   [4] p. 94.   [5] See Varro ap. Gell. l.c.

[6] Aediles were used in the trial of Coriolanus (Dionys. vii. 26, see p. 98); Gracchus sent one of his *viatores* to drag his colleague Octavius from the Rostra (Plut. *Ti. Gracch.* 12). Cf. Liv. xxv. 4 (case of Postumius 212 B.C.) "tribuni . . . ni vades daret . . . prehendi a viatore . . . jusserunt."

[7] Varro, as an antiquarian, refused to obey such a summons on the ground of its illegality (Gell. xiii. 12.)

The first ground of conflict was religious and arose from a use, or rather misuse, of the auspices, which we have hitherto refrained from discussing because it is only indirectly connected with the *jus auspiciorum.* It arose from a power possessed not by the magistrate only but by every Roman citizen. It was the duty of any one who was the witness of an evil omen (e.g. one of the *dirae* belonging to the class of *auspicia oblativa*) to give notice of this occurrence to any magistrate about to embark on an important undertaking. The most frequent occasion on which such *obnuntiatio*[1] was employed was the holding of the *comitia.* The respect paid to this announcement by the magistrate guiding the proceedings naturally depended on the position which the announcer held in the state. The notice of a private and unknown citizen might be received with suspicion; that given by an augur, who actually waited by the *comitia* to watch for such signs,[2] or by another magistrate, would usually be respected. But, while the *obnuntiatio* of the augur, the plebeian magistrate, and the private citizen depended on chance, that of the patrician magistrate could be the result of design. Observation of the heavens was, as we saw, the favourite form of *spectio* of the urban magistrate, and the belief was strongly held that, if he asked a sign, the sign would come. The lightning which appeared might be a lucky or unlucky omen for the magistrate himself; but, whether it appeared on the left or right, it was, as an *auspicium oblativum,* unfavourable to the holding of the *comitia.*[3] A patrician magistrate had, therefore, only to give out that "he would observe the heavens" (*se servaturum de coelo*) to suspend all meetings of the *comitia* and of the *concilium.*[4] Hence the edict by which the consuls summoned the *comitia centuriata* contained the words "ne quis magistratus minor de coelo servasse

[1] Donatus *ad Ter. Ad.* iv. 2, 9 "qui malam rem nuntiat, obnuntiat, qui bonam adnuntiat; nam proprie obnuntiare dicuntur augures, qui aliquid mali ominis scaevumque viderint." Cf. Cicero *Phil.* ii. 33, 83; *de Div.* i. 16, 29 (*dirarum obnuntiatio*).
[2] The plebeian magistrates sometimes watched for such signs, for purposes of obstruction, and were then improperly said *servare de coelo* (Cic. *ad Att.* iv. 3, 3). The words are properly used only of the *spectio.* See Greenidge, "The Repeal of the Lex Aelia Fufia" in *Class. Rev.* vii. p. 158.
[3] p. 163.
[4] Cic. *pro Sest.* 36, 78; Dio Cass. xxxviii. 13. To discuss, as has been done, whether the patrician magistrates' *obnuntiatio* was valid against the tribunes is to raise rather an idle question. The *lex Aelia Fufia* could not have artificially regulated religious belief, and the Plebs was as susceptible to *auspicia* as the Populus (see p. 39).

velit." [1]   The patrician *obnuntiatio* was a powerful weapon in politics, the counterpoise to the plebeian *intercessio*.

The uncertainty respecting the necessity for observing most of these religious messages called for legislation; and about the year 153 B.C. two laws, the *lex Aelia* and the *lex Fufia*, were passed which, amongst other comitial regulations,[2] professed to give rules for the *obnuntiatio*.[3]   The import of these rules is quite uncertain, but they seem to have recognised the right of the magistrate to watch the skies to the detriment of public business, and to have attempted to define the value of the announcement made by plebeian magistrates, augurs, and perhaps even by private individuals.   The scandalous use made of the auspices by the consul Bibulus in the year 59 B.C. was a shock to the national conscience, and the ineffectiveness of his procedure gave courage to the enemy.   In the next year the tribune P. Clodius abrogated at least that portion of the law which bolstered up the misuse of the *spectio;* the *obnuntiatio* was frequently employed as a political engine after this date, but its authors are tribunes and augurs,[4] which shows that it was in these cases based on the professed chance observation of *auspicia oblativa.*

The other modes of conflict were based on powers inherent in the magistracy; these were the right of prohibition possessed by the higher magistrates over the lower, and the right of veto possessed by superiors over inferiors or by colleagues with equal powers over one another.

The right of prohibition was an outcome of *major potestas* and was possessed by all higher over all lower magistrates.   The tribune had it against all officials except the dictator; the consul against the praetor and against all magistrates with the exception of the dictator and the tribune.   The magistrate's right to forbid differed from the magistrate's intercession in that the latter was levelled against a completed act and *rendered it invalid;* the former was merely a prohibition based on some power which the superior magistrate had in reserve; this power was the *coercitio,* the use of which was threatened if the command was disobeyed;

---

[1] Gell. xiii. 15 ; *minor* here simply means "inferior to the consul."
[2] They regulated the precedence of the *comitia* for elections and for laws (Cic. *ad Att.* i. 16, 13).
[3] Cic. *in Pis.* 4, 9 ; *de Prov. Con.* 19, 46 ; *in Vat.* 7, 18.
[4] Cic. *Phil.* ii. 32, 80 and 38, 99 ; *ad Att.* iv. 9, 1 ; 16, 7, etc.   See *Class. Rev.* vii. p. 160.

hence, if the *coercitio* was not effectively put forward, *the act which contravened the command was valid*.[1]

The scope of the exercise of this power was conditioned by circumstances; most frequently the prohibition was directed against certain specific acts. The intercourse of a lower magistrate with the people, which had not the approval of his superior, might be hampered by this means; thus the higher magistrate had the right *avocare contionem* from the lower.[2] The tribune possessed it in a supreme degree, and it was a grave infringement of his majesty when any other official called away a portion of the people whom he was addressing.[3] The consul might hinder the praetor from introducing a *rogatio*,[4] and to guard against the possibility of the *obnuntiatio* when he himself was holding the *comitia* consistently forbade him to consult the heavens on that day.[5] Other more glaring misuses of magisterial power were hindered in this way, such as the attempt to triumph without the consent of Senate or people,[6] or the effort to prolong a magistracy beyond its appointed tenure.[7]

But the prohibition might, under special circumstances, be far more sweeping than this; it might extend to the suspension of all the functions of a magistrate, or even to the enforced cessation of almost all the active life of the state.

A higher magistrate, although he could not take away office from an inferior or even force him to abdicate, could visit a misuse of his functions by prohibiting all further action on his part. This power, practically amounting to a suspension from office, is found twice in our annals directed by the consul against the praetor—in one case for a breach of respect, in the other for revolutionary proceedings.[8] Nor was the power confined to

---

[1] The exercise of the *coercitio* might of course be vetoed, and in this case the prohibition was of no avail. See Liv. ix. 34 (n. 7). [2] p. 159.

[3] Liv. xliii. 16 (169 B.C., P. Rutilius tr. pl.) "C. Claudio diem dixit, quod contionem ab se avocasset."

[4] ib. xxvii. 5 (210 B.C.). The consul declined to question the people on the nomination of a dictator, "quod suae potestatis esset," and forbade the praetor to do so. [5] p. 172.

[6] Cf. the story in Suet. *Tib.* 2, "Etiam virgo vestalis fratrem (App. Claudius, consul 143 B.C.) injussu populi triumphantem, adscenso simul curru, usque in Capitolium prosecuta est, ne vetare aut intercedere fas cuiquam tribunorum esset."

[7] Liv. ix. 33-34. P. Sempronius, tribune, attempted to compel App. Claudius, who was trying to prolong his censorship beyond eighteen months, to abdicate. He tried to imprison the censor but was resisted by the veto of three colleagues.

[8] *Auct. de vir. illustr.* 72, 6 (for the occasion see p. 171); the consul "ne quis ad eum (praetorem) in jus ire edixit." Dio Cass. xlii. 23; amongst the

Rome. The provincial governor had a similar capacity for dis-missing officials, who disgraced his administration, from the country under his control.[1]

A far more comprehensive act was the edict of a magistrate with *major potestas* that all lower magistrates should suspend the exercise of their functions. Such a cessation of public business was known as *justitium*, a name derived from the suspension of that department of business which was the most constant sign of the active life of the state, the courts of law (*juris statio*). The decree was usually pronounced by the highest magistrate present in Rome who possessed the *imperium*, by the dictator,[2] or by the consuls[3]; and, as a rule, the *justitium* was proposed on a vote of the Senate[4] and to meet certain definite contingencies. The most usual circumstances which called for it were a sudden war, or a rising within the confines of Italy and its neighbourhood (*tumultus*),[5] or a public mourning following on a national disaster, or the death of a distinguished man.[6] The cessation of the *justitium* (*justitium remittere*[7]) was pronounced by a decree of the magistrate who had enjoined it.

Although such a prohibitive order suspended the whole administration of justice both civil and criminal, was accompanied by the closing of the *aerarium*,[8] and even by the cessation of the sittings of the Senate, it necessarily did not interrupt all the business of the state, for it might be declared for the purpose of directing exclusive attention to some special sphere of administration. Thus in time of danger the military levy went on,[9] and during the social war, while all other judicial business was suspended, the Varian commission still sat to perform its vindictive work on the friends of the allies.[10]

other penalties imposed by Servilius Isauricus on Caelius Rufus (see p. 171) was the transference of his functions to another praetor, τά τε προσήκοντα τῇ ἀρχῇ αὐτοῦ ἄλλῳ τῳ τῶν στρατηγῶν προσέταξε.

[1] Cic. *in Verr.* iii. 58, 134 "quaestores, legatos, praefectos, tribunos suos, multi missos fecerunt et de provincia decedere jusserunt, quod illorum culpa se minus commode audire arbitrarentur, aut quod peccare ipsos aliqua in re judicarent."   [2] Liv. iii. 27; vii. 9.   [3] *C.I.L.* vi. n. 895.
[4] Liv. iii. 3; Cic. *Phil.* v. 12, 31.   [5] Liv. iii. 5; vi. 7; Cic. l.c.
[6] Mommsen conjectures that, on the occasion of every public funeral in the forum, a short *justitium* was declared (*Staatsr.* i. p. 251 n. 4).   [7] Liv. x. 21.
[8] Cic. *de Har. Resp.* 26, 55 "justitium edici oportere, jurisdictionem inter-mitti, claudi aerarium, judicia tolli." Cf. Plut. *Ti. Gracch.* 10; Cic. *pro Plancio* 14, 33.   [9] Liv. vi. 7.
[10] Cic. *Brut.* 89, 304 "exercebatur una lege judicium Varia, ceteris propter bellum intermissis."

Such was the constitutional employment of this exceptional power. But its value as a political weapon was too obvious for it to fail to be part of the armoury of the tribunes. We have seen the use to which it was put by the tribune Licinius;[1] and his example was followed in the last century of the Republic by his great successor in agrarian agitation, Ti. Gracchus. In 133 he published an edict "prohibiting all other magistrates from transacting business until the voting on his law was finished; he put his own seals on the temple of Saturn, that the quaestors might not draw money out or pay money in; he announced a fine that he would inflict on praetors who ventured to disobey, so that each in terror abandoned the administration which had been confided to him."[2] The higher patrician magistrates, the consul and praetor, could employ no such direct weapon. They could, however, indirectly check the passing of a *plebiscitum* by assigning to a comitial day one of those movable feasts, the date of which was fixed by their authority,[3] and thus making it a *dies fastus*.

Intercessio, though sometimes employed to describe the power of prohibition which we have just discussed,[4] is more properly applied to the power possessed, not only by higher magistrates, but by those of equal authority, of vetoing acts already performed by magistrates of equal or lower authority. It was an outcome, therefore, not only of *major* but of *par potestas*, and its invariable consequence was the invalidity of the act against which it was levelled. The intercession accompanied the *par potestas* of the consuls; with the creation of lower magistrates the conception of *major potestas* as giving this power arose, and the culminating point in the history of the intercession was the creation of the tribunate. It was the great safeguard against illegal or inequitable acts performed by magistrates, who were irresponsible during their year of office, and the tribune's *major potestas* over every magistrate made him the guardian of the interests, originally of the Plebs and later of the whole community.

A veto to be valuable should imply some knowledge of the business vetoed; and thus we are not surprised to find that, except in the case of the tribune, the *intercessio* was generally confined within the limits of colleagueship. Thus the dictator

---

[1] p. 119.　　　　　　　　　　　　　　[2] Plut. *Ti. Gracch.* 10.
[3] "(Feriae) imperativae sunt, quas consules vel praetores pro arbitrio potestatis indicunt" (Macrob. *Saturn.* i. 16, 6).　　　[4] e.g. by Livy (x. 37).

possessed it against the consul, the consul against the praetor; although it is not improbable that the consul could veto the acts of the aedile and quaestor who were not his colleagues.[1]

The tribune, outside the bounds of his own college, could employ the intercession against all the patrician magistrates except the dictator — against the consul, praetor, aedile, and quaestor.   The growth of the Roman constitution, however, created magistrates between whom no relation which justified the veto could be imagined to exist; none, for instance, could be established between the aedile and quaestor or between the consul and censor, and accordingly these magistrates had no power of impeding one another's actions.

Three general limitations existed, which alone made this strange power a practical working principle of the constitution. The first, which was necessary to prevent utter confusion, was the finality of the intercession.   The veto could not be vetoed, and the act which had been declared void could not be again made valid by the exercise of this power.   A second was its purely *civil* character; in the field divided command was not tolerated, and the intercession, therefore, did not exist.   A third was that the veto could only be directed against what was clearly the act of a magistrate.   We shall find instances of this rule in the special applications of the intercession; an important consequence of it was that neither the verdict of a *judex* in civil cases, nor, after the growth of the standing criminal courts, of the *judices* in these *quaestiones* could be quashed by a magistrate.

The intercession may conveniently be considered from the point of view of three spheres of magisterial power against which it was directed — the decree (*edictum* [2]), the *rogatio*, and the *senatus consultum*.

(i.) The intercession might be directed against decrees of any kind—against those issued in the course of civil jurisdiction by the praetor, in the course of criminal jurisdiction by the consul, aedile, or quaestor, or in the exercise of other departments of administration such as the military levy.   Intercession in all these cases rested on *appellatio*, the request for help

---

[1] No instance of such a veto being exercised at Rome is known; but it is recognised in the municipal law of Salpensa (Bruns *Fontes*) c. 27.

[2] Or *decretum*.   The formal difference is slight; by the end of the Republic *edictum* is a general, *decretum* a more special (and generally judicial) command.

N

(*auxilium*) made by the individual who felt himself injured by
the decree.   The appeal had to be made personally to the
magistrate and the *intercessio* exercised personally by him.   Thus
we find tribunes tracking the footsteps of consuls to offer help
on the occasion of an expected levy,[1] and a praetor taking up
his position close to the chair of his colleague, waiting for
appeals from his decisions.[2]   In civil jurisdiction the *intercessio*
might be employed at any stage of the proceedings before the
magistrate (*in jure*) ; the appeal was usually from one of the
city praetors to another, although they might possess different
judicial departments (*provinciae*).[3]   The general principle was to
give the mutual right of veto to magistrates possessing somewhat
similar authority and knowledge.   But this rule did not apply
to the tribune.   His interference was directed against both civil[4]
and criminal jurisdiction, and against the exercise of administrative power, especially that of the consul.   In such cases as
the consular conscription or the quaestor's collection of the taxes,[5]
it is not the general decree that is opposed by the tribune, but
its application to individual cases by the *coercitio* of the
magistrate.   An appeal of this kind made to the tribunes
sometimes became the subject of a quasi-judicial process,
especially if it had been made to the whole college.[6]   A
picture of this process, which has been preserved, shows the
appeal made from a consular levy ; the appellants and the
magistrate appealed against appear before the benches of the
tribunes (*ad subsellia tribunorum*) ;[7] the *collegium* weighs the
arguments and then gives its verdict, sometimes with the grounds
of its decision.[8]   It is possible that the college may in these
cases have agreed to give the finding by a majority of votes,

[1] Liv. iv. 55.
[2] Caes. *Bell. Civ.* iii. 20 (Caelius Rufus) "tribunal suum juxta C. Treboni
praetoris urbani sellam collocavit, et si quis appellavisset . . . fore auxilio pollice-
batur." For the consequent necessity of the presence of the tribunes in Rome
see p. 94.
[3] Thus Verres, who was *praetor urbanus*, had his decisions vetoed by Piso,
who was probably *praetor peregrinus*, in cases where Verres had decided contrary
to his own edict. Cic. *in Verr.* i. 46, 119 ; cf. Caes. l.c.
[4] Of the four private-law speeches of Cicero, two, those for Quinctius and
Tullius, show the request for tribunician interference with the praetor's jurisdiction.
Cf. Cic. *Acad. Prior.* ii. 30, 97 "postulant ut excipiantur haec inexplicabilia.
Tribunum aliquem censeo adeant (*al.* videant) ; a me istam exceptionem nunquam
impetrabunt."   [5] Liv. xxxiii. 42.
[6] The tribunes promise "cognituros se de quo appellati essent" (Liv. xlii. 32).
[7] Liv. xlii. 33.   [8] Ascon. *in Milon.* p. 47.

although, if one tribune persevered in the veto, he might over-
rule the assent of all his colleagues.

(ii.) The intercession against a *rogatio*, as contrasted with the
power of forbidding a magistrate to question the people,[1] became
at a very early period of the Republic the exclusive right of the
tribune. It might be pronounced in any of the assemblies and
against any kind of measure brought before these assemblies—
against elections,[2] against *leges*, including formal acts such as
the *lex curiata*,[3] and against *plebiscita*.[4] Custom had caused the
intercession against a *rogatio* to be guided by certain formalities;
it seems to have been irregular to pronounce the veto before
the day of voting had arrived,[5] and indeed before the speeches
for and against the law had been made.[6] In the case of laws,
the correct time for interposing the veto seems to have been the
moment when the introductory acts of the magistrate were
over and before the voting had commenced;[7] in elections we
find the tribune interceding after the first tribe had voted.[8]

(iii.) The intercession against a decree of the Senate (*senatus
consultum*) was in theory a veto of the magistrate's decree on
which he had taken advice. It resided originally with the *par
majorve potestas*. It was exercised by the tribune against the
tribune,[9] consul,[10] and praetor,[11] and throughout the greater part
of the history of the Republic by the consul against the consul.[12]
The tribune possessed the right of vetoing senatorial decrees at
the time when he had not only no power of summoning the
Senate, but not even a seat in the House. In early days he
placed his bench before the open doors for the purpose of
examining decrees which were passed out to him and signifying
his approval or dissent.[13] But, when in course of time the

[1] p. 174.   [2] Liv. iv. 50 ; xxv. 2.
[3] Cic. de Leg. Agr. ii. 12, 30.   [4] Plut. Ti. Gracch. 10.
[5] Cic. ad Att. iv. 16, 6 ; Ascon. in Cornel. p. 58.
[6] Liv. xlv. 21 "cum ita traditum esset, ne quis prius intercedat legi, quam
privatis suadendi dissuadendique legem potestas facta esset."
[7] Momms. Staatsr. i. p. 285.   [8] Liv. xxvii. 6.
[9] Cic. pro Sest. 31, 68.   [10] ib. 34, 74.
[11] Cic. ad Fam. x. 12, 3 and 4.
[12] Liv. xxx. 43. Consular intercession against the praetor was unnecessary,
since the praetor did not usually summon the Senate while the consul was at
Rome.
[13] Val. Max. ii. 2, 7 "Illud quoque memoria repetendum est, quod tribunis
plebis intrare curiam non licebat, ante valvas autem positis subselliis decreta
patrum attentissima cura examinabant, ut, si qua ex eis improbassent, rata esse
non sinerent. Itaque veteribus senatus consultis C. litera subscribi solebat,

tribune gained the right of taking part in debate and of summoning the Senate, his intercession came to replace that of the consuls ; and although the consular veto of a *senatus consultum* continued to be employed long after that against a *rogatio* had ceased to be recognised, it is not found after the time of Sulla (81 B.C.).[1] Here again the tendency was to make the tribunate the sole prohibitive power, and the tribune the sole guardian of the law.

The exercise of the veto in the Senate was simplified by the magistrate, who intended to impede the resolution, signifying his intention beforehand. This is the meaning of the declaration often made by a magistrate in the Senate, e.g. by the consul, that " he would not allow any business to proceed " (*non passurum quicquam agi*).[2] This declaration saved the time of the House, since the veto was not pronounced during the debate, but usually after the voting on the measure[3] or while the voting was in progress.[4] Hence the veto did not interrupt the procedure, nor even the threat of the veto suspend the particular business. The motion on which the veto had been put was, if approved by a majority of the Senate, drawn up as a resolution of the House (*senatus auctoritas*). It had lost its binding legal force as a decree, but it remained as an opinion for the guidance of any magistrate who cared to respect it. Sometimes the Senate requested the magistrate to suspend the intercession (*intercessionem remittere*),[5] and sometimes attached to a particular decree a general vote of censure on any magistrate who should veto it.[6] The intercession on certain kinds of *senatus consulta* might be forbidden by law. Thus the *lex Sempronia* (*de provinciis consularibus*) of 123 B.C. forbade the employment of the veto on the senatorial assignment of the consular provinces.[7]

eaque nota significabatur illa tribunos quoque censuisse." In *S.C.C.* translated into Greek it appears as ἔδοξεν (*S.C.C. de Thisbaeis*, Bruns *Fontes*). In those given in Cic. *ad Fam.* viii. 8, 6, the letters " i. n." (sometimes interpreted "intercessit nemo ") are probably a corruption for *censuere*.

[1] Momms. *Staatsr.* i. p. 282 n. 7 ; combated by Willems *Le Sénat* p. 200 n. 2.
[2] Liv. xxvi. 26 ; xxx. 40 ; cf. xlii. 10 "Popillius . . . prae se ferens si quid decernerent, intercessurum, collegam deterruit."
[3] Val. Max. ii. 2, 7.
[4] Cic. *ad Fam.* x. 12, 3.   [5] Liv. xxxvi. 40.
[6] Cic. *ad Fam.* viii. 8, 6 "qui impedierit prohibuerit, eum senatum existimare contra rem publicam fecisse."
[7] Cic. *de Prov. Con.* 8, 17 ; *pro Domo* 9, 24. Intercession in jurisdiction and administration is sometimes forbidden in municipal laws : *Lex Rubria* i. 50 ; *Lex Ursonensis* c. 72 (Bruns *Fontes*).

It is needless to say that, with this conflict of authority, there was no true theory of responsibility in the Roman magistracy; for that implies a unity of power. But a description of what may be called the second element of responsibility, the capacity for being punished, or for being forced to give compensation, for a misuse of functions, will form a fitting complement to the history of the intercession.

The civil and criminal responsibility of magistrates was enforced by the same courts and the same processes by which ordinary citizens were tried. The only privilege which they enjoyed was that, as a rule, they could not be tried for a criminal offence during their year of office, and that none but the magistrates without the *vocatio* and *prensio* (i.e. the quaestors and aediles) could be summoned into the praetor's court.[1] There was no special category of political offences which the magistrate alone could commit, although it is true that he was more specially liable than ordinary citizens to be tried for certain crimes; his greater capacity for doing harm to the state by cowardice or ignorance would expose him more than the ordinary citizen to a charge of *perduellio;* but the *judicium populi* tried him as a citizen, not as a magistrate, and the general rule that a magistrate was exempt from prosecution during his year of office made him, in fact, a *privatus* when he stood his trial. The commission of delicts, which were not cognisable by the popular courts, would have brought him before the ordinary civil tribunals. If he robbed a citizen, it was *furtum;* if he assaulted him in a manner not justified by his power of *coercitio,* it was *injuria.* There was indeed one delict which only a magistrate or an official could commit—appropriation of the state funds. In very early times this may have been brought under the expansive conception of *perduellio,* and punished criminally.[2] A few early laws, such as the fifth century *lex de ambitu,* were directed exclusively against magistrates or candidates for a magistracy; these laws doubtless specified the

---

[1] Varro ap. Gell. xiii. 13 "Qui potestatem neque vocationis populi viritim habent neque prensionis, eos magistratus a privato in jus quoque vocari est potestas." The context shows that they were practically as exempt as the higher magistrates.

[2] Nothing is known of the early history of *peculatus.* The word itself, "the misappropriation of cattle," which had been collected as fines, shows the antiquity of the offence described by Varro (*L.L.* v. 95) as *peculatus publicus.* For the early procedure see Mommsen *Strafrecht* p. 768.

penalty to be imposed,[1] but their interpretation was left to the ordinary organs of criminal justice, the *comitia*.

But, as the foreign activity of Rome increased, and greater individual responsibility devolved on commanders distant from the centre of affairs and severed from all collegiate control, the possibilities of magisterial wrong-doing became too great to allow of the continuance of this simple system. The original theory was not, indeed, abandoned; the magistrate was tried before the same civil and criminal courts as the ordinary citizen; but the first step in the differentiation of ordinary from political jurisdiction was made when the initiatory steps in criminal proceedings against the magistrate were made the duty of a special office. It was the tribunes who were now used by the state—that is, by the Senate—as public prosecutors in criminal matters. It was a rough kind of justice which they meted out; the various charges which they brought could hardly be described by specific names, and in few cases was a penalty fixed by law. They formulated a punishment and brought it before the people, appearing as accusers either before the tribes or, when the penalty they proposed was a capital one, before the centuries, and the people, by a special legislative act, accepted or rejected their proposal.[2] Their superior *potestas* and, when the injury was done to their person, their *sacrosanctitas* gave them the legal right to coerce any magistrate into appealing or to bring him to trial during his year of office; but so strong was the feeling against this indignity to the magistracy that the veto of a colleague postponed the decision until the expiry of the official functions of the delinquent.[3] This political jurisdiction was not, however, directed solely against magistrates, but against any individuals who held an official position, against

---

[1] In Polybius' time bribery was a capital offence at Rome (Polyb. vi. 56).

[2] Polyb. vi. 14. The people are often judges of money penalties, when the offence can be valued in money, καὶ μάλιστα τοὺς τὰς ἐπιφανεῖς ἐσχηκότας ἀρχάς, θανάτου δὲ κρίνει μόνος. Cf. c. 15. The greatest source of the power of the people is that ἀποτιθεμένους τὴν ἀρχὴν ἐν τούτῳ δεῖ τὰς εὐθύνας ὑπέχειν τῶν πεπραγμένων.

[3] Liv. xxiv. 43 (214 B.C., the tribune Metellus prosecutes the censors Furius and Atilius) "Sed novem tribunorum auxilio vetiti causam in magistratu dicere dimissique fuerant"; Suet. *Caes.* 23 (Caesar on leaving for Gaul) "a L. Antistio, tr. pl., postulatus, appellato demum collegio, obtinuit, cum reipublicae causa abesset, reus ne fieret." In the case of the trial of the censors of 169 B.C. (Liv. xliii. 16) the accused agree to be put on their trial during their tenure of office.

the staff-officers (*legati*) of a general,[1] against envoys [2] and senators,[3] and even against the farmers of the revenue (*publicani*).[4] The usual victims, however, were consuls and praetors, and the offences charged were mainly such as came under the conceptions of treason,[5] or were open violations of the rules governing the magistracy;[6] but sometimes they were wrongs done to individuals, such as might have come before the civil courts.[7]

The growth of Rome's provincial territory made the continuance of this clumsy and casual jurisdiction impossible. The creation of the standing criminal courts (*quaestiones perpetuae*), with their presidents and juries, was the reaction of the provinces on Rome. We shall speak elsewhere of the mixed character of these courts, which were formed of a fusion of ideas borrowed from the criminal and civil law. The earliest which were created supplied a readier redress and severer punishments for the delicts of magistrates than the civil courts could give. Others were based on the classification of political offences. The great codification of the criminal law effected by Sulla (81 B.C.) rendered the tribunician jurisdiction superfluous, although it still reappeared at intervals during the party struggles of the close of the Republic.

We have now reviewed every important aspect of the magistracy in general; but before going on to describe the separate functions of the magistrates in administration, so far as these have not been already anticipated, it will be convenient to touch slightly on the formal conditions requisite for holding office at Rome. These conditions often illustrate the magistrate's position in the state, and they sometimes create real limitations on his power.

The qualifications for public office (*jus honorum petendorum*)

---

[1] Liv. xxix. 22 (204 B.C.). Pleminius and his colleagues were "producti ad populum ab tribunis."

[2] ib. vi. 1 "Q. Fabio . . . ab Cn. Marcio tribuno plebis dicta dies est, quod legatus in Gallos, ad quos missus erat orator, contra jus gentium pugnasset."

[3] ib. *Ep.* 69 " L. Appuleius Saturninus . . . Metello Numidico, eo quod in eam (the agrarian law) non juraverat, diem dixit."

[4] ib. xxv. 3 (Postumius a *publicanus*, for shipwrecking and false reports of shipwreck).

[5] e.g. waging war without authorisation (Ascon. *in Cornelian.* p. 80, 104 B.C.), disgraceful flight imperilling the safety of others (Liv. xxvi. 2, 211 B.C.).

[6] Exceeding the legal duration of a magistracy, in this case the dictatorship (Cic. *de Off.* iii. 31, 112). The instance, though typical, is not historic.

[7] Liv. xliii. 7, 8 (170 B.C.).

were based on the general principle that for patrician magistracies any citizen was eligible,[1] for plebeian only those of plebeian birth.[2] But to this general rule there were certain limitations based partly on the idea of the dignity of office, partly on the view that experience of a certain kind was necessary for the fulfilment of such responsible functions.

In the first place, citizenship had not its private-law connotation. Freedmen may not have been *de jure* excluded from office;[3] but the lists of magistrates show that not only were the sons of freedmen ineligible, but that the magistracy was practically reserved to those who could boast a free grandfather.[4]

In the second place, certain careers were considered as a necessary preliminary to, others as a necessary disqualification from, the magistracy. In a military city like Rome one is not surprised to find that a certain amount of military service was demanded of one who might have to lead the armies of the state, and that during the greater part of the Republic the *capite censi* were wholly excluded from the magistracy. The length of service required from the infantry soldier is unknown; from the *eques equo publico* it was ten years' service "in the camp or the province,"[5] as late as the time of C. Gracchus (124 B.C.).[6] This military qualification gives us a minimum age of twenty-eight as being necessary for the holding of the quaestorship. In the Ciceronian period, on the other hand, the age was thirty,[7] and the military qualification, although it still partially survived in municipal law,[8] seems to have been abolished for Rome. Conversely, the exercise of any trade or profession for which payment was received was a disqualification for office, as long

---

[1] Tac. *Ann.* xi. 22 "apud majores . . . cunctis civium, si bonis artibus fiderent, licitum petere magistratus."

[2] Festus p. 231 "plebeium magistratum neminem capere licet, nisi qui ex plebe est." Cf. Suet. *Aug.* 10.

[3] This seems shown by Suet. *Claud.* 24 (see p. 135).

[4] Momms. *Staatsr.* i. p. 488. Exceptional elections of the sons of freedmen are found in 304 B.C. (Liv. ix. 46, Cn. Flavius (see p. 185) as aedile) and in the year 100 B.C. (App. *B.C.* i. 33).

[5] *Lex Julia Municipalis* (Bruns *Fontes*) l. 92 "in castreis inve provincia."

[6] Plut. *C. Gracch.* 2.

[7] There is also evidence for this as the minimum age at a period earlier than Cicero's political career; see Cic. *in Verr.* ii. 49, 122.

[8] In Caesar's municipal law (45 B.C.) the qualification for a municipal magistracy is either thirty years of age or a certain length of service—six years on foot or three on horseback (*L.J.M.* l. 89).

as the trade or profession was exercised.[1] This was, to some extent, an outcome of the prejudice against βαναυσία found amongst all military peoples;[2] but, as offices at Rome were unpaid, it was also a necessary provision for securing due attention to the discharge of the duties of the magistracy.

Thirdly, access to the magistracy might be hindered by the past moral delinquencies of an individual or his criminal condemnation. It is a mistake to suppose that there was a definite class of *infames* excluded from office at Rome. Certain criminal laws made temporary or permanent exclusion from the magistracy one of their sanctions. Exclusion on kindred grounds— notorious moral lapses of the candidate, his previous condemnation in a disgraceful civil suit, the fact that a prosecution for a crime was at that moment hanging over his head—was entirely the work of the magistrate who presided over the elections. He acted entirely on his own discretion, although naturally on the advice of a *consilium* of experienced men, in declining to receive the name of such a candidate.[3] This remarkable power was the outcome of the still surviving theory that the magistrate nominated his successor, and that the election by the people was only a complementary act.

Other limitations to the attainment of magistracy were determined by the previous holding of office. The magistrate who presided over the filling up of a vacancy in the regular magistracies might not return himself as elected;[4] and two laws further provided that, if a new office was established by statute, neither the *rogator* of the measure nor his colleagues or relatives should be eligible to the post.[5]

---

[1] Liv. ix. 46 (of the election of Cn. Flavius to the curule aedileship) "Invenio in quibusdam annalibus, cum adpareret aedilibus . . . neque accipi nomen, quia scriptum faceret, tabulam posuisse et jurasse, se scriptum non facturum."

[2] Cic. *de Off.* i. 42, 150; in later Roman law spoken of as *vilitas;* see Greenidge *Infamia in Roman Law* pp. 12, 193.

[3] Cic. *pro Cluent.* 42, 119; Schol. Bob. in Cic. *pro Sulla* 5, 17, p. 361 Orell.; Cic. *pro Rosc. Com.* 6, 16; Tertull. *de Spect.* 22; Ascon. *in orat. in Tog. Cand.* p. 115; *Lex Julia Munic.* l. 104; *Dig.* 48, 7, 1. All these passages are discussed in Greenidge *Infamia in Roman Law* pp. 18-40 and 187.

[4] Liv. iii. 35 "Ars haec erat, ne semet ipse creare posset; quod praeter tribunos plebi (et id ipsum pessimo exemplo) nemo unquam fecisset." The revolutionary period shows Cinna and Carbo nominating themselves consuls for two successive years (Liv. *Ep.* 83) and Caesar as dictator presiding over his own election to the consulship (Caes. *B.C.* iii. 1, 1).

[5] Cic. *de Leg. Agr.* ii. 8, 21 "Licinia est lex atque altera Aebutia, quae non modo eum, qui tulerit de aliqua curatione ac potestate, sed etiam collegas ejus, cognatos, affines excipit, ne eis ea potestas curatiove mandetur."

The continuation and accumulation of magistracies were also forbidden by *plebiscita* of the year 342 B.C., which enacted that at least ten years must elapse between the tenures of the same magistracy, and that two magistracies should not be held together in the same year.[1]   Such legislation was the starting-point for a series of measures known as *leges annales*, which specified the order in which the various magistracies must be held (*certus ordo magistratuum*),[2] the age which qualified for each, the interval which must elapse between the holding of any two, and that which must intervene between the holding of the same, magistracies.   In the year 180 B.C. the *lex Villia*, a *plebiscitum* of a comprehensive character, was passed, which specified the age at which each magistracy might be held;[3] it appears also to have fixed the interval which must elapse between the holding of two patrician magistracies, since from about this period we find the beginning of the rule, which held good in Cicero's day, that a biennial interval must be observed between the patrician offices in the *gradus honorum*.[4]   Finally, Sulla in 81 B.C. re-enacted the rules about the *certus ordo* and the interval between the same magistracies by declaring that the quaestorship must be held before the praetorship, and the praetorship before the consulate, and that ten years must elapse before the resumption of the same magistracy.[5]

The validity of election was dependent on the observance of certain forms, the first of which was concerned with the

[1] Liv. vii. 42 "aliis plebiscitis cautum ne quis eundem magistratum intra decem annos caperet; neu duos magistratus uno anno gereret." Cf. x. 13.

[2] Cic. *de Leg. Agr.* ii. 9, 24 "ne in iis quidem magistratibus quorum certus ordo est."

[3] Liv. xl. 44 "eo anno rogatio primum lata est ab L. Villio tr. pl., quot annos nati quemque magistratum peterent caperentque." It probably accepted the age of twenty-eight for the quaestorship ; the minimum age for the consulship in the time of Cicero was forty-three (*Phil.* v. 17, 48) ; that for the praetorship is quite unknown ; thirty-five and forty have been conjectured.

[4] Cic. *ad Fam.* x. 25, 2 "non est annus hic tibi destinatus, ut, si aedilis fuisses, post biennium tuus annus esset" (i.e. for election to the praetorship). To be elected in the earliest year, when one is qualified by the interval, is to attain a magistracy "anno sibi destinato" (l.c.) or "suo anno" (Cic. *pro Mil.* 9, 24). Momms. *Staatsr.* i. pp. 527, 529. The principle of at least one year's interval seems to have applied to the transition from plebeian to patrician magistracies in the form that candidature during the holding of any office was forbidden (Momms. *Staatsr.* i. p. 533).

[5] App. *B.C.* i. 100 καὶ στρατηγεῖν ἀπεῖπε πρὶν ταμιεῦσαι καὶ ὑπατεύειν πρὶν στρατηγῆσαι, καὶ τὴν ἀρχὴν τὴν αὐτὴν αὖθις ἄρχειν ἐκώλυσε πρὶν ἔτη δέκα διαγενέσθαι.

presiding magistrate.   While the tribune alone could be the
president at the election of plebeian magistrates, the consuls and
praetors created the *magistratus populi*, but, as we have already
shown in connexion with the *interregnum*, none but a consul
could preside at the consular and praetorian elections.

The first act of the candidate was to send in his name
(*profiteri*) to the magistrate destined to preside.   This *professio*
had to be made three weeks (*trinum nundinum, intra legitimos
dies*)[1] before the date of election.   A list of the candidates
was then prepared for the people[2] after the magistrate had
examined their names and satisfied himself of the qualifications of the competitors.   Up to the middle of the last century
B.C. the candidates need not be in Rome ; but after the year
63 B.C. some unknown law enacted that they should make the
professio in person,[3] and a similar clause was again inserted in
Pompeius' law *de jure magistratuum* of 52 B.C.[4]   During the interval
between the *professio* and the election, canvassing, which had
commenced long before the open profession of candidature, became
brisker.   Legitimate *ambitio* almost rose to the dignity of a
formal act.   The aspirant, in a dazzlingly whitened robe (*candidatus*), surrounded by a cortège and accompanied by a slave
with a good memory for names (*nomenclator*), affably saluted all
the citizens whom he met, and shook hands warmly with the
rustic voter.   Rome's habit of extending her franchise made the
country vote always of some importance ; but after the social
war the canvassing that followed the *professio* was as nothing
compared with that which had preceded it.   The municipal
voters, who could not come up for ordinary legislative business,
flocked to Rome for the elections in the summer ; and to secure
success all Italy had to be sounded from the Padus to the
Lacinian promontory.   Canvassing on this gigantic scale required

---

[1] Cic. *ad Fam.* xvi. 12, 3 "se praesentem trinum nundinum petiturum " ;
Sallust, *Cat.* 18 "post paulo Catilina pecuniarum repetundarum reus prohibitus
erat consulatum petere, quod intra legitimos dies profiteri nequiverit."   The
interval was probably twenty-four days.   See the section on the *comitia*.

[2] Plut. *Aem. Paul.* 3 ; *Sull.* 5.

[3] Cic. *de Leg. Agr.* ii. 9, 24 (63 B.C.) "praesentem profiteri jubet, quod nulla
alia in lege unquam fuit, ne in iis quidem magistratibus quorum certus ordo est " ;
Suet. *Caes.* 18 (60 B.C.) "cum edictis jam comitiis ratio ejus haberi non posset . . .
et ambienti ut legibus solveretur multi contradicerent, coactus est triumphum,
ne consulatu excluderetur, dimittere."   Cf. Plut. *Caes.* 13.

[4] Dio Cass. xl. 56 (Pompeius) τὸν περὶ τῶν ἀρχαιρεσιῶν νόμον τὸν κελεύοντα
τοὺς ἀρχήν τινα ἐπαγγέλλοντας ἐς τὴν ἐκκλησίαν πάντως ἀπαντᾷν, ὥστε μηδένα
ἀπόντα αἱρεῖσθαι, παρημελημένον πῶς ἀνενεώσατο.

time and an elaborate organisation. We find Cicero beginning
to canvass on 17th July 65 B.C. for the consular elections in
64; and men better circumstanced in birth, wealth, and rank
commenced operations by setting in motion a vast machine,
which had as its head some noble coterie at Rome (*sodalitas*),
and as its instruments the election agents (*divisores*), each of
whom took charge of a portion of a tribe. The means used
were not necessarily illegitimate, although the names of the
divisores became associated with bribery,[1] and a series of laws—
not longer, however, than the chain of enactments which Rome
usually devoted to some special theme—strove by ever-increasing
penalties to stamp out an evil which disappeared only with the
popular assemblies themselves.

After the people had chosen the new magistrate by their
suffrage, a final duty had to be performed by the president in
the shape of the *renuntiatio*, or formal announcement of the
result of the election. That this was not a purely formal act is
shown by the president's power to refuse to return a legally,
or even morally, unqualified candidate who had slipped through
the previous stages of election.[2]

If we believe that the king during his lifetime nominated
his successor,[3] there must from the first have been an interval
between appointment to and entrance on office. This interval
existed throughout the Republic for most of the annual magistracies; only the dictator, the censors, the magistrates created
as the result of an interregnum (*ex interregno*), or those elected
to fill up a place that had become vacant (*suffecti*), entered office
immediately on their election. For the ordinary magistrates
there was a more or less considerable interval between election
and entrance on office; for the patrician magistracies it had
originally been short, for the elections were one of the last acts
of the consul's annual reign, and the new consuls and praetors
entered office from the close of the third century on 15th March,[4]

---

[1] Hence their association with *sequestres*—the agents in whose hands the
candidate deposited money. Cic. *pro Planc.* 18, 19 ; Q. Cic. *de Pet. Cons.* 14, 57.

[2] *Lex Jul. Munic.* l. 132 "neve quis ejus rationem comitieis conciliove
[habeto, neive quis quem, sei adversus ea comitieis conciliove] creatum est,
renuntiato." In 67 B.C. the consul Piso, questioned "Palicanum num suffragiis
populi consulem creatum renuntiaturus esset," answered "non renuntiabo"
(Val. Max. iii. 8, 3).

[3] p. 47.

[4] Mommsen (*Staatsr.* i. p. 599) places this change in 222 B.C. Liv. xxxi. 5, etc.

from 153 B.C. on 1st January.[1] But in the closing years of the Republic—perhaps in consequence of a change introduced by Sulla—the elections were universally held in the month of July ; and this gave a six-months' interval between election and entrance on office for the consuls and praetors, and one of more than four months for the quaestors and tribunes, who assumed their functions on 5th and 10th December respectively.[2]

During this interval the magistrate elect was *designatus*, and, though his *imperium* or *potestas* was necessarily dormant, he had a distinct position in the state and could exercise certain official functions preparatory to the magistracy, such as issuing edicts, which would be binding after his entrance on office.[3] Even before the *renuntiatio* he had taken an oath of fealty to the state [4] —one, however, that could only have been exacted when the candidate was present at the election.

The entrance on office was signalised by another promise on oath to respect the laws (*in leges*)—a custom which probably grew out of the power of the people to bind either present or future magistrates by an *execratio* to respect a certain *lex*.[5] Refusal to take it within the period of five days was followed by loss of office ; [6] only the Flamen Dialis, who might not swear, could claim exemption, and with the people's consent take the oath by deputy.[7] During the later Republic we also find evidences of an oath which closed the tenure of office ; the magistrates, on the expiry of their functions, addressed the people and swore that, during their period of rule, they had wilfully done nothing against the interest of the state but striven their utmost to promote its welfare.[8]

The assumption of the magistracy carried with it the right—

---

[1] *Fasti Praenestini* (*C.I.L.* i. p. 364) "'[ann]us nov[us incipit], quia eo die mag[istratus] ineunt : quod coepit [p. R.] c. a. DCI."

[2] Quaestors (Cic. *in Verr.* Act. i. 10, 30 ; *Lex de XX. quaest.* in Bruns *Fontes* l. 15) ; tribunes (Dionys. vi. 89).

[3] Dio Cass. xl. 66 ; Cic. *in Verr.* i. 41, 105 ; Liv. xxi. 63.

[4] The *execratio* is given by Pliny (*Paneg.* 64), "explanavit verba quibus caput suum, domum suam, si sciens fefellisset, deorum (Jupiter and the Dii Penates) irae consecraret."

[5] Cic. *ad Att.* ii. 18, 2 "habet . . . Campana Lex (of the consul Caesar in 59 B.C.) execrationem in contione candidatorum."

[6] Liv. xxxi. 50 ; if we may argue from municipal law (*Lex Salpens.* c. 26), omission to take it due to mere neglect was visited in the first instance by a fine.

[7] Liv. l.c.

[8] Cic. *ad Fam.* v. 2, 7 ; *pro Sulla* 11, 34 ; *in Pison.* 3, 6 ; *pro Domo* 35, 94. Cicero, at the close of 63, varied the oath by swearing that he had saved the state.

and indeed the duty—to exhibit certain external marks of
dignity which distinguished the masters of the community from
their subjects.　The lictors and the fasces were a survival from
the monarchy, and were employed as a token of dignity and for
the enforcement of the *coercitio* by the magistrates with *imperium*,
on a scale, as will be seen when we describe the different magistracies, proportioned to the strength of the *imperium*.　The
other magistrates possessed only the servants—*scribae, praecones,
accensi, viatores, servi publici*—necessary for the carrying out of
their behests.

Like the lictors, the purple robe—the almost universal symbol
of royalty in the ancient world—and the curule chair were inherited by the Republican magistrate ; but the royal robe could
be used only in the triumphal procession, where the other regal
insignia were revived,[1] or for the celebration of festivals.[2]　In
the garb of peace of the curule magistrates the purple had become
a narrow hem (*praetexta*) round the toga.　The quaestors, who
were not included in this list, seem to have worn no special
dress ; while the tribunes and plebeian aediles showed, by their
complete lack of magisterial *insignia*, that they were never
regarded as magistrates of the community.

In the dress of war the regal colour also reappears.　Once
outside the *pomerium* the magistrate may don the scarlet military
cloak (*paludamentum*) worn over his armour.　The dagger (*pugio*)[3]
worn round his neck or on his waist, and the axes, which can
now be enclosed in the fasces, were added signs of the un-
trammeled *imperium*.

The *insignia* were not mere empty signs that bolstered up a
power which won no true respect.　If the Senate appeared to
the envoy of Pyrrhus to be an assembly of kings, he was looking
at a body the members of which had for some period of their
lives received the homage due to kings.　The reverence for office
as a holy trust, which is such a characteristic feature of Republican forms of government, was heightened in the Roman
mind by its genius for abstraction, which saw in the individual
holder of power not the magistrate but the magistracy, and by
its almost superstitious veneration for the forms of law.　It
was an obvious thing to Romans that they must spring from their

---

[1] p. 45.　　　　　　　　　　　　[2] Liv. v. 41.

[3] The dagger is mentioned more frequently than the sword (*gladius*) as the
distinctive sign of military power.　Momms. *Staatsr.* i. p. 434 n. 1.

horse when they met a magistrate riding,[1] that they must make room for him on the path, that they must rise from their seat as he passed by, and that they must stand bareheaded before him in the *contio* or the *comitia*. The occasional Roman, to whom these things were not obvious, was soon reminded of his duties by the *coercitio* of the magistrate, who had the fullest means of protecting his own dignity ; his life had been made by the law as sacred as the life of the state itself, for an attempt on the safety of a Roman magistrate was treason (*perduellio*).

§ 2. *The Individual Magistracies*

After this general review of the magistracy, we may glance at the precise place in the state administration assigned to the separate magistrates, so far as the record of their duties has not been already anticipated.

The Dictator

The only true mode of creating a dictator (*dicere dictatorem*) was through nomination by one of the consuls,[2] who, as we have seen, to avoid unfavourable omens, pronounced his selection between midnight and morning.[3] The question, which consul was to exercise this power, was decided either by the possession of the fasces, which belonged only to the acting consul, or by one of the two favourite modes of settling questions of collegiate action, agreement (*comparatio*) or the use of the lot (*sortitio*).[4] But this purely consular function came in time, like all extra-ordinary acts of administration, to be usurped by the Senate. At what period this result was attained we cannot say ; for the annalists have transferred the constitutional observances of the

---

[1] Hence such phrases as *decedere via, descendere equo, adsurgere sella, caput aperire*. The senators were in the habit of rising from their seats when the consul entered the Curia (Cic. *in Pis.* 12, 26).

[2] A decree of the augurs in 426 B.C. declared the consular tribunes capable of this nomination (Liv. iv. 31).

[3] p. 165.

[4] Liv. viii. 12 "Aemilius, cujus tum fasces erant, collegam dictatorem dixit " ; iv. 26 "Sors, ut dictatorem diceret (nam ne id quidem inter collegas convenerat) T. Quinctio evenit " ; iv. 21 " Verginius, dum collegam consuleret, moratus, permittente eo, nocte dictatorem dixit."

third century B.C. to the earliest times.[1] Finally, the point was
reached at which the Senate not only suggested the advisability
of nomination but·the name of the nominee;[2] opposition to
these instructions was constitutionally possible,[3] but was borne
down by the *de facto* power of the Senate with the tribunate as
its instrument.   By the close of the fourth century B.C. custom
had further fixed the rule that the person created should be
a past holder of the consulship.[4] The ancient provision that
the dictator could be nominated only on Roman soil was found
impossible of observance, since the consul, when he received the
Senate's message, was often far distant from the city, and *ager
Romanus* was, in true Roman fashion, liberally interpreted to
include the whole of Italy.[5] After the nomination of the new
magistrate his *imperium* was confirmed by a *lex curiata*.[6] The
insignia of the dictator were in one respect greater even than
those of the king.   As the consul had inherited the twelve regal
lictors, the dictator, in order that his higher *imperium* might be
more clearly shown, was preceded by twenty-four;[7] and the
axes were seen with the fasces even within the walls.[8] The
dictator appointed to meet an emergency either of war or revolution[9] bore no special designation which had reference to this
emergency, but was aptly described as created for carrying on
the business of the state (*rei gerundae causa*).[10] But minor needs
of peace might lead to the nomination of a dictator for a special
purpose; we find a dictator appointed for holding elections

[1] Liv. iv. 17 "senatus . . . dictatorem dici Mam. Aemilium jussit " ; vii. 12
"dictatorem dici C. Sulpicium placuit.   Consul ad id adcitus C. Plautius dixit."
[2] ib. xxii. 57 (216 B.C.) "dictator ex auctoritate patrum dictus M. Junius."
[3] ib. *Ep.* 19 ; Suet. *Tib.* 2 (the enforced abdication of Claudius Glicia,
nominated by Claudius Pulcher).   In Liv. iv. 26 the *coercitio* of the tribune is
represented as employed against the consuls who disobey.
[4] Mommsen in *C.I.L.* i. p. 557.
[5] Liv. xxvii. 5 (210 B.C., on the proposal of the consul to nominate a dictator
in Sicily) "patres extra Romanum agrum (eum autem in Italia terminari) negabant
dictatorem dici posse."   [6] ib. ix. 38-39.
[7] Polyb. iii. 87 ; but, as a rule, he was preceded by only twelve within the
walls (Liv. *Ep.* 89 "Sulla, dictator factus, quod nemo umquam fecerat, cum
fascibus viginti quatuor processit").
[8] Liv. ii. 18 "Creato dictatore primum Romae, postquam praeferri secures
viderunt, magnus plebem metus incessit."
[9] p. 85.
[10] e.g. the dictator named by Livy (ix. 26) as "quaestionibus exercendis" (314) is
mentioned in the *Fast. Capitol.* as "rei gerundae causa" (Momms. *Staatsr.* ii. p.
157 n. 2) ; a dictator "seditionis sedandae et rei gerundae causa" is found in the
Fasti for 368.

(*comitiorum habendorum causa*),[1] on one occasion for making out
the list of the Senate (*legendo senatui*),[2] and others for purely
ceremonial or religious purposes—for the celebration of games
(*ludorum faciendorum causa*)[3] and the ordering of festivals
(*feriarum constituendarum causa*),[4] and for driving the nail (*clavus
annalis*) into the temple of Jupiter (*clavi figendi causa*),[5] an act of
natural magic which was supposed to be a specific against pestilence.   These dictators *imminuto jure*, appointed for a special
purpose, were expected to retire as soon as the function was
completed.[6] The six months' tenure of the dictator *rei gerundae
causa*[7] was never legally exceeded, but it might be shortened,
for it seems to have been necessary for the dictator to resign
when the consul who had nominated him retired from office.[8]

    The creation of a dictator did not abolish the other magis-
tracies of the people; it merely suspended their *independent*
activity. The dictator was a *collega major* given to the consuls,
who still continued under his direction to command armies,[9] and
even those troops which were levied by the dictator took the
oath of obedience to the consuls as well.[10] The praetors still sat
in the courts, and lesser officials continued to perform the subordinate functions of government. But it was felt that under a
dictator all magistrates existed on sufferance, with the exception
of those of the Plebs.[11] It is certain that the presence of a

---

[1] Liv. vii. 24 "qui aegris consulibus comitia haberet." Cf. c. 26 (absence
of consuls in the field) and ix. 7.

[2] ib. xxiii. 22. In 216 B.C. M. Fabius Buteo was appointed dictator "qui
senatum legeret."   [3] ib. viii. 40.

[4] ib. vii. 28 (for establishment of *feriae* on the occasion of a *prodigium*); "dictator
Latinarum feriarum causa" in *Fast. Cap.* (*C.I.L.* i. p. 434) for the year 257 B.C.

[5] The first instance was on the occasion of the great pestilence in 363 B.C.
(Liv. vii. 3 "Lex vetusta est . . . ut, qui praetor maximus sit, Idibus Septem-
bribus clavum pangat "). Cf. Fest. p. 56.

[6] Cic. *de Off.* iii. 31, 112 (see p. 183); cf. Liv. vii. 3. L. Manlius, appointed
"clavi figendi causa," acted "perinde ac reipublicae gerendae . . . gratia creatus
esset," and was forced to abdicate.   [7] p. 84.

[8] This is Mommsen's interpretation (*Staatsr.* ii. p. 160 n. 4) of Liv. xxx. 39.
C. Servilius Geminus had been appointed dictator *comitiorum causa*—"Saepe
comitia indicta perfici tempestates prohibuerunt. Itaque, cum prid. Id. Mart.
veteres magistratus abissent, novi subfecti non essent, respublica sine curulibus
magistratibus erat."

[9] Liv. iv. 41. The consul is here said "auspicio dictatoris res gerere."

[10] ib. ii. 32 "quamquam per dictatorem dilectus habitus esset, tamen, quoniam
in consulum verba jurassent, sacramento teneri militem rati."

[11] This view has led to the exaggerated statement of Polybius (iii. 87) that, on
the establishment of a dictator, παραχρῆμα διαλύεσθαι συμβαίνει πάσας τὰς ἀρχὰς
ἐν τῇ Ῥώμῃ πλὴν τῶν δημάρχων : which has been copied by later Greek writers.

dictator brought no legal diminution to the powers of the tribune ; it is equally certain that constitutional custom dictated that the *auxilium* of these city magistrates should not be effective when the state was under martial law.[1] Collision was necessarily rare since the duties of the dictator took him far afield.

This extraordinary power had yet some normal limitations. The dictator never meddled with civil jurisdiction ; and he had not the power, possessed by the consuls while in Rome, of taking money from the *aerarium* without a decree of the Senate.[2] The government was naturally unwilling that a magistrate to all intents and purposes a king should wage war out of Italy ; and there is but one example of a dictator commanding in the extra-Italian world.[3]

A further limitation to his original powers, and one of the greatest consequence, was subsequently introduced. The dictator was made subject to the *provocatio* within the city,[4] probably by the *lex Valeria* of 300 B.C.[5]—a change which, while not hampering the power of this magistracy in the field, prevented its being used for ruthlessly crushing a so-called sedition in Rome. Although we here see the commencement of the infringement of its civil power, the military authority of the office persisted for a century longer. It was not until the Hannibalic war that the two weakening elements of popular election and colleagueship were introduced into this magistracy. In the year 217 B.C., when, after the disaster at the Trasimene lake, it was difficult to communicate with the sole surviving consul, Q. Fabius Maximus

---

[1] This is clearly shown by the attitude of the dictator L. Papirius Cursor when pursuing his disobedient master of the horse (Liv. viii. 34). The dictator hopes that the veto will not be employed ("optare ne potestas tribunicia, inviolata ipsa, violet intercessione sua Romanum imperium"). Zonaras expresses the fact and not the law (vii. 13 οὔτ' ἐγκαλέσαι τις αὐτῷ οὔτ' ἐναντίον τι διαπράξασθαι ἴσχυεν οὐδὲ οἱ δήμαρχοι).

[2] Zonar. vii. 13 οὔτε ἐκ τῶν δημοσίων χρημάτων ἀναλῶσαι τι ἐξῆν αὐτῷ, εἰ μὴ ἐψηφίσθη.

[3] Liv. *Ep.* 19 (249 B.C.) "Atilius Calatinus primus dictator extra Italiam exercitum duxit"; Dio Cass. xxxvi. 17 (the dictatorship was limited to Italy) καὶ οὐκ ἂν εὑρεθείη δικτάτωρ οὐδεὶς ἄλλοσε, πλὴν ἑνὸς ἐς Σικελίαν, καὶ ταῦτα μηδὲν πράξαντος, αἱρεθείς.

[4] Festus p. 198 "optima lex in magistro populi faciendo, qui vulgo Dictator appellatur, quam plenissimum posset jus ejus esse significabatur . . . postquam vero provocatio ab eo magistratu ad populum data est, quae ante non erat, desitum est adici 'ut optima lege,' ut pote imminuto jure priorum magistrorum."

[5] p. 168. It could not have been a consequence of the Valerio-Horatian laws of 449 B.C. (see p. 109).

was elected dictator,[1] presumably at the *comitia centuriata* under the guidance of a praetor. In the same year the distrust and misplaced confidence of the people raised M. Minucius, the master of the horse, to an equality of command with Fabius.[2] Both acts were signs that the office was felt to be an anachronism, and the next year (216) marks the last instance of the military dictatorship.[3] The last dictator (*comitiorum habendorum causa*) was appointed in 202 ;[4] for the application of the name to Sulla and Caesar was the transference of the title of a constitutional office, in the first instance to a constituent authority, in the second to a monarchy, and in neither case was even the ancient mode of nomination preserved.[5]

The Magister Equitum

Every dictator, no matter for what purpose appointed,[6] nominated as his delegate a master of the horse,[7] who, unlike other delegates, possessed the *imperium*, six fasces,[8] and a rank equal to the praetor.[9] These distinctions justify the assertion that he was a magistrate,[10] and apparently one of curule rank, even though his tenure of power was strictly dependent on that of his nominator.[11] Like a magistrate he asked for a *lex curiata*

---

[1] Liv. xxii. 8.

[2] Livy (xxii. 25) describes it as a *rogatio* "de aequando magistri equitum et dictatoris jure." Cf. c. 26 "de aequato imperio."

[3] Liv. xxii. 57, M. Junius Pera.   [4] *Fast. Capitol.*

[5] Sulla was nominated by an interrex (though his powers were conferred by law), Caesar by a praetor. Plutarch (*Marc.* 24) says that the praetor could nominate the dictator, a proceeding which is declared by Cicero to be wholly unconstitutional, *ad Att.* ix. 15, 2 (49 B.C.) "volet (Caesar) . . . vel ut consules roget praetor vel dictatorem dicat, quorum neutrum jus est. Etsi si Sulla potuit efficere, ab interrege ut dictator diceretur, cur hic non possit ?" The nomination of Caesar was regular in so far as a special *lex* was passed which empowered the praetor to nominate (Caes. *B.C.* ii. 21 ; Dio Cass. xli. 36).

[6] An exception is found in 216 B.C. M. Fab. Buteo was appointed "dictator sine mag. eq. senatus legendi causa" (see p. 193).

[7] In the single case of the election of a dictator, the *magister equitum* was also elected (Liv. xxii. 8).

[8] Dio Cass. xlii. 27 ; Antonius, as Caesar's *magister equitum*, had six lictors.

[9] Cic. *de Leg.* iii. 3, 9 "equitatumque qui regat, habeto pari jure cum eo, quicumque erit juris disceptator."

[10] Pompon. in *Dig.* 1, 2, 2, 19 "et his dictatoribus magistri equitum injungebantur sic, quo modo regibus tribuni celerum : . . . magistratus tamen habebantur legitimi."

[11] Liv. iv. 34 "jussoque magistro equitum abdicare se magistratu, ipse deinde abdicat."

for the ratification of his *imperium*,[1] and he seems to have had power to question the people and to transact business with the Senate.[2] In these three respects the office differed from that of the *tribuni celerum* of the monarchy. As the dictator was a lesser king, the *magister equitum* was a greater lieutenant; but, in spite of the theoretical independence of his position, his services were entirely at the disposal of the dictator, who could enforce obedience to his commands, if necessary, by capital punishment.[3] Although originally employed, as the name signifies, for the sole leadership of the *equites* under the higher *imperium* of the dictator, and always to some extent preserving his character of a cavalry general, he could be entrusted by his absent superior with full command either in the camp or in Rome.[4] The office was a useful one, as it gave two generals of tried military capacity to Rome in time of danger, and obviated the disadvantages that might follow from the dictator's having to use incompetent consuls or praetors as his subordinates. This consideration also explains why, in order to secure experienced men for the post, the custom became fixed of choosing ex-consuls or ex-praetors.[5]

The Consuls

The consuls, after their election at the *comitia centuriata*, could at least in later times assume the *insignia* of their rank, and transact all the ordinary official business within the state without waiting for the consent of the *curiae*. Their first act was the taking of the auspices; these were always favourable, for the *haruspex* who stood by[6] announced, as a matter of form, that lightning had been seen upon the left. Armed with this consent they assumed the praetexta, and, preceded by their lictors, performed the first significant act of authority. This act

---

[1] Liv. ix. 38 "Papirius C. Junium Bubulcum magistrum equitum dixit : atque ei, legem curiatam de imperio ferenti, triste omen diem diffidit."

[2] Cic. *de Leg.* iii. 4, 10 ; see p. 160.

[3] Liv. viii. 32 sq. ; cf. xxii. 27 "in . . . civitate, in qua magistri equitum virgas ac secures dictatoris tremere atque horrere soliti sint."

[4] ib. iv. 27 "relictoque (at Rome) L. Julio magistro equitum ad subita belli ministeria."

[5] ib. ii. 18 ; Dio Cass. xlii. 21 (Caesar τὸν Ἀντώνιον, μηδ' ἐστρατηγηκότα, ἵππαρχον προσελόμενος).

[6] Dionys. ii. 6 τῶν δὲ παρόντων τινὲς ὀρνιθοσκόπων μισθὸν ἐκ τοῦ δημοσίου φερόμενοι.

was the summons of the Senate,[1] and was one which showed that they were the magistrates who stood highest in the Roman executive. For, indeed, throughout Republican history, the consulship—though in power it often yielded to the tribunate or dictatorship, and in the reverence it inspired to the censorship —was the highest titular office in the state.[2] The rank of the consuls is sufficiently exhibited by the fact that it was chiefly by their names that the years were dated,[3] and by the ceremonial respect which was paid to them by the other magistrates.[4]

In considering the functions of the consuls we must distinguish between two periods of the history of the Republic. The first extends from their institution to the year 81 B.C.; the second from this year, when the reforms of Sulla introduced a change in their position which was felt as long as consuls continued to exist. This change caused no alteration in their powers, but only in the scope of their activity. During the first period they are the heads of the whole state, and are found ruling wherever Roman energy extends; during the second they are practically the chief magistrates only of the city of Rome and of Italy.

The theory of colleagueship—that each individual member of a college was vested with the fullest power of action subject to the veto of his assessor—did not necessitate a united activity of the consuls in every department of state. They divided their functions, sometimes before their entry on office,[5] and in early times there are traces of the fundamental division of competence expressed by the terms *domi* and *militiae*, one consul occasionally taking the field at the head of an army, while the other remained at home to transact the business of civil administration.[6] This arrangement, which divested colleagueship of its meaning as a safeguard against the rule of a single man, was, however, very unusual, and, as a rule, the consuls were present together in Rome or undertook a joint command abroad. But joint activity in the city—even after the duties of registration had been given

---

[1] Cic. *post Red. ad Quir.* 5, 11. The first meeting of the Senate was in early times held by the elder of the two consuls (ὁ πρεσβύτερος τῶν ὑπάτων Dionys. vi. 57).

[2] Cic. *pro Planc.* 25, 60 "honorum populi finis est consulatus."

[3] App. *B.C.* ii. 19. In formal dating the names of the two chief praetors were added. See the *Senatus Consultum de Asclepiade* (Bruns *Fontes*).

[4] Suet. *Tib.* 31 ; see p. 191.

[5] Liv. xliv. 17 (169 B.C.) "designatos extemplo sortiri placuit provincias."

[6] ib. ii. 33 "consul alter Romae mansit, alter ad Volscum bellum missus"; cf. Dionys. vi. 91 ; Liv. ix. 42.

to the censor and those of civil justice to the praetor—was in some departments almost impossible.   It was obviated by a principle of rotation, which gave the administration and the fasces for a single month to each consul in turn,[1] the elder of the two being given the symbol of power first, and the one who possessed it at the moment being described as *consul major*.[2] This distinction never wholly vanished; for Caesar, we are told, revived in his consulship (59 B.C.) an old custom by which the lictors walked behind the consul who had not the fasces.[3]   But long before Caesar's time positive co-operation between the consuls in the city was common.   They summoned the Senate together, and many consular laws bear the names of two rogators.   There remained, however, several important acts which, while they, morally if not legally, demanded the assent of both consuls, could yet be performed only by one.   Such were the election of magistrates and the nomination of a dictator. In these cases the question as to which consul should act was often decided by agreement (*comparatio*) or by lot (*sortitio*).

In all domestic matters, with the exception of civil jurisdiction and finance, the consuls were the heads of the administration,[4] and this, in the developed Republic, meant that they were the chief servants of the Senate.   It was the consuls who regularly consulted this body, who expressed its decrees, as well as commands which they had a constitutional right to issue on their own authority, in the form of edicts, and who brought legislative measures, which had received senatorial approval, before the *comitia* of the centuries and of the tribes.   It was they, too, who represented the state to foreign kings and nations and introduced their envoys into the Senate.

Consular jurisdiction was of two kinds, administrative and criminal.   The administrative justice of the Republic was concerned chiefly with financial matters touching the interests of the community, such as pecuniary claims made by the state on individuals or by individuals on the state.   The regular discharge of this duty passed to the censors; but in the gaps between the censorships it reverted to the consuls.   We also find them

[1] Cic. *de Rep.* ii. 31, 55.

[2] Festus p. 161 "majorem consulem L. Caesar putat dici, vel eum penes quem fasces sint, vel eum, qui prior factus sit." The first explanation is doubtless the correct one.

[3] Suet. *Caes.* 20.

[4] Polyb. vi. 12 πασῶν εἰσι κύριοι τῶν δημοσίων πράξεων.

adjudicating on questions of property between the cities of Italy.[1] In this matter they doubtless acted on the instructions of the Senate.

The criminal jurisdiction of the consuls was expressed in three ways. It was for centuries, as exercised through the quaestors, the regular capital jurisdiction for ordinary, as opposed to political, crimes; it was asserted, as part of their *coercitio*, with or without appeal according to the nature of the sentence imposed;[2] or it might be jurisdiction without appeal delegated by the people. We shall trace elsewhere the growth of a custom by which the *comitia* assigned jurisdiction on certain crimes to special commissioners. The people, who in this delegation were acting on the advice of the Senate, generally left the appointment of the commission to that body, and the Senate selected either a consul or a praetor.[3] We also find the consul presiding over a criminal inquiry (*quaestio*) raised by a point of international law, such as the question whether the repudiation of a treaty by the people should have as its consequence the surrender of the general guilty of concluding it.[4]

The unlimited *imperium* of the consul in the field (*militiae*), which was asserted when he had crossed the *pomerium*[5] and required the sanction of the *lex curiata*, was, in the early Republic when wars were confined to Italy, generally exercised by both the consuls together. To avoid the inconvenience and danger attending the rule of two commanders-in-chief of equal power, the principle of rotation was adopted, each consul having the supreme command for a single day.[6] But this device was necessary only when military considerations dictated that all the

---

[1] Cicero furnishes an instance for the year 54 B.C., *ad Att.* iv. 15, 5 "Reatini me ad sua Τέμπη duxerunt, ut agerem causam contra Interamnates apud consulem et decem legatos, quod lacus Velinus . . . in Nar defluit."

[2] p. 167.

[3] Selection of a consul, Cic. *de Fin.* ii. 16, 54, in 141 B.C., "decreta a senatu est consuli quaestio"; of a praetor, Liv. xlii. 21, in 172 B.C., "C. Licinius praetor consuluit senatum quem quaerere ea rogatione vellet. Patres ipsum eum quaerere jusserunt."

[4] Cic. *de Rep.* iii. 18, 28 (of the year 136 B.C.) "Consul ego quaesivi, cum vos mihi essetis in consilio, de Numantino foedere." Mommsen (*Staatsr.* ii. p. 112 n. 3) thinks that the *consilium* was formed by the Fetiales (cf. Cic. *de Leg.* ii. 9, 21).

[5] For the question whether the *pomerium* or the first milestone was the limit of the full *imperium* see p. 79.

[6] For the rotation of the *imperium* before Cannae (216 B.C.) see Polyb. iii. 110, Liv. xxii. 41.

Roman forces should act together. Frequently the Roman armies had been simultaneously directed against various points of Italy, and the custom naturally suggested itself that each consul should command half of the regular army of four legions, and thus have an independent sphere of operations (*provincia*).[1] In a defensive war, such as that against Hannibal, Italy would naturally fall into two consular provinces;[2] but the practice became even more essential when the Roman arms extended beyond the peninsula, and in the period of the acquisition of the empire, from the beginning of the first Punic war to the close of the struggle with Greece (264–146 B.C.), *Italia* as a whole, and some foreign country such as Greece or Macedon, are the regular *provinciae* held by the consuls.[3] The arrangements which were made for the permanent government of provinces, first through praetors and afterwards through pro-magistrates, tended to arrest their employment for this purpose; but down to the time of Sulla (81 B.C.) a consul might at any time be appointed to a transmarine province.[4]

The consuls settled the distribution of *provinciae* by agreement or by lot,[5] the *sortitio* becoming in time the more usual practice. Occasionally the Senate ventured to suggest that one of the consuls was better qualified for a special department, and in this case the inevitable consent of his colleague enabled him to assume it *extra sortem*.[6] But, as Rome's activity extended, and the available magistrates with *imperium* increased, the important question came to be, not who should have one of two departments, but which should be the consular provinces. This power to nominate the provinces (*nominare provincias*) had, by the close of the Hannibalic war, become the undisputed prerogative of the

---

[1] Liv. xxii. 27 "Ita (Fabius, after the appointment of Minucius as his colleague in 217 B.C.) obtinuit uti legiones, sicut consulibus mos esset, inter se dividerent."

[2] ib. xxx. 1 (203 B.C.) "censuerunt patres, ut consules inter se compararent sortirenturve, uter Bruttios adversus Hannibalem, uter Etruriam ac Ligures provinciam haberet."

[3] Italy and Macedonia (ib. xxxii. 8, xlii. 31, xliii. 12), Italy and Greece (xxxvii. 1).

[4] Italia and some foreign country are still consular *provinciae* in 112 and 111 B.C. (Sall. *Jug.* 27, 43). When a consul was appointed to one of the old praetorian provinces, he did not supplant the praetor but commanded with and over him.

[5] Liv. xxx. 1 "ut consules inter se compararent sortirenturve." Cf. ib. xxxii. 8, xxxvii. 1, and the other passages cited in note 3.

[6] ib. viii. 16 ; cf. Cic. *pro Domo* 9, 24. In 205 B.C. Scipio was given Sicilia *extra sortem* because his colleague was *pontifex maximus* (Liv. xxviii. 38).

Senate,[1] and one of its surest modes of controlling the consuls. This *de facto* power was formally recognised by a law of the tribune C. Gracchus in 123 B.C., although it scarcely required legal recognition, and the purport of the *lex Sempronia* was to weaken the discretionary power of the Senate by enacting that the consular provinces should be fixed before the election of the consuls who were to hold them.[2] At this period the consular departments were almost invariably foreign commands ; but, after the close of the social war and the reforms of Sulla, they were held by their recipients as proconsuls after their year of office at Rome had expired.

We do not know the exact tenor of the *lex Cornelia de provinciis ordinandis*. Sulla did nothing to infringe the military *imperium* of the consuls ; after as before his law it was legal for them to "approach any province" ;[3] but he devised some means of separating home from foreign commands, which, by crystallising the established custom, restricted the consuls and praetors to the civil government of Rome and Italy, and sent them out after their year of office as proconsuls and propraetors to the provinces. The powers conferred by the military *imperium*[4] were thenceforth lost, and the consul at the close of the Republic had less specific functions than any magistrate ; even his criminal jurisdiction had vanished before the establishment of the permanent courts. Yet still the consul, who observed constitutional forms, was the chief interpreter of the Senate's will ; while one who, like Caesar in 59 B.C., violated all these forms, might exercise an almost monarchical power. The possession of the consulship was the great annual prize, contested and almost equally secured by the conservative and the reform parties from the time of the Gracchi to the close of the Republic,[5] and the competition was not wholly directed to secure the military *imperium* which lay beyond it. The civil office might still make

[1] Liv. xxi. 17 (218 B.C.) "nominatae jam antea consulibus provinciae erant ; tum sortiri jussi." Cf. ib. xxviii. 38.

[2] Sall. *Jug.* 27 ; Cic. *pro Domo* 9, 24.

[3] Cic. *ad Att.* viii. 15, 3 "consules quibus more majorum concessum est vel omnes adire provincias." Lucullus went as consul to Asia in 74 B.C.

[4] p. 153.

[5] That staunch conservative Q. Catulus was wont to reflect with pleasure "non saepe unum consulem improbum, duos vero nunquam, excepto illo Cinnano tempore, fuisse" (Cic. *post Red. in Sen.* 4, 9). By *improbi* Catulus meant "radicals."

a capable man, supported by a powerful following, the guide of the destinies of the state.[1]

The Praetors

We have seen how the functions of civil jurisdiction were given to a minor colleague of the consuls, and how a second colleague was subsequently added to try cases in which the interests of *peregrini* were involved.[2] The needs for judicial magistrates could not end here. The provinces of Sicily and Sardinia, acquired as a consequence of the first Punic war, required jurisdiction, and two praetors were given them about the year 227 B.C.; two more were added in 198 B.C. for the two newly acquired Spanish provinces, thus bringing up the full number to six. A *lex Baebia* (*circa* 180 B.C.) enacted that four and six praetors should be elected in alternate years, probably for the wise purpose of making the praetorian government of the difficult Spanish provinces biennial; but this law was soon suspended, and six praetors continued to be annually elected until the time of Sulla (81 B.C.).[3] It is true that between 198 and 81 many provinces had been added to the Roman Empire; but the principle of administration by pro-magistrates had gained recognition while these were being created; the praetors were becoming, like the consuls, more and more city officials, and the necessity for adding to their number came from the development of the criminal law. At least eight praetors were needed for the presidency of the civil and criminal courts at Rome, and consequently two were added by Sulla to the original six.

The variety of functions performed by the praetors was due to their having a general and a special character. On entering office, after election by the centuries, they were at once, as inferior colleagues of the consuls, capable of any of the duties which flowed from the *imperium*. They were then assigned some special office, some definite *provincia*; but the exercise of

[1] The consul was the "legitimus tutor" of the state (Cic. *post Red. ad Quir.* 5, 11) and "quasi parens bonus aut tutor fidelis" (*de Or.* iii. 1, 3).

[2] p. 120.

[3] Two praetors for Sicily and Sardinia (Liv. *Ep.* xx.), two more for the Spanish provinces (Liv. xxxii. 27). For the *lex Baebia* see Liv. xl. 44. For the restoration of the number six see Vell. ii. 16. Pomponius says that four were added by Sulla (*Dig.* 1, 2, 2, 32), but eight are found in 47 B.C. (Dio Cass. xlii. 51).

this did not destroy their capacity for general action. For command in war, as well as for the exercise of at least civil jurisdiction—both attributes of the full *imperium*—they required a *lex curiata*. Each had the right to six lictors, and appeared with the full number when controlling a province outside the city; but, in the exercise of his jurisdiction at home, he employed, or was allowed, only two.[1]   The praetor's specific title was derived from his province ; of the two original home praetors one was known as the *praetor qui inter cives jus dicit*, or, in the colloquial phrase which became titular, as *praetor urbanus;* the other as the *praetor qui inter peregrinos jus dicit*, known finally as the *praetor peregrinus*. But both the home praetors were often spoken of as having *urbanae provinciae* and exercising *urbana jurisdictio*.[2] Their rank was higher than that of their colleagues—hence their names were, like those of the consuls, used for dating [3]—and of the two the *praetor urbanus* was regarded as holding the more distinguished position.[4] His duties were naturally far more engrossing than those of his colleague, and the law that he must not be absent more than ten days from Rome during his year of office [5] made him more of a distinctly civic official.

The powers of the praetors, taken in their natural order, may be divided into (i.) their general administrative duties at Rome, and (ii.) the duties of their special departments. In the first of these spheres they acted in virtue of their own *imperium* but *vice* the consuls, and generally, therefore, when the consuls were absent from the city. If they acted when the consul was present, it was by authority of the Senate, and legally the consuls might prohibit this action.[6]   Such an injunction by the Senate was a

---

[1] The praetor had a right to six lictors (στρατηγὸς ἑξαπέλεκυς, App. *Syr.* 15 ; cf. Polyb. iii. 40) and appears with the full number in the province (Cic. *in Verr.* v. 54, 142 "sex lictores circumsistunt ") ; but, in the exercise of his jurisdiction within the city, he employed, or was allowed, only two (Censorinus *de Die Nat.* 24, 3 ; cf. Cic. *de Leg. Agr.* ii. 34, 93).

[2] *Praetor urbanus* (*S. C. de Bacch.* ll. 5, 8, 17, 21), *praetor qui inter cives jus dicet* (*lex Agraria* of 111 B.C.), *provincia* or *sors urbana* (Liv. xxiv. 9, xxv. 3, xxvii. 7, xxviii. 10, xxix. 13), *jurisdictio urbana* (ib. xxxii. 28, xlii. 31)—*praetor qui inter peregrinos jus dicet* (*lex Acil.* ll. 12 and 89 ; *lex Jul. Munic.* ll. 8 and 12), *jurisdictio inter peregrinos* (Liv. xl. 1), *provincia peregrina* (ib. xxvii. 7, xxviii. 10). Both these praetors, as distinct from those in foreign command, are said to have *urbanae provinciae* (ib. xliii. 11), *provincia urbana* (xxxii. 1), *jurisdictio urbana* (xxv. 41, xxx. 1).

[3] p. 197.
[4] App. *B. C.* ii. 112.
[5] Cic. *Phil.* ii. 13, 31.   [6] p. 174.

constitutional mode of coercing the consuls into doing their
duty. In this way the praetors might summon the Senate,[1]
propose a *rogatio*,[2] hold the levy,[3] and exercise criminal jurisdiction
delegated by the people.[4] Usually, however, such duties were
performed by them only in the absence of the consuls, and the
praetor urbanus generally took the lead,[5] although the summons
of the Senate by both home praetors, and even by a provincial
praetor, was not unknown.[6]

The special functions of the praetors were always assigned
by lot (*sortitio*). During the period when some of the praetors
governed provinces, a regular sortition took the form of an
assignment of the two urban *provinciae* to two, and of the foreign
provinces to two and afterwards to four members of the college.[7]
But in the third and early part of the second centuries, before
prorogation of command became the normal principle, and when
Rome had few magistrates with *imperium* at her disposal, this
regular sortition could not always be observed. Sometimes the
two urban praetorships were combined,[8] or the *praetor peregrinus*
might be given an Italian command, such as Cisalpine Gaul.[9]
In this way a praetor could be spared for the command of the
fleet or in Gaul (at Ariminum). This disturbance of the *sortitio*
and the appointment of a praetor *extra ordinem* [10] were naturally
the work of the Senate. After Sulla the two civil and six of
the criminal courts were assigned to the eight praetors by lot.

The civil jurisdiction, whether of the urban or provincial
praetors, still adhered to the ancient form by which the ruling in
law (*in jure*) was the duty of the magistrate, and the judgment
on the question of fact (*in judicio*) was the function of a single

[1] Liv. xlii. 21.   [2] ib. xxvii. 5.   [3] ib. xliii. 14.
[4] ib. xlii. 21 ; see p. 199.
[5] e.g. in the *dilectus* (ib. xxv. 22, xxxix. 20, xlii. 35).
[6] After Cannae the two urban praetors summoned the Senate (ib. xxii. 55).
In 197 B.C., on the news of troubles in Spain, "decreverunt patres ut, comitiis
praetorum perfectis, cui praetori provincia Hispania obvenisset, is primo quoque
tempore de bello Hispaniae ad senatum referret" (ib. xxxiii. 21).
[7] The *provinciae* assigned to the four praetors are *urbana, peregrina*, Sicilia,
Sardinia (ib. xxviii. 10), to the six praetors the same with the addition of the
two Spains (ib. xxxii. 28, xl. 1).
[8] ib. xxv. 3 (212 B.C.) "Et praetores provincias sortiti sunt ; P. Cornelius
Sulla urbanam et peregrinam, quae duorum ante sors fuerat." Cf. ib. xxxvii.
50 (189 B.C.).
[9] ib. xxix. 13 (204 B.C.) "M. Marcio urbana, L. Scribonio Liboni peregrina
et eidem Gallia."
[10] ib. xxiv. 9 (215 B.C.) "comitiis praetorum perfectis, senatus consultum
factum ut Q. Fulvio extra ordinem urbana provincia esset."

judex or, in matters requiring rapid decision, of a bench of "recoverers" (*recuperatores*). The rulings of the *praetor urbanus* had originally followed the forms of the *legis actio*, but in matters affecting *peregrini* a custom had grown up for the praetor to devise formularies of action (*formulae*) which bound the *judex* in his decision. The convenience of this procedure extended its use to almost all cases, and by a *lex Aebutia* of uncertain date the simpler formulary procedure almost wholly replaced the more complicated provisions of the *legis actiones*.[1] The *formula* was a conditioned acquittal or condemnation; the praetor said to the *judex*, "If it appears that a debt is due, an obligation has been incurred, etc., condemn the defendant in a certain amount or in a sum left to your estimate; if the condition is not apparent, acquit him" (*si paret . . . condemna; si non paret, absolve*). The *judex* by his finding changed the conditioned sentence into one that was categorical and final.

In most communities such rulings as those of the praetors would be occasional expositions of a fixed code or of an uncertain body of statute and customary law. At Rome a useful practice was adopted which brought the living law, as opposed to the dead letter of her only code and to statutes which had fallen into disuse, before the eyes of all the people. The praetors announced by means of edicts, issued on their entrance on office, what their rulings would be in any given case. The edict was the "living voice of the civil law";[2] and it is not surprising to find that by the time of Cicero it had taken the place of the "song" of the Twelve Tables in the legal education of the Roman youth.[3] The profession of the edict was interpretation of the law of Rome; but it was an interpretation that took the form of "assisting, supplementing, and even correcting the civil law."[4]

---

[1] Gaius *Inst.* iv. 30 "per legem Aebutiam et duas Julias sublatae sunt istae legis actiones; effectumque est ut per concepta verba, id est, per formulas, litigaremus"; Gell. xvi. 10, 8 "cum . . . omnis . . . illa duodecim tabularum antiquitas nisi in legis actionibus centumviralium causarum lege Aebutia lata consopita sit."

[2] Marcian in *Dig.* 1, 1, 8 "nam et ipsum jus honorarium viva vox est juris civilis."

[3] Cic. *de Leg.* i. 5, 17 "Non ergo a praetoris edicto, ut plerique nunc, neque a XII Tabulis, ut superiores . . . hauriendam juris disciplinam putas." Cf. *de Leg.* ii. 23, 59 "discebamus enim pueri XII, ut carmen necessarium: quas jam nemo discit."

[4] Papinian in *Dig.* 1, 1, 7, 1 "jus praetorium est, quod praetores introduxerunt adjuvandi vel supplendi vel corrigendi juris civilis gratia propter utilitatem publicam."

It was, therefore, not the *jus civile* of Rome, but the valid modifications of this expressed in what was currently known as magistrates' law (*jus honorarium*). The civil law was of course presumed as the background of these documents; it found expression in many formulae which the magistrates continued to give, and the *album* itself probably contained a line of separation which showed where the formulae based on *jus civile* ended and those founded on magisterial promises began. The most typical language of the *jus honorarium* is one of command veiled under the form of promises; the praetor asserts "under certain given circumstances I will grant or will not grant a case" (*judicium, actionem dabo . . . non dabo*). Less frequently the language is more imperative: "I will compel payment or an oath" (*solvere aut jurare cogam*); before the question of right is decided, "I forbid force to be used" (*vim fieri veto*).

A consideration of judge-made law, the consequence it may be of precedents drawn from already decided cases, and therefore merely the recognition of practice which had already crept into use,[1] but still expressed, as it is in this case, in a purely abstract form, suggests many questions. First, as to its validity. The edict was law that held good for a year (*lex annua*):[2] a limitation that would have produced a most unsatisfactory uncertainty as to its validity for future litigants and subsequent magistrates, had it not been for the facts that it was actually continuous, and that it was received, only to be slightly modified in accordance with legislative changes or with the demands of convenience, by successive wielders of civil jurisdiction. To use technical language, the edict was *perpetuum et tralaticium*.[3] Secondly, we must consider the limitation on the magistrate and the forces that bound him to observe his own promulgated law. At Rome the veto operated successfully for this purpose[4] even before the passing of the *lex Cornelia* of 67 B.C., which obliged a magistrate to adhere to the rulings of

---

[1] For the edict as the expression of customary law see Cic. *de Invent.* ii. 22, 67 "Consuetudine autem jus esse putatur id, quod voluntate omnium sine lege vetustas comprobarit . . . Quo in genere et alia sunt multa et eorum multo maxima pars, quae praetores edicere consuerunt."

[2] Cic. *in Verr.* i. 42, 109 "qui plurimum tribuunt edicto, praetoris edictum legem annuam dicunt esse."

[3] Ascon. *in Cornel.* p. 58; Cic. *in Verr.* i. 44, 114. *Perpetuum* means "continuous," *tralaticium* "transmitted."

[4] Cic. *in Verr.* i. 46, 119. Cf. p. 178.

his own edict.[1] In the shaping of the edictal rules the mere
fact of publicity in a community so legally gifted as that of the
Romans must have sufficed to keep the magistrate within the
bounds of prudence; when he was conscious of little legal training,
the assistance of eminent jurisconsults must have frequently
been called in.

The edict is the source of most of our modern Roman law;
the titles of Justinian's *Digest* are often commentaries on its
rubrics excerpted from the writings of the scientific jurists, and
that it should become the prototype of the world's law was only
natural when we consider the way in which it was built up.
It was not only the collective work of generations of gifted men,
who were fortunately not professing lawyers, but it was the
outcome of an adjustment of Roman law first with that of Italy
and then with that of the provinces. The beginnings of a
recognition of a "law of the civilised world" (*jus gentium*) must
be older than the institution of the *praetor peregrinus*, since
for more than a century the *praetor urbanus* had been issuing
edicts not merely for *cives* but also for *peregrini;* but, when a
separate comprehensive edict was issued for *peregrini*, equity
found a more systematic expression, and its reaction on the
comparatively rigid forms of the urban edicts was necessarily
great; but the power of this reaction was possibly even surpassed
by that of the provincial edict (*edictum provinciale*), issued
originally by the foreign praetors and then by the proconsuls
and propraetors in each of Rome's dependencies.

The connexion of the praetors with criminal jurisdiction was,
apart from the rare occurrence of a special judicial commission,
due to the growth of the standing courts. These *quaestiones
perpetuae* or *judicia publica* were to a large extent modelled on
the civil procedure by which compensation was exacted through
a court of *recuperatores*. Hence the praetors seemed their most
appropriate presidents, and the size of the college was, as we
have seen,[2] increased by Sulla to meet the growing number of
these courts. For criminal jurisdiction six praetors were available, whose provinces were possibly determined by the Senate
and were certainly distributed amongst the designated magistrates

---

[1] Ascon. *in Cornel.* p. 58 "Aliam deinde legem Cornelius, . . . tulit, ut
praetores ex edictis suis perpetuis jus dicerent, quae res . . . gratiam ambitiosis
praetoribus, qui varie jus dicere assueverant, sustulit." Cf. Dio Cass. xxxvi. 23.
[2] p. 202.

by the use of the lot.[1] Although the general principle of distribution made each praetor preside over the jurisdiction ordained by a single law which created a *quaestio*, yet the spheres of jurisdiction were by no means fixed. Groups of *quaestiones* or of their branches[2] might be rearranged every year, and it may not even have been necessary for a single praetor to maintain a particular sphere of jurisdiction throughout the whole tenure of his office. The general administrative functions of the office might interfere with jurisdiction, and a readjustment of the original distribution of *provinciae*, probably with the consent of the Senate, seems to have been sometimes necessary.[3]

The Aediles

The junction of the plebeian and curule aedileships into a single office is testified by their being spoken of together where their duties are mentioned or prescribed by law,[4] and the fusion was so complete that it is sometimes impossible to discover whether a historical reference applies to the plebeian or to the patrician magistracy. But in their respective qualifications for office, forms of election and *insignia*, the separation was still complete. The plebeian aediles must still be plebeians, while the curule aediles belonged in alternate years to either order;[5] the former were elected by the Plebs, the latter by the *comitia tributa* of the people; the former sat on the modest bench of the plebeian officials and had no distinctive dress, the latter sat on the curule chair and wore the *praetexta;*[6] the anomaly remained that the one office was not a magistracy at all, the other a magistracy proper which gave its holder a claim to a seat in the Senate. The one peculiar privilege of the plebeian aediles—the

---

[1] Cic. *in Verr.* Act. i. 8, 21 ; *pro Mur.* 20, 42. The fullest account that we possess of the distribution of such functions amongst the members of the college refers to the year 66 B.C. (ib. *pro Cluent.* 53, 147 ; Ascon. *in Cornel.* p. 59).

[2] e.g. the *lex Cornelia de sicariis et veneficis* took cognisance of murder, poisoning, and arson, that *de falsis* of the forgery of documents and of wills as well as of coining.

[3] After the *sortitio* for 62 B.C. the praetor Q. Metellus Celer was given the province of Cisalpine Gaul (Cic. *ad Fam.* v. 2, 3, and 4). During his praetorship (63 B.C.) he had been summoned to a command in northern Italy.

[4] Cic. *de Leg.* iii, 3, 7 "Suntoque aediles, curatores urbis, annonae ludorumque sollemnium : ollisque ad honoris amplioris gradum is primus ascensus esto." Cf. *lex Jul. Munic.* 1. 24.   [5] p. 122.

[6] Cic. *in Verr.* v. 14, 36.

sacrosanctitas which they shared with the tribunes—vanished as a consequence of their employment as officials of the state.[1]

The general position now assumed by the aediles was that of assistants to the consuls in the administration of the city; in the fulfilment of which task they had certain special spheres of competence assigned them.[2]

(1) Their care of the state archives—originally possessed to a limited extent by the plebeian aediles [3]—was still continued, and they divided in some unknown way with the quaestors the custody of *senatus consulta* in the *aerarium Saturni*.[4]

(2) The *cura urbis* involved a series of duties connected with the public sites, buildings, and functions of the city. The aediles had to see to the paving of the streets, to insist on individuals keeping the pathways before their own houses in repair, and to lease out at the public cost the renewal of such thoroughfares as were connected with public buildings.[5] They saw that all public places, such as roads and squares, were kept clean and clear of obstacles, partly from a sanitary motive, partly for the purpose of preventing the encroachments of private buildings on public sites.[6] They controlled the water-supply and prohibited private persons, with the connivance of the water-inspectors (*aquarii*), taking more than their fair share from the public conduits.[7] Their control of public buildings and temples was limited to inspection and supervision, for the repair of such buildings, at least when undertaken on a large scale, was leased out by the censors. Closely connected with this *aedium sacrarum procuratio*[8] was their control of the *cultus* of the community, which obliged them to see that no foreign innovations crept into the primitive form of Roman worship.[9] Their police duties are shown by the edicts which they issued for keeping order at the

---

[1] Livy (iii. 55), in stating the ineffectiveness of the *sacrosanctitas* granted by law and not by oath, says "itaque aedilem prendi ducique a majoribus magistratibus, etc." Cf. Gell. xiii. 13.

[2] Cic. *de Leg.* iii. 3, 7, cited p. 208.

[3] p. 98.   [4] Dio Cass. liv. 26.

[5] *Lex Jul. Munic.* ll. 20, 32-45, 29, 46.

[6] Suet. *Vesp.* 5 ; *lex Jul. Munic.* l. 68.

[7] Cic. *ad Fam.* viii. 6, 4 (Caelius Rufus, curule aedile in 50 B.C., says) "nisi ego cum tabernariis et aquariis pugnarem, veternus civitatem occupasset." ·

[8] ib. *in Verr.* v. 14, 36 "mihi sacrarum aedium procurationem, mihi totam urbem tuendam esse commissam."

[9] Liv. xxv. 1 (on the spread of foreign superstitions in Rome in 213 B.C.) ' incusati graviter ab senatu aediles triumvirique capitales, quod non prohiberent." Cf. Cic. *de Har. Resp.* 13, 27.

P

public games,[1] and by their control of private places of utility or amusement to which the public were admitted, such as baths, taverns, and the like.[2] The aediles possessed the usual means of *coercitio* for enforcing their decrees ; they seized pledges (*pignora*) and imposed fines (*multae*).[3] When the latter surpassed the limit of the *multa suprema*, the case went on appeal to the people ; the plebeian aediles defended their fines before the *concilium plebis*, the curule before the *comitia tributa*. From the *cura urbis* also sprang an anomalous civil jurisdiction which was confined to the curule aediles ; in one form of civil action which survived in their edict as codified under Hadrian—that, namely, arising from the damage done by wild beasts on the public roads—it was they who gave the *formula* and appointed the *judex* or *recuperatores*.[4]

(3) Their care of the market is typified by Cicero in the most important of its subdivisions—the care of the corn-supply (*cura annonae*).[5] Their duty was to regulate prices as far as possible, especially by the prevention of monopolies ; the aediles often sold corn at a moderate price fixed by the state, although sometimes ambition led them to incur the loss themselves ;[6] and it was they who as a rule presided over the distributions ordained by the later *leges frumentariae*.[7] The supply of corn to an army in Italy from the city magazines was also one of their cares.[8] Other duties springing from their control of the market were the enforcement of the sumptuary laws,[9] the inspection of

[1] Macrob. *Sat.* ii. 6 "lapidatus a populo Vatinius cum gladiatorium munus ederet, obtinuerat ut aediles edicerent ne quis in arenam nisi pomum misisse vellet."

[2] Seneca *Ep.* 86, 10 "hoc quoque nobilissimi aediles fungebantur officio intrandi ea loca quae populum receptabant exigendique munditias et utilem ac salubrem temperaturam." Cf. Suet. *Claud.* 38 ; Tac. *Ann.* ii. 85.

[3] Tac. *Ann.* xiii. 28 (56 A.D.) "cohibita artius et aedilium potestas statutumque quantum curules, quantum plebei pignoris caperent vel poenae inrogarent."

[4] *Dig.* 21, 1, 40-42 (from the edict of the curule aediles) "ne quis canem, verrem vel minorem aprum, lupum, ursum, pantheram, leonem . . . qua vulgo iter fiet, ita habuisse velit, ut cuiquam nocere damnumve dare possit."

[5] p. 208 n. 4.

[6] Liv. xxiii. 41 ; xxxi. 50 ; xxxiii. 42. Cic. *de Off.* ii. 17, 58 "ne M. quidem Sejo vitio datum est, quod in caritate asse modium populo dedit : magna enim se et inveterata invidia, nec turpi jactura, quando erat aedilis, nec maxima liberavit."

[7] Cic. *ad Fam.* viii. 6, 5 (from Caelius Rufus in 50 B.C.) "alimentariam (legem), qua jubet aediles metiri, jactavit (Curio)."

[8] Liv. xxvi. 10 (211 B.C., when Hannibal was at the gates of Rome) "Fulvius Flaccus . . . inter Esquilinam Collinamque portam posuit castra. Aediles plebis commeatum eo comportarunt."

[9] For this there is no direct evidence, but the aediles complain about the transgression of sumptuary laws in Tac. *Ann.* iii. 52-55.

weights and measures with the maintenance of their normal standard,[1] and the regulation of the sale of slaves and cattle. This power found expression in civil jurisdiction, which was in this case also confined to the curule aediles. It was they who gave the *formula* for the return of slaves and cattle sold under false representations, and appointed the *judex* in such cases.[2]

(4) The *cura ludorum* of the aediles was not the mere presidency of festivals such as was possessed by other magistrates, but the establishment of regularly recurring games, very largely at their own expense. The games were given jointly by the respective pairs of colleagues,[3] the oldest festival, the *ludi Romani*, being in the hands of the curule,[4] the *ludi plebeii* in those of the plebeian aediles.[5] The other festivals established from time to time—*Megalesia, Cerealia, Floralia*—increased the burden of the aedileship. The Megalesia apparently fell to the lot of the curule aediles,[6] the others seem to have been given indifferently by either pair.

The aediles are sometimes found exercising functions of criminal jurisdiction, all of which cannot be brought into close connexion with any of their special powers, and which, therefore, do not spring from the ordinary *coercitio*. This criminal jurisdiction was, like the civil jurisdiction of the curule aediles, an anomaly, for these magistrates did not possess the *imperium*. It is to be explained partly as a survival (for some jurisdiction of the kind had been exercised by the plebeian aediles) and partly as the result of considerations of convenience. Before the institution of the *quaestiones perpetuae* there was a great lack of criminal courts at Rome. The *quaestores* were at hand for the trial of grave capital crimes against individuals, and the tribunes for political jurisdiction. What was needed was a magistracy for bringing ordinary and lesser crimes involving a money penalty (*multa*) before the people, and this was found in the aedileship. It is true that the aediles were not prohibited from undertaking the prosecution of political crimes that might be

---

[1] Momms. *Staatsr*. ii. p. 499. He takes "cum tabernariis pugnarem" (Cic. *ad Fam*. viii. 6, 4, cited p. 209) in this sense.

[2] *Dig*. 21, 1, 1 ; Gell. iv. 2.

[3] Cic. *in Verr*. v. 14, 36.

[4] Liv. x. 47 ; xxvii. 6. They were shared by both colleagues (Suet. *Caes*. 10).

[5] Liv. xxiii. 30.

[6] Dio Cass. xliii. 48 (44 B.C.). Here by a decree of the Senate the Megalesia are celebrated by the plebeian aediles.

met by a fine, such as a mild case of *majestas*[1] or the bribery of a bench of *judices;*[2] and judgment on a breach of the peace (*vis*) was in harmony with their police duties.[3] But as a rule it is a class of ordinary crimes, somewhat beneath the dignity of tribunician prosecution, that we find them visiting. Such were adultery committed either by men or women,[4] usury,[5] illegal speculations in corn,[6] and the offence of exceeding the amount of domain-land which the laws permitted an individual to possess.[7] The aediles were stimulated to a career of prosecution by the singular custom which permitted them to retain the fines collected and to apply them to any public purpose which they pleased. We find them expended on buildings and adornments of the city, and by the plebeian aediles on their games.[8]

The Quaestors

We have already spoken of the criminal investigators (*quaestores parricidii*), whom tradition attributes to the monarchy,[9] and of the more certain assistants of the consuls for criminal jurisdiction and finance (*quaestores parricidii et aerarii*), who are assigned to the early Republic.[10] We have seen that, first nominated by the consuls, they were soon elected by the tribes,[11] and we have witnessed the opening of the office to Plebeians when, in 421 B.C., the number of quaestors was raised from two to four, and one of these officials was assigned to each consul in the field.[12] About the year 267 B.C. four more were added for the purposes of Italian administration, and no further change is recorded

---

[1] When during the first Punic war Clodia uttered her ill-omened wish about the Roman people, "C. Fundanius et Ti. Sempronius, aediles plebei, multam dixerunt ei aeris gravis viginti quinque milia" (Gell. x. 6). Cf. Suet. *Tib.* 2.

[2] Cicero promises, as aedile, to prosecute those "qui aut deponere aut accipere aut recipere aut pollicere aut sequestres aut interpretes corrumpendi judicii solent esse" (*in Verr.* Act. i. 12, 36).

[3] An instance is furnished by Clodius' prosecution of Milo in 56 B.C. (Cic. *pro Sest.* 44, 95 ; *ad Q. fr.* 2, 3). A prosecution by the aedile in defence of his own dignity or person is an outcome of his *coercitio.* An instance is furnished by Gell. iv. 14.

[4] Liv. viii. 22 ; xxv. 2.

[5] ib. xxxv. 41.

[6] ib. xxxviii. 35. Here the offence was *annona compressa* by the corn-dealers.

[7] Condemnation "quia plus, quam quod lege finitum erat, agri possiderent" (ib. x. 13). Condemnation of *pecuarii* (x. 47). Cf. xxxiii. 42.

[8] ib. xxxviii. 35 ; x. 23.

[9] p. 63.   [10] p. 80.   [11] p. 81.   [12] p. 117.

until Sulla raised their number to twenty,[1] although some inter-
mediate increase is not improbable.

After the quaestorship had become an independent magistracy,
its tenure continued to be annual; but the consular quaestor is
so much a part of his superior that, after the prolongation of
the *imperium* had become usual, a biennial tenure, held partly in
Rome, partly in a province, must have been the rule.[2] The
rank of the quaestor was the lowest in the *cursus honorum*,[3] and
he had none of the *insignia* of the curule magistrates. Coins
exhibit him on a straight-legged chair, with a money-bag or
money-chest, and a staff the significance of which is unknown.

The quaestorian *provinciae* were determined, before these
magistrates entered on their office, by a decree of the Senate,[4]
and the individuals were then assigned to their several departments by lot; although, probably always by a special grace of
the Senate, there are instances of commanders selecting their
own assistants.[5]

The departments may be grouped under the three heads of
urban, military, and Italian.

(i.) The general duty of assistance which the two urban
quaestors (*quaestores urbani*) rendered to the consuls was curtailed
of one of its attributes by the loss of their criminal jurisdiction
about the middle of the second century B.C.; for they could no
longer have been needed as delegates in *parricidium* after the
first *quaestio de sicariis* had been established.[6] Their functions
were henceforth, as they had for some time mainly been, financial.
Their old association with the *aerarium* gave them the custody
of the keys of this treasury,[7] the guardianship of the standards
that were kept there,[8] and, above all, of the great mass of state
papers and archives which it held. These contained laws[9] and

---

[1] Tac. *Ann.* xi. 22 "post lege Sullae viginti creati supplendo senatui."

[2] C. Gracchus served as quaestor for three years; one was spent in Rome and
two in Sardinia (Plut. *C. Gracch.* 2).

[3] Cic. *in Verr.* Act. i. 4, 11 "quaestura primus gradus honoris."

[4] ib. i. 13, 34 "quaestor ex senatus consulto provinciam sortitus es."

[5] Liv. xxx. 33 "Laelium, cujus . . . eo anno quaestoris extra sortem ex
senatusconsulto opera utebatur" (Scipio in 202 B.C.); Cic. *ad Att.* vi. 6, 4
"Pompeius . . . Q. Cassium sine sorte delegit, Caesar Antonium; ego sorte
datum offenderem?"

[6] The first trace of a *quaestio de sicariis* is in 142 B.C. (Cic. *de Fin.* ii. 16, 54).

[7] Polyb. xxiv. 9*a*, 1.

[8] Liv. iii. 69 "signa . . . a quaestoribus ex aerario prompta delataque in
campum."

[9] Cic. *de Leg.* iii. 20, 46.

decrees of the Senate,[1] the list of *judices*,[2] the public accounts
(*tabulae publicae*), which included the statements of moneys voted
to magistrates [3] and the reckoning of provincial governors with
the *aerarium* in respect to direct tribute paid them by the provincials. Connected with this financial custody were the quaestors'
duties of collection. To them the *publicani* usually paid the sums
which they had guaranteed for the leasing of the public revenues.[4]
The collection of fines imposed by the *judicia populi*, and exacted
by the *quaestiones* for peculation and extortion, was also in their
hands.[5]

The quaestors also conducted sales on behalf of the treasury—
not of those large portions of the public domain which were
alienated by the censors, but of current acquisitions, such as those
of slaves and booty captured in war,[6] and of that portion of
conquered land which was brought immediately under the
hammer (*ager quaestorius*).[7] This threefold function of guardianship, collection, and sale gave the urban quaestors an unequalled
grasp of the state of the public revenues, and as they were
annual, while the censors—the budget-makers—were merely
occasional officials, we are not surprised to find them making
financial statements in the Senate.[8]

(ii.) The general assistance which the quaestors were meant
to render to the consuls was extended, as we saw,[9] in the year
421 B.C. to their activity in the field. Each consul or praetor
who assumed a military command was given a particular quaestor
(the dictator being exempted from what was regarded as a
limitation on the discretionary powers of the magistrate), and,

---

[1] Liv. xxxix. 4. It was the duty of the quaestors to see that they were
genuine. Cato the younger required the oath of the consuls that a certain
decree had been passed (Plut. *Cat. Min.* 17).

[2] Cic. *Phil.* v. 5, 15.

[3] ib. *in Verr.* iii. 79, 183 "eorum hominum (the *scribae* of the quaestors)
fidei tabulae publicae periculaque magistratuum committuntur."

[4] The security was given to the *aerarium* ("subsignare apud aerarium"
Cic. *pro Flacco* 32, 80) ; hence the money was probably paid into that treasury.

[5] Liv. xxxviii. 58 "Hostilius et Furius damnati (for *peculatus* in 187 B.C.)
praedes eodem die quaestoribus urbanis dederunt." In the *lex Acil. Rep.* (l. 57)
it is said of the man convicted "q(uaestori) praedes facito det."

[6] Plaut. *Capt.* i. 2, 111 ; ii. 3, 453.

[7] Hygin. *de Cond. Agr.* p. 115.

[8] *Auct. ad Herenn.* i. 12, 21 "Cum L. Saturninus legem frumentariam de
semissibus et trientibus laturus esset, Q. Caepio, qui per id temporis quaestor
urbanus erat, docuit senatum aerarium pati non posse tantam largitionem."

[9] p. 117.

after the custom had grown up of extending the *imperium*, these assistants accompanied the proconsuls and propraetors to their provinces. The term of the quaestorship was prolonged with that of the office with which it was associated,[1] for the connexion between the superior and inferior was regarded as being of almost as personal a character as that between father and son.[2] We shall examine the relation more minutely when we come to deal with provincial organisation. It is sufficient to remark here that, though the quaestors' functions were mainly financial, they were in all other respects true administrative delegates of the magistrates with *imperium*,[3] and were constantly employed on judicial and military business.

(iii.) The quaestors of Italy were probably identical with those of the fleet (*classici*), and were a result of the organisation of Italy which followed the war with Pyrrhus (267 B.C.). For the purposes of the Pyrrhine war twelve quaestors were created, whose number, when they were given permanent stations, was reduced to four.[4] Three of these stations can be approximately determined. One was Ostia, and the tenure of this post was burdened with the duty of the supply of corn to Rome.[5] The second appears to have been the woods and forests (*calles*) of Italy.[6] The third was in Cispadane Gaul,[7] perhaps at Ravenna

[1] p. 213. If the quaestor was lacking through death or any other cause, the governor appointed one of his *legati* as *pro quaestore* (Cic. *in Verr.* i. 36, 90).

[2] Cic. *pro Planc.* 11, 28 "morem illum majorum qui praescribit in parentum loco quaestoribus suis praetores esse oportere."

[3] ib. *in Verr.* i. 15, 40 "Tu, cum quaestor ad exercitum missus sis, custos non solum pecuniae sed etiam consulis, particeps omnium rerum consiliorumque fueris."

[4] Lydus *de Mag.* i. 27 κρινάντων Ῥωμαίων πολεμεῖν τοῖς συμμαχήσασι Πύρρῳ τῷ Ἠπειρώτῃ κατεσκευάσθη στόλος καὶ προεβλήθησαν οἱ καλούμενοι κλασσικοὶ (οἱονεὶ ναύαρχαι) τῷ ἀριθμῷ δυοκαίδεκα κυαίστωρες. Lydus may be right about the original number, although it has been sometimes thought a confused reminiscence of the raising of the number from four to eight.

[5] Vell. ii. 94 ; cf. Cic. *pro Mur.* 8, 18 "tu illam (provinciam habuisti), cui, cum quaestores sortiuntur, etiam acclamari solet, Ostiensem non tam gratiosam et illustrem quam negotiosam et molestam."

[6] Tac. *Ann.* iv. 27. In 24 A.D. a rising near Brundisium was repressed by "Curtius Lupus quaestor, cui provincia vetere ex more calles evenerant." Mommsen (*Staatsr.* ii. p. 571), following Lipsius, would read Cales, the oldest Latin colony in Campania, and therefore supposes that this quaestor's functions extended over the whole of South Italy. The woods and forests was the *provincia* which the Senate destined for Caesar as proconsul (Suet. *Caes.* 19 "opera optimatibus data est ut provinciae futuris consulibus minimi negotii, id est, silvae callesque, decernerentur").

[7] Plut. *Sert.* 4.

or Ariminum. The fourth is unknown, but was perhaps the quaestorship at Lilybaeum in Sicily, which, after the creation of the first Sicilian praetor in 227 B.C., would have become a provincial post. The other three survived the Republic as spheres of Italian administration.[1] The functions of these quaestors were chiefly the levying of contingents from the allies in ships and men,[2] the protection of the coasts, and at Ostia, as we have seen, the supply of corn for the capital.

A further quaestorian department is mentioned by Cicero—the *provincia aquaria*, which was probably concerned with the water supply of the capital. It is uncertain whether this function was attached to one of the Italian quaestorships.[3]

The Censors

We have already described the institution of the censorship in 443 B C.,[4] and have seen that patrician rank was originally a necessary qualification for the post. The first mention of a plebeian censor is in 351 B.C.[5] One of the Publilian laws of 339 B.C. is said to have extended to the censorship the provision of the Licinian law about the consulship, and to have enacted that one censor must be a Plebeian;[6] but it is not until the year 131 B.C. that we find two plebeian censors.[7]

The election to this office, like that to the other higher magistracies, took place in the *comitia centuriata*[8] under presidency of the consul. The election was then ratified, not, as in the case of other magistrates, by a *lex curiata*, but by a *lex*

---

[1] The last to remain were the Gallic and Ostian, which, as Italian *provinciae*, were abolished by the Emperor Claudius in 44 A.D. (Suet. *Claud.* 24).

[2] So Sertorius, as Gallic quaestor in the Marsic war, was instructed στρατιώτας . . καταλέγειν καὶ ὅπλα ποιεῖσθαι (Plut. *Sert.* 4).

[3] Cicero speaks of Vatinius, when holding this post, being sent to Puteoli on some other business (*in Vat.* 5, 12), but this does not show that he was holding an Italian quaestorship. See Momms. *Staatsr.* ii. p. 573 n. 3.

[4] Liv. iv. 8 ; see p. 115.

[5] ib. vii. 22 (C. Marcius Rutilus) ; cf. x. 8.

[6] ib. viii. 12 "ut alter utique ex plebe, cum eo [ventum sit] ut utrumque plebeium fieri liceret, censor crearetur." Madvig and Mommsen would omit "ventum sit," and so make the Publilian law open both places in the college to Plebeians.

[7] ib. *Ep.* lix. "Q. Pompeius Q. Metellus tunc primum utrique ex plebe facti censores lustrum condiderunt."

[8] Messala ap. Gell. xiii. 15, 4.

centuriata,[1] a form of statutory approval which marks the censors as peculiarly the officials concerned with the organisation of the *exercitus*.

In rank the censor occupies an anomalous position. Although lacking the *imperium* and the right of summoning people and Senate, he is reckoned amongst the *majores magistratus*, he has the "highest *auspicia*,"[2] he sits in the curule chair, wears the purple-striped toga, and (an honour accorded to no other magistrate) is buried in the full purple of the king.[3] Politically the censorship was the apex of a career. Often held in its earlier period by ex-consuls, it became practically confined to the consular, and its enormous powers, its lofty ethical significance, and its comparative infrequency made it the goal of those who had already attained the chief titular dignity of the state.

Four attributes of the office are very important in determining its character. The first gave it the necessary authority, the others created a healthful limitation of its powers.

(1) The censorship was an irresponsible office.[4] Its holders could not be called to account for any act done in connexion with the *census*, any act that was an outcome of the *censoria potestas* ratified by the *lex centuriata;* and although the *lectio senatus* was a later addition to their functions, this power seems to have been included in the indemnity. This principle of immunity was stated in a decree of the Senate of the year 204 B.C.,[5] and, although often challenged by the tribunes, was maintained until the close of the Republic. One of the effects of the Clodian *plebiscitum* of 58 B.C., which limited the discretionary power of the censors in the *regimen morum*,[6] would have been to make them judicially responsible for a breach of its provisions; but this law was soon repealed. The censors were also free from the usual limitation created by the tribunician intercession; it

[1] Cic. *de Leg. Agr.* ii. 11, 26 "majores de singulis magistratibus bis vos sententiam ferre voluerunt : nam cum centuriata lex censoribus ferebatur, cum curiata ceteris patriciis magistratibus, tum iterum de eisdem judicabatur."

[2] Messala ap. Gell. xiii. 15.

[3] Polybius (vi. 53) says that the *imago* of the censor at a funeral was clad in purple. As all the *insignia* of the other magistrates that he mentions are those of their life-time, this should be true of the censors. Perhaps the complete purple was worn for certain ceremonial purposes. Mommsen (*Staatsr.* i. pp. 411 and 446) thinks they were only buried in it.

[4] ἀρχὴ ἀνυπεύθυνος (Dionys. xix. 16).

[5] Liv. xxix. 37 ; Val. Max. vii. 2, 6.

[6] Ascon. *in Pison.* p. 9.

was clearly invalid against the particular *potestas* exercised at the *census*,[1] although the *obnuntiatio* could be employed against the summons of the people to the *census* and the *lustrum*, as against any other *contio*.[2]

(2) The limitation of tenure to eighteen months caused a break in the continuity of the magistracy, and was a symbol that the office was merely occasional. The censorial ordinances were valid for the whole quinquennial period of the *lustrum*, but, whatever may have been the original intention of the limitation of tenure, it was continued as an effective guarantee against such enormous powers being exercised for a continuous period of four or five years.[3]

(3) Re-election to the censorship was forbidden, for a continuous moral control exercised by the same men would have been intolerable.[4]

(4) The collegiate principle operated here as in other offices, but nowhere was the check of the veto more necessary and more healthy than in its influence on the arbitrary moral judgments of the censors. Without it the Senate might have been packed by a single man, and degradation from the highest positions and on the scantiest evidence might have been due to caprice, and followed by the unpopularity which divided responsibility renders less intense.[5] The collegiate relation was, indeed, closer in this than in any other magistracy. Its holders must be elected together, the name of the singly-appointed censor not being returned;[6] and, whether from grounds of convenience or

---

[1] Hence the helplessness of the tribune against censorial animadversion. Cf. Liv. xliv. 16 "multis equi adempti, inter quos P. Rutilio, qui tr. pl. eos violenter accusarat: tribu quoque is motus et aerarius factus."

[2] Cic. *ad Att.* iv. 9, 1.

[3] For the later mode of regarding this limitation see Liv. iv. 24 "grave esse iisdem per tot annos magna parte vitae obnoxios vivere." But, if the tenure was fixed by the *lex Aemilia* (of the dictator Mamercus Aemilius, 434 B.C., Liv. l.c.), it originated before the censorship had become a dangerous power.

[4] Liv. xxiii. 23 "nec censoriam vim uni permissam et eidem iterum." The prohibition is attributed to a law of Marcius Rutilus Censorinus, censor 294 and 265 B.C. (Plut. *Cor.* 1; cf. Val. Max. iv. 1, 3); but it could not have been his work, at least as censor, for this official had not the *jus rogandi*. See Momms. *Staatsr.* i. p. 520.

[5] It is Cicero's business in the *pro Cluentio* (43, 122) to represent this divergence of view as a weakness in the censorship; cf. Liv. xlii. 10 (173 B.C.) "concors et e re publica censura fuit . . neque ab altero notatum alter probavit." But it was a necessary condition of the continuance of the office in a free state.

[6] Liv. ix. 34 "cum ita comparatum a majoribus sit ut comitiis censoriis nisi duo confecerint legitima suffragia, non renuntiato altero comitia differantur."

from a religious scruple, it was enacted that, if one post was vacated by abdication or death, the holder of the other should resign.[1]

The original and specific powers of the censors, various as they seem, form a perfect unity. Their work is briefly that of numbering and purifying the people. The accompaniments of this *census* are (i.) registration, i.e. the assignment of individuals to their proper state-divisions; (ii.) the decision of the incidence of financial burdens, based on an estimate of the property of individuals; (iii.) the consideration of the moral worth of individuals with reference to their fitness to exercise various functions of state, known generally as the *regimen morum*; (iv.) the purification (*lustrum*), perhaps to avert the anger of the gods from the iniquity of numbering the people, perhaps merely a regularly recurring atonement for involuntary sin, the voluntary sinners being first removed by the exclusion effected by the *cura morum*.

To this aggregate two functions were added: first, the *lectio senatus*, which, although no part of the *census*, is an outcome of the same activity and forms an integral part of the *regimen morum*; secondly, financial duties, such as the leasing of taxes and *opera publica*—functions that any of the supreme magistrates could perform. They are not an integral part of the *census*, and this portion of the censors' business is conducted under senatorial supervision.[2]

I. The *lectio senatus*, although in the eyes of the censors and of the world the first of their charges, was but a late attachment to their office. Even in the year 311 B.C. the consuls could still venture to set aside a censorian list and return to the practice of selecting their own *consilium*,[3] and later still (216 B.C.) a dictator could be chosen for the purpose of filling up gaps in the order.[4] A *lex Ovinia*, a *plebiscitum* of uncertain date, may have made the

---

[1] Tradition attributed the origin of this rule to a religious scruple, "quia eo lustro (in which a *suffectus* was appointed) Roma est capta: nec deinde unquam in demortui locum censor sufficitur" (Liv. v. 31).

[2] Cicero mixes up the earlier and later functions in his pseudo-law, which expresses all the activities of the censors (*de Leg.* iii. 3, 7), "Censores populi aevitates, suboles, familias pecuniasque censento: urbis, tecta, templa, vias, aquas, aerarium, vectigalia tuento: populiquè partes in tribus discribunto: exin pecunias, aevitates, ordines partiunto: equitum peditumque prolem discribunto: caelibes esse prohibento: mores populi regunto: probrum in senatu ne relinquunto."

[3] Liv. ix. 30.   [4] ib. xxiii. 22; see p. 193.

censors mainly responsible for the *lectio*, but the fragmentary
paraphrase of its contents, which has been preserved, merely
limits their discretionary power in the exercise of their choice.
The censors are to choose "the best men," a direction which,
interpreted by our knowledge of later methods of selection,
implies at the least that ex-curule magistrates must be chosen,[1]
at the most that the whole list of magistrates (including the
plebeian aediles and the quaestors) should be scrutinised before
censorian nominees were appointed.[2]

The framing of the Senate's list was, in accordance with the
estimate of its importance, the first work of the censors after
their entrance on office. It was accomplished rapidly, for there
was no summoning of the Senate as a corporation, or even of
individuals, as at the *census*. Facilities may have been offered
to a senator of clearing himself of charges,[3] but formal procedure
was dispensed with, and nowhere was the arbitrary power of the
censors more manifest than in the execution of this the gravest
of their duties.

Rejection took the form of affixing marks (*notae*) against
names in the register; these names were omitted in the revised
list. Then took place the *sublectio* of new names, and here the
censure was pronounced by omitting those who had a claim to
a seat in the house.[4] The veto, which operated in its constantly
negative manner, which enabled one censor to retain a name
omitted by the other,[5] or even perhaps to hinder the election
of a new member selected by his colleague, and the written
grounds for censure appended to the rejected name (*sub-*

---

[1] In the great *sublectio* after Cannae (216 B.C.) the ex-curule magistrates not
already on the list were chosen in the order of their tenure of power ; then the
ex-aediles, ex-tribunes of the *plebs* and the *quaestorii*, lastly men of distinction
who had held no magistracy (Liv. xxiii. 23).

[2] Festus p. 246 "Ovinia tribunicia intervenit, qua sanctum est ut censores
ex omni ordine optimum quemque jurati (*Cod.* curiati, *Mommsen* curiatim) in
senatum legerent."   If "ex omni ordine" means "from every grade of the
magistracy," the second interpretation is necessary.

[3] The *oratio* of Cato as censor against L. Quinctius Flaminius was delivered *post
notam* (Liv. xxxix. 42) ; but it suggests that the censors felt themselves bound at
times to give reasons for their actions.

[4] The phrases for rejection and omission are *movere, ejicere, praeterire*. The
last applies both to existing and to expectant senators, and has reference to the
public reading of the list (*recitatio*) (Cic. *pro Domo* 32, 84 "praeteriit in recitando
senatu").

[5] Liv. xli. 57 "retinuit quosdam Lepidus a collega praeteritos" ; cf. Cic.
pro Cluent. 43, 122.

scriptio censoria),[1] were some guarantees against capricious exclusion.

The automatic method of recruiting the Senate introduced by Sulla produced a modification in the censorian selection. The magistrates seem to have lost the power of rejecting applicants, their right of exclusion being confined to names already on the list. It is not known whether the censors at a subsequent *lustrum* still retained the power of reversing an *infamia* once pronounced ; but the usual mode in which a seat was regained by an ejected senator was to seek popular election and to enter the Senate through a magistracy.[2]

II. The *census* opened with a summons to the people to meet the censors in the Campus Martius. It was the army as exhibited in the centuriate list that the censors wished primarily to examine, and, consequently, it was the members of this body that they summoned to appear in person ; the *capite censi*, with their votes in the tribes and their taxable capital, might be represented only by the *curatores tribuum*,[3] although the censor could summon any member of the burgess community whom he pleased.[4]

The financial examination at each *census*, which had as its object the rating for the *tributum*, was based on the returns of the last scrutiny. There was, therefore, some means of checking the declarations now made on oath by each head of a family, and in doubtful cases external evidence must have been taken. The returns were made in accordance with the instructions of a general formula (*lex censui censendo*) which the censors had published ;[5] but their general conditions must always have been the same. First came a declaration of the size of the property, then of its value. But the estimate of the individual owner need not be accepted by the censors ; they often attached an exaggerated estimate to articles of luxury,[6] or expressed their disapprobation

---

[1] For a type of *subscriptio* see Ascon. *in or. in Tog. Cand.* p. 84 "Antonium Gellius et Lentulus censores . . senatu moverunt causasque subscripserunt, quod socios diripuerit, quod judicium recusarit, quod propter aeris alieni magnitudinem praedia manciparit bonaque sua in potestate non habeat."

[2] Usually the praetorship or quaestorship. Momms. *Staatsr.* i. p. 521 n. 3.

[3] See the formula of summons in Varro (*L.L.* vi. 86), "omnes Quirites pedites armatos, privatosque curatores omnium tribuum, si quis pro se sive pro altero rationem dari volet, vocato in licium huc ad me."

[4] Mommsen believes in a special summons to the *capite censi* (*Staatsr.* ii. p. 366).

[5] Liv. xliii. 14.

[6] Cato in 184 assessed articles of luxury at ten times their value (Liv. xxxix. 44 ; Plut. *Cat. Maj.* 18).

of social or moral offences by an arbitrary and excessive rating of the goods of the offenders.[1]

All the property thus assessed must be the object of quiritarian ownership. Originally it had been but the land and the animals associated with it (*res mancipi*),[2] such objects as had been conveyed by mancipation, and for the evidence of the transfer of which from hand to hand the mancipation witness could be summoned. But the growing mercantile community had to take account of movables, and throughout the historical period all objects of property, corporeal or incorporeal, which constituted *pecunia* in the later sense of the word, were subject to valuation and taxation.[3] After the time when direct taxation ceased in Italy (167 B.C.) the valuation was no longer made for the *tributum ;* but property was still for a time the determinant of the kinds of military service and voting rights, and the censors had still to scrutinise the professions of the assessed, although the scrutiny was perhaps conducted with less rigour than before.

As it was the head of the family alone that could give an account of property, so it was to him that the censor put the requisite questions as to the persons dependent on his care. The respondent gave not only his own name, his father's and his age, but made similar declarations about his son, his daughter, and his wife.[4] Inquiries about the female members of the family were chiefly undertaken on moral grounds ; they were of no importance for the work of registration, whose object was to assign voting rights and military burdens. Of the three subdivisions of the Roman state—the *curia*, the tribe, the century —the first was not considered by the censor, for the *curia*, like the *gens*, was inherited. The assignment of the tribe varied at different periods. If there was never a time in the history of the censorship when it had been confined to land-holders,[5] the possessor of an allotment was naturally registered in the *tribus*

---

[1] Liv. iv. 24 " Mamercum . . . tribu moverunt octuplicatoque censu aerarium fecerunt "; Val. Max. ii. 9, 1 "Camillus et Postumius censores aera poenae nomine eos, qui ad senectutem caelibes pervenerant, in aerarium deferre jusserunt."   [2] See p. 69.

[3] Cic. *de Leg.* iii. 3, 7 "familias pecuniasque censento " ; *lex Jul. Munic.* l. 147 "rationem pecuniae . . . accipito." *Pecunia* here applies to both *res mancipi* and *nec mancipi.*

[4] Cic. l.c. " aevitates suboles . . . censento"; *lex Jul. Munic.* l. 145 "eorum . . . nomina, praenomina, patres . . . et quot annos quisque eerum habet . . . accipito."   [5] p. 68.

which contained his plot of ground, the non-possessor in that
wherein he dwelt.   But, by the year 312 B.C., the landless
citizens had already been confined to the four urban tribes; the
radical censor of that year distributed them even over the
country tribes, to increase the voting power of this *forensis
factio;*[1] but in 304 B.C. the landless proletariate was again confined to the *tribus urbanae,*[2] and hence arose the permanent
distinction between the more honourable country and the less
distinguished city tribe.   As a matter of fact, this distinction
between the landed and the landless citizen could not continue
when all property, personal as well as real, became of equal
value at the *census,* and membership of the tribe became practically hereditary.   But it was a heredity which might be broken
by the censor at every period of registration.   He might, as we
shall see, arbitrarily transfer an individual from his paternal
country tribe to one of the four urban divisions, which, partly
from historical reasons, partly because they contained the freedmen, were accounted less distinguished.

The distribution into centuries naturally followed the distinctions of property and age which qualified for those bodies.   The
list which set forth this distribution was still pre-eminently an
army list, but the table of seniors (*tabulae seniorum*) undoubtedly
contained the names of those who were past the age of compulsory service.   The *sexagenarii,* although the young bloods might
object to their voting for a war in which they were not to share,[3]

[1] Liv. ix. 46 "forensis factio App. Claudi censura vires nacta, qui . . .
humilibus per omnes tribus divisis forum et campum corrupit." Cf. Diod. xx.
46 (App. Claudius) ἔδωκε τοῖς πολίταις ὅποι προαιροῖντο τιμήσασθαι. Mommsen
imagines that it was in this year that the landless citizens *first* found a place in
the tribes (*Staatsr.* ii. 392 sq., 402 sq.).

[2] Liv. l.c. "aliud integer populus . . . aliud forensis factio tendebat. . . .
Fabius simul concordiae causa, simul ne humilimorum in manu comitia essent,
omnem forensem turbam excretam in quattuor tribus conjecit urbanasque eas
appellavit."

[3] *Sexagenarius de ponte.* Cf. Cic. *pro Rosc. Amer.* 35, 100 "Habeo etiam
dicere, quem contra morem majorum, minorem annis LX de ponte in Tiberim
dejecerit"; Festus p. 334 "quo tempore primum per pontem coeperunt comitiis
suffragium ferre, juniores conclamaverunt ut de ponte dejicerentur sexagenari, qui
jam nullo publico munere fungerentur, ut ipsi potius sibi quam illi deligerent
imperatorem." If *pons* could be taken literally, a curious parallel is furnished
by early Slavonic procedure. "The vechés passed whole days in debating the
same subjects, the only interruptions being free fights in the streets. At Nov-
gorod these fights took place on the bridge across the Volchov, and the stronger
party sometimes threw their adversaries into the river beneath" (Kovalevsky
Modern Customs and Ancient Laws of Russia p. 138).

or electing a general by whom they would not be led, still had the right of taking part in the deliberations of the *comitia centuriata*.

It is obvious that the complete census of tribes and centuries included every voting unit of Rome, and, in spite of the fact that an individual scrutiny of the *aerarii* may not have taken place,[1] we must suppose that there was a tribal list of *all* the citizens which proved the right to vote at the *comitia tributa* and the *concilium plebis*. But it is almost certain that, when an historian mentions a census of Republican times, he is reproducing merely the army list,[2] the vital element in registration for a military state. All under the military age are excluded, and it has even been concluded that in the historical lists the *seniores* themselves are not entered.[3] The *proletarii* are potentially, and in a sense actually, members of the Roman army;[4] but it is very questionable whether they appear in the Republican lists. It was, perhaps, not until the Principate that the census contained the names of all male Romans above the military age.[5]

III. *The recognitio equitum.*—The word *equites* primarily and properly applied only to the citizen cavalry of 1800 men, serving on horses supplied by the state.[6] These formed the *centuriae equitum equo publico*, and this class was the *ordo equester* in the strict sense.

It is true that *equites* had come to have a wider meaning than this. About the close of the fifth century, individuals possessing a certain census and not included in the equestrian centuries were permitted to serve as cavalry with their own horses.[7] They were no definite body, but were selected for a particular service by the commander, if the censors had admitted their pecuniary qualification.[8] The consequence was that the terms

---

[1] p. 221.
[2] " Eorum qui arma ferre possent " (Liv. i. 44), τῶν ἐχόντων τὴν στρατεύσιμον ἡλικίαν (Dionys. xi. 63), τῶν ἐν ταῖς ἡλικίαις (Polyb. ii. 24).
[3] Momms. *Staatsr.* ii. p. 411.
[4] p. 72.
[5] Beloch *der Italische Bund* p. 78.
[6] p. 73.
[7] The change is put by tradition at the time of the siege of Veii (403 B.C., Liv. v. 7 "quibus census equester erat, equi publici non erant adsignati . . . senatum adeunt factaque dicendi potestate equis se suis stipendia facturos promittunt "). Livy here assumes a *census* as existing for the *equites equo publico*, but it is questionable whether it was not transferred from these new *equites* (*equo privato* as they are called by modern historians) to the old equestrian centuries.
[8] Polyb. vi. 20 πλουτίνδην αὐτῶν γεγενημένης ὑπὸ τοῦ τιμητοῦ τῆς ἐκλογῆς.

eques and even *ordo equester* were transferred to these potential knights, and came to specify all who possessed a certain census, which, in the Principate and probably in the later Republic, was 400,000 sesterces.[1]   The censorship was only concerned with this wider body of knights as the authority which proved the monetary qualification of its individual members.   The only body of *equites* which it recognised and treated as a corporation was that of the eighteen centuries.

The review of the knights (*equitum census*,[2] *recognitio equitum*[3]) took place, not like that of the rest of the citizens in the Campus Martius, but in the Forum.   The whole corps filed past the censor man by man, each knight leading his horse by the bridle, as the herald called his name.[4]   The first question considered by the censors was that of discharge.   While the knights were still the cavalry of Rome, the service was a burden, and a burden that from the close of the second century of the Republic was made incompatible with a seat in the Senate.[5]   In the Gracchan period, as we have seen, ten years' service had to be proved before the knight could claim his dismissal.[6]   The discharge was usually granted, if the conditions had been fulfilled, but the censors, as a penal measure, claimed the right of not allowing past service to count, and even of imposing additional service at the knight's own expense.[7]   Ignominious discharge, before the completed term of service, was a consequence of military negligence, as shown, for instance, by the shabby condition of the public horse (*impolitia*),[8] or of any moral blemish, which in other ranks of life would have entailed dismissal from the Senate or the tribes.   The form of dismissal was "sell your horse" (*vende*

---

[1] There is no direct authority for this particular *census* earlier than the Principate.   The fact that a *census*, approximating to or identical with the equestrian, was required for *judices* under the Gracchan law, and the specification that these should not be senators or members of senatorial families, led to these judges being called "knights."   They were selected from a class practically identical with that of the *equites equo privato*.

[2] Cic. *pro Cluent.* 48, 134.   [3] Suet. *Claud.* 16.

[4] Val. Max. ii. 9, 7.

[5] Cic. *de Rep.* iv. 2, 2.   So Pompeius, a consul who had never been a senator (70 B.C.), claims and obtains his discharge before he enters on his office (Plut. *Pomp.* 22).

[6] Plut. *C. Gracch.* 2.   See p. 184.

[7] Liv. xxvii. 11 (209 B.C.) "(Censores) addiderunt acerbitati (the deprivation of the public horse) etiam tempus, ne praeterita stipendia procederent eis, quae equo publico meruerant, sed dena stipendia equis privatis facerent."

[8] Gell. iv. 12 ; Festus p. 108.

Q

equum), of retention "lead it on" (*traduc equum*).[1] The censors' final duty was to fill up the vacant gaps in the centuries. This was done by the enrolment, at their own discretion, of qualified members from the infantry (*pedites*).

This procedure was but one example of that wider censure which was directed against the citizen body at the time of its registration in the Campus Martius. This scrutiny was preceded by an edict in which the censors declared some of their moral canons — canons, we may believe, that were transmitted from college to college and seldom departed from — while they animadverted on new evils which they believed to be undermining the life of the state.[2] The acts which called forth their censure may be conveniently considered under four heads.

(i.) Those concerned with family life and private relations. The father as the domestic magistrate or judge[3] was wholly responsible for the conduct of the little world of the family, and the censor exercised his control over women vicariously through their husbands.[4] The objects of censorian animadversion were the cruel punishment of slaves,[5] the wrong done to a client, which had been formerly punished by pontifical law,[6] the bad education of children, whether it took the form of undue harshness or of over-indulgence,[7] and the non-performance of the *sacra* of the clan.[8] The censors discountenanced celibacy,[9] imposing additional taxation on persistent bachelors.[10] They discouraged *mésalliances* such as unions between free-born citizens and freedwomen,[11] and checked the legal freedom of divorce. In the usual marriage by *consensus* a mere repudiation on the part of the husband was sufficient to dissolve the tie;[12] but the censors

---

[1] Cic. *pro Cluent.* 48, 134; Liv. xxix. 37. Removal from the ranks is described as a deprivation of the horse (*adimere equum*, Liv. xxiv. 18, xli. 2, 7).

[2] A fragment of a censorian edict of 92 B.C. directed against the "Latini rhetores" has been preserved. It contains the words "Haec nova, quae praeter consuetudinem ac morem majorum fiunt, neque placent neque recta videntur" (Suet. *de Clar. Rhet.* 1; Gell. xv. 11, 2).

[3] "Judex domesticus," "domesticus magistratus" (Sen. *Controv.* ii. 3; *de Benef.* iii. 11).

[4] Cic. *de Rep.* iv. 6, 16 "Nec vero mulieribus praefectus praeponatur, qui apud Graecos creari solet; sed sit censor qui viros doceat moderari uxoribus."

[5] Dionys. xx. 13.   [6] p. 55.   [7] Dionys. l.c.

[8] Festus p. 344.

[9] Cic. *de Leg.* iii. 3, 7 "coelibes esse prohibento."

[10] Val. Max. ii. 9, 1 "Camillus et Postumius censores aera poenae nomine eos, qui ad senectutem coelibes pervenerant, in aerarium deferre jusserunt."

[11] Liv. xxxix. 19.   [12] Cic. *Phil.* ii. 28, 69.

restrained a reckless exercise of this power, and we find a senator
degraded for divorcing his wife without taking advice of the
family council.[1] They also punished bad husbandry, neglect of
property,[2] and luxurious living,[3] and enforced good faith (*fides*)
in the execution of informal contracts which were not yet
protected by the sanctions of the civil law. This was especially
the case with guardianship (*tutela*),[4] but their scrutiny extended
to all legal relations that were held to involve *bona fides*, such as
those of partnership, mandate, and deposit.[5]

(ii.) Disqualifications were pronounced as a consequence of
certain modes of life, trades, or professions. Actors were per-
petually disqualified from all civic privileges,[6] and gladiators
were probably subject to a similar degradation.[7] Amongst dis-
honourable employments was reckoned that of a money-lender
who exacted an excessive rate of interest.[8]

(iii.) Breaches of political duty in any sphere called down
the censor's displeasure. The magistrate might be degraded for
cruelty or insubordination in the exercise of his office,[9] for the
neglect of constitutional formalities,[10] for a misuse of the auspices,[11]
or even for the passing of a law likely to injure the morals of
the community.[12] The *judex* might be punished for accepting

---

[1] Val. Max. ii. 9, 2 "M. Val. Maximus et C. Junius Brutus Bubulcus
censores . . . L. Annium senatu moverunt, quod, quam virginem in matrimonium duxerat, repudiasset, nullo amicorum in consilio adhibito "

[2] Plin. *H.N.* xviii. 3, 11.

[3] Plut. *Ti. Gracch.* 14 ; Val. Max. ii. 9, 4. For excessive taxation imposed
on articles of luxury see Liv. xxxix. 44 ; Plut. *Cat. Maj.* 18 ; and p. 221.

[4] Cf. Gell. v. 13 " M. Cato in oratione, quam dixit apud censores in Lentulum,
ita scripsit : 'quod majores sanctius habuere defendi pupillos quam clientem non
fallere.'"

[5] Greenidge *Infamia in Roman Law* p. 67.

[6] Even amateur performances might call down the *nota*. See Suet. *Dom.* 8
(Domitian) "suscepta correctione morum . . . quaestorium virum, quod gesticulandi saltandique studio teneretur, movit senatu."

[7] The *lex Julia Municipalis* excludes them, like actors, from the municipal
senate ; the *lex Acilia repetundarum* from the bench of *judices*.

[8] Suet. *Aug.* 39 "notavitque aliquos quod, pecunias levioribus usuris mutuati,
graviori foenore collocassent."

[9] Plut. *Cat. Maj.* 17 ; *C. Gracch.* 2.

[10] Gell. xiv. 7 "opus etiam censorium fecisse existimatos, per quos eo tempore
(i.e. at an unlawful time) senatus consultum factum esset."

[11] Cic. *de Div.* i. 16, 29 "Appius . . . censor C. Ateium (tribune 55 B.C.)
notavit, quod ementitum auspicia subscriberet."

[12] Val. Max. ii. 9, 5 " M. autem Antonius et L. Flaccus censores (97 B.C.)
Duronium senatu moverunt, quod legem de coercendis conviviorum sumptibus
latam tribunus plebi abrogaverat."

bribes,[1] the soldier or officer for shirking service or for showing cowardice or disobedience,[2] and the voting citizen for a misuse of his judicial or elective power.[3] Disgraceful conduct in a court of law might also entail the censure. It visited the collusion of a prosecutor with the accused or malicious prosecution in a criminal case (*praevaricatio, calumnia*),[4] and attended false witness and false oaths. Since there was no secular punishment for perjury, its visitation was peculiarly the work of the censors.[5]

(iv.) The censors sometimes pronounced disqualifications as the result of a judicial sentence.[6] Theft and other private delicts were attended with infamy, and sometimes the censure was independent of the judgment of a court.[7] The censure, which followed a criminal condemnation, might be either one of the censors' own creation[8] or the mere fulfilment of a disqualification already enjoined by law. Of the second kind were the disabilities pronounced by the *lex Cassia* of 104 B.C.[9] or by the *lex Calpurnia de ambitu* of 67 B.C., the latter of which enjoined perpetual exclusion from the Senate as a result of condemnation.[10]

IV. The effects of the censorian *infamia* depended partly on the rank of the person disqualified, but were always regulated to some extent by the gravity of the offence. The senator was removed from the list, the knight from the equestrian centuries, the commoner is said *tribu moveri* or *aerarius fieri*, or both.[11] "Removal

[1] Cic. *pro Cluent.* 42, 119 ; 48, 121 ; Suet. *Dom.* 8.
[2] Liv. xxiv. 18 ; xxvii. 11 and 25.
[3] In 204 B.C. the censor M. Livius disfranchised for the purposes of the *comitia centuriata* (*aerarios reliquit*) thirty-four out of the thirty-five tribes "quod et innocentem se condemnassent et condemnatum consulem et censorem fecissent" (Liv. xxix. 37).
[4] *Lex Jul. Munic.* l. 120.
[5] Cic. *de Off.* iii. 31, 111 "indicant (the sanctity of the oath in former times) notiones animadversionesque censorum, qui nulla de re diligentius quam de jure jurando judicabant."
[6] To this form of disqualification the name "mediate *infamia*" has been given by modern jurists.
[7] Cic. *pro Cluent.* 42, 120 "quos autem ipsi L. Gellius et Cn. Lentulus duo censores . . . furti et captarum pecuniarum nomine notaverunt, ii non modo in senatum redierunt, sed etiam illarum ipsarum rerum judiciis absoluti sunt."
[8] Liv. xxix. 37 (in 204 B.C., Claudius Nero) "M. Livium (his colleague), quia populi judicio esset damnatus, equum vendere jussit."
[9] It enacted "ut quem populus damnasset cuive imperium abrogasset in senatu ne esset" (Ascon. *in Cornelian.* p. 78).
[10] Dio Cass. xxxvi. 21.
[11] Liv. xlv. 15 "omnes iidem ab utroque et tribu remoti et aerarii facti" ; xliv. 16 "tribu quoque is motus et aerarius factus" ; xxvii. 11 ; xxix. 37 "aerarios reliquit."

from the tribe" has two meanings : either that of the milder penalty of relegation from a higher to a lower tribe, or of the severer punishment of total exclusion from the tribes, while *aerarium facere* implies exclusion from the centuries.[1]

V. *The lustrum.*—After the ranks of the various orders had thus been purified, the lustral sacrifice (*lustratio*) was offered for the whole assembled army in the field of Mars.[2] The ox, the sheep, and the pig (*suovetaurilia*), which were led round the host and then sacrificed to the god, were at once an atonement for sin and a thanksgiving for blessings prayed for at the preceding *lustrum* and since vouchsafed.[3] The completion of this ceremonial marked the close of the censor's functions, at least of those connected with the *census*.

VI. *Other functions of the censors.*—The necessity for the division of functions, which had created the censorship, led to financial duties, analogous to but unconnected with those of the *census*, being taken from other magistracies and attached to that office. These were the leasing of the public revenues, the maintenance of public property, and the administrative jurisdiction connected with these duties.

The Roman state, in its administration of the public property, had always favoured the system of contracting out. The system was that of purchase or lease by middlemen (*publicani*) of a prospective source of revenue, which the individual or the company farmed at its own risk or profit. Sometimes the middleman was himself the occupant (*possessor*) of, or the contractor (*conductor*) for, the source of wealth from which the revenue was derived. This principle was applied to limited sources of wealth or those requiring particular industrial appliances, such as fisheries, salt-works, mines, and forest-land. This system of direct farming was sometimes applied to domain-land both in Italy and the provinces. The *ager Campanus* was dealt with in this way, and the royal domains of the kings whom Rome had supplanted were, with the confiscated territory of Corinth, let on long leases

---

[1] See Greenidge *Infamia in Roman Law* pp. 106-110. Mommsen (*Staatsr.* ii. pp. 402 ff.) makes the expressions *tribu movere* and *in aerarios referre* identical after 312 B.C. and interprets both as signifying the removal from a higher to a lower tribe.   [2] Liv. i. 44 ; Dionys. iv. 22.

[3] At each *lustrum vota* were offered "quae in proximum lustrum suscipi mos est" (Suet. *Aug.* 97). Before the censorship of Scipio Aemilianus it had been the custom to pray "ut populi Romani res meliores amplioresque facerent" ; after it, on his initiative, "ut eas perpetuo incolumes servent" (Val. Max. iv. 1, 10).

to *publicani*,[1] who doubtless in most cases sublet these territories to smaller holders. Such contracts were put up to auction, and their terms were fixed by a *lex censoria* dictated by the censor as the representative of the state. This *lex*, besides specifying the revenue which the lessee was required to pay, also fixed the conditions under which the contract was to be undertaken.[2]

The second kind of tax-farmer is a true middleman.[3] The *publicanus* here is not himself employed in working the source of wealth; he is not a *possessor* or occupant, but one who has bought from the state the right to collect revenue from such an occupant. The right is put up to auction and bought for a fixed sum, for which the company of successful contractors furnishes security. Their gains depend on the prospective surplus of the revenue which they propose to farm over the sum which they have agreed to pay. This was the method of dealing with the public land which had been left open for occupation by squatters (*occupatorius ager*). It was either tilled land (*ager*) enjoyed by a *possessor*, or pasture land (*silva pascua, saltus*) over which the *pastor* grazed his flocks. Both occupants were tolerated by the state on condition that they paid a fixed due for their precarious tenure.[4] The *publicani* were the men who had the right to collect this *vectigal* from the user of the land, and the dues which they might collect were determined by the *lex dicta* under which the censor sold the right.[5] A further class of revenues collected in this manner were the harbour dues (*portoria*). They were based on the same leading idea of the use of public ground by a private occupant; he pays

---

[1] Cic. *de Leg. Agr.* ii. 19, 50 and 51 ; 29, 81. The leases were sometimes of considerable duration (Hyginus p. 116 Lachm. "Ex hoste capti agri postquam divisi sunt per centurias . . . qui superfuerunt agri vectigalibus subjecti sunt, alii per annos [quinos], alii per annos centenos pluresve : finito illo tempore iterum veneunt locanturque ita ut vectigalibus est consuetudo ").

[2] e.g. a *lex censoria* enjoined that not more than five thousand workmen should be employed in the gold mines of Vercellae by the contractor who worked them (Plin. *H.N.* xxxiii. 78).

[3] The jurists inform us that this is the true sense of *publicanus;* the *conductores* are only *publicanorum loco* (*Dig.* 39, 4, 12, 13). In common parlance, however, both are *publicani*, and this usage is etymologically justifiable, since they are both concerned with a *publicum*, a word which denotes state revenue and state service (*Dig.* 39, 4, 1 ; Tac. *Ann.* xiii. 51 ; Liv. xxiii. 49, 1).

[4] *Vectigal* (ἀποφορά Plut. *Ti. Gracch.* 8 ; cf. App. *B.C.* i. 7). In the case of pasture land it was called *scriptura* (Festus p. 333).

[5] *Lex agraria* l. 85 "ex lege dicta, quam . . censores . . deixerunt, publicano dare oportuit."

for this use, and the right of collecting this *vectigal* within a given area is sold to a company of *publicani*. A great extension was given to this system of tax-farming by its application to provincial administration. The Roman translated the tithe (δεκάτη, *decuma*) which he found in Sicily and Asia into his own familiar *vectigal*, but for a time he adhered to the existing conditions of local collection, and in Sicily the tithes were sold in the island itself in accordance with the *lex Hieronica*.[1] Asia was the first province to which the experiment of a collective sale of the taxes in Rome was applied.[2] The system was apparently extended to the Asiatic provinces organised by Pompeius, and the censorship was the normal vehicle through which the revenues of a vast kingdom could be purchased by a company of Roman speculators.

The censors exercised great discretionary powers in the conclusion of these contracts, but a revision of such as had already been concluded belonged not to them but to the Senate.[3] Their merely executive capacity is an explanation of the fact that they could not alienate the property of the Roman people. Wherever the sale of public lands or buildings by these officials is described, we must assume the concurrence of the people or the Senate.

The extent of the censors' control of the property of the state made their registers (*tabulae*) assume the proportions of a budget, which must have been the guide of the state's expenditure. Although only quinquennial, this budget was tolerably stable, for the varying returns (as opposed to the invariable revenues, such as the fixed tribute of some of the provinces) were estimated for the interval that elapsed between one *lustrum* and another. An unusual increment, such as that from booty, which might appear in any year, would have formed the ground for a statement made by the quaestors, the permanent officials of the *aerarium*.

But, although estimates were made by the censor, he had little to do with general expenditure. He had no concern with the provinces and the army, and was limited to the maintenance

<hr/>

[1] Cic. *in Verr.* ii. 26, 63 ; 60, 147 ; iii. 7, 18.
[2] ib. iii. 6, 12 and 14.
[3] Polyb. vi. 17. The Senate can συμπτώματος γενομένου κουφίσαι καὶ τὸ παράπαν ἀδυνάτου τινὸς συμβάντος ἀπολῦσαι τῆς ἐργωνίας. Cf. the section on the Senate's control of property. In 169 and 59 B.C. we find the people releasing from an oppressive contract (Liv. xliii. 16 ; App. *B.C.* ii. 13).

and extension of the public property of the state. He was
either a maker or a repairer of *opera publica*, such as roads,
aqueducts, temples, and public buildings.[1] Such buildings or
repairs were leased out to contractors, the state here becoming
the debtor of a private company and seeking to obtain the
lowest estimate for the work.[2] For the purpose of repairs or
new works a credit (*pecunia attributa*) was granted by the Senate,
which directed the quaestors to employ this money at the
discretion of the censors.[3] Within the limits of this sum they
could act at their own discretion with respect to the modes of
expenditure, although they doubtless took the advice of the
Senate. These grants and the purposes to which they were
applied were known by the strange name of *ultro tributa*,[4] a
designation which may be a relic of a time when such *opera* were
not leased, but were burdens (*munera, moenia*), owed as a voluntary
tribute by the community.[5]

These financial functions of the censors gave rise to an
administrative jurisdiction. In their guardianship of public
places they decided where private buildings had encroached on
state property,[6] or where public buildings had been usurped by
privati.[7] They may at times have pronounced on the pecuniary
penalties meant to enforce the rights of public property, for
they sometimes exercised their coercive power and proclaimed
varying penalties (*multae*) to compel obedience;[8] but such
quasi - criminal jurisdiction must have been exercised more
frequently by the aediles, and, where the amount of the fine
necessitated the appeal, it must have been pronounced and

---

[1] Cic. *de Leg.* iii. 3, 7 "templa, vias, aquas . . tuento"; *ad Fam.* xiii. 11, 1
"sarta tecta (i.e. the repairs of walls and roofs) aedium sacrarum locorumque
communium tueri."

[2] Cf. Liv. xxxix. 44 "ultro tributa infimis (pretiis) locaverunt."

[3] ib. xliv. 16 "ad opera publica facienda cum eis (censoribus) dimidium ex
vectigalibus ejus anni attributum ex senatus consulto a quaestoribus esset";
xl. 46 "censoribus deinde postulantibus ut pecuniae summa sibi, qua in opera
publica uterentur, attribueretur, vectigal annuum decretum est."

[4] *Lex Jul. Munic.* l. 73 ; Liv. xxxix. 44 (quoted n. 2).

[5] Mommsen (*Staatsr.* ii. p. 446) takes the phrase to mean something "voluntarily granted" by the Senate to the magistrate.

[6] Liv. xxxix. 44. The later tendency, however, was for such public rights
to be protected by the praetor's interdicts.

[7] ib. xl. 51 "complura sacella publica quae fuerant occupata a privatis
publica sacraque ut essent paterentque populo curarunt."

[8] ib. xliii. 16 "censores ad pignora capienda miserunt multamque pro
contione privato dixerunt."

defended by the latter magistrates.   Jurisdiction bearing a
resemblance to that of civil law was concerned with the *ultro
tributa*, when the question arose whether a contract had been
carried out satisfactorily or not, and with disputes about the
public land, the controversy in the latter case lying most
frequently between the *publicanus* and the *possessor*,[1] but sometimes, no doubt, between one who claimed to be an owner on
the one hand and the middleman or an occupant on the other.
The form of this jurisdiction varied.   Sometimes, when the
dispute lay between the state and an individual, as in the
controversies about the *ultro tributa*, the sentence was the result
of a purely magisterial cognisance, although we may suppose
that the censor could, if he pleased, give a *judex* in such a case.
Where the dispute lay between two *privati*, even though one
of them had the quasi-official position of a *publicanus*, the granting
of a *judex* or *recuperatores* was, at least in the later Republic,
usual.[2]

The plebeian Magistrates

The accidental preservation of the tribunate, through the
failure of the decemvirate to do its work, and consequently of
the plebeian assembly in all its purity, led to the persistence
of a magistracy chosen only by and only from the Plebs.   But
the plebeian aedileship was welded with the curule office of
the same name into practically a single magistracy, which has
already been discussed ;[3] while the tribunate is so intimately
bound up with every phase of the constitutional development
and organisation of Rome, that every one of its leading functions
has already been considered.

We have seen the method of its institution and the singular
religious basis on which its power rested,[4] and we have observed
the numbers of the holders of the office rising from two to
four, and finally to ten.[5]   The right of eliciting resolutions from
the Plebs and the coercive power and jurisdiction possessed by
this office have also been described.[6]   We have further dwelt on
the anomalous duality of the office, and seen how in a certain
sense it is not a magistracy, the tribune lacking both the
requisite *insignia*[7] and the right of taking *auspicia impetrativa*,[8]

---

[1] *Lex agraria* ll. 35, 36.   [2] ib.   [3] p. 208.
[4] p. 93.   [5] p. 94.   [6] pp. 95 ff.   [7] p. 190.   [8] p. 162.

but how, on the other hand, it becomes practically a magistracy of the people, when functions originally purely plebeian come to be used in the interest of the whole state. The right of acting with the Plebs gave the tribunes the power of initiating legislation when *plebiscita* had been raised to the level of *leges* ;[1] in their elective capacity they not only presided over the appointment of their successors and of the plebeian aediles, but through the Plebs they might not only create a minor magistracy such as the triumvirate *agris dandis assignandis*,[2] but in the closing years of the Republic actually conducted the election of such officials.[3] Their power of prohibition and their right of veto,[4] limited for a moment by Sulla but soon restored in all its plenitude,[5] became, when constitutionally employed, a guardianship of the whole state against the illegal or unconstitutional proceedings of other magistrates, and formed the chief basis of the Senate's authority. Their association with the Senate, from being merely prohibitive, grew to be positive,[6] and they finally shared the presidency of that body. Lastly, their powers of coercion and jurisdiction widened into a judicial control of the magistracy ; they were the prosecutors of faulty officials, and, up to the time of the development of the *quaestiones*, represented the chief means which the state possessed of enforcing criminal responsibility on its executive.[7]

The minor Magistrates

Prominent amongst the minor magistrates (*minores magistratus*)[8] stands a group known finally, and perhaps in Republican

---

[1] p. 126.

[2] Cic. *de Leg. Agr.* ii. 7, 17 "toties legibus agrariis curatores constituti sunt triumviri quinqueviri decemviri." Cf. ib. ii. 12, 31 "eodem jure . . . quo habuerunt (pullarios) tresviri lege Sempronia."

[3] ib. ii. 7, 16 "jubet enim (the agrarian law of Rullus) tribunum plebis, qui eam legem tulerit, creare decemviros per tribus septemdecim, ut, quem novem tribus fecerint, is decemvir sit."   [4] pp. 174, 177.

[5] The nature of the Sullan limitations is unknown. Caesar says "Sullam nudata omnibus rebus tribunicia potestate tamen intercessionem liberam reliquisse" (*B.C.* i. 7), and Cicero "Sullam probo, qui tribunis plebis sua lege injuriae faciendae potestatem ademerit, auxilii ferendi reliquerit" (*de Leg.* iii. 9, 22). He probably formulated cases in which it could not be employed. There are instances of the tribunician veto between 81 B.C. and 70 B.C., the date of the restoration of the tribune's power. See Momms. *Staatsr.* ii. p. 308 nn. 1 and 2.

[6] p. 162.   [7] p. 182.   [8] Cic. *de Leg.* iii. 3, 6.

times, as the *viginti-sex-viri*.[1] This group was merely a collection of small colleges and not itself a *collegium*. It is probable that most of its members were originally nominated by superior magistrates ; in later times they were all elected in the *comitia tributa*, although doubtless a separate elective act was required for each college.

(*a*) The *IIIviri capitales*, sometimes called by the less technical name of *IIIviri nocturni*, probably from their duty of extinguishing fires, were introduced as a standing institution about the year 289 B.C.[2] Their general function was that of assistance to the other magistrates in criminal jurisdiction. After the judgment had been pronounced, they guarded the prisoners and carried out the death sentence.[3] Their duties preliminary to a criminal trial were the preventive imprisonment of the accused and the conduct of a first examination after a criminal charge had been made.[4] They also heard ordinary police-court charges, such as those of vagrancy or nocturnal disturbance of the peace,[5] and they exercised police duties in the town, such as that of preserving order in the streets.[6] When acting as magistrates who could give a final judgment, their dealings seem to have been with slaves and foreigners. There is no evidence that they possessed any right of sentencing citizens or any higher jurisdiction which would bring them into contact with the people.

(*b*) The triumvirate of the masters of the mint (*IIIviri monetales*),[7] originally an occasional, first becomes a standing office about the time of the social war.[8]

(*c*) Six sanitary commissioners, acting probably as subordinates to the aediles and bearing the titles *IVviri viis in urbe purgandis* (or *viarum curandarum*), *IIviri viis extra propiusve urbem Romam passus mille purgandis*, are first mentioned in Caesar's Municipal Law (45 B.C.). The first looked to the cleansing of the streets within Rome, the second perhaps of those within the radius of a mile from the walls.[9]

---

[1] Festus p. 233 ; Dio Cass. liv. 26.   [2] Liv. *Ep.* xi.
[3] Cic. *de Leg.* iii. 3, 6 ; Sall. *Cat.* 55.
[4] Val. Max. vi. 1, 10 ; Cic. *pro Cluent.* 13, 38.
[5] Ascon. *in Milon.* p. 38.   [6] Plaut. *Amph.* 1. 1, 3.
[7] Pompon. in *Dig.* 1, 2, 2, 30. The full official title which first appears in 44 B.C. is *a(uro) a(rgento) a(ere) f(lando) f(eriundo)*. For this title and its variants see Momms. *Staatsr.* ii. p. 602 n. 3.
[8] Momms. *Staatsr.* ii. p. 601.
[9] Verbally the second title might, and perhaps should, refer to the *viae* of Italy. But the office is probably an urban magistracy. See ib. p. 604.

(*d*) The *xviri stlitibus judicandis* have a strange history; for, from being simple *judices*, they become minor magistrates of the people. They are doubtless the decemvirs who were rendered sacrosanct by the Valerio-Horatian laws of 449 B.C.,[1] the reason for this protection being that they were the jurors who decided in cases of freedom, that ultimate plebeian right which, as the story of Verginia shows, might sometimes be assailed. By Cicero's time they are still judges in *liberales causae*, but they have risen to the rank of independent magistrates.[2]

(*e*) The *iiiiviri praefecti Capuam Cumas*[3] were the elected delegates who represented the jurisdiction of the praetor in the *municipia* and colonies of the Campanian district. Their functions may be more appropriately discussed when we are dealing with the organisation of Italy.

Certain judicial and military posts were also filled by popular election. The paucity of criminal judges at Rome after the institution of the *quaestiones perpetuae*[4] led to the appointment of an annual president of the chief court which tried ordinary crimes—that, namely, which dealt with murder and kindred offences (*quaestio de sicariis*). The magisterial position of these *judices quaestionis* is shown both by the fixed qualification—it is generally, perhaps always, an ex-aedile that is appointed[5]—and by the fact that, like the magistrate who takes the oath *in leges*,[6] these *judices* swear to observe the special law which they are administering.[7] They were probably elected by the people in the *comitia tributa*.[8]

Subordinate military posts were also in the people's gift, and we have already noticed how the tribunate of the legions became in part a quasi-magistracy.[9] In the year 311 B.C. the appointment of consular delegates for the command and maintenance of the fleet was also entrusted to the tribes.[10] These *iiviri navales*

---

[1] Liv. iii. 55.

[2] Cic. *de Leg*. iii. 3, 6. For their jurisdiction in cases of freedom in the Ciceronian period see Cic. *pro Caec*. 39, 97 ; *pro Domo* 29, 78.

[3] Festus p. 233.

[4] p. 207.

[5] This was the case with C. Claudius Pulcher (*O.I.L.* i. p. 279), C. Junius (Cic. *pro Cluent*. 29, 79), and C. Julius Caesar (Suet. *Caes*. 11).

[6] p. 189.

[7] Cic. *pro Cluent*. 33, 91.

[8] Mommsen inclines to think that the office followed as a matter of course on the aedileship (*Staatsr*. ii. p. 590).

[9] p. 155.   [10] Liv. ix. 30.

were not annual officials, but, in obedience to the occasional character of the Roman fleet, came into existence when a war required its creation. The office seems to have become extinct by the second century B.C.

More occasional still was the creation by the *comitia tributa*, in later times occasionally by the *concilium plebis*,[1] of minor magistrates with extraordinary functions. Such were the officials for conducting a colony (*coloniae deducendae*), for the assignment of land (*agris dandis assignandis*), or for the dedication of a temple (*aedi dedicandae*). To this category belong the occasional *curatores* for the corn-supply and the roads (*annonae, viarum*).

[1] p. 234.

CHAPTER V

THE PEOPLE AND ITS POWERS

WE have already noticed the duality of procedure by which the powers of the people were exercised, and seen that every popular act was dependent on a *rogatio*.[1] But different spheres of popular activity may conveniently be distinguished. They may be divided into (i.) legislative or quasi-legislative acts; (ii.) elective; (iii.) judicial.

(i.) With respect to legislation proper, the Roman, like every other government which recognises the theory of parliamentary sovereignty and has no provision for a constituent assembly, drew no distinction between constitutional and other laws. But in our enumeration we may conveniently distinguish between those ordinances which altered the structure of the constitution and affected public rights, and those which dealt merely with the private relations of the citizens to one another.

In constitutional legislation the power of the people was unlimited. They could create new parliaments, as they did the *comitia tributa populi*;[2] they could delegate full powers of legislation to parliaments already existing, as they did to the *concilium plebis*.[3] They could devolve powers almost amounting to sovereign rights on an individual, as they devolved them ultimately on the Princeps. They might suspend the constitution and set up a provisional government, as they did when they gave constitutive powers to the decemvirs or to Sulla.

They might also observe or create rules which limited their own power of utterance. A result of observance of a rule is a *formula* which appears in Roman laws declaring their operation invalid in so far as they conflict with any fundamental obligation

---

[1] p. 13. [2] p. 102. [3] p. 126.

—the *fas* or *jus* which lies at the background of the state and which the people themselves dare not infringe. The scruple was expressed in the saving clause—

SI QUID JUS NON ESSET ROGARIER, EJUS EA LEGE
NIHILUM ROGATUM.[1]

Primarily this clause guarded a law against being a breach of a religious obligation ;[2] but, as interpreted by Cicero, it was a profession of respect even for certain ultimate secular rights— the right, for instance, to the possession of citizenship.

The creation of limitations may be instanced by the provision of the Twelve Tables, which forbade enactments to the detriment of individuals (*privilegia*),[3] and by a principle—perhaps rather a rule of procedure analogous to the formalities of legislation— which forbade laws on different subjects to be passed *en bloc* (*per saturam*), a provision re-enacted by a *lex Caecilia Didia* of 98 B.C.[4]

The creation of new magistracies was also within the power of the people, and, originally, the extension of an office beyond its proper term. In the year 327 B.C., at the commencement of the second Samnite war, the consul Q. Publilius Philo had his *imperium* prolonged by a *plebiscitum;*[5] although, as early as 308 B.C., in the prorogation of the command of the consul Q. Fabius Maximus, the Senate alone is mentioned as giving its sanction.[6]

The establishment of special judicial commissions to decide without appeal, in cases where the ordinary authorities were felt to be unable to cope with crime or conspiracy, was, in the strict theory of the constitution, entirely in the people's hands. Commissions

---

[1] Cic. *pro Caec.* 33, 95 ; cf. *pro Domo* 40, 106 "Quae tua fuit consecratio ? Tuleram, inquit, ut mihi liceret. Quid ? Non exceperas ut, si quid jus non esset rogari, ne esset rogatum ?"

[2] Valerius Probus gives the formula which emphasises this religious aspect of the saving clause. It was SI QUID SACRI SANCTI EST QUOD NON JURE SIT ROGATUM, EJUS HAC LEGE NIHIL ROGATUR.

[3] See p. 107.

[4] Cic. *pro Domo* 20, 53 "quae (est) sententia Caeciliae legis et Didiae nisi haec, ne populo necesse sit in conjunctis rebus compluribus aut id quod nolit accipere aut id quod velit repudiare ?" The principle had existed as early as the *lex Acilia Repetundarum* of 122 (l. 72). See Mommsen *Staatsr.* iii. p. 336.

[5] Liv. viii. 23.

[6] ib. ix. 42. Compare, however, x. 22 (296 B.C.), where the *plebiscitum* and the *senatus consultum* are both mentioned in connexion with the prorogation of the command of L. Volumnius. For the recognition of the *imperium* of the consul for a single day to enable him to triumph, see p. 158.

of this kind are found in 187,[1] 172,[2] and 141 [3] B.C.   In all these
cases there was co-operation between the Senate and people, and
it is not until the revolutionary period that the people ventures
on its own authority to establish a commission for criminal
investigation.[4]

The public rights of the individual were also under the
control of the *comitia*, and the conferment of citizenship was
solely the people's gift.   As originally the patrician *comitia* could
alone coopt patricians,[5] so in later times the assembly of the
whole Populus could alone admit new partners to its rights.
Civic rights could be conferred on individuals or communities,
in whole or in part, and the Plebs was for this purpose equally
competent with the Populus.[6]   A mediate grant of the citizenship could be made by the conferment of the power by the people
on a magistrate entrusted with the founding of a settlement,
as when the *lex Appuleia* of 100 B.C. granted the right to Marius
to raise three persons to the citizenship in any colony which he
planted.[7]   Citizenship might also be conferred by an imperator for
good service in the field ; but the power had to be given, or perhaps
in some cases the grant retrospectively sanctioned, by the people.
Such a power was given by law to Pompeius after the war with
Sertorius ;[8] but Pompeius may provisionally have conferred the
citizenship during the campaign.   Marius granted the boon on
the field of battle ;[9] he may have already had the power given
him by the people,[10] or he may have calculated on the subsequent
ratification of his act.

Deprivation of the citizenship of a community, the legality
of which by any power was questioned in the later Republic,[11]
could be effected, if at all, only by the people, and the people

[1] Liv. xxxviii. 54-60.   [2] ib. xlii. 21 and 22.
[3] Cic. *de Fin.* ii. 16, 54.
[4] The *quaestio Mamilia* of 110 B.C. (Sall. *Jug.* 40).
[5] p. 14.
[6] The *lex Plautia Papiria* (Cic. *pro Arch.* 4, 7 ; see p. 311) was the work of
two tribunes.
[7] Cic. *pro Balbo* 21, 48 "lege Appuleia . . . qua lege Saturninus C. Mario
tulerat, ut in singulas colonias ternos cives Romanos facere posset."
[8] ib. 8, 19 "lege quam L. Gellius Cn. Cornelius (coss. 72 B.C.) ex senatus
sententia tulerunt . . . videmus satis esse sanctum ut cives Romani sint ii, quos
Cn. Pompeius de consilii sententia singillatim civitate donaverit."
[9] Val. Max. v. 2, 8 "(C. Marius) duas . . . Camertium cohortes mira virtute
vim Cimbrorum sustinentis in ipsa acie adversus condicionem foederis civitate
donavit."
[10] Momms. *Staatsr.* iii. p. 135 n. 5.   [11] Cic. *pro Caec.* 35 101.

might in this particular be represented by the Plebs.   It was this body which pronounced on the fate of Capua in 210 B.C., and their decision entailed a criminal condemnation, the penalty of being sold into slavery.   The people, however, did not itself pronounce deprivation of citizenship, but left the fate of the Capuan burghers to the Senate.[1]

The people might also give the right of voting to those who already possessed citizenship without it.   This was so entirely a popular gift that even the previous deliberation of the Senate was not considered necessary for such a conferment.   When a tribune proposed to grant the right of suffrage to the *municipia* of Formiae, Fundi, and Arpinum in 188 B.C., he was met by the veto of four of his colleagues, who insisted that the Senate's judgment should first be taken.   But, yielding to instruction on the true principle of such gifts, they eventually withdrew their opposition.[2]

The deprivation of voting power—*tribu movere* in the extreme sense—seems to have been retained by the censor,[3] although a protest against its use to disfranchise a whole class was raised in 169 B.C.[4]   The people alone could impose a new burden on itself, and taxation belonged wholly to the *comitia*.[5]

Passing to legislation on private matters, we find that any fundamental change in the legal relations of citizens to one another must be effected by the people.   The law of the Twelve Tables is itself a *lex centuriata*, and we need only think of laws, such as those

---

[1] Liv. xxvi. 33 (speech of M. Atilius Regulus) " ' Per senatum agi de Campanis, qui cives Romani sunt, injussu populo non video posse. Idque et apud majores nostros in Satricanis factum est (319 B.C.), cum defecissent, ut M. Antistius tribunus plebis prius rogationem ferret scisceretque plebs uti senatui de Satricanis sententiae dicendae jus esset. Itaque censeo cum tribunis plebis agendum esse ut eorum unus pluresve rogationem ferant ad plebem qua nobis statuendi de Campanis jus fiat.' L. Atilius tribunus plebis ex auctoritate senatus plebem in haec verba rogavit . . . Plebes sic jussit, 'Quod senatus juratus, maxima pars, censeat, qui adsidetis, id volumus jubemusque.' "

[2] ib. xxxviii. 36 "edocti populi esse, non senatus, jus suffragii quibus velit impertiri, destiterunt incepto."

[3] p. 229.

[4] Liv. xlv. 15 (169 B.C. ; on the proposal of the censor Sempronius to disfranchise the freedmen, his colleague Claudius) "negabat . . . suffragii lationem injussu populi censorem cuiquam homini, nedum ordini universo adimere posse : neque enim, si tribu movere posset, quod sit nihil aliud quam mutare jubere tribum, ideo omnibus quinque et triginta tribubus emovere posse, id est civitatem libertatemque eripere."

[5] In Liv. vii. 16 (357 B.C.) we find the account of the creation of the *vicesima manumissionis* by the *comitia tributa populi*.

R

on usury, or the *lex Voconia* on inheritance, as types of a multitude of others. In the matter of civil procedure also a fundamental change, such as that permitting the use of the *formula* in place of the *legis actio* in cases falling under the *jus civile*, required legislation.[1] Yet we feel that it is only a question of degree whether such changes are effected by the people or by the authority of individuals. In matters of substantive law immense changes were brought about by the interpreting authority of the praetor;[2] while in procedure also much was left to the discretion of pontiffs, magistrates, and jurists. The same principle of division of authority applies to police regulations. Wide as were the coercive powers of the magistrates, sweeping infringements on individual liberty, such as those created by the sumptuary laws, were the work of the people.

We may pause here to examine the form of a *lex*, and especially that portion of it which secured its validity—its sanction. A complete law contained three parts: (1) its preamble (*praescriptio*), which described the formal circumstances of its enactment;[3] (2) the text, in which a minute and exhaustive formalism was rigorously preserved; (3) the sanction, which contained the pains and penalties pronounced against those who violated the provisions of the enactment. A *poena*, however, was not of itself sufficient to constitute a perfect law. A *lex perfecta* was one which declared an act invalid and imposed a penalty for disobedience. The imposition of a penalty without the declaration of invalidity constituted a *lex minus quam perfecta*.[4] A law without a sanction was *imperfecta*.[5] The method of repeal most frequently practised at Rome was rather that of supersession than of the declaration of the nullity of the former enactment. Hence the sanction of laws often gives impunity to those who by obedience incur the pains and penalties pro-

---

[1] This change was effected by a *lex Aebutia* (Gell. xvi. 10, 8 ; Gaius iv. 30).

[2] p. 205.

[3] The fullest *praescriptio* which has been preserved is that of the *lex Quinctia de aquaeductibus*, a consular law of 9 B.C. (Frontinus *de aquaeductibus* 129). It runs : "T. Quinctius Crispinus consul populum jure rogavit populusque jure scivit in foro pro rostris aedis divi Juli pr(idie) [k] Julias. Tribus Sergia principium fuit, pro tribu Sex. . . . L. f. Virro [primus scivit]."

[4] Ulpian *Reg. praef.* 2 "Minus quam perfecta lex est, quae vetat aliquid fieri et, si factum sit, non rescindit, sed poenam injungit ei qui contra legem fecit." The Licinio-Sextian agrarian law of 367 was apparently of this kind.

[5] Macrob. *Comm. in Somn. Scip.* ii. 17, 13 "inter leges quoque illa imperfecta dicitur, in qua nulla deviantibus poena sancitur."

nounced by some previous measure.¹ Repeal might be either
complete or partial, and a series of technical terms was evolved
to express this difference.² The attempt of certain laws to secure finality by prohibiting
repeal was necessarily futile, as opposed to the whole theory of
parliamentary sovereignty.³ It is possible, however, that the
leges sacratae of the early Republic, such as that which made
the tribune sacrosanct, were regarded as unalterable. The
execratio, which was their sanction, may have been regarded as
a fundamental religious obligation, and have been held, as such,
to be one of those sacred rights which, as we have seen,⁴ no law
professed to infringe.

The sovereign privilege of exempting individuals from laws
was naturally possessed at first by the legislative body itself;
but by a curious revolution, which we shall trace elsewhere,⁵
this singular privilege became a prerogative of the Senate.

The people's control of external matters, although it is still,
from a juristic point of view, legislative, bears a closer resemblance to the administrative functions of a Greek or modern
government. Here the magistrate was empowered to act in all
matters of detail, and we shall see how this magisterial sphere
was usurped by the Senate. The people had only the control
of the fundamental relations of Rome with foreign states. Their
activity was confined to the declaration of war, the making of
treaties, and the giving of charters.

A declaration of war was, according to Roman notions,
strictly necessary only when treaty relations, or even at times
relations which approximated to those of a treaty,⁶ had been

---

¹ Cic. *ad Att.* iii. 23, 2 "alterum caput est tralaticium de impunitate SI QUID
CONTRA ALIAS LEGES EJUS LEGIS ERGO FACTUM SIT."
² Ulpian *op. cit.* 3 "Lex aut rogatur, id est, fertur ; aut abrogatur, id est,
prior lex tollitur ; aut derogatur, id est, pars primae (legis) tollitur ; aut sub-
rogatur, id est, adjicitur aliquid primae legi ; aut obrogatur, id est, mutatur
aliquid ex prima lege." Cf. the clause in a law cited by Cicero (*ad Att.* iii. 23,
3) "SI QUID IN HAC ROGATIONE SCRIPTUM EST, QUOD PER LEGES PLEBISVE SCITA
PROMULGARE, ABROGARE, DEROGARE, OBROGARE SINE FRAUDE SUA NON LICEAT."
³ Cic. l.c. 23, 2 "neque enim ulla (lex) est, quae non ipsa se saepiat difficultate
abrogationis. Sed, cum lex abrogatur, illud ipsum abrogatur, quo modo eam
abrogari [*non*] oporteat."
⁴ p. 239.   ⁵ See the section on the Senate.
⁶ Livy describes a controversy whether from this point of view an armistice
(*indutiae*) rested on a level with a *pax*: (iv. 30) "cum Veientibus . . . indutiae,
. . . non pax facta . . . ante diem rebellaverant . . . controversia inde fuit utrum
populi jussu indiceretur bellum an satis esset senatus consultum. Pervicere tribuni
. . . ut Quinctius consul de bello ad populum ferret : omnes centuriae jussere."

broken. Such a declaration could be made only by the people.[1] But the international point of view was not the only dominant one in this matter. The people must have been consulted in many cases where there were no treaty relations, and the reason would have been simply the advisability of its declaring its will on a matter which might be of vital importance to the community. The *comitia centuriata* seems invariably to have represented the people in this capacity.[2] With respect to the conclusion of international relations, we shall touch elsewhere on the controverted question[3] whether the magistracy had the right of binding the popular conscience by a sworn treaty, or whether this required the consent of the people. The survival of the controversy into as late a period as that of the Jugurthine war seems to prove that the federative power was once a magisterial privilege ; and the fact is also attested by the inclusion in agreements made by commanders of a clause specifying that the agreement should only be valid if ratified by the people.[4] In the middle Republic there was no question that treaty relations were the prerogative of the people,[5] and, unlike the case of the declaration of war, the Plebs is here included in the conception of the people.[6] By the nature of the case it could only be the outlines of an agreement that were thus laid before the *comitia*, and details of settlement were left to the commander, assisted by a commission.[7] The organisation of a province and the *lex provinciae* that followed the subjection of a district were not usually interpreted in the light of treaty relations ; they were

---

[1] Polyb. vi. 14 ὑπὲρ εἰρήνης οὗτος (ὁ δῆμος) βουλεύεται καὶ πολέμου.

[2] Mommsen *Staatsr.* iii. p. 343.

[3] See the section on the Senate.

[4] Polyb. i. 62 (agreement between Lutatius Catulus and the Carthaginians in 241 B.C.) ἐπὶ τοῖσδε φιλίαν εἶναι Καρχηδονίοις καὶ Ῥωμαίοις, ἐὰν καὶ τῷ δήμῳ τῶν Ῥωμαίων συνδοκῇ. The people rejected the treaty, but it was subsequently maintained that, but for this saving clause, it would have been binding (ib. iii. 29).

[5] ib. vi. 14 καὶ μὴν περὶ συμμαχίας καὶ διαλύσεως καὶ συνθηκῶν οὗτος (ὁ δῆμος) ἐστιν ὁ βεβαιῶν ἕκαστα τούτων καὶ κύρια ποιῶν ἢ τοὐναντίον.

[6] Liv. xxix. 12 (205 B.C., peace with Philip of Macedon) "jusserunt . . . omnes tribus " ; xxx. 43 (201 B.C., peace with Carthage) "De pace . . . omnes tribus jusserunt " ; xxxiii. 25 (196 B.C., peace with Philip of Macedon) "ea rogatio in Capitolio ad plebem lata est. Omnes quinque et triginta tribus, uti rogas jusserunt."

[7] So on the conclusion of the second Punic war (Liv. xxx. 43 "M'. Acilius et Q. Minucius tribuni plebis ad populum tulerunt 'Vellent juberentne senatum decernere ut cum Carthaginiensibus pax fieret, et quem eam pacem dare quemque ex Africa exercitum deportare juberent'").

the work of a commander and a senatorial commission. On the
other hand, cities with treaties (*civitates foederatae*) and cities with
charters (*civitates liberae*) have their rights given them by the
people. In the one case the rights are guaranteed by an irrevocable agreement sworn to by the *fetiales;* in the other by a
revocable charter (*lex data*), which as late as 71 B.C. is still an
utterance of the people (*lex rogata*).[1] We shall see, in dealing
with the Senate, that, even in this matter of granting treaties or
charters to separate states, senatorial authority encroached on
that of the people.

(ii.) We have already seen how in theory the popular power
of election was a modification of a principle of nomination;[2]
after its recognition the principles regulating it were practically
those of legislation, the magistrate questioning and the people
commanding. The representation of the dual community is
here rather more marked than in the case of legislation; for
while a *plebiscitum* is often spoken of as a *lex*, no one credits the
tribune with the position of a *magistratus populi*, and however
wide his powers may have become, he always remains in theory
the head of the plebeian community. The preliminaries to
election necessary to the candidate for office have already been
considered,[3] and the further process of election will be dealt with
when we describe the procedure of the *comitia* as a whole.

(iii.) The origin of the jurisdiction of the people is, as we
have seen, obscure; but it is probable that it did not spring
wholly from the *provocatio*,[4] and even in cases where it did, the
appeal tended to become extinct, from the fact that a magistrate
who recognised the restrictions imposed on his *imperium* by law
would not pronounce a sentence, but would bring the case
immediately before the people. A trial before the people
(*judicium populi*) took place when a magistrate recognised the
limitations on his power; the *provocatio*—an extremely rare
occurrence in the later Republic—was required to start the
same procedure when the magistrate refused to recognise these
limitations.

The judicial competence of the different magistrates and
comitia was determined partly by law, partly by custom. Two
fundamental principles were recognised :—

(1) That capital cases should be reserved for the centuries.

[1] See *lex Antonia de Termessibus* (Bruns *Fontes*).
[2] p. 47.   [3] p. 187.   [4] p. 63.

To this there is the exception furnished by the special capital jurisdiction of the Plebs.[1]

(2) That a case initiated by a magistrate could be tried only in that assembly which the magistrate was competent to approach. To this principle there were two exceptions: first, the consular delegates—the quaestors and the *duumviri perduellionis* — although possessing no *jus agendi cum populo*, yet guided the assemblies in which an appeal from their decision was made;[2] and secondly, the tribune, when conducting a capital prosecution before the *comitia centuriata*, approached, and perhaps had the presidency of, this body.[3]

But, as a rule, the official character of the magistrate who conducts the prosecution, and the nature of the penalty which he proposes, are signs of what assembly passes its final judgment on the case.

The capital jurisdiction of the consuls, expressed through the quaestors, was exercised in the *comitia centuriata;* an appeal against the *coercitio* of consuls and praetors, when the fine which they imposed passed the limit of the *multa suprema*,[4] came before the *comitia tributa populi*. The jurisdiction of the aediles[5] was always exercised before the tribes; the curule aediles as *magistratus populi* must have brought their case before the *comitia tributa populi;* the plebeian aediles, who, as magistrates of the Plebs, had no right of approaching the people, appeared before the *concilium plebis*. With regard to the tribunes, where their jurisdiction was capital, it may in certain cases have been exercised by the *concilium plebis*, but usually necessitated an appearance before the *comitia centuriata;*[6] where it was pecuniary, the tribune would invariably have brought the case before his own assembly of the Plebs.

The procedure in a *judicium populi* consisted of two stages. In the first, the magistrate who intended to impose a sentence which was beyond the limits of his personal jurisdiction held a preliminary examination (*anquisitio*).[7] This is conducted with the fullest publicity before an informal assembly or *contio* which

[1] See below on the competence of the *concilium plebis*.
[2] See Momms. *Staatsr.* i. p. 195; ii. p. 618.   [3] See p. 161.
[4] p. 169.   [5] p. 211.   [6] p. 161.
[7] *Anquisitio* (a variant of the *quaestio* of the magistrate when he investigates on his own authority) perhaps means an "inquiry on both sides," i.e. through accusation and defence (Lange *Röm. Alt.* ii. p. 470; cf. Festus p. 22 "anquirere est circum quaerere").

he has summoned. This preliminary investigation is repeated three times, on days not necessarily consecutive. The magistrate is represented as a prosecutor, and his expressions of opinion at these meetings are spoken of as *accusationes*. His final judgment, consequent on the proceedings of the third *contio*, is a bill (*rogatio*), which he gives notice of his intention to bring before the *comitia*. The penalty proposed in this bill need not be that originally suggested, for the investigation may have led the magistrate to amend his original proposal.[1]

The legal interval for promulgation—three weeks—then elapsed, and at its close the proposal was brought by the magistrate before the *comitia*. It was then either accepted or rejected (necessarily without amendment) by the assembled people. This formal assembly (*comitia*) was, in judicial as in legislative acts, preceded by a *contio*; and the magistrate's final statement of his proposal before this *contio* is spoken of as his "fourth accusation" (*quarta accusatio*).[2] If, through any chance, such as evil auspices, the bill was not carried through the *comitia*, a fresh promulgation, with another interval of three weeks, was necessary for a revival of the trial. This necessity made a repetition of a prosecution by the same magistrate on the same charge very infrequent.[3]

Hitherto we have been treating the case of a *judicium populi* consequent on the magistrate's recognising the limitations on his power. But there is a possibility of his refusing this recognition, and in this case the matter can be brought to the people only by means of an appeal (*provocatio*) lodged by the accused. This contingency was, in the middle and later Republic, unusual but not unknown, for the jurisdiction of the *duumviri perduellionis* was, as we know from the case of Rabirius,[4] regulated at times in such a manner that an appeal to the people was an essential part of the procedure.

---

[1] Liv. ii. 52 (the tribunes) "cum capitis anquisissent, duo milia aeris damnato multam edixerunt"; xxvi. 3 (a pecuniary penalty having been proposed during the first two days) "tertio . . . tanta ira accensa est ut capite anquirendum contio subclamaret."

[2] Cic. *pro Dom.* 17, 45 "cum tam moderata judicia populi sint a majoribus constituta . . . ne inprodicta die quis accusetur, ut ter ante magistratus accuset intermissa die quam multam irroget aut judicet, quarta sit accusatio trinum nundinum prodicta die, quo die judicium sit futurum." Cf. App. *B.C.* i. 74.

[3] Cic. l.c. "si qua res illum diem aut auspiciis aut excusatione sustulit, tota causa judiciumque sublatum sit."   [4] Dio Cass. xxxvii. 27.

In such a case there were two magisterial investigations instead of one. The first was the *quaestio*, as a result of which the magistrate had pronounced the appellable sentence; the second was the *anquisitio* before the people preceding the decision in the *comitia*. It must occasionally have happened that different magistrates conducted these two stages of procedure; for if an individual appealed against the decision of a magistrate in a province or in the field, this magistrate might himself be unable to conduct the case at Rome.

The people is represented from a very early time as rescinding its own sentences.[1] This rescission was simply the repeal of a law, and was perhaps not regarded originally as the revision of its own sentence by a court. No provision was made that the particular assembly which had pronounced the sentence should repeal it. This was, indeed, sometimes the case. Popilius, for instance, who had been held responsible for the judicial murders following the fate of Ti. Gracchus, was both banished and restored by *plebiscita*.[2] But, on the other hand, Metellus, "interdicted" by a consular bill, which must have been passed at the *comitia centuriata*,[3] was restored by the *rogatio* of a tribune,[4] while Cicero himself, banished by a tribunician enactment, was recalled from exile by a consular law passed at the *comitia centuriata*.[5]

A further step in the exercise of this power was taken when attempts were made to rescind the decisions of the *judices* of criminal commissions by decrees of the people. This was first attempted in 88 B.C. by the tribune P. Sulpicius Rufus, who carried a *plebiscitum* for the restoration of exiles who had been condemned by the Varian commission.[6] Other tentative steps in the same direction led up to Caesar's bill of 49, by which he effected the restoration of those who had been condemned under the Pompeian laws of 52 B.C.[7] The instances of

[1] Cic. *pro Domo* 32, 86 "at vero . . . Kaeso ille Quinctius (cf. Liv. iii. 13) et M. Furius Camillus et M. Servilius Ahala (cf. Liv. iv. 16, 21) . . . populi incitati vim iracundiamque subierunt ; damnatique comitiis centuriatis cum in exilium profugissent, rursus ab eodem populo placato sunt in suam pristinam dignitatem restituti."
[2] Cic. *Brut.* 34, 128 ; *post Red. in Sen.* 15, 38.
[3] App. *B.C.* i. 31.
[4] Cic. *pro Planc.* 28, 69 ; *post Red. in Sen.* 15, 38.
[5] Cic. *ad Att.* iv. 1, 4.
[6] *Auct. ad Herenn.* ii. 28, 45.
[7] Caes. *B.C.* iii. 1 "praetoribus tribunisque plebis rogationes ad populum ferentibus . . . in integrum restituit." Cf. Suet. *Caes.* 41 ; Dio Cass. xliii. 27.

this period generally illustrate the rescission of the decrees of special commissions, which were themselves political weapons evoked by party conflict, but M. Antonius when tribune is said to have effected the restoration of a man who had been condemned for an ordinary crime,[1] and, therefore, presumably by an ordinary *quaestio perpetua*, and it seems clear that by Cicero's time this power of restitution by the *comitia* had come to be regarded as practically one of pardon.   Each of the three legislative assemblies was competent to "restore" (*restituere*).   The proposals are usually tribunician, but Caesar also employed praetorian rogations (probably before the *comitia tributa*) for the purpose.[2]

Two powers analogous to that of the rescission of a sentence are the remission of outlawry and amnesty.

The outlawry referred to is not that following on *aquae et ignis interdictio*, which was an act of the people and the confirmation of a criminal sentence, but that consequent on a decree of the Senate, which had pronounced individuals to be *hostes*. Although we might have expected that the Senate, which passed, would be the body to rescind such a decree, we find the belief that the restitution of the outlawed required a *lex* or *plebiscitum*. Marius pretended that such a permit was necessary for his entrance into Rome in 87 B.C.,[3] and Octavian in 43 B.C. had a law passed which rescinded the outlawry of Dolabella.[4]

Amnesty is an act which implies that no trial and no condemnation, whether pronounced by a court or other body, have taken place ; it gives immunity from the consequence of criminal acts that have not yet been judged.   This, however, is a prerogative, not of the people, but of the Senate.   It was a decree of this body that gave an immunity (not subsequently respected) to Caesar's murderers in 44 B.C.,[5] and a similar act in 33 B.C. granted an amnesty to senators who had during the civil war raised troops at their own cost.[6]

The occasional grounds of invalidity of these legislative or quasi-legislative acts of the people have already been incidentally considered.   We have spoken of the conditions of the auspices and the intercession,[7] neglect of either of which made a law *ipso*

[1] "de alea condemnatum" (Cic. *Phil.* ii. 23, 56), that is, probably, under the *lex Cornelia de falsis* (Rein *Criminalrecht* p. 833).
[2] See p. 248.
[3] Plut. *Mar.* 43 ; cf. Vell. ii. 21 ; App. *B.C.* i. 70.
[4] App. *B.C.* iii. 95.   [5] Vell. ii. 58 ; cf. Cic. *Phil.* i. 1, 1.
[6] Dio Cass. xlix. 43.   [7] pp. 166, 179.

jure invalid, and the same consequence followed a breach of the
formal rules which the people had made for its own guidance,
such as the rules of promulgation which we shall soon discuss,
or the provision against the union of heterogeneous measures in
the same bill.[1] In the earlier period of Republican history such
invalid ordinances were, when they took the form of election,
subjected to a procedure resembling repeal, and there are many
instances of magistrates *vitio creati* forced to abdicate their office,
a renewal of the elective procedure following on their abdication ;[2]
and even in the case of laws which offended against fundamental
principles of the constitution, it was at all times considered safer
to secure their formal repeal.[3] But the more logical idea of
absolute nullity, which required no repeal, subsequently prevailed,
and we shall find that it is the Senate which, as the guide of the
executive power, pronounces enactments to be invalid in consequence of formal flaws.

When we turn from the " people " in general to its manifestations in the separate *comitia* and in the *concilium* of the Plebs, we
find that, although historically we are dealing with different
parliaments, practically we are treating the Roman community
engaged with different orders of the day under different formal
rules. The people require to be organised in one way for one
function, in another way for another,[4] but under the changing
forms there is a unity of personnel which forbids us regarding the
different assemblies as different sovereigns.[5] The only disturbance
to this unity is found in the fact that the Patricians were always
excluded from the *concilium* of the Plebs.[6]

The *comitia curiata*, the oldest sovereign in Rome, was a mere
shadow of its former self. Its main constitutional function was that

---

[1] p. 239.
[2] When **Varro says** (*L.L.* vi. 30) "magistratus vitio creatus nihilo secius
magistratus " he is reflecting the practical procedure—hardly the constitutional
theory, unless the *dictum* implies that repeal is impossible because unnecessary,
and that there is no authority for determining the nullity of the election.
[3] Cicero says, with respect to the law exiling him, that there was some point
in its being held invalid as a *privilegium*, " sed multo est melius abrogari " (*ad
Att.* iii. 15, 5).
[4] Laelius Felix ap. Gell. xv. 27, 5 "Cum ex generibus hominum suffragium
feratur, ' curiata ' comitia esse, cum ex censu et aetate ' centuriata,' cum ex
regionibus et locis, ' tributa.' "
[5] How easily one *comitia* could melt into another is shown by the words of
Cicero [*ad Fam.* vii. 30 (44 B.C.)] " Ille autem (Caesar), qui comitiis tributis
esset auspicatus, centuriata habuit."
[6] See Appendix on the *comitia tributa*.

of passing the *lex curiata*, which was necessary for the ratification originally of the *imperium* [1] and, with the creation of fresh patrician magistracies, of the *potestas* which these involved.[2] Yet although in theory no magistracy was properly constituted (*justus*) until its holder had received the ratification of the *curiae*, we know that in the case of those with *imperium*, and we may conclude that in that of others, most of the ordinary functions could be exercised without this sanction. It was only the full exercise of the *imperium*, whether in jurisdiction, in military command, or in the transmission of office, that was in suspense until the *lex* had been elicited. Without it the praetor could not give justice from his tribunal,[3] the consul could not hold an assembly for the creation of his successor,[4] and whether as magistrate or promagistrate could not exercise the full *imperium* in the field,[5] until the ambiguous wording of the *lex Cornelia de provinciis ordinandis* made the requirement in this last particular a doubtful point.[6]

For the purpose of this conferment the *comitia curiata* was in Cicero's day often represented by but thirty lictors,[7] and the same scanty attendance may have sufficed for the other formal acts which it retained from antiquity. These are the acts of the *comitia calata*.[8] The public will and testament made at this assembly was extinct at the close of the Republic; but the *comitia* still met, under the presidency of the *pontifex maximus*, for the inauguration of the *rex sacrorum* and the *flamines*, and under the same guidance for the *detestatio sacrorum* made by one who passed from his *gens* either by an act of adrogation or by transition from the patrician to the plebeian order.[9]

---

[1] p. 49.

[2] Messala ap. Gell. xiii. 15, 4 "Minoribus creatis magistratibus tributis comitiis magistratus, sed justus curiata datur lege."

[3] Dio Cass. xxxix. 19.   [4] ib. xli. 43.

[5] Cic. *de Leg. Agr.* ii. 12, 30 "consuli, si legem curiatam non habet, attingere rem militarem non licet."

[6] Sulla's law had said that the magistrate should retain *imperium* until he re-entered the city, apparently without mentioning the *lex curiata*. App. Claudius, consul for 54 B.C., who had been prevented by the tribunician veto from getting his *lex curiata* passed, presumed on this silence and said "legem curiatam consuli ferri opus esse, necesse non esse ; se, quoniam ex senatus consulto provinciam haberet, lege Cornelia imperium habiturum quoad in urbem introisset" (Cic. *ad Fam.* i. 9, 25).

[7] Cic. *de Leg. Agr.* ii. 12, 31.   [8] p. 26.

[9] Gell. xv. 27, 1 "'calata' comitia esse, quae pro conlegio pontificum habentur aut regis aut flaminum inaugurandorum causa. Eorum autem alia esse 'curiata,' alia 'centuriata'. . . . Isdem comitiis, quae 'calata' appellari diximus,

The *comitia centuriata*, once known as the "greatest of the comitia" (*comitiatus maximus*),[1] not only from its importance as expressing the sovereign will, but from the possibility of enforcing the attendance of the assembled army, always retained something of its military character and its association with the *imperium*. Its summons and presidency belong by right only to the magistrates with *imperium*. The consuls are its normal presidents for elections and for laws ; the praetor approaches it for purposes of jurisdiction, and the interrex for the election of a consul. The election of magistrates with *imperium* and of the censors was confined to this body, and we have already seen how its supreme judicial authority was asserted and infringed.[2] The army alone could declare war,[3] but its legislative power, though never lost, was infrequently asserted after the recognition of sovereignty in the two assemblies of the tribes which were more easily summoned and organised.

But not only did the tribe assemblies infringe the power of those of the centuries, they became the later model of the latter, and the tendency to detract from the influence of wealth was shown in the reorganisation of the *comitia centuriata* on a tribal basis.[4] The date of this change is unknown ; but, as the redistribution of the centuries in its final form assumes the existence of thirty-five tribes, the alteration may not be earlier than the year 241 B.C. The leading principle of the new arrangement was that the five classes were distributed over all the tribes in such a manner that there were two centuries of each class—one century of *seniores* and one of *juniores*—in a single tribe. Each class thus had two votes in a tribe and seventy votes

---

et sacrorum detestatio et testamenta fieri solebant." It is not known what particular acts were reserved for the " comitia calata " assembled *centuriatim ;* Mommsen thinks the inauguration of the Flamen Martialis outside the city (*Staatsr.* iii. p. 307).

[1] p. 107.   [2] pp. 107, 246.   [3] p. 244.

[4] Liv. i. 43 "Nec mirari oportet hunc ordinem, qui nunc est post expletas quinque et triginta tribus duplicato earum numero centuriis juniorum seniorum-que, ad institutam ab Servio Tullio summam non convenire." Cf. Dionys. iv. 21. The description of Cicero (*de Rep.* ii. 22, 39 and 40) probably refers to the Servian arrangement, although Mommsen (*Staatsr.* iii. p. 275) holds that it refers to the reformed *comitia.* The description given in the text is in essentials that of Pantagathus (died 1567) *ap. Ursinum in* Liv. i. 43. For the different systems that have been adopted see Willems *Le Droit Public* p. 97. Mommsen (l.c.) admits the 70 votes for the 70 centuries of the first class, but thinks that the 280 centuries of the other classes were so combined as to form but 100 votes ; the total votes being $70 + 100 + 5 + 18 = 193$, as before.

in all. The eighteen centuries of knights still stood outside the tribe ; so did the four centuries of *fabri, accensi, tibicines* and *cornicines,* and the fifth century of *proletarii* which probably existed at this time.[1] The total number of centuries would thus be 373 (350 + 18 + 5). The majority of this number is 187, but the first class and the *equites* together now have but 88 votes, thus losing their preponderance in voting power. In spite of this arrangement by tribes there is no tribal vote. The unit of voting is still the century, and it is the number of centuries that decides the question. The organisation is still by classes, the seventy centuries of each class voting as distinct bodies.[2] The *equites* seem still to have had the right of voting first,[3] and the first class took precedence of the others ; for the lot which designated the *centuria praerogativa*[4] seems to have been cast only amongst the seventy groups of *seniores* and *juniores* belonging to this class.[5]

The restoration by Sulla of the older method of voting (88 B.C.)[6] was not a permanent reform. It disappeared during the Cinnan reaction, and it is questionable whether it was renewed by the dictator. If it was, it soon vanished with other items of his aristocratic reorganisation.

The *comitia tributa* was the most handy of all the assemblies of the full Populus, and was, consequently, the most frequently employed for the passing of *leges.* Its presidents were the patrician magistrates, usually the consuls and praetors and, for purposes of jurisdiction, the curule aediles. It elected these aediles and other lower magistrates of the people, as well as the twenty-four tribunes of the first four legions. Its jurisdiction was limited to pecuniary penalties.

The *concilium plebis,* practically the sovereign body of the state, differed from this last assembly in two respects. It could

---

[1] p. 73.

[2] Cic. *Phil.* ii. 33, 82 " Ecce Dolabellae comitiorum dies : sortitio praerogativae : quiescit. Renuntiatur, tacet. Prima classis vocatur : renuntiatur. Deinde, ita ut assolet, suffragia ; tum secunda classis."

[3] Liv. xliii. 16 "cum ex duodecim centuriis equitum octo censorem condemnassent, multaeque aliae primae classis." It would seem as though the *sex suffragia* (p. 73) voted with or after the first class. Drakenborch would read *octodecim* for *duodecim,* but this would seem to give too small a number of condemnatory votes amongst the *equites.*   [4] Cic. *pro Planc.* 20, 49.

[5] Hence such expressions as *Aniensis juniorum, Veturia juniorum, Galeria juniorum* (Liv. xxiv. 7 ; xxvi. 22 ; xxvii. 6).

[6] App. *B.C.* i. 59.

be summoned only by plebeian magistrates and it never included the Patricians.[1] Besides issuing universally valid decrees (*plebiscita*), it elected the magistrates of the Plebs, and in its judicial capacity was the body which considered the penalties which they had formulated. By the strict letter of the Twelve Tables this jurisdiction should have been limited to the imposition of fines,[2] but, besides instances of its capital jurisdiction at an early period of its history, it continued to possess the unquestioned right of pronouncing outlawry (*aquae et ignis interdictio*) against any one already in exile,[3] and after the time of Caius Gracchus there are traces of an independent capital jurisdiction which it exercised against magistrates who had violated the *provocatio*.[4]

The freedom of this plebeian assembly was for a time limited by Sulla's ordinance (88 B.C.) directing that no measure should be brought before it which had not received the previous sanction of the Senate;[5] but the old powers of unimpeded legislation were restored in 70 B.C. If Sulla also took the right of prosecution from the tribune,[6] the higher jurisdiction of the Plebs was restored by the enactment which gave it back its legislative power, for tribunician prosecutions continue to the end of the Republic.

An anomalous use of the popular suffrage was made in the case of elections to the priestly colleges. Formerly they had been kept distinct from the secular life of the state, and even when the reforming spirit dictated that they should be submitted to the voice of the people, a religious scruple forbade the intervention of the *comitia*. The electoral body was composed of seventeen tribes selected by lot from the thirty-five, and this

[1] See Appendix on the *comitia tributa*.
[2] p. 107.
[3] Liv. xxv. 4 (212 B.C.) "Tribuni plebem rogaverunt plebesque ita scivit, 'Si M. Postumius ante K. Maias non prodisset citatusque eo die non respondisset neque excusatus esset, videri eum in exilio esse, bonaque ejus venire, ipsi aqua et igni placere interdici"; ib. xxvi. 3 (211 B.C.) "Cn. Fulvius exulatum Tarquinios abiit. Id ei justum exilium esse scivit plebs."
[4] When Plutarch says (*C. Gracch.* 4) that C. Gracchus gave the right of trying such cases τῷ δήμῳ, this word may include the Plebs. Gracchus at least seems to have banished the ex-consul Popilius by means of a *plebiscitum* (Cic. *pro Domo* 31, 82 " ubi enim tuleras ut mihi aqua et igni interdiceretur? quod Gracchus de P. Popilio . . tulit ").
[5] App. *B.C.* i. 59.
[6] This conclusion has been drawn from the words of Cicero (*in Verr.* Act i. 13, 38) "judiciis ad senatorium ordinem translatis sublataque populi Romani in unum quemque vestrum potestate."

body, which was *not* the Populus,[1] was presided over by a pontiff.[2] This organisation was probably first applied about the middle of the third century B.C. to the creation of the *pontifex maximus ;* it received a great extension at the close of the second century. A Domitian law, a *plebiscitum* of 104 B.C., applied election in a modified form to the religious *collegia*—probably to the four great guilds of pontiffs, augurs, quindecemvirs, and epulones. The college in question presented, the people elected and gave to the college again a *congé d'élire*, whereupon the chosen candidate was solemnly coopted by the members of his guild.[3] Sulla abolished this mode of appointment, and perhaps with it the popular election of the chief pontiff, restoring the aristocratic mode of cooptation ; but appointment by the seventeen tribes was restored again in 63 B.C., through a plebiscite of the tribune Labienus.[4]

Our final task in connexion with the people and its powers will be to describe the preliminaries to the meetings of the *comitia* and the *concilium*, and the mode in which business was transacted at these gatherings.

The legal days of meeting (*comitiales dies*) were those which were neither holy (*nefasti*) nor dedicated to the work of justice (*fasti*). The 194 days thus left clear were further broken into by the *nundinae*, the first days of the eight-day week, on which not even a *contio* could be held,[5] and by the movable festivals (*feriae conceptivae*) which were fixed by the magistrates. These rules of time were binding on all meetings of Populus and Plebs ; those of place differed for the various assemblies. The assembly of the *curiae* met within the *pomerium*, usually in the Comitium on the north-west of the Forum.[6] The centuries, on the other hand, must meet without the walls, and their place of assembly was usually the Campus Martius, but meetings are sometimes

[1] Cic. *de Leg. Agr.* ii. 7, 18 "Quod populus per religionem sacerdotia mandare non poterat, ut minor pars populi vocaretur."
[2] For this presidency by the youngest pontifex (the one, i.e., who stood the least chance of election) see Liv. xxv. 5 (212 B.C.). From Cic. *ad Brut.* i. 5, 4 it follows that the consuls had something to do with arranging the elections, but not that they were ever the presidents.
[3] Cic. *de Leg. Agr.* ii. 7, 18 ; Vell. ii. 12, 3.
[4] Dio Cass. xxxvii. 37.
[5] Macrob. *Sat.* i. 16, 29 "Julius Caesar XVI auspiciorum libro negat nundinis contionem advocari posse, id est cum populo agi ideoque nundinis Romanorum haberi comitia non posse."
[6] Varro *L.L.* v. 155 "comitium ab eo quod coibant eo comitiis curiatis et litium causa."

found in other places such as "the Peteline grove outside the
river-gate," and an unknown site called the Aesculetum.[1] The
two assemblies of the tribes were originally bound to no locality,
except for the fact that the plebeian, as purely city, magistrates
could not easily find their way outside the walls. But the
eliciting of a *rogatio* from the tribes by the consul in his camp at
Sutrium in 357 B.C. led, through the fear of military influence, to
the rule that no resolution should be elicited from the people
in the military domain,[2] and since that date the two assemblies
of the tribes were held within the first milestone. The open
space of the Capitol (*area Capitolii*) was at one time their usual
resort both for elections and for laws, but in the later period of
the Republic it was found convenient to conduct the elections
both of the lower and plebeian magistrates in the Campus
Martius, while the Rostra in the Forum, the usual centre of
demagogic strife and the ordinary gathering place for *contiones*,
was chosen as the site for the legislation of the tribes.[3]

The first step in the intercourse of a magistrate with the
people, which was to produce a binding act, was the setting
forth by the former of a decree specifying the day of meeting,[4]
and describing the nature of the act which he meant to introduce.
This promulgation[5] assumed various forms in accordance with
the purpose of the projected meeting. In prosecutions it contained the name of the accused, the nature of the charge, and
the penalty proposed; in elections at least the places to be filled,
but probably in later times a list of the candidates as well;[6]
in legislation the text of the law which was to be the subject of
the *rogatio*. No provision seems to have been made that the
text should remain unaltered until a Licinio-Junian law of
62 B.C. provided that a copy of the promulgated enactment
should be deposited in the *aerarium* as a guarantee that no
amendment was inserted before the people was asked to accept it.[7]

---

[1] Liv. vi. 20 ; Plin. *H.N.* xvi. 10, 37.   [2] Liv. vii. 16.

[3] The change to the Forum is perhaps post-Gracchan ; see Momms. *Staatsr.*
iii. p. 385.   Cf. the prescription of the *lex Quinctia de aquaeductibus* (p. 242).

[4] Gell. xiii. 15, 1 " In edicto consulum, quo edicunt quis dies comitiis centuriatis futurus sit."   "Comitia edicere" (Liv. xxiii. 31) and "comitia indicere"
(Liv. iv. 6) are employed as descriptive of this act.

[5] Festus p. 224 "promulgari leges dicuntur cum primum in vulgus eduntur,
quasi provulgari."   [6] Momms. *Staatsr.* iii. p. 370.

[7] Schol. Bob. to Cic. *pro Sest.* 64, 135 (p. 310) "(lex) Licinia et Junia . . . illud
cavebat ne clam aerario legem ferri liceret."   For registration in the *aerarium* at
the time of promulgation cf. Cic. *de Leg.* iii. 4, 11.   Clodius' law exiling Cicero

The minimum interval between the promulgation and the meeting was the space of three *nundina*, i.e. 24 days, and this condition was as necessary for jurisdiction and elections as for laws.[1] On the appointed day the first act of the magistrate, who meant to guide a meeting of the Populus, was the *auspicatio* in the sacred enclosure (*templum*) which formed the centre of the gathering. Celestial signs alone [2] seem to have been the object of this morning watch; but no such observation was necessary for plebeian gatherings; they were disturbed only by *auspicia oblativa*.[3] The auspices had been taken before sunrise, and if they were favourable the herald was then sent round the walls inviting the people to meet the magistrate at dawn.[4] This was sufficient for the *comitia* of the tribes.[5] For the centuries more elaborate preparations were necessary. Proclamation of the meeting was made from the Rostra, and the red flag flew from the Janiculum to show that it was guarded while the army was busy in the Campus.[6] The military horn was blown on the *arx* and round the walls, and, if the summons was for a court of justice, before the house of the accused.[7]

When the people were assembled the president opened with a prayer,[8] and the *rogatio* was read with the request whether the quirites "will and order it" (*velitis, jubeatis*). The magistrate is now addressing a *contio*, and the *rogatio* is subjected to a limited discussion. The president explains and advises it, and the officials or senators whom he has assembled express their support or dissent.[9] This discussion always preceded acts of legislation.[10] When the *comitia* met for jurisdiction there may

in 58 B.C. was amended (Cic. *ad Att.* iii. 2 " praesertim nondum rogatione correcta "), but whether before or after promulgation is not clear.

[1] Dionysius, Plutarch, and Priscian explain *trinum nundinum* as the third market-day, an interval of *trinarum nundinarum*, i.e. seventeen days; but Mommsen has made out a good case for its being three *nundina*, i.e. intervals of eight days (*Staatsr.* iii. p. 375).   [2] p. 164.   [3] p. 38.

[4] Varro *L.L.* vi. 91 "comitiatum praeco populum vocet ad te, et eum de muris vocet praeco."

[5] The herald is not mentioned in connexion with the *concilium plebis*. The *comitia curiata* were summoned by a *lictor curiatius*. See Momms. *Staatsr.* iii. p. 386.

[6] Gell. xv. 27 ; Dio Cass. xxxvii. 27.

[7] Varro *L.L.* vi. 92 ; Plut. *C. Gracch.* 3.

[8] " Sollemne carmen precationis " (Liv. xxxix. 15).

[9] Cic. *de Leg.* iii. 4, 11 "qui agent . . . rem populum docento " ; Quintil. *Inst. Or.* ii. 4, 33 "Romanis pro contione suadere ac dissuadere moris fuit."

[10] Except perhaps at the *comitia centuriata* (Momms. iii. p. 395), but this body had almost ceased to be a legislative assembly.

S

have been some debate even in the *quarta accusatio*;[1] it was
probably only at elections that it was wholly absent.

When the discussion was over the *contio* was dissolved.
Those who had no votes were dismissed from the enclosure;[2]
to those with votes the magistrate said, "Si vobis videtur,
discedite, quirites,"[3] thus asking them to divide up into their
separate compartments, whether tribes or curiae or centuries.
The enclosure was deemed large enough to hold all the privileged
citizens, although where such a space could have been found on
the Capitol or in the Forum is one of the mysteries of Roman
topography.   This enclosure was divided longitudinally into
as many compartments (*consaepta*) as there were voting divisions.
Each division was connected with the magistrate's tribunal
through a gallery (*pons*) running the whole length of the enclosure, this high gallery being connected with the various
voting compartments by separate descending *pontes*.

The votes in each compartment were taken singly, and were
given at the exits of the various *pontes*.   During the greater
part of Republican history votes were given verbally, the tellers
(*rogatores*) marking them off on tablets by means of points (*puncta*).[4]
In legislation the affirmative answer was *uti rogas*, the negative
antiquo; in jurisdiction acquittal and condemnation were pronounced by *libero* and *damno*; in elections *dico* and *facio* seem to
have been employed.[5]   But in the latter half of the second
century of the Republic the ballot was introduced.   The change
was gradual.   Secrecy was first secured for elections by the *lex
Gabinia* of 139, and for jurisdiction, with the exception of cases
of treason (*perduellio*), by the *lex Cassia* of 137.   The *lex Papiria*
of 131 extended the principle to legislation, and finally the *lex
Caelia* of 107 admitted it for cases of treason.[6]   In legislation
and jurisdiction the old formulae were retained, the tablets
which were distributed being marked V and A, or L and C.
For the purpose of elections blank tablets were distributed on
which the voters wrote the names.[7]   The *tabellae* were now

[1] p. 247.   [2] Originally *licium*, later *saepta* or *ovile*.
[3] Liv. ii. 56 ; cf. Asc. *in Cornel.* p. 70 "discedere, quod verbum . . .
significat . . . [ut] in suam quisque tribum discedat, in qua est suffragium
laturus."
[4] Hence the expression *ferre punctum* (Cic. *pro Planc.* 22, 53).
[5] Liv. v. 13 ; iii. 21.
[6] Cic. *de Leg.* iii. cc. 15, 16.
[7] Hence the discovery of a fraud at an election through tablets being μιᾷ
χειρὶ γεγραμμέναις (Plut. *Cat. Min.* 46).

thrown into an urn (*cista*) at the exit of each *pons*. The reckoning
of the votes (*diribitio*) was in the hands of tellers who were
sometimes called by the old name *rogatores*, but were also spoken
of as *diribitores*.[1] The *cistae* were watched by public *custodes*,
and in the case of elections the candidates were allowed to
place one guardian at each urn.[2]

The issue was decided by the vote of the groups. In the
assemblies of the curiae and the tribes the voting of the groups
took place simultaneously, in that of the centuries in the order
which we have already described.[3] In the two former assemblies
the order in which the votes of the groups were proclaimed had
thus to be decided by lot.[4] The reading (*pronuntiatio, recitatio*)
was continued only to the point at which an absolute majority
for or against the measure had been obtained. When sixteen
curiae or eighteen tribes were found to have given the same
vote, it ceased, and the formal announcement of the result
(*renuntiatio*) was then made by the magistrate. In the *comitia
centuriata* the announcement of the result might be reached
without all the centuries being called on to vote, since the
result of each vote was proclaimed immediately after the group
had given it, and the needful majority might be reached before
all the groups had voted. The absolute majority was required in
elections as well as in legislative acts, and hence the candidate
who gained a mere relative majority was not returned.[5]

Records of the voting were kept for some time in case the
decision should be challenged.[6] The promulgated *lex* was, as
we saw, deposited in the *aerarium*, as laws which had passed
must have been long before this provision was made, but they
were kept without order or method, and skilled assistants were
required to ferret out the desired enactment.[7] Little regular

[1] Cic. *cum Sen. Gr. eg.* 11, 28 ; *in Pis.* 15, 36.
[2] Plin. *H.N.* xxxiii. 2, 31 ; Cic. *cum Sen. Gr. eg.* 7, 17.   [3] p. 253.
[4] The first curia or tribe is the *principium*. See the prescription of the *lex Quinctia* (p. 242). Even after the ballot was introduced the name of the first voter in a division was specified (*primus scivit*, l.c.).
[5] *Tribus* or *centurias non explere* is said of such candidates (Liv. iii. 64 ; xxxvii. 47). Cf. Liv. xxii. 35.
[6] Cic. *in Pis.* 15, 36 "hoc certe video quod indicant tabulae publicae vos rogatores, vos diribitores, vos custodes fuisse tabularum." It is the list of votes as certified by the guardians and tellers rather than the separate voting tablets that Cicero here speaks of. But the tablets themselves were kept for a time in *loculi* (Varro *R.R.* iii. 5, 18).
[7] Cic. *de Leg.* iii. 20, 46 "Legum custodiam nullam habemus. Itaque eae leges sunt quas apparisores nostri volunt ; a librariis petimus."

provision seems to have been made for the publication even of
recent measures; but those which were considered important
were originally painted on wood and later engraved on bronze,
and fixed in temples or other public places.[1]

[1] See the evidences collected by Mommsen (*Staatsr.* iii. pp. 418-419). It is
from this practice that *figere* and *refigere* are used of the publication and annulling
of laws.

CHAPTER VI

THE Roman constitution, in the form in which we have left it
at the close of the period of its growth, was the chaotic result
of attempts to arrest internal revolution, and of feeble and
misdirected efforts to readjust the relations of outworn powers.
A state in which three popular assemblies have each the right
of passing binding acts of parliament, in which twenty magistrates with clashing authority have each the right of eliciting
the sovereign will of the people, possesses no organisation which
can satisfy the need for which constitutions exist—the ordered
arrangement of all the wants of civic life by means of a series
of uniform acts possessing perpetual validity. It is true that
the search for a personal authority is the object of theoretic,
not of practical, inquiry. The average man, who is fortunately
the power that in the long run determines the shape that politics
shall assume, seeks law alone and cares nothing for its source.
The vagueness of the ultimate power does not affect him, if the
rules it lays down are rigid and binding; he will accept principles
in place of persons, and by doing so he proves that he is more
scientific than the scientists. But the fundamental principles
that lie behind the personal power in a state are too vast in
their scope to apply immediately to the needs of human life.
They require interpretation by means of legislative and executive
authorities; and if these acts of interpretation are to have the
character of principles, the dictating authorities must have a
fixed character and a permanent life, and there must be some
guarantee that they shall submit their judgments to the
accumulated experience of the past. No such character and no
such guarantee were to be found in the existing elements of
the Roman state which had strict legal recognition. The *comitia*

could, like a parliament in a modern state where no provision
for a constituent assembly exists, go on in an endless career
of constitution-making; the magistrates could interpret the laws
at their own will, and by fighting out the merits of their rival
interpretations amongst themselves paralyse the state or plunge
it into anarchy. It was felt that a central power must reside
somewhere, a power which should guide the people and control
the magistrates, a power which should above all avert the
terrible conflicts between rival authorities so amply encouraged
by the existing law.

It was scarcely necessary, at any one point in the growth of
the Roman constitution, to raise the question where this power
was to be found. A chain of circumstances, some internal and
some external, had provided a body of men possessing the three
main qualifications necessary for the exercise of central authority
—permanence, experience, and the free power of deliberation.
With every step in the professed extension of popular privilege
the power of the Roman Senate had increased; and the explanation of this anomaly is to be found in the fact on which we
have already dwelt, that the distribution of authority amongst
the popular assemblies, and the increase in the number of the
magistracies, had involved such a weakening of the authority
of magistrates and people as to render both incapable of any
pretence at effective rule. The long series of wars in which
Rome was engaged, from the commencement of the struggle
with Pyrrhus to the close of the third contest with Carthage,
and the new duties of administration entailed by the
organisation of Italy and of the earlier provinces, exhibited this
incapacity in a still more glaring light. But the growth of the
Senate's authority cannot be attributed mainly to the necessities
of external administration; for the fundamental changes which
conditioned its pre-eminence had come when Rome was little
more than a city-state, and the Senate would have ruled had
Rome continued to govern a tract of territory no larger than
that possessed by a Cretan city. The Empire was the final
ratification, the seal of the Senate's authority; but the origin of
this authority is to be found, not in the accident of conquest, but
in the working of the Roman mind itself.

The circumstances which determined the growth of the power
of this great council of state are connected, firstly, with the
constitution of the council itself; secondly, with the changes in

its presidency ; and thirdly, with its absorption of isolated powers, some of which it drew from the incompetent hands of magistrates and people, others of which it created.

(i.) A nominee body, such as the Senate had originally been, may be moulded by the will of the nominator. The personal selection by the consuls of their intimate friends, the habit of omitting, at the annual revision of the list, the names of those who were alien to them in sympathy, while favouring the dignity of the aristocracy by making it appear as though exclusion were based on arbitrary preference and not on censure, yet diminished the independence and lessened the prestige of the councillors thus arbitrarily selected. It is true that the work of selection was performed by two consuls, and the judgment of the one might be balanced by the prejudice of the other ; it is also true that public opinion would have been shocked by the choice of unworthy members of the magisterial council, and that the aristocracy itself would have resented the omission of a name distinguished by the great deeds of its possessor while in office ; but the self-existence of this council could only be secured by the one great device of taking from the magistrate, whose duty it was to consult, the selection of the men whose duty it was to furnish him with advice. An opportunity for effecting this change was offered by the institution of the censorship. The selection of the Senate (lectio senatus) is indeed no part of the census, nor do we know when this highest of all the privileges of the censors was transferred to the new authority. But by the year 312 not only, as we have seen,[1] had the transference been effected, but conditions of selection had been imposed which made the Senate partly a body of ex-curule magistrates, partly of nominees who had done good service to the state in the lesser grades of the magistracy or the higher ranks of the army. The vista that lay before the eyes of all aspirants to office was now no longer the annual magistracy, temporary in its nature and hampered by restrictions of every kind, but the seat in the Senate to which it was the stepping-stone. Within the charmed circle the grades of rank were still of importance, and the "servants of the order,"[2] as the magistrates now tended to become, could find in

---

[1] p. 219.
[2] Cic. pro Sest. 65, 137 "senatum reipublicae custodem, praesidem, propugnatorem collocaverunt (majores) ; hujus ordinis auctoritate uti magistratus et quasi ministros gravissimi consilii esse voluerunt."

the magnificent displays of the aedile, the high judicial functions of the praetor, the military leadership of the consul, and the moral control of the censor, the graduated satisfaction of the most diverse ambitions. But, even before the point of transition marked by the curule magistracy had been passed, the Roman noble tended to identify his interests with those of the house to which fate and the inevitable suffrages of the people had destined him. Interest even more than conviction would sanction such a choice ; the vast nominal powers of the magistracy he could wield but for a year ; of the clique of Three Hundred he was a life-long member. And the depressing influence, which contact with some scores of middle-aged and experienced men must have over youth even when blessed with genius, completed the work which interest and a vague class sympathy had begun. The new member moved in that narrow circle of ideas which through its very narrowness was strong enough to baffle Pyrrhus, Hannibal, and Philip, and to half complete the organisation of the world. The men that rose above it—Scipio, the Gracchi, Caesar—found endless difficulties in their path, and originality of conception, which is conspicuous by its absence in the organisation of the Roman Empire, led its possessors to exile, death, or monarchy. But the restraining influence was felt only in the essential principles of politics ; in the control of details a free hand was still given to the administrator, and individuality of a uniform, decorous, and sober kind, combined with a high average level of practical ability, is to be found in the Roman senator of the best period. The narrowness of interest, the selfishness and the corruption, which are the besetting sins of a corporation with an assured tenure of rule, were also weakened in the case of the Roman Senate by the fact that, through the elective principle, it was always in constant touch with the people. It is true that the Senate was a parliament, the members of which were elected for life—a parliament, therefore, that might easily cease to represent the wishes of the electorate ; but each member, until he obtained the coveted prize of the consulship, was ever submitting himself to the suffrages of the people in order to pass from grade to grade of honour. The susceptibilities of the " great tame beast " had to be respected ; its eyes must be dazzled by occasional popular measures, by military achievements, at the worst by private bounty or by brilliant shows. The coterie system that worked the elections could do much, but it could not do everything; the race for honours provided *stimuli* sufficient—even when the public opinion of his own order failed—to keep a counsellor of Rome up to a high level of efficiency.

An order of nobility that is practically hereditary tends to attach to itself titles of nobility and external distinctions of dress. The democratic nomenclature of the Romans prevented the development of the first, and although within the Senate the grades of rank were clearly marked, and the distinctions between *consulares, praetorii, aedilicii* and the former holders of lesser magistracies were observed in the order of debate, these designations were not employed as constant epithets. But the desire of emphasising difference of functions by external signs, which is such a strongly marked feature in Roman public life, revealed itself fully in the senatorial garb. The present or past holder of curule office wore the purple-striped toga of the magistrate, the ordinary senator bore on his tunic a stripe of the same colour, which during the last century of the Republic was distinguished by its breadth from that worn by the order of the equites. Still more distinctly a part of the senatorial *insignia* is the senatorial shoe of red leather (*calceus mulleus*), which, distinct in shape as well as in colour, was worn by no other members of the state. The origin of the distinction is obscure; tradition explained the sandal as the royal footgear,[1] which continued to be worn by the patrician senators in their character of potential kings (*interreges*).[2] The gold ring the senators shared with the members of the equestrian order. Since the nobility of a senator ended with his life, it is needless to remark that the *insignia* could not be transmitted to descendants. Yet, as some of them— the gold ring and perhaps the *latus clavus*—had merely a social sanction, it is not improbable that the practically hereditary nature of the nobility had led to their being worn by members of senatorial families destined to follow their fathers' career. There is, at least, no reason to suppose that the youthful order of *laticlavii* was an invention of the Emperor Augustus.[3]

[1] Festus p. 142 " mulleos genus calceorum aiunt esse, quibus reges Albanorum primi, deinde patricii sunt usi."

[2] Hence the distinction between the patrician and plebeian form of shoe (Mommsen *Staatsr.* iii. p. 891). In the time of Cato the elder this footgear was only worn by the plebeian senator "qui magistratum curulem cepisset " (Festus l.c.).

[3] For an investiture of boys with the *latus clavus* earlier than the rule of Augustus, see Suet. *Aug.* 94.

The identification of the magistracy with the Senate, which had been practically complete by the close of the third century of the Republic, was perfected in law by the dictator Sulla. The quaestorship was now made the stepping-stone to the Senate ;[1] the personal selection by the censors—which, in the face of unwritten custom, had been growing weaker year by year— was dispensed with; while their more important right of rejecting unworthy members could be resorted to only when the censorship was occasionally galvanised into new life. An automatic mode of recruiting the order should, if the power and dignity contemplated by the reactionary legislator were to be secured, have been accompanied by an equally automatic method of divesting of their rank those who had proved unworthy of it. But no such system was devised, and the morals of the Senate were for the first time left to chance, or rather to the reasonable hope that after the age of thirty-one (the lowest period of life at which senatorial dignity could be held) the character once formed would not deteriorate.

A more important factor in the change introduced by the Cornelian legislation was the permanent increase in the numbers of the Senate. Doubled by the immediate action of the dictator, the body continued to maintain its complement of about 600 members ; for twenty annual additions of ex-magistrates of the usual quaestorian age would enable it to retain this normal level. The large size thus given to the senatorial body is one of its most surprising features, when we consider the business with which it had to deal. Secrets that are uttered with bated breath in a modern cabinet were proclaimed aloud at Rome to an assembly of the size of a modern parliament. But there were no reports of proceedings for the eyes or ears of the outside world, and secrecy about reasons for policy was sometimes only too well kept. Such secrecy was often treated as suspicious by the professed leaders of the people at the close of the Republic, and the consciousness of danger felt in the Senate seemed mere weakness to the mob. The history of the Senate, if it does not show the futility of secret diplomacy, may yet prove it to be unnecessary that this diplomacy to be effective should be entrusted to a few.

(ii.) The freedom and power of a deliberative assembly

[1] Tac. *Ann.* xi. 22 "post lege Sullae viginti (quaestores) creati supplendo senatui."

depends very largely on the unrestricted right of debate and
initiative possessed by its individual members.   In theory the
Roman senator was sorely hampered in the exercise of both of
these powers.   The body to which he belonged ever retained its
formal character of a council of advisers; the magistrate might
summon it or not at his discretion, might refuse to lay a
particular question before the house, or decline to elicit the
opinions (*sententiae*) of some suspected members, opinions which
they had no power to give unasked.   So long as these powers
were in the hands of two consuls, a conspiracy of silence might
easily impede the expression of the Senate's judgment; but
when the right of summoning and of laying business before the
house became the property of the praetors in virtue of their
imperium, and was subsequently, by an anomalous recognition of
a revolutionary power, extended to the tribunate, the number
of possible presidents was increased to twenty, and the Senate
again drew its strength from the dissensions of the magistrates.
Twenty men, even if they all represent a nobility, must also
represent different shades of opinion, and will attempt to elicit
views corresponding to their own, which may then be submitted
to the approval and the votes of the house.   The practice
having early arisen that it was only a definite expression of
opinion coming from some quarter of the house that should be
submitted to the approval of its members, the magistrate, eager
to put the desired motion (*relatio*), is now to a large extent
dependent on the senator.   And the few gaps that still remain
in the latter's power of initiative are filled up by ingenious
fictions of debate.   The senator would rise, unburden his soul
of cherished views on matters alien to the debate,[1] and then
make his speech conform to the rules of the house by concluding
with a formal opinion on the direct issue put before it by the
magistrate.   In one instance at least we find the method reversed; the great political crime of Carthage's destruction was
prepared by the famous *sententia* of Cato,[2] often repeated in
speeches on unrelated topics, and having no connexion with the
issue that was directly before the house.

To understand the facilities for information and the freedom

---

[1] Gell. iv. 10, 8 "Erat . . jus senatori ut sententiam rogatus diceret ante
quicquid vellet aliae rei et quoad vellet." For this practice of *egredi relationem*
see Tac. *Ann.* ii. 33.

[2] "Delenda est Carthago" (Florus ii 15); cf. App. *Lib.* 69.

of debate possessed by the Senate, we must have a clear view of
the functions of its presidents and of the position of the ordinary
magistrates in that assembly. The right of summons and the
right of laying business before the body were inseparable; both
were possessed by three orders of magistrates—consuls, praetors,
and tribunes. But law, in the shape of the power given by the
major potestas, made it impossible for the praetor to exercise his
right of summons in defiance of the consul; while custom
dictated that even the tribune should not exercise this right
when the consul was at Rome. But, once the summons has
been issued and obeyed, the convoker of the council is not its
only president. The three classes of magistrates have each the
right of reference, and each in an order prescribed by customary
law. The consuls' motions come first; they are followed by
those of the praetors, and then the tribunes have their turn.[1]
This system of priority, although necessary to prevent confusion,
was under ordinary circumstances a matter of comparative un-
importance. It could only become a serious hindrance to the
freedom of debate if the consul abruptly dismissed the meeting
before a decision had been reached on some question of pressing
importance,[2] or if a method of systematic obstruction were
adopted by some senator, who wasted the hours with prolix
oratory until the setting of the sun made a suspension of business legally necessary. But the former device was revolutionary
in its character, and on the occasion of its use a fit preparation
for a revolution; while the latter seems to have been employed,
as by the younger Cato during Caesar's consulship, as a weapon
against an offensive *relatio* already before the house.[3] The
president himself had ample powers for meeting such designs;
in the case in question the consul had the obstructive stoic
haled from the room.[4]

A more serious danger would have been the absence of
information from the officials who succeeded the consul in
putting motions before the house; but this was obviated by the

[1] An attempt to violate this order was made in 56 B.C., "cum Lupus tribunus
pl. . . . intendere coepit ante se oportere discessionem facere quam consules.
Ejus orationi vehementer ab omnibus reclamatum est; erat enim et iniqua et nova"
(Cic. *ad Fam.* i. 2, 2).

[2] The consul Marcellus thus dismissed the Senate in 50 B.C. on its favouring
the proposal that both Pompeius and Caesar should lay down their commands
(App. *B.C.* ii. 30).

[3] Gell. iv. 10, 8.   [4] ib. l.c.; Suet. *Caes.* 20.

power which magistrates had of speaking (*verba facere*) without invitation at any period of the debate. This power was possessed as an admitted right by those magistrates who were themselves presiding; the quaestors, whose financial statements were indispensable, and the aediles may have exercised it only on sufferance. This privilege was the more necessary as the presiding magistrates at least could not be asked their opinion by the official who held the attention of the house; they could not give advice, for they were themselves seeking it of others.

Custom had determined with equal care the method by which opinions should be elicited from the unofficial and advising members of the house. The question "what is your advice?" (*quid censes?*) was put by the president to each senator in an order corresponding to his official rank. In the days of the activity of the censorship, it was this magistracy which had determined the president's first selection; the censors had placed at the head of their list the name of some distinguished man (often himself an ex-censor), and it was this "chief of the Senate" (*princeps senatus*) whose opinion was first sought. But, after Sulla's reform in the constitution of the order, there is, in spite of the occasional revival of the censorship, no certain evidence of the perpetuation of this dignity. Henceforth a body of *consulares* holds the first place, and from these the presiding magistrate—at least the consul who opens the business of the house—chooses his first adviser, according to no settled rules, but with due regard to seniority or personal distinction.[1] The only exception to this practice was to be found in the latter half of the year, when the consuls elect, either in virtue of their quasi-magisterial position or because they might themselves have to carry out the decrees which were being discussed, took precedence of the consulars.[2] From the latter the question passed down through the *praetorii* to the men of aedilician or

[1] Gell. xiv. 7, 9 (from the *Commentarius* of Varro) "singulos autem debere consuli gradatim incipique a consulari gradu. Ex quo gradu semper quidem antea primum rogari solitum qui princeps in senatum lectus esset; tum autem, cum haec scriberet, novum morem institutum refert per ambitionem gratiamque ut is primus rogaretur quem rogare vellet qui haberet senatum, dum is tamen ex gradu consulari esset." For this *novus mos* cf. Cic. *ad Att.* i. 13, 2 (61 B.C.) "Primum igitur scito primum me non esse rogatum sententiam praepositumque esse nobis pacificatorem Allobrogum" (C. Calpurnius Piso, a relative of the presiding consul).

[2] Sall. *Cat.* 50 (in the debate on the Catilinarian conspirators) "D. Junius Silanus primus sententiam rogatus quod eo tempore consul designatus erat."

tribunician rank, and so finally to the lowest grade of all—the
ex-quaestors ; and it is probable that, in every grade, the rule
of consulting a designated magistrate before an ex-magistrate
was observed. It is obvious that this procedure, when rigidly
adhered to, left the non-curule members of the Senate only an
infinitesimal chance of a share in the debate. These had always
been known as *pedarii*, in contradistinction to the *curules;*
originally nominees of the censors, they included after the time
of Sulla the former tribunes and plebeian aediles, and the
members of quaestorian rank. As they were rarely reached in
the debate, they seldom had the opportunity of expressing an
opinion, and hence arose the erroneous notion of some antiquarians that the *pedarii* were given the right of voting but not
the power of debate.[1] But restrictions of this kind, arising from
practice and not from law, were never pressed by the Romans.
The repute of a man who had not reached curule rank might
exceed that of all the other senators ; the principle that would
open the lips of a Bibulus and close those of a Cato was
recognised as mischievous in certain emergencies, and it was
the latter who as tribune elect—that is, as a *pedarius*—moved
the resolution which condemned the Catilinarian conspirators to
death.[2]

From the mass of opinions elicited in the course of the
debate, the president might choose any that he pleased to submit
to the judgment of the house. The safeguard of the individual
senator was here found in the number of the presiding magistrates.
As a rule the same order was followed in putting *sententiae* to
the vote as had been observed in eliciting them ; but out of an
aggregate of opinions that, with differences of detail, gave
practically the same advice, the president might choose that
which he considered most to the point or best worded as the one
to be submitted to his council. It was certainly an unusual
step when, in the historic debate of December 5 in the year

---

[1] Festus p. 210 "(Pedarius senator) ita appellatur quia tacitus transeundo ad
eum, cujus sententiam probat, quid sentiat indicat." Cf. Gell. iii. 18. The
explanation cited by Festus is true only so far as it expresses a usual circumstance
of debate. The name *pedarius* is probably derived from the absence of the
curule chair (Gavius Bassus ap. Gell. l.c).
[2] Vell. ii. 35 "Hic tribunus plebis designatus . . . paene inter ultimos
interrogatus sententiam"; Cic. *ad Att.* xii. 21, 1 "Cur ergo in sententiam
Catonis? Quia verbis luculentioribus et pluribus rem eandem (i.e. the opinion
already expressed by *consulares*) comprehenderat."

63 B.C., Cicero put to the vote the *sententia* of Cato in place of the similar but weaker resolutions of the *consulares* ;[1] but the consul in this exercise of his discretionary choice was acting well within his rights.

One is sometimes surprised, considering the rigidity of the procedure and the size of the body, at the amount of business that appears to have been transacted at a single meeting of the Senate. But both the rules of procedure and the Roman temperament account for the rapidity of the debate. As regards the former it must be remembered that no motion could be put unless pressed by a magistrate, that there was no distinction between substantive motions and amendments, that alternative proposals, therefore, had not to be submitted in detail to a division, that the carrying of one motion generally swept all *sententiae* on the same subject aside, that motions for adjournment did not take precedence of other motions, and that the business of the house was not interrupted by this modern device for wasting time. We must also remember that a division in the modern sense of the word was rare, and that it appears seldom to have been necessary to take the numbers of the members who respectively supported or were adverse to a motion.[2] The estimate of the voting was in fact going on during the debate; it was the custom of the senator, often without rising, to express a few words of assent to a former speech,[3] and it was not unusual to leave one's bench and take up a position near the man whose opinion one supported.[4] The sense of the house could thus often be taken before the debate had ended; where it was not obvious the consul urged to a division (*discessio*);[5] even then it is improbable that recourse

[1] See p. 270 n. 2.
[2] In a rough estimate of the house (61 B.C.) Cicero mentions 15 on one side of a question, "quite 400 " on the other (*ad Att.* i. 14, 5). On Curio's proposal in 50 B.C. that both Pompeius and Caesar should lay down their commands, 22 dissented, 370 approved (App. *B.C.* ii. 30). In the latter case there seems to have been no formal division (see p. 268 n. 2); and in both the small numbers may be the result of exact computation, the large either of a guess or of a deduction drawn from an already counted quorum.
[3] "Verbo adsentiri" (Sall. *Cat.* 52); cf. Cic. *ad Fam.* v. 2, 9 "sedens iis adsensi."
[4] "In alienam sententiam pedibus ire" (Gell. iii. 18, 1).
[5] The invitation to divide on the *sententia* was couched in the form "Qui hoc censetis, illuc transite : qui alia omnia, in hanc partem" (Festus p. 261). Hence the colloquial phrase "ire in alia omnia" for negativing a proposal at the Senate (Cic. *ad Fam.* i. 2, 1).

was had to counting, unless the parties on either side were very evenly balanced. Other reasons for rapidity were to be found in the Roman temperament and in the intellectual atmosphere of the house. The Roman, until his better nature was corrupted by the schools of Athens and Rhodes, was a man of few words; the Senate was the least likely body in the world to be swayed by florid eloquence; clearness and brevity were the qualities most in demand, and even at the close of the Republic, when the Senate had surrendered itself to the perilous pleasure of listening to carefully woven sentences, the "paint pots" of Cicero [1] were still in all probability the exception and not the rule.

The voice of the majority of the Senate was embodied in a resolution (*senatus consultum*). Considered as the mere advice of the magistrates' council it had no legal validity whatever; its binding character sprang from the fact that it was a decree of the magistrate applying to a sphere in which he was himself competent to issue such injunctions. Hence, as we have seen, [2] the veto pronounced on a decree of the Senate by the colleague or superior of the magistrate who has elicited it, is no exception to the rule that the acts of corporations or of private individuals were not subject to this form of invalidation. So little was this the case that, when the decree had been vetoed, the advice of the Senate still remained unimpaired. The annulled resolution was still drawn up, but it had become an *auctoritas* merely.[3] It was still of sufficient potency to bind constitutionally-minded magistrates, but it no longer imposed the duty of obeying it on the community. The *consultum* or *auctoritas* was drawn up at the place of meeting soon after the resolution which it embodied had been passed. As there were no permanent officials of a responsible character to see to its redaction, a small committee was appointed by the president to attest the genuineness of the document;[4] this consisted usually of the author of the resolution and of some of his supporters.

(iii.) The Senate exerted its developed authority under

---

[1] Cic. *ad Att.* i. 14, 3 "totum hunc locum, quem ego . . . soleo pingere, de flamma, de ferro—nosti illas ληκύθους."

[2] p. 179.

[3] Cic. *ad Fam.* viii. 8, 5 ff. In § 6 we find the formula "Si quis huic s. c. intercesserit, senatui placere auctoritatem perscribi."

[4] ib. l.c. § 6 " Pr. Kal. Octobres in aede Apollinis scrib. adfuerunt L. Domitius Cn. f. Fab. Ahenobarbus," etc.

two different aspects. It was the body which exercised the
power of previous deliberation on matters which must be
submitted to the judgment of a nominally higher authority, the
people, and it was a council which professed to give final direc-
tions to the magistrates on the conduct of their administrative
duties. It possessed no sphere of its own in which it could act
unassisted by magistrates and people, and thus its formal independence is far less than that possessed by such a body as the
Athenian *Boulê*. The only department of state in which it
seems to have independent authority—the power of perpetuating
the very life of the *civitas* by the appointment of an interrex—
belongs strictly not to the Senate but to its patrician members ;
and even for the exercise of this right during the Republic the
motive power had to spring ultimately from a magistrate of the
Plebs.[1]

The Senate by exercising a probouleutic authority showed its
sense of its own limitations. Occasionally, as we shall see, it
usurped isolated powers that belonged of right to the people; but
as a rule its final authority was only felt in that vast sphere
of executive influence that had been formerly entrusted to the
magistrates. It could control, but it might not usurp, the
sovereign powers of the people ; it elected no magistrates ; it
possessed no legislative authority ; it could not declare war or
make peace ; it dared not extend the limits of Roman citizenship
by the conferment of the franchise ; it made no claim to the
exercise of jurisdiction or of the still more sovereign right of
pardon.

Yet, when it is remembered that the activity of the *comitia*
in all these matters could only be set in motion by the magistrate,
and that the Senate's advice had grown into a real power of
control, it is easy to see that the first step in every measure of
importance must come under the cognisance of this all-pervading
council. Its probouleutic authority was based on the observance
by the magistrate of certain unwritten rules, which regulated
the exercise both of his positive and of his negative powers. It
was held that no magistrate should question the people on any
important matter without the Senate's advice, and that he should
not decline to exercise this power at its request ; that the power
of veto should be employed only at the discretion of the council,
and that the request for its exercise should not be refused.

[1] p. 148.

T

These unwritten principles were, as a rule, strong enough to fetter a magistrate's action by his conviction of their necessity; when this conviction was not sufficiently strong, the Senate resorted to its last constitutional weapon, the veto of a friendly magistrate. For this purpose the tribunician college was usually employed; its size offered the largest scope for differences of opinion, for of the ten legally supreme magistrates of the state one at least could generally be found to whom the Senate's word was law. The blocking of legislation through the *intercessio* of a senatorial tribune may be illustrated by the attempt of Octavius to negative the agrarian legislation of the elder Gracchus :[1] the effort to annul an administrative order of a sweeping kind by the veto pronounced against the proposal of the praetor Juventius when, without consultation of the Senate and without previous intimation to the consuls, he attempted to urge the *comitia* of the people into a declaration of war with Rhodes.[2]

In dealing with the powers of the Senate two courses lie open before us ; we may either treat them in the order of their growth and show how the successive usurpations were effected, or we may describe them as they existed in their developed form. The first method would have more of an historical interest, but, apart from its difficulty and obscurity due to the frequent lack of evidence, it would result in a wholly unsystematic classification of the aggregate of acquired rights. It is preferable, therefore, to deal with the Senate's powers in their developed form, with a preliminary warning that they were gained at very lengthy intervals and by very different means. Some, such as the control of finance, were usurped from the magistrate ; others, such as the dispensation from laws, were stolen from the people ; to others again, such as the control of the details of provincial government, the Senate had an altogether peculiar right, such powers being created during the period of the growth of its ascendency.

With the election of magistrates the Senate of the later Republic had no direct concern, and the people alone claimed the perhaps not wholly constitutional right of deposing them.

[1] Plut. *Ti. Gracch.* 10 ; App. *B.C.* i. 12.

[2] Polyb. xxx. 4. For the motive of the veto see Liv. xlv. 21 "M. Juventius Thalna . . . praetor novo maloque exemplo rem ingressus erat, quod, ante non consulto senatu, non consulibus certioribus factis, de sua unius sententia rogationem ferret vellent juberentne Rhodiis bellum indici, cum antea semper prius senatus de bello consultus esset, deinde ex auctoritate patrum ad populum latum."

But towards the close of its tenure of power, when the struggle
for existence caused it to strain its prerogatives to the utmost
limit, we find the Senate claiming the very analogous right of
suspending a magistrate from the exercise of the functions of his
office. A charge of turbulent proceedings was the motive for
the suspension of Caesar from the praetorship, and of Metellus
Nepos from the tribunate in 62,[1] and Caelius Rufus was ejected,
on the allegation of similar misconduct, from the curule chair of
the praetor in 48.[2]   The use of this power against the praetor,
or indeed against any magistrate subject to the *major potestas* of
the tribune, is comprehensible; for the latter might, at the
bidding of the Senate, inhibit any official from the exercise of
his customary functions; how the power could be employed
against the tribunate itself is one of the hidden mysteries of
senatorial usurpation.

The power of legislating, that is of establishing fundamental
changes in civic relations, was never claimed by the Senate; nor
had it ever possessed any legal right to suggest or impede the
making of a law.   The *patrum auctoritas*, like the *interregnum*,
had resided only with the patrician members of that body; and
the power of previous deliberation claimed by the later Senate as
a whole was merely one of the inevitable results of the balance
of power within the magistracy.   Such slight approximations to
law-making as are found were simply the result of consultation
by the magistrates on questionable points.   The Senate reaffirmed
an ancient principle that the confession of a slave which might
doom his master to death or exile should not be wrung from him
by torture ;[3] it might even infringe so much on the freedom of
contract as to suggest a current rate of interest[4]—a principle
which the praetor might respect if he cared or if his colleague
obliged him to do so.

But here again we meet with the strange anomaly that the
Senate can destroy where it cannot create.   It claimed the

[1] Suet. *Caes.* 16 (Caesar supported Metellus in carrying) "turbulentissimas
leges adversus collegarum intercessionem . . . donec ambo administratione
reipublicae decreto patrum submoverentur."
[2] In this case the prohibition was effected through the coercive power of the
consul springing from his *majus imperium* (Dio Cass. xlii. 23).
[3] Tac. *Ann.* ii. 30 "vetere senatus consulto quaestio in caput domini
prohibebatur."
[4] Cic. *ad Att.* v. 21, 13 (50 B.C.) "cum senatus consultum modo factum sit . .
in creditorum causa, ut centesimae perpetuo faenore ducerentur."

sovereign privilege of exempting individuals from the operation
of the laws, and the claim which was an admitted usurpation
was sanctioned by custom.   Formerly the sovereign people could
alone grant such dispensations, but the motion submitted to the
people was first approved by the Senate.   Very gradually the
second stage in the proceedings was dropped, for it was considered the merely formal sanction of an already accomplished
act; and the senatorial right of dispensation was assured until it
was attacked by the tribune Cornelius (67 B.C.).   The proposal
that it should be restored to the people was successfully resisted,
but a compromise was arrived at by which it was agreed that no
act of dispensation should be valid which had not been approved
by a house of at least two hundred members.[1]   This provision,
evidently meant to prevent the abuse of the power for purely
personal or party ends, did not fulfil its purpose, for *senatus
consulta* of this kind were gained by influential men on the
slightest pretexts and for the most unworthy objects.[2]

An observance of certain forms had always been necessary for
the legislative activity of the people to be regular and valid.   In
countries which recognise the sovereignty of parliament, the
guardian of such forms is in the first instance the legislative
chamber itself, in the second the courts of justice, which can, or
should, be allowed to refuse to put into effect any law that has
been passed in disregard of such formalities.   This was the case
at Rome.   The laws themselves contained clauses which pronounced their ineffectiveness in case they should be found to
violate the principles of the constitution, and the courts of
justice had the courage to resist the enactments even of the
provisional government of the dictator Sulla.   But the executive
authority might also have doubts about the propriety of putting
into force a measure which it recognised to be irregular; and of
this executive authority the Senate was the guide.   Hence its
well-established claim to point out a flaw in a legislative enactment, to establish the fact that the magistrate had questioned
the people improperly, and that the answer of the people was
therefore null and void.   The exercise of this revising power

---

[1] Ascon. *in Cornel.* p. 58.

[2] M. Brutus had gained from the Senate the validation of a bond (*syngrapha*),
by which an exorbitant rate of interest was demanded from the government of
Salamis in Cyprus.   Bonds of this kind, through which obligations were incurred
by provincials at Rome, had been rendered illegal by a *lex Gabinia* of 67 B.C.
(Cic. *ad Att.* v. 21, 12).

once led to the greatest upheaval that Roman history records. It was by pointing out that the law of the younger Livius Drusus, which contained amongst its other clauses the gift of *civitas* to the allies, was irregular as contravening the condition fixed by a *lex Caecilia Didia* (98 B.C.) that wholly different enactments should not be contained in the same *rogatio*,[1] that the Senate brought to a head the formidable conspiracy which culminated in the outbreak of the social war. History also brings to our notice the attempted reversal by this means of a popular judgment of a far smaller kind. It was suggested in the Senate that a notice of the alleged irregularities of Clodius' *plebiscitum* should be made the ground of Cicero's recall; but the exiled orator, while thinking that there was "something in the notion," yet preferred the far safer form of an abrogation of the enactment by the popular voice itself.[2]

When we turn from legislation to its complement of jurisdiction we find little direct interference by the Senate with the regular course of either civil or criminal procedure. On exceptional occasions it might decide the sphere of the praetor's activity,[3] and by its practical weight in the declaration of a *justitium* it might suspend the operation of the business of the courts; but it did not interfere in the details of such business, and the appeals to the vetoing magistrates were left to their own discretion.

With respect to the criminal jurisdiction of the regular courts, although the Senate never assumed a faculty for determining the procedure or the sentence, it sometimes took the initiative in a prosecution by suggesting that a charge should be brought, and this implication *might* be contained in a senatorial judgment that a certain course of action was *contra rem publicam*.[4]

---

[1] Cic. *pro Domo* 16, 41 "judicavit senatus M. Drusi legibus, quae contra legem Caeciliam et Didiam latae essent, populum non teneri." The account that the Livian laws were shelved as *contra auspicia* (Ascon. *in Cornel.* p. 68 "Philippus cos. . . . obtinuit a senatu, ut leges ejus omnes uno s. c. tollerentur. Decretum est enim contra auspicia esse latas neque eis teneri populum") may contain one of the grounds of their abrogation.

[2] Cic. *ad Att.* iii. 15, 5 "Quod te cum Culleone scribis de privilegio locutum, est aliquid, sed multo est melius abrogari."

[3] p. 204.

[4] Liv. xxv. 4; Sall. *Cat.* 50; Ascon. *in Milon.* p. 44. The Senate in this way sometimes interprets a criminal law and extends its incidence. See Cic. *de Har. Resp.* 8, 15 "decrevit senatus eos qui id fecissent (i.e. who had disturbed the rebuilding of Cicero's house) lege de vi, quae est in eos qui universam rem publicam oppugnassent (i.e. vi publica) teneri."

With respect to an extraordinary commission, the true theory of the Republic was that it could be established only by the people. The procedure adopted against Clodius for the violation of the rites of the Bona Dea is typical of the constitutional method that should always have been employed. The offence which he had committed—though vaguely designated "incest"—was one that in that particular form was unknown to Roman law. First the college of pontiffs is consulted, and pronounces the act an offence against religion (*nefas*); then a decree of the Senate is framed specifying the crime and the procedure, which is modelled as closely as possible on that of the ordinary criminal courts. This decree is then submitted for ratification to the judgment of the people.[1] Acts of attainder are a lamentable confession of weakness in a political, social, and legal system; but it was right that this weakness should not be remedied by an administrative authority representing a single caste.

But there were certain emergencies which it was thought could not be met, even by the establishment of a special judicial commission. Epidemics of crime, such as poisoning, arson, murder, seemed to demand the immediate exercise of the magistrate's *imperium*, and for this exercise the Senate is the directing and controlling force. Such an exercise of magisterial *coercitio* at the behest of the Senate is practically a declaration of martial law, although the Senate by its decree does not create a new power, but simply urges the magistrate to set free the forces latent in his *imperium*. The earlier Republic had provided a suspension of constitutional procedure in the form of the dictatorship as a means of meeting such an emergency; the later constitution had no such provision, and the burden of responsibility fell on the joint shoulders of Senate and magistrates. Whether the exercise of such summary capital jurisdiction was legal depended on the status and sex of the victims. If the 170 women put to death for poisoning in 331 B.C.[2] were executed by magisterial decree, the act was legal, for women had no right of appeal. Similar legality attended its exercise over provincials;[3] and, if similar sentences were inflicted on Italian

---

[1] Cic. *ad Att.* i. 13, 3 "Credo enim te audisse, cum apud Caesarem pro populo fieret, venisse eo muliebri vestitu virum . . . mentionem a Q. Cornificio in senatu factam . . postea rem ex senatus consulto ad pontifices relatam, idque ab iis nefas esse decretum ; deinde ex senatus consulto consules rogationem promulgasse."

[2] Liv. viii. 18.

[3] ib. xl. 43 (180 B.C.) "A. C. Maenio praetore (cui, provincia Sardinia cum

allies,˙ it was a gross violation of treaty obligations, but not of
the laws of Rome. The male citizen alone might not be put to
death in this summary fashion; and if the Roman members of
the great criminal society of the Bacchanalian guild were executed
without appeal,[2] this was a judicial murder only justified by the
horror excited in the public mind by the blackest crimes
masquerading under the guise of religion. We still possess a
fragmentary copy of the decree by which this "conspiracy" was
repressed; in it the Senate thinks that "capital punishment
should be inflicted,"[3] but the decree does not by its wording
suspend the ordinary laws of appeal.

This guardianship of the state against conspiracies (conjura-
tiones) may have been the precedent for a power, the legality of
which, as exercised by the Senate during the last century of the
Republic, was hotly contested. This was the power of declaring
the existence of a condition of things which the Greeks would have
denominated στάσις, of singling out a party in the state and its
leaders as enemies (hostes) to the Republic, the latter being professedly represented by the Senate itself and the magistrates who
happened to be friendly to it, and of advising the magistrates
who were its presidents, above all the magistrates with imperium,
and sometimes even the pro-magistrates,[4] to employ every means
of summary coercion to ward off the impending danger. The
formula for thus entrusting the guardianship of the community
to a clique of friendly magistrates was expressed in the words
"that the consuls, praetors, and tribunes of the Plebs (with the
addition at times of other officials with the imperium) should see
that the state took no harm."[5] After the passing of this decree

evenisset, additum erat ut quaereret de veneficiis longius ab urbe decem
millibus passuum) literae adlatae se jam tria millia hominum damnasse."
  [1] Liv. xxxix. 41 (184 B.C.); cf. ix. 26 (314 B.C.) and the instance cited
in the next note. In such instances of quaestiones extended to Italy, it is not
clear whether socii as well as cives were executed summarily by Roman
magistrates.
  [2] ib. xxxix. 18.   On this point see Zumpt Criminalrecht der Römer i. 2 p. 212.
  [3] C.I.L. i. n. 196 (a letter from the consuls to some unknown magistrates of
the ager Teuranus in Brutii) l. 24 "eorum (i.e. the Senate) sententia ita fuit 'sei
ques esent, quei avorsum ead fecisent, quam suprad scriptum est, eeis rem
caputalem faciendam censuere.'"
  [4] The consul was armed against C. Gracchus, the consuls in 63; the consuls,
praetors, and tribunes in 100 B.C.; the interrex, proconsul, and all other magistrates with imperium in 77 B.C.
  [5] The decree proposed to meet the threatened revolution of M. Lepidus in
77 B.C. ran as follows : "quoniam M. Lepidus exercitum privato consilio paratum

the responsibility of the Senate ceases; the magistrates act at
their own peril and cannot again devolve any responsibility for a
judicial murder they may have committed in the execution of
their instructions by again consulting the Senate on the guilt of
their victims or on the method of execution to be employed.[1]
There were obvious reasons which rendered it impossible for this
power to be based on any distant precedent; like the power last
discussed it was a substitute for the vanished dictatorship, which
was an integral part of the constitution, and subsequently to the
decline of this office there was no revolution in Rome antecedent
to that which was held by conservatives to have been inaugurated
by the legislation of the Gracchi. But, even apart from the
question of precedent, the absurdity of the Senate's claim to be
guardian of the Republic is manifested by the fact that the
opposite party in the *stasis* might more truly represent the
theory of the constitution, as the Gracchan party did, than the
Senate's government itself; a broad line separates political
opposition, even with the utmost force to back it, from criminal
conspiracy against society, and by the passing of this " ultimate
decree " the Senate declared itself the *author* of a revolution.
The controversy as to right is here insoluble : the insolubility
depends on the fact that there was no permanent government at
Rome except that of convention and of force.

Yet Roman sentiment would have declared that there were
times when the decree and its consequences were justified.
Force can only be met by force, and a gathering such as Catiline's
army in Etruria was a fair object of attack by the executive
authorities ; but sentiment would not have allowed the execution
without appeal of a few prisoners captured within the city, however grave the danger. A state of war must be recognised,

cum pessimis et hostibus rei publicae contra hujus ordinis auctoritatem ad urbem
ducit, uti Appius Claudius interrex cum Q. Catulo pro consule et ceteris, quibus
imperium est, urbi praesidio sint operamque dent ne quid res publica detrimenti
capiat" (from speech of Philippus in Sall. *Hist.* lib. i. frgt. 77, § 22). The
historical instances of the employment of this power are against C. Gracchus and
his adherents in 121 B.C., in the tumult of Saturninus (100), the first Sullan
restoration (88), by the anti-Sullans (82), at the threatened revolution of M.
Lepidus (77), in the Catilinarian conspiracy (63), during the disturbances raised by
Q. Metellus (62), and those preceding the sole consulship of Pompeius (52), against
Caesar (49), against Dolabella and M. Antonius (43).

[1] Cf. Sall. *Cat.* 50 " consul . . . convocato senatu refert quid de eis fieri
placeat, qui in custodiam traditi erant. Sed eos paulo ante frequens senatus
judivcaerat contra rem publicam fecisse."

but there was no power in the Roman state that could declare martial law and execute its consequences.

The exercise of this unprecedented power evoked a vigorous protest from the true government, the people.[1] The plebiscite passed by the younger Gracchus was aimed more directly at the magistrates, and it improved on the Valerian laws by enacting "that no *judicium* should be exercised on the *caput* of a Roman citizen without the consent of the people."[2] But it is possible that it made senators individually responsible for the decree authorising such conduct on the part of the magistrates,[3] and it is almost certain that it abrogated a clause in the law of the Twelve Tables by declaring that the Plebs might exercise capital jurisdiction against a magistrate guilty of violating the provisions of the measure.[4] Henceforth there could be no question of the illegality of the *ultimum senatus consultum*, for Cicero's quibble that the Gracchan law only protected the lives of *cives*, and that individuals specified by the Senate had been declared *hostes*,[5] is an argument in a circle. It is this latter possibility which the Gracchan law denied ; and though common sense might interpret certain overt acts as a sign of war against society, no degree of treason could *ipso jure* make a citizen into an enemy unless that treason had been proved in a court of law.

More justifiable than the power which we have just con-

---

[1] Although the *ultimum senatus consultum* had not been passed against Ti. Gracchus, the condemnation of his adherents without appeal (Vell. ii. 7 ; Val. Max. iv. 7, 1) was the exercise of the jurisdiction of martial law. It was this jurisdiction which elicited the *plebiscitum* of C. Gracchus.

[2] Cic. *pro Rab.* 4, 12 "C. Gracchus legem tulit ne de capite civium Romanorum injussu vestro judicaretur."

[3] Schol. Ambros. p. 370 " Quia sententiam (wrongly for "legem" ; see Zumpt *Criminalrecht* i. 2 p. 73) tulerat Gracchus ne quis in civem Romanum capitalem sententiam diceret." Cf. Cic. *pro Sest.* 28, 61 "Consule me, (Cato), cum esset designatus tribunus plebis, obtulit in discrimen vitam suam : dixit eam sententiam, cujus invidiam capitis periculo sibi praestandam videbat." So Dio Cassius (xxxviii. 14), in speaking of the first bill of Clodius against Cicero, says ἔφερε μὲν γὰρ καὶ ἐπὶ πᾶσαν τὴν βουλήν, ὅτι τοῖς τε ὑπάτοις τὴν φυλακὴν τῆς πόλεως . . . προσετετάχει.

[4] Plut. *C. Gracch.* 4 τὸν δὲ (νόμον εἰσέφερε), εἴ τις ἄρχων ἄκριτον ἐκκεκηρύχοι πολίτην, κατ' αὐτοῦ διδόντα κρίσιν τῷ δήμῳ. δῆμος here may mean either *populus* or *plebs* ; but Gracchus, as tribune, put his own law into force against Popilius (Cic. *pro Domo* 31, 82).

[5] Cic. *in Cat.* iv. 5, 10 " At vero C. Caesar intelligit legem Semproniam esse de civibus Romanis constitutam ; qui autem rei publicae sit hostis eum civem esse nullo modo posse."

sidered was the police-control which the Senate exercised in
Rome.   Here, as in other matters of administration, its attention
was confined to great and exceptional emergencies.   In the
absence of all facilities for the expression of public opinion in
Rome, except through the medium of a magistrate, the ancient
trade guilds (*collegia artificum*) formed convenient centres for
electioneering in the democratic interest.   The fact that towards
the close of the Republic their weight was thrown into the anti-
senatorial scale led the government to regard their existence as
inimical to public order.   A decree of the Senate of the year
64 B.C. summarily dissolved all but the most venerable guilds
which were supposed to derive their origin from Numa ;[1] and
this sudden suppression may be regarded as a last step in a long
career of administrative interference, no record of which has been
preserved by history.   Private political clubs, on the other hand,
such as were known by the names of *sodalitates* and *decuriati*, did
not come under the immediate cognisance of the magistrate ; for
their coercion the Senate had to procure the passing of a law.[2]
But minor details connected with bribery and corruption were
within its competence.   It infringed the inviolability of the
magistrate's house by allowing search to be made there for
incriminating proof of corruption, and it directed that whoever
should be guilty of harbouring professional election agents
(*divisores*) at his dwelling should be liable to a vote of censure
and possible prosecution.[3]

If we now turn from the corrective to the administrative
activity of the Senate, we shall find that this was exhibited
chiefly in the departments of foreign relations, finance, and
religion.

The primary spheres of foreign activity are the declaration
of war, the making of peace, and the framing of alliances.   All
these powers belonged of right to the people, and, as regards
the first, there was never any question that the Senate's position
was merely that of a constant adviser.   The two latter powers

[1] Cic. *in Pis.* 4, 9 ; *pro Sest.* 25, 55 ; Dio Cass. xxxviii. 13.
[2] Cic. *ad Q. fr.* ii. 3, 5 (56 B.C.) "senatus consultum factum est ut sodalitates
decuriatique discederent lexque de iis ferretur ut, qui non discessissent, ea poena
quae est de vi tenerentur."   The *sodalitates* were clubs of the type of the Greek
ἑταιρεῖαι, the *decuriati* probably electioneering associations.
[3] Cic. *ad Att.* i. 16, 12 (61 B.C.) "senatus consulta duo jam facta sunt odiosa
. . . unum, ut apud magistratus inquiri liceret, alterum, cujus domi divisores
habitarent, adversus rem publicam."

merge into one another, for a state that was not on some terms
of alliance with Rome was, according to the rude notions of the
prevailing international law, an enemy of the Republic. There
appear at intervals during the Republic signs of a keen but
advantageous controversy as to whether the right to conclude
binding treaties in the name of the Republic was possessed by
the *imperator* in the field, as well as by Senate and people. To
profit by the oath of a general when it entailed success, to dis-
avow it when it meant failure, and in this case to hand the
unfortunate commander, who had saved Roman lives but not
Roman honour, bound and naked as a scapegoat to the enemy,
were the convenient results of this condition of juristic doubt.
The Caudine Forks in Samnium, Numantia in Spain, and the
neighbourhood of Suthul in Numidia saw Roman generals and their
deluded adversaries equal victims of this controversy.[1] But the
opinion finally prevailed that without the consent of the Senate
and the people no sworn treaty (*foedus*) could be binding.[2] The
practice as to the division of this authority between the council
and the assembly varied from time to time. In the earliest
period a treaty of peace seems to be within the competence of
the magistrate, and therefore of the Senate; in the constitution
of the middle Republic, as revealed to us by Polybius, such an
agreement is always submitted to the people for ratification,[3]
but the close of Republican history shows cases where the
Senate alone is mentioned as the deciding authority.[4]

But the people had at all times merely the final ratifying
authority in these matters. The diplomatic negotiations that
preceded the conclusion of an agreement with a foreign nation
had ever been in the hands of the Senate. When envoys
approached an *imperator* in the field, his duty was to send them
on to the consuls and their council; how far he himself entered
into preliminary negotiations with them depended on his own
discretion, but in the best days of the Republic he could make

[1] Liv. ix. 8-12 ; Plut. *Ti. Gracch.* 7 ; Cic. *de Off.* iii. 30, 109 ; Sall. *Jug.* 39.
[2] Sall. *Jug.* 39 "senatus ita, uti par fuerat, decernit suo atque populi injussu nullum potuisse foedus fieri."
[3] Polyb. vi. 14 ὑπὲρ εἰρήνης οὗτος (ὁ δῆμος) βουλεύεται καὶ πολέμου. καὶ μὴν περὶ συμμαχίας καὶ διαλύσεως καὶ συνθηκῶν οὗτός ἐστιν ὁ βεβαιῶν ἕκαστα τούτων καὶ κύρια ποιῶν ἢ τοὐναντίον.
[4] The Gaditani approach the Senate for the renovation of a treaty made with a pro-magistrate in 78 B.C. Cicero questions its validity (*pro Balbo* 15, 34) on the ground that the people was not consulted. The passage illustrates both the Senate's exercise of this power and the continuance of a controversy as to its right.

no definite agreement. The mode in which the Senate received the envoys from a state differed according as the community had already treaty relations with Rome, or was in a state of natural war. The permanent representation of a friendly nation —except through the vague relationship with a noble Roman house—was a device as yet unknown; but the concession was made to the envoys of such a state of receiving them within the town.[1] The representatives of the enemy, on the other hand, had no claim to reception within the walls.[2] The embarrassment inspired by the approach of the suspected Eumenes of Pergamus in 166 B.C. caused a passing regulation to be framed that no kings (the "carnivorous animals" of Cato) should be received at Rome in person.[3] Towards the close of the Republican period (67 B.C.) a demand for the better ordering of business, as well as the suspicion created by the dealings of envoys lingering in Rome with the political coteries, caused a law to be passed that the month of February should be devoted to the reception of legations.[4] As most of the envoys at this time came from states within the Roman sphere of influence, it was an advantage to the provincials to have a definite season set apart in which they could air their grievances.

The most pressing demand for entering into new relations with states naturally accompanied the organisation of a province. For the immediate attention to this demand the conquering general was competent, although he was sometimes assisted by ten commissioners (*legati*) appointed by the Senate.[5] The whole work of organisation, known as the law of the province (*lex provinciae*), bore the name of the *imperator*, and the *lex Rupilia* of Sicily, the *lex Pompeia* of Bithynia, and the law of Metellus in Crete preserved the memory of individual victors and organisers.

---

[1] Hence the institution of the *Graecostasis.* Varro (*L.L.* v. 155) describes it as "sub dextra hujus (the Rostra) a comitio locus substructus ubi nationum subsisterent legati, qui ad senatum essent missi; is Graecostasis appellatus a parte ut multa."

[2] So the Numantian envoys in 36 B.C. are received ἔξω τοῦ τείχους (Dio *fr.* 79). As a rule the appeal was made to the nearest *imperator*, and his representations might accord such legati a reception within the city. See Momms. *Staatsr.* iii. 2 p. 1150.

[3] Liv. *Ep.* xlvi. "in commune lex lata est ne cui regi Romam venire liceret." Cf. Polyb. xxx. 17.

[4] Cic. *ad Q. fr.* ii. 13, 3 "Appius interpretatur . . . quod Gabinia sanctum sit, etiam cogi ex Kal. Febr. usque ad Kal. Mart. legatis senatum quotidie dare."

[5] Polyb. xxii. 24; Liv. xlv. 17.

The *lex* in this case is a charter (*lex data*), not a comitial act (*lex rogata*), and when we remember that the organisation of the provinces took place during the period of senatorial ascendency, we are not surprised at the omission of the formality of the consultation of the people.

The assignment of external spheres of rule (*provinciae*) to magistrates was one of the most important powers connected with the senatorial administration of the provinces. We have already seen how the original theory that a magistrate chose his department gave way to senatorial selection. In spite of the fact that the provinces were not assigned to specified individuals, but to holders of certain offices, this right of bestowal put great patronage in the hands of the Senate; it might reward or punish consuls or proconsuls by the assignment of more or less important districts,[1] and the lot (*sortitio*) by which the individual holders were determined was often tampered with.[2]

The final organisation of Italy and the provinces also gave fresh spheres of influence to the Senate. The free cities, which extended over the whole of Italy, and were found as privileged units in the provinces, were subject to its controlling power. These had given up all claim to the exercise of external authority, and it was the Senate that adjusted the conflicting claims of states both within and without the bounds of Italy.[3] When the rights of a free city were held, not by treaty, but by a precarious charter, the Senate might cancel certain grants, which, by the terms of the charter, were revocable at pleasure.[4] In the details of provincial government and the relations of the subject cities to the governor the Senate seems seldom to have interfered directly. But we must remember that in every province the governor was accompanied by a senatorial committee in the form of a *consilium* composed of his legates and of any senator who happened to be in the province.[5] It was

---

[1] For the attempt made by the *lex Sempronia* to obviate this power see p. 201.

[2] Cic. *ad Fam.* v. 2, 3 (to Metellus Celer, proconsul of Cisalpine Gaul, 62 B.C.) "Nihil dico de sortitione vestra: tantum te suspicari volo nihil in ea re per collegam meum me insciente esse factum." Cf. *ad Att.* i. 16, 8.

[3] Liv. xlv. 13; Dittenberger n. 240. The Senate sometimes referred questions respecting the internal affairs of these states to Roman *patroni*, with whom they had entered into relations of clientship (Liv. ix. 20; Cic. *pro Sulla* 21, 60).

[4] *lex de Termessibus* ii. 6 "Nei quis magistratus . . . meilites . . . introducito . . . nisei senatus nominatim . . . decreverit."

[5] Sall. *Jug.* 62 "Metellus propere cunctos senatorii ordinis ex hibernis accersi jubet: eorum et aliorum, quos idoneos ducebat, consilium habet." Cf.

his duty to refer every important matter to this council, and the most important questions it bade him reserve for the judgment of the Senate at home.[1]

The power of the purse, which has been the guarantee of so many popular liberties, was not possessed by the people at Rome. By escaping so early the incidence of direct taxation they lost a formidable weapon with which they might have fought the Senate. For this reason the admitted incapacity of the latter body to impose a new tax on the community was no great limitation to its powers after the year 167 B.C., when the Italian *tributum* disappeared.[2] The control of the details of finance, which had never belonged to the people but always to the executive, was the mainstay of its power in this department. The circumstance that the control of estimates had been given to occasional officials, the censors, and that the details of expenditure had been taken from the hands of the consuls and placed in those of the most subordinate of all magistrates, the quaestors, sufficiently explains the growth of a central directing authority, which may be considered in its three relations to the property of the state, the estimates, and the expenditure.

The chief property of the state in the later Republic was the income derived from the provinces, and it is obvious that the Senate determined its amount when it ratified the terms of the *lex provinciae*. But the older source of revenue—the public domains of the state—was also subject to its control. It granted the occupation or the use of public lands and decreed their alienation by sale or gift.[3] It also accepted or rejected gifts and bequests to the state, and the proposal of Ti. Gracchus that the people should deal with the movable property left by Attalus III., king of Pergamus,[4] struck at one of the most undisputed of senatorial prerogatives.

The most important estimates of those items of revenue and

c. 104 "Marius . . . Sullam (the quaestor) ab Utica venire jubet, item L. Bellienum praetorem, praeterea omnes undique senatorii ordinis, quibuscum mandata Bocchi cognoscit."

[1] Cic. *ad Att.* ii. 16, 4 "Illud tamen, quod scribit (Q. Cicero, governor of Asia) animadvertas velim, de portorio circumvectionis ; ait se de consilii sententia rem ad senatum rejecisse."

[2] Cic. *de Off.* ii. 22, 76 "tantum in aerarium pecuniae invexit (Paulus) ut unius imperatoris praeda finem attulerit tributorum." Cf. Plut. *Paul.* 38.

[3] Momms. *Staatsr.* iii. 2 pp. 1112-20.

[4] Plut. *Ti. Gracch.* 14 οὐδὲν ἔφη τῇ συγκλήτῳ βουλεύεσθαι προσήκειν, ἀλλὰ τῷ δήμῳ γνώμην αὐτὸς προθήσειν.

expenditure which varied from time to time were, as we have
seen,[1] made every five years by the censors. But the Senate
exercised the right of directing, even of reversing, the arrangements made by these officials ; the appeal against an oppressive
contract was made to them,[2] and during the vacancy in the
censorship they designated the magistrates who were to preside
over new financial assignments.[3]

The control over the treasury, both in the voting of large
supplies or in detailed expenditure for definite purposes, was
complete. The provincial budget, comprising the allowances for
the different governors, was voted by the Senate, and this *senatus
consultum de provinciis ornandis*[4] was one of its most effective
means of controlling the magistracy. The special sums voted
for military or any other purposes were either directly paid[5] or
credited by the quaestors to the commanders abroad or to the
home officials.[6] We have already seen that it was only the
consul who could order the quaestors to pay without a permit
from the Senate ;[7] but, as the consul after the time of Sulla
rarely took the field, the Senate's control of expenditure was
finally uninterrupted even by this survival.

If we pass from the most material to the most spiritual
element in human life, we find this also directed to a certain
extent by the Senate. Although religion in its various departments was under the control of special guilds, yet these colleges
possessed little power of initiative, and an executive authority
was necessary to carry out their will. The announcement of
prodigies was met by the Senate with forms of expiation suggested
by the priestly colleges. In the Sibylline books above all
answers might be discovered whose political was even greater
than their religious import. When the dangerous annexation

---

[1] p. 229.
[2] The Senate invalidated the *locationes* of the censors of 184 B.C. (Liv. xxxix.
44 "locationes cum senatus precibus et lacrimis publicanorum victus induci et
de integro locari jussisset "). A vain appeal was made by the *publicani* of Asia
to remit their contracts in 60 B.C. (Cic. *ad Att.* i. 17, 9 ; cf. ii. 1, 8).
[3] The business of draining the Pomptine marshes is entrusted to a consul
(Liv. *Ep.* xlvi.), the building of an aqueduct to a praetor (Frontin. *de Aquaed.* 7).
[4] Cic. *ad Att.* iii. 24.
[5] This was necessary when the supplies were destined for the army. See Sall.
Jug. 104 "(Rufus) qui quaestor stipendium in Africam portaverat." Compare
the section on provincial government.
[6] The phrase for opening this credit is *attribuere.* See Liv. xliv. 16 "ad
opera publica facienda cum eis (censoribus) dimidium ex vectigalibus ejus anni
(169 B.C.) attributum ex senatus consulto a quaestoribus esset."   [7] p. 194.

of Egypt could be staved off by a few lines on these mysterious leaves,[1] it is no wonder that their own guardians, the *decemviri*, scarcely dared to unfold them without the authorisation of the Senate. The activity of the *comitia* was sometimes hampered by the Senate's habit of decreeing extraordinary festivals (*feriae*),[2] while the successful general was dependent on its will for the duration of the thanksgivings (*supplicationes*) which followed his victory.[3] The reception of a new god into the Roman Pantheon was probably in strict law a popular right,[4] but it is one that seems to have been tacitly conceded to the Senate.[5]

[1] Cic. *ad Fam.* i. 1 sq.

[2] Cic. *ad Q. fr.* ii. 6, 4 and 5 (56 B.C.) "consul est egregius Lentulus . . . Dies comitiales exemit omnes. Nam etiam Latinae instaurantur : nec tamen deerant supplicationes. Sic legibus perniciosissimis obsistitur."

[3] In the later Republic these periods of thanksgiving had reached the inordinate length of fifteen, twenty, and even fifty days (Caes. *Bell. Gall.* ii. 35 ; iv. 38 ; Cic. *Phil.* xiv. 11, 29). At this period the *supplicatio* was considered the usual preliminary of a triumph ; but Cato explains to Cicero that this was not always the case (*ad Fam.* xv. 5, 2 "Quodsi triumphi praerogativam putas supplicationem et idcirco casum potius quam te laudari mavis, neque supplicationem sequitur semper triumphus," etc.).

[4] Cic. *pro Domo* 49, 127 "video . . . esse legem veterem tribuniciam quae vetat injussu plebis aedes, terram, aram consecrari." The *jussus plebis* probably implies that of the *populus* as well. See Momms. *Staatsr.* iii. 2 p. 1050.

[5] The Senate alone is mentioned as decreeing the reception of the *Magna Mater* in 205 B.C., and as ordaining the erection of her temple (Liv. xxix. 10 and 11 ; xxxvi. 36).

CHAPTER VII

THE INTERNATIONAL RELATIONS OF ROME AND THE INCORPORATION OF ITALY

THE peoples of Greece and Italy offer, amidst many general points of similarity, some striking differences in their conceptions of international relations. The pan-Hellenic sentiment, which created a shadowy law of nations, has no pan-Italic counterpart. Outside the Greek city-state there was but the sentiment of nationality to create rules for human conduct; but, for this very reason, the rules, when created, were of pan-Hellenic validity. In Italy we get narrower but closer groupings; its history is the history of leagues, and the inevitable result of this more concentrated life was a closeness of international ties between the federated members which stood in marked contrast to the vagueness of the relations between the isolated groups.

The ties of religion and of ethnic affinity, as expressed in an obvious similarity of institutions, were, in Italy as elsewhere, the strongest connecting forces between states; but in Italy they were but the first rude ligaments that gave place to a stronger political bond and that crumbled to pieces when the more enduring chain had been forged. The festival of the Alban Mount became to the Latins, as the sacred centre of Volsinii to the Etruscans, but the religious symbol of a lasting league. Beyond the limits of the league the national and religious sentiment was weak. There was no Delphi to direct the Italian peoples, and no Olympia at which they might meet.

This isolated grouping of the Italian peoples may have been partly due to the great mixture of the populations of Italy south of the Alps and south even of the Apennines; but the earliest Italian history reveals the fact that even the closely-related races of Latins, Umbrians, and Sabellians were not connected by much

U

closer ties of an international character than those which bound
each to the Etruscan, the Iapygian, the Gaul, and the Greek.
It is true that with the progress of time something like an ethnic
sentiment was created in the purely Italian group, with vast
consequences to the history of the world. After the Umbrian
power, which had once extended from sea to sea, had been
weakened, on the left by the Etruscan, on the right by the Celt,
Rome becomes the great frontier power, the bulwark of the
group of blood-related nations against the foreign-speaking
Tuscan and the Gaul whose kinship with herself she had forgotten; but the relation soon became political, and, therefore, more
than international. That aggregation of vague human sentiments,
which is called International Law, was not juristically stronger
within the sphere of the blood-related than it was within the
sphere of the Italian group of peoples.

Within this wider sphere of humanity, that was not yet
"Italian," there are traces of the observance by Rome of customs
relating to the conduct of war and to negotiations for procuring
peace—customs which by their very existence show that, though
the early Roman employed the same word to designate the
stranger and the enemy, a state of war was not considered as
the permanent relation even between *hostes;* which prove, by
their elaboration, the antiquity of some sense of international
obligation, and which exhibit, by the constancy with which
they were applied, the existence of reciprocal forms and duties
owed by the hostile state to Rome. The functions of the
Fetiales, the priestly ambassadors (*oratores*)[1] who demand reparation, declare war and ratify a peace, seem never to have been
confined to those peoples with whom Rome had treaty relations,
but to have been extended to any nation which had not by
specific acts waged war on Rome. Four of the priestly guild of
Fetiales were appointed to seek redress. These elected one of
their number to become their representative, to be for the time
the "ratifying father of the Roman people" (*pater patratus populi
Romani*). At the borders of the offending tribe the *pater* with
many imprecations called Jupiter to witness that the grievance
was established, the demand reasonable. Three times did he
make the same appeal—to the first sojourner he met in the
stranger's territory, to the sentinel at the gate, and to the magistrate within the walls. Thirty days were allowed for the reply;

[1] See p. 56.

on the first of these the standard was hoisted on the citadel of
Rome, and the burgess army gathered for the threatening war.
If an appeasing answer were not returned within these days of
grace, the *pater* again set forth and launched a charred spear (the
prehistoric weapon of hardened wood) into the territory of the
offender, with words setting forth the menace of war.[1] When
the struggle was over it was he who struck the peace and the
sacrificial victim with a flint-stone which symbolised the watchful
Jupiter (*Jupiter lapis*).[2] The sanctity of envoys, other than these
priestly messengers, was as rigorously observed in the Italian as
in the Greek world. A violent death on an embassy was a
martyrdom deserving of immortality, and the ancient Rostra in
the Comitium showed a group of statues erected to those who
had met their fate in the cause of peace.[3] The neutrality of
ambassadors was exacted with equal care, and the disaster of the
Allia might be looked on as a retribution for the impious pre-
cipitancy of the Fabii who, forgetting their sacred character,
fought in the ranks of Clusium against the Celtic hordes.[4]

In the agreements made by generals and envoys with a
foreign people, the idea, common to most primitive minds, that
it is the oath which makes the promise binding is strikingly
present. We have already touched on the vast constitutional
import of this conception in its connexion with the question,
posed but never completely answered by the too patriotic
jurists : "Who could take the oath on behalf of the Roman
people ? " But the theory which on the whole prevailed, that
it could not be taken by a general in the field, not only
nullified the promise so made and rendered it a mere agreement (*sponsio*), valid between citizens but not between strangers,
but exposed the rash swearer to the extremest penalties.
With a strange inconsistency of judgment it was held that the
oath, which was no oath, laid the guilt of perjury on the conscience of the people, unless the man who had caused the people

[1] Dionys. ii. 72 ; Liv. i. 32 ; cf. Plin. *II.N.* xxii. 2.
[2] Polyb. iii. 25 ; Liv. i. 24. Yet the ceremonies they describe are different.
In that related by Polybius the stone has a passive signification ; the priest hurls
it from him and prays, "May I only be cast out, if I break my oath, as this stone
is now."   In that described by Livy, "the pig represents the perjurer, the flint-
knife the instrument of divine vengeance " (Strachan-Davidson's Polybius, *Proleg.*
viii.), and Jupiter is here to strike the *people* that fails in the compact.   Possibly
the two forms of ritual were used in different kinds of treaties ; the first, perhaps,
in commercial compacts, the second in agreements that closed a war.
[3] Liv. iv. 17 ; Middleton *Ancient Rome* i. p. 245.   [4] Liv. v. 36.

unwittingly to sin was offered up as an atoning sacrifice.
Naked and bound, like the sacrificial human victim of prehistoric times prepared for the altar, the *imperator* was surrendered
to the offended people.   It is not surprising that the latter
—whether Samnites, Spaniards, or Numidians [1]—refused to take
the worthless gift from the hands of the *pater patratus*, and preferred to continue the conflict with a people still convicted of
sin.   The individual oath to return, made by a prisoner of war
released on parole, though binding on his soul alone and, as a
religious obligation, not punishable by the civil arm, was enforced by the public conscience.   One—others said more than
one—of the Roman captives sent by Hannibal after Cannae to
negotiate an exchange of prisoners declined to return on the
negotiations falling through.   The pretext was that they had
revisited the camp of the conqueror *after* the oath had been
taken.   Tradition varied as to the punishment imposed by Rome ;
some spoke of a summary arrest and enforced return to the
Phoenician camp, others of a degradation by the censor and of a
public detestation that drove the perjurer to suicide.[2]

Such are some of the isolated specimens that have been
handed down to us of rules of international right which Rome
thought due to every nation.   But, apart from such universal
duties, the Roman mind, with its simple dichotomy of the world
into enemies (*hostes*)[3] and friends (*amici*), recognised varying
degrees of obligation as due to either class.   The *hostes* were all
states or individuals with whom Rome had no treaty relations.
With these there was no presupposition even of constant
diplomatic relations, and their absence was symbolised by the
manner in which envoys from such states were received.   The
tradition of "speaking with one's enemy in the gate" was
rigorously preserved to the end of the Republic, and the Senate
had to meet a messenger from the enemy outside the walls.[4]
The friends of Rome were those with whom she had any relations
that approximated to a federative character.   There might be no
definite treaty, no specified interchange of obligations ; but the
vague term *amicitia* with kindred titles of affection was applied

[1] See p. 283.
[2] Liv. xxii. 61.
[3] Varro *L.L.* v. 3 "multa verba aliud nunc ostendunt, aliud ante significa-
bant, ut hostis : nam tum eo verbo dicebant peregrinum qui suis legibus uteretur,
nunc dicunt eum quem tum dicebant perduellem." Cf. Cic. *de Off.* i. 12, 37.
[4] p. 284.

to the vaguest association as well as to the closest alliance with
Rome; it was indifferently a symbol of the greatest independence or of the practical subjection of the contracting state.
The members of the military symmachy in Italy could share
this title with distant Carthage,[1] and even the barbarous Aedui
are "kinsmen and brothers" of the Roman people.[2]   Even
in the case of these communities the perpetual representation of
mutual interests by means of permanent ambassadors—an institution still in its infancy in the seventeenth century of our era
—was naturally unknown; but their recognition as friends
granted their envoys or representatives an entrance and an
audience of the Senate within the walls.[3]

Closer relations between Rome and her "friends" were
generally conditioned by ethnic and their corresponding
religious ties.   But the foreign element in early Rome shows
that this was not universally the case.   The rape of the Sabine
women in its least significance reveals the fact of the close tie of
intermarriage between Rome and a non-Latin community; the
first treaty with Carthage reveals commercial relations, which
were accompanied by some form of international jurisdiction,
with a Phoenician power.[4]

The first, because the most universal, ties which attract our
attention as based on treaty relations are those of commerce.
Commercial treaties with the foreigner led, in the very infancy
of Roman history, to the development both of common courts
and of a common code.

In the later Republic and in the Empire we have frequent
mention of a civil court which was believed to have had an
international origin.   Attempts have been made to assign to
this court of *recuperatores* a purely Roman source;[5] but its
essential peculiarities—the large uneven number of jurors, three
or five, when the ordinary civil courts knew but one; the
rapidity and simplicity of the procedure; the *formula* framed by

[1] Polyb. iii. 22.
[2] "Aeduos, fratres consanguineosque saepe numero a senatu appellatos" (Caes.
B.G. i. 33).
[3] Cf. p 284 for this rule and for the exception to it made in 166 B.C.
[4] In the first treaty with Carthage two kinds of legal satisfaction are given to
Roman traders.   In Libya and Sardinia the state guarantees the debt; in the
Sicilian cities under the Carthaginian protectorate Romans and Carthaginians are
on an equal footing (Polyb. iii. 22).
[5] Hartmann (O. E.) *Der ordo judiciorum und die judicia extraordinaria der
Römer* Thl. i. pp. 229 ff.

a magistrate and not taken from the *legis actiones* of the civil law —are best explained as survivals of a time when it was a mixed court of international jurisdiction.[1] The two or four jurors probably represented the contracting states in equal proportions, the third or fifth may have been an arbitrator chosen from another community; the magistrate who gave the *formula* would have been an official of the town in which the mixed court sat.

But the *formula* implied a system of legal principles, and these could not easily be furnished by the civil law (*jus civile*) of each contracting state. It was not Roman pride that prevented the foreigner from participating in her native law; it was the unwillingness of the foreigner to be made subject to a code characterised by excessive cumbrousness, by danger and by delay, and the counter-objection of the Roman to be the victim of similar disadvantages in the contracting state. No merchant, to whom time meant money, would adopt the cumbrous form of conveyance known as the *mancipatio*, when ownership could be acquired by the simple transfer (*traditio*) known of all nations; none would care to repeat a *formula* (to be learnt only of the Roman pontiff), the least error in the utterance of which was sufficient to extinguish his claim ; and the symbolic acts performed before the praetor, though possibly dear to the Roman mind, could not have been attractive to the foreigner. Convenience dictated a compromise, and this was found in the gradual collection of a body of rights (*jus*) from the customs of "the world" (*gentes*) as known to the Romans. This *jus gentium*, or body of rights possessed by man as a citizen of the world, was a code of private international law, and it cannot be regarded as being even purely Italian. A nation that borrowed its alphabet from a Chalcidian city, that imitated the military organisation of the Hellenes, that traded in the sixth century with Sicily, Sardinia, Libya and Carthage, must have been deeply imbued with the customs of the Greek and Phoenician world. Nor was this code a growth of Rome's supremacy, for her commercial preceded her political greatness. Its origin dates back to a time probably anterior to the Republic, certainly far earlier than the institution of the praetorship. We have already

---

[1] Festus p. 274 "Reciperatio est, ut ait Gallus Aelius, cum inter populum et reges nationesque et civitates peregrinas lex convenit quomodo per reciperatores reddantur res reciperenturque resque privatas inter se persequantur." See Keller *Civilprocess* p. 36 ; Rudorff *Rechtsgeschichte* ii. p. 34.

noticed how for more than a century the same civil judge administered both laws, that of the state and that of the *gentes*,[1] and how the *jus civile* was insensibly modified by contact with its younger relative.

But closer relations than those of commerce might exist between Rome and states connected with her by neighbourhood or kindred. The interchange of the rights of private law, of ownership and of marriage, which the Greeks called ἰσοπολιτεία, was a natural out-growth of the Italian tendency to close political association. Such communion rendered each member of the contracting states in private law a *civis* of the other; the *conubium* carried with it the *patria potestas* and all the family rights that flowed from this power; the *commercium* allowed the citizen of the contracting state to own Roman land, to convey property by Roman forms, to make a contract by the ceremonial of the *sponsio*, to inherit from a Roman or to make a Roman his heir, while it gave the citizen of Rome corresponding rights in the alien city. There could be no question here of mixed tribunals or of private international law. The courts of each state were fully competent; if we may judge from the early relations of Rome with the Latin cities, the place in which the contract had been concluded, or, in other words, the forms of the contract, determined the competence of the court.[2]

Still more definite bonds of union than these relations of private law (although often their primary condition) were certain political creations which made the ties between the states something more than international. It was a nucleus approaching a federal government which gave the first impulse to the extension of Roman power in Italy. Rome, as known to us in legend, is never quite a city-state. She is an offshoot of Alba Longa, the titular head of the Latin league. Tradition says that her conquest of her mother city led to her occupying a singular position with respect to the thirty cities of this league. She was one of the contracting parties, the cities were the other; she was the equal, not the member, of the group. The acceptance of this position by the confederate cities shows their eagerness for the protection of the frontier town; but the protectorate

[1] p. 207.
[2] In the treaty supposed to be the work of Spurius Cassius and to date from 493 B.C. the following clause was found: τῶν τ᾽ ἰδιωτικῶν συμβολαίων αἱ κρίσεις ἐν ἡμέραις γιγνέσθωσαν δέκα, παρ᾽ οἷς ἂν γένηται τὸ συμβόλαιον (Dionys. vi. 95).

became burdensome, a war ensued, and Roman rule was shaken off only to be reimposed on firmer, lines by the strong hand of the Etruscan dynasty represented by the Tarquins. Rome now became one at least of the religious centres of the league, and the Diana of the Aventine symbolised the lasting union of the Latin folk.[1]   The expulsion of the kings, while it stripped Rome of territory, shook for a time the allegiance of the league, and it was not until 493 B.C. that the old conditions were renewed ; for the details that might in historical times be read in the treaty attributed to Sp. Cassius were doubtless but a replica of the old terms of the alliance. Eternal peace was enjoined, mutual support was to be given in war, and each contracting party was to share equally in the booty. The supreme command in war was to be held now by the Roman general, now by the commander of the confederate forces.[2]   But the closest bond was that of ἰσοπολιτεία,[3] the mutual participation in *commercium* and doubtless also in *conubium*, which was accompanied by the proviso that the court of the state, in which the contract had been concluded and the case was therefore tried, should give speedy satisfaction to the claimant from each community.[4]   Reciprocity such as this was naturally accompanied by freedom in choice of domicile. The Roman settled in the Latin city and the Latin in the Roman retained the private rights of both communities. It is doubtful whether at this period the transference of residence was accompanied by a share in the voting rights of the state in which the immigrant sojourned.[5]

To this association a third factor was soon added in the Hernican league.[6]   The extension of the confederation beyond its ethnic limits was a grand strategic move ; for by the inclusion of the Hernici, Rome now presented a compact chain of fortresses against her enemies of the east and south, the Aequi and the Volsci. Their military importance explains why the newly admitted members were raised to the level of the older allies.

---

[1] Dionys. iii. 34, 51.
[2] ib. vi. 95 ; Festus p. 241.
[3] Dionys. viii. 70, 74.   [4] p. 295.
[5] App. *B.C.* i. 23. Dionysius (viii. 72) speaks of the Latins and Hernicans exercising voting privileges (ψηφοφορία) in Rome in the year 486 B.C. But it is impossible that they could have been enrolled in the centuries, which was a Roman army list, and no assembly of the tribes had yet received state recognition.
[6] Dionys. viii. 69, 72, 74.

They boasted the same reciprocity of private rights with Rome, they shared in a third part of the spoils of war, and they joined with Romans and Latins in the work of common colonisation.

This colonisation was at once a military and social measure, and the means by which the league extended its geographical and political limits. The custom of war, which permitted the Italian tribes to annex a third of all conquered land, had ever been used as a means of expansion by the powerful league. And this expansion was a very real one ; for the Latin colonies (*coloniae Latinae*), as they were called, were full members of the society that gave them birth. Such towns as Suessa Pometia, Cora, and Velitrae had been military outposts in the territory of the Volsci; and now the Volscian, the Rutulian, and even the Etruscan were oppressed with the weight of new foundations by the three great powers. But the year 384 seems to mark a strange and unaccountable break in the history of this extension. Of all the Latin colonies founded after that date, but one is mentioned as a member of the confederacy—a circumstance which has led to the conclusion that Rome (whether with or without the consent of the other members) had cut off all future joint foundations from the religious and federal privileges of the league. Otherwise the consequences of this exclusion were not great ; the new towns were military allies of the league, not of Rome, and their citizens still possessed those private rights which always remained of the essence of *latinitas*. Forty-seven cities—partly old Latin towns, partly Latin colonies earlier than 384—still participated in the Latin festival ; that within this circle a distinction was drawn between thirty voting and seven-teen not-voting members is an insecure conclusion based on the attempts of the annalists to reconstruct the traditional number of thirty Latin cities ; there may still have been thirty votes, but these may well have been distributed in some way over the forty-seven cities of the league. That the closing of the Latin confederacy was due mainly to Roman pressure is perhaps shown by the series of dangerous revolts amongst its cities, which often sided with their ancient enemies the Volsci. The Hernicans were as eager to shake off the yoke ; but Rome emerged from both crises with her power strengthened and her commonwealth enlarged. The latter result was due to a renewed employment of her old device of absorption. Tusculum in 381, and Satricum not long afterwards, had their commonwealths destroyed, and were forced, as a penal measure, to accept the full or partial Roman citizenship.[1] At the close of the struggle in 358 the leagues were renewed and the relations of Rome with the two groups of states remodelled, probably on harder terms. In the Samnite war which followed, the Latin cities first clung to Rome, for they preferred a native to a Sabellian hegemony; but Rome's rapid conclusion of a treaty of peace and alliance with the Samnites, which the league was asked to accept and not to ratify, was taken as the final proof of actual subjection concealed under the name of a hegemony. The Latins made their last demands; they gave up their position as a military confederacy, but they did not wish to be absorbed into the body politic of Rome. They asked for the golden mean—a system of federal government, but one that should still preserve the fundamental distinction between Rome and the confederate cities. One of the consuls was to be a Roman, the other a Latin, and half the Senate was to be chosen from Latium. But the civic feeling was too strong at Rome; she would not herself surrender the communal constitution which she had so often wrested from others; she rejected the alternative which would have paralysed her power as a conquering state and made of her but a federal capital. Her "No!" to the Latins was one of the turning-points in the history of Italy and of the world.

The battles of Veseris and Trifanum gave her the victory, but she was sorely puzzled as to the use to be made of it. The league was to be broken up, its members isolated, and this work of disintegration was carried through with thoroughness; not only were the federal assemblies (*concilia*) abolished, but no right of intermarriage or of commercial intercourse (*jus conubii et commercii*) was permitted between the cities.[2] But how to deal with the individual communities was a far harder problem. The incorporation which had been the punishment of isolated

---

[1] Livy, by attributing *civitas* to Tusculum (vi. 26) and calling the Tusculans *cives* (vi. 36), seems to imply that they were full citizens. In this case the city could not have been from the first a *municipium*, the name it bears later ("municipium antiquissimum " Cic. *pro Planc.* 8, 19). Festus, however (p. 127), includes Tusculum amongst the states with *civitas sine suffragio*, i.e. amongst the true *municipia*, and we know that Livy (x. 1) uses *civitas* for *civitas sine suffragio*. The Satricani are *cives Romani* in 319 B.C. (Liv. ix. 16). Satricum had formerly belonged to the thirty Latin cities (Dionys. v. 61).

[2] Liv. viii. 14 "Ceteris Latinis populis (i.e. other than those with whom special arrangements were made) conubia commerciaque et concilia inter se ademerunt."

revolt could not be applied to the *disjecta membra* of a whole league, for it would have changed the city-state into a nation. Hence the plan adopted was a compromise between the old policy of absorption and a new principle—that of alliance. Aricia, Pedum, and Lanuvium lost their independence and received the full Roman franchise ; while Tibur, Praeneste, Lavinium were compelled to conclude separate treaties (*foedera*) with Rome, and formed the nucleus of the ever-growing class of *civitates foederatae*. Thirty years later (306 B.C.) a similar fate befell the remaining league of the Hernici. Their loyalty had not stood the test of the second Samnite war ; but there were degrees of guilt amongst the cities. Anagnia, the chief centre of the revolt, and other incriminated towns, were given merely the private rights of citizenship ; the full citizenship was indeed offered to the three loyal towns of Aletrium, Ferentinum, and Verulae, but, on their expressing a preference for their own local constitutions and codes, they were permitted to retain an autonomy guaranteed by separate treaties.[1] The break up of the Hernican league was only an incident in a triumphant career of conquest that was never followed by annexation. The Samnite wars and the struggle with Pyrrhus had ended in the acknowledgment of Rome's supremacy by every nation south of the Macra and the Rubicon. The three civilisations of Greece, Tuscany, and Italy furnished her indifferently with allies ; the town and the tribal union were alike represented in her symmachy. Tibur and Praeneste in Latium, Aletrium and Ferentinum amongst the Hernici, ·Volaterrae and Clusium in Etruria, Iguvium in Umbria, the Picentes, Marsi, and Peligni amongst the Sabellians, and Greek cities like Neapolis in Campania or Rhegium amongst the Bruttii, are types of the states and peoples that she numbered amongst her *socii*.

The effect of this unification, and of the tendencies which had preceded it, was to divide the inhabitants of Italy into two broad classes—those of citizens (*cives*) and those of allies (*socii*) of Rome. The first class (far the smaller numerically) represented the earlier effort at incorporation ; the second was the

---

[1] Liv. ix. 43 "Hernicorum tribus populis, Aletrinati, Verulano, Ferentinati, quia maluerunt quam civitatem, suae leges redditae ; conubiumque inter ipsos, quod aliquamdiu soli Hernicorum habuerunt, permissum. Anagninis, quique arma Romanis intulerant, civitas sine suffragii latione data : concilia conubiaque adempta, et magistratibus, praeterquam sacrorum curatione, interdictum."

consequence of the later policy which founded a military league. Minuter distinctions of rights, which necessitate cross-divisions in the classification of the states, sometimes obscure this fundamental analysis; but it was never lost sight of and was the guiding light to the Roman lawyer, as it is to us, in his path through the labyrinth of the complex organisation of Italy.

The *cives* of Rome bear this name either in a full or a partial sense; they may be citizens with voting rights or citizens in private law alone (*cives sine suffragio*). If we fix our attention on the first of these classes, we find that historically there were two modes in which the *civitas* was gained by a commune outside the city. It might be due to the incorporation of an already existing state, or it might be the consequence of the planting of a Roman colony. The merging of some of the Latin communities in Rome [1] has already furnished instances of the former mode of conferment; the Roman colonies which illustrate the second (*coloniae civium Romanorum*) were outlying fragments of the Populus, planted as a defensive garrison on the third of the conquered land, which was the legitimate spoil of the invader. A social was from the first combined with the military object; but the enforced exodus of portions of the burgess body on some occasions [2] proves that, in this form of colonisation, the interest of the state came before that of the individual. It was, in fact, a military levy ordained by law, although voluntary profession usually took the place of the compulsory summons of the regular *dilectus*. In military array, with standards flying,[3] the squadron marched to the appointed place under the leadership of the commissioners appointed by the people. When a new town was to be founded, or an old one reconstituted, it was done with the imposing ceremonies that marked the birth and enlargement of Rome. After the will of the gods had been tested and happy omens gained, the commissioners, with veiled heads and loins girt up, guided a plough, to which were yoked an ox and a cow. They thus drew the *pomerium* of the state, only staying the furrow where the gates of the city were to be.[4] The greater number of these settlements of Roman citizens were for the protection of the Italian coasts, and the members of the

---

[1] p. 299.   [2] Dionys. vii. 13; Plut. *Cor.* 13.

[3] Hyginus p. 176 "cum signis et aquila et primis ordinibus ac tribunis deducebantur"; Tac. *Ann.* xiv. 27 "non enim, ut olim, universae legiones deducebantur cum tribunis et centurionibus et sui cujusque ordinis militibus."

[4] Varro *L.L.* v. 143; Serv. ad *Aen.* v. 755.

maritime colonies (*coloniae maritimae*) were allowed exemption from active military service.[1] Few in numbers (often but a handful of 300 men), and settled in an already existing political society, the colonists formed a privileged patriciate amongst its older members. The town-council, and such subordinate magistrates as Rome allowed them to possess, were probably chosen from the new settlers alone ; but, as the autonomy which they enjoyed was not great, as they possessed no high judicial magistrates of their own, and as their voting power at Rome was more a potential than an actual right, they differed little from the native inhabitants, who as *cives sine suffragio* came equally under the jurisdiction of the Roman courts and their representatives.

Whether the commune of Roman citizens had had a natural or artificial growth, it was never in early times a true state (*civitas*). Roman law knew of ἰσοπολιτεία, but not of the closer bond of συμπολιτεία ; and the principle that no Roman citizen could be a full member of another state, although in the later Republic it had given place to the theory of the municipal independence of the *civis*, was always maintained in international relations with states of the outer world.[2] As the negation of state life implied the negation of communal independence, we are not surprised to find that none of these communities of Roman citizens possessed a true civic organisation of its own. We cannot define the rights of their town-councils, we cannot assert the absolute non-existence of popular gatherings for certain purposes ; but the absence of the *imperium* and of a true judicial magistracy is clearly discerned. These communes fell under the immediate civil jurisdiction, originally of the consuls, later of the *praetor urbanus*. Originally it may have been necessary for every case not settled by voluntary arbitration to be brought to Rome, but the distance of some of these towns from the capital would have soon rendered this principle of jurisdiction impossible. The modern solution, that the judge should go on circuit, could not be thought of in a state where the bench consisted of a single man, and where this individual was prohibited by law from leaving the city for more than ten days during his

[1] Liv. xxvii. 38 (207 B.C.) "colonos etiam maritimos, qui sacrosanctam vacationem dicebantur habere, dare milites cogebant"; xxxvi. 3 (191 B.C.) "contentio orta cum colonis maritimis . . . nam, cum cogerentur in classem, tribunos plebei appellarunt."

[2] Cic. *pro Balbo* 11, 28 ; *pro Caec.* 34, 100.

year of office.[1]   The only alternative was furnished by the
favourite Roman device of delegation.   The praetor nominated
praefects for jurisdiction (*praefecti juri dicundo*), and these were
sent, sometimes as standing magistrates, sometimes perhaps as
mere circuit judges, through the Roman towns, which were thence
known as *praefecturae*.[2]   Delegation implies either a division of
competence or, in the case of the lower court possessing full
jurisdiction, an appeal to the delegating authority.   There is
no trace of the latter practice at Rome, and a systematic division
of authority, although motives of convenience may sometimes
have led the praetor to permit it, is inconsistent with the Roman
idea of jurisdiction flowing direct from the *imperium.*   Possibly
the praetor permitted the praefect to regulate almost every kind
of contentious jurisdiction, subject to his own right of summoning
any case he pleased from the delegate to Rome.   By a legal
fiction the courts of the *praefecturae* were held to be within the
praetor's sphere of competence, i.e. within a single milestone of
the city; they were, to use the technical Roman expression,
judicia legitima.   No trace whatever has been preserved of the
criminal procedure applied to such communities.   The fact that
the praefect was the delegate of a civil magistrate would not
prove that he was incapable of exercising criminal jurisdiction,
for *jurisdictio* of every kind is latent in the praetor's *imperium.*
All higher jurisdiction was reserved for the people; but there
was only one *populus Romanus*, that of the city of Rome.   Hence
when the citizen of Ostia or Tusculum was accused of an offence,
the penalty for which demanded a popular sanction, we may
assume that he could either make the appeal, through a fiction
like that underlying the civil jurisdiction, in spite of his local
separation from Rome, or that he stepped, or was brought within,
the first milestone of the city, the limit inside which the *provocatio* could legally be made.

The second type of *cives* are those without the right of
suffrage (*sine suffragio*).   There can be little question that the

---

[1] p. 203.

[2] Festus p. 233 "Praefecturae eae appellabantur in Italia, in quibus et jus
dicebatur et nundinae agebantur; et erat quaedam earum res publica, neque
tamen magistratus suos habebant; in quas legibus praefecti mittebantur quodannis, qui jus dicerent.   Quarum genera fuerunt duo: alterum, in quas solebant
ire praefecti quattuor, [qui] viginti sex virum numero populi suffragio creati erant
. . . alterum, in quas ibant quos praetor urbanus quodannis in quaeque loca
miserat legibus."   Amongst the *praefecturae* which he enumerates are the Roman
colonies of Volturnum, Liternum, Puteoli, and Saturnia.

idea of this *status* was derived from Rome's relations with the cities of the Latin league ; in her process of absorption, however, she conferred it on towns to which she did not grant the other typically Latin rights ; in this way she made of it an independent *status*. The Etruscan town of Caere is said to have won this right in 353 as a gift for good service to Rome. After the dissolution of the Latin league in 338 B.C. a group of Campanian townships, Capua, Cumae, Atella, and Calatia, were with (the then Latin) Fundi and Formiae brought into this relation with the now dominant city of Latium ;[1] others nearer home, such as Arpinum of the Volsci, were similarly rewarded or absorbed (303 B.C.),[2] while the *status* was imposed as a means of degrading and reducing to impotence rebellious townships such as Anagnia, the leading city of the Hernici.[3]   The motive of the conferment, although it might make a difference to the rights of the towns, produced none in the relations of their respective *cives* to Rome.

The *civis sine suffragio* was known as a *municeps*, and the state, all of whose full members enjoyed this *status*, derived from its occupants the name of *municipium*. The name of this type of citizen — the "taker up of burdens" — aptly expresses his subjection to the chief duties (*munera*) of Roman citizenship, such as service in the Roman legions, forced labour in raising defences, the payment of the war-tax (*tributum*), and his exclusion from the usually corresponding rights of suffrage and of office ;[4] it emphasises the fact, strange to the early Roman mind, of public duties not balanced by public rights, but it contains no implication of the strangest characteristic of the *municeps*—one almost unknown in ancient legal systems—the possession of a personality in private which is not the result of a personality in public law. The *municeps* possesses *commercium*

---

[1] Liv. viii. 14 "Campanis . . . Fundanisque et Formianis . . . civitas sine suffragio data. Cumanos Suessulanosque ejusdem juris conditionisque, cujus Capuam, esse placuit." For Atella and Calatia see Festus pp. 131, 233.
[2] Liv. x. 1.   [3] ib. ix. 43, quoted p. 299.
[4] Festus p. 131 "municipes erant qui ex aliis civitatibus Romam venissent, quibus non licebat magistratum capere sed tantum muneris partem, ut fuerunt Cumani, Acerrani, Atellani, qui et cives Romani erant et in legione merebant, sed dignitates non capiebant"; cf. p. 127 "participes . · . fuerunt omnium rerum ad munus fungendum una cum Romanis civibus praeterquam de suffragio ferendo aut magistratu capiendo." The words "qui ex aliis civitatibus Romam venissent" in the first definition do not describe the *municipes* of historical times ; they suggest a possible origin for the institution. These rights were first conditioned by domicile in Rome, but the condition was subsequently removed.

with all its consequences; he possesses *conubium* with Rome; he is, from the point of view of private law, in every sense a citizen.

This possession of citizenship carried with it as a necessary consequence his subjection to the praetor's court. His home, the *municipium*, is therefore, equally with the community of full Roman citizens, a *praefectura*, and the rules of jurisdiction were the same in both classes of states. To the praefects nominated by the praetor were in course of time added others elected by the *comitia tributa*, and reckoned amongst the minor magistrates known as the *viginti-sex-viri*.[1] These latter were the four praefects of Capua, Cumae, and the Campanian coast; but, in regard to the mode of election, there is no difference discernible between the judicial magistrates of the *municipia* and those of the communities of Roman citizens. Elected praefects visited the *municipium* of Capua and the Roman colony of Puteoli, while nominated praefects held their court in the colony of Saturnia and the municipal town of Anagnia.[2]

But the praefect was far from representing the higher functions of government in every *municipium*. These towns fall into two broad divisions, not according to the rights which they receive, but according to the rights which they retain. The *civitas sine suffragio* might be granted *honoris causa* to a state which maintained its complete independence or its communal autonomy. It was thus conferred on Capua, Cumae, Formiae, and Fundi,[3] and the gift of the partial citizenship under these conditions was a valued privilege. It enabled a Capuan to own Roman land, to settle on the *ager publicus*, to marry into the noble houses of Rome, and to serve, not in the auxiliary cohort, but in her army or in the legion raised from the *municipes*. But meanwhile his own magistrate, the *meddix tuticus*, administers in the Campanian courts the native Sabellian law,[4] his senate deliberates, and his popular assembly decides. Sometimes, as in the case of Capua, the state is still bound by treaty relations to Rome, and the two conflicting principles of armed alliance and of absorption are for once commingled.[5]

---

[1] p. 235.   [2] Festus p. 233, quoted p. 302.
[3] Liv. viii. 14.   [4] ib. xxiv. 19; xxvi. 6.
[5] The language of Livy makes it doubtful whether he conceives the *foedus* to have continued after the *civitas* had been conferred. They are different stages of rights, but he may mean them to be cumulative. In xxxi. 31 we read "cum . . . ipsos (Campanos) foedere primum, deinde conubio atque cognationibus,

Yet, in spite of their independence, there is every reason to believe that the inevitable praefects visited these states. We must assume, at least in the cases where autonomy reached the grade which is visible in Capua, that a dual system of law prevailed in these communities; the court and the procedure would follow the form of contract, whether Sabellian or Roman, and the parties might appear indifferently before the Capuan *meddix* or the Roman praefect. In other cases, where a large measure of administrative autonomy is visible, but where no magistrate with a higher rank than that of aedile is found within the state,[1] it is possible that Roman law alone prevailed and that the Roman praefect was the only judge.

The lower class of *municipia* was represented by states "whose whole commonwealth had been merged in that of Rome."[2] Of this class Anagnia, the degraded town of the Hernici, was a type.[3] Stripped of all the active rights of citizenship, and under the direct government of a Roman praefect, the members of such towns possessed no personality in public law at all. Their position was that of the free Plebeians previous to their admission to the *suffragium* and the *honores*.

The second principle in Rome's Italian policy, first projected after the close of the Latin war and carried to its completion after the struggle with Pyrrhus, resulted in a great military hegemony over states, whose treaty relations enabled them to call themselves the "allies" (*socii*) of Rome. Collective names were soon devised to indicate the closeness of the union thus formed; at first the confederates were "wearers of the toga" (*togati*), a name that applied equally to the Latin, Sabellian, and Etruscan. But the introduction of the Greek *pallium* into the league destroyed this basis of classification; and the later term *Italici* was evolved, a word whose geographical signification emphasises the idea of a territorial limit to certain rights—one which, as we shall see, was not rigorously preserved, but which

postremo civitate nobis conjunxissemus" (cf. xxiii. 5). The *civitas* here is probably the full citizenship conferred on individual Capuans. They are spoken of as *socii* in 216 B.C. (xxiii. 5), and though the word is sometimes loosely used, it harmonises in its literal sense with the great constitutional privileges of the town.

[1] As at Arpinum (Cic. *ad Fam.* xiii. 11, 3).
[2] Festus p. 127 "quorum civitas universa in civitatem Romanam venit."
[3] It did not possess any magistracy for secular purposes (Liv. ix. 43 "magistratibus, praeterquam sacrorum curatione, interdictum ").

marks the distinction, valid alike for the Republic and the Principate, between Italy as the privileged and the provinces as the unprivileged world.

The condition of a conquered town, whether in Italy or the provinces, before its alliance with Rome, is described by the word *deditio*, a term which implies absolute surrender to the power (*ditio, potestas*)[1] or to the honour (*fides*)[2] of the Roman people, the two latter expressions being to the Roman mind legally equivalent.[3] Such a *dediticia civitas* is in the negative condition of an absolute suspension of rights, and remains in this case until some are given back by Rome with a guarantee of their permanence. *Deditio* is, therefore, a temporary *status*, although it might be occasionally prolonged as a penal measure, as it was in the case of the revolted Bruttii after the Hannibalic war.[4] In Italy, as a rule, the terms that Rome dictated were those of a military alliance, the conditions for membership of this being, firstly, external sovereignty (*libertas*), as conditioned by the terms and objects of the league;[5] secondly, internal independence—a condition which the Greek cities called αὐτονομία, and which, in a Latin charter to a provincial town, appears in the form of the permit *suis legibus uti ;*[6] thirdly, a basis for these rights, as also for the obligations which these states owed to Rome. In dealings with the extra-Italian world this basis was either a charter (*lex data*), given by the Roman people and revocable by them, or a treaty (*foedus*), equally sanctioned by the people but irrevocable, as being sworn to by the two contracting parties ; its revocation could only be the consequence of a genuine *casus belli*. In the first case the state is a *libera civitas*, in the second a *libera et foederata civitas*,[7] or, in its more general and briefer designation, a *foederata civitas*.[8] In Italy positive evidence furnishes us only with the *foederatae*, but the existence of the *liberae civitates* must be assumed, since, immediately on the beginning of provincial organisation in Sicily, this *status* is adopted.

[1] "in ditionem" (Liv. xxxvii. 45), "in potestatem" (xxxix. 54).
[2] "in fidem" (ib. viii. 2).
[3] Polyb. xx. 9, 12 παρὰ Ῥωμαίοις ἰσοδυναμεῖ τό τε εἰς τὴν πίστιν αὐτὸν ἐγχειρίσαι καὶ τὸ τὴν ἐπιτροπὴν δοῦναι περὶ αὐτοῦ τῷ κρατοῦντι.
[4] Gell. x. 3, 19.
[5] *Dig.* 49, 15, 7, 1 "liber populus est is qui nullius alterius populi potestati est subjectus."
[6] *Lex Antonia de Termessibus* i. 8.
[7] Plin. *Ep. ad Traj.* 92 (93).
[8] Cic. *in Verr.* iii. 6, 13 ; cf. App. *B.C.* i. 102 (ἐπὶ συνθήκαις ἔνορκοι).

In Italy also there was doubtless the distinction between the higher and the lower kind of *foedus*—the *foedus aequum* and the *foedus iniquum*.   In all treaties concluded between Rome and cities in her symmachy there was a recognition of partial dependence in the latter ; but some of these treaties contained a "suzerainty" clause to the effect that the state in question should "in a friendly spirit respect the majesty of the Roman people." This clause did not diminish the *libertas* of the state accepting it, but merely strengthened the position of Rome.[1]   It was a characteristic of the *iniquum foedus*.[2]

The duties of the federate cities expressed in their name (*socii*, σύμμαχοι) were primarily the furnishing of requisitions whether in men or ships.   The latter were demanded from the Greek cities of the coast, but Italy as a whole furnished the auxiliary land armies of Rome, the *togati* liable to the levy.[3] Every state had to keep a register of its effective strength in accordance with a principle of assessment (*formula*).[4]   The general demands of Rome were specified in the treaties ; the special levies required at any given time were dictated by the Senate and consuls.[5]

Military requisitions necessarily involve pecuniary burdens. But these were all indirect.   Each city had complete control of its own finances ; no tribute was imposed by Rome, and the antithesis to the *socius* is the *stipendiarius*.[6]   This immunity was originally based on the theory of treaty relations ; later, when the view had grown up that the tribute paid by the stipendiary states was the result of their precarious tenure as *possessores*, the Italians were held to be owners of their land.   The *jus Italicum* of the Principate confers on any state to which it is granted quiritarian ownership, and, therefore, immunity from taxation on land.

---

[1] *Dig.* 49, 15, 7, 1 "hoc adjicitur, ut intellegatur alterum populum superiorem esse, non ut intellegatur alterum non esse liberum." Cf. Cic. *pro Balbo* 16, 35 "Id habet hanc vim, ut sit ille in foedere inferior."

[2] *Dig.* l.c. "is foederatus est item sive aequo foedere in amicitiam venit sive foedere comprehensum est ut is populus alterius populi majestatem comiter conservaret."

[3] *Lex Agraria* l. 21 "socii nominisve Latini, quibus ex formula togatorum [milites in terra Italia inperare solent]."

[4] Liv. xxii. 57 ; xxvii. 10 "milites ex formula paratos esse."

[5] The number of troops required was decreed every year by the Senate (Liv. xli. 5 etc.), the consuls fixing the amount which each state was to send in proportion to its fighting strength.   [6] Cic. *pro Balbo* 9, 24.

Enjoyment of their own laws and control of their own courts were other symbols of the autonomy of the allies. Rome could not legislate for the Italian *socii*, and they were beyond the judicial authority of the Roman magistrate in Italy.

But the necessities of social and commercial intercourse rendered it advisable that the Italian allies—more especially the Latins—should be brought into close legal relations with Rome, and the acceptance by the latter of innumerable civil laws of the central state is attested by Cicero.[1] The Italians are known to have been bound by a *plebiscitum* concerning loans [2]—this, however, only made contracts of a certain kind between them and Romans invalid, and may not have demanded their consent; but their formal acceptance must have been required for the Didian law, which extended the sumptuary regulations of the *lex Fannia* to all the *Italici*.[3] The "free" as well as the "federate" city has the right to accept or decline a legislative proposal put before it by the Roman government.[4]

Closest of all to Rome were the Latins. As members of federate cities they were amongst the *socii*,[5] and it is only as a class with special privileges that they are distinguished from the latter.[6] *Latinitas* had, through the efforts of colonisation, long lost its geographical and ethnic significance. It was the name for a *status* often accepted by Roman citizens, which combined the anomalies of sovereignty and a partial Roman citizenship. The sovereign rights are those possessed by the *socii*, the civic privileges were originally those held by the *municipia*; but it is possible that on and after the foundation of Ariminum and the last twelve Latin colonies [7] *commercium* alone was granted, *conubium*

---

[1] Cic. *pro Balbo* 8, 21 "innumerabiles aliae leges de civili jure sunt latae ; quas Latini voluerunt, adsciverunt."

[2] Liv. xxxv. 7 (193 B.C.) "M. Sempronius tribunus plebis . . . plebem rogavit plebesque scivit ut cum sociis ac nomine Latino creditae pecuniae jus idem quod cum civibus Romanis esset." The enactment was produced by the discovery that Roman creditors escaped the usury laws by using Italians as their agents.   [3] Macrob. *Sat.* iii. 17, 6.

[4] Cic. *pro Balbo* 8, 20 "foederatos populos fieri fundos oportere . . . non magis est proprium foederatorum quam omnium liberorum." For the formula of acceptance ("fundi—i.e. auctores—facti sunt") cf. Festus p. 89.

[5] Cic. *pro Balbo* 24, 54 "Latinis, id est foederatis."

[6] The distinction is expressed in the familiar *socii ac nominis Latini* (Liv. xli. 8), *socii et Latinum* (Sall. *Hist.* i. 17), and perhaps in *socii Latini nominis*, if this last expression is to be regarded as an asyndeton.

[7] These twelve colonies, with the dates of their foundations, are—Ariminum (268 B.C.), Beneventum (268), Firmum (264), Aesernia (263), Brundisium (244).

refused.[1]   The most distinctive privilege of the Latin had been the concession of facilities for acquiring Roman political rights. A Latin who migrated from his town and became a domiciled immigrant (*incola*) of Rome had retained his civic rights in private law, and gained a limited power of suffrage.[2]   He could even by complete expatriation (*exilium*) surrender his own *civitas* and attain the full Roman citizenship.   But the conditions subsequently imposed on this right[3] were evaded, immigration continued unchecked, and there was a danger of the depopulation of the districts from which the exiles came.   This evil suggested the later method, which gave the Latins admission to the *civitas*. The holder of a magistracy in his native town was, by the mere fact of his position, to become a full citizen of Rome.   It is improbable that this right replaced the right of exile possessed by already existing Latin towns, and the date of its origin is unknown ; but it possibly accompanied the remodelling of Latin rights in 268 B.C., and is henceforth the typical privilege of the Latin colony.[4]   Another mode in which the individual Latin could acquire the Roman *civitas* was by conducting a successful prosecution under the Acilian and Servilian laws of extortion.[5]

The freedom of the cities, whether Latin or Italian, seems to

Spoletium (241), Cremona and Placentia (218), Copia (193), Valentia (192), Bononia (189), Aquileia (181).

[1] The later Latin colonists have of right no *conubium* with Rome (Ulp. *Reg.* v. 4 "Conubium habent cives Romani cum civibus Romanis ; cum Latinis autem et peregrinis ita si concessum sit "). The change may have come with this last outburst of Latin colonisation in Italy ; but it may be as late as the extension of *latinitas* to the provinces. For the right of *commercium* possessed by these colonies see Cic. *pro Caec.* 35, 102 "jubet enim (Sulla Volaterranos) eodem jure esse quo fuerint Ariminenses, quos quis ignorat duodecim coloniarum fuisse et a civibus Romanis hereditates capere potuisse ? "

[2] Appian (*B.C.* i. 23), speaking of C. Gracchus' proposal to extend the citizenship, suggests a Latin right ψῆφον ἐν ταῖς 'Ρωμαίων χειροτονίαις φέρειν. Livy, with reference to the year 212 B.C., speaks of the *sortitio* as to the tribe or tribes in which the Latins should vote (xxv. 3, in the trial of Postumius "sitella . . . lata est ut sortirentur ubi Latini suffragium ferrent ").

[3] Liv. xli. 8 "Lex sociis ac nominis Latini, qui stirpem ex sese domi relinquerent, dabat ut cives Romani fierent."

[4] This was the *latinitas* given to Cisalpine Gaul in 89 B.C. by a law of the consul Cn. Pompeius Strabo.   Ascon. *in Pison.* p. 3 "Pompeius enim non novis colonis eas (Transpadanas colonias) constituit, sed veteribus incolis manentibus jus dedit Latii, ut possent habere jus quod ceterae Latinae coloniae, id est ut gerendo magistratus civitatem Romanam adipiscerentur."   Consequently when Caesar refounded Comum in this district, in accordance with the *lex Vatinia* (59 B.C.), the new *civitas* possessed this right (App. *B.C.* ii. 26).

[5] *Lex Acilia* 1. 77 ; Cic. *pro Balbo* 24, 54.   The probable dates of these laws are 122 and 111 B.C. respectively.

have won rigid respect from Rome and her magistrates. The
burdens of military service were, indeed, unevenly distributed
between the central city and her allies,[1] while the spoils of war
were mainly for the Roman. But it was a shock and a surprise
when in 173 B.C. a consul made personal requisitions on the
federate city of Praeneste.[2] The lesson once learnt was only
too faithfully followed, and the illegal demands of Roman
officials were accompanied by acts of capricious violence.[3] But
the burden of service and the misuse of power were not the only
motives urging the allies to seek the *civitas* of Rome ; nor was it
merely a sentimental desire to be invested with the Roman
name. The citizenship had a positive value both as a protection
and a source of gain. The protection against capital or corporal
penalties tacitly accorded to Romans by provincial governors
could not be claimed by the allies, and, although there is no
evidence that Rome, in her final organisation of the Italian
confederacy, continued her early policy of inhibiting *commercium*
between the towns, yet citizenship had a commercial value.
Ownership of land in the provinces was protected by the praetor
and the proconsul, but only when it was held by a Roman. To
the Roman trade with the barbarian was secure, to the Italian
precarious ; and everywhere he had to face the competition of
the commercial companies of Roman knights. The grounds of
interest coincided with those of sentiment in producing a demand
which the progressive party amongst the Romans strove to meet.
The first attempt was made through a law of the consul Flaccus
in 125 B.C.,[4] the second by one of C. Gracchus in 121, the
latter law probably offering citizen rights to the Latins and
Latin rights to the other allies.[5] The final proposal of Livius

---

[1] The allies before the social war reckon as their chief grievance "per omnes
annos atque omnia bella duplici numero se militum equitumque fungi" (Vell.
ii. 15).
[2] Liv. xlii. 1 "(L. Postumius Albinus) . . . literas Praeneste misit, ut sibi
magistratus obviam exiret, locum publice pararet, ubi deverteretur, jumentaque,
cum exiret inde, praesto essent. Ante hunc consulem nemo unquam sociis in
ulla re oneri aut sumptui fuit . . . Injuria consulis . . . et silentium . . .
Praenestinorum jus, velut probato exemplo, magistratibus fecit graviorum in dies
talis generis imperiorum."   [3] C. Gracchus ap. Gell. x. 3, 3.
[4] App. *B.C.* i. 21 and 34. According to Valerius Maximus (ix. 5, 1) Flaccus
proposed to give the *provocatio* to those "qui civitatem mutare noluissent."
[5] App. *B.C.* i. 23. Plutarch makes it a simple proposal of citizenship for the
allies (*C. Gracch.* 5). The geographical limits of these proposed extensions are
unknown. Velleius (ii. 6) remarks vaguely, with respect to the Gracchan law,
"dabat civitatem omnibus Italicis, extendebat eam paene usque Alpis."

Drusus in 91 was probably an unmodified extension of the *civitas*,[1] and it was the failure of this measure that led to the Italian revolt. A new suggestion for a solution of the problem of the relations of Rome to Italy sprang from the organisation of the hostile states. A federal capital, Corfinium, now Italica, was created, and a provisional federation of eight states formed, one which was intended ultimately to embrace the whole of Italy. The Roman, or rather Italian, pattern was follow'ed in the new constitution; it possessed two consuls, twelve praetors, and a senate of five hundred;[2] but both the magistracies and the senate were of a federal type. The issue of the war was to determine whether Rome should remain the leading state or become a mere member of an Italian confederation, although the unlikelihood of the giant city's settling down to this position may have appealed to some of the federal leaders.[3] Unless a redistribution of territory and population had been effected, Rome would have been the Thebes of the league, and the fate of the Empire would have been in suspense, for a federal government's capacity for imperial rule had yet to be tested. By timely concessions Rome saved her position as the head of the confederacy. By the *lex Julia* (90 B.C.) all the Italian states that had not revolted were offered the *civitas*,[4] and this was followed by the *lex Plautia Papiria* (89 B.C.), which offered the *civitas* to the *socii* and *incolae* of the allied cities in revolt.[5] These measures effected a considerable extension of the citizenship, but other means, of which we are ignorant, must have been adopted for the gradual incorporation of communities, many of which still remained for a considerable time in rebellion against Rome.[6]

[1] App. *B.C.* i. 35; he promised to reintroduce the law περὶ τῆς πολιτείας. Liv. *Ep.* lxxi. "socios et Italicos populos spe civitatis Romanae sollicitavit"; Vell. ii. 14 "Tum conversus Drusi animus . . . ad dandam civitatem Italiae."

[2] Diod. xxxvii. 2.

[3] Cf. the words of Pontius Telesinus, the Samnite leader in the later struggle at the Colline gate (Vell. ii. 27), "eruendam delendamque urbem . . . nunquam defuturos raptores Italicae libertatis lupos, nisi silva, in quam refugere solerent, esset excisa." This, however, is an expression of Samnite rather than of Italian feeling.   [4] App. *B.C.* i. 49; Cic. *pro Balbo* 8, 21.

[5] Only one clause of this law is known—that by which the *civitas* was granted to *incolae* enrolled on the registers of federate communities; they were to have the citizenship, if they made profession to the praetor within sixty days (Cic. *pro Arch.* 4, 7). It is difficult to believe that this cumbrous rule applied to the citizens of the towns.

[6] The gradual nature of the incorporation is attested by the expression of Velleius (ii. 16), "paulatim deinde recipiendo in civitatem, qui arma aut non ceperant aut deposuerant maturius, vires refectae sunt."

The work of incorporation immediately raised two problems. The first was the question of the voting rights of the new citizens. These rights were at first grudgingly accorded to prevent the new citizens swamping the old. The *novi cives* were enrolled in but eight of the existing tribes.[1] But this compromise could not last long ; redistribution became a party cry, and even the conservatives felt the damage done to their cause by a prolonged opposition to the Italian vote. The measure of Sulpicius (88 B.C.), which distributed the new citizens over all the tribes, was indeed repealed with his other laws ; but its principle seems to have been adopted in a decree of the Senate of 84 B.C.,[2] and the equality of the Roman and Italian vote was henceforth never questioned. The vote itself was not of the importance anticipated. It was, in the first place, rendered ineffective through lack of a system of representation. Even had such a system, planned on a small scale by Augustus,[3] been realised, it is questionable whether it could have saved the Republic. The Empire had to be garrisoned by professional armies, and these could not be found in Italy. The military and the civil power would in any case have been opposed, and the conflict must have ended in a victory for the former. But, so far as the extension of the *civitas* did affect future politics, it was only to create a dualism between the Roman proletariate and the Italian country voters. They had different ideals and different leaders. But the former were on the spot, ready for any legislative work, and in the troubled politics that ushered in the monarchy it was they who supported those champions of freedom who replaced senatorial

---

[1] Vell. ii. 20 "Itaque cum ita civitas Italiae data esset, ut in octo tribus contribuerentur novi cives, ne potentia eorum et multitudo veterum civium dignitatem frangeret plusque possent recepti in beneficium quam auctores beneficii, Cinna in omnibus tribubus eos se distributurum pollicitus est." Appian (*B.C.* i. 49) seems to speak of the creation of ten new tribes(δεκατεύοντες ἀπέφηναν ἑτέρας ἐν αἷς ἐχειροτόνουν ἔσχατοι). The attempt to reconcile these accounts by supposing that they refer to different classes of allies or are the respective products of the two acts of legislation (Kubitschek *Imp. Rom. trib. descr.*; Beloch *der Italische Bund*) receives some epigraphic support, but rests either on a correction of Appian's text or on the assumption that his account refers to ten of the *old* tribes.

[2] Liv. *Ep.* 84 "Novis civibus senatus consulto suffragium datum est," a careless phrase of the epitomiser or copyist for the distribution through the tribes (Drakenborch). Sulla, in spite of his rescission of the rights of certain rebel towns, did not disturb this arrangement.

[3] Augustus formed the plan of giving to the senates (*decuriones*) of the twenty-eight colonies which he founded in Italy the right of voting for the magistrates at Rome. They were to send their votes under seal (Suet. *Aug.* 46).

rule by a military despotism. The ideal of the Italian was quiescence; the scattered voters with no corporate organisation were more prone to look to persons than to causes; sometimes there was a wave of municipal enthusiasm, but many an Italian township recognised no leader but its Roman patron, and saw in his success at the polls the highest use to which they could put their suffrage.

The second great problem was that of the future administrative relations of Rome to these incorporated townships. The growth of the municipal idea was not a new one. Even as early as the beginning of the second century B.C. the possibility had been demonstrated of combining active internal independence with the possession of the full Roman *civitas*. Arpinum had received the full citizenship in 188 B.C., and its citizens vote henceforward ,in the Cornelian tribe;[1] but its internal autonomy was not destroyed, for the town was still legislating for itself in 115 B.C.[2] Meanwhile there are signs that a higher type of organisation was being given to Roman colonies; at least duovirs, who may be *duoviri juri dicundo*, are found at Puteoli in 105 B.C.[3] This idea of some political and judicial independence being enjoyed by townships, which had become a part of Rome, was worked out on the grandest scale after the social war; but the turbulent times which followed were not suited to comprehensive municipal legislation, and it is not likely that a definite system, which adjusted local to central powers, was developed before the Augustan period. Something had however been done in Cicero's time. Here and there we find a local constitution remodelled,[4] and there is evidence that there was already some division of competence between the local magistrate and the *praetor urbanus* in civil jurisdiction—the defendant being in some cases compelled to give bail (*vadimonium*) to bring his case to Rome.[5]

---

[1] Liv. xxxviii. 36.

[2] Cicero says that his grandfather, in or just before the consulship of Scaurus (115 B.C.), "restitit M. Gratidio . . . ferenti legem tabellariam" (*de Leg.* iii. 16, 36).   [3] *C.I.L.* i. p. 163.

[4] A fragment of a constitution of Tarentum, dating apparently from a time not long subsequent to the *lex Julia* of 90 B.C., has been preserved (*Fragmentum Tarentinum* in *L'Année Épigraphique*, 1896, pp. 30, 31). Arpinum was undergoing reorganisation in 46 B.C. (Cic. *ad Fam.* xiii. 11, 3).

[5] Cic. *in Verr.* v. 13, 34 "unum illud, quod ita fuit illustre notumque omnibus, ut nemo tam rusticanus homo L. Lucullo et M. Cotta consulibus (74 B.C.) Romam ex ullo municipio vadimonii causa venerit quin sciret jura omnia praetoris urbani nutu . . . Chelidonis . . . gubernari."

This principle of a limitation of the power of the local courts is found fully developed in a *lex Rubria* which deals with the organisation of Cisalpine Gaul. This district had held an anomalous position from the time of the social war. Although still a province, its towns had been given Latin rights in 89 B.C.[1] This was interpreted by the democratic party as a forecast of the citizenship, for Gallia Cisalpina was certainly enrolled in Rome by the revolutionary government of Cinna or his successors.[2] The grant, however, was not approved at the Sullan restoration, and its validity was disputed until Caesar renewed the gift in 49 or 48 B.C.[3] Two or three years earlier he had busied himself with the creation of an Italian organisation in the Gallic towns;[4] but, even after his conferment of the citizenship, the incorporation of the district into Italy was not immediately accomplished. It remained technically a province until 42 B.C., when Octavianus gained the consent of the Senate to its "autonomy,"[5] i.e. to its recognition as a group of Italian townships. It is doubtful whether the *lex Rubria* belongs to the epoch of the Julian or the Augustan organisation;[6] but it is practically certain that it extends an already existing Italian system to the new district. The chief characteristic of the system is a division of power between the praetor at Rome and the magistrate in the municipal town. In the fragment of the law which we possess this division is manifested in two particulars. The right of declaring bankruptcy (*missio in possessionem*) is reserved for the praetor, although the provisional arrest of the debtor (*duci jubere*) may be ordered by the local magistrate. Again, in the action for the recovery of a loan and in those

---

[1] Ascon. *in Pison.* p. 3.

[2] This is proved both by the attempt of Crassus, as censor in 65 B.C., to place the Transpadanes on the register of citizens (Dio Cass. xxxvii. 9), and by Cicero's comment on Marcellus' action in scourging a citizen of Novum Comum in 51 B.C. (Cic. *ad Att.* v. 11, 2 "Marcellus foede in Comensi : etsi ille magistratum non gesserit, erat tamen Transpadanus ").

[3] Dio Cass. xli. 36.

[4] Cic. *ad Att.* v. 2, 3 "eratque rumor de Transpadanis, eos jussos IIIIviros creare. Quod si ita est, magnos motus timeo."

[5] App. *B.C.* v. 3 τήν τε γὰρ Κελτικὴν τὴν ἐντὸς Ἄλπεων ἐδόκει Καίσαρος ἀξιοῦντος (i.e. Octavianus after Philippi) αὐτόνομον ἀφιέναι, γνώμῃ τοῦ προτέρου Καίσαρος. Cf. iii. 30 and Dio Cass. xlviii. 12.

[6] The name given to the district in the law *Gallia Cisalpeina, Gallia cis Alpeis* (cc. 22 and 23) suits both epochs equally well, for Caesar had not made it a part of Italy. The fact that the *praetor urbanus* is the central authority in jurisdiction (cc. 21 and 22) suits the Augustan epoch better.

arising from some other obligations, all cases involving a sum
over 15,000 sesterces must be remitted to Rome, the local
magistrate having the right to enforce on the parties bail
(*vadimonium*) for their appearance there.[1]   These fragmentary
notices are an index to a principle which was doubtless fully
elaborated in the Augustan legislation.

A tolerable degree of uniformity was also secured in the
political structure of the towns of Italy.   It was but a
development of the typical Italian constitution of magistrates
(*magistratus potestatesve*),[2] senate (*senatus, curia*, composed of
decuriones conscriptive), and popular assembly (*comitia conciliumve*,
composed of *municipes* and sometimes of *incolae*) ; and the *lex
Julia municipalis* of Caesar (45 B.C.) ordains a uniform qualification for the local magistracies and senates, and enjoins that the
local census shall be taken in conjunction with that of Rome.
But, though the general lines of organisation were the same, this
uniformity was chiefly the result of growth, not of creation.   No
effort was made at securing a common nomenclature either for
the states or for their officials.   Caesar's municipal law shows
municipia, coloniae and *praefecturae* existing side by side,[3] while
inscriptions show titles for officials, such as dictator or praetor,
which may be as old as those of Roman magistrates.[4]

[1] *Lex Rubria* cc. 21 and 22.   For the *vadimonium* cf. Cic. *in Verr.* v. 13,
34 (quoted p. 313).
[2] Generally *quattuorviri*, this board being usually divided into two magistrates
with higher jurisdiction (*duumviri juri dicundo*) and two police officials (*duumviri
aediles*).   Sometimes we find *IIIIviri juri dicundo*, perhaps a designation for the
joint board, or, where the magistrates with aedilician power alone are referred
to, *IIIIviri aediles* or *aedilicia potestate*.   See Wilmanns *Index* pp. 620-622.
[3] *Lex Julia mun.* 1. 84.   Cf. Cic. *in Pis.* 22, 51 "neque enim regio ulla fuit,
nec municipium neque praefectura aut colonia, ex qua non ad me publice
venerint gratulatum."
[4] Wilmanns *Index* p. 618.

CHAPTER VIII

WHEN Rome had asserted her supremacy over the greater part of Sicily at the close of the first Punic war, a new problem in organisation was presented to her. She held, perhaps rightly, that these new dependencies, with their transmarine position, fickle politics, and in some cases Carthaginian sympathies, could not safely be included in the military symmachy of Italy; so she substituted tribute for military service, placed the command of the cities of a wide district under the guidance of the personal *imperium*, and created the first permanent external department of administration (*provincia*). The government which had been adopted for Hellenic cities was still more necessary for the barbarians of Spain, a country which Rome had not sought but which military exigencies alone warned her not to leave. The recognition of Empire in the West was rapid and easy, for the effective government of Italy seemed to involve the control of the Tyrrhenian Sea. The Senate showed greater hesitancy in accepting a similar Adriatic policy, and declined to recognise that Rome had permanent interests even in eastern Europe of a magnitude that should lead to Empire. War followed war, Greece was once and Macedon twice at her feet, but on every occasion she declined to annex. It was not until experience had proved the costliness and the danger of a protectorate that in 146 B.C. Macedonia was recognised as a province with Achaea as its annexe. The troublesome relations with Carthage had meanwhile ended in war and annexation, and what had hitherto been rather a distant problem—Rome's relations with the potentates of Asia—became, as the years rolled on and as Roman trade struck deeper roots in the East, one of paramount concern. The history of eastern Europe was repeated in Asia, and although Rome had already a foothold in Anatolia through her acceptance of the kingdom of Pergamus, the death-blow to the protectorate system in these regions was first struck by Pompeius' organisation of the East at the close of the Mithridatic wars (65-63). Further extensions in the West and North, which resulted in the conquest of further Spain and of Gaul, were due to the enterprise of individual commanders, or to the search for a frontier which should be a permanent protection against barbarian invasion; and at the close of the Republic the list of Roman provinces had risen to fifteen.[1]

The idea of a province was that of an aggregate of states (*civitates*); where Greek or Phoenician civilisation had penetrated, these states were cities, but sometimes, as in Gaul and Spain, they were cantons or tribes. Natural political associations were usually chosen as the units of government, although formidable combinations were broken up, and the numerical regulation of the government centres in a province was an integral part of its organisation. Thus the number of communal unions was in Sicily 68,[2] in Asia 44,[3] and 64 in Transalpine Gaul.[4] Such aggregates probably include the free and federate states, which, although geographically, were not juristically within the province at all. The cities which were *liberae* and those which were *liberae et foederatae* differed, sometimes perhaps in the degree, but always in the basis, of their rights. The latter had the grant of their rights embodied in a sworn treaty (*foedus*), which was the product in the earlier Republic of Senate and people, in the later of either of these powers,[5]—a guarantee which was meant to be perpetual, and the breach of which was either an act of war or its result. A charter (*lex data*), on the other hand,[6] which made a city only "free" might be revoked at any moment. The rights common to both groups of states are practically those of the Italian communes[7]—a control of their

---

[1] Sicily, Sardinia, Hither and Further Spain, Illyricum, Macedonia and Achaea (separated by Caesar), Africa, Asia, Gallia Narbonensis, Gallia Cisalpina, Bithynia, Cyrene with Crete, Cilicia and Syria.

[2] The number is given by Pliny (*H.N.* iii. 88). In Cicero's time there was about this number. He speaks of the appointment of 130 censors (*in Verr.* ii. 55, 137), two for each state (ib. 53, 133).

[3] Cassiodorus *Chron.* ad A.U.C. 670 "Asiam in XLIIII. regiones Sulla distribuit."

[4] Tac. *Ann.* iii. 44. This division may be the work of Augustus.

[5] pp. 244, 283.   [6] p. 245.

[7] Except that ownership of the soil is not always, as in Italy, the ground of exemption from taxation. On the free city of Termessus in Pisidia "free possession" is alone conferred.

own finances, a free enjoyment of their land which exempted
them from the payment of tribute, and above all a use and
enjoyment of their own native law [1]—and both agree in being
entirely outside the sphere of the governor's jurisdiction.[2] He
could enter such a privileged city only as a guest, and although
for purposes of convenience great central cities which were
free, as Antioch in Syria and Thessalonica in Macedonia, were,
from their position as natural capitals, chosen as the residence of
the governor, he merely exercised jurisdiction in these towns,
not over their citizens. More distant still from provincial rule
were the allied kings (reges socii) on the frontiers. Their independence was less conditioned than that of the free and allied
cities, for they were bound to furnish less definite assistance to
Rome in time of need, and their foreign activity was not wholly
destroyed. But the chief reason why in a list of Rome's friends
they appear in a separate category [3] is that a treaty with a king
was not, like one with a Republic, regarded as eternal. It was
a personal obligation, and its perpetual validity depended on its
renewal with each successive occupant of the throne.

States which belonged to neither of these categories were
subject or, as the phrase ran, tributary (stipendiariae), the test of
subjection being the normal one in the ancient world of the
payment of a tax to a superior. Yet these too had their rights
and their charter. The guarantee, however, was no longer
individual but collective, and was contained in the law of the
province (lex provinciae). This law was usually the work of the
conquering general himself, assisted by ten senatorial commissioners (decem legati) appointed by the Senate, and it continued to bear the name of its chief creator, as we see in the
cases of the lex Rupilia of Sicily,[4] the lex Aemilia of Macedonia,[5]
and the lex Pompeia of Bithynia.[6] While it re-established the
states of a conquered district, it also gave them certain ultimate
rights. It defined the burden of the tribute, specified the

[1] See the lex Antonia de Termessibus (71 B.C.), especially the clause which
confers autonomy "so far as is consistent with this charter" (i. l. 7 "eique
legibus sueis ita utunto . . . quod advorsus hanc legem non fiat").
[2] Cic. de Prov. Cons. 3, 6. For the weakening of this respect for αὐτονομία in
the Ciceronian period and Caesar's attempt to strengthen it by law (probably the
lex Julia repetundarum of 59 B.C.) see Cic. in Verr. iii. 89, 207 ; in Pis. 16, 37
(' lege Caesaris justissima atque optima populi liberi plane et vere erant liberi ").
[3] Festus p. 218.   [4] Cic. in Verr. ii. 13, 32 ; 15, 37 ; 16, 39 ; 24, 59.
[5] Liv. xlv. 17 and 32.   [6] Plin. ad Traj. 79 (83), 1.

particular circuit-courts which the citizens of the various towns
were to attend, and framed regulations, which the governor was
expected to observe, about national and international jurisdiction.
But these regulations, slight and general as they were, are no
sufficient test of the amount of autonomy, in administration and
jurisdiction, actually enjoyed by the subject towns. Much of
their independence was permissive and based on the will of the
governor. But the ruler, whether honest or dishonest, was
practically bound to grant it, for the Roman government had
provided him with no staff which could take over the minuter
duties of administration; if he was an enlightened man, he
cherished the fiction that the states were free;[1] if unenlightened,
he at least knew that by permitting self-government he was
saving himself trouble. In the case of the eastern cities the
neglect of the governor was almost as great an evil as his
exactions.[2]

The theory of Roman taxation was in origin that it was a
war indemnity. This accounts for the fact that in the early
days of Rome's dealings with conquered peoples a tax might be
imposed even on nations which were declared free,[3] and for the
name *stipendium* ("payment for the army") which was borne by
the direct taxation imposed by Roman commissioners on provincials.[4] This equitable theory, that the taxes collected should
merely defray the expenses of the military occupation and
administration of a province, seems to have been realised in
practice where the Roman government took the trouble to
organise a system of its own. The Macedonians were made to
pay but half of what they had paid to their kings,[5] the Spanish
provinces must have cost more than they brought in, and in

[1] As Cicero did in his government of Cilicia. See *ad Att.* vi. 2, 4 "omnes
(civitates), suis legibus et judiciis usae, αὐτονομίαν adeptae, revixerunt"; vi. 1,
15 "multaque sum secutus Scaevolae (governor of Asia *circa* 98 B.C.); in iis
illud, in quo sibi libertatem censent Graeci datam, ut Graeci inter se disceptent
suis legibus . . . Graeci vero exsultant quod peregrinis judicibus utuntur."
[2] This we may gather from Cicero's account of the proceedings of the native
magistrates in Cilicia (*ad Att.* vi. 2, 5 "Mira erant in civitatibus ipsorum furta
Graecorum, quae magistratus sui fecerant : quaesivi ipse de iis, qui annis decem
proximis magistratum gesserant ; aperte fatebantur").
[3] On the conquest of Epirus in 167 B.C., although all the Illyrians were
declared *liberi*, only some were pronounced "non solum liberi sed etiam immunes"
(Liv. xlv. 26).
[4] Cf. Tac. *Hist.* iv. 74 "nam neque quies gentium sine armis neque arma sine
stipendiis neque stipendia sine tributis haberi queunt."
[5] Liv. xlv. 29.

Cicero's time it was only the Asiatic provinces, where taxes were imposed on quite a different system, that yielded a surplus.[1]   It was this system, which the Romans found existing in Sicily, Sardinia, and Asia, and with their characteristic negligence elected to preserve, which changed the whole theory of Roman taxation. The principle was that of the payment by the cultivator (*arator*) of a tithe (*decuma*) of the produce of his land. It was inevitable that the Roman lawyer should associate this due with the *vectigal* paid by the occupants of *ager publicus*, and should evolve from the comparison the strange theory that land in the provinces was not owned but merely "possessed" by its holders.[2] The chief practical consequences of the tithe system were a surplus to the treasury, and the exactions of the middlemen (*publicani*) through the indirect system of collection which it involved.

The direct tax (*stipendium*) was collected by a tribute assessed either on the land (*tributum soli*) or on the personalty of individuals (*tributum capitis*).[3] The Romans of the Republic seem never to have attempted to form an accurate estimate of the resources furnished by the land and personal wealth of a province; doubtless in Hellenised districts they employed the systems which they found existing, such as the schedules which formed the bases of the εἰσφοραί: in Spain amongst other rough expedients they seem to have adopted a valuation tax on a proportion of the produce of the soil;[4] while elsewhere, as in Macedonia,[5] they fixed a total on the existing basis of collection.

---

[1] Cic. *pro Leg. Man.* 6, 14 "ceterarum provinciarum vectigalia, Quirites, tanta sunt ut iis ad ipsas provincias tutandas vix contenti esse possimus, Asia vero tam opima est et fertilis ut . . . facile omnibus terris antecellat."

[2] Gaius ii. 7 "in eo (provinciali) solo dominium populi Romani est vel Caesaris, nos autem possessionem tantum vel usumfructum habere videmur." The theory is perhaps as old as the Gracchan period. C. Gracchus' association of the Asiatic taxes with the censor (cf. p. 231) must have done a good deal to develop it. It is no wonder that this theory led to the view that the provinces were "quasi quaedam praedia populi Romani" (Cic. *in Verr.* ii. 3, 7).

[3] These expressions are known only from the literature of the Empire ; it may be a mere accident that in Republican literature *tributum* seems never to be used of imperial taxation. The form *stipendium* is preferred. In Liv. xxiii. 32 we have the *tributum* of Sardinia mentioned with reference to Republican times. The *venditio tributorum* and the ὠναί of Cilicia (Cic. *ad Fam.* iii. 8, 5 ; *ad Att.* v. 16, 2) probably refer to local taxes improperly sold to *publicani*.

[4] Liv. xliii. 2 "(Hispani) impetraverunt ne frumenti aestimationem magistratus Romanus haberet."

[5] p. 319.

The direct tax was usually collected by the communes themselves and paid to the governor's quaestor.

The tithe (*decuma*) was collected on the contract system, and the difference in its mode of collection in the *vectigales provinciae* depended on whether the site of the auction was in the province itself, where local companies or even communities [1] could compete for its collection, or whether the tithes of the whole province must be put up to auction in Rome, in which case the province was likely to become the prey of a single Roman company.   In Sicily the first system was adopted in accordance with the principles laid down by Hiero, its last great king (*lex Hieronica*) ; [2] the second system was devised by C. Gracchus for Asia and was doubtless extended to eastern provinces subsequently organised such as Cilicia.[3]   The pretext for the change was no doubt the incapacity of the Asiatic cities to collect their own dues,[4] and was welcome to the weakness of the states, which liked to have near them a body of Roman capitalists from whom they could borrow in emergency ; but it created a pernicious connexion between capitalism and administration which made the government of the Asiatic dependencies the gloomiest scene of Roman rule.   The tithe system in Asia, and perhaps in other provinces where it prevailed, was abolished by Caesar in 48 B.C.[5]   The harbour and frontier dues (*portoria*), the source of revenue next in value to the direct tribute or the tithe, were collected by private companies (*portitores*) perhaps throughout the whole imperial world, as they had been from the earliest times in Italy.[6] Other dues demanded from the province were paid for by the Roman government.   Such were the corn supplied for the praetor and his retinue (*frumentum in cellam* or *frumentum aestimatum*),[7] and the second *decuma* sometimes required by the state (*frumentum emptum*) and raised by command of the Senate

---

[1] Cic. *in Verr.* iii. 33, 77.   [2] ib. ii. 13, 32 ; 26, 63, etc.
[3] ib. iii. 6, 12 "inter Siciliam ceterasque provincias . . . in agrorum vectigalium ratione hoc interest, quod ceteris aut impositum vectigal est certum . . . aut censoria locatio constituta est, ut Asiae lege Sempronia."
[4] Cf. Cic. *ad Q. fr.* i. 1, 11, 33 "nomen autem publicani aspernari non possunt, qui pendere ipsi vectigal sine publicano non potuerint, quod iis aequaliter Sulla discripserat." The reference is to Sulla's temporary abolition of the Gracchan principle of collection.
[5] App. *B.C.* v. 4 ; Dio Cass. xlii. 6.
[6] Nothing seems to be known about the conditions of sale of the provincial *portoria*, e.g. whether those of Asia were put up at Rome like the *decumae*.
[7] Cic. *in Verr.* iii. cc. 81-96, 188-222.

Y

and people.[1] In both these cases a reasonable price was fixed by the Roman government.

We pass now to the governor and his staff. The early institution of praetors and the later use of the pro-magistracy for provincial government have already been described.[2] But we have seen that even Sulla did not formally dissociate the consulship and praetorship from provincial rule.[3] The consequences of this continued association were curious. By a law of C. Gracchus, which aimed at destroying one of the most valuable pieces of patronage which the Senate had at its disposal, the consular provinces must be assigned before the election of their holders.[4] They are strictly consular, and are technically entered on by their possessors on March 1 of their year of office, although no definite agreement need be come to as to their partition until the following December [5]—the earliest date at which the consuls of the later Republic could quit their urban duties. March 1 was the beginning of the military and provincial year, as since 152 B.C. January 1 had been of the year of civil office at Rome. The reason why the 1st of March of the year of office at Rome was chosen, and not the same date in the following year, was that the pro-magistracy was not yet recognised as a separate office, and that, if this second solution had been adopted, the interval between December 29 and March 1 would have caused a break in the *imperium*.[6] The anomaly resulted that a provincial governor held his command only for two months in his own right, and for ten months while waiting for his successor. It was harmless in practice, inasmuch as Sulla's law had ordained that the governor should retain his *imperium* until he returned to Rome, and need only quit his province thirty days after the arrival of his successor,[7] and was

---

[1] Cic. *in Verr.* iii. 70, 163. Cf. Liv. xxxvi. 2 "idem L. Oppio de alteris decumis exigendis in Sardinia imperatum." Sometimes this enforced sale of corn (*frumentum imperatum*) was required from free cities such as Halaesa, Centuripae, and Messana in Sicily (Cic. *in Verr.* iii. 73, 170 ; iv. 9, 20).

[2] pp. 201, 202.   [3] p. 201.

[4] Sall. *Jug.* 27 ; Cic. *de Prov. Cons.* 2, 3 ; *pro Domo* 9, 24.

[5] Cic. *ad Fam.* i. 9, 25.

[6] Cf. Cic. *de Prov. Cons.* 15, 37 (if the consul of 55 B.C. succeeds Caesar on March 1, 54 B.C.) "Fuerit toto in consulatu sine provincia, cui fuerit, antequam designatus est, decreta provincia ? Sortietur, an non ? Nam et non sortiri absurdum est, et quod sortitus sis non habere. Proficiscetur paludatus ? Quo ? Quo pervenire ante certam diem non licebit. Januario, Februario provinciam non habebit. Kalendis ei denique Martiis nascetur repente provincia."

[7] Cic. *ad Fam.* i. 9, 25 ; xii. 4, 2.

only accidentally disastrous as leading to the quarrel between
Caesar and the Senate, and thence to the downfall of the Roman
Republic. The pro-magistracy was first raised into a separate
office by a Pompeian law of 52 B.C., which enacted that governors
should seek their provinces five years after holding office at
Rome. It was a law that, by diminishing the nearness of the
prize, was intended to make the consulship and praetorship less
an object of illegitimate ambition at Rome. It might, therefore,
have conferred a slight indirect benefit on the provincials, but
the speedy collapse of the Republican government prevented its
adequacy being tested. The tenure of a provincial governorship
was nominally annual, but, even after Sulla had raised the
number of praetors to eight, there were but ten magistrates
available for fifteen provinces, and we know of three propraetors
—Verres in Sicily, Q. Cicero in Asia, and Fonteius in Narbonese
Gaul—who severally held their provincial commands for three
years in succession.

The chief members of the governor's staff were one subordinate
magistrate, the quaestor, and certain senatorial commissioners
(*legati*), one of whom was usually assigned to a praetorian, and
three to a consular province. The magisterial position of the
quaestor did not entitle him to an independent sphere of duties.
It is true that he was, in the main, a financial official, was
entrusted by the Senate with money or a credit for meeting the
expenses of the administration of his province,[1] received the
revenues from the *stipendium*, and had at the end of the year to
give an account of income and expenditure in his own name
and that of his superior;[2] but even here the real responsibility
was incurred by the governor, whose commands were irresistible,
and in all other respects the quaestor is the merest delegate,
who exercises jurisdiction, or any kind of administrative work,
in obedience to a voice that was supposed to convey a paternal
authority.[3] He might even, like the legates, be dismissed for
incompetence or maladministration before the term of his office

---

[1] Cic. *in Verr.* i. 13, 34 "pecunia attributa, numerata est. Profectus est
quaestor in provinciam (Verres). Venit exspectatus in Galliam ad exercitum
consularem cum pecunia."

[2] *Rationes referre* (Cic. *in Verr.* i. 13, 36). In accordance with a *lex Julia*
(perhaps *repetundarum*) of Caesar's, the accounts had to be deposited at the
aerarium, and two copies in two cities of the province (Cic. *ad Fam.* v. 20, 2;
Plut. *Cato Min.* 38).

[3] p. 215.

had expired.[1]   The *legati* had originally been representatives of
the government in Rome, but, to avoid friction, the custom grew
up of allowing governors to suggest individuals for the post.[2]
Yet to the end of the Republic their names were submitted to
the Senate, and they were supposed to be subordinate officials
of the state.   No special departments were, however, assigned
them; any power which they exercised was delegated by the
governor, whether it took the form of the command of a legion
or the presidency of a court.   A still more independent selection
was made of the unofficial members of the staff.   The "comrades"
(*comites*) of the governor were young men, whom he initiated in
the mysteries of official and diplomatic life, and whose services
he employed for any purpose for which they seemed competent.[3]
But, however many instruments the governor might use, there
was such a complete unity of responsibility that, in dealing with
the administration of a province, we are treating of the powers
of a single man.

These powers were exercised chiefly in three spheres—-military,
administrative, and judicial.   In a province that seethed with
war the summer months were spent in camp, the winter in more
peaceful duties; but in a settled district the governor could
map out his circuits as he pleased, and devote some time to the
ungenial task of inspecting the affairs of the municipalities under
his control.   Apart from the necessary diplomatic intercourse
with neighbouring potentates or protected chiefs, the amount of
administrative work which the governor undertook was as much
or as little as he pleased.   Its quantity depended on his view
as to how far self-government was a symptom of health or of
disease.   That it sometimes had the latter character is shown by
the startling discovery made by Cicero when he undertook an
unexpected investigation into the financial affairs of his subject
states.   He found that the native Greek magistrates of Cilicia

---

[1] Cic. *in Verr.* iii. 58, 134 "Quaestores, legatos . . . multi missos fecerunt
et de provincia decedere jusserunt, quod illorum culpa se minus commode audire
arbitrarentur aut quod peccare ipsos aliqua in re judicarent."

[2] The transition is marked in 169 B.C. (Liv. xliv. 18 "Senatus Cn. Servilio
consuli negotium dedit, ut is in Macedoniam, quos L. Aemilio videretur,
legaret").

[3] Cicero delegates even jurisdiction to one of his *comites*, Volusius (*ad Att.* v.
21, 6).   Other members of his retinue were his son Marcus and his brother
Quintus.   These intimates of the governor were spoken of as *contubernales, cohors
amicorum*, even as *cohors praetoria* (Cic. *ad Q. fr.* i. 1, 4, 12), although this title
was properly applied to the governor's military guard.

had been plundering their respective treasuries for the last ten years.[1] But the possibility of such a discovery is itself a testimony to the best aspect of provincial rule in the Republic—its noble but sometimes misguided belief in the capacity of people to govern themselves.

There was, however, one systematic function to which most of the governor's energies were directed in time of peace, and that was jurisdiction, both civil and criminal. General regulations concerning jurisdiction were made in the charters of the provinces; but these could not be the same for every country, since the judicial machinery of some groups of states was far more perfect than that of others. Sicily, the only province the details of whose *lex* are known, was peculiarly favoured, and its privileges may be taken as the best type of those offered by Rome. It was ordained that, in a suit between two citizens of the same state, the trial should be held in that state and according to its laws,[2] a regulation which certainly guaranteed the native *judex* and the native code, but which did not, perhaps, inhibit an appeal to the governor or take away his right of interpreting the law. The charter then provides for cases of inter-political jurisdiction. If a Sicilian of one state sues a Sicilian of another, the governor is to provide by lot the *judex* or *judices*,[3] who are perhaps in this case to be Roman citizens.[4] When litigation arises between an individual and a community not his own, the Senate of some third state should be the judge, when either litigant has challenged one of three senatorial bodies proposed.[5] In suits between Roman citizens and Sicilians the *judex* was to be of the nationality of the defendant.[6] In all other matters *judices* chosen by the magistrate (*selecti*) were to be appointed from the Roman citizens dwelling within the assize.[7]

[1] p. 319, note 2.
[2] Cic. *in Verr.* ii. 13, 32 "Siculi hoc jure sunt ut, quod civis cum cive agat, domi certet suis legibus."
[3] ib. "quod Siculus cum Siculo non ejusdem civitatis (agat), ut de eo praetor judices ex P. Rupilii decreto . . . sortiatur."
[4] It is possible, however, that the principle here adopted was that the *judex* should be of the nationality of the defendant.
[5] Cic. l.c. "quod privatus a populo petit aut populus a privato, senatus ex aliqua civitate, qui judicet, datur, cum alternae civitates rejectae sunt."
[6] ib. "quod civis Romanus a Siculo petit, Siculus judex datur, quod Siculus a civi Romano, civis Romanus datur."
[7] ib. "ceterarum rerum selecti judices ex conventu civium Romanorum proponi solent."

In Sicily it is clear that the *peregrinus judex* was a standing institution. Elsewhere, even in the Hellenised East, his existence was more dependent on the grace of the governor. Cicero, in his government of Cilicia, following the precedent of Mucius Scaevola, the ideal governor of Asia, allowed the greatest freedom to the native laws, courts, and judges, and remarks on the quickened life which their use inspired in the provincials.[1] The attempt, indeed, to substitute her own for the native law was abhorrent to the political sense of Rome, and her most ambitious representatives never attempted to make their edicts into codes. The importance of the edict was chiefly felt in matters of private international law, administrative jurisdiction, and procedure. It stated principles which should regulate the relations between members of different states or between provincials and Romans, it issued rules for the settlement of claims made by the *publicani*, and it supplemented the law of the province by framing regulations for the conduct of private suits. The edict of each province was a separate entity, and drew its name from the country to which it directly applied,[2] and it had a continuous existence, although the unity and continuity of its life depended too much on the discretion of the individual governor.[3] The edict might be composed at Rome,[4] and its author might copy from more than one original. The rulings of his predecessor would doubtless be well known; there were the edicts of other provinces, the work of famous administrators of the past;[5] and, as a fruitful source of general rules of procedure, there was the *edictum perpetuum* of the capital. In Cicero's own edict, of which he furnishes a brief description, the principles regulating business and trading relations (especially as existing between Roman companies and provincials) were clearly and fully set forth. As much attention was

---

[1] Cic. *ad Att.* vi. 1, 15 "multaque sum secutus Scaevolae; in iis illud, in quo sibi libertatem censent Graeci datam, ut Graeci inter se disceptent suis legibus . . . Graeci vero exsultant quod peregrinis judicibus utuntur"; *ad Att.* vi. 2, 4 "omnes (civitates), suis legibus et judiciis usae, αὐτονομίαν adeptae, revixerunt."

[2] "Edictum Siciliense" (Cic. *in Verr.* i. 45, 117).

[3] Extreme changes might be made a ground of complaint by the departing governor. Thus Cicero writes from Cilicia (50 B.C.) "Appius enim ad me ex itinere bis terve . . . literas miserat, quod quaedam a se constituta rescinderem" (*ad Att.* vi. 1, 2).

[4] Cic. *ad Fam.* iii. 8, 4.

[5] Thus Cicero, governor of Cilicia, followed in some respects the edict of Mucius Scaevola, the former governor of Asia (Cic. *ad Att.* vi. 1, 15).

devoted to the general rules of inheritance and bankruptcy, such as had been evolved by the *imperium* at Rome, and which were doubtless meant not to supersede the customs of the various communities, but to be a common law for the province as a whole. But much remained that could not be formulated. A province had boundless surprises in store, and Cicero found it wiser to leave the third part of his edict "unwritten." The principles of the urban praetor were to be drawn upon as occasion required.[1]   The civil jurisdiction of the governor, which was based on the edict, was either personal or delegated, and in both cases required the visitation of circuits (*conventus*, διοικήσεις),[2] into which the province had been divided at the time of its organisation. A programme of the assize was drawn up, the stay in each circuit was accurately determined,[3] and the governor held a court (*forum egit*) in each of them in turn.[4]

Delegated jurisdiction was performed usually by the quaestor and the legates; in both cases it was due to the mandate of the governor,[5] who could assign them lictors, if he pleased,[6] and could always control their sentences.[7]

The governor possessed an unfettered criminal jurisdiction over the members of the stipendiary states; but it cannot be supposed that he often exercised it. He might summon any case into his court, but ordinary crimes he doubtless left to the judicial machinery of the states themselves.[8]   On the other

---

[1] Cic. *ad Att.* vi. 1, 15 "unum (genus) est provinciale, in quo est de rationibus civitatum, de aere alieno, de usura, de syngraphis; in eodem omnia de publicanis. Alterum, quod sine edicto satis commode transigi non potest, de hereditatum possessionibus, de bonis possidendis vendendis, magistris faciendis: quae ex edicto et postulari et fieri solent. Tertium, de reliquo jure dicundo ἄγραφον reliqui. Dixi me de eo genere mea decreta ad edicta urbana accommodaturum."

[2] Cic. *ad Fam.* iii. 8, 6.   [3] Cic. *ad Att.* v. 21, 9.

[4] Cic. *ad Att.* v. 20, 1; *ad Fam.* iii. 8, 4 and 5.

[5] Suet. *Caes.* 7 "'Quaestori (Caesari) ulterior Hispania obvenit; ubi cum, mandatu praetoris, jure dicundo conventus circumiret, etc." Quaestorian jurisdiction was more frequent in Sicily than in other provinces, on account of the presence of the second quaestor at Lilybaeum.

[6] Cic. *ad Fam.* xii. 30, 7 "Illud non nimium probo quod scribis . . . te tuis etiam legatis lictores ademisse."

[7] Thus Verres quashes either a decision, or the execution of a decision, given by his quaestor (Cic. *Div. in Caec.* 17, 56 "Lilybaeum Verres venit postea: rem cognoscit: factum improbat: cogit quaestorem suum pecuniam . . . adnumerare et reddere").

[8] Possibly certain kinds of criminal jurisdiction were guaranteed to cities by the *lex provinciae*. The Senate of Catina in Sicily tried a slave (Cic. *in Verr.* iv. 45, 100).

hand, it was held that an offence might be of such import as
to transcend even his competence; and although there was no
legal means of escaping his jurisdiction, it was considered
advisable that he should send cases of a grave political
character—those, for instance, connected with sedition or a
popular rising—to be tried at Rome.[1] The only restraining
influence on the governor's jurisdiction was the necessity, imposed
by custom, of consulting a council of advisers.[2] This *consilium*,
however, was purely Roman, being composed of Roman citizens
residing in the *conventus* and of members of the governor's
retinue,[3] and although a council composed wholly of the latter
was usually avoided, there was no legal hindrance to such a
narrow selection.[4]

Over Roman citizens in the provinces the governor possessed
the same autocratic power; for his jurisdiction here is on a
level with that of the camp, and he gives judgment in a sphere
to which the *provocatio* does not extend.[5] Yet a strong customary
law, which was seldom disobeyed, directed that he should remit
to Rome all cases in which Roman citizens were to be tried on
a capital charge, and that, if he pronounced judgment himself,
he should inflict on them no degrading punishments.[6]

Almost every item in the provincial organisation that we
have sketched shows where its inherent weakness lay. It
resided in the uncontrolled power of the governor. Yet it was
a weakness more apparent in practice than in theory. There
were many controlling forces at work which the organiser and
the government hoped would be effective. There were the
charters of cities and of provinces, and in the province a
constant, if improvised, committee of the Senate, which the
governor was supposed to consult before he ventured on any

---

[1] Cic. *in Verr.* i. 33, 84 (of an *émeute* at Lampsacus) "Non te ad senatum
causam deferre . . . non eos homines, qui populum concitarant, consulum literis
evocandos curare oportuit?"

[2] The council was not, however, legally necessary. Cf. Cic. *in Verr.* ii. 30, 75
"Reus plorare . . . ut cum consilio cognosceret."

[3] ib. ii. 29, 70 ; 30, 75.

[4] ib. ii. 30, 75 "hominem innocentem de sententia scribae, medici haruspicis-
que condemnat."

[5] For the threat of capital punishment on a Roman citizen see Cic. *ad Q. fr.*
i. 2, 5 ; for its apparent execution, Diod. xxxvii. 5, 2.

[6] Cic. *in Verr.* v. 66, 170 "Facinus est vincire civem Romanum ; scelus,
verberare : prope parricidium, necare : quid dicam in crucem tollere?" Cf. *pro
Rab.* 5, 17.

important step.[1]   There was an unparalleled amount of legislation intended for the protection of provincials and expressed in
enactments dealing with the ordering of the provinces, the rights
of magistrates, and with extortion (*de provinciis ordinandis, de jure
magistratuum, repetundarum*) ; and, lastly, there was the criminal
responsibility supposed to be enforced by the courts which
carried out these laws.   Some of these checks—the charters of
the favoured cities, the senatorial commission—were real, but
were not far-reaching enough seriously to affect the form of
provincial rule.   Those of the laws were almost nugatory, for
though the government that proposed them had a collective
conscience, its individual members who were bound by them
had none, and the courts that were supposed to enforce these
laws became the prey of party strife and the weapon of party
fanatics.   But a government that depends on protective legislation and the enforcement of criminal responsibility must be in a
perilous state.   The defect must be in the principle of rule, not
merely in its working.   And in truth the Republican theory of
provincial rule represents a fundamental inconsistency of idea.
The theory aimed at the impossible combination of martial law
with municipal independence.   Had the rights of all the states
been provided with better safeguards, their self-government
might have been more real, and the autocracy of the governor
might have been proportionately checked.   But this solution
would have been an offence to the idea of the unlimited *imperium*,
a clinging superstition which the Romans had inherited from the
history of their own state and her days of conquest.   The
Roman Empire had been developed from a protectorate ; it bears
to the end of the Republican period the traces of its origin, and,
in its lack of organisation, conveys the suggestion of being a
merely provisional government.   The merits of such system as
there was cannot be ignored.   The unrestricted *imperium* was
necessary in time of war and, under a benevolent despot, might
be useful even in days of peace, while the very absence of
organisation betrays the noble belief that the aggregate of states
which formed a province was rather a confederated suzerainty
than an integral part of an empire.   But its defects are more
glaring and are to be found in the absence of some central
authority at home, not interested in provincial misrule, which

[1] See p. 285.

might enforce responsibility on governors; in the existence of annual commands, and the exaggeration of routine which rendered extraordinary appointments, such as that of Pompeius, inevitable ; and in the lack of an organised civil service, which, with its mechanical routine and its self-evolved rules, is perhaps the surest of all checks on autocracy.

CHAPTER IX

THE party of reform which, during the last century of the Republic, gave a new development to the elastic Roman constitution, by gradually creating a stronger executive organ than had been known since the time of the monarchy, had two distinguishing features. One was an opposition, sometimes rational, sometimes blind, to the senatorial government; the other the exposition of a positive programme for remedying evils which all but the most callous or careless could see. The nature of their attack varied with the assailable features presented by its object. At first it was directed against the assumed indifference of the Senate to internal reform and its failure to suggest hasty remedies for economic grievances. This was the essential feature of the Gracchan movement; but, although its example was perilous, the immediate effects of this first revolution were transitory in the extreme. The Senate emerged from the attack shaken but victorious. Italy was but of little account when the world lay at the feet of the noble families who composed the great council of state, and the Senate could be made to appear the only true government for an empire. Unfortunately this theory was rudely shaken. A miserable war in a protected state, into which the government was most unwillingly dragged, was thought sufficient to show that the merits of the senatorial administration of the empire were an illusion. The epoch of the Jugurthine war is the turning-point of the history of this period. A reforming party with an imperial policy must associate itself with the military power. The change was rapidly effected. Tribunes, commons, assemblies still represent the nominal sovereigns, but their weapons—too powerful for the users—are the *imperator*, the

army, and the camp. Henceforth we find a perpetual association of militarism with democracy which could have but one
issue, a monarchy resting on the sword.

But to the reformers of the times the ultimate solution of the
constitutional problem was something far less present than the
programme of reform, which was being handed on from leader to
leader with scarcely an item altered since the time when the
genius of C. Gracchus had given it birth. It contained agrarian
laws, measures for corn distribution and for colonies beyond the
sea, means for relieving social distress and the plethora of the
great capital, and at times it admitted—the most pressing need
of all—proposals for remedying the iniquitous relations that the
law permitted to exist between debtor and creditor. A new and
unexpected development was given to the activities of the party
by the introduction into their programme of proposals for
enfranchising the Italians. This was a measure that, like so many
others in popular programmes, was a creation of the demagogue
and was profoundly distasteful to his followers. Its acceptance
by the Liberals (*populares*) was a pure accident—one due to the
desire of breaking a formidable weapon employed by the Whig
opposition, who, like Scipio Aemilianus, had adopted the somewhat dangerous policy of playing off Italian rights against those
of the city proletariate. But, as belief usually follows acceptance, there is some reason for regarding the franchise question
as, at least finally, a plank in the democratic programme. In
the multiform efforts of the discontented we can also discern
the spasmodic attempt to create a competent central military
authority for Rome, as the only means of securing corn,
commerce, and the empire.

It was by no means a homogeneous party which developed
this programme and attempted to replace a government which
they deemed incompetent. Even its more thorough-going
members cannot be described by a single name. Amongst the
populares were many Liberals who had nothing to gain by
revolution ; but amongst them were also to be found many who
were democrats by necessity as well as by conviction, the
revolutionary element which was often a thorn in the side of
the reforming constitutionalists, the class of *improbi* which
supplied Catiline's so-called " conspiracy " and made it a genuine
democratic movement, and whose aspirations were subsequently
represented by Caelius Rufus and Dolabella. Nor must it be

supposed that there was any clear line of demarcation between *populares* and senators. Nowhere was the Senate more bitterly attacked than from within its own body. The leaders of the extreme party had attained the magistracies that entitled them to a seat in the Curia, and elections, so far as they were not gained by family influence or bribery, were fought on party lines. Nor even amongst the constitutionalists was there a lack of would-be reformers of a more moderate type. The elder Cato and the Scipionic circle, while eager to maintain senatorial ascendency, had been conscious of some of its defects ; and, as the cry for innovation gathered in strength, a party was formed which, by borrowing wholesale from the radical programme, attempted to reconcile the privileges of their order with concessions to Italy, purity in imperial administration, and care for the poor of Rome. This attempt was shattered by the fate of the younger Drusus, and henceforth there is no senatorial party of reform. Even Cicero, with his wide sympathies and his acute sense of the evils of the time, can suggest only a *concordia ordinum*, merely a means of bolstering up the existing constitution by means of a union of the propertied and therefore "loyal" classes (*boni*). The municipal statesman did, indeed, wish to see an "Italian" rather than a "Roman" government, but he had no scheme by which Italy could have secured representation at Rome, and before the close of his life he had accepted the inevitable solution of personal rule. There was to be a *moderator rei publicae*, a *princeps civitatis ;* [1] but this monarchy is not to destroy the constitution ; his prince is to be a loyal coadjutor of the Senate, not the exponent of a military despotism.

It is probable that with parties so evenly balanced as the *populares* and *optimates* no very decisive result would have been attained, had it not been for the existence in the state of a perfectly homogeneous body of men with few ideals but very decided wants. This was that upper middle class of large and moderate capitalists which, through an accident in nomenclature, had come to be known as *equites*.[2] It was a class that possessed the tradesman's narrow honesty and complete indifference to all politics not connected with business. Like all classes, they were quite willing to plunder the provinces while state officials did the same ; but they desired strong government more than

---

[1] Cic. *de Rep.* v. 6, 8 (*ad Att.* viii. 11, 1) ; v. 7, 9.   [2] p. 224.

plunder. They longed for an administration which should secure them adequate protection in the conquered world over which they had spread the network of their trade, and which should also ensure a freedom from revolution at home. Hence their wavering and yet always decisive attitude. To secure their first end they join the attacking party, to secure their second they attach themselves to the government, and their adherence or disaffection always turns the fortune of the day. It was the *equites* who helped the democrats to raise Marius to power, who forced their own creature to abandon his revolutionary colleague Saturninus, who ruined the schemes of the younger Drusus and set the Varian commission on the track of his adherents ; it was their hostility that proved equally fatal to the schemes of Sulla and of Catiline, their commercial instincts which lifted Pompeius into power and led them at the crisis of 60 B.C. to abandon the Senate and give their whole support to Caesar. There is something tragic in the ruthless massacre of *equites* which ushers in the Augustan monarchy ; for no class had done more for its existence and to none did it prove a greater boon.

To appreciate the issue of this struggle in which all parties were engaged, we must recognise its two-fold aspect as a struggle for social and political renewal, and consider separately the fate of the detailed programme of reform and the change in the constitution to which the attacks on the Senate led. From the first point of view the efforts of the democratic party ended in an unqualified success ; for every item of its programme was carried out, with the requisite modifications, by Caesar and the Principate. The agrarian question reached as near an approach to settlement as such eternal questions can attain, especially when it became absorbed into the movement of transmarine colonisation which was employed in the Principate for poorer citizens and for veterans. The extension of the franchise was completed, so far as the territory south of the Alps was concerned, by Caesar's renewal of the gift of citizenship to the Transpadanes and Augustus' incorporation of their territory as a part of Italy,[1] while the Principate was liberal with the conferment of Latin rights on provinces, such as Sicily, the Maritime Alps, and Spain, and the full citizenship gradually won its way in the provincial

---

[1] p. 314.

world by individual grants and recruiting for the legions. The laws of debt were emended by the just bankruptcy laws of Caesar and Augustus, and even the *leges frumentariae* required but a slight modification to make them a genuine scheme of poor-relief.[1] The *equites*, too, the class to whom C. Gracchus had given an official recognition, became a still more recognised order under the Principate and a most useful wheel in the administrative machinery.

It is more difficult to decide whether the radical change of government to which the agitation led can be considered a genuine triumph for the reformers. Military monarchy may be regretted by those who see in it a confession of incapacity to combine imperial government with Republican institutions; but, from the point of view of the reforming party, it was only a disappointment if we conceive that their leaders thought that government by *comitia* might replace the rule of the Senate. But there is hardly a trace of this idea. No effort was made throughout the whole of this period to make the *comitia* a work-able or really democratic institution; and personal rule, as the only expression of democracy, had asserted itself at the be-ginning of the movement. The only open question was whether it should be a Periclean *tyrannis* of the type enjoyed by C. Gracchus or a Napoleonic rule such as that of Caesar. As a matter of fact the Principate learnt a lesson from both solutions —that of the Gracchan and that of the Marian epoch—and established itself on a joint basis of the *tribunicia potestas* and the *proconsulare imperium*.

If we look round for other possible solutions, we find two faintly foreshadowed, but both doomed to failure. The first was a reformed Senate, not merely the existing body artificially bolstered up, as it had been by Sulla, but a body really made representative of Italy through the free inclusion of *novi homines*. The idea was held by Cicero, but no scheme was ever considered which would have made it a reality. For such an object to be attained, election to those magistracies from which the Senate was recruited must cease to be in the hands of the Roman *comitia*; but no one to our knowledge, with the exception of the Emperor Augustus, thought of the possibility of election by

---

[1] Caesar reduced the number of the recipients of the corn-dole from 320,000 to 150,000 (Suet. *Caes.* 41). In the Principate it stood at about 200,000. See Marquardt *Staatsverw.* ii. p. 118.

the municipal towns.[1] Help might also have been looked for from a reformed assembly, one that had been made representative of the whole Italian people. The allies nearly worked out this means of salvation for themselves,[2] but the magnitude of Rome was itself a stumbling-block to the solution of the problem on federal lines. We can hardly blame the thinkers of the day for not seeing the possibility of a representative assembly of a national kind; for the Italian, like the Greek mind, though familiar enough with the idea of the representation of cities, had not advanced to the conception of the representation of individuals through electoral districts.

The reason why the creation of an Italian senate or an Italian assembly might have warded off the monarchy is that such a body might have commanded respect even from the army of the provinces. This correspondence in sentiment might, it is true, have required that the army should remain mainly Italian; and Augustus' attempt to give Italy something of a representative character may have been abandoned through fear of a conflict between an army which was becoming provincial in personnel and an Italian proletariate, when the choice of a Princeps had to be decided. Yet, although circumstances were hostile to a fusion of Italy and the provinces, and the Principate was not to be Italian, one should not forget that it had something of a popular character. The Roman citizens of the legions who made the Princeps[3] were of a better type than the *plebs urbana* of Rome; for not only was the freedman element eliminated, but discipline had with them replaced demoralisation, their life was lived under healthier influences, and although they were often moved to their selection by a mere *esprit de corps*, they generally succeeded in placing a very capable man on the throne.

Caesar was the first sole ruler of Rome; and we might be inclined to imagine that the powers which he enjoyed were consciously assumed merely as those of a provisional government, were there not signs that towards the close of his life he was satisfied with the solution which he had adopted. The early dictatorships of 49 and 48 B.C., the second and longer of which was only for the term of a year,[4] were merely efforts for tiding

[1] p. 312.   [2] p. 311.
[3] It is true, however, that the Princeps was often made by *an* army, not by *the* army.
[4] Dio Cass. xlii. 20. The dictatorship of 49 B.C. had been held only for eleven days and was probably conferred merely *comitiorum habendorum causa.* See p. 193.

over a crisis; and the same may perhaps be said of a later
tenure of this office, which was conferred on him for ten years
in 46 B.C.[1] But in the last year of his life (44 B.C.) he entered
on a perpetual dictatorship,[2] a revival of the Roman monarchy
both in reality and in name. It is true that the title *rex* was
not assumed, out of deference to the feelings of the masses who
saw in it merely a synonym of oriental despotism; and for the
same reason the diadem was declined.[3] But every educated
Roman knew that the Roman monarchy had been nothing else
than the unlimited *imperium*, and many may have believed that
dictator or "master of the people" was the most significant of
the titles of the king. It was, therefore, a *regnum* under which
Rome was living,[4] and there was no concealment of its military
character, for the title *imperator* was now borne by the regent
within the walls.[5] This designation was a mere symbol of
military command and the fullest jurisdiction; it was no description of a basis actual or future on which Caesar's power could
rest, for the unqualified *imperium* had no existence to the Roman
mind, and, if it was to be unlimited, it must be either regal or
dictatorial.

With respect to the other powers which Caesar assumed, the
praefectura morum, given for three years in 45 B.C.,[6] has the
appearance of a special conferment for a given purpose; but the
tribunicia potestas was granted early in his period of rule (48 B.C.)
and given for life; it must have been regarded even now as the
ideal complement of a lasting *imperium*, valuable for the inviolability it conferred and for the "civil" and popular colouring
which it gave its holder. To realise the nature of Caesar's
authority by an inspection of the bases of his power needed
some reflection; but none was wanted to mark the external
symbols of royalty—the triumphal robe, the portrait-head on
coins, the statue placed amongst those of the seven kings in the
Capitol. These were the symbols that were taken as tests of

[1] Dio Cass. xliii. 14 and 33. It has been interpreted as a dictatorship *rei
publicae constituendae causa*.
[2] *C.I.L.* i. p. 452.
[3] Plut. *Caes.* 61; *Ant.* 12; Cic. *Phil.* ii. 34, 85.
[4] Cf. Cic. *ad Fam.* xi. 27, 8 "si Caesar rex fuerit . . . quod mihi quidem videtur."
[5] Dio Cass. xliii. 44. Caesar probably used it after his name and not as a
praenomen, as stated by Suetonius (*Caes.* 76). It became with him a kind of
cognomen, and Augustus, who inherited it, changed its position in the order of
his names.
[6] Dio Cass. xliii. 14.

Z

what the future monarchy was to be, and which reduced, not merely rigid constitutionalists, but even moderates and men of compromise, to despair. With Caesar conciliation was not accompanied by its requisite complement, compromise; he was tender of everything but sentiment, and did not care to estimate the force of what he must have considered mere prejudice; but, in spite of the modifications introduced into his theory of government by Augustus, it was he who pointed out that the necessary basis for the future Principate was the tribunician power combined with some kind of military *imperium*.

The murder of Caesar had, in words of the time, abolished the *rex* but not the *regnum*,[1] and the Triumvirate of 43 B.C. was but a suspension of hostilities between the rival claimants. In form it was a provisional government, like that of the early Decemvirate, for the reform of the constitution, and received the sanction of the people;[2] but so purely was it an agreement between the contending personalities that its renewal was contrived in 38 B.C. without any reference to the *comitia*.[3] For ten years (38-28 B.C.) Octavian's position was far more irregular than that of Caesar had ever been, and, even after the defeat and death of Antonius, his sole claim to power was an *imperium*, which had never been conferred, irregularly continued from a usurped Triumvirate. These indefinite powers resting, as he himself describes them, "on universal consent,"[4] were essential to the accomplishment of the work that had to be done before the forms of the constitution were restored. The consulships which he held did not give the requisite authority, and the value of the *tribunicia potestas*, which he had possessed from 36 B.C.,[5] was negative rather than positive. In the course of his sixth consulship (28 B.C.) he considered the time to be ripe for a final settlement. It assumed the form of a surrender. He issued a solemn decree in which he cancelled the irregular ordinances of the Triumvirate,[6] and he fixed January 1, 27 B.C. as the date

[1] Cic. *ad Fam.* xii. 1, 1 "nam, ut adhuc quidem actum est, non regno, sed rege liberati videmur."
[2] *Monumentum Ancyranum* i. 8-9 "Populus . . . me . . . trium virum rei publicae constituendae creavit."   [3] App. *B.C.* v. 95.
[4] *Mon. Anc.* vi. 13-15 "In consulatu sexto et septimo, bella ubi civilia exstinxeram, per consensum universorum potitus rerum omnium, rem publicam ex mea potestate in senatus populique Romani arbitrium transtuli."
[5] Dio Cass. xlix. 15.
[6] Tac. *Ann.* iii. 28 "sexto . . . consulatu . . . quae triumviratu jusserat abolevit."

THE TRANSITION TO THE PRINCIPATE 339

on which he would divest himself of his extraordinary power.[1] On this day "he gave back the commonwealth to the discretionary power of Senate and people."[2] A return was expected, and had doubtless been arranged, but the gift made by the grateful Senate seemed small in comparison with what had been surrendered. It was enough, however, to make the abdicating monarch a very powerful head of the executive of the state. Augustus, as he was now for the first time designated,[3] was given *imperium* for ten years with the government of certain specified provinces,[4] while at the same time he was made commander-in-chief for life of all the forces of the state, with the sole right of raising levies and of making war and of declaring peace.[5] Yearly consulships were still the chief basis of his dignity, if not of his authority, in the capital, while the tribunician power still continued but was as yet sparingly employed.

Such was the settlement that was greeted, officially and unofficially, as a restoration of the Republic,[6] but which later writers held, with equal reason, to be the commencement of the legitimate monarchy.[7] The weak point in the arrangement was the authority of the prince within the capital. The consulship had admirable Republican associations, but was hemmed in by awkward limitations. Its jurisdiction had become almost extinct, its initiative was fettered by colleagueship, it was technically not the highest power in the state, and the constant usurpation by the Princeps of one of the two offices of highest titular rank was a bar to the legitimate ambition of aspiring nobles. Hence the need for the new settlement which was attained in 23 B.C. The details of the change, which gave the Principate its final form,

[1] Cf. Tac. *Ann.* i. 2 "posito triumviri nomine."
[2] *Mon. Anc.* l.c.
[3] ib. vi. 16 (after the words on p. 338 note 4) "Quo pro merito meo senatus consulto Aug. appellatus sum."
[4] Dio Cass. liii. 12. Augustus uses the expression *consulare imperium* for his position at this time (*Mon. Anc.* ii. 5, 8). It resembled a pro-consular command, but was held within the city. Compare the position of Pompeius in 52 B.C.
[5] Strabo p. 840 ἡ πατρὶς ἐπέτρεψεν αὐτῷ τὴν προστασίαν τῆς ἡγεμονίας καὶ πολέμου καὶ εἰρήνης κατέστη κύριος διὰ βίου.
[6] In the Calendar we find for January 13 (the day of the settlement) "quod rem publicam P. R. restituit" (*C.I.L.* i. p. 312). Cf. Ovid *Fasti* i. 1. 589 "redditaque est omnis populo provincia nostro"; Vell. ii. 89 "prisca illa et antiqua rei publicae forma revocata."
[7] Dio Cass. lii. 1 ἐκ δὲ τούτου μοναρχεῖσθαι αὖθις ἀκριβῶς ἤρξαντο. In the *Cenotaphia Pisana* (A.D. 2) ii. l. 12 Augustus is called "custos imperi Romani totiusque orbis terrarum praeses" (Wilmanns n. 883).

will be described elsewhere. Its essential features were that the constant investiture with the consulship was dispensed with, that the *tribunicia potestas* was shifted from the background to become the chief symbol of authority for the Princeps in Rome and Italy, and that an *imperium*, which must now be described as *proconsulare*, was renewed and perhaps increased.[1] Further isolated grants were made to fill up the gaps in this heterogeneous association of powers, and to elevate the new extraordinary magistrate of the Republic to the requisite height above the ordinary officials of the state.

[1] Dio Cass. liii. 32.

CHAPTER X

§ 1. *The Powers of the Princeps*

WE have seen that the powers on which Augustus based his position as Princeps were the *proconsulare imperium* and the *tribunicia potestas*. In the theory of a constitution which he presented to the world the first of these prerogatives was supposed to establish his power outside Rome and Italy, the second, with its purely civic traditions, to be the basis of his influence within the central state. His object in exalting the tribunician power to the first place in Rome and her Italian dependencies now merged in the city, was to conceal as carefully as possible the military basis of his rule. The unlimited *imperium* was to be felt only by his army and his provincial subjects.

It needed little reflection to show that this principle, although in appearance the most important that underlay the Principate, was practically unworkable. Government in Rome was inconceivable without an *imperium*, and supreme government impossible without one of such an indefinite character that it should seem to stand out of relation to the regular and limited *imperia* of consuls and praetors. This power was secured by an easy juristic device. By a special exemption, which had its prototypes in Republican history, the Emperor was allowed to *retain* the full *imperium* within the walls;[1] and lawyers were careful not to declare explicitly what was implied in this retention. It might have meant—as it would have meant during the Republic—that the Emperor was not debarred by his presence in Rome from holding command abroad. It

[1] Dio Cass. liii. 32.

might signify that the limitations imposed by the city walls now rendered the pro-consular a quasi-consular *imperium*, and this was perhaps the ruling theory. But a different line of interpretation would have rendered it easy to show that the *imperium* here as elsewhere was unlimited. The nebulous atmosphere of this mockery of a magistracy was as well suited to the despot as to the constitutional ruler. In the actual position of the Princeps within Rome we find traces of all these theories. As a provincial ruler he governs from the capital; as commander-in-chief he keeps his praetorian guards in Italy and his fleets at Ravenna and Misenum; while as the wielder of an undefined but civic *imperium* he gives justice, as a court of first instance or a court of appeal, and issues edicts to supplement the laws.

But the recognition of an *imperium* within Rome was not alone sufficient. Even when this was joined to the tribunician power, great gaps were left in the position which should be held by a true head of the state. To fill these up, and thus supply a solid foundation for autocracy, fresh grants of isolated powers were necessary; and these grants, though in theory occasional, soon became permanent in practice. The Emperor, like the tribune, possessed no distinctive official dress while he resided in Rome : hence the consular *insignia* had to be conferred;[1] he possessed in virtue of his tribunician power only the right of making the third proposal at the Senate: hence the grant of the *jus primae relationis*.[2] Such grants admitted of indefinite extension, and the stage which they had reached by the date of the accession of Vespasian is partially known to us from the only official document which throws light on the powers of the early Principate. In the existing fragment of this charter, which appears to be a decree of the Senate meant to be submitted to the people for their formal assent,[3] we find the Emperor credited with the heterogeneous powers of making treaties, extending the *pomerium*, commending candidates for magistracies, and issuing edicts as interpretations of law human and divine. The measure further exempts him from the operation of certain enactments and gives him certain privileges, not

---

[1] Dio Cass. liv. 10.   [2] ib. liii. 32.

[3] *C.I.L.* vi. n. 930. It describes itself as a law and is generally known as the *lex de imperio Vespasiani*. But its wording bears more analogy to that of a *senatus consultum*. See Mommsen *Staatsrecht* ii. p. 878.

possessed by the other magistrates, in his relations with the Senate. These powers cannot be brought under any single legal designation ; but, as most of them are more or less directly connected with some kind of *imperium*, the view that they were tacked on to the bill conferring the tribunician power, which received the formal ratification of the Plebs, is improbable. On the other hand, they cannot be said to have belonged originally to a law conferring the *imperium ;* for the imperial biographies frequently speak of the gift of the *proconsulare imperium* (by the Senate) and of the *tribunicia potestas* (by Senate and People) without any hint of a general law conferring the "imperium." [1] Yet the gift of the *imperium* is sometimes mentioned,[2] and if the passages of jurists of the second and third centuries, which speak of *imperium* being conferred through a *lex*,[3] are genuine, we must conclude that the centre of gravity in the powers of the Princeps had shifted with the course of years. Originally the casual collection of powers, which appears in the law sanctioning Vespasian's rule, must have been a mere supplement to the two leading prerogatives—the proconsular and the tribunician powers. But it is quite possible that in the course of time the vast development and the great importance of these added privileges may have caused the enactment containing them, now known as the *lex de imperio*, to overshadow the other sources of the imperial authority.

There was one source, however, most distinctively expressive of the character of the Principate, which found no expression in legal enactments. The military oath (*sacramentum*), which during the closing years of the Republic was tending to become a bond of personal allegiance between a legion and its chief, was naturally taken in the Principate by the whole army to its sole

---

[1] *Vitae Macrini* 7 ; *Alexandri* 8 ; *Probi* 12 ; *Maximi et Balbini* 8.

[2] "Dato imperio" (*Vita Veri* 4), "accepit imperium" (*Vita Alexandri* 1). It is possible, however, that these are references merely to the reception of the title *imperator ;* cf. *Vita Juliani* 3 "imperator est appellatus" ; *Vita Probi* 12 "nomen imperatorium." For the view that there was always a *lex de imperio* see Karlowa *Römische Rechtsgeschichte* i. pp. 493 ff.

[3] Gaius *Inst.* i. 5 (on the imperial *constitutio*) "nec unquam dubitatum est quin id legis vicem obtineat, cum ipse imperator per legem imperium accipiat" ; Ulpian in *Dig.* 1, 4, 1 "Quod principi placuit, legis habet vigorem : utpote cum lege regia, quae de imperio ejus lata est, populus ei et in eum omne suum imperium et potestatem conferat." The view that these passages are interpolations is possible but hazardous. A genuine expression of belief in the *lex regia* appears in Justinian (*Cod.* i. 17, 1. 7).

commander.[1]   But on the very first transference of the throne
a new departure was made.   At the accession of Tiberius the
oath of fealty was taken voluntarily by the civil orders ;[2] it was
administered by provincial governors and was renewed twice a
year, on the first of January and on the anniversary of the
Emperor's accession.[3]   The fact that a soldier's oath bound the
whole Roman world was the fittest expression of the military
character of the new despotism.

A classification of the Emperor's powers in detail, with an
attempt to deduce each of them from a prerogative conferred on
him at his accession, is rendered difficult by the facts that no
Roman lawyer cared or dared to evolve a complete theory of
the Imperial constitution, and that here, as in so many other
departments of Roman history, we are dealing with an office
which, as it grew, gradually absorbed into itself fresh spheres of
influence.   The Principate, in fact, finally absorbed the state,
and the only adequate formula for its authority which later
jurists could find was that the people had committed its sovereign
power to its delegate.   But yet, when we examine the spheres
of the Emperor's activity, it becomes clear that, while some are
connected with an *imperium*, others are attached more closely
to the tribunician power, while others again are associated with
the relics of Republican offices held by the Princeps, or flow from
certain extraordinary rights conferred on him by statute.

(i.) The first rights connected with the *imperium* that strike
our attention are those exercised in the military sphere —
rights which, on a vast scale, reflect and extend the powers
possessed by the *imperator* of the Republic.   The Princeps has
the right to raise levies,[4] to nominate officers, and to confer
military distinctions.   In declaring war he has replaced the
comitia of the centuries ; and the statutory recognition of his
right to conclude a treaty [5] settled a vexed question of Republican

---

[1] For the monopoly of the *sacramentum* possessed by the Princeps compare the
charge brought against Agrippina after her death (59 A.D.), "Adiciebat crimina
. . . quod consortium imperii juraturasque in feminae verba praetorias cohortes
. . . speravisset" (Tac. *Ann.* xiv. 11).

[2] "Romae ruere in servitium consules, patres, eques" (Tac. *Ann.* i. 7).

[3] Tac. *Hist.* i. 55 "Inferioris tamen Germaniae legiones sollemni Kalen-
darum Januariarum sacramento pro Galba adactae." For the renewal of the oath
on the anniversary of accession see Plin. *ad Traj.* 52.

[4] Cf. Tac. *Hist.* iii. 58 (Vitellius) "vocari tribus jubet, dantes nomina sacramento adigit."

[5] *Lex de imp. Vesp.* 1 "foedusve cum quibus volet facere liceat." These

procedure.¹ This recognition of the federative power was not
earlier than the reign of the first Claudius,² but had already
become a permanent element in the imperial authority by the
accession of Vespasian. The right to extend the *pomerium* of
the city, which dates also from the reign of Claudius, is also
found amongst the list of imperial prerogatives in 69 A.D.³

The Republican general had often followed up a successful
campaign by assigning lands and planting colonies. These acts
had been done at the mandate of the people; but the new
commander-in-chief needed no such permit. The Princeps
divides territories that belong to the Roman people and
establishes colonial settlements at his will. The gift of the
franchise had also been entrusted at times to the Republican
commander,⁴ and now it is placed wholly in the hands of the
Emperor. He grants these gifts both to communities and to
individuals. He gives Latin rights to *peregrinae civitates*,⁵ and
citizenship to Latin towns, while he may alter the nominal *status*
of a community by changing a *municipium* into a colony, or a
colony into a *municipium*.⁶ His right of conferring citizenship
on individuals was equally unquestioned,⁷ and he might remedy
the defect of birth by giving *ingenuitas* to a freedman.⁸

With the *imperium* too is obviously connected the administration of those provinces which were peculiarly entrusted to
the care of the Princeps. The government of these provinces,
as well as the maintenance of the army, necessitated a financial
administration, separate from that of the state and peculiar to
himself, and this was accompanied by a right of coinage.
His criminal and civil jurisdiction over citizens as well as
soldiers are also connected with some undefined idea of the
imperium, while his power of legal interpretation, although

powers are summed up by Dio Cassius liii. 17 (as imperators the Emperors have
the right) καταλόγους τε ποιεῖσθαι . . . πολέμους τε ἀναιρεῖσθαι καὶ εἰρήνην
σπένδεσθαι.   ¹ p. 283.

² Dio Cass. lx. 23 (after Claudius' conquest of Britain) ἐψηφίσθη τὰς συμβάσεις
ἁπάσας, ὅσας ἂν ὁ Κλαύδιος ἢ καὶ οἱ ἀντιστράτηγοι αὐτοῦ πρός τινας ποιήσωνται,
κυρίας, ὡς καὶ πρὸς τὴν βουλὴν τόν τε δῆμον εἶναι.

³ *Lex de imp. Vesp.* 15 "utique ei fines pomerii proferre promovere cum ex
republica censebit esse, liceat ita, uti licuit Ti. Claudio Caesari Aug(usto) Germanico." Cf. Tac. *Ann.* xii. 23.

⁴ p. 240.   ⁵ Gaius *Inst.* i. 96.
⁶ Gell. xvi. 13, 5.   ⁷ Gaius *Inst.* iii. 72 and 73.

⁸ This was effected, either indirectly by the gift of the gold ring (*jus
aureorum anulorum*), or directly by the fiction of a *natalibus restitutio*. See
Dig. 2, 4, 10, 3; 40, 11, 2; Plin. *ad Traj.* 72 and 73.

specially conferred, does not differ essentially from that of the praetor, and is to be traced to the same source. The detailed consideration of these powers must be deferred until we treat of that separation of authority between Caesar and the Senate which gave its formal character to the Principate.

(ii.) The *tribunicia potestas*, which had been granted to Augustus in 36, reconferred in 30, and made the chief outward support of his authority in 23 B.C.,[1] continued to serve the Emperors as the ostensible means by which all other magistracies were subject to their control,[2] and possessed an artificial prominence from its employment as a means of dating the years of their reign. Positively it conferred the *sacrosanctitas*, which had encompassed the Republican tribune,[3] the right of approaching the assembly of the Plebs, which was of value as long as the Emperors deigned to legislate through popular channels, and perhaps the only strictly constitutional power which they possessed of transacting business with the Senate.[4] But its negative were now, as ever, of more value than its positive powers. The *intercessio* made its possessor the moderator of the state,[5] and the severest means of tribunician coercion could be employed against every recalcitrant official ; while this veto, when used in the Senate, became either a means of suspending the jurisdiction of that body or a method of pardoning the criminal whom it had condemned.[6] The right of help (*auxilium*)[7] based on the appeal (*appellatio*) becomes also, as we shall see, one of the means of establishing the first true appellate jurisdiction which the Roman world had seen.

(iii.) With respect to other Republican offices in which the

[1] Dio Cass. xlix. 15 ; li. 19 ; liii. 32. See pp. 338, 340.

[2] Tac. *Ann.* iii. 56 "id summi fastigii vocabulum Augustus repperit, ne regis aut dictatoris nomen adsumeret ac tamen appellatione aliqua cetera imperia praemineret."

[3] Dio Cass. xlix 15 καὶ τὸ μήτε ἔργῳ μήτε λόγῳ τι ὑβρίζεσθαι· εἰ δὲ μή, τοῖς αὐτοῖς τὸν τοιοῦτό τι δράσαντα ἐνέχεσθαι οἷσπερ ἐπὶ τῷ δημάρχῳ ἐτέτακτο.

[4] The *additional* rights granted to the Emperor in connexion with the Senate (see p. 348) assume a right of intercourse with it.

[5] Dio Cass. liii. 17 (the tribunician power) δίδωσί σφισι τά τε γιγνόμενα ὑφ' ἑτέρου τινός, ἂν μὴ συνεπαινῶσι, παύειν.

[6] Tac. *Ann.* iii. 70 "recipi Caesar (Tiberius) inter reos vetuit . . . perstititque intercedere" ; xiv. 48 "credebaturque haud perinde exitium Antistio quam imperatori gloriam quaeri ut condemnatum a senatu intercessione tribunicia morti eximeret" (Nero).

[7] ἀμύνειν (Dio Cass. li. 19) ; cf. Tac. *Ann.* i. 2 (of Augustus) "ad tuendam plebem tribunicio jure contentum."

Princeps was directly interested, we have only to consider the consulship and the censorship, for they were the only two whose titles or powers were sufficient to warrant their assumption by the head of the state.

The consulship was no intcgral part of the imperial power after Augustus had ceased to employ it in this way;[1] but it was frequently assumed as an occasional office by the Princeps, who held it for a short time, generally at the beginning of his rule.

The censorship had disappeared as a Republican office, and we might have expected that its vast powers combined with its Republican traditions would have made it a valuable supplement to the authority of the Prince. But there were reasons against its assumption. In its pure form it was an occasional office, and its permanent tenure might have shocked Republican sentiment; while the fact that the assessment of the Roman people for the *comitia* and the army soon ceased to be necessary made its absence scarcely felt. On the analogy of the *tribunicia potestas*, the powers of the office without the office itself were, in the form of a *cura legum et morum*, offered to Augustus, but declined by him.[2] There was no constitutional difficulty about exercising some of the functions of the censorship through the *imperium*, whether consular or quasi-consular, and this was done by Augustus when he revised the list of the Senate in 29 and 18 b.c.[3] Two of the succceding Principos, howcvor, Claudius and Vespasian, thought fit to assume the office in its old temporary form, and Domitian carried out the design of making it an integral part of the Principate by assuming the position of censor for life (*censor perpetuus*).[4] His precedent was not followed because it was unnecessary. The revision of the list of the Senate and *equites*—the only meaning that the *cura morum* now had—was established by consent as an admitted right of the Princeps,[5] and even the power of creating Patricians came to be recognised as one inherent in his office. This power had been conferred on

[1] p. 340.

[2] The statement of Suetonius (*Aug.* 27 " Recepit et morum legumque regimen aeque perpetuum ") is not borne out by the *Monumentum Ancyranum* or by Augustus' titular designations.

[3] Suet. *Aug.* 35 ; *Mon. Anc.* ii. 5 "consulari cum imperio lustrum solus feci."

[4] Dio Cass. lxvii. 4 τιμητὴς δὲ διὰ βίου πρῶτος δὴ καὶ μόνος καὶ ἰδιωτῶν καὶ αὐτοκρατόρων ἐχειροτονήθη.

[5] ib. liii. 17 καὶ τοὺς μὲν καταλέγουσι καὶ ἐς τὴν ἱππάδα καὶ ἐς τὸ βουλευτικόν, τοὺς δὲ καὶ ἀπαλείφουσιν, ὅπως ἂν αὐτοῖς δόξῃ.

Caesar and Augustus by law ; Claudius and Vespasian exercised it as censors ; [1] but, apparently without further enactment, this power of ennobling, extinct since the beginning of the Republic [2] and no part of the Republican census, became an admitted imperial prerogative. It was only when the destined Princeps was himself a Plebeian that this honour, which was considered a necessary qualification for his office, was conferred on him by the Senate.[3]

(iv.) The chief of the extraordinary rights conferred on the Princeps by special enactment were those which had relation to the Senate, the right of recommendation to office (*commendatio*) and a dispensation from the operation of certain laws.

The special privileges which distinguished the Emperor from other magistrates in transacting business with the Senate were three in number. First, he has not merely the power to put a motion (*referre*) when present in the house, but he can send a written recommendation (*relationem facere*) when the Senate meets under the presidency of another magistrate.[4] In such a meeting the Emperor as a rule only claims priority for one item in a single sitting (*jus primae relationis*); hence we sometimes find, as a special privilege, the right of priority given him for three, four, or five.[5] The power which he possesses of dividing the house upon his motion without debate (*senatus consultum per discessionem facere*) is not a new one, but one that might be exercised by the consul of the later Republic. Secondly, the Emperor has the power to withdraw a *relatio* of his own which is already before the house (*relationem remittere*); and thirdly, the privilege of ordering the Senate to meet under the presidency of another magistrate.

The second special right has reference to the elections of

[1] Tac. *Ann.* xi. 25 "Isdem diebus in numerum patriciorum adscivit Caesar (Claudius as censor) vetustissimum quemque e senatu aut quibus clari parentes fuerant . . . exhaustis etiam quas (familias) dictator Caesar lege Cassia et princeps Augustus lege Saenia sublegere." Cf. Suet. *Otho* 1 ; and for Vespasian's censorship *Vita Marci* 1 "Annius Verus . . . adscitus in patricios . . . a Vespasiano et Tito censoribus."

[2] p. 14.

[3] *Vita Juliani* 3 "in patricias familias relatus"; *Macrini* 7 "senatus . . . Macrinum . . . in patricios allegit novum hominem." Cf. Dio Cass. lxxviii. 17.

[4] *Lex de imp. Vesp.* l. 3 "utique ei senatum habere, relationem facere, remittere, senatus consulta per relationem discessionemque facere liceat." In l. 7 we find the right of the Princeps to summon the Senate *ex mandatu*.

[5] *Jus tertiae relationis* (*Vita Probi* 12), *quartae* (*Vita Pertinacis* 5), *quintae* (*Vita Marci* 6, *Alexandri* 1).

magistrates, and introduces us to the question how far the
Princeps could control them. Two functions are attributed
to him by our authorities, that of nomination and that of
commendation; but the effects of the two are very different.
The *nominatio* is merely the negative power possessed by the
Republician magistrate of receiving names and excluding unqualified aspirants from candidature. With respect to most
offices—the praetorship, for instance—it was exercised by the
Princeps conjointly with the consuls, and the number of candidates whom he nominated was, at least in the early Principate,
limited.[1] The practical effect of the Prince's nomination on the
election might be great, but its legal influence was *nil*.[2] *Commendatio*, on the other hand, a privilege developed from the
Republican practice by which candidates were recommended by
distinguished persons for election, is a right legally conferred,
and one which absolutely secures the choice by the electing
body of the person so commended.[3] The extent to which it
might be employed differed with the various magistracies; thus
in Tiberius' reign, out of at least twelve candidates for the
praetorship only four were commended by the Emperor.[4] Magistrates, who had gained their position by this act of imperial
favour, were designated *candidati Caesaris*.[5] The highest office
of all, the consulship, seems, at least in the early Principate,
never to have been awarded on a formal imperial recommendation; for the description of the method by which Tiberius
filled up this post at his pleasure shows that the Emperor
effected his object by a clever use of the nomination.[6] This
may have been a limitation of practice, not of theory, for the

---

[1] Tac. *Ann.* i. 14 "candidatos praeturae duodecim nominavit (Tiberius),
numerum ab Augusto traditum, et hortante senatu ut augeret jure jurando ob-
strinxit se non excessurum."

[2] This practical effect seems sometimes to have been obviated by the Emperor's
selecting his candidates for nomination by lot (Dio Cass. lviii. 20). See Mr.
Strachan-Davidson in Smith *Dict. of Antiq.* ii. p. 237.

[3] *Lex de imp. Vesp.* 1. 10 "utique quos magistratum potestatem imperium
curationemve cujus rei petentes senatui populoque Romano commendaverit,
quibusque suffragationem suam dederit promiserit, eorum comitis quibusque
extra ordinem ratio habeatur." Cf. Tac. *Ann.* i. 15 "sine repulsa et ambitu
designandos." For the precedent set by Caesar's use of it see Suet. *Caes.* 41.

[4] Tac. *Ann.* i. 15 "moderante Tiberio ne plures quam quattuor candidatos
commendaret, sine repulsa et ambitu designandos."

[5] e.g. *praetor, tribunus, quaestor candidatus* (Wilmanns *Index* pp. 551 ff.).

[6] Tac. *Ann.* i. 81 "plerumque eos tantum apud se professos disseruit,
quorum nomina consulibus edidisset: posse et alios profiteri, si gratiae aut

words of the law as we have it exempt no office from this imperial control, and it is certain that from the time of Vespasian onwards the consulship too was subject to the *commendatio*.[1]

The Princeps, according to the enactment which confers powers on Vespasian, was dispensed from certain laws (*legibus solutus*).[2] There is no implication here of an exemption from the operation of the ordinary civil and criminal law. The Princeps is not above the laws, nor are the courts of the community his courts; and, if he was exempt from prosecution during his year of office, this was the normal privilege of the Republican magistrate. What is meant is the dispensation from certain principles of the constitution or enactments, which the Principate as a magistracy necessarily violated or which were found inconvenient to the Princeps. Such were the *leges annales*, or the rule forbidding the holding of the *imperium* within the walls. In choosing an heir the Emperor was also exempted from following the precise formalities of adrogation;[3] he could manumit without the *vindicta*[4] and was not subject to the disabilities of the Julian and Papian law.[5]

(v.) The separation of religious from political duties, which had been a characteristic of the Republic, was continued theoretically under the Principate. The Emperor was in no sense a high priest, and ritual was still a function of the sacerdotal colleges. But he was a member of the great religious guilds which dealt with augury and with the *jus divinum*,[6] and the law gives him the power to carry out the orders of such societies if he thinks it to be in the interest of the state.[7] We have not, however, merely the phenomenon of the civil assisting the religious arm, for the

meritis confiderent." It may have been a person so appointed who inaccurately describes himself as "per commendation(em) Ti. Caesaris Augusti ab senatu co(n)s(ul) dest(inatus)" (*Inscr. Reg. Neap.* n. 4762 ; *C.I.L.* ix. n. 2342).

[1] *C.I.L* xiv. n. 3608 "hunc . . . Caesar Aug. Vespasianus iterum cos. fecit " ; Plin. *Paneg.* 77 (of Trajan) "praestare consulibus ipsum qui consules facit." Mommsen (*Staatsr.* ii. p. 925) thinks that the change came with Nero.

[2] *Lex de imp. Vesp.* l. 22 "utique quibus legibus plebeive scitis scriptum fuit, ne divus Aug(ustus), Tiberiusve Julius Caesar Aug(ustus), Tiberiusque Claudius Caesar Aug(ustus) Germanicus tenerentur, iis legibus plebisque scitis imp(erator) Caesar Vespasianus solutus sit."

[3] Tac. *Hist.* i. 15 (Galba to Piso on the latter's adoption) "si te privatus lege curiata apud pontifices, ut moris est, adoptarem."

[4] Paulus in *Dig.* 40, 1, 14, 1.   [5] Ulpian in *Dig.* 1, 3, 31.

[6] Dio Cass. liii. 17 ἐν πάσαις ταῖς ἱερωσύναις ἱερῶσθαι.

[7] *Lex de imp. Vesp.* l. 17 "utique quaecunque ex usu rei publicae majestateque divinarum . . . rerum esse censebit, ei agere facere jus potestasque sit."

Prince, as *pontifex maximus*, represents both in his own person. The chief pontificate was specially conferred on him with the other imperial powers; he may originally have been invested, like the pontifex of the Republic, by the assembly of the seventeen tribes,[1] but later the creation seems to have been wholly the work of the Senate, although a formal announcement of the result (*renuntiatio*) was still made before the assembly.[2] When the Principate came to admit the principle of colleagueship, only one of the Augusti was made chief pontiff,[3] and the association of the highest religious and civil power continued until the stole was rejected by the piety of Gratian.[4]

It is obvious that the attempt to keep the rôles of pontiff and Princeps apart, even if made, could never have been successful. Where crime was also sin the pontiff could now utter authoritative law and exercise coercion; the lay and the religious character are strangely mixed in the methods adopted by Domitian for the punishment of incest,[5] and when the *jussio principis* speaks on a question of burial law,[6] it must have been difficult to tell whether it was the Prince or the pontiff who was giving his decision.

Apart from its influence on law, the chief pontificate was valuable for its powers of patronage. Few distinctions were more earnestly sought by young nobles than admission to the religious colleges, and the door to them lay chiefly through the Princeps. His influence might be exercised by his right of nomination or by his commendation to the electing body.[7]

§ 2. *Titles, Insignia, and Honours of the Princeps*

In dealing with the titles of the Princeps, it is as well to begin with those which were not in the list of official titles, for, impressed on the ruler, as they were, by current usage, they were often the most significant. The word *Princeps*, although it

[1] p. 254.   [2] Mommsen *Staatsr.* ii. p. 31.
[3] Dio Cass. liii. 17. In the decrees to Maximus and Balbinus the *pontificatus maximus* is mentioned (*Vita* 8), and it is possible that it was held by both these emperors conjointly.   [4] Zosimus iv. 36.
[5] Suet. *Dom.* 8 "Incesta Vestalium virginum . . . varie ac severe coercuit: priora capitali supplicio; posteriora, more veteri."
[6] Ulpian in *Dig.* 11, 7, 8.
[7] Dio Cass. liii. 17; Tac. *Hist.* i. 77 "Otho pontificatus auguratusque honoratis jam senibus cumulum dignitatis addidit"; Plin. *ad Traj.* 13 (8) "rogo dignitati, ad quam me provexit indulgentia tua, vel auguratum vel septemviratum, quia vacent, adicere digneris."

described no office or peculiar authority, was yet a semi-official designation ; even as employed in the later Republic it had signified a political pre-eminence over other citizens,[1] and now it denoted not so much the "chief citizen" as the "head" or "chief man" in the state, the director of the Republic, to whom all looked for guidance, who was responsible for its failures and credited with its successes, even when these were the result of the actions of other magistrates.[2]   It was above all a title which tended to emphasise the continuance of the life of the Republican government under the new *régime*, and suggested a mental contrast, at once to the Emperor's position as the commander of his legions, expressed in the title *imperator*, and to that absolute headship which, as exercised in family life at Rome, was known as *dominium*.[3]   The name, indeed, of *dominus* inspired such a horror in the mind of Augustus that he disliked this mode of address (a familiar one from the members of a family to its head) to be employed even by his sons and grandsons,[4] and Tiberius insisted that he was *dominus* only to his slaves.[5]   But the language of courtly life, perhaps at times of real affection, forced the title into use, and the younger Pliny employs it constantly in his correspondence with Trajan.   It is not, however, until the time of Severus that it appears on the public addresses of corporations, and Aurelian is the first emperor who is *dominus* on his coins.[6]   It is probable that these niceties of western nomenclature were always lost on the oriental mind.   To it the Principate is a monarchy, and Caesar, when he is not a god, is either αὐτοκράτωρ or βασιλεύς.

If we turn now to the titular designation of the Princeps, we find that this consists partly of titles of office, partly of those of honour.   The word *imperator* occupies a doubtful place between

---

[1] Cic. *ad Att.* viii. 9, 4 "nihil malle Caesarem quam principe Pompeio sine metu vivere"; *ad Fam.* vi. 6, 5 "esset hic quidem (Caesar) clarus in toga et princeps." Cf. Vell. ii. 124 "una tamen veluti luctatio civitatis fuit, pugnantis cum (Tiberio) Caesare senatus populique Romani, ut stationi paternae succederet, illius, ut potius aequalem civem quam eminentem liceret agere principem."

[2] Tac. *Ann.* iii. 53 (Tiberius says) "non aedilis aut praetoris aut consulis partes sustineo, majus aliquid et excelsius a principe postulatur."

[3] Dio Cass. lvii. 8 (see note 5) ; Ovid *Fasti* ii. 142 "Tu (Romule) domini nomen, principis ille (Augustus) tenet."

[4] Suet. *Aug.* 53.

[5] Dio Cass. lvii. 8 δεσπότης μὲν τῶν δούλων, αὐτοκράτωρ δὲ τῶν στρατιωτῶν, τῶν δὲ δὴ λοιπῶν πρόκριτός εἰμι.   Cf. Tac. *Ann.* ii. 87.

[6] See Mommsen *Staatsr.* ii. p. 760.

the two; for while denoting no office, it signifies the possession
of an active and untrammelled *imperium.* It occupies a twofold
place in the list of titles. Augustus employed it as a *praenomen,*
perhaps in accordance with the view that he had inherited the title
from his uncle, who had borne it (apparently as a *cognomen*[1]) during
the later years of his life, and as a *praenomen* it was used by most
succeeding emperors.[2]   But it appears a second time in the titular
designation of the Princeps with its old Republican significance—
that of an appellation borne by a commander who had been
acclaimed after a victory.[3]   As so employed it was qualified by
numerals to mark the number of the salutations; amongst these
was reckoned that which had acclaimed him Emperor, and, consequently, after the first victory won under his auspices, he
appears as *imperator II.*

A more distinctive title of office is that of *proconsul.* Although
it merely expresses the fact of a *proconsulare imperium,* it was a
designation that was avoided by the early Principes, probably out
of deference to the senatorial administration of the public
provinces, which was exercised through proconsuls, and it was
first employed by Trajan. Its employment hints at the practical
disappearance of the dual control abroad, and suggests the all-
embracing nature of the Emperor's *imperium.*

Amongst the honorary appellations of the Emperor, *Caesar*
and *Augustus* take the foremost place. The latter, although
appended to the Emperor's name like a *cognomen,* was never
looked on as a family designation. It was the highest of all
personal titles of honour, since it expressed the sanctified majesty
of the Prince alone,[4] and was not borne even by that subordinate
partner on the throne (*consors imperii*), the holder of the *proconsulare imperium* or *tribunicia potestas,* through whose assistance the
earlier emperors sometimes lightened the burden of their administration. It was not until the collegiate principle was fully
recognised in 161 A.D. that the *duo Augusti* appear.

Caesar, on the other hand, was in origin purely a family
designation, since it was the hereditary *cognomen* of that branch

---

[1] Caesar had been *imperator* since his first salutation in Gaul; but the right to
use the title as a *nomen* seems first to have been granted him in 45 B.C. after the
victory of Munda (Dio Cass. xliii. 44 ἐκείνῳ τότε πρώτῳ τε καὶ πρῶτον, ὥσπερ τι
κύριον, προσέθεσαν). It does not seem, however, that he employed it as a
praenomen, as is stated by Suetonius (*Caes.* 76). Cf. p. 337.

[2] Dio Cass. l.c.   [3] p. 156.

[4] Dio Cass. liii. 16 Αὔγουστος ὡς καὶ πλεῖόν τι ἢ κατὰ ἀνθρώπους ὢν ἐπεκλήθη.

of the Julian house which had ascended the throne, and all the
emperors to Caligula could claim a legitimate right to it whether
by descent or adoption. Even Claudius and Nero, connected as
they were with the extinct family of Caesars, might use it with
some show of family right. It is only with Galba and his successors that *Caesar* becomes strictly an appellative; it is an
assertion of a fictitious dynastic claim such as that which led the
princes of the house of Emesa to adopt the revered name of
Antoninus, and may be indirectly connected with a claim to
succeed to the crown property.[1] The name, even when thus
artificially employed, continued to be a *cognomen;* it was shared
by the ruling Princeps with his sons and grandsons.

With Hadrian's reign we find the beginning of a limitation of
its use. The Caesar is now the presumptive successor to the
throne;[2] the elective monarchy has been recognised as one that
is, if not hereditary, at least capable of transmission through
nomination, and the choice of the bearer of the name is made
by the reigning Emperor, although it may be suggested by the
Senate.[3] After the beginning of the third century the name
appears as *nobilissimus Caesar,* Geta being the first prince to bear
this title. The recognition of the dual monarchy rendered it
inevitable that two Caesars might be simultaneously designated
for the throne.

Other honorary *cognomina*, such as *Germanicus, Pius, Felix,*
were, even when transmitted, purely personal, although their
adoption was now reserved for the Emperor, and such designations were no longer borne by the other nobles in the state.
The designation *pater patriae* has more distinct reference to the
political position of the Princeps. A title once conferred by
popular acclamation on Cicero, it is now equally in the gift of the
people as represented by the Senate. As its conferment was not
necessary to the powers of the Principate, the grant of this
designation, however much it might be the result of flattery, was
always regarded as the reward of merit.[4]

The order of the imperial titles admits of variations, but, as
finally fixed, was usually *pontifex maximus, tribunicia potestate*

---

[1] Karlowa *Rechtsgeschichte* i. p. 508.

[2] *Vita L. Veri,* 2.

[3] Mommsen *Staatsr.* ii. p. 1140.

[4] App. *B.C.* ii. 7 οὐδὲ γὰρ τοῖσδε καίπερ οὖσι βασιλεῦσιν εὐθὺς ἀπ' ἀρχῆς ἅμα
ταῖς ἄλλαις ἐπωνυμίαις, ἀλλὰ σὺν χρόνῳ μόλις ἥδε ὡς ἐντελὴς ἐπὶ μεγίστοις δὴ
μαρτυρίᾳ ψηφίζεται: *Vita Hadriani* 6 " patris patriae nomen delatum sibi

(II. III. etc.), *imperator* (II. III. etc.), *consul* (II. III. etc.), *censor* (when this office was assumed, as it was by Claudius, Vespasian, Titus and Domitian), *proconsul* (a title adopted by Trajan and occupying the last place after the reign of Hadrian).[1]

The usual *insignia* of the Princeps are those of a Republican magistrate. Within the walls he wears the scarlet-striped gown (*toga praetexta*) ; outside them he may don the scarlet *paludamentum*. But the laurel crown, which he might wear anywhere and at any time,[2] and the laurel-wreathed *fasces*[3] are peculiar to him. At festivals and games the embroidered robe of triumph (*vestis triumphalis*) might also be assumed. Like other magistrates he has lictors[4] and *viatores*, but he also boasts a special bodyguard as well, other than the praetorian cohorts. This guard was composed of mounted foreign mercenaries, usually of German horsemen.

But other peculiar honours seemed to lift the Princeps to more than magisterial rank. Regular vows (*vota*) were offered for him, as for the state,[5] by the consuls and the colleges of priests ; his birthday and the days of his victories were celebrated as public festivals ;[6] his statue and image are sacred and may not be profaned even by juxtaposition with unclean things ;[7] his *genius* is the most binding power by which a man can swear ; for while perjury in the name of the gods is punished only by heaven, to swear falsely by the Emperor's name is treason on

statim, et iterum postea, distulit quod hoc nomen Augustus sero meruisset." It was declined altogether by Tiberius (Suet. *Tib.* 26 and 67) and was not borne by the transitory emperors Galba, Otho, and Vitellius. See Mommsen *Staatsr.* ii. p. 780.

[1] See Mommsen *Staatsr.* ii. pp. 782-786. As typical instances we may cite an inscription of Vespasian giving the *praenomen imperatoris :* "Imp. Caesar. Vespasianus Aug. pontif. max. tribunic. potest. vi. imp. xiiii. p.p., cos. vi. desig. vii. censor " (Wilmanns n. 855), and one of Caracalla showing the title *proconsul :* " M. Aurellius Antoninus Pius Felix Augustus . . . pontif. max., trib. pot. xviii. imp. iiii. cos. iiii. p.p. procos." (ib. n. 2868). *Pater patriae* appears sometimes before, sometimes after *consul*.

[2] Dio Cass. xlix. 15.

[3] On Gordian's revolt in Africa the laurelled *fasces* were immediately assumed (Herodian vii. 6 ; *Vita Maximini* 14).

[4] Originally twelve, later twenty-four (Dio Cass. lxvii. 4).

[5] Dio Cass. li. 19.   [6] ib.

[7] For the reverence to the statue of the deified Emperor see Suet. *Tib.* 58 "genus calumniae (sc. majestatis) eo processit ut haec quoque capitalia essent : circa Augusti simulacrum servum cecidisse, vestimenta mutasse, nummo vel annulo effigiem impressam latrinae aut lupanari intulisse." For the right of *asylum* attaching to the living Emperor's image see Tac. *Ann.* iii. 36 ; Gaius *Inst.* i. 53.

earth.[1] Coins, whether struck by the Senate or the Emperor, show only his head or that of members of the imperial house.

The *domus Caesaris* was, in fact, raised far above the position of the other noble houses in the state. It was especially the agnatic descendants of the founder of the dynasty that were thus honoured, and the Roman idea of the unity of the household even led to the inclusion of the name of Caesar's relatives in the soldier's oath of fealty.[2] Their effigies, too, appear on coins—a right originally restricted to such members of the family as actually shared in the government, but which was in later times granted as a compliment to ladies of the imperial house.[3] Caesar's relatives might also be distinguished by commands which could be interpreted as a promise of the succession. We shall speak elsewhere of this meaning which might be read into the gift of the proconsular or tribunician power, and almost equally significant was the appointment of some young member of the family to the honorary command of the corps of *equites* (*princeps juventutis*).[4] There was, indeed, one title which seemed to signify a dignity absolutely equal to that of the Princeps himself. This was the name *Augusta*, which was borne by certain ladies of the ruling family. It was originally reserved for a single member, such as the mother, the grandmother, or the wife of the reigning Emperor, and may have originally implied some share in the throne. The Principate was not a regular magistracy, and there was no valid constitutional ground for excluding women from the throne, although the actual influence of queen-mothers, such as Livia, Agrippina, or Mamaea, however powerful it may have been, was wholly informal.[5] The name *Augusta* came, however, to be employed merely as an honorary designation, to be borne by such a woman as Marciana, the unaspiring sister of Trajan.[6] A stranger title was developed by the ambition

[1] Tertull. *Apol.* 28 " citius ... apud vos per omnes deos quam per unum genium Caesaris pejeratur." In the official oath taken by the magistrates of Salpensa and Malaca the deified Caesars and the genius of the living Caesar come between Jupiter and the *di Penates*. (Bruns *Fontes*.)

[2] On Seneca's question with reference to Agrippina (59 A.D.) "an militi imperanda caedes esset," the answer is "praetorianos toti Caesarum domui obstrictos . . . nihil . . . atrox ausuros." Caligula specifically included the names of his sisters in the *sacramentum* (Dio Cass. lix. 9)

[3] Mommsen *Staatsr.* ii. p. 831.

[4] *Mon. Ancyr.* iii. 5 ; Dio Cass. lix. 8.

[5] The name *Augusta* as assumed by Victorina in Gaul (A.D. 268) certainly meant that she claimed to be Empress.   [6] Plin. *Paneg.* 84.

of ladies of the second and third century. Faustina, wife of
Marcus Aurelius, and Julia Domna, wife of Septimius Severus,
were both designated "mothers of the camp" (*mater castrorum*).
One important and disastrous result of this elevation of the
imperial house was that its members were protected, like its
head, against all the attacks of *laesa majestas*. As even the
most indirect reflection on the Princeps was treason, because he
represented the state, a similar view was taken of constructive
wrongs to members of the imperial family, because they were
one with the Princeps. This view was too purely Roman to
need time to develop. Even in the reign of the second Princeps
we find that a poet has to expiate by death the folly of an
obituary poem on the Emperor's living son.[1]

As the Princeps was not a king he had no court, and
"Augustus or Trajan would have blushed at employing the
meanest of the Romans in those menial offices which, in the
household and bedchamber of a limited monarch, are so eagerly
solicited by the proudest nobles of Britain."[2] Yet, although
the *entourage* of the early Principes was simplicity itself, the
stately life of the Republican noble had already furnished precedents for distinguishing the grades and privileges of those
who sought the Emperor's presence. The younger Gracchus
and Livius Drusus had, at the daily *salutatio*, drawn distinctions
amongst their numerous adherents; at the morning audience
some were received singly, others in larger or in smaller
groups;[3] and it is not surprising that this distinction should
have been revived for the great throng of callers who filled the
hall of the imperial palace. The *amici* of the Princeps were
those "received at court," and were divided into friends of the
first and second "audience."[4] From this body were selected
the judicial and administrative advisers of the Emperor (*consilium*)
as well as the comrades (*comites*) whom he took with him when
he quitted Italy on business of state. From the latter, who

---

[1] Tac. *Ann.* iii. 49-51.
[2] Gibbon ch. iii.
[3] Seneca *de Ben.* vi. 34, 2 "Apud nos primi omnium Gracchus et mox Livius
Drusus instituerunt segregare turbam suam et alios in secretum recipere, alios cum
pluribus, alios universos. Habuerunt itaque isti amicos primos, habuerunt
secundos, numquam veros."
[4] Seneca *de Clem.* i. 10 "cohortem primae admissionis"; *Vita Alex.* 20
"moderationis tantae fuit . . . ut amicos non solum primi aut secundi loci sed
etiam inferioris aegrotantes viseret."

consisted of senators or knights, he selected a group for a special journey,[1] and employed them as delegates in matters administrative, judicial, and military.

§ 3. *Creation, Transmission, and Abrogation of the Principate*

The Principate was, in the theory of the constitution, an elective office, and one based on the principle of occasional delegation. It was necessary for the life of the state that there should be a magistracy,[2] but it was not necessary that there should be a Princeps. Hence there was no institution such as the Republican *interregnum* to fill up the gap left by the vacancy of the throne,[3] and the fact that such gaps did occur in the history of the Principate shows that the possibility of government by magistrates, senate, and people was no mere fiction. The abstract idea of a Principate was indeed perfectly realised at the death of the very first Princeps, in so far as responsible men in the Roman world had a perfectly definite idea of the precise powers that must be vested in an individual in order to save that world from anarchy. Yet Tiberius can pretend to hesitate, not merely about assuming the office, but about the nature of the office which he assumes;[4] and, although on the accession of his successor, Gaius Caesar, the *soliti honores* were conferred *en bloc*, yet the idea that the creation of a Princeps was an act of special investiture always clung to the office. It was obvious so far as the choice of the person was concerned, but it even affected the powers conferred, and we have seen that the grants made to Emperors of the second and third centuries were in all probability different, both in form and in matter, from those made to Emperors of the first.[5]

The electing body was the Roman people, chiefly represented by the Senate but still retaining in its own hands the formal ratification of most of the powers conferred. But the powerlessness of this sovereign is of the very essence of the history of

---

[1] Hence such titles as "comes divi Hadriani in oriente," "comes Imp. Antonini Aug. et divi Veri bello Germanico" (Wilmanns nn. 1184, 637).

[2] p. 147.

[3] *Interregnum* might be used metaphorically of the interval between the death of one Princeps and the accession of another. See *Vita Taciti* 1.

[4] Tac. *Ann.* i. 12 "dixit forte Tiberius se ut non toti rei publicae parem, ita quaecunque pars sibi mandaretur, ejus tutelam suscepturum."

[5] p. 343.

the Principate.   As a rule, all that it can do is to recognise an
imperium already established by the army, whether this establishment be due to the tacit consent of praetorians or legionaries
or to the active use of their swords.   The crucial point in the
creation of an emperor is his salutation by his army as
imperator.   Such a salutation did not mean that the general
who accepted it was Princeps; it meant only that he was
a candidate for the Principate.   The act itself was one of
revolution; its legality depended upon its success.   Did the
legions in other provinces accept the candidature, the Senate
immediately fulfilled its formal task; did rival aspirants meet
in battle, it was always ready to welcome the survivor.   To be
truly a Princeps was to receive the customary honours and
offices from the Senate, and Vitellius was acting in the true spirit
of the constitution when he adopted as the formal date of his
accession (*dies imperii*) the day on which his claims had been
ratified by the fathers.[1]   Vespasian was acting contrary to that
spirit when he regarded as the beginning of his the moment
at which he had been saluted *imperator* by the legions of Egypt.[2]

   Yet although the history of the Empire furnishes an unparalleled series of successful revolutions, it must not be supposed
that the importance of the Senate's formally transmitting the
succession was ever questioned or obscured.   The Senate's
authority was rendered stable by the many peaceful instances of
dynastic succession; it was rendered creditable by such a stand
as that made against the tyrant Maximin; it was kept alive by
the fact that when, in the days of the "thirty tyrants," the
Empire was breaking up, Italy was still the only formal centre of
a world power; it was bound up with the magic name of Rome,
and even in the third century was welcomed with relief by an
army sick of its own lawless violence.[3]

   But whether we lay more stress on the *de facto* or the *de jure*
element in the act of election, we must admit that the elective

[1] Henzen *Act. Fr. Arv.* p. 64. Hadrian, after his salutation by the soldiers,
wrote to the Senate that he had been *praepropere* addressed as *imperator* (*Vita
Hadriani* 6).   Pertinax, after his appointment had been accepted by the
praetorian guards, laid down his power in the Senate and was elected again (Dio
Cass. lxxiii. 1).
[2] Suet. *Vesp.* 6.
[3] *Vita Taciti* 2 (after the murder of Aurelian) "exercitus, qui creare imperatorem raptim solebat, ad senatum literas misit . . . petens ut ex ordine suo
principem legerent.   Verum senatus, sciens lectos a se principes militibus non
placere, rem ad milites rettulit, dumque id saepius fit, sextus peractus est mensis."

principle was not the sole determinant in the transmission of the Principate. It was crossed by two others, both of which were typically Roman. These were the principles of nomination and of hereditary succession.

Nomination took the form of designation by some significant act. One of the most significant modes in which the Princeps could point to his choice of a successor was to invest an individual with an approximation to those powers which were of the essence of the Principate, and thus to make him in a sense a colleague in the Empire (*collega, consors imperii*). The powers chosen were the *proconsulare imperium*, the *tribunicia potestas*, or both. It was thus that Augustus at different times designated Agrippa and Tiberius for the throne,[1] that Tiberius pointed to Germanicus and Drusus as his destined successors, that Nerva nominated Trajan, Trajan Pius, and Pius Marcus Aurelius.[2] Although such a position is described as one of colleagueship in the imperial power, yet it did not confer, as regards the *imperium*, the most characteristic rights of the Principate. The colleague did not possess joint command over the praetorian guard or the fleet, nor joint administration over all the Caesarian provinces,[3] unless these rights were conferred by special mandate, as they were on Tiberius during the closing years of Augustus' life;[4] nor had the colleague, although in possession of an independent *imperium*, any right to triumph, except by the will of the Princeps,[5] for his victory had been due to legions which had

---

[1] In 13 B.C. Agrippa received *tribunicia potestas* for five years (Dio Cass. liv. 12). For Tiberius' claims see Tac. *Ann.* i. 3 "filius, collega imperii, consors tribuniciae potestatis adsumitur."

[2] Tac. *Ann.* i. 14 (Tiberius on his accession, A.D. 14) "Germanico Caesari proconsulare imperium petivit"; iii. 56 (A.D. 22) "Tiberius mittit literas ad senatum quis potestatem tribuniciam Druso petebat." For Trajan see Plin. *Paneg.* 8 "ante pulvinar Jovis optimi maximi adoptio peracta est . . . simul filius, simul Caesar, mox imperator et consors tribuniciae potestatis"; *Vita Pii* 4 "adoptatus est (Pius) . . . factusque est patri et in imperio proconsulari et in tribunicia potestate collega"; *Vita Marci* 6 (Marcus before he came to the throne) "tribunicia potestate donatus est atque imperio extra urbem proconsulari."

[3] Mommsen *Staatsr.* ii. p. 1158.

[4] Vell. ii. 121 "cum . . . senatus populusque Romanus postulante patre ejus, ut aequum ei jus in omnibus provinciis exercitibusque esset quam erat ipsi, decreto complexus esset."

[5] Agrippa twice declined a triumph offered him by Augustus (Dio Cass. liv. 11 and 24), and the Senate conferred the title of *Imperator* only on the proposal of the Princeps (Tac. *Ann.* i. 58, Germanicus in A.D. 15, "exercitum reduxit nomenque imperatoris auctore Tiberio accepit").

taken the *sacramentum* to another. The name *imperator* was not borne by this assistant to the throne unless it was specially conferred, as it was by Vespasian on Titus and by Hadrian on Antoninus Pius.[1] It is uncertain whether the possessor of the *tribunicia potestas* and of the *proconsulare imperium* in its lower form had to have these powers reconferred on his accession to the throne. In the case of the *imperium*, since it fell short of that required for the imperial position, reconferment is probable. But yet the possession of such a power seemed to create a continuity in the Principate, and the state seemed never to have lost its head.

A second mode of nomination was effected by the Princeps designating his intended successor as his heir. It was not merely that this was an effective way of showing one's will, but it actually pointed to a transmission of the crown property (*patrimonium*) which accompanied the Principate. Gaius attempted to employ this mode of designation in favour of his sister Drusilla,[2] and Tiberius showed either that he had left the succession open, or that he contemplated a joint Augustate, by making his great-nephew Gaius and his grandson Tiberius Gemellus joint heirs.[3]

Adoption was as effective a means of emphasising one's intentions. Such an adoption by the Princeps might be by testament, but it need not follow the legal forms, and required only a public announcement through a *contio* whether in the Forum, the Senate, or the camp.[4] It was thus that Galba named Piso as his successor, but adoption usually accompanied the gift of quasi-imperial power, as in the cases of Tiberius, Trajan, Antoninus Pius, and Marcus Aurelius.[5]

We have already noticed the method by which the Princeps, sometimes with the help of the Senate, could announce his wishes as to the succession by the gift of the name of Caesar.[6] This

---

[1] Mommsen *Staatsr.* ii. p. 1154.

[2] Suet. *Gaius* 24 "(Gaius Drusillam) heredem quoque bonorum atque imperii aeger instituit."

[3] ib. 14. Compare Domitian's contention after the death of Vespasian "relictum se participem imperii sed fraudem testamento adhibitam" (Suet. *Dom.* 2).

[4] Tac. *Hist.* i. 15 (see p. 350) ; i. 17 (of the adoption of Piso by Galba) "consultatum inde pro rostris an in senatu an in castris adoptio nuncuparetur"; Suet. *Galba* 17 "(Galba Pisonem) perduxit in castra ac pro contione adoptavit." Nerva proclaims on the Capitol his adoption of Trajan (Dio Cass. lxviii. 3).

[5] See p. 360, n. 2.   [6] p. 354.

was a constitutional recognition of a principle of designation which had hitherto been informal.

Three of the modes of nomination which we have mentioned —those by heirship, adoption, and the gift of the name of Caesar —obviously approach very closely to the principle of hereditary succession. Adoption especially created to the Roman mind a tie only less strong than that of natural birth ; and, whichever of the three methods was employed, it would have been considered almost inconceivable that a man should pass over his own son or agnatic descendant in favour of a stranger. Just as in the Republic son had succeeded father in office, so in the Principate it was easy to gain recognition for a dynasty ; and, as a rule, it was only when the last of a line had, for misgovernment or other reasons, been violently overthrown, that the principle of selection found free play. The magic of the name of Caesar could call even Claudius to the throne ; Vespasian, the *novus homo*, found it easy to transmit his power ; the dynasty founded by Severus ran through four generations in spite of the murder of Caracalla and the scandal of Elagabalus' rule ; the death of the two elder Gordians made the accession of the third inevitable ; and Carus, the last of the rough soldier emperors, could be succeeded by the gentle Numerian and the extravagant Carinus.

The lack of any definite principle of succession combined with the warring forces within the Empire to make the position of a ruling Emperor one of dazzling uncertainty. The possibility of election by the legions created a rude standard of merit, and it is questionable whether any really incapable man ever sat on the Roman throne. But usurpation was often followed by dethronement, tyranny by death or posthumous disgrace ; and although such expulsions, executions, and censures were practically the work of the army, it is of some importance for the constitutional theory of the Principate to determine the legal form which dethronement or condemnation assumed.

As it was the Senate, representing the people, which gave, so it was this power which took away the Principate ; and the act of deposition is attested in the cases of Nero, Didius Julianus, and Maximin.[1] Deposition was followed by death, and then came the condemnation of the reign, one that might follow even

---

[1] Plut. *Galba* 7 (a messenger announces that) ὁ δῆμος καὶ ἡ σύγκλητος αὐτοκράτορα τὸν Γάλβαν ἀναγορεύσειεν : Herodian ii. 12 (the Senate) ψηφίζεται τὸν μὲν (’Ιουλιανὸν) ἀναιρεθῆναι, ἀποδειχθῆναι δὲ μόνον αὐτοκράτορα τὸν Σεουῆρον : *Vita*

when the death of the tyrant had not been directly ordered by
the government.[1]   In its extremest form this was a condemnation of the memory (*damnatio memoriae*) of the late ruler on the
ground that he was a traitor (*perduellis*).[2] His *acta* were rescinded, his name erased from the records.   A milder form of
censure was the mere neglect of his *acta* in the form that no
oath to observe them was sworn by magistrates and senators.[3]
In the latter case there was no wholesale rescission of the acts,
and each special case in which the late Emperor had decided
was approved on its individual merits.

On the other hand the acceptance of a reign took the two-
fold form of an oath to observe the *acta* of the dead Emperor [4]
and a vote to assign him a place amongst the deified Caesars.
The prospect of this posthumous recognition of the merits of a
reign must often have exercised a stimulating influence on the
occupant of the throne,[5] although it was somewhat spoilt by the
consciousness that the decision of the Senate would, to a large
extent, be guided by the wishes of his successor in office.

§ 4. *The other Powers in the State—the Magistracy, the Comitia,
and the Senate*

(1) *The Magistracy*

As the Republican constitution continued in form unimpaired,
so its most essential feature, the magistracy, although subjected

Maximini 15 "Ubi haec gesta sunt (i.e. after the recognition of the Gordians)
senatus magis timens Maximinum aperte ac libere hostes appellat Maximinum et
ejus filium."
    [1] This was the case with Caligula, although the *damnatio* was incomplete.
See Suet. *Claud.* 11 "Gaii quoque etsi acta omnia rescidit, diem tamen necis,
quamvis exordium principatus sui, vetuit inter festos referri."
    [2] The deposed Nero was thus treated as a traitor (Suet. *Ner.* 49 "codicillos
praeripuit legitque se hostem a senatu judicatum et quaeri ut puniatur more
majorum ").
    [3] The *acta* of Tiberius were not sworn to (Dio Cass. lix. 9), although his
memory was not condemned.   His reign appears amongst the legitimate precedents for the authority of Vespasian in the *lex de imperio*, those of Gaius, Nero,
Galba, Otho, and Vitellius being omitted.
    [4] Dio Cass. lvii. 8 (Tiberius) ἐπὶ ταῖς τοῦ Αὐγούστου πράξεσι τούς τε ἄλλους
πάντας ὥρκου καὶ αὐτὸς ὥμνυε.
    [5] Tiberius characteristically enough would not have his *acta* sworn to during
his lifetime (Tac. *Ann.* i. 72 ; Suet. *Tib.* 67), and some thought the motive was
"ne mox majore dedecore impar tantis honoribus inveniretur " (Suet. l.c.).   His
objection to his own deification was interpreted by some as a sign "degeneris
animi " (Tac. *Ann.* iv. 38).

to modification, was still an integral element in the administration of Rome and Italy during the Principate. Few radical differences were introduced into the magisterial qualifications or career ; the innovations affected only the age for office, the starting point in the *cursus honorum*, and one of the steps in the *certus ordo magistratuum*. The minimum age for the quaestorship was now twenty-five years,[1] for the praetorship thirty,[2] and two new qualifications were necessary before the quaestorship could be held. One was membership of the vigintivirate, the aggregate of lower magistracies to which the *sex-et-vigintiviratus* of the Republic had now shrunk.[3] The other, perhaps originally a practical rather than a legal qualification, was the tenure of the military tribunate,[4] the latter being held generally after one of the magistracies in the vigintivirate had been administered. This change, though apparently formal, meant a fundamental alteration in the spirit of the new nobility. The possibilities of culture, to be acquired in the schools of Athens and Rhodes, were now almost extinct. From the age of eighteen the aspirant to the highest honours in the State might be serving with Caesar's legions on the frontier. It was through the Emperor's grace that he attained a military position which was at least a practically necessary qualification for the magistracy ; at the age of twenty-five the young soldier entered on the race for higher honours ; as an ex-praetor, even at times as an ex-quaestor, he might be made the general of a brigade (*legatus legionis*), and from thence proceed to the government of a military, or the administration of a civil, province. Nothing shows more clearly the true military character of the new monarchy than the fact that even its civil and Republican posts were administered by

---

[1] Dio Cass. lii. 20. Here it is made the age for entrance into the Senate ; but the completion of the twenty-fifth year is meant. Cf. Quintil. *Inst. Or.* xii. 6, 1 "quaestoria aetas."

[2] Dio Cass. l.c. Dispensations from these rules might be given by the Senate, in accordance with the *jus liberorum* ("ut singuli anni per singulos liberos remittantur" *Dig.* 4, 4, 2), or to members of the imperial house (Tac. *Ann.* iii. 29 "Per idem tempus (A.D. 20) Neronem e liberis Germanici jam ingressum juventam (Tiberius) commendavit patribus, utque munere capessendi vigintiviratus solveretur et quinquennio maturius quam per leges quaesturam peteret . . . postulavit").

[3] Dio Cass. liv. 26 ; cf. Tac. *Ann.* iii. 29, quoted in the last note.

[4] In inscriptions of the early Principate the vigintivirate is sometimes not found in the list of *honores*. But it is more probable that it is omitted than that it was an alternative to the military tribunate. See Mommsen *Staatsr.* i. p. 544 n. 4.

soldiers; nothing explains more adequately the subservience of
the Senate than the fact that it was composed mainly of ex-
officers, trained in the habits of rigid obedience and in un-
wavering respect to the *sacramentum*—of men to whom Caesar
was not Princeps but Imperator.

With respect to the steps in office which followed the quaestorship, a further change was due to the unwillingness of candidates to burden themselves with the aedileship, now that its
powers of bribery were of no avail, and with the now undis-
tinguished tribunate of the Plebs. The rule was laid down that
between the quaestorship and praetorship a Patrician must hold
the curule aedileship, a Plebeian one of the two aedileships or
the tribunate.[1] An exemption from this lengthy course could,
however, be given by an exercise of the imperial right of *adlectio*.
This was the conferment of an artificial magisterial rank. In
form it was a power exercised in the revision of the list of the
Senate and elevated from a lower to a higher grade within that
order. But the *adlectio* also had the effect of qualifying for the
magistracy immediately above the rank thus artificially assigned.
One who was *adlectus inter quaestorios* was qualified for the
tribunate, one *adlectus inter tribunicios* for the praetorship, and
one *adlectus inter praetorios* for the consulship. The consulship
was amongst civic magistracies still the crown of a political
career; hence the rarity of adlection *inter consulares*.[2]

A smaller honour was the conferment by the Senate, generally
on the proposal of the Princeps, of the *ornamenta* of a magistracy
(*quaestoria, praetoria, consularia*) on one who had not held the
magistracy itself. This honour gave no right of entry into the
Senate, and none of holding the magistracy next in rank to that
whose ornaments were conferred,[3] but merely the privilege of
wearing the *insignia* of an office at festivals and on other public
occasions;[4] it may, however, have given the right of voting with
the class of senators whose *ornamenta* were conferred, if the
person honoured was already provided with a seat at the Senate.[5]

---

[1] Dio Cass. lii. 20.
[2] Its use by Macrinus in the third century excited opposition (Dio Cass. lxxviii.
13). See Mommsen *Staatsr.* ii. p. 942.
[3] Dio Cass. liv. 19 (of Tiberius in 16 B.C.) ἐστρατήγησε γάρ, καίπερ τὰς στρατηγικὰς τιμὰς ἔχων (Tiberius had received the *ornamenta praetoria* in 19 B.C.,
see c. 10); c. 32 Drusus ἀγορανόμος . . . καίπερ τὰς στρατηγικὰς τιμὰς ἔχων
ἀπεδείχθη : cf. c. 22.
[4] Suet. *Aug.* 35 ; Dio Cass. lviii. 12.   [5] Mommsen *Staatsr.* i. p. 458.

This distinction was by no means reserved for persons legally qualified for the, magistracy ; it might be granted to knights high up in the imperial service, such as the praefects of the guard[1] and of the watch,[2] or to provincial procurators.[3] Claudius granted it to imperial freedmen,[4] and we find that even senators excluded from the curia were sometimes left the *ornamenta* of their rank.[5]

The permission to use the ornaments of a triumph (*ornamenta triumphalia*) was the result of the limitation of the right to the actual triumph. The application of the principle that this right was inconsistent with a subordinate *imperium*,[6] had, when applied to the Principate, the effect of legally confining triumphs to the Princeps alone ; for the governors of his own provinces were merely his delegates, while those of senatorial provinces, though nominally in independent authority, had as a rule no armies at their command.[7] The triumphal *insignia* might, however, be granted by the Senate on the proposal of the Princeps.[8]

The election to the magistracies will be more fitly treated in connexion with the *comitia* and the Senate. The obligations to which their holders bound themselves on their appointment were those of the Republic, with the exception that the *jus jurandum in leges* was amplified by the inclusion of the valid *acta* of the Princeps—those, that is, of a living or a previous emperor whose binding character had been recognised by oath.[9]

---

[1] The consular *insignia* were granted to Nymphidius and to Crispinus under Nero (Tac. *Ann.* xv. 72 ; xvi. 17) ; the praetorian *insignia* to Sejanus and to Macro under Tiberius (Dio Cass. lvii. 19 ; lviii. 12).

[2] Quaestorian *insignia* were granted to Laco under Tiberius (Dio Cass. lviii. 12).

[3] Tac. *Ann.* xii. 21 "consularia insignia Ciloni (procurator of Pontus) . . . decernuntur"; Suet. *Claud.* 24 "ornamenta consularia etiam procuratoribus ducenariis indulsit."

[4] As the praetorian *insignia* to Pallas, the quaestorian to Narcissus (Tac. *Ann.* xii. 53 ; xi. 38). Cf. Suet. *Claud.* 28.

[5] Suet. *Aug.* 35 (Augustus) "quosdam ad excusandi se verecundiam compulit : servavitque etiam excusatis insigne vestis et spectandi in orchestra epulandique publice jus." [6] p. 156.

[7] In an exceptional case, such as Junius Blaesus' command in Africa, the proconsul might be saluted *imperator* on the permission of the Princeps (Tac. *Ann.* iii. 74), and the first condition of a triumph be fulfilled. But this incident, dating from A.D. 22, was the last of its kind on record.

[8] Suet. *Aug.* 38 "super triginta ducibus justos triumphos et aliquanto pluribus triumphalia ornamenta decernenda curavit"; Wilmanns n. 1145 l. 19 "senatus . . . triumphalibus ornamentis honoravit auctore imp. Caesare Augusto Vespasiano"; *Index* p. 609.

[9] Dio Cass. lix. 9. The obligation to swear *in acta Caesaris* had, with reference to the acts of the first Caesar, begun in 45 B.C. (App. *B.C.* ii. 106), and had been

If we turn now to the individual offices, we find that the
CONSULS are still the officially recognised heads of the Republic
and of the Senate. On the suspension of the Principate they
are the representatives of the state,[1] and we find them acting in
accordance with this character. It was the consuls who, on the
deposition of Nero, sent despatches to Galba with the news of
his selection,[2] and it was by the surrender of his dagger to a
consul that the abdication of Vitellius was effected.[3] The dignity
of the office is shown by the fact that it was the only one in
which a citizen might have the Princeps as a colleague, and still
more by the view of a gracious emperor that, when he was
performing the functions of that office, the vast dignity of the
Principate was for a moment lost in that of the consulship.[4] As
presidents of the Senate the consuls were partners in its nominal
sovereignty. They guided its jurisdiction, both in civil and in
criminal matters, and in the former may have acted as its commissioners. They also possessed in their own right high judicial
functions—in matters of trust (*fidei commissa*), for instance—
which were originally delegated to them by the Princeps, and of
which we shall treat elsewhere.

But the very fact that the consulship was such a prize, as
well as the fact that its occupation led to the filling of other
high offices—the government of certain senatorial and imperial
provinces and the praefecture of the city—induced a shortening
of its tenure and a consequent multiplication of the individuals
who might enjoy its privileges and become qualified for other
duties. The expensiveness of the office may also have contributed to this end; for the increase in the number of occupants
would lessen the pecuniary burden imposed by the celebration
of games.[5] Even the half-yearly consulships of the early
Principate become in course of time very infrequent, and we

renewed during the triumvirate (Dio Cass. xlvii. 18), the formula running *se
nihil contra acta Caesaris facturum*. For the obligation as continued in the
Principate cf. p. 363.
[1] Herodian (ii. 12), with reference to the downfall of Didius Julianus, speaks
of the consuls οἱ τὰ τῆς Ῥώμης διοικεῖν εἰώθασιν ὁπηνίκα ἂν τὰ τῆς βασιλείας
μετέωρα ᾖ.   [2] Plut. *Galba* 8.   [3] Tac. *Hist.* iii. 68.
[4] Plin. *Paneg.* 77 "comitia consulum obibat ipse (Trajanus); tantum ex
renuntiatione eorum voluptatis quantum prius ex destinatione capiebat . . .
Adibat aliquis ut principem; respondebat se consulem esse."
[5] On the consuls was laid the burden of certain newly-established festivals
such as those celebrating the *Natalia* of Augustus and the victory of Actium (Dio
Cass. lvi. 46; lix. 20).

subsequently find a tenure of but four or two months.[1] Those
appointed for 1st January were *ordinarii*, the others *suffecti*,[2] and
the whole year was dated by the names of the former.

The number of the PRAETORS varied under Augustus and his
successors from ten to eighteen. Twelve, fourteen, fifteen, and
sixteen are found at various times, and the final limit of eighteen
was still maintaining itself in the time of Hadrian.[3] The reason
for this expansion of their numbers was their utility for the
enlarged jurisdiction of the period. The Republican functions
of the *praetor urbanus* and the *praetor peregrinus* continued,
until those of the latter became extinct, perhaps soon after the
conferment of citizenship on the whole Roman world by Caracalla (212 A.D.);[4] while other praetors were guides of the
quaestiones perpetuae, until the disappearance of these commissions
towards the close of the second century.[5] But new spheres of
extraordinary jurisdiction claimed the attention of others. Thus
Claudius instituted two praetors for adjudication on trusts
(*fidei commissarii*),[6] Nerva one for the decision of cases arising
between the *fiscus* and private individuals (*fiscalis*),[7] and Marcus
Aurelius another for the granting, and perhaps for the control,
of guardians (*tutelaris*).[8] For a short time the administration of
the *aerarium* was also in the hands of praetors.[9]

Most of the specific functions, which the AEDILES had exercised during the Republic, now passed to other hands or were
shorn of their importance. The history of the later Republic
had shown how incompetent these officials were to exercise an
adequate control of the market, and the *cura annonae* passed to
the Princeps and to the praefecture established by him. Their
police functions were to a large extent absorbed by the praefecture of the city, but they still destroyed books condemned by the

---

[1] See Mommsen *Staatsr.* ii. pp .84-87. The climax was reached with twenty-
five consulships in a single year (189 A.D.) under Commodus (Dio Cass. lxxii. 12 ;
Vita Commodi 6).

[2] *Vita Alexandri* 43.   [3] Pompon. in *Dig.* 1, 2, 2, 32.

[4] Marini *Atti Arvali* p. 784.

[5] Dio Cassius, lii. cc. 20, 21 (speech of Maecenas), may mean to imply their
existence in his own time. Geib (*Criminalprocess* pp. 392-397) assigns their disappearance to the end of the first century.

[6] Pompon. in *Dig.* 1, 2, 2, 32 "divus Claudius duos praetores adjecit qui de
fidei commisso jus dicerent, ex quibus unum divus Titus detraxit : et adjecit divus
Nerva qui inter fiscum et privatos jus diceret."   [7] See last note.

[8] *Vita Marci* 10 "praetorem tutelarem primus fecit, cum ante tutores a consulibus poscerentur, ut diligentius de tutoribus tractaretur."

[9] See § 5.

Senate,[1] and attempted to carry out the sumptuary laws.[2]   The *cura urbis* still entailed on them the duty of keeping clean the streets of Rome [3] and a supervision over places of public resort.[4] Much of their criminal jurisdiction must have lapsed with the disappearance of trials before the *comitia*, but they still retain a power of inflicting fines and seizing pledges—one which was limited and regulated during the reign of Nero [5]—and the special civil jurisdiction of the curule aediles still continues.[6]

The QUAESTORS still maintained their functions as financial officials and general assistants to the magistrates.   Their number had been raised by Caesar to forty, but was again reduced to twenty by Augustus.[7]   For a time two quaestors had the guardianship of the *aerarium*,[8] and others were in the public provinces the financial and judicial assistants of the proconsuls.[9] Four more were assigned to the consuls, two to each, as their agents and assistants;[10] while the Princeps himself employed two, commended by himself (*quaestores Augusti, quaestores candidati principis*), chiefly for the purpose of reading his despatches to the Senate.[11]   During the reign of Claudius a step was taken which " put up the quaestorship for sale," [12] and associated it with a function that clung to it longer than any other.   This was the exhibition of gladiatorial games at the cost of the exhibitor,[13] a

---

[1] On the condemnation of the history of Cremutius Cordus in A.D. 25 "libros per aediles cremandos censuere patres " (Tac. *Ann.* iv. 35).

[2] Tac. *Ann.* iii. 52-55 (A.D. 22).

[3] We hear of Vespasian during the reign of Caligula ἀγορανομοῦντός τε . . . καὶ τῆς τῶν στενωπῶν καθαρειότητος ἐπιμελουμένου (Dio Cass. lix. 12). Cf. Suet. *Vesp.* 5.

[4] Tac. *Ann.* ii. 85 (A.D. 19) " Vistilia praetoria familia genita licentiam stupri apud aediles vulgaverat."

[5] ib. xiii. 28 (A.D. 56) "cohibita artius et aedilium potestas statutumque quantum curules, quantum plebei pignoris caperent vel poenae inrogarent."

[6] Gaius *Inst.* i. 6 (of the *jus edicendi*) "amplissimum jus est in edictis duorum praetorum . . . item in edictis aedilium curulium."   Their edict was codified under Hadrian, and appears in *Dig.* 21, 1.

[7] Karlowa (*Rechtsgesch.* i. p. 532) thus distributes them—two urban, four of the consuls, twelve for the public provinces, and two attached to the Emperor.

[8] See § 5.   [9] See chap. xi.

[10] The practice first began in 38 B.C. (Dio Cass. xlviii. 43). Cf. Tac. *Ann.* xvi. 34 " Tum ad Thraseam in hortis agentem quaestor consulis missus."   They were selected by the consuls themselves (Plin. *Ep.* iv. 15, 8).

[11] *Dig.* 1, 13, 1, 2 and 4 "sane non omnes quaestores provincias sortiebantur, verum excepti erant candidati principis . . . qui . . . epistulas ejus in senatu legunt."

[12] Tac. *Ann.* xi. 22 (A.D. 47) "quaestura . . . velut venundaretur."

[13] The obligation imposed in 47 was modified in 54 A.D. (Tac. *Ann.* xi. 22 ; xiii. 5), but was renewed under Domitian (Suet. *Dom.* 4).

2 B

pecuniary burden which henceforth fell on every aspirant for higher office, until Severus Alexander ordained that only the *quaestores candidati* should themselves defray the expenses of these spectacles, the cost of the games given by the others being defrayed from the *fiscus*.[1]

The TRIBUNES OF THE PLEBS were not colleagues of the Princeps, for the *tribunicia potestas* was not the tribunate, and the actions in virtue of it were not even theoretically subject to the tribunes' veto. But their great negative powers were still occasionally exercised in some departments of state during the first century of the Principate. Like the office itself, however, they were but a shadow of those of the Republic.[2] The *intercessio* against decrees of the Senate might be attempted when unimportant matters, such as the right to scourge actors, were under discussion,[3] or might be employed as a warning to the Senate that the Princeps should be consulted on the business in hand.[4] In higher matters of state its exercise might mean danger or death to the tribune who mistook the fictitious for the real Republic, or who, recognising the tyranny, chose to brave the anger of the Emperor.[5] The right of *auxilium* was still exercised against a praetor in 56 A.D.,[6] and appealed to by an Emperor in 69.[7] But this, too, soon disappeared to leave no trace. In the early Principate the tribunes seem to have possessed some

---

[1] *Vita Alexandri* 43 "quaestores candidatos ex sua pecunia jussit munera populo dare . . . arcarios vero instituit, qui de arca fisci ederent munera eademque parciora."

[2] The tribunate is to the younger Pliny "inanis umbra et sine honore nomen " (*Ep.* i. 23).

[3] Tac. *Ann.* i. 77 (A.D. 15, on the proposal of *jus virgarum in histriones*) "intercessit Haterius Agrippa tribunus plebei increpitusque est Asinii Galli oratione, silente Tiberio, qui ea simulacra libertatis senatui praebebat."

[4] Tac. *Hist.* iv. 9 (A.D. 69, on the praetors of the *aerarium* announcing a deficit) "cum perrogarent sententias consules, Volcatius Tertullinus tribunus plebis intercessit, ne quid super tanta re principe absente statueretur." This is the last recorded instance of the *intercessio* (Momms. *Staatsr.* ii. p. 309 n. 1).

[5] Tac. *Ann.* vi. 47 [53] (in A.D. 37 a woman was accused of *majestas*) "qua damnata cum praemium accusatori decerneretur, Junius Otho tribunus plebei intercessit, unde . . . mox Othoni exitium." Rusticus Arulenus, a *flagrans juvenis*, offered to veto the decree of the Senate which condemned Thrasea Paetus in A.D. 66 (xvi. 26).

[6] ib. xiii. 28 "inter Vibullium praetorem et plebei tribunum Antistium ortum certamen, quod immodestos fautores histrionum et a praetore in vincla ductos tribunos omitti jussisset."

[7] Tac. *Hist.* ii. 91 (Vitellius, when Emperor, attacked by Helvidius Priscus in the Senate) "commotus . . . non tamen ultra quam tribunos plebis in auxilium spretae potestatis advocavit."

right of summoning civil cases from the Italian towns to Rome,[1]
probably through an exercise of the veto; and, although their
criminal jurisdiction had disappeared with the *comitia*, they
retained some power of inflicting fines (*multae*), which was limited
during the reign of Nero.[2]   There is also evidence that they still
possessed the right of veto in civil jurisdiction.[3]   Amongst positive powers their presidency of the Senate still survives, as we
shall see in dealing with that body.

The office of tribune, since it conferred little distinction, was
by no means an object of ambition; and the difficulty of getting
the ten places filled led to the inclusion of this magistracy, as
one of the necessary steps, in the *cursus honorum*,[4] and sometimes
to more drastic measures such as the selection of ex-quaestors by
lot under Augustus,[5] or the reception of members of the equestrian order under Claudius.[6]   Yet, with all its disadvantages,
the tribunate survived the Principate, and tribunes are named in
imperial despatches of the fourth century.[7]

(2) *The Comitia*

An element in the restoration of the Republic by Augustus,
after the provisional government of the Triumvirate was over,
was a renewal of the life of the popular assemblies.[8]   But it was
impossible that their purely local character could be reconciled
with the imperial interests of the day, or that their popular
character should be consistent with the rule of the Princeps and
his nobility.   For a moment they remained to a certain extent a
reality, and throughout the Principate they exercised the shadow
of power which was sufficient to express the still surviving theory
of popular sovereignty.

From the first a considerable portion of the powers of the

[1] In A.D. 56 they were forbidden " vocare ex Italia cum quibus lege agi posset "
(Tac. *Ann.* xiii. 28).   See Appendix.   [2] Tac. l.c.
[3] Juvenal vii. 228 " Rara tamen merces, quae cognitione tribuni Non egeat."
The words doubtless mean "which does not lead to the *appellatio*."   In such a
case even the Republican tribunes took "cognisance" of the merits of the appeal.
The explanation that the tribunes were now given some extraordinary jurisdiction
in civil cases is unnecessary.
[4] p. 365.   [5] Dio Cass. liv. 26.   [6] ib. lx. 11.
[7] e.g. *Cod.* 6, 60, 1 (A.D. 319) "Imp. Constantinus A. consulibus, praetoribus
tribunis plebis senatui salutem."
[8] Suet. *Aug.* 40 "Comitiorum quoque pristinum jus reduxit."

comitia had been transferred wholly to the Princeps; for to him belonged the rights of declaring war, of making peace, and of forming alliances;[1] while the criminal jurisdiction which the people exercised at the end of the Republic was no longer necessary, for while the more definite portion of it was handed over to the *quaestiones*,[2] the more indefinite now fell under the extraordinary cognisance of the Senate. Legislative power tended to centre more and more in the Princeps and Senate, and it is only during the first century that enactments are mentioned which have the true forms of *leges* and *plebiscita*.[3] The right of election was the most permanent of the popular prerogatives. Under Augustus the people still chose its magistrates, although the choice was considerably influenced by the Princeps;[4] and after Tiberius in the first year of his reign had caused all the real elements of election—the profession, the nomination, the vote—to be transferred to the Senate,[5] the formal *renuntiatio* of the successful candidates (an integral part of the election)[6] still continued to be made to the people down to the third century.[7] It is only in respect to the consulship that there is a doubt whether, during the first century A.D., more than the mere announcement of the result was not effected in the *comitia*. The evidence is conflicting, but the indications of a formal popular control of these appointments are on the whole outweighed by those which refer to the Senate the real elements of election—rendered nugatory at times by the way in which the Princeps exercised his powers of nomination.[8] There can be little question, how-ever, that in the later Principate the consular, like all other,

---

[1] p. 344.

[2] Dio Cass. lvi. 40 (Augustus) ἐκ . . . τοῦ δήμου τὸ δύσκριτον ἐν ταῖς διαγνώ-σεσιν ἐς τὴν τῶν δικαστηρίων ἀκρίβειαν μεταστήσας.

[3] e.g. the Julian laws passed by Augustus in the *concilium plebis*, the *lex Junia Norbana* of the reign of Tiberius, *plebiscita* of Claudius. The last known *lex* is an agrarian law of Nerva (*Dig.* 47, 21, 3, 1).

[4] Dio Cass. liii. 21 (when the election was entrusted to the people, Augustus) ἐπεμελεῖτο ὅπως μήτ' ἀνεπιτήδειοι μήτ' ἐκ παρακελεύσεως ἢ καὶ δεκασμοῦ ἀπο-δεικνύωνται. Cf. Tac. *Ann.* i. 15 "potissima arbitrio principis, quaedam tamen studiis tribuum fiebant."

[5] Tac. *Ann.* i. 15. The change was, we are told by Velleius (ii. 124), in accordance with the instructions of Augustus.

[6] p. 188.　　　　　　　　　　　　[7] Dio Cass. lviii. 20.

[8] p. 349. In *C.I.L.* vi. 10213 we find a notice of "improbae comitiae in Aventino, ubi (Sej)anus cos. factus est." We find Vitellius canvassing for his candidates in the circus (Tac. *Hist.* ii. 91 "comitia consulum cum candidatis civiliter celebrans omnem infimae plebis rumorem in theatro ut spectator, in circo ut fautor adfectavit"). On the other hand, we have *ab senatu destinatus* in

elections were vested in the Senate. The survival of the *comitia* into the third century, whether for the purpose of the *renuntiatio* or for that of ratifying the powers of the Princeps, was no mere mass-meeting informally assembled. The stately forms of the Republic were preserved, and when the centuries were assembled the red flag still flew from the Janiculum.[1]

(3) *The Senate*

It was through the Senate of the Principate that the idea of popular sovereignty was most practically and even most formally expressed ; and, as the Principate claimed and even tried to be nothing more than the extraordinary magistracy of a Republic, the most infinite pains was taken with this body to give it dignity, stability, and weight. We shall speak elsewhere of the senatorial "order" which was created during the Principate ; it was from this order that the Senate was recruited, and the will of the Princeps could be very distinctly asserted in the selection of members of the great council. Entrance was, as in the Republic, chiefly through the magistracy, the tenure of the quaestorship qualifying for a seat at the board. When, therefore, the Senate became itself the electing body, the principle of entrance was one of cooptation ; and as the Princeps did not, to any great extent, influence the selection of quaestors by his *commendatio*,[2] the principle was something more than a mere theory. But we shall see that he often gave the *latus clavus* which admitted to the senatorial order; we have seen that he advanced to the military tribunate, which became one of the qualifications for the quaestorship ;[3] he might also have exercised an influence in the formal nomination of candidates for this office ; while his right of *adlectio*,[4] when exercised with reference to persons who had not been magistrates, gave him the power of actually creating senators.

The qualifications for the Senate had reference to age, wealth, and birth. As twenty-five was the minimum age for the quaestorship, a man might be a senator at twenty-six.[5] The

---

the inscription quoted on p. 349 n. 6. Dio Cassius (lix. 20), in speaking of the temporary restoration of popular elections by Caligula, mentions them in connexion with the consulship.

[1] Dio Cass. xxxvii. 28.

[2] p. 369.   [3] p. 364.   [4] p. 365.

[5] p. 364. Hence the expression "nondum senatoria aetate" (Tac. *Ann.* xv. 28 ; *Hist.* iv. 42).

census required, though it varied from time to time during the reign of Augustus, was finally fixed at a million sesterces.[1] *Ingenuitas* was required—Claudius even demanded free birth through three generations[2]—and it was counted one of the abuses of tyrannical rule when the favour of Emperors admitted freedmen into the Senate.[3] For a time the council maintained its mainly Roman character, but "new men" from Italy and the provinces crept in with the censorships of Claudius and Vespasian,[4] and the former Emperor even granted admission to the Gallic Aedui, perhaps by an employment of his right of *adlectio*.[5] The reception of provincials finally became so frequent that, to give them an Italian interest, it was decreed by Trajan that one-third of their property must be invested in land in Italy,[6] a quota that was changed by Marcus Aurelius to one-fourth.[7]

Removal from the Senate belonged to the Emperor either as censor, when he exercised the discretionary moral judgment which had been associated with the Republican *lectio*,[8] or in virtue of that power of revision which, as we have seen, became associated with the Principate.[9] The chief grounds of exclusion were lack of the requisite census, refusal to take the oath *in acta Caesaris* which was demanded of senators as of magistrates,[10] or condemnation for crime. The Senate itself, in the exercise of its judicial power, could add to the sentence which it inflicted on a senator the penalty of expulsion from the house;[11] it might even make this expulsion a punishment for calumnious accusation.[12] The revised list of the Senate (*album senatorium*) was

[1] Dio Cass. liv. 17, 30 ; Tac. *Ann.* i. 75, ii. 37.
[2] He declared "non lecturum se senatorem nisi civis Romani abnepotem" (Suet. *Claud.* 24).
[3] *Vita Commodi* 6 "ad cujus (Cleandri) nutum etiam libertini in senatum atque in patricios lecti sunt " ; *Vita Elagabali* 11 " Fecit libertos praesides, legatos, consules, duces."
[4] Tac. *Ann.* iii. 4 "simul novi homines e municipiis et coloniis atque etiam provinciis in senatum crebro adsumpti" ; Suet. *Vesp.* 9 "Amplissimos ordines . . . purgavit supplevitque, recenso senatu et equite . . . honestissimo quoque Italicorum ac provincialium adlecto."
[5] Tac. *Ann.* xi. 25 ; Prof. Pelham in *Classical Review* ix. p. 441.
[6] Plin. *Ep.* vi. 19.   [7] *Vita Marci* 11.
[8] For the infliction of such a *nota* by Domitian see Suet. *Dom.* 8, "quaestorium virum, quod gesticulandi saltandique studio teneretur, movit senatu."
[9] p. 347.
[10] Tac. *Ann.* iv. 42 (Tiberius) "Apidium . . . Merulam, quod in acta divi Augusti non juraverat, albo senatorio erasit."
[11] ib. iii. 17 ; vi. 48.
[12] ib. iv. 31 ; xii. 59.

posted up publicly every year,[1] and the Emperor appeared at
the head of this list as *princeps senatus*.[2] The number of the
Senate was fixed by Augustus at 600,[3] and, as there seems to
have been little or no alteration in the number of the quaestors,
the size of the body into which they passed may have been
fairly constant. Augustus also instituted fixed days for meeting.
These regular meetings (*senatus legitimi*) took place twice a
month, on the Kalends and the Ides, except during the autumn
months of September and October, and attendance on these days
was compulsory.[4] Even to these meetings, however, there was
a summons through an edict.[5] Extraordinary sittings (*senatus
indicti*) could also be held whenever the magistrate deemed
them necessary.[6] The presidency and summons belonged chiefly
to the consuls, but, as in the Republic, were possessed also by
the praetors and tribunes.[7] When the Senate had been summoned, the Princeps shared in the presidency as a magistrate,
and it is very questionable whether he ever appeared at the
board in the character of a simple senator.[8] As a magistrate he
might address the house at any moment, and, during the early
Principate at least, custom dictated that there should be a pause
at the opening and at the close of a debate which the Princeps
might fill up with an expression of opinion if he pleased.[9] We
have already noticed the singular privileges which he possessed
in the matter of bringing business before the house.[10]

[1] Dio Cass. lv. 3 ; Tac. *Ann.* iv. 42.
[2] Dio Cass. liii. 1 (Augustus in 28 B.C. during the censorship of himself
and Agrippa) ἐν αὐταῖς (ταῖς ἀπογραφαῖς) πρόκριτος τῆς γερουσίας ἐπεκλήθη :
cf. lxxiii. 5, where Pertinax πρόκριτος . . . τῆς γερουσίας κατὰ τὸ ἀρχαῖον
ἐπωνομάσθη : an expression which seems to show that it was not a constant
designation of the Princeps at this period.
[3] ib. liv. 13, 14.
[4] ib. lv. 3 ; Suet. *Aug.* 35 ; Merkel ad Ovid. *Fast.* p. vi.
[5] *Lex de imp. Vesp.* l. 9 "ac si e lege senatus edictus esset habereturque."
[6] *Vita Gordianorum*, 11 ; *Vita Hadriani*, 7 ; Dio Cass. liv. 3.
[7] For the summons by a praetor see Tac. *Hist.* iv. 39 ; by tribunes, Dio Cass.
lvi. 47, lx. 16, lxxviii. 37 ; by tribunes and praetors, ib. lix. 24.
[8] The doubt is raised by Piso's address to Tiberius during a trial for *majestas*,
"quo . . . loco censebis, Caesar ? Si primus, habebo quod sequar : si post omnes,
vereor ne imprudens dissentiam " (Tac. *Ann.* i. 74). Dio Cassius also says of
Tiberius (lvii. 7) καὶ γὰρ αὐτὸς ψῆφον πολλάκις ἐδίδου. But neither writer may
be using strictly technical language ; and it is not certain that the Princeps could
be *asked* his opinion. On the other hand, when Caesar put the question, the other
magistrates gave *sententiae* (Tac. *Ann.* iii. 17). The question is not of much
importance for the Principate as a whole, as in its later period the Emperor
usually consulted the Senate by letter. See p. 369.
[9] See Tac. *Ann.* i. 74, quoted in the last note.   [10] p. 348.

Amongst the powers of the Senate, that which was formally the greatest was the creation and deposition of the Princeps. We have already seen how this right was limited in practice;[1] but its nominal exercise was an expression of the view that the sovereignty of the Roman people now found its chief exponent in the ancient council. The same idea is expressed in the senatorial power of dispensation from laws—whether in favour of the Princeps and members of his house,[2] or in administrative matters such as the right of forming associations.[3] The elective power which the Senate enjoyed from the beginning of the reign of Tiberius[4] is also a sign of its perpetuating the powers of the people.

Over foreign administration, once the great bulwark of its power, the Senate has now but little control. Although it still receives messages of the victories of the Princeps, and grants him a triumph,[5] it has lost all independent rights of war, peace, and alliance. But it receives envoys from the provinces which are under its control,[6] and from the towns of Italy,[7] and, at least in the first century of the Principate, it may act as the advising body of the Princeps in spheres which pertain wholly to him. Tiberius consulted the Senate on military questions;[8] Vespasian waived an embarrassing offer of help from the Parthians by urging them to send an embassy to the Senate; and Decebalus, after his conquest by Trajan, obtained his final terms of peace by the same means.[9] Such concessions were doubtless acts of grace on the part of the Princeps, but they also represent a constitutional principle which finally disappeared—the principle of consulting the representatives of the people on questions that were of paramount interest to the state.

The other powers of the Senate, which express its sovereignty or its partnership of administration with the Princeps, we must

---

[1] p. 359.   [2] p. 350.

[3] The formula for the formation of a *collegium legitimum* runs 'quibus senatus c(oire) c(onvocari) c(ogi) permisit e lege Julia ex auctoritate Augusti" (*C.I.L.* vi. n. 4416).

[4] p. 372.

[5] Dio Cass. lxviii. 29.

[6] Tac. *Ann.* iii. 60 ; xii. 62.   [7] ib. xiii. 48.

[8] "de legendo vel exauctorando milite, ac legionum et auxiliorum descriptione" (Suet. *Tib.* 30).

[9] Tac. *Hist.* iv. 51 ; Dio Cass. lxviii. 9, 10. In 49 A.D. during the reign of Claudius we also read of a reception of Parthian envoys in the Senate (Tac. *Ann.* xii. 10).

reserve for the next section, in which we shall attempt to
illustrate the theory of a dual control which pervades the constitution of the Principate.

§ 5. *The Chief Departments of the State ; the Dual Control of
Senate and Princeps*

We have already seen that, in the most essential fact of
sovereignty—the creation of the Principate—the Senate and
people, or rather the Senate as representing the people, was
theoretically supreme.[1] The attribute of sovereignty that comes
nearest to this is the power of legislation, for it is one that the
"determinate human superior" generally retains in his own
hands. The other functions that are usually associated with the
highest authority in a community, such as the control of general
administration, jurisdiction, finance, cultus and coinage, may
more easily be delegated. If the delegation is temporary, there
is no division of sovereign power ; if perpetual, there is such a
division unless the legislative power be thought of as capable of
recalling the mandate. We have already seen to what a large
extent the people had delegated its powers to the Princeps, and
we have also seen that this delegation was, in fact though not in
theory, perpetual.[2] But, in the spheres of authority which we
are now about to examine, there is neither the theory of complete
retention, nor that of complete delegation, of sovereign power.
The sovereign has partly retained and has partly delegated in
perpetuity every one of the functions of government which we
have enumerated, and this singular dualism affects, not only the
administrative, but even the legislative activity of the state.

(i.) *Legislation.*—With respect to legislation it has already been
shown how the *comitia* still uttered their general mandates until
a period at least as late as the reign of Nerva.[3] But, even before
the legislative power of the people became extinct, this power
had been passing to the Senate ; and in the strict theory of the
constitution, true legislative authority is to be finally found only
in the great council which represents the people.

The origin of this senatorial legislation is doubtless to be
sought in the advice on legal points which the Republican Senate
had often tendered to the magistrate, and in the interpretation of

[1] p. 358.   [2] p. 358.   [3] p. 372.

customary law or of enactments which often accompanied this advice.[1] It has, indeed, been noted that the *senatus consulta* of the Principate, which prescribe general commands such as in the Republic would have been the subject of *leges*, are often expressed in this advisory form ;[2] decrees of the Senate never attained the formal structure of a law ;[3] they also lack its imperative mode of utterance, and for these two reasons they were never described as *leges*. The highest degree of validity which the jurist could give them was "the binding force of laws";[4] but this force was sufficient to make them sources of the *jus civile*,[5] and down to the third century such general commands as tended to alter the fundamental legal relations of Roman citizens to one another, were generally expressed in the form of *senatus consulta*.

The Princeps, on the other hand, is not credited directly with any power of legislation ; but the faculty for making *jus*, which was inherent in the *imperium* of every Roman magistrate, and especially apparent in that of the praetor, was manifested by the Princeps in an unexampled degree. His methods of utterance are through the edict, the decree, and the rescript. The *edictum* is, like that of the praetor, technically an interpretation of law ; but the creative power associated with interpretation is here pushed to its extremest limits, and statute law supplemented this faculty inherent in the *imperium* by explicitly declaring that whatever ordinances the Princeps might lay down should (with certain limitations fixed by precedents) be considered valid.[6] Whether the edict of one Princeps bound his successor must have depended to some extent on the degree of formality in the utterance. Tiberius professes respect even for the *obiter dicta* of

---

[1] p. 275.

[2] Thus the *S. C. Velleianum*, which limited the obligations which women might incur, begins, "Quod Marcus Silanus et Velleus Tutor consules verba fecerunt . . . quid de ea re fieri oportet, de ea re ita censuere" (*Dig.* 16, 1, 2, 1) ; cf. *Dig.* 36, 1, 1, 2 (*S. C. Trebellianum*), 14, 6, 1 (*S. C. Macedonianum*), and see Kipp *Quellenkunde des röm. Rechts* p. 27.

[3] The jurists refer to them by the names of their proposers ; hence such designations as *Velleianum*, *Trebellianum* (see last note). But such designations are not official. The *S. C. Macedonianum* is called after the offender who had been the occasion of the decree.

[4] Gaius i. 4 "Senatus consultum est, quod senatus jubet atque constituit : idque legis vicem obtinet, quamvis fuerit quaesitum."

[5] *Dig.* 1, 1, 7 ; 1, 3, 9.

[6] *Lex de imp. Vesp.* l. 17 "utique quaecunque ex usu rei publicae majestateque divinarum humanarum publicarum privatarumque rerum esse censebit, ei agere facere jus potestasque sit, ita uti divo Augusto . . . fuit."

Augustus ;[1] but this reverence was exaggerated, and none but the
formal edicts expressed in written form could, as a rule, have
been included in the *acta*.   It is by no means certain that even
these were always included in the *acta* to which the oath was
taken ;[2] but if an edict had been recognised as valid by several
succeeding Principes and was then abandoned, some formal method
of repudiation seems to have been necessary.[3]

   The *decretum* was, in its strict sense, the sentence of the
Princeps when sitting as a high court of justice ;[4] as a *res judicata*
it necessarily possessed absolutely binding force for the case in
which it was issued, and prevented any renewal of this process ;
but, unless formally rescinded in a succeeding reign, its validity
as a precedent seems not to have been questioned, and the
words *Caesar dixit* appeal to the jurists almost with the force
of law.[5]

   The third mode of utterance is by means of the letter (*epistola*)
or rescript (*rescriptum*).[6]   These letters contained instructions
either on administrative or on judicial matters.   In their first
character they might be addressed either to individual officials
subordinate to the Emperor or to the provincial diet,[7] the scope
of their application depending on the Emperor's discretion at the
time of the issue, and on the interpretation of the rescript after
his death.   In matters of justice, whether addressed to the
judge or to the litigant, they might settle doubtful points
of law or extend a principle to new cases.   The power of
interpretation is at least as great in the rescript as in the edict ;
but the rescript was the more powerful vehicle for law-making.
It kept the Princeps in constant touch with the provincial world,

----

[1] Tac. *Ann.* i. 77 "divus Augustus immunes verberum histriones quondam
responderat, neque fas Tiberio infringere dicta ejus."

[2] p. 363.

[3] Paulus in *Dig.* 28, 2, 26 "Filius familias, si militet . . . aut heres scribi aut
exheredari debet, jam sublato edicto divi Augusti, quo cautum fuerat ne pater
filium militem exheredet."

[4] It was sometimes used in a more general sense for *constitutio principis*, as
when Papinian says "Jus . . . civile est quod ex legibus, plebis scitis, senatus
consultis, decretis principum, auctoritate prudentium venit" (*Dig.* 1, 1, 7).

[5] *Dig.* 4, 2, 13 " Exstat enim decretum divi Marci in haec verba, etc. . . .
Caesar dixit, etc."

[6] "Rescript" is properly an *answer* to a letter, but it soon came to be used as
equivalent to *epistola*.   See Kipp *op. cit.* p. 37.

[7] Cf. *Dig.* 1, 16, 4, 5 "imperator noster Antoninus Augustus ad desideria
Asianorum rescripsit " (on the mode in which the proconsul should arrive at the
province of Asia).

and was the chief mode in which the uniformity of its administration and its law was moulded. The rescripts also had, on account of the precision and permanence of their form, a more unquestioned validity, as perpetual enactments, than either the edict or the decree. When the *acta* of an emperor are referred to, it is chiefly these, together with the charters or privileges (*leges datae, beneficia*) that he may have conferred on states, that are intended. The rescripts might be elicited either by the *consultatio* of a doubtful official who was subordinated, either as an administrator or as a judge, to the Emperor, or they might be written in answer to the petition (*libellus, supplicatio*) of one of the parties to a suit. In the latter case they were often a convenient substitute for the personal appearance of the appellant in the Emperor's court.

The edicts, decrees, and rescripts came eventually to be described as "imperial constitutions" (*constitutiones principum*), and although, as we have seen, different degrees of permanence might attach to each of these methods of utterance, to a jurist of the second century they all had the force of law.[1] From this category of enactments with binding force one important class of imperial ordinances seems formally to have been exempted. This class consisted of the *mandata*, or general instructions which the Princeps gave to officials subordinate to himself. In the early Principate they were for the most part issued to the governors of Caesar's provinces, but the gradual encroachment of the Emperor's powers on senatorial administration led to the mandates being issued to proconsuls as well. When the mandate dealt with a precise point of the *jus civile* and was repeated by successive emperors, it doubtless came to have the force of a rescript;[2] but it was more often concerned with the general administrative duties of subordinates, directing them in the doubtful cases of the moment, and, therefore, not necessarily laying down rules of perpetual validity. In one sense the man-

---

[1] Gaius i. 5 " Constitutio principis est, quod imperator decreto vel edicto vel epistola constituit ; nec unquam dubitatum est quin id legis vicem obtineat." Cf. Ulpian in *Dig.* 1, 4, 1, 1 "Quodcumque . . . imperator per epistulam et subscriptionem statuit vel cognoscens decrevit . . . vel edicto praecepit, legem esse constat. Haec sunt quas vulgo constitutiones appellamus."

[2] Thus the soldier's testament was created by a series of mandates : "divus Julius Caesar concessit . . . divus Titus dedit : post hoc Domitianus : postea divus Nerva plenissimam indulgentiam in milites contulit : eamque et Trajanus secutus est et exinde mandatis inseri coepit caput tale. Caput ex mandatis, etc." (Ulpian in *Dig.* 29, 1, 1).

date stands higher than the rescript, for it is as a rule more general in form, and a *mandatum* may be the result of a series of *rescripta* on the same point; but in another sense it stands lower, since it was understood that it might be recalled at any moment by the Princeps who had issued it, and that it might not be observed by his successor. The remarkable differences of treatment to which the Christians were subjected during the Principate was due chiefly to the fact that, so far as this treatment was a concern of the central government at all, it was one directed by mandate.

A review of the powers of the Princeps as exercised through his "constitutions" and his mandates shows that he was not regarded as a true legislative authority, and that the binding force of his ordinances was technically inferior to that possessed by decrees of the Senate. But the theory of legislation was never of much practical importance at Rome. The Romans had lived for centuries mainly under the rule of interpreted or judge-made law, and now the Roman world, enlarged and unified, looked for guidance, not to the *comitia*, which were in decay, or to the Senate, whose contact with the provinces was ever becoming less, but to the one interpreter who was known to every judge and every litigant, and whose utterances could be heard at the farthest ends of the earth. It was the force of circumstances, not any constitutional theory, which made the Princeps the highest of all legislative, because the greatest of all interpreting, authorities.

(ii.) *Jurisdiction.*—If we turn from the legislative to the judicial sphere, we find the same theoretical assertion of a dual control. But it is complicated in this instance by the fact that the Senate is not the sole representative of the Republican side of the administration. The state still asserts itself through old organs such as the praetors and the *judices*, while it has acquired a new organ in the joint activity of consuls and Senate. In a sphere parallel to theirs the Princeps works, sometimes exercising a jurisdiction that is all his own, at other times infringing on their powers, but always occupying a position that exhibits him to the provincial mind as the highest court in the Roman world. The jurisdiction of these several courts must be treated in its separate aspects of civil and criminal, of jurisdiction in the first instance and by way of appeal. The power of reversing sentences and the right to pardon must also be considered.

The civil jurisdiction of the Republic, with its division into *jus* and *judicium*, continued during the greater part of the period of the Principate, and the praetor still gave his legal rulings in the shape of a formula which he submitted to a *judex*. But these *judicia ordinaria* tended gradually to be replaced by the personal cognisance (*cognitio*) of the magistrate, which, exercised on a limited scale by the praetor during the Republic, became a feature of the Emperor's own jurisdiction from the very beginning of the Principate, and was soon extended to provincial governors and to his great delegates, the praefects. This jurisdiction was described as *extra ordinem*, and, like the other form, it admitted of a distinction between magistrate and *judex*. But the new *judex extra ordinem datus*[1] is wholly different in character from the *judex ordinarius* of the older form of process. The new procedure does not admit the distinction between *jus* and *judicium ;* the *judex* is a true delegate, is appointed without a *formula*, and decides on the law as well as on the facts of the case. The sphere of the *cognitio* of the Princeps was probably unlimited in theory, and may have been conferred on the first Emperor by statute.[2] It was a voluntary jurisdiction which any one might request and which the Emperor might refuse. In case of such refusal the case was taken by the praetor. The early Principes, however, showed an unwillingness to interfere with the common-law jurisdiction of the ordinary courts, and confined their attention to cases of equity, such as those springing from matters of trust (*fidei commissum*) and guardianship (*tutela*). But the number even of these cases soon became too vast for the cognisance of the Emperor and his occasional delegates, and we have seen how special praetors were successively appointed to share in this equitable jurisdiction.[3]

The civil courts of appeal existing under the Principate are partly due to a survival of the Republican principle of *appellatio* to a magistrate with the right of veto, partly to the principle (new for Rome, though not for the provinces) of delegated jurisdiction, and partly to a wholly novel principle of an appeal which can com-

---

[1] Gell. xii. 13, 1 "Cum Romae a consulibus judex extra ordinem datus pronuntiare . . . jussus essem."

[2] Dio Cass. li. 19 (in 30 B.C. it was decreed) τὸν Καίσαρα τήν τε ἐξουσίαν τὴν τῶν δημάρχων διὰ βίου ἔχειν . . . ἔκκλητόν τε δικάζειν. It is probable that the last words only describe the establishment of the Princeps as a high court of voluntary jurisdiction. See Greenidge in *Classical Review* viii. p. 144.

[3] p. 368.

pletely reverse the decisions of a lower court, which has its origin
mainly in an attempt at centralising the higher provincial
jurisdiction in Rome. From the decision of a *judex* in the *judicia
ordinaria* there is now, as formerly, no appeal to any authority,
although, as we shall see, the sentences of *judices* might, under
certain conditions, be reversed by the authority either of the
praetor or the Princeps. From the decision of the praetor *in
jure* an appeal lies as before to an equal or higher authority,[1] and
the veto in virtue of the *major potestas* or *majus imperium* is
naturally possessed by the Princeps. When we find Tiberius
present in the praetor's court, he may be there for the purpose of
over-ruling that magistrate's decisions.[2] His presence seems to
show that the limitations of the old *auxilium*—which must be
offered in person[3]—were preserved. Whether the veto was
pronounced in virtue of the *imperium* or in virtue of the *tribunicia
potestas* is a matter of indifference ; how the veto operated is the
really important point. On the analogy of the Republican intercession its effects should have been purely cassatory, and perhaps in
the early Principate this principle was observed. But it must be
remembered that the Princeps is in a very different position
to the vetoing consul or tribune of the Republic, or even to the
Republican praetor who presides over a department other than
that which he controls by his veto. These magistrates can
negative a decision of a lower court, but they cannot replace this
negatived decision by a positive judgment of their own. The
Princeps, on the other hand, has a theoretically unlimited power
of civil jurisdiction.[4] He can, therefore, supplement his negative
by a positive judgment, and this unique combination of the power

---

[1] Paulus in *Dig.* 5, 1, 58 "Judicium solvitur vetante eo qui judicare jusserat
vel etiam eo qui majus imperium in eadem jurisdictione habet." The veto in
virtue of *par potestas* is here omitted on account of its disappearance in the time
of Paulus (*circa* 200 A.D.). See Merkel *Gesch. der klassichen Appellation*
ii. p. 19.

[2] Tac. *Ann.* i. 75 "judiciis adsidebat in cornu tribunalis, ne praetorem curuli
depelleret ; multaque eo coram adversus ambitum et potentium preces constituta" ;
Dio Cass. lvii. 7 ἐπεφοίτα δὲ καὶ ἐπὶ τὰ τῶν ἀρχόντων δικαστήρια, καὶ παρα-
καλούμενος ὑπ' αὐτῶν καὶ ἀπαράκλητος, καὶ ... ἔλεγεν ὅσα ἐδόκει αὐτῷ, ὡς πάρεδρος.
The civil courts are here meant, or at least included ; but it is possible that
Tiberius may often have appeared in them as a self-constituted adviser, not as an
authority to be appealed to ; cf. Suet. *Tib.* 33 "magistratibus pro tribunali
cognoscentibus plerumque se offerebat consiliarium ; adsidebatque juxtim vel
exadversum in parte primori." According to Suetonius (l.c.) he exercised a similar
influence over the jurisdiction of the *quaestiones*.
[3] p. 178.   [4] p. 382.

of vetoing and the power of judging is almost unquestionably the basis of that appeal to Caesar which leads to the reformation of a sentence. It is not improbable that the appeal came to operate in this way even against the praetor, although, even if it did not, the effect of Caesar's veto would really be reformatory. Even the tribunes of the Republic could put pressure on a praetor to induce him to alter his formula,[1] and we can hardly imagine the praetor withstanding the suggestion accompanying a veto pronounced by the holder of the *tribunicia potestas*. The jurisdiction of the municipal towns of Italy was, so far as it was "ordinary" jurisdiction, still under the control of consuls, praetors, and tribunes, at least as late as the reign of Nero.[2] These municipal courts were technically those of the *praetor urbanus*, and the Princeps probably interfered (if at all) with their jurisdiction only through his control of the rulings of the praetor in Rome. We shall trace elsewhere the mode in which the extraordinary jurisdiction of one of Caesar's delegates, the praefect of the city, came to encroach on the ordinary jurisdiction of the Roman courts.

Another method of appeal springs from the principle of delegated jurisdiction. Caesar, when he cares to exercise civil jurisdiction, can perform it either personally or through mandataries, and there is necessarily an appeal from the mandatary to the higher authority, unless this authority distinctly asserts that no appeal will lie.[3] The appeal in such a case, if it is upheld, issues not merely in the veto but in the reform of the sentence of the mandatary. Caesar may, of course, employ such delegates as he pleases. Augustus used the *praetor urbanus* and *consulares* for home and foreign *appellationes*,[4] a word which in this context

---

[1] Cic. *pro Tullio* 16, 38 "quid attinuit te tam multis verbis a praetore postulare ut adderet in judicium 'INJURIA,' et, quia non impetrasses, tribunos plebis appellare et hic in judicio queri praetoris iniquitatem quod de injuria non addiderit?" So the tribunician veto might be employed to elicit an exception. Cic. *Acad. Prior.* ii. 30, 97 "Tribunum aliquem censeo adeant [*al.* videant]: a me istam exceptionem nunquam impetrabunt."

[2] Tac. *Ann.* xiii. 28 (A.D. 56). See Appendix.

[3] Dio Cass. lix. 8 ὁ μὲν γὰρ Τιβέριος οὕτως αὐτὸν (Silanus) ἐτίμησεν, ὥστε μήτ' ἔκκλητόν ποτε ἀπ' αὐτοῦ δικάσαι ἐθελῆσαι, ἀλλ' ἐκείνῳ πάντα αὖθις τὰ τοιαῦτα ἐγχειρίσαι. We do not know what position Silanus held. If, as is generally supposed, he was consul, the reference may be to appeals from jurisdiction in *fidei commissa* delegated by the Princeps to the consul.

[4] Suet. *Aug.* 33 "Appellationes quotannis urbanorum quidem litigatorum praetori delegabat urbano: at provincialium consularibus viris, quos singulos cujusque provinciae negotiis praeposuisset." That the conjecture *praefecto*

probably means simply "requests for cognisance" made to the Princeps. The imperial jurisdiction in matters of trust (*fidei commissa*) was delegated to consuls or to praetors.[1]   But, apart from this regular delegation, the Emperor might instruct any one to be his *judex extra ordinem*, when he did not care to take the case himself.

The appeal from provincial governors was, so far as the public or senatorial provinces were concerned, the result of a conscious striving after unity of administration, although it was not wholly unconnected with Republican precedents; with respect to Caesar's provinces, it was a direct consequence of the fact that the governors of these provinces were merely his legates, although the frequency with which the appeal was allowed shows the same striving for a centralised jurisdiction. The principle which in the early Principate regulated appeals from the public provinces was that these should come invariably to the Senate, and this principle of the dyarchy, which tended to be disregarded, was emphatically restated by Nero at the commencement of his reign.[2]   It was probably a development of a Republican custom in accordance with which certain important cases had been summoned from the provinces to Rome by the consuls and Senate (*Romam revocatio*);[3] but this principle seems to have been now extended to include true cases of appeal as well as cases of denial of jurisdiction. When such appeals in civil matters came to Rome, it is probable that the Senate delegated the hearing of them to the consuls.

The fact that this principle of the appellate jurisdiction of the Senate required restatement in 54 A.D. prepares us for the ultimate neglect into which it fell. It is certain that by the close of the second and beginning of the third century, Caesar, or his great delegate the praefect of the praetorian guard, is the universal court of appeal for the whole provincial world. This result cannot be attached to any power possessed by the Princeps

delegabat urbis is untenable has been pointed out by Mommsen (*Staatsr.* ii. p. 985 note 1).

[1] For the delegation to praetors see p. 368 ; for that to consuls cf. Quint. *Inst. Or.* iii. 6, 70 "Non debes apud praetorem petere fidei commissum sed apud consules, major enim praetoria cognitione summa est."

[2] Tac. *Ann.* xiii. 4 "teneret antiqua munia senatus, consulum tribunalibus Italia et publicae provinciae adsisterent."

[3] Cic. *in Verr.* iii. 60, 138 ; *ad Fam.* xiii. 26, 3 ; *Fragmentum Atestinum* (Bruns *Fontes*) l. 10.

over the proconsuls of the public provinces; for the statement that he possessed *majus imperium* over such governors[1] can only mean that in any collision of authority the Princeps is not inferior to the proconsul. The world-wide appellate jurisdiction of the Princeps was a thing of very gradual growth, and it originated, not from any idea of his prerogative, but from the irresistible tendency of provincial governors, senatorial as well as imperial, to refer their difficulties to the highest interpreting authority in the Roman world, the Princeps and his *consilium* of judicial advisers. It is no wonder that the man who became the central source of law should also become the universal authority for its interpretation in detail.

When we turn to criminal jurisdiction, we find that here too there are three sources of *jus*. The Republic is represented by the *quaestiones perpetuae* with their praetors and equestrian *judices*, and also by the new criminal jurisdiction which has been attached to the consuls and the Senate; the Principate is represented by the jurisdiction of the Princeps and his delegates. The jurisdiction of the *quaestiones*, so long as it continued,[2] proceeded on the old lines. They judged except where the case, through a request of the parties accepted by a higher court, was exempted from their jurisdiction. The higher courts, which might stop their jurisdiction by accepting a case, were those of the Senate and the Princeps. Both of these were high courts of voluntary jurisdiction, and no appeal was permitted from one to the other.[3] Voluntary jurisdiction is by its nature difficult to define; but custom tended to limit the Senate's cognisance to certain classes of cases. These classes were determined either by the position of the accused or the nature of the offence. The Senate tried ordinary crimes, such as murder, adultery, incest, when they were committed by the members of the upper classes in society,[4] and there was a growing feeling, which subsequently

---

[1] When the Senate granted the *proconsulare imperium* to Augustus in 23 B.C. ἐν τῷ ὑπηκόῳ τὸ πλεῖον τῶν ἑκασταχόθι ἀρχόντων ἰσχύειν ἐπέτρεψεν (Dio Cass. liii. 32). Cf. Ulpian in *Dig.* 1, 16, 8 [" (proconsul) majus imperium in ea provincia habet omnibus post principem"] and in 1, 18, 4. It is a passive rather than an active *majus imperium* that is here contemplated. The whole scheme of the provincial dyarchy rested on the assumption that there should be no relations between the proconsul and the Princeps. [2] p. 368.

[3] Ulpian in *Dig.* 49, 2, 1, 2 "sciendum est appellari a senatu non posse principem, idque oratione divi Hadriani effectum." It was doubtless the original principle, confirmed and not created by Hadrian.

[4] Tac. *Ann.* iii. 14, xvi. 8; Suet. *Aug.* 5.

obtained something like legal recognition, that a senator should be tried by his peers.[1] But the character of the offence was the chief determinant of the Senate's jurisdiction. Any offence of a directly political character, even in the early Principate a breach of a treaty by a foreign prince,[2] tended to come before it. It was the usual court for extortion or other misuse of powers by provincial governors ;[3] it judged offences against the majesty of the state ;[4] and when the majesty of the Princeps had become identified with that of the state, it might be employed as a convenient engine of judicial tyranny.[5] Its utility was assisted by the unlimited and arbitrary character of its jurisdiction. It interpreted while it judged ; it might extend the incidence of a law and frame new penalties ; it might even punish in cases where no penalty was fixed by law ;[6] and the principle, forbidden in the *quaestiones*, of uniting several crimes in the same charge, was here admitted.[7] This jurisdiction was technically,

---

[1] There was no legal principle of the kind. According to Dio Cassius (liii. 17) the monarchical power extended so far ὥστε καὶ ἐντὸς τοῦ πωμηρίου καὶ τοὺς ἱππέας καὶ τοὺς βουλευτὰς θανατοῦν δύνασθαι, and a senator, like Calpurnius Piso in 20 A.D., might be brought before the Emperor (Tac. *Ann.* iii. 10). But Septimius Severus permitted a *senatus consultum* to be passed that the Emperor should not be allowed to put a senator to death without the will of the Senate (Dio Cass. lxxiv. 2 ; *Vita Severi* 7). The principle had been stated earlier by Hadrian (*Vita Hadriani* 7 "juravit se nunquam senatorem nisi ex senatus sententia puniturum ").

[2] Augustus in 29 B.C. brought Antiochus of Commagene, Tiberius in A.D. 17 Archelaus of Cappadocia before the Senate (Dio Cass. lii. 43, lvii. 17 ; Tac. *Ann.* ii. 42). In A.D. 19 Rhescuporis of Thrace was accused there (Tac. *Ann.* ii. 67).

[3] Cases of extortion are to be found in Tac. *Ann.* iii. 66, xii. 59 ; *Hist.* iv. 45. In A.D. 23 we find the imperial *procurator* (*patrimonii*) of Asia brought before the Senate for exceeding his powers (Tac. *Ann.* iv. 15).

[4] Tac. *Ann.* iv. 13 (A.D. 23) "Carsidius Sacerdos, reus tamquam frumento hostem Tacfarinatem juvisset, absolvitur, ejusdemque criminis C. Gracchus."

[5] Amongst the prosecutions for treason against the Princeps which disfigure the reign of Tiberius we may mention those against Libo Drusus (Tac. *Ann.* ii. 27 ff.), against Cremutius Cordus (ib. iv. 34, 35), and against Sejanus (Dio Cass. lviii. 9, 10).

[6] In A.D. 37 we find that a mother, who had caused her son to commit suicide, "accusata in senatu . . . urbe . . . in decem annos prohibita est " (Tac. *Ann.* vi. 49). In A.D. 61 we find interdiction from Italy pronounced against a man for a kind of *praevaricatio*, "quod reos, ne apud praefectum urbis arguerentur, ad praetorem detulisset " (ib. xiv. 41).

[7] Quintil. *Inst. Or.* iii. 10, 1 ; vii. 2, 20. For instances see Tac. *Ann.* ii. 50, iv. 21 ; Plin. *Ep.* ii. 11, 3 ff. In the last passage we find the question of the legality of this procedure raised ("Respondit Fronto Catius deprecatusque est ne quid ultra repetundarum legem quaereretur . . . Magna contentio, magni utrimque clamores, aliis cognitionem senatus lege conclusam, aliis liberam solutamque dicentibus ").

perhaps, a *cognitio* of the consuls.[1] But the Senate was their constant advising body, and the sentence took the form of a *senatus consultum*. We shall soon see how the Emperor's presence at the board enabled him to influence a jurisdiction which was technically independent of his control.

The voluntary jurisdiction of the Princeps in criminal matters was theoretically unlimited, and could be exercised at any time or in any place. It rested with him whether he would undertake the cognisance (*cognitionem suscipere*) at the request of one of the parties,[2] or refer the case to the ordinary court, that is, to the *quaestio* competent to try it. The relations of the two high courts of voluntary jurisdiction to the ordinary court of necessary jurisdiction, are admirably exemplified by the procedure adopted in the trial of Piso for the murder of Germanicus (A.D. 19-20). It is at the outset assumed that the case, which is one of poisoning, will come before the special commission established by the *lex Cornelia de veneficis*. But the Emperor's cognisance is sought by the prosecutor, and Tiberius and his *consilium* actually listen to the preliminaries of the trial. But the Emperor soon sees how invidious it will be to pronounce judgment in a case in which the murder of his own nephew and adopted son is the subject of investigation, and he, therefore, sends the matter unprejudiced to the Senate with a request that they should exercise their voluntary jurisdiction — a request which, coming from the Princeps, it was practically, although not legally, impossible for the Senate to decline.[3]

But, although any request for cognisance might be listened

---

[1] It is possible, however, that the Senate was held to continue the extraordinary criminal jurisdiction of the *comitia*. Tacitus certainly regards the *cognitio* as belonging to the Senate (*Ann.* ii. 28 "Statim corripit reum, adit consules, cognitionem senatus poscit").

[2] Plin. *Ep.* vi. 31, 8 (in a case of a forgery of a will) "Heredes, cum Caesar ('Trajanus) esset in Dacia, communiter epistula scripta, petierant ut susciperet cognitionem."

[3] Tac. *Ann.* ii. 79 "Marsus . . . Vibius nuntiavit Pisoni Romam ad dicendam causam veniret. Ille eludens respondit adfuturum, ubi praetor, qui de veneficiis quaereret, reo atque accusatoribus diem prodixisset"; ib. iii. 10 "petitum . . . est a principe cognitionem exciperet ; quod ne reus quidem abnuebat, studia populi et patrum metuens . . . haud fallebat Tiberium moles cognitionis quaque ipse fama distraheretur. Igitur paucis familiarium adhibitis minas accusantium et hinc preces audit integramque causam ad senatum remittit." " Remittit " does not imply that the Senate was bound to take the case. For the technically voluntary nature of its jurisdiction cf. ib. iv. 21, xiii. 10, where we find the expressions "receptus est reus," "recepti sunt inter reos."

to, the Princeps usually confined his personal jurisdiction to certain spheres. These included serious crimes committed by members of the upper ranks in society, but especially offences committed by imperial servants or by the officers of the army.[1] The Emperor might, of course, delegate this jurisdiction, although the delegation of special cases seems to have been unusual.[2] On the other hand, the regular delegation of certain kinds of offences is frequent enough, and is the basis of the criminal jurisdiction of the Emperor's servants, the various praefects who presided over the city, the praetorian guard, the corn-supply, and the watch.[3]

A peculiar right of the Princeps to try cases from the provinces in which the lives of Roman citizens were involved may, perhaps, have grown up during the Principate. It certainly does not exist during the early portion of this period. Instances of the maintenance of the Republican principle, that capital charges against Roman citizens should be sent to Rome, are indeed furnished by such cases as those of the Bithynian Christians in the reign of Trajan,[4] and perhaps of St. Paul's appeal in the reign of Nero ;[5] and perhaps such a demand for a trial at Rome was accompanied by a request, usually accepted, to be tried before the Princeps ; but there are as many instances which prove the unlimited jurisdiction of the provincial governor, at least when dealing with ordinary crimes. Thus Marius Priscus scourged and strangled a Roman knight in the province of Africa, and Galba, when governor of Tarraconensis, crucified a guardian, who was a Roman citizen, for poisoning his ward.[6] There are, however, signs that the right to kill (*jus gladii*), if this expression refers to ordinary as well as to military jurisdiction, was specially

---

[1] Dio Cass. lii. 22, 33. A case of adultery of a centurion with a tribune's wife comes before the Emperor. Trajan stated the ground on which he tried this case (Plin. *Ep.* vi. 31, 6 "Caesar et nomen centurionis et commemorationem disciplinae militaris sententiae adjecit, ne omnes ejusmodi causas revocare ad se videretur ").

[2] An instance is mentioned by Pliny (*Ep.* vii. 6, 8 "mater, amisso filio . . . libertos ejus eosdemque coheredes suos falsi et veneficii reos detulerat ad principem judicemque impetraverat Julium Servianum ").

[3] See the section on the functionaries of the Princeps (p. 406 sq.).

[4] Plin. *ad Traj.* 96, 4 " quia cives Romani erant, adnotavi in urbem remittendos."

[5] It is not properly an appeal but a denial of jurisdiction. But on what ground the jurisdiction of the procurator was denied is not clear. The Roman citizenship, in virtue of which St. Paul claimed exemption from scourging at Philippi and Jerusalem, is not mentioned here. See *Class. Rev.* x. p. 231.

[6] Plin. *Ep.* ii. 11 ; Suet. *Galba* 9.

given by the Emperor at least to the administrators of his own provinces,[1] which shows that the frequent requests of one who stood "before Caesar's judgment seat" to be tried by Caesar had issued in some standing rule. At a later time, when the universal criminal appeal to Caesar had grown up, certain persons —senators, officers, and decurions—are exempted from capital or severe penalties pronounced by provincial governors,[2] and this jurisdiction, reserved for the Princeps, was exercised by the *praefectus praetorio* without appeal.

The Princeps was (especially in the early Principate) by no means a universal court of criminal appeal for the whole Roman world. There was no appeal to him from the *quaestiones perpetuae*, although he may have had some right of rescinding the inequitable judgments of such courts (*in integrum restitutio*) ; nor is there theoretically any appeal from the Senate, although the Princeps possesses, through the *tribunicia potestas*, a practical power of rescinding the judgments of that body.[3] In the matter of jurisdiction delegated to his praefects, the appeal lies unless he wills it away, as he does in favour of the *praefectus praetorio*. With respect to the provinces, the principle of the dual control, which we have illustrated with reference to civil jurisdiction,[4] must have originally been supposed to hold good with reference to criminal jurisdiction as well ; but the dyarchy was, in this particular, ultimately dissolved. By the end of the second century Caesar, represented in most cases by his inappellable praetorian praefect, was the highest court of criminal appeal for the whole Roman world.

Besides the right of appeal, there is in most political societies a power residing somewhere which is, or approximates to be, a

---

[1] For its attachment to procurators and to persons with extraordinary commands see the instances given by Mommsen (*Staatsr.* ii. p. 270). So the praefectures of the guard, the *vigiles* and the fleet, are *honores juris gladii* (*Vita Alex.* 49). In the case of ordinary provincial governors it is, perhaps, safer to say that the *jus gladii* is possessed by them, or permitted to them, rather than that it was attached to them by the Princeps (Ulp. in *Dig.* 1, 18, 6, 8 "qui universas provincias regunt, jus gladii habent et in metallum dandi potestas iis permissa est").

[2] Dio Cass. lii. 22, 33 ; *Dig.* 48, 19, 27, 1 and 2.

[3] Even by Tiberius' reign this procedure had become so formal that a rule was framed for its exercise. A definite interval was prescribed within which the Princeps might consider the request for the intercession (Tac. *Ann.* iii. 51 [A.D. 21] "factum senatus consultum, ne decreta patrum ante diem *decimum* ad aerarium deferrentur idque vitae spatium damnatis prorogaretur" ; cf. Dio Cass. lvii. 20 ; Suet. *Tib.* 75).

[4] p. 385.

power of pardon. It is sometimes regarded as a signal attribute of sovereignty, but somewhat improperly, since the power of rescinding sentences or of ordering a new trial may reside in a mere executive authority, such as a court of cassation, which possesses none of the other attributes which we usually associate with a sovereign. In the constitution of the Principate it is certainly not regarded as a sovereign right, for the power is limited and, like most of the manifestations of public life, is theoretically divided between the organs of the Republic and the Princeps.

The Senate possessed no general power of pardon beyond the right, inherited from the Republic, of annulling charges and thus releasing people, who are on their trial, on certain public and festal occasions.[1] This right of declaring *abolitiones publicae* was one expression of its right of amnesty.[2] But the Senate had besides, as a high court, the right of rescinding its own former sentences (*in integrum restitutio*).[3] It might also be occasionally consulted by the Princeps on the advisability of his rescinding the sentences of the imperial courts—those, as a rule, which had been pronounced by former Emperors.[4] But such consultation was not a right of the Senate, but merely a concession of the Emperor.

The Emperor, in his relation to the courts of Rome, possessed the full power of *restitutio* only over his own sentences and those of his predecessors in office.[5] He had no right of interference in the way of *restitutio* with the judgments of the Senate, for the power which he possessed, of preventing the reception of the charge[6] or the execution of the judgment, was merely a

---

[1] "Ob laetitiam aliquam vel honorem domus divinae vel ex aliqua causa, ex qua senatus censuit abolitionem reorum fieri " (Ulp. in *Dig.* 48, 16, 12 ; cf. 48, 3, 2, 1). Domitian by an edict declared that such *abolitiones* did not extend to slaves who were in custody awaiting trial (*Dig.* 48, 16, 16 ; cf. 48, 3, 2, 1).

[2] p. 249.

[3] Ulp. in *Dig.* 3, 1, 1, 10 "De qua autem restitutione praetor loquitur ? Utrum de ea quae a principe vel a senatu ? Pomponius quaerit : et putat de ea restitutione sensum, quam princeps vel senatus indulsit."

[4] It is said of Claudius (Suet. *Claud.* 12) "neminem exulum nisi ex senatus auctoritate restituit " ; and of Antoninus Pius (*Vita* 6) "His quos Hadrianus damnaverat in senatu indulgentias petit, dicens etiam ipsum Hadrianum hoc fuisse facturum."

[5] Such acts are mentioned under Claudius (Dio Cass. lx. 4), Otho (Tac. *Hist.* i. 90 ; Plut. *Otho* 1), Vitellius (Tac. *Hist.* ii. 92), Vespasian (Dio Cass. lxvi. 9), Nerva (Plin. *Ep.* iv. 9, 2), Antoninus Caracalla (*Vita* 3), and Gordian (Herodian vii. 6, 4).

[6] Tac. *Ann.* ii. 50 "(Tiberius) liberavit . . . Appuleiam lege majestatis, adulterii graviorem poenam deprecatus."

practical and accidental consequence of the application of the tribunician power to a decree of the Senate.[1] Nor is there any distinct evidence of his possessing the power of rescinding the sentences of the *quaestiones perpetuae*, although interference with these on equitable grounds is not improbable, and seems, where permitted, to have taken the form of consent to a new trial (*retratactio*).[2] With respect to the ordinary civil courts, the praetor possessed the power of equitable restitution,[3] but there is evidence that the Princeps, also as a court of equity, might rescind inequitable sentences both of ordinary *judices* and of *centumviri.*[4]

The Princeps also possessed a power of quashing indictments (*abolitio*), which does not seem to have been confined to his own jurisdiction, but to have been extended to other criminal courts as well.[5] Its origin may be explained on two grounds. The first depends on the fact that it was possible to have any case brought to the Emperor's court, on the request either of the prosecutor or of the accused. The Emperor might, after listening to the preliminaries, refuse to hear such a case without "remitting" it to another court,[6] and it is very improbable that any other authority would listen for a moment to a prosecution to which the Emperor had declined to attend. The dismissal of the case by the Princeps was practically a power of abolition ; but the right might have been exercised even more directly. Republican history furnishes an instance of a tribune prohibiting the president of a *quaestio* from receiving a charge,[7] and it is obvious that the *tribunicia potestas* of the Princeps might have been exercised in the same way to impede the first step in the jurisdiction of every criminal court.

With respect to the provinces, just as the criminal appeal finally passes to the Emperor,[8] so the revision of the sentences of

---

[1] p. 390.

[2] Gordian is spoken of as παλινδικίαν διδοὺς τοῖς ἀδίκως κατακριθεῖσι (Herodian vii. 6, 4).

[3] Ulp. in *Dig.* 3, 1, 1, 10.

[4] Suet. *Claud.* 14 "(Claudius) iis, qui apud privatos judices pius petendo formula excidissent, restituit actiones"; *Dom.* 8 "(Domitianus) ambitiosas centumvirorum sententias rescidit."

[5] This power was employed by Augustus (Suet. *Aug.* 32 "Diuturnorum reorum . . . nomina abolevit"), Gaius (Suet. *Calig.* 15 "criminum . . . si quae residua ex priore tempore manebant, omnium gratiam fecit"; cf. Dio Cass. lix. 6), Vespasian (Dio Cass. lxvi. 9), and Domitian (Suet. *Dom.* 9).

[6] p. 388.   [7] Cic. *in Vat.* 14, 33.   [8] p. 390.

the local courts, where revision is suggested by the judge,[1] as well as the infliction of punishments denied to the judge—such as the capital penalty on decurions or deportation on any one[2] —centre finally in the hands of the Princeps. All right of revision and restitution is not, indeed, denied to the provincial governor,[3] but while this was finally restricted by certain well-defined rules, the Emperor's power of restitution appears ulti-mately to have been unlimited. "This power might be so employed by the Emperor as to take the form of a free pardon,[4] but theoretically it was merely an equitable assistance. As a legally unlimited power of rescinding sentences, it approaches very nearly to a power of pardon ; but it is an executive duty rather than a sovereign right, and we search in vain in the Principate for a power of pardon regarded as an admitted con-stitutional right of a sovereign."[5]

(iii.) *Administration.*—The principle of a dual control is as manifest in administrative matters as in any other. The spheres of administration are Rome, Italy, and the Provinces. With respect to the first two it is clear that one of the few justifications for the maintenance of Republican government was that, by leaving the ordinary administrative duties connected with Rome and Italy to the Senate and ordinary magistrates, it enabled the Princeps to concentrate his attention on his proper sphere, the foreign and provincial world. But even the provinces did not deserve the undivided attention of the Princeps. Those whose administration presented no special difficulties, and which required no military force, might still be left to the care of the Roman

---

[1] *Dig.* 48, 19, 9, 11 "referre ad principem debet, ut ex auctoritate ejus poena aut permutetur aut liberaretur."

[2] The capital punishment of decurions was prohibited by Hadrian (*Dig.* 48, 19, 15), and the earliest *mandata*, directing the procedure of governors in such cases, proceed from the *divi fratres* (ib. 48, 19, 27, 1 and 2). The punishment of deportation had been confined to the Princeps and the praefects of the prae-torian guard and the city by the time of Septimius Severus (ib. 48, 19, 2, 1 and 48, 22, 6, 1 ; cf. § 7).

[3] Pliny often raises this question in his correspondence with Trajan (31 [40], 4 ; 56 [64], 3 ; 57 [65], 1). The passages seem to show (i.) that there was at the time no fixed rule defining the governor's power of *restitutio*, at least in public provinces ; (ii.) that *restitutio* by a governor was felt to be permissible in certain cases.

[4] A passage in Justinian's *Code* (9, 51, 1) shows us Antoninus (Caracalla) saying to a man, who had been deported to an island, "Restituo te in integrum provinciae tuae."

[5] Greenidge in *Classical Review* viii. p. 437.

people. This division of responsibility might have continued a reality had the Principate continued to be what it was in origin—a provisional government by an individual who had little personal assistance at his command. But as this rule gradually assumed the form of a huge government department, overshadowing all others, with an organised civil service which replaced the assistance furnished by freedmen and slaves, it not unnaturally tended to encroach on the Republican spheres of administration. The motive for the tendency was chiefly the fact that the Princeps was, in the eyes of all men, not the head of a department but of the state, and a responsibility, which he would gladly have disclaimed, for the acts of all officials, even those of Republican departments, was thus thrust upon him.[1] There is no particular ground for believing that the Princeps managed departments such as Rome or Italy better than the Republican officials. The important fact was that public opinion forced him to manage them, whether for good or ill.

(iv.) *Finance.*—Finance at Rome was always so intimately bound up with provincial control, that the division of the provinces into public and imperial implied of itself the existence of two separate financial departments. The Senate still asserts control over the *aerarium*, and gives instructions to the guardians of the chest. The qualification of these guardians varied from time to time. The dictator Caesar had in 45 B.C. given the charge to two aediles, but quaestors seem again to have been the presidents of the treasury[2] until Augustus in 28 B.C. instituted two *praefecti aerarii Saturni*, chosen yearly from the ex-praetors by the Senate.[3] Even this change was short-lived, and the praefects were soon replaced by two of the praetors of the year who received their *provincia* by lot.[4] Claudius in 44 A.D. restored the Republican method of administration through quaestors; but these were no longer to be annual officials designated by lot, but to be chosen by the Emperor for a period of three years.[5] Finally under Nero (56 A.D.) the elements of

---

[1] Cf. Tac. *Ann.* iii. 53 (quoted p. 352).
[2] Dio Cass. xliii. 48 ; Momms. *Staatsr.* ii. p. 557.
[3] Tac. *Ann.* xiii. 29 ; Dio Cass. liii. 2 ; Suet. *Aug.* 36.
[4] Tac. l.c. ; Dio Cass. liii. 32.
[5] Tac. l.c. ; Dio Cass. lx. 24 ; Suet. *Claud.* 24. For the election by the Princeps see the inscription to Ti. Domitius Decidius "electo (Mommsen, "adlecto" Wilmanns) a T. Claudio Caesare . . . qui primus quaestor per triennium citra ordinem praeesset aerario Saturni " (Wilmanns n. 1135).

the Augustan and the Claudian arrangements were combined [1] in the provision that two ex-praetors should be appointed as praefects of the treasury, but that these should be named, generally for three years, by the Princeps.[2] The fact that the Princeps appointed the guardians of the public chest was by no means an assertion that he controlled its funds, and, although his indirect influence on the *aerarium* was unquestionably great, this treasury still remained in principle under the direction of the Senate alone. Even in the second century it voted a loan to Marcus Aurelius for carrying on a war.[3]

The Princeps was rendered financially independent of the Senate through the possession of his own treasury (*fiscus* or *fiscus Caesaris*),[4] into which flowed the revenues from his own provinces, certain dues owed by the public provinces, and some extraordinary revenues, such as the confiscated goods of condemned criminals or lapsed inheritances (*bona damnatorum, bona vacantia*), in the claim to which the *fiscus* finally replaced the *aerarium*. The Princeps was the owner of the *fiscus*, but was regarded as a trustee of the wealth which it contained. To sue the *fiscus* was to sue the Princeps; but, although he was the sole subject of rights in relation to this treasury, he did not regard the money which it contained as though it were his own private property. Even in the early Principate there is evidence of the existence of crown property (*patrimonium* or *patrimonium privatum*), the use of which for private purposes was vested in the Princeps.[5] The *patrimonium* doubtless commenced by being the strictly personal property of the first family of Caesars, and much of it was acquired by bequest;[6] but, when the Principate had ceased to be hereditary in the Julian line, it seems to have

---

[1] Momms. *Staatsr.* ii. p. 559.

[2] Tac. l.c. ; Mommsen l.c.

[3] Dio Cass. lxxi. 33 καὶ χρήματα ἐκ τοῦ δημοσίου ᾔτησε τὴν βουλήν.

[4] For the meaning of the word—the great basket in which money was kept in the state treasuries—see Mommsen *Staatsr.* ii. p. 998 n. 1. At the beginning of the Principate there were, perhaps, *fisci* rather than a *fiscus* (cf. Suet. *Aug.* 101), although there must always have been a central controlling department.

[5] Tiberius in 23 B.C. says of Lucilius Capito, procurator of Asia, "non se jus nisi in servitia et pecunias familiares dedisse" (Tac. *Ann.* iv. 15). He was doubtless a "procurator patrimonii." Cf. Tac. *Ann.* xii. 60 ("cum Claudius libertos, quos rei familiari praefecerat, sibique et legibus adaequaverit") ; xiii. 1 "P. Celer eques Romanus et Helius libertus, rei familiari principis in Asia inpositi."

[6] Marquardt *Staatsverwaltung* ii. p. 256.

been looked on as crown property, which was heritable only by the successor to the throne. The bequeathal of this property, which was implied when the Princeps selected an heir, might thus be regarded as a mode of designation; although, if the destined heir did not succeed, the *patrimonium* passed to his successful rival. It was probably due to the uncertainty of the tenure of the *patrimonium* that with Septimius Severus we find the creation of a new aggregate of private property, the *res privata*,[1] the administration of which was kept quite distinct from that of the *patrimonium*. All Caesar's property, whether held in trust for the state or for the crown, or applied to the needs of his family, was equally administered by his own private servants. Of these we shall speak when we deal with the functionaries of the Princeps as a whole.

Another treasury under imperial control, which served a public purpose, was that established for supplying pensions to discharged soldiers. The want of it had been severely felt in the last years of the Republic, when the mercenary army looked for its final rewards to plunder or the political influence of its generals; and, when Augustus created a professional army by the introduction of the long-service system, he found it necessary to establish a pension fund for those who had given twenty of the best years of their life to the practice of arms. The result was the *aerarium militare*, which the Emperor endowed with a large capital,[2] and to which, as fixed sources of revenue, the two taxes of the *vicesima hereditatum* and the *centesima rerum venalium* were assigned.[3] The administration of this chest was given to three praefects (*praefecti aerarii militaris*), who remained three years in office, and were chosen from ex-praetors, originally by lot but later by the Princeps.[4]

---

[1] *Vita Severi* 12 "interfectis innumeris Abani partium viris . . . omnium bona publicata sunt . . . Tuncque primum privatarum rerum procuratio constituta est." The ordinarily accepted view of the relations of these two departments to one another is that of Hirschfeld and Marquardt, viz. that the *patrimonium* was the inalienable crown property, the *res privata* the strictly personal property of the Princeps. Karlowa (*Rechtsgeshichte* i. p. 505) takes an exactly oppositive view of their relations, based partly on the fact that extant inscriptions show the *procurator rationis privatae* to have had a higher rank than the *procurator patrimonii*.

[2] *Mon. Anc.* iii. 39 "HS milliens et septingentiens (170 million sesterces) ex patrimonio meo detuli."

[3] Dio Cass. lv. 25 ; Tac. *Ann.* i. 78.

[4] Dio Cass. l.c.; cf. Tac. *Ann.* v. 8 (vi. 3).

(v.) *Cultus.*—In matters of religion and worship the dyarchy
is again apparent. So far as the state had a religious head, the
Princeps, in virtue of the chief pontificate, occupied this position,
and we have seen the influence which this headship gave him.[1]
But the Senate had not lost all its control over the cultus of
the community or its right to pronounce on foreign worships,
when their social merits or their legality were in question.
It is the Senate that is consulted on the growth of Egyptian
and Jewish worship at Rome,[2] and on the right of asylum
in the provinces.[3] Claudius questions it on the subject of the
restoration of the college of *haruspices*,[4] and Aurelian asks it
for a pontifex to dedicate the great temple of the sun-god at
Palmyra.[5] So far as the appointment to the great priestly
colleges was not controlled by the Princeps, the gift of this
honour was now in the hands of the Senate.

(vi.) *Coinage.*—The right of coinage, although its possession
by a state may be taken as a mark of sovereign rights being
enjoyed by that community, is scarcely a significant mark of the
sovereignty within a state. Whether the Senate or the Princeps
possessed this right would make little difference to the theory
of the constitution. As a fact, the right was possessed by both
powers, and was an additional illustration of the principle of the
dyarchy. From the year 15 B.C. the Princeps undertakes the
gold and silver coinage, the Senate that of copper. The possession of the latter was a privilege in so far as the exchange value
of copper was higher than its intrinsic value, and payments of
any amount could be made in what was really a token currency.[6]

We have now exhibited the system of dual control as it
existed in all the chief departments of the state. It would be
easy to prove that in almost every particular it might be made
a fiction. The senatorial power of legislation is directed to so
large an extent by the imperial initiative that the *oratio* of the
Princeps is sometimes cited in place of the decree of the Senate
to which it gave birth;[7] the independence of senatorial jurisdiction is often infringed by the tribunician power of the

---

[1] p. 351.   [2] Tac. *Ann.* ii. 85.   [3] ib. iii. 61.
[4] ib. xi. 15.   [5] *Vita Aurel.* 31.
[6] Mommsen *Römisches Münzwesen* pp. 742 ff. He shows that the transitory
usurpation of the copper coinage by Nero was due to the same desire of making a
profit as his reduction of the value of silver.
[7] *Dig.* 2, 15, 8 "divus Marcus oratione in senatu recitata effecit ne, etc." Cf.
24, 1, 23 ; 27, 9, 1.

Emperor, while his authority is directly or remotely in conflict with that of the other courts at every turn; his praefects tend to usurp the administration of Rome and Italy, while his procurators are a check on the activity of the proconsuls of the public provinces; his influence over the *aerarium* can be asserted whenever he cares to take the trouble to initiate or support in the Senate the proposal of a grant of money to himself.[1] But such a control of departments, if wisely asserted, by no means rendered the dyarchy nugatory. Under a judicious prince the Republican constitution was sufficient for its own sphere in perhaps ninety-nine cases out of every hundred; because in the hundredth some pressure was felt from the head of the state, we cannot pronounce the dyarchy to be a fiction. If the control by the Princeps is brutally and unwisely, however legally, asserted, he is by common consent not a Princeps but a tyrant. We must judge the Principate by its best names, by a Nerva, a Trajan, a Marcus Aurelius, an Alexander, a Decius. In the reigns of all these princes the dyarchy is a living thing. If it is objected that it becomes a living thing merely through a concession of the Princeps, the answer is that this concession was certainly not pictured by these Emperors to themselves as an act of grace, but was regarded as mere obedience to the constitution; and to maintain the theory that a constitution which demands obedience from the wise is a palpable fiction because it cannot enforce obedience on the headstrong, is to wring a strange admission from political science.

§ 6. *The Senatorial and the Equestrian Nobility*

Although the authority of the Princeps rested virtually on the support of the army, his position might have been unsafe, and would have been embarrassing, had he not secured for the work of administration at home and abroad an official class, that was dependent to some extent on imperial creation and, therefore, worked in harmony with himself. The old Republican nobility, so far as it had not been extinguished, might be utilised; but it could be employed only by being kept in fetters, and by power being given to the Princeps to recruit its ranks at his will. We

[1] Tacitus (*Ann.* vi. 2 [8]) remarks, with reference to proposals carried in the Senate in 32 A.D., "et bona Sejani ablata aerario ut in fiscum cogerentur, tanquam referret."

have already considered his control of office, his right of *adlectio*, and his power of creating Patricians. But a wider power, cognate to the gift of the Patriciate, was needed, to make him the patenter of a nobility from which alone senators and magistrates were to be chosen. Such a power had been usurped by Augustus, and the recognition of a " senatorial order " was its result. Perhaps in the later Republic society had already recognised the right of the prospective senator to wear the broad scarlet stripe (*latus clavus*) on his tunic, but the right became more clearly defined with the commencement of the Principate; and the *laticlavii* are prospective senators and holders of Republican offices, either recognised as such by the Princeps or endowed by him with the symbol of senatorial rank. The senator's son possesses the right to wear the *latus clavus* and to attend the meetings of the *curia*, in which he will one day take an active part;[1] the eques to whom the symbol has been given may qualify for the Senate through the vigintivirate and the quaestorship. The first steps to office and to the Senate were, as we have seen, usually through the army; but the young soldier who was destined for the Senate differed, in service and in title, from his purely equestrian compeer. The *tribuni laticlavii*[2] are a special class of officers, who may often have started their service, as mounted officers of the legions, with the brevet rank of tribune, and whose service was shorter than that of the other equites in order that they might be qualified for the quaestorship by the age of twenty-five.[3] The possessors of the *latus clavus* must always have been expected to pursue a senatorial career;[4] by the time of Claudius they might be compelled to this course, the penalty of refusal being the deprivation of the broad stripe, but sometimes of equestrian rank as well.[5]

[1] Suet. *Aug.* 38 "Liberis senatorum, quo celerius rei publicae assuescerent, protinus . . . latum clavum induere et curiae interesse permisit."

[2] Wilmanns *Index* p. 602 ; cf. Suet. *Dom.* 10.

[3] Augustus had given the post of *praefectus alae* as well as that of *tribunus militum* to senators' sons (Suet. *Aug.* 38). Mommsen (*Staatsr.* i. p. 548) thinks that after Tiberius these *laticlavii*, as a rule, filled the office of tribune alone. They could scarcely have been given a real command when they first joined the standards.

[4] The poet Ovid, who assumed the *latus clavus* by right of birth, took the first steps towards a senatorial career by filling two posts in the vigintivirate, but he went no further and subsided into equestrian rank (Ovid *Trist.* iv. 10, 29 ; *Fasti* iv. 383).

[5] Suet. *Claud.* 24 "Senatoriam dignitatem recusantibus equestrem quoque ademit."

Great care was taken to preserve the dignity and purity of this senatorial order. The *latus clavus* was granted only to those who could trace free birth through four generations, and Claudius was forced to excuse his conduct in giving it to a freedman's son.[1] The Julian marriage laws prohibited marriage with freed-women or actresses, not only to senators, but to their sons, grandsons, and great-grandsons.[2] "The order" was reckoned to include the wives of senators and all descendants in the male line,[3] together with adoptive children, until they were emancipated, and even those natural children who had been emancipated.[4] The commercial disabilities of senators were perpetuated and sharpened. The Republican prohibition that they should not be purchasers of public contracts[5] was renewed by an edict of Hadrian.[6] They were permitted to invest capital at a moderate rate of interest, but at times even this was disallowed.[7]

These disabilities were, however, to some extent compensated by privileges. As the senators ceased to be purely Roman, the question of their duties to their native states had to be considered, and the rule was fixed that, while they were allowed to retain their domicile of origin (*origo*), they owed no public duties (*munera*) to the cities of their birth.[8] We have already mentioned the growth of the principle which reserved criminal jurisdiction on a senator to the senatorial court.[9]

In the early Principate there was no distinct title reserved for the order, but after the close of the first century the epithet *clarissimus* came to be applied to its members, and the title *clarissima* is even given to women of senatorial rank.[10] A distinction in office and dignity but no distinction in rank separates

---

[1] Suet. *Claud.* 24 "Latum clavum (quamvis initio affirmasset non lecturum se senatorem nisi civis Romani abnepotem) etiam libertini filio tribuit, sed sub conditione si prius ab equite Romano adoptatus esset." Claudius then appealed to the famous precedent set by his ancestor Appius Caecus.

[2] *Dig.* 23, 2, 44.   [3] ib. 1, 9, 8 ; 50, 1, 22, 5.

[4] ib. 1, 9, §§ 5, 6, 7, 10.

[5] Asc. *in or. in Tog. Cand.* p. 94.

[6] Dio Cass. lxix. 16 ἐνομοθέτησε δὲ . . . ἵνα μηδεὶς βουλευτὴς μητ' αὐτὸς μήτε δι' ἑτέρου τέλος τι μισθῶται.

[7] Severus Alexander at first forbade the taking of interest, but subsequently allowed 6 per cent (*Vita* 26). For investment by a senator at an earlier period cf. Plin. *Ep.* iii. 19, 8 " sum quidem prope totus in praediis, aliquid tamen fenero."

[8] *Dig.* 50, 1, 23 "municeps esse desinit senatoriam adeptus dignitatem, quantum ad munera ; quantum vero ad honorem, retinere creditur originem." Cf. ib. 1, 9, 11 ; 50, 1, 22, 5 ; *Cod.* 10, 40 [39], 8.

[9] p. 387.   [10] Friedländer *Sittengesch.* i. 3.

the Princeps from the senators. They are his "peers" (ὁμότιμοι),[1] and this peerage is chiefly shown in their sole participation in Republican offices. They might, indeed, be delegates of the Princeps, but not his servants in the sense in which the procurators were. Besides filling the regular offices of state, senators possessed a monopoly of provincial government, where the country governed was a true *provincia* and not a department assigned temporarily or permanently to a procurator or praefect; they were the sole commanders of the legions, and, as Caesar's nominees, they filled the office of praefect of the city and the various commissionerships (*curationes*) for duties which he had undertaken, such as the care of the water-supply, of the roads, of public works, and of the banks and channel of the Tiber (*curatores aquarum, viarum, operum publicorum, alvei et riparum Tiberis*).[2]

We have already spoken of the military training and attitude of this nobility,[3] and also of its gradually increasing provincial character.[4] Both these characteristics were in harmony with its sphere of duties, which were mainly provincial. A successful member of the order could have seen but little of Rome or Italy until his declining years. If his early military service was real and not nominal,[5] he spent most of the years between eighteen and twenty-five in the camps and on the frontiers. If he had shown military ability, he might be sent back as an ex-quaestor to take command of a legion, although such a legateship was usually reserved to men of praetorian rank.[6] The praetorship and consulship qualified him for long terms of service in successive Caesarian provinces, and for the annual governorship of those still under the control of the Senate.[7] This identification with provincial life was an identification with the Principate, for there were few Republican associations to impress the mind when the bounds of Italy had been passed. The principles of selection,

[1] Dio Cass. lii. cc. 7, 15, 31; lxvii. 2.   [2] See p. 413.
[3] p. 364.   [4] p. 374.
[5] Suet. *Claud.* 25 "stipendiaque instituit (Claudius) et imaginariae militiae genus, quod vocatur 'supra numerum,' quo absentes et titulo tenus fungerentur."
[6] In A.D. 16 a proposal was made in the Senate "ut . . . legionum legati, qui ante praeturam ea militia fungebantur, jam tum praetores destinarentur" (Tac. *Ann.* ii. 36).
[7] Galba's is a good instance of a distinguished senatorial career. He obtained office *ante legitimum tempus;* after the praetorship he governed Aquitania, after the consulship Upper Germany; he was then proconsul of Africa, and finally for eight years legate of Tarraconensis. See Suet. *Galba* 6, 7, 8.

2 D

training, and habituation to which this nobility was subject
were thus directed to inspire it with a belief in, if not with an
enthusiasm for, the accepted order of things.

The second order which supported the throne and did the
work of the Empire was that of the Equites. The word *eques*
has now, as in the Republic, a dual signification. Tacitus
employs it to describe the capitalist class, presumably the
possessors of a census of 400,000 sesterces,[1] and it is obvious
that current terminology did not accept the restrictions which
the Principate may have wished to impose on the use of the
term. It is uncertain what these restrictions were, for literature
and inscriptions mention two methods of conferring equestrian
rank, and it is not known whether these methods—the gift of
the rank through the gold ring and through the public horse—
were sometimes alternative or always concurrent. But the grant
of knighthood to freedmen is described as having been effected
by the gift of the gold ring[2]—a gift which, as early as the time
of Hadrian, had come to confer free birth (*ingenuitas*) merely and
not equestrian rank,[3] and it cannot be shown that the public
horse was always given to members of this class when they were
endowed with the *insignia* of knighthood.[4] It is not improbable,
however, that when the gold ring had lost its earlier signification
and become merely a means of conferring free birth, only one
order of official equites was recognised, and that the title in its
proper sense was restricted to the order whose members had,
from the time of Augustus, been pre-eminently the bearers of
the name. This order was the old one of the *equites equo publico*,

---

[1] Tac. *Ann.* iv. 6 "(the state contracts) societatibus equitum Romanorum agitabantur."

[2] Dio Cass. liii. 30. On Antonius Musa, who had saved Augustus' life, was conferred τὸ χρυσοῖς δακτυλίοις (ἀπελεύθερος γὰρ ἦν) χρῆσθαι: ib. xlviii. 45 (Augustus, on the reception of Menas the former freedman of Sex. Pompeius) δακτυλίοις τε χρυσοῖς ἐκόσμησε καὶ ἐς τὸ τῶν ἱππέων τέλος ἐσέγραψε. These words *may* mean that Menas was made an *eques equo publico* as well.

[3] A rescript of Hadrian is quoted with reference to the *ingenuitas* conferred by the gold ring (Ulp. in *Dig.* 40, 10, 6). For other references to this right see *Dig.* 38, 2, 3 ; Justin. *Nov.* 78.

[4] The usurpation of the gold ring by freedmen, which was repressed by Claudius (Suet. *Claud.* 25) and Domitian, and the inspection in the theatre instituted by the latter (Martial v. 8) seem to refer to a civil class ; at least there is no evidence that such people claimed to be *equites equo publico*. When Dio Cassius (lvi. 42) speaks of οἵ τε ἱππεῖς, οἵ τε ἐκ τοῦ τέλους καὶ οἱ ἄλλοι, it is not clear who "the others" are, but the passage shows that persons other than those in the corps were called "equites."

which was reorganised and vastly extended in scale at the very beginning of the Principate. We are told that even under Augustus the annual parade might witness the appearance of five thousand knights,[1] and these could have been but a portion of the order, for many members of the corps must have been detained on financial, administrative, and military duties in the provinces. This increase in numbers seems to have led to the abandonment of the old centuriate organisation, for the equites of the Principate are grouped in *turmae* and commanded by *seviri*.[2] Selection for the order was entirely in the hands of the Princeps,[3] and probably any one with the requisite qualifications —free birth, good character, and a property of 400,000 sesterces —could get this patent of nobility from the Emperor's hands. At the times when the censorship was revived in the person of the Princeps,[4] the selection and elimination of equites may have followed the rules prevailing under the Republican system of revision;[5] but, as the censorship was no part of the constitution of the Principate, some department must have existed from the first for the purpose of registering the names of applicants. We find a permanent bureau eventually established for this purpose. It bore the title *a censibus equitum Romanorum*, and seems to have been a branch of the general department of petitions (*a libellis*).[6] Although this office was concerned primarily with the duty of admission to the order, yet its holders must have pointed out to the Princeps cases where the qualifications requisite for knighthood had ceased to exist, and they must thus have acted as the board that really controlled the tenure of the rank. The formal control in this particular was, however, effected, now as in the Republic, by a solemn and public act. The act, although a Republican survival, was not employed with its Republican meaning. The parade of the knights (*transvectio equitum*) on the Ides of July had, during the Republic, been a mere procession; it was now given the significance of the censorian review in the

---

[1] Dionys. vi. 13.

[2] The *seviri* would seem to show that there were six *turmae*. See Hirschfeld *Verwaltungsgesch.* p. 243 n. 1.

[3] Hence such expressions as *a divo Hadriano equo publico honoratus* (Wilmanns 1825), *equo publico exornatus ab Impp. Severo et Antonino Augg.* (ib. 1595).

[4] p. 347.

[5] p. 225. It is probable that the revision of the knights described in Suet. *Claud.* 16, *Vesp.* 9 refers to the censorship of these emperors.

[6] *a censibus equitum Romanorum* (Wilmanns 1275), *a censibus a libellis Aug.* (ib. 1249 *b*), *a libellis et censibus* (ib. 1257).

Forum,[1] and became the means of testing the qualifications of members of the order (*probatio equitum*).[2] The knights now passed on horseback, not on foot ; they could not ask for their discharge (*missio*), for the tenure of their rank was no longer conditioned by military service, although Augustus finally permitted all members of the age of thirty-five, who were unwilling to continue in the corps, to return their public horses ;[3] but the knights were still questioned and made to give an account of their conduct,[4] and those whose answers were unsatisfactory were dismissed from the ranks.[5] That Augustus took this duty seriously is shown by the fact that he more than once asked the Senate for committees, whether of three or ten members, to assist him in the work.[6] But, although this parade is found in the reigns of subsequent Emperors,[7] and can be traced as late as the fourth century A.D.,[8] the serious duty of rejection was probably exercised more and more by the permanent bureau which admitted to the order.

The eighteen centuries of Roman knights had, even at the end of the Republic, never lost touch with the army. They had ceased to be the citizen cavalry, but they were composed of the young nobility who furnished the mounted officers of the legions. This secondary military character was retained by the corps in the Principate ; but it had an additional significance as well. There can be no doubt that it was from the *equites equo publico* that the Emperors chose those members of the official hierarchy —procurators and praefects—who were of equestrian rank. It is less certain whether this corps furnished all the *judices* during the early Principate. Jurisdiction, whether civil or criminal, was a burden (*munus*), and this may have been imposed on all who possessed the requisite census, whether they had made profession for the order or not.[9]

[1] p. 225.

[2] Suet. *Aug.* 38 "equitum turmas frequenter recognovit, post longam intercapedinem reducto more transvectionis."

[3] ib. 38 "mox reddendi equi gratiam fecit eis, qui majores annorum quinque et triginta retinere eum nollent."

[4] ib. 39 "Unum quemque equitum rationem vitae reddere coegit."

[5] Suet. *Calig.* 16 "palam adempto equo, quibus aut probri aliquid aut ignominiae inesset." [6] Suet. *Aug.* 37, 39.

[7] In those of Caligula (Suet. *Calig.* 16) and Nero (Dio Cass. lxiii. 13), and perhaps in those of Vitellius (Tac. *Hist.* ii. 62) and Severus Alexander (*Vita* 15).

[8] Zosimus ii. 29.

[9] By the side of such titles as *equo publico judex selectus ex V decuriis* (Wilmanns 2110) and *equum publicum habens adlectus in V decurias* (ib. 2203)

It was natural that an order thus definitely constituted, and which became more rigid as time went on, should end by enjoying titles of honour peculiar to itself. This stage had been attained by the second century ; but the titular designations are not strictly those of the equestrian order, but of the grades of office to which it led. After the reign of Marcus Aurelius the equestrian hierarchy was divided into three classes; the first contained only the praefect of the praetorian guard who was called *vir eminentissimus ;* the second the other equestrian praefects and higher procurators, who bore the title *perfectissimi ;* the third —the possessors of all other equestrian posts—were *egregii.*[1] The equestrian officers of the army were not graduated on a similar scale of rank, and the municipal knights of Italy are designated only by the old Republican and non-official epithet of *splendidi.*[2] The more definite, but equally non-official, epithet of *illustris* may have been applied to individuals who possessed the senatorial census and the *latus clavus,* but who were passing through the equestrian service in the army (*equestris militia*), which was preparatory to entrance into the Senate.[3] But the name more particularly designated men who, possessed of a senatorial fortune, preferred to retain their equestrian rank, and even perhaps any equites of fortune and dignity such as the holders of the great praefectures.[4]

§ 7. *The Functionaries of the Princeps*

The Princeps, since he is not a king, has neither magistrates nor ministers subject to his will ; but he possesses a number of delegates and servants who assist in the performance of his vast duties of administration. Some of these, such as the legates,

we find the title *quin. decur. judi*(*cum*) (*inter*) *quatringenarios* (Henzen 6469), in which a purely monetary qualification is expressed.

[1] Wilmanns nn. 1639, 2841, *Index* p. 564 ; Mommsen *Staatsr.* iii. p. 565.

[2] Wilmanns n. 2858 ; Mommsen ib. n. 3.

[3] These might have been included in the *equites illustres* whom Augustus forbade to set foot in Egypt (Tac. *Ann.* ii. 59 "vetitis nisi permissu ingredi senatoribus aut equitibus Romanis illustribus "), but the knights chiefly referred to here are doubtless distinguished permanent members of the order.

[4] The variants used by Tacitus would apply to both of these classes. He uses *insignis* (*Ann.* xi. 5) and speaks of *primores equitum* (*Hist.* i. 4). Two ex-praefects of the praetorian guard are described as *equites Romani dignitate senatoria* (*Ann.* xvi. 17). Cf. note 3.

praefects, and curators, find analogies in the Republican constitution; others, such as the procurators and secretaries of
departments, are borrowed from the organisation of a Roman
household and are transferred from the life of the palace to that
of the state. We may neglect for the moment the legates and
provincial praefects, who will be considered in the section dealing
with the organisation of the provinces, and fix our attention on
the offices of the central government, which are either peculiar
to Rome and Italy or common to them and the provincial world.

(i.) *The Praefects.*—The four great praefectures, which were
concerned originally with the administration of Italy and Rome,
were those of the city (*urbi*), the praetorian guard (*praetorio*), the
corn-supply (*annonae*), and the watch (*vigilum*). Of these the first
stands entirely out of relation to the others so far as the career
and qualification of its holders were concerned; for, while the
praefecture of the city was a senatorial post, all the others were,
during the greater part of the Principate, equestrian. Of the
three latter offices the praefecture of the praetorian guard was the
highest in rank, next came that of the corn-supply, and thirdly
that of the watch.[1]

The praefecture of the city was the continuation in name, and
to some extent in functions, of one of the oldest offices in Rome;[2]
but the historical continuity is rendered somewhat imperfect by
the fact that the ancient praefecture, which had originated with
the kings and had ceased to be a reality only with the appointment of the first praetor,[3] still continued in a shadowy form during
the Principate as the praefecture created when the days of the
Latin festival drew the magistrates away from Rome.[4] But the
new office of the Principate was, in a sense, a continuation of the
old one of the monarchy. Both were products of personal rule
and were based on the theory of delegation; the later office was
suggested by the earlier, and both had much the same sphere of
administration. The link between the Republican office and that
of the Principate is found in the arrangements of the dictator
Caesar and in the earlier procedure of Augustus. The link was
broken when, under Tiberius, the praefecture became a permanent
and not an occasional office. In 46 B.C. Caesar had left six

---

[1] For the promotions from one praefecture to another, see Mommsen *Staatsr.*
ii. p. 1042 n. 1.

[2] p. 61.   [3] p. 120.

[4] Tac. *Ann.* vi. 11 [17] "duratque simulacrum, quotiens ob ferias Latinas
praeficitur qui consulare munus usurpet."

praefecti in Rome to administer the affairs of the city during his absence;[1] Maecenas had had a similar, though less definite, position given him by Augustus;[2] and when the latter became Princeps, the praefecture between the years 27 and 24 B.C. became a more regular, although still an occasional office, and was renewed from time to time by Augustus during his absences from the capital.[3] Tiberius' long periods of retirement made it practically perpetual,[4] and under subsequent reigns the praefect remains in office even when the Princeps is present in Rome.[5] It was, perhaps, due to its associations with the Republican magistracy that this office was filled by a senator and a consular.[6] The same associations may account for the facts that the praefect of the city, although a delegate of the Princeps and nominated by him for an indefinite period,[7] is yet accounted a magistrate, and is even credited with *imperium.*[8]

One of the early occupants of the office[9] sent in his resignation six days after his appointment on the ground that he had held an *incivilis potestas;* and indeed the scope of the praefect's duties and the extent of summary jurisdiction and coercive power which they involved, might easily lead a sensitive mind to shrink from such un-Republican authority. The praefect was briefly the guardian of the city (*custos urbis*), and nothing that could be construed as a part of that *tutela*[10] was exempt from his control. It was his duty to keep order everywhere, at the

[1] Suet. *Caes.* 76 "praefectos . . . pro praetoribus constituit, qui absente se res urbanas administrarent"; Dio Cass. xliii. 28 πολιανόμοις τισίν ὀκτώ, ὥς τισι δοκεῖ, ἢ ἕξ, ὡς μᾶλλον πεπίστευται, ἐπιτρέψας.

[2] Tac. *Ann.* vi. 11 [17].

[3] Tac. l.c.; cf. Dio Cass. liv. 19.

[4] In Tac. *Ann.* vi. 10 [16] it is said of L. Piso (died 32 A.D.) "praefectus urbi recens continuam potestatem et insolentia parendi graviorem mire temperavit."

[5] We find Maximus as praefect during Caligula's presence in Rome in 39 A.D. (Dio Cass. lix. 13).

[6] Tac. *Ann.* vi. 11 [17] "(Augustus) sumpsit e consularibus."

[7] *Vita Commodi* 14 "praefectos urbi eadem facilitate mutavit"; *Vita Pii* 8 "successorem viventi bono judici nulli dedit nisi Orfito praefecto urbi, sed petenti." For the frequent life-long tenure of the office see Dio Cass. lii. 24.

[8] Paulus in *Dig.* 5, 1, 12, 1 "(Judicem dare possunt) hi quibus id more concessum est propter vim imperii, sicut praefectus urbi ceterique Romae magistratus"; contrast Pompon. in *Dig.* 1, 2, 2, 33 "nam praefectus annonae et vigilum non sunt magistratus, sed extra ordinem utilitatis causa constituti sunt."

[9] Messala Corvinus, praefect *circa* 25 B.C. (Jerome in Euseb. *Chron.* a. 1991).

[10] Seneca *Ep.* 83, 14 "L. Piso urbis custos . . . officium . . . suum, quo tutela urbis continebatur, diligentissime administravit."

games as in the market, and for this purpose he had at his disposal the city cohorts (*cohortes urbanae*) established by Augustus,[1] three divisions of which were quartered in Rome during the reign of Tiberius.[2] But the preservation of order implied interference with a great many departments of civic life. The praefect controlled the theatre, the money-changers, the sale of meat, the trading and religious guilds; he listened to the grievances of slaves or to the complaints of *patroni* about their freedmen, and finally even had cognisance of serious offences committed by guardians.[3] The criminal jurisdiction, which was the complement of his authority, was so indefinite that at a very early period it crossed that of the *quaestiones perpetuae*,[4] and, as the tendency of the Principate was to make the latter give way before the former, we are not surprised at the unlimited criminal jurisdiction described by Dio Cassius and recorded in the *Digest* as vested in the praefect in the third century A.D.[5] He might at this time inflict the severest punishments, even deportation or condemnation to the mines.[6] His police control and criminal jurisdiction extended to the limit of a hundred miles from Rome.[7] Within the city he might judge in person; jurisdiction in Italy he exercised through delegates.[8] He also possessed a certain civil jurisdiction connected with his functions of preserving order,[9] and finally became the court of appeal, in civil cases, from officials in Rome.[10] But he was not a final court, for a further appeal lay from the praefect to the Emperor.

[1] Suet. *Aug.* 49.   [2] Tac. *Ann.* iv. 5.   [3] *Dig.* 1, 12.

[4] Tac. *Ann.* xiv. 41 (A.D. 61) "pari ignominia (interdiction from Italy) Valerius Ponticus adficitur, quod reos, ne apud praefectum urbis arguerentur, ad praetorem detulisset, interim specie legum, mox praevaricando ultionem elusurus."

[5] Dio Cass. lii. 21 καὶ τὰς δίκας, τάς τε παρὰ πάντων ὧν εἶπον ἀρχόντων ἐφεσίμους τε καὶ ἀναπομπίμους καὶ τὰς τοῦ θανάτου, τοῖς τε ἐν τῇ πόλει, πλὴν ὧν ἂν εἴπω, καὶ τοῖς ἔξω αὐτῆς μέχρι πεντήκοντα καὶ ἑπτακοσίων σταδίων οἰκοῦσι κρίνῃ : Ulp. in *Dig.* 1, 12, 1 "Omnia omnino crimina praefectura urbis sibi vindicavit [a praefectura urbis sibi vindicari, *Momms.*], nec tantum ea, quae intra urbem admittuntur, verum ea quoque, quae extra urbem intra Italiam [intra c̄ lapidem, *Momms.*, cf. 1, 12, 1, 4] epistula divi Severi ad Fabium Cilonem praefectum urbi missa declaratur."   [6] *Dig.* 1, 12, 3 ; 48, 19, 8, 5.

[7] *Collatio* 14, 3, 2 ; *Dig.* 1, 12, 1, 4.   Cf. note 5.

[8] Ulp. in *Dig.* 1, 12, 3 "Praefectus urbi, cum terminos urbis exierit, potestatem non habet : extra urbem potest jubere judicare."

[9] *Dig.* 1, 12, 1, 6 "Sed et ex interdictis quod vi aut clam aut interdicto unde vi audire [aut unde vi adiri, *Momms.*] potest."

[10] Dio Cass. lii. 21 (quoted n. 5) ; *Cod.* 7, 62, 17 (Constantine, A.D. 322) "si apud utrumque praetorem, dum quaestio ventilatur, ab aliqua parte auxilium provocationis fuerit objectum, praefecturae urbis judicium sacrum appellator observet."

The *praefectus praetorio* was in origin the commander of the
Emperor's bodyguard. This *corps d'élite*, which even in the
Republic had grouped itself round a commander in the field, was
given a definite existence and organisation in the year 28 B.C.,[1]
and became the police of Italy, the selected home force composed,
unlike the legions, mainly of Italian citizens,[2] and the protector,
often the transmitter, of the throne. Its praefects at this early
stage represent the military character of the despotism perhaps
more purely than any other officials, and even the reign of the
second Caesar could show in Sejanus one of the most formidable
of those praefects who were almost partners of the throne. The
danger threatened by the office illustrates its power, and this
was recognised when Vespasian sought security by giving the
praefecture to his own son Titus,[3] or Severus married his elder
son to the daughter of his praefect Plautianus.[4] A more
favourite method was to increase the number of its holders.
Two were frequently appointed, and three are found on two
occasions since the time of Commodus.[5] Gradually the military
functions of the office ceased to be the most important, although
its military history had determined its character. The praefect
of the guard had always been the man who stood next the
throne ; he was a truer *alter ego* of the Princeps than the
praefect of the city, for his activity was not confined to Rome
and Italy. It was he who issued rapid injunctions for the
organisation of the army or for the guidance of the civil service
throughout the Empire, and at times we find two praefects, such
as Adventus and Macrinus in the reign of Caracalla, representing
respectively the military and civil spheres. But jurisdiction,
the most constant of the Emperor's cares, and the framing of
legal decrees, also demanded the attention of the praefect, and
hence it was necessary to entrust the office to the first jurists of
the Empire. Papinian, Ulpian, and Paulus were all praefects of
the guard. The change in the character of the office perhaps
began with Hadrian ; it was carried on during the reigns of the
Antonine Emperors, and finally achieved in that of Septimius

---

[1] Dio Cass. liii. 11.
[2] Tac. *Ann.* iv. 5. Otho speaks of the corps as "Italiae alumni et Romana
vere juventus" (Tac. *Hist.* i. 84).
[3] Suet. *Tit.* 6.   [4] *Vita Severi* 14.
[5] Two are regarded as the normal number by Dio Cassius (lii. 24). Three are
found under Commodus, Didius Julianus, and Severus Alexander. See Mommsen
Staatsr. ii. p. 867.

Severus.   The judicial aspect of the office was now paramount.
The praefect has become the highest criminal judge in Italy
outside the hundredth mile-stone;[1] he is the court of appeal
in criminal cases from all provincial governors,[2] and judges in
those cases which the provincial governor was not competent to
decide.[3]   He is also the court of appeal from provincial governors
in civil cases.[4]   This extensive jurisdiction was a result of the
centralisation of judicial power in the Emperor, which we have
already traced.[5]   It had to be delegated, and no fitter delegate
could be found than the praefect.   Convenience also dictated
that the delegation should be final, and the principle was finally
arrived at that there should be no appeal from the praefect to
the Emperor.[6]   This did not mean that the Emperor ceased to
judge; for at any moment he might displace his praefect and
hear the case himself.   As the praefect judged *vice principis*, it
is natural to suppose that he presided over the imperial
consilium,[7] which attained a definite organisation in the reign of
Hadrian;[8] and this probability is scarcely shaken by the fact
that we find special *consiliarii* nominated for the praefect,[9]
for he exercised a varied jurisdiction and might be holding
a court at the same time as the Emperor.   Apart from jurisdiction, his general mandates and ordinances had legal force,

[1] *Collatio* 14, 3, 2.   The right was given by constitutions ("jam eo perventum
est constitutionibus").   The citation is from Ulpian, and this jurisdiction had
doubtless been attained before the time of Caracalla.   Cf. *Vita Alex.* 21.
[2] *Cod.* 9, 2, 6, 1 (Gordian, A.D. 243, with reference to appeal against a *praeses
provinciae* on the ground of condemnation in absence) "praefectos praetorio
adire cura."
[3] ib. 4, 65, 4, 1 (Alexander, A.D. 222) "si majorem animadversionem exigere
rem deprehenderit (praeses provinciae), ad Domitium Ulpianum praefectum
praetorio et parentem meum reos remittere curabit "; cf. 8, 40 [41], 13.
[4] *Dig.* 12, 1, 40 "Lecta est in auditorio Aemilii Papiniani praefecti praetorio
juris consulti cautio hujusmodi "; cf. 22, 1, 3, 3.
[5] p. 386.
[6] *Dig.* 1, 11, 1, 1 (Arcadius in early part of fourth century A.D.) "praefectorum
auctoritas . . . in tantum meruit augeri ut appellari a praefectis praetorio non
possit.   Nam cum antea quaesitum fuisset an liceret . . . et extarent exempla
eorum qui provocaverint, postea publice sententia principali lecta appellandi
facultas interdicta est;" *Cod.* 7, 62, 19 (Constantine, A.D. 331) "a praefectis
autem praetorio provocare non sinimus."
[7] Cf. *Vita Marci* 11 "habuit secum praefectos, quorum et auctoritate et
periculo semper jura dictavit."
[8] See below on the *consilium*.
[9] Karlowa *Rechtsgesch.* i. p. 549.   A knight of the third century is appointed
in consilium praef. praet. item urb(i) ex sacra jussione (Henzen 6519).   Cf.
Mommsen *Staatsr.* ii. p. 1122 n. 1.

provided that they did not conflict with laws or imperial constitutions.[1]

During the greater part of the Principate equestrian rank was a necessary qualification for this praefecture. Senators first began to hold this office from the time of Severus Alexander, who gave his praefects *senatoria dignitas* and the title *clarissimus*,[2] for it was held that one who pronounced judgment on a senator should himself be of senatorial rank.[3] At the time when the praefect was a knight, dismissal from office often took the form of making him a senator or a member of the senatorial order.[4]

The *praefectus annonae* was the final product of a question that had never ceased to agitate Rome from the close of the Punic wars. Anxiety about the supply of corn to the capital had raised Pompeius to an extraordinary position in 57 B.C.,[5] and in 43 the Senate, alarmed at the possible designs of Antonius and Octavian, had agreed that no individual *curator* for corn should again be appointed.[6] In the early Principate the duty belonged technically to the *aediles cereales* instituted by Caesar;[7] but epochs of scarcity led to its being taken over by the Princeps. Augustus accepted the task in 22 B.C.,[8] but whether as a permanent *cura* is uncertain,[9] and in 18 B.C. and 6 A.D. experiments were made to carry it through by the appointment of *curatores* of praetorian or consular rank.[10] Finally, as a definite *cura* of the Princeps, it was given to a praefect. The *cura annonae* as undertaken by the Princeps involved two charges; firstly, the gratuitous distribution of corn to the poorer classes at Rome, and secondly, the placing of corn on the Roman market for purchasers as well as recipients. It was with the latter of these duties that the praefect was chiefly, perhaps exclusively, con-

---

[1] *Cod.* 1, 26, 2 (Alexander, A.D. 235) "Formam a praefecto praetorio datam, etsi generalis sit, minime legibus vel constitutionibus contrariam, si nihil postea ex auctoritate mea innovatum est, servari aequum est."

[2] *Vita Alex.* 21.

[3] ib. "Alexander autem idcirco senatores esse voluit praef. praet., ne quis non senator de Romano senatore judicaret."

[4] ib. "si quis imperatorum successorem praef. praet. dare vellet, laticlaviam eidem . . . summitteret"; cf. *Vita Commodi* 4; *Vita Hadriani* 8 "cum Attianum ex praefecto praetorii ornamentis consularibus praeditum faceret senatorem."

[5] Cic. *ad Att.* iv. 1, 7; Dio Cass. xxxix. 9.

[6] Dio Cass. xlvi. 39.   [7] *Dig.* 1, 2, 2, 32.

[8] Dio Cass. liv. 1; *Mon. Anc.* Gr. iii. 6.

[9] Mommsen *Staatsr.* ii. p. 1038 n. 1; Hirschfeld *Verwaltungsgesch.* p. 130 n. 1; Karlowa *Rechtsgesch.* i. p. 553.

[10] Dio Cass. liv. 17; lv. 26.

cerned.[1] He had to see that the requisite mass of grain was brought to the market, and that it was sold at a moderate and stable price.[2] Assistance was furnished him by subordinate officials in Rome itself, in the harbours of Italy, and in the provinces, senatorial as well as imperial ; but the number of these procurators was not large, since the lower departments of the corn-supply were managed by guilds, such as those of the *mensores* and *navicularii*,[3] "associations that originally leased their services to the state and finally became its instruments."[4] The praefect possessed a jurisdiction arising from his administrative duties. He listened to criminal informations touching the public supply of corn,[5] and seems even to have heard certain civil actions arising out of the corn trade.[6] The appeal from his judgment went immediately to the Emperor.[7]

The institution of the *praefectus vigilum* was equally the result of the Emperor's undertaking a special department of administration that had formerly belonged to Republican magistrates. The guardianship of the town against fires and nocturnal disturbances had belonged chiefly to the *triumviri capitales*,[8] and in a more general way to the aediles. But the Republican appliances were found insufficient, and Augustus formed an early scheme for giving the curule aediles a fire-brigade of six hundred slaves.[9] Even this did not prove satisfactory, and in A.D. 6 he undertook the new *cura*—an undertaking which was followed by the establishment of seven cohorts of *vigiles*, one for every two of the fourteen regions of the city, and the creation of a praefect set over the tribunes who were commanders of these divisions.[10] This praefecture was, like that of the corn-supply, equestrian, and the two differ little in rank ; for, although the *praefectura annonae* was reckoned superior, direct promotion from the command of the *vigiles* to that of the praetorian guard is found.[11] The

---

[1] *Praefecti frumenti dandi* are found, apparently for the purpose of distribution, as late as the second century. They were generally ex-praetors and appointed *ex senatus consulto*, probably because the *aerarium* bore or contributed to the cost. See Mommsen *Staatsr.* ii. p. 673 ; Karlowa *Rechtsgesch.* i. p. 553.
[2] Dio Cass. lii. 24 ; Seneca *de Brev. Vitae* 19, 1.
[3] Hirschfeld in *Philologus* 1870, pp. 79 ff.
[4] Karlowa *Rechtsgesch.* i. p. 556.
[5] *Dig.* 48, 2, 13 ; cf. 48, 12, 1.   [6] ib. 14, 5, 8 ; 14, 1, 1, 18.
[7] ib. 14, 5, 8 "sententiam (praefecti annonae) conservavit imperator " ; cf. Dio Cass. lii. 33.
[8] p. 235.   [9] Dio Cass. liv. 2.
[10] Paulus in *Dig.* 1, 15, 1 and 3.   [11] Karlowa *Rechtsgesch.* i. p. 558.

praefect protected the town and patrolled the streets by night, and he exercised a jurisdiction closely connected with his police functions, and resembling, in a lower degree, that of the praefect of the city. He tried cases of arson, robbery, burglary, and thefts in baths;[1] but the higher jurisdiction in such cases belonged to the *praefectus urbi*, and the praefect of the watch could not try Roman citizens on capital charges.[2] In the third century he possessed some civil jurisdiction in matters connected with leases and house-rent.[3]

(ii.) *The Curators.*—There were certain *curae* undertaken by Augustus which he did not give to equestrian praefects, but to senatorial *curatores*. These *curae* of the roads of Italy, of the public works, of the public water-supply, and of the channel and banks of the Tiber (*viarum, operum publicorum, aquarum publicarum, alvei et riparum Tiberis*), were filled by nomination of the Princeps, but their holders were perhaps, like the praefects of the *aerarium*, regarded as officials of the people or of the Senate rather than of the Emperor ; the reason for this view probably being that the care of the roads, *opera publica*, and the like was concerned with *solum publicum*, and " the public soil in Rome and Italy was, even after the foundation of the Principate, not the property of the Emperor but of the people or the Senate."[4] Hence in the early Principate the pecuniary means for this administration was guaranteed from the *aerarium*, the *fiscus* merely contributing.[5] Hence too the occupation of these posts by senators and their method of appointment. In 11 B.C. Augustus nominated *curatores aquarum* with the consent of the Senate (*ex consensu senatus, ex senatus auctoritate*) ;[6] the *curatores operum publicorum* and *viarum* were perhaps nominated in the same way, and the *curatores* of the Tiber were in Tiberius' reign appointed by lot.[7]

---

[1] *Dig.* 1, 15 ; cf. 12, 4, 15 ; 47, 2, 57 [56], 1.
[2] ib. 1, 15, 3 and 4 ; *Cod.* 1, 43, 1.
[3] *Dig.* 19, 2, 56 ; 20, 2, 9. *Praefecti vigilum* (one of whom is the jurist Herennius Modestinus) take part in a controversy which has come down to us known as the *lis fullonum* (Bruns *Fontes ; C.I.L.* vi. n. 266). The case has been discussed by Bethmann-Hollweg *Civilprozess* ii. p. 767 n. 60 and Mommsen in *C.I.L.* l.c. ; *Staatsr.* ii. p. 1058 n. 3.
[4] Karlowa *Rechtsgesch.* i. p. 539.
[5] Coins of 16 B.C. exist (Eckhel vi. 105) with the inscription " s. p. q. R. imp. Cae(sari), quod v(iae) m(unitae)s (unt) ex ea p(ecunia) q(uam) is ad a(erarium) de-(tulit) " ; cf. *Vita Pert.* 9 "aerarium in suum statum restituit. Ad opera publica certum sumptum constituit. Reformandis viis pecuniam contulit."
[6] Frontinus *de Aquaed.* 100 and 104.   [7] Dio Cass. lvii. 14.

(iii.) *The Procurators.*—The quasi-magisterial position of the occupants of the higher imperial posts could not be reflected in the lower grades of office. So far as the detailed *ministeria principatus*[1] were concerned, the Princeps adopted the analogy of the Roman house, not of the Roman state, and employed either general agents (*procuratores*) or assistants designated by the secretarial or other duty which they performed (*ab epistulis*, *a rationibus*, etc.). There was always a distinction between the two classes, which was still preserved now that they had become official. The agent of domestic life might indeed approximate to the condition of a mere bailiff, and might be a slave; but the necessity for representing the absent *dominus* in courts of law had made it convenient that the procurator should be a free man; and the idea of agency, usually of general agency (*procuratio omnium rerum*),[2] was closely associated with the word. On the other hand, the slaves and freedmen of the household who copied and kept accounts, were not agents; and, in accordance with this distinction, the officials of the Principate who bear such titles as *ab epistulis*, *a libellis*, *a rationibus*, are not spoken of as procurators, although one of these posts might rise to the dignity of a procuratorship, as that *a rationibus* did.

Although from the point of view of functions the two classes must be kept distinct, from that of qualification they may be discussed together. In both we observe the tendency for the household to become a bureau, for the freedman and slave to give place to the Roman knight. Tiberius' household consisted mainly of freedmen,[3] and their influence reached its zenith in the reign of Claudius. An Emperor who sought popularity might, like Vitellius, transfer the *ministeria* of the Principate to Roman knights;[4] but no comprehensive attempt seems to have been made to reorganise the bureaucracy on this footing until the time of Hadrian.[5] Henceforth the higher grades were held as a rule by knights, only the lower being possessed indifferently by equites or freedmen.[6] The procuratorship was the patent of

---

[1] Tac. *Hist.* i. 58.   [2] Cic. *pro Caec.* 20, 57.
[3] Tac. *Ann.* iv. 6 "intra paucos libertos domus."
[4] Tac. *Hist.* i. 58 "Vitellius ministeria principatus per libertos agi solita in equites Romanos disponit." In Otho's reign we find a mention of Secundus the rhetor ἐπὶ τῶν ἐπιστολῶν γενόμενος (Plut. *Otho* 9).
[5] The evidence for Hadrian's change is mainly epigraphic. See Hirschfeld *Verwaltungsgesch.* i. p. 32. Two instances of it are found in *Vita Hadr.* 22 "ab epistulis et a libellis primus equites Romanos habuit."   [6] Dio Cass. lii. 25.

equestrian nobility (*equestris nobilitas*),[1] and we have seen that titles were finally devised to express the differences in procuratorial rank.[2] The civil service now became closely connected with the army, and the occupants of civil posts were mainly retired officers, men who had held at least one of the three positions in the equestrian service,[3] and who, after the second century, had generally filled every grade before they took the procuratorship.[4] This militarising of the administrative service is one of the most curious features of the Principate. It gave that service its precision, its rigidity, its tendency to work as a smooth machine almost independently of personal control. This tendency was a blessing in so far as it was calculated to diminish the influence due to the idiosyncrasies of the Princeps, or of any individual holder of office ; but one cannot help suspecting that a great deal of the administrative tyranny, which darkened the closing years of the Principate and weakened the Empire, was due to the ineradicable habits of routine inspired by a military life, and that the Greek or Graeco-Asiatic freedman, although a more corrupt, was, on the whole, a more capable administrator. The military supply was not, however, altogether sufficient, and from the time of Hadrian a civil career was also open, which gave a chance to the aspiring lawyer.

Theoretically the procurator's duties were those of mere agency, and he had little discretionary authority and no general official power. Tiberius' emphatic statement that his procurator's business was merely to manage the Emperor's slaves and personal property[5] is echoed in the language of the *Digest*, which tells us that the duties of these servants of the Emperor were strictly defined, that they were accountable to their master for the use made of the finances or property under their care, that they could not give, sell, or transfer it, and that "careful management" was the limit of their power.[6] It was only when they kept within these bounds that their acts had all the authority

---

[1] Tac. *Agric.* 4 "Cn. Julius Agricola . . . utrumque avum procuratorem Caesarum habuit, quae equestris nobilitas est."
[2] p. 405.
[3] i.e. the posts of *praefectus cohortis*, *tribunus militum*, *praefectus alae*. See Suet. *Claud.* 25.
[4] Hirschfeld *op. cit.* p. 248.
[5] Tac. *Ann.* iv. 15. See p. 395.
[6] Ulp. in *Dig.* 1, 19, 1, 1 "si venditionis vel donationis vel transactionis causa quid agat, nihil agit : non enim alienare ei rem Caesaris, sed diligenter gerere commissum est"

of those of the Princeps himself.[1]   But the extending spheres
of their operations rendered it impossible for these limits to be
rigorously preserved.   Claudius asked and obtained that his
procurators should be permitted jurisdiction within their own
financial departments [2]—an almost necessary result of the fact
that in the provinces (and especially in those under senatorial
management) there was no convenient court of arbitration to
decide when money was or was not owing to the Princeps.[3]
The consent of the Princeps, also, to the procurator's acts must
eventually have meant the consent of the chief bureau at Rome ;
for, in spite of the extraordinary capacity for personal government possessed by the Roman Emperors, the fiscal system was
too complicated for every detail to reach their ears.

The chief duties of the procurators were financial, and most
of these agents can be summed up under the title *procuratores
fisci.*   A number of titles are met with which clearly have reference to the central department at Rome.   Such are *procurator
summarum* found in an inscription of Nero's time and borne by
a freedman,[4] *procuratores rationum summarum,*[5] *rationalis summae
rei,*[6] *dispensator* or *dispensator summarum,*[7] and *vilicus summarum.*[8]
The titles belong to different epochs, and it is difficult to establish
their precise import.   It is generally agreed that from the time
of Claudius the title *a rationibus* was reserved for the chief
controller of the *fiscus.*   After the reign of Hadrian this post
was reserved for equites,[9] and the members of the central bureau
had a higher standing than the financial agents in the provinces.
The title *procurator rationum summarum,* which belongs to the
second century, denotes some highly placed official connected
with this central chest ; but, as it does not seem to be identical
with the title *a rationibus,* it has been thought to represent a
subordinate controller perhaps instituted by Marcus Aurelius.[10]

---

[1] *Dig.* 1, 19, 1.
[2] Suet. *Claud.* 12 "ut . . . rata essent, quae procuratores sui in judicando
statuerent, precario exegit" (from the Senate).   Tacitus exaggerates the nature
of the change when he says that " Claudius libertos, quos rei familiari praefecerat,
sibique et legibus adaequaverit" (*Ann.* xii. 60).
[3] Cf. Ulp. in *Dig.* 1, 16, 9 (with reference to the duties of a proconsul) "sane
si fiscalis pecuniaria causa sit, quae ad procuratorem principis respicit, melius
fecerit, si abstineat."

[4] Henzen 6525.
[6] *Cod.* 3, 26, 7.
[8] *C.I.L.* v. n. 737.
[10] ib. p. 35.

[5] Wilmanns 1259, 1262.
[7] Suet. *Vesp.* 12 ; Henzen 6396.
[9] Hirschfeld *Verwaltungsgesch.* i. p. 32.

The title *rationalis*, which was often identical with *procurator*,[1] seems at some period within the third century to have replaced *a rationibus* as the designation of the chief officer of the *fiscus*.[2]

Amongst provincial procurators we may enumerate first those who were confined to the imperial provinces. The procurator here occupied the position which the quaestor held in the public provinces; he was the chief officer of the provincial *fiscus*, collected the taxes due to it, and managed the disbursement of its funds. There was also a treasury connected with the military station in the province (*fiscus castrensis*), and at the head of it a *procurator castrensis*, who superintended the payments made to the soldiers,[3] and military expenses in general. Other procurators were common to all the provinces; for even those that were "public" paid certain dues to the Emperor.[4] Such were lapsed legacies and the goods of the condemned (*bona caduca* and *damnatorum*), after the *fiscus* had asserted its claim to these revenues,[5] and the taxes owed by Roman citizens everywhere, such as the *vicesima hereditatum* and the *centesima rerum venalium*. But the public provinces owed more direct dues to the Princeps as well. Thus Africa, a corn-supplying but not an imperial province, was brought into the closest relation with his *cura annonae*, and even the most peaceful districts must have defrayed the expense of the necessary military protection, and surrendered certain revenues to be collected by imperial officials.

Common, too, to all the provinces were the agents who managed the imperial estates (*procuratores patrimonii* or *patrimonii privati*).[6] We have already noticed that after the time of Severus a distinction was drawn between the *res privata* and the *patrimonium* of the Emperor.[7] From this time onward the *procurator rerum privatarum* is distinct from the *procurator patrimonii*.[8]

---

[1] Cf. the title of *Dig.* 1, 19 " De officio procuratoris Caesaris vel rationalis."

[2] Hirschfeld, *op. cit.* p. 37 ; Liebenam *Beiträge zur Verwaltungsgesch.* p. 32.

[3] Strabo iii. p. 167. The title *a copiis militaribus* is found in inscriptions (Orelli 2922, 3505)

[4] Tac. *Ann.* ii. 47. Here it is said of cities of Asia, "quantum aerario aut fisco pendebant, in quinquennium remisit (Caesar)." The *procurator Asiae* of *Ann.* iv. 15 is probably a *procurator patrimonii*. See p. 395.

[5] p. 395. For procurators *ad bona damnatorum* see Wilmanns 1278, 1291. For a *procurator a caducis, C.I.L.* iii. n. 1622.

[6] Wilmanns 1257, 1272, 1273, 1275, 1285.

[7] p. 396.

[8] Timesitheus, the father-in-law of Gordian, was *proc. tam patrimoni quam rat. privatar.* in one district, *proc. ration. privat.* in another (Wilmanns 1293).

2 E

The non-financial procurators, who were actually governors of districts, will be discussed when we are dealing with the organisation of the provinces.

The tenure of office by a procurator was indefinite, and depended on the imperial pleasure. Technically their posts expired when the Princeps who had appointed them died,[1] and the renewal of their office by his successor, although it must have been the rule, was treated as a new appointment. The posts were well paid and procurators bore the titles *trecenarius, ducenarius, centenarius,* and *sexagenarius,* according as their salaries varied from 300,000 to 60,000 sesterces. The salaries of the procurators at Rome were probably higher than those belonging to the same departments in Italy and in the provinces. Thus the *procuratio rationis privatae* was probably in Rome a *trecenaria,* in the provinces a *ducenaria,* in Italy, where it would be merely a branch of the central office, a *centenaria procuratio.*[2] Promotion seems to have been determined chiefly by merit, and one of the strong points of the system was that there was no mechanical system of advancement. It was possible for a secretary, who had never been a procurator proper, to be appointed to a praefecture,[3] but, as a rule, several procuratorships were passed through before this summit of equestrian ambition was attained.[4]

(iv.) *Personal Assistants.*—The secretariate of the Principate was, as we have seen, but the business side of the organisation of a Roman household, but so rapidly did the importance and official aspect of these posts develop that already by Nero's reign a Roman noble, who kept assistants with such titles as *ab epistulis* and *a libellis,* might be suspected of treasonable designs.[5] These

[1] Herodian vii. 1 (Maximin) τήν τε θεραπείαν πᾶσαν, ἣ συγγεγόνει τῷ Ἀλεξάνδρῳ τοσούτων ἐτῶν, τῆς βασιλείου αὐλῆς ἀπέπεμψε : cf. *Vita Pert.* 12 "Sane nullum ex eis, quos Commodus rebus gerendis imposuerat, mutavit, exspectans urbis natalem, quod eum diem rerum principium volebat esse."

[2] Liebenam *op. cit.* p. 55.

[3] *Vita Nigri* 7 "cum unus ad memoriam, alter ad libellos paruisset, statim praefecti facti sunt (Paulus et Ulpianus)."

[4] This may be illustrated by the careers of Burrus (*proc. Augustae, proc. Ti. Caesaris, proc. divi Claudii, praefecto praetori, C.I.L.* xii. 5842), of Vibianus Tertullus (*ab epistulis Graecis, proc. a rationibus, praefectus vigilum, C.I.L.* iii. 6574) and of Sex. Var. Marcellus (*proc. aquarum, proc. Brittaniae, proc. rationis privatae, vice-praefectus praetorio,* Orelli 946).

[5] Tac. *Ann.* xv. 35 (under Nero, in A.D. 64, Torquatus Silanus was forced to death on various grounds) "quin eum inter libertos habere, quos ab epistulis et libellis et rationibus appellet, nomina summae curae et meditamenta"; cf. ib. xvi. 8 (A.D. 65) "Ipsum dehinc Silanum increpuit isdem quibus patruum ejus

secretaryships became, in fact though not in law, great offices of state. They required more highly trained ability than most of the procuratorships, and, as they brought their holders into close relations with the Princeps, the influence and the power of patronage which they conferred must have been enormous. The official *ab epistulis* put into shape all the decisions of the Princeps which took the form of letters, so far as these were not written personally by the Princeps himself. The answers to the *consultationes* of officials, to the despatches of generals and provincial governors, or to deputations from foreign communities, together with the nomination of officials and officers and the conferment of privileges, passed through his hands.[1]

The official *a libellis* drew up the answers to petitions (*preces, libelli*)[2] made by private individuals to the Emperor. The answer was generally given in a short *subscriptio* appended to the document.[3] The framing of such replies required considerable legal knowledge; hence it is not surprising to find that jurists like Papinian and Ulpian held this post.

The official *a cognitionibus* was the adviser of the Emperor on legal points, which were settled by imperial decree. The points on which advice was given were perhaps wholly those of civil jurisdiction, and were probably such as did not need to come before the imperial *consilium*.[4] The office was in existence at the beginning of the third century,[5] but is thought to have been subsequently merged in that *a libellis*.[6]

The official *a memoria* is first mentioned about the time of the Emperor Caracalla. His function was probably to put into form and reduce to writing (often by dictation to a secretary)[7] such

Torquatum, tanquam disponeret jam imperii curas praeficeretque rationibus et libellis et epistulis libertos."
  [1] Dio Cass. lii. 33 ; Stat. *Silv.* v. 1, esp. 83-107 ; Justinus xliii. 5, 12 ; Suid. s.v. Διονύσιος.
  [2] Seneca *Cons. ad Polyb.* vi. 4 and 5.
  [3] *Vita Carini* 16 "fastidium subscribendi tantum habuit ut inpurum quendam . . . ad subscribendum poneret." The Princeps himself may not have written more than his signature. See *Vita Commodi* 13 "ipse Commodus in subscribendo tardus et neglegens, ita ut libellis una forma multis subscriberet."
  [4] Karlowa *Rechtsgesch.* i. p. 545.
  [5] Dio Cass. *Ep.* lxxviii. 13.
  [6] Karlowa l.c.
  [7] *Vita Carini* 8 " Julius Calpurnius, qui ad memoriam dictabat." He attended the Princeps with the other secretaries ; see *Vita Alex.* 31 "Postmeridianas horas subscriptioni et lectioni epistularum semper dedit, ita ut ab epistulis, a libellis et a memoria semper adsisterent."

speeches and verbal decisions of the Emperor as did not fall under the competence of the other officials.

(v.) *The Consilium.*—The *consilium* of the Princeps [1] was merely a renewed manifestation of that eternal principle of Roman public life which directed that a magistrate should seek advisers. A council was necessary for public confidence, but an imperial *consilium* was originally no part of the constitution of the Principate. Tiberius imitated Augustus in seeking advice before coming to a decision on important matters; [2] yet when he sat as a high court of criminal jurisdiction, his board of assessors could be described as consisting of a " few friends." [3] The board may have become more determinate in succeeding reigns, but the first Princeps whom we hear of as giving it a definite organisation was Hadrian. That Emperor, we are told, when he held a court of justice, summoned as his advisers jurisconsults approved by the Senate. [4] It is only a *judicial* council that is here described, and there is nothing to show that these legal experts were necessarily consulted on administrative matters. The basis, however, was laid for a permanent council of state, and the *consiliarii Augusti* of this period became a definite and salaried class. [5] They included both senators and equites, [6] and some bore the title *jurisperiti.* [7] Others may not have been gifted with special knowledge of the law, and may have been employed in cases where general ability or experience may have been of more value than juristic training. Actual jurisdiction was not, however, the only

---

[1] This *consilium* must not be confused with the committee of the Senate which had been employed by Augustus and Tiberius, but was subsequently discontinued. This board, composed of some of the magistrates and a number of senators chosen by lot, had given a preliminary consideration to the business to be submitted to the Senate (Suet. *Aug.* 35 ; *Tib.* 55 ; Dio Cass. liii. 21). Something like it was devised by Mamaea in the reign of Severus Alexander (Dio Cass. lxxx. 1 ; Herodian vi. 1).

[2] Dio Cass. lv. 27 ; lvii. 7.

[3] Tac. *Ann.* iii. 10 "paucis familiarium adhibitis" (in the trial of Piso, A.D. 20). In Nero's trial of Octavia in A.D. 62 his body of advisers ("amicos quos velut consilio adhibuerat princeps" Tac. *Ann.* xiv. 62) may have been regarded as a *consilium domesticum.*

[4] *Vita Hadr.* 18 "cum judicaret, in consilio habuit non amicos suos aut comites solum, sed juris consultos . . . quos tamen senatus omnes probasset."

[5] Hirschfeld *Verwaltungsgesch.* i. p. 215. Probably only the equestrian members of this board received salaries (Mommsen *Staatsr.* ii. p. 990).

[6] Cf. *Vita Hadr.* 8 "erat . . . tunc mos, ut, cum princeps causas agnosceret, et senatores et equites Romanos in consilium vocaret et sententiam ex omnium deliberatione proferret."

[7] e.g. "centenario consiliario Aug(usti) . . . juris perito" (Wilmanns 1286).

occasion on which legal knowledge was indispensable in an adviser. The help of the jurist had to be sought in the framing of the imperial *constitutiones*,[1] and we are told that for this purpose Severus Alexander was assisted by twenty *jurisperiti* out of a *consilium* numbering seventy in all.[2]   A difference of personnel for different branches of administration is easily comprehensible, for it is improbable that the Emperor needed to summon all his councillors on every occasion on which he took advice.[3]   The mode of consultation was wholly informal and depended on the discretion of the Princeps.   Augustus in the exercise of his jurisdiction distributed voting tablets (*tabellae*) to his councillors, on which they could inscribe acquittal or condemnation or a modified verdict.[4]   We cannot imagine that the votes were reckoned as in the jury system.   The *tabellae* were for the enlightenment of the Princeps, and he may have decided according to the weight of the names of those who handed them in.   Nero, we are told, took opinions on paper, and, after reading them, gave his own judgment as though it were that of the majority of his advisers.[5]   Under Severus Alexander opinions were given verbally and taken down in short-hand.[6]

We have already shown that it is probable that the imperial *consilium* in its developed form was employed by the praefect of the praetorian guard when he gave judgment *vice* the Princeps.[7]

[1] p. 380.
[2] *Vita Alex.* 16 "neque ullam constitutionem sacravit sine viginti jurisperitis et doctissimis ac sapientibus viris isdemque disertissimis non minus quinquaginta."
[3] In Maecenas' supposed advice to Augustus, which in this, as in other respects, probably reflects the practice of the time of Dio Cassius, it is said of the *consilium* ἄλλοι ἄλλοτε διαγινωσκέτωσαν (Dio Cass. lii. 33).
[4] Suet. *Aug.* 33.
[5] Suet. *Nero* 15.
[6] *Vita Alex.* 16 "ut iretur per sententias singulorum ac scriberetur quid quisque dixisset."
[7] p. 410.

CHAPTER XI

§ 1. *The Organisation of Italy*

THE chief feature of the organisation of Italy during the early Principate was the completion of the efforts made during the later Republic at incorporating its towns with Rome. The unity aimed at was chiefly that of jurisdiction, but we have no evidence of the steps which Augustus took to perfect the system of judicial centralisation, which had been devised at the close of the Republic.[1] At the same time this Emperor adopted a device which, though its full details and effects are unknown, seemed to foreshadow the later principle of a close administrative unifi- cation of Italy with the capital. He divided the peninsula, exclusive of the immediate territory of Rome, into eleven regions (*regiones*).[2] The immediate purpose contemplated by this division is unknown ; but it laid the basis for subsequent distributions of many branches of Italian administration. The public domains, taxes paid by Roman citizens such as the *vicesima hereditatum*, and the results of the census, were organised or calculated by regions.[3] They were employed, therefore, for work which neces- sarily fell on the central government, and this organisation so far implied no infringement on the communal autonomy of the towns. Such infringement came as a necessary result of the influence of the personality of the Princeps, which finally domi- nated Italy as effectually as it controlled Rome. But its coming was very gradual. The final change may be illustrated by the

---

[1] p. 314.
[2] Plin. *H.N.* iii. 46 "nunc ambitum ejus (Italiae) urbesque enumerabimus, qua in re praefari necessarium est auctorem nos divum Augustum secuturos, descriptionemque ab eo factam Italiae totius in regiones XI."
[3] See the references in Marquardt *Staatsverw.* i. p. 220.

disappearance of the municipal *comitia*, the limitation of local jurisdiction, the loss of an independent system of local finance, and the control ultimately assumed by the central government of the actual administration of many of the Italian states.

Of these changes, the downfall of the *comitia* is perhaps less remarkable than their continuance for so long a period after the assemblies had ceased to be a reality at Rome. A Latin colony in the time of Domitian still elects its magistrates at a *comitia curiata*,[1] and the transference of this principle to Spain shows its prevalence at the time in Italy. The paucity of inscriptions of the early Principate which speak of elections by the only alternative body, the local Senate, is remarkable, and there are clear indications of the survival of the principle of popular election until the time of Antoninus Pius.[2] It doubtless retained its hold on Italy as late as it did on the western provinces; its disappearance from the whole municipal sphere was the result of a new system of creating magistrates, the characteristics of which will be traced when we are dealing with the provinces of this period.[3] The elective power of the assemblies no doubt survived all their administrative functions. The tendency even of the early Principate was to confine these to the local Senates, which were accounted more responsible bodies, and were far better instruments of the central controlling power of Rome.

The limitation of the local courts of law cannot be fully illustrated, but it is to some extent connected with the establishment of high individual authorities for jurisdiction in Italy, which begins with Hadrian. That Emperor divided Italy into four great circuits, and placed each of them under a *consularis*.[4] These magistrates were replaced under Marcus Aurelius by *juridici*[5] of praetorian rank, whose purely civil jurisdiction was finally concerned with that portion of Italy which was separated from the *urbica dioecesis*, the sphere of the praetor's competence.[6]

---

[1] *Lex Malacitana* c. lii. ff.

[2] Kuhn *Verfassung des römischen Reiches* i. pp. 236, 237. In an inscription of Hadrian's time we find in Ostia *II. vir . . . in comitiis factus* (*C.I.L.* xiv. 375). For this and other instances see Liebenam *Städteverwaltung* p. 479.

[3] p. 438.

[4] *Vita Hadr.* 22 "quattuor consulares per omnem Italiam judices constituit." Of Antoninus Pius, who was one of these, it is said "cum Italiam regeret" (*Vita Anton.* 3). Cf. App. *B.C.* i. 38.

[5] *Vita M. Anton.* 11 "datis juridicis Italiae consuluit ad id exemplum, quo Hadrianus consulares viros reddere jura praeceperat."

[6] Ulpian in *Fragmenta Vaticana* 205, 232, 241.

These officials are mentioned only in connexion with extraordinary
jurisdiction concerned with trusts, the nomination of guardians,[1]
or questions of administrative law, such as a controversy
concerning the qualification for the decurionate.[2] But, as extraordinary jurisdiction was gaining the upper hand of the *jus ordin-
arium*, and as such administrative questions would at an earlier
period have been settled by the municipalities themselves,[3] the
powers of the *juridici* may be regarded as a very real limitation
of those of the local magistrates and senates. We have already
seen that all the higher criminal jurisdiction of these towns had
disappeared. Within the limit of a hundred miles from Rome
such cognisance belonged to the praefect of the city, outside this
limit to the praefect of the guard.[4]

The financial difficulties under which many of the Italian
towns laboured, invited a further system of imperial control.
This took the form of the institution of *curatores rei publicae*, of
senatorial or equestrian rank, whose existence is traceable from
the close of the first century A.D., and who were given by the
Princeps as extraordinary commissioners to reinvigorate the
financial life of poverty-stricken municipalities.[5]

But an even more vigorous control was impending, which was
to bring Italy nearer to the condition of a province. The extraordinary commissioners known as *correctores* (διορθωταί), whom
the Principate often gave to free cities or districts in the provinces,[6] were finally transferred to Italy.[7] When its municipalities
were placed under this tutelage, there was little more than a
formal difference between their condition and that of the subject
towns, and nothing but a more regular system of administration and the imposition of direct taxation was wanted to change
Italy into a province. Both these changes were effected under
the rule of Diocletian. Italy was, it is true, not divided into

---

[1] Ulp. l.c. ; *Dig.* 40, 5, 41, 5.

[2] Fronto *ad Amicos* ii. 7.

[3] Marquardt (*Staatsverw.* i. p. 227) remarks that such a question as the qualification of a decurion belongs under Caesar's legislation (*lex Ursonensis* c. 105) to
the municipal courts.

[4] pp. 408, 410.

[5] Mommsen *Staatsr.* ii. p. 1082, Liebenam *Städteverw.* p. 480, and in *Philologus* lvi. 290 ff. How far this curatorship became a standing office is uncertain.

[6] p. 428.

[7] The first official *ad corrigendum statum Italiae* belongs to the year 214 A.D.,
while the provincial *corrector* goes back to the time of Trajan (Marquardt *Staatsverw.* i. pp. 228, 229).

provinciae, but its districts were placed under regularly-appointed *correctores*, and its lands supplied revenues to the imperial court and to Rome. This climax of centralisation was probably the inevitable result of the imperial system and the external circumstances of the time. To the Princeps Italian and provincial problems were the same; Italy was not always the country in which the Emperor established his permanent residence, and, as the onset of the barbarians threatened even the Italian frontier, there was no possible reason why Italy should not pay its quota to the general taxation. But economic and social evils may have contributed to the imperial encroachments on Italian administration. The weaknesses which led to imperial control may have been those which the Emperors sought to cure. These were poverty and depopulation, and how earnestly they were grappled with may be seen by a glance at the system of state support known as the *alimentarium*. The leading idea of this institution is the endowment of a state or district with a fund which should give partial support to children, and by this means encourage production and relieve the responsibilities of parents or guardians. Such charitable efforts had, at an early period, been made by individuals;[1] and from the reign of Nerva the state, as represented by the Princeps, took up the enterprise. Nerva's example was followed by Trajan,[2] who extended and organised the system, and similar efforts were made by Hadrian, Antoninus Pius, Marcus Aurelius, and Severus Alexander.[3] The form usually taken by the endowment was an advance by the Princeps of funds which were deposited on good landed security at moderate interest, 5 or $2\frac{1}{2}$ per cent. From this interest a certain number of boys and girls were to be supported, by the gift either of a certain amount of corn or of a sum of money— twelve, sixteen, or twenty sesterces—per month. This support was guaranteed until the boys had attained their eighteenth and the girls their fourteenth year.[4] The details of this organisation

[1] See the inscription of Atina of the time of Augustus (Wilmanns 1120), "T. Helvio . . . legato Caesaris Augusti, qui Atinatibus HS . . . legavit, ut liberis eorum ex reditu, dum in aetatem pervenirent, frumentum et postea sestertia singula millia darentur."

[2] Victor *Epit.* 12 ; Dio Cass. lxviii. 5.

[3] Marquardt *Staatsverw.* ii. pp. 143, 144. Pius, in honour of his wife Faustina, created a fund for *puellae Faustinianae* (*Vita* 8) ; Alexander, in honour of his mother, one for *pueri puellaeque Mammaeani* (*Vita* 57).

[4] Our knowledge of this institution is derived chiefly from two metal tables, the *Tabula Veleias* (of Veleia in Cisalpine Gaul) and the *Tabula Baebianorum* (of

were supervised in each locality by a *quaestor alimentorum*, while the general control of the funds over a large district was usually entrusted to the curators of the roads [1] which ran through that domain, who sometimes bore the title *praefectus*, sometimes that of *curator alimentorum*.[2] This wise method of charitable relief, which inspired an interest in agriculture while it relieved poverty and encouraged the growth of population, continued in force until the close of the Principate, and the *praefecti*, who administered this department, can be traced till the time of Diocletian.[3]

§ 2. *The Organisation of the Provinces*

The imperial problem of the later Republic—the task of finding a frontier—occupied the unceasing energy of the early Principes, and in this, as in similar cases in the history of the world, delimitation involved extension. Sometimes the views as to the proper boundary altered, and advance was at times succeeded by retrogression. Thus Augustus sought the Elbe only to fall back on the Rhine, and Trajan adopted against the great eastern power a heroic policy of annexation which did not commend itself to his successor. In one instance, too—that of Britain—a forward movement was made which can scarcely be explained as the search for a scientific frontier. But, on the whole, the slow and ordered progress was one that sought not territories, but boundaries, and the movement necessitated expansion, whether it took the form of the annexation of the wild districts to the south of the Danube, or the gradual absorption of the kingdoms and principalities which intervened between the old Asiatic provinces and the Euphrates or the African dominions and the sea. The Danube, the Rhine, and the German Ocean; the Euphrates and the Syrian Desert; the Ethiopian kingdoms, the Sahara, and the Atlantic, were the limits within which

the Ligures Baebiani near Beneventum). See E. Desjardins *De tabulis alimentariis*, Mommsen in *I.R.N.* 1354, Wilmanns 2844, 2845. On the institution see Marquardt *Staatsverw.* ii. pp. 141-147, Liebenam *Städteverw.* pp. 105, 360.

[1] p. 413.

[2] e.g. *curator viae Appiae, praefectus alimentorum: curator viarum et praefectus alimentorum Clodiae et coherentium : curator viae Aemiliae et alimentorum* (Wilmanns 1189, 1215, 1211). See Marquardt, Liebenam ll.cc., and Mommsen *Staatsr.* ii. p. 1079. In districts not pierced by the great roads, procurators (*alimentorum, ad alimenta*) were employed. [3] Marquardt l.c. p. 147.

the Principate was to strive to make the best of the means left by the victorious Republic for the government of the world. The Republic had indeed laid a solid foundation for ordered rule, and although we are accustomed to think of the Roman Empire chiefly in connexion with the three peaceful centuries of the Principate, it should not be forgotten that the work of the latter was chiefly the introduction, not of original ideas, but of those slight but decisive modifications which are sufficient to change a clumsy into a workable machine. A more effective, although far from perfect, system of military defence, a greater division of authority amongst the organs of government, a more careful estimate of provincial burdens, a competent although perhaps over-rigid civil service,—these were the immediate gifts of the Principate to the world. The results were comfort and peace ; but a comfort that was too often divested of even local patriotism, and a peace that was singularly devoid of intellectual ideals. A universal citizenship was also amongst the hidden treasures of the Empire, but it was a gift conferred in proportion to its valuelessness, and the Princeps whose edict was to make the world a city was a calculating spendthrift bent only on increasing the taxes of his subjects. But, since the golden mean of Empire had yet to be found, we cannot blame the Principate for doing too much that which the Republic did too little. Every reaction is violent, and in this instance at least over-government was intended to be in the interest of the subject. The subject acclaimed it, at least in its initial stages,[1] although his descendant was to find it a burden in comparison with which the yoke of the Republican proconsul would have seemed a trifle.

Augustus with characteristic modesty and discretion reserved his strength for the most difficult of the provinces—those on the frontier which demanded military occupation and unusual vigilance in administration—and thus created the distinction between Caesar's provinces and those which were public (*publicae*) and were entrusted to the care of the Senate and people.[2] There were occasional interchanges of provinces between the co-rulers.

---

[1] Tac. *Ann.* i. 2 " Neque provinciae illum rerum statum abnuebant, suspecto senatus populique imperio ob certamina potentium et avaritiam magistratuum, invalido legum auxilio, quae vi, ambitu, postremo pecunia turbabantur."

[2] δῆμος καὶ γερουσία (Dio Cass. liii. 12). These provinces are " propriae populi Romani" as opposed to those " propriae Caesaris " (Gaius ii. 21).

Thus Achaea and Macedonia were relinquished by the Senate in A.D. 15, but restored to it in A.D. 44,[1] and Marcus Aurelius took over or surrendered districts according to the necessities of war.[2] But in the middle of the Principate the Senate possessed but eleven,[3] the Princeps twenty-one under regular governors,[4] nine administered by procurators,[5] one, Egypt, ruled by an equestrian praefect.

As in the Republic, the only true provincial *civitates* were those which were *stipendiariae*. The free or free and allied communities were still technically exempt from the governor's control. But the free cities were lessened in number and restricted in privileges. The supposed abuse of its self-governing powers by a *foederata civitas* might cause the treaty to be rescinded and the state to be brought under direct provincial rule ;[6] while, even when *libertas* was retained, its merits might be suspected, and the state might be placed under the financial tutelage of *curatores* (λογισταί) or the administrative care of *correctores* (διορθωταί) appointed by the Princeps.[7] It is also certain that *libertas* no longer conferred immunity from taxation. We know that, of the cities of Asia which are described as tributary in the reign of Tiberius,[8] two, Magnesia ad Sipylum and Apollonidea, were *liberae*,[9] while Byzantium, which had been in alliance with Rome during the Republic, also paid tribute in the reign of Claudius.[10] This change, which is specially noticeable in the East, has been with great probability attributed to Pompeius. While granting or renewing charters and privi-

---

[1] Tac. *Ann.* i. 76 ; Dio Cass. lx. 24 ; Suet. *Claud.* 25.

[2] *Vita Marci* 22 "Provincias ex proconsularibus consulares (i.e. governed by consular *legati*) aut ex consularibus proconsulares aut praetorias pro belli necessitate fecit."

[3] Asia, Africa, Baetica, Narbonensis, Sardinia and Corsica, Sicilia, Macedonia, Achaea, Creta and Cyrene, Cyprus, Bithynia.

[4] Tarraconensis, Germania superior, Germania inferior, Brittania, Pannonia sup., Pannonia inf., Moesia sup., Moesia inf., Dacia, Dalmatia, Cappadocia, Syria, Lusitania, Aquitania, Lugdunensis, Belgica, Galatia, Pamphylia and Lycia, Cilicia, Arabia, Numidia. See Marquardt *Staatsv.* i. p. 494.

[5] Alpes Maritimae, Alpes Cottiae, Alpes Poeninae, Raetia, Noricum, Thracia, Epirus, Mauretania Tingitana, Mauretania Caesariensis. See Marquardt l.c.

[6] Suet. *Aug.* 47, *Claud.* 25, *Vesp.* 8.

[7] Mommsen *Staatsr.* ii. p. 858 ; Marquardt *Staatsverw.* i. p. 358. The earliest known commissioner dates from the time of Trajan. He was "missus in provinciam Achaiam . . . ad ordinandum statum liberarum civitatum" (Plin. *Ep.* viii. 24).

[8] Tac. *Ann.* ii. 47.

[9] Strabo xiii. p. 621 ; Cic. *pro Flacco* 29, 71.

[10] Tac. *Ann.* xii. 63.

leges, he reserved to Rome the right to tax,[1] and thus dissociated the ideas of *libertas* and *immunitas*, which had hitherto been inseparable. The new principle was so fully accepted by the Principate that even the possession of Latin rights could not have exempted a state from taxation,[2] and the immunity of cities became more of an exceptional political privilege. Sometimes it took the form of exemption only from a special tax, such as the freedom from the port dues of Illyricum claimed by the state Tyras in Moesia.[3] Less frequently it was a freedom from all external burdens, such as that enjoyed, on account of its historical associations, by the town of Ilium.[4] But the favourite means of granting immunity to a state was to confer the right known as the *jus Italicum*—a right which implied that the members of the city were, like the inhabitants of Italy, in quiritarian ownership of their soil, and, therefore, exempt from the land-tax. This right generally accompanied the honorary designation of the town as a *colonia*, although the title might be conferred without the right,[5] or be accompanied by only a partial immunity.[6] Many states in Lusitania, Gaul, Germany, Syria, and Phoenicia were made *coloniae* and granted the *jus Italicum*.[7]

The two great problems in taxation which confronted the early Principate were the formation of an estimate of the resources of the Empire, and the apportionment of burdens by reference to the capacities of the various countries. Both tasks were undertaken vigorously by Augustus. To both belong his budget of the resources of the Empire,[8] the geographical works undertaken under the auspices of Agrippa,[9] and the comprehensive assessments made in various provinces. The right of making such assessments belonged to the Princeps,[10] and seems not to have been limited to his own provinces, although it is to these that our definite information chiefly refers. The first known

---

[1] Mommsen *Staatsr.* iii. p. 684.

[2] Mommsen points out (ib. p. 685) that, if it did, Spain after the time of Vespasian would have paid no taxes.   [3] *C.I.L.* iii. n. 781.

[4] *Dig.* 27, 1, 17 ; cf. Suet. *Claud.* 25.

[5] *Dig.* 50, 15, 8, 5 "Divus Antoninus Antiochenses colonos fecit salvis tributis."

[6] ib. 7 "Divus Vespasianus Caesarienses colonos fecit non adjecto ut et juris Italici essent, sed tributum his remisit capitis ; sed divus Titus etiam solum immune factum interpretatus est."   [7] *Dig.* l.c.

[8] "Rationes imperii" (Suet. *Cal.* 16), λογισμοὺς τῶν δημοσίων χρημάτων (Dio Cass. lix. 9). Cf. Tac. *Ann.* i. 11.

[9] Marquardt *Staatsverw.* ii. pp. 207-211.   [10] Dio Cass. liii. 17.

census of the kind was that undertaken in the three Gauls in 27 B.C.,[1] which we find renewed in the years 14, 17, and 61 A.D.[2] There is a trace of an Augustan census in Spain,[3] and a similar task was undertaken in Syria.[4] When these great preliminary estimates were over, provision had to be made for a periodical revision of the assessment. This was done under imperial control and for each province separately. A special imperial decree was issued, and under it the commissioner (*censor, censitor, ad census accipiendos*)[5] made a renewed estimate, with the assistance of delegates, in the shape of equestrian officers and procurators, for the special communities or districts in the provinces subject to the census. Originally the chief officials were of senatorial rank, but after the end of the second century equestrian procurators were generally entrusted with the census[6]—a circumstance which is probably to be accounted for by the fact that in the course of years the duty of making out the returns had become more automatic and therefore simpler.[7] It is not known whether there were fixed dates for the regular recurrence of the census in each province;[8] but there were taxes, such as the *tributum capitis* in Syria, paid only by people of an age that fitted them for labour,[9] which would have demanded renewed registration at somewhat short intervals; and in Egypt there was a cycle of fourteen years for the payment at least of the poll-tax, which goes back to the time of Tiberius and perhaps of Augustus.[10] The careful nature of the estimate of the land-tax is shown by the official form of the schedule of returns (*forma censualis*), which has been preserved. This specified the community and *pagus* in which the farm was

---

[1] Liv. *Ep.* 134; cf. Dio Cass. liii. 22.

[2] Tac. *Ann.* i. 31 and 33; ii. 6; xiv. 46.

[3] Dio Cassius (liii. 22), after saying that Augustus made ἀπογραφαί in the Gallic provinces, adds κἀντεῦθεν ἔς τε τὴν Ἰβηρίαν ἀφίκετο, καὶ κατεστήσατο καὶ ἐκείνην.

[4] St. Luke ii. 2; Joseph. *Antiq.* xvii. 355.

[5] See the inscriptions collected by Kubitschek in Pauly-Wissowa *Real-Encyclopädie*, s.v. *census*.

[6] The *tres Galliae* honour a procurator as "primus umquam eq(ues) R(omanus) a censibus accipiendis" (Wilmanns 1269). The inscription is attributed to the joint rule of Severus and Caracalla.   [7] Kubitschek l.c.

[8] The chief evidence that there was comes from the province of Dacia. In a document of sale from Alburnum Majus, dated May 6, 159 A.D., the purchaser of a house binds himself "[uti] . . . pro ea domo tributa usque ad recensum dep[e]n[dat]" (Bruns *Fontes*).

[9] *Dig.* 50, 15, 3 "in Syriis a quattuordecim annis masculi, a duodecim feminae usque ad sexagensimum quintum annum tributo capitis obligantur."

[10] Grenfell and Hunt *Oxyrhynchus Papyri* ii. pp. 207 ff.

situated, the names of two neighbours, and the character of the land assessed.[1] The taxes were either imposts on the land (*tributum soli*) or on the person (*tributum capitis*). The land-tax was in most provinces paid either in money or grain, more usually in the former; but in certain minor districts it was delivered wholly, or almost wholly, in kind. Cyrene sent its famous silphium, the Sanni in Pontus wax, and the Frisii of Germany the skins of oxen.[2] The personal tax might be one on professions, income, or movable property. It was rarely a poll-tax pure and simple, although this is found in Egypt[3] as a relic of the Ptolemaic organisation; amongst the Jews, when the δίδραχμον had been diverted from the Jewish temple to that of Jupiter Capitolinus;[4] in Britain,[5] where it would have been difficult to collect any other personal tax from the mass of the people; and in the tiny island of Tenos,[6] whose poverty probably forbade any other method of assessment. It may, however, have existed in many provinces by the side of other personal taxes as a burden imposed on those whose property fell below a certain rating.

The collection of the chief imperial taxes was now direct, since the system of *decumae* with the accompanying tax-farmers (*decumani*) had been abolished.[7] But there seem to have been different degrees of directness in the method. A distinction is drawn between the *stipendium* of the public and the *tributum* of Caesar's provinces,[8] and as this distinction can scarcely be one of a method of taxation, it must be one based on the method of collection. Perhaps in the public provinces the taxes were still collected by the states themselves and paid by them to the

[1] *Dig.* 50, 15, 4 "Forma censuali cavetur, ut agri sic in censum referantur. Nomen fundi cujusque: et in qua civitate et in quo pago sit: et quos duos vicinos proximos habeat. Et arvum . . . vinea . . . olivae . . . pratum . . . pascua . . . silvae caeduae."
[2] Plin. *H.N.* xix. 40; xxi. 77; Tac. *Ann.* iv. 72.
[3] Josephus *Bell. Jud.* ii. 16, 4; cf. Grenfell and Hunt l.c.
[4] Josephus *Bell. Jud.* vii. 6, 6. The Jews seem, however, to have paid other personal taxes as well. See App. *Syr.* 50; Marquardt *Staatsverw.* ii. p. 202.
[5] Boadicea is made to say that, besides the land-tax, τῶν σωμάτων αὐτῶν δασμὸν ἐτήσιον φέρομεν (Dio Cass. lxii. 3).
[6] *C. I. Gr.* 2336.
[7] p. 321.
[8] Gaius ii. 21 "(*provincialia* praedia) quorum alia stipendiaria, alia tributaria vocamus. Stipendiaria sunt ea, quae in iis provinciis sunt quae propriae populi Romani esse intelliguntur. Tributaria sunt ea, quae in his provinciis sunt quae propriae *Caesaris esse* creduntur."

quaestor, while in the imperial provinces the procurator came into direct contact with the tax-payer. But much was still left to the efforts of private companies, and the abolition of the *decumani* was perhaps the sole infringement made on the vast operations of the *publicani*. The extent to which the system of contracting out was still employed may be illustrated by the facts that "companies of Roman knights" are said still to have gathered in the *pecuniae vectigales*—by which the *portoria* are chiefly meant—and other *publici fructus*—the revenues from mines, salt-works, quarries, and the like—during the reign of Tiberius,[1] that in the reign of Nero severe measures had to be taken to repress the exactions of the *publicani*,[2] and that these state middlemen have a title devoted to them in the *Digest* of Justinian.[3] Even a tax which fell to an imperial treasury, such as the *vicesima hereditatum*, was collected by contractors in the reign of Trajan.[4] The contracts were no longer leased by a central authority in Rome, but by the official who controlled the department with which the tax was concerned. In most cases it was an imperial procurator who leased the tax, and perhaps to some extent supervised its collection.[5] The direct taxes were paid to the quaestor in the public provinces, and in the imperial were collected by the procurators, of whose functions and operations we have already spoken.[6] In connexion with the fiscus of each province there was a bureau (*tabularium*)[7] in which the assessments were kept.

The method of government in the public provinces underwent considerable modifications, but suffered little formal alteration. The tenure of office was still annual, and the regulation that a five years' interval must elapse between home and foreign command,[8] which had been neglected by Caesar,[9] was revived by Augustus,[10] but considerations of fitness and another method of determining seniority considerably interfered with the application

---

[1] Tac. *Ann.* iv. 6 "frumenta et pecuniae vectigales, cetera publicorum fructuum, societatibus equitum Romanorum agitabantur." Cf. "societates vectigalium" (xiii. 50). [2] ib. xiii. 50, 51.
[3] *Dig.* 39, 4. [4] Plin. *Paneg.* 37.
[5] *Procuratores* and *publicani* are found concerned with the same taxes in the same province, e.g. *procurator IIII. publicorum Africae* (*C.I.L.* iii. 3925 ; Wilmanns 1242), *conductor IIII. p. Afr.* (*C.I.L.* vi. 8588).
[6] p. 417.
[7] *Tabularium censuale* (*C.I.L.* ii. 4248). For the officials connected with it, called *tabularii*, see Wilmanns *Index* p. 572.
[8] p. 323. [9] Dio Cass. xlii. 20. [10] ib. liii. 14.

of the latter principle. Some qualified candidates were set aside by the Senate either on its own motion or by the advice of the Emperor,[1] and the *jus liberorum* admitted some to the *sortitio* in preference to others.[2] All the governors of public provinces were now called proconsuls, whether they had previously held the consulship or not,[3] in order to distinguish them from the legates of Caesar's provinces, who all bore the title *pro praetore.* The two greatest of the public provinces, Asia and Africa, were always given to *consulares,* while the other governments might be held by men of praetorian rank. A definite allowance (*salarium*) was now given to the governor,[4] which must have removed some of his temptation to extortion. Each proconsul was attended by lictors and had the other *insignia* of his rank. But the *proconsulare imperium* was in many respects a mere shadow of its former self. Its possessor did not wear the sword or the military dress,[5] to show that his command was not a military one, and in deference to the full *proconsulare imperium* possessed by the Princeps. It was an exception to this rule that until the time of the Emperor Gaius the legion in Africa was under the command of the governor of that province;[6] but even here, where the employ-ment of active military power was needed, the appointment of the proconsul was thrown practically on the Princeps.[7] The governor was also hampered by assessors[8] more carefully selected than the *legati* of Republican times. The *legati proconsulis pro praetore,* three of whom were assigned to the higher class of provinces, such as Asia and Africa, and one to the lower, such as Sicily and Baetica, although nominally selected by the proconsuls themselves, had to be approved by the Princeps; and the fact that they bear a title which suggests the *imperium* shows, that although they were still delegates of the governor, their juris-diction was more definite and independent in the dioceses assigned them than it had been in Republican times. Even the quaestor now bears the title *quaestor pro praetore,*[9] and exercises, besides his

---

[1] Tac. *Ann.* iii. 32. In A.D. 22 it was determined afresh that the Flamen Dialis might not leave Italy, "ita sors Asiae in eum qui consularium . . . proximus erat coulata" (ib. iii. 71).
[2] Dio Cass. liii. 13.   [3] ib. .
[4] "Salarium proconsulare" (Tac. *Agric.* 42).
[5] Dio Cass. l.c.   [6] Tac. *Hist.* iv. 48.
[7] Tac. *Ann.* iii. 35 (on the outbreak of the war with Tacfarinas in A.D. 21) "Tiberius . . . M'. Lepidum et Junium Blaesum nominavit, ex quis pro consule Africae legeretur."
[8] πάρεδροι (Dio Cass. liii. 14).   [9] Wilmanns *Index* p. 553.

2 F

financial functions, a definite judicial charge—the kind of jurisdiction which was in the hands of the curule aedile at Rome.[1]
We have already shown the possibilities of imperial interference
with the administration and jurisdiction of proconsular governors
through the presence of procurators in their provinces, and
through the tendencies which led to the Emperor's becoming a
court of appeal for the whole provincial world.[2]

In his own provinces Caesar was the only possessor of the
proconsulare imperium.[3] Hence his governors were merely legates
(*legati Caesaris pro praetore*). They were not, however, regarded
as mere delegates. They exercised an independent jurisdiction,
which they could delegate to their subordinates—a proceeding
of which the mere mandatary is incapable.[4] Their military
command was delegated, but some at least of them exercised the
power of life and death over the soldiers in their province.[5]
All the legates wore the military dress and sword,[6] since all
governed provinces in which legions were quartered. But even
their military discretion was to some extent limited by the fact
that the legions now had their own regular commanders (*legati
legionum*), while their civil authority was lessened by the circumstances that the financial affairs of the province were chiefly in
the hands of a procurator responsible to the Princeps or to a
bureau, and that in many provinces after the time of Hadrian
and the Antonines we find a special legate appointed for jurisdiction (*legatus juridicus*),[7] who, though inferior to the governor
in rank, was a delegate not of him but of the Princeps.

One of the secrets of the better administration of Caesar's
provinces was the length of time during which one of these
legates might be kept in a single province. Thus in Tiberius'
reign Sabinus governed Moesia for twenty and Silius Gaul for
seven years,[8] while somewhat later Galba was in Spain for eight.[9]
In every case the tenure of such commands depended on the
Emperor's discretion,[10] and the holders drew fixed salaries from

---

[1] Gaius i. 6. On the changed position of these assistants of the proconsuls, see
Bethmann-Hollweg *Civilprozess* ii. p. 102 ; Greenidge in *Class. Rev.* ix. p. 258.
[2] pp. 417, 385.
[3] Except when a colleague was occasionally appointed. See p. 360.
[4] *Dig.* 1, 21, 5.
[5] Dio Cassius (lii. 22) attributes this power ἐς μόνον τὸν ὑπατευκότα ἄρχοντα,
i.e. to a *legatus consularis*.
[6] Dio Cass. liii. 13.   [7] Wilmanns *Index* p. 559.
[8] Tac. *Ann.* i. 80 ; vi. 39 ; iv. 18.   [9] Plut. *Galba* 4.
[10] Dio Cass. liii. 13 ; Tac. *Ann.* i. 80.

the imperial treasury.[1] To the higher class of provinces, such as Syria, *consulares* were sent ; those of a lower class, such as Aquitania and Galatia, might be governed by men of praetorian rank.

The sphere of imperial rule included a class of dependencies which had not yet become, or were not thought worthy of being, organised as definite provinces and placed under senatorial legates. They were governed by personal agents of Caesar, who were in this case known as *procuratores Caesaris pro legato*.[2] Some of these districts, such as the three Alpine provinces, were comparatively small ; but others, such as the Mauretanias, Thrace, Judaea,[3] were of considerable size, and the presence of mere procurators in such countries must be accounted for by the fact that they were not important military stations but defended by some great command in a neighbouring province.   The procurator was, indeed, sometimes under the partial control of the neighbouring imperial legate ; thus Judaea was in some way attached to the larger province of Syria, and Pilate was deposed from office by Vitellius its governor.[4] But even in this case the procurator is the delegate, not of the governor, but of the Princeps.   Thus, when St. Paul appealed against the jurisdiction of Festus, the appeal was made directly to Caesar.

Anomalous methods of government were adopted for the two greatest military and strategic positions in the Empire—Germany, which was divided into an upper and a lower province, and Egypt. The two strips of land west of the Rhine, which contained the garrisons not merely of the river frontier but of Gaul, were not placed under the ordinary provincial legates.   The two consular *legati*, not of the separate legions, but of the armies, were themselves the governors of the districts ; they bore the title *pro praetore*,[5] and, except when the supreme command over Gaul and the Germanies was assumed by a colleague of the Emperor,[6] were

---

[1] Dio Cass. liii. 23

[2] Wilmanns 1267 ; *procurator vices agens legati* (ib. 1622 *a*). The title *procurator et praeses* was also applied to them. The *procurator vice praesidis* was an ordinary procurator holding an *interim* command for the regular governor of a province (Wilmanns *Index* p. 568).

[3] See p. 428 ; and cf. Tac. *Hist.* i. 11.

[4] Josephus *Antiq. Jud.* xviii. 4, 2.

[5] *Leg. pro pr. exercitus Germanici superioris, legato pro pr. Germaniae super(ioris) et exercitus in ea tendentis* (Wilmanns 867, 1186). Cf. Tac. *Ann.* vi. 30 "Gaetulicus ea tempestate superioris Germaniae legiones curabat."

[6] Tac. *Ann.* i. 31.

not under the control of any governor of the neighbouring Gallic provinces. Egypt, in a sense a private domain of the Princeps,[1] and, as the key of land and sea, guarded even from the approach of a man of senatorial rank,[2] was entrusted to an equestrian praefect (*praefectus Aegypti*), who exercised the reality without the name of the *imperium*,[3] wielded all the powers of a governor,[4] and had an army under his control.

The Romanisation of the provinces was still effected by the insensible channels which had been operative during the Republic—social intercourse, commerce, and the forms of the provincial edict. But more conscious efforts in the same direction were made in the Western world. The foundation of municipalities of an Italian type, the encouragement given to a Latin-speaking foreigner to find a career in the imperial service, the state support given to Roman systems of education—all tended to make portions of provinces, such as Gaul and Spain, centres of as pure a Latinity as could be found in Italy itself. Even when the full *civitas* was not at once conceded, preparation for it was made by the grant of Latin rights which were now conferred on whole provinces, such as Sicily, the Maritime Alps, and Spain,[5] and made the dwellers in these regions participants in all the private rights of Roman law. The general tendency was to elevate the West at the expense of the East, or rather perhaps to decline the struggle with Hellenic civilisation, and to rest content with Romanising the barbarism of the lands that encircled Italy. In spite of this, the greatest triumphs of the legal genius were to be found in the East; the gift for theory seemed to be still peculiarly a property of the Greek or Oriental mind, and it was Asia, Phoenicia, and Syria that produced the names of Gaius, Ulpian, and Papinian. Such men had the signal advantage of comparing and even practising two perfected systems;

[1] Tac. *Hist.* i. 11 "Aegyptum copiasque, quibus coerceretur, jam inde a divo Augusto equites Romani obtinent loco regum : ita visum expedire provinciam aditu difficilem, annonae fecundam . . . domi retinere."

[2] Tac. *Ann.* ii. 59 "Augustus . . . vetitis nisi permissu ingredi senatoribus aut equitibus Romanis illustribus, seposuit Aegyptum, ne fame urgueret Italiam, quisquis eam provinciam claustraque terrae ac maris . . . insedisset."

[3] Ulpian (in *Dig.* 1, 17, 1) speaks of his having an "imperium . . . ad similitudinem proconsulis."

[4] Tac. *Ann.* xii. 60 "divus Augustus apud equestres, qui Aegypto praesiderent, lege agi decretaque eorum proinde haberi jusserat, ac si magistratus Romani constituissent."

[5] Cic. *ad Att.* xiv. 12, 1 ; Tac. *Ann.* xiii 32 ; Plin. *H.N.* iii. 30.

for until the beginning of the third century, Graeco-Oriental forms were the common law of the Eastern half of the Empire, and the edict of Caracalla, which by the grant of the *civitas* implied the future currency of Roman forms, must have created something like a legal revolution in this part of Rome's dominions.[1]

The omnipresence of Roman law was a fitting consequence and symbol of the even, harmonious, uneventful working of provincial life, and of the uniform machinery which was eliminating national characteristics and reducing all provinces to the same level of excellence or decadence.   But, in spite of the highly organised character of provincial administration, it was the city-state (*civitas*) that was still the unit, and the character of its public life remained at all times the test of the effectiveness of the Roman system.

Amidst the brilliant variety of the urban life of the Empire, some uniformity had been secured even during the days of the Republic by Rome's leaning to aristocratic types of organisation. But a slight modification of existing forms of constitution was all that was needed to bring the local machinery into harmony with that of the central government, and there was no effort made to create a uniform type of administration or to regard the provincial state as a mere municipality adapted only to serve the purposes of the imperial system.   The Principate ushers in this latter tendency, but at first it is very gradual.   In its initial stages it manifests itself in the light of a paternal interest, whether on the part of governors or Emperors, in the affairs of local corporations, in minute regulations as to the responsibilities of magistrates, the use of public funds, and the care of public property.[2]   Perhaps for a time such measures were beneficial ; certainly for nearly two centuries, in spite of the fact that there is here and there observable a tendency to shirk municipal office as a burden,[3] the vitality of the towns, fostered by peace and the large revenues of commerce, was strong enough to resist the enervating effects of this interference, and hundreds of inscriptions show us a wealth, a splendour, a generosity in endowment, and a thirst for municipal fame, that seem a sufficient reward for

---

[1] See Mitteis *Reichsrecht und Volksrecht.*

[2] Cf. Plin. *Epp. ad Traj.* 17 (28), 37 (46), 39 (48), 47 (56), 54 (62), 111 (112).

[3] The *lex Malacitana* (the charter of a Latin colony in Spain founded between 81 and 84 A.D.) contains (c. li.) elaborate provisions for forcing candidates to come forward for office (Bruns *Fontes*).   Trajan in a letter to Pliny speaks of those " qui inviti fiunt decuriones " (Plin. *Ep. ad Traj.* 113 [114]).

the untiring exertions of an anxious government. But this government finally came to lean on what it had fostered. The same tendencies, still very imperfectly understood, which changed professions into corporations, trades into guilds, and made even military service a hereditary burden, fastened on the towns, and the government sought to find in them a class which would be solely responsible for local and imperial duties. This was found ultimately in the local Senate—the order of *decuriones* or *curiales* — which had always formed the pivot of municipal administration controlled or created by Rome, but which now tended to become sharply severed from the other classes in the communities, and, while solely endowed with the privileges of office, held these privileges at a tenure which it would gladly have surrendered. The legal texts of our period do not yet show the crushed and broken aristocracy of a later date ; but they reveal the beginning of the movement which was to lead men to regard membership of the Senate as certain ruin, and to flee from office as though it were the plague. In the first place, the local magistracy was ceasing to be a stepping-stone to the Senate. There is a tendency to recruit the order through an *adlectio* of otherwise unqualified members,[1] a tendency which reveals an anxiety to preserve the maximum numbers of the order. This admission is effected by the board itself, and prepares us for the practice of the later Empire by which the order recruits itself from all qualified persons who are bound to serve. In another way also the earlier relation of magistrate to senate was being reversed. The principle of the earlier law, in accordance with which the previous possession of office is a necessary qualification for the *curia*,[2] has been changed for one in accordance with which none but a decurion can be a magistrate. A definite grade of municipal nobility has been evolved, an official caste has been created, and the decurions are sharply severed from the Plebs.[3]

---

[1] See Marquardt *Staatsverw.* i. p. 190 ; Kuhn *Verfassung des römischen Reichs* i. p. 238.   Cf. Plin. *ad Traj.* 112 (113) "ii quos indulgentia tua quibusdam civitatibus super legitimum numerum adicere permisit." Contrast with this the principle of admission to local senates recognised by the *lex Julia Munic.* l. 85 "nei quis eorum quem . . . legito neve sublegito . . . nisi in demortuei damnateive locum."

[2] *Lex Julia Munic.* l. 135 "II vir(atum) IIII vir(atum) aliamve quam potestatem, ex quo honore in eum ordinem perveniat."

[3] Paulus in *Dig.* 50, 2, 7, 2 "Is, qui non sit decurio, duumviratu vel aliis honoribus fungi non potest, quia decurionum honoribus plebeii fungi prohibentur."

Each class has its burdens, and, though the severest of these
were ultimately to fall on the *curiales*, the municipal law of the
Digest calls on all members of the communes to do their duties
to their state and to the Empire.   Each class has its appropriate
duties ; to the decurions belong the higher branches of administration, but every category of citizens has its *munera congruentia*.[1]
The legal writers divide the burdens of public life into two
categories.   The *munera personalia* are those that demand the
activity of the person ; the *munera patrimonii* those that are
incumbent on wealth.[2]   To the former belong the functions of
public officials such as those concerned with the finances of the
state, with the inspection of the market, roads, buildings and
aqueducts, with the maintenance of the peace or the representation of the interests of the city.   But municipal duties by no
means exhausted the category of such burdens.   The state
finally saddled the municipalities with the returns for the census
and the raising of the revenue in corn or money, and made the
collectors responsible for any deficit.[3]   The cost of the imperial
transport and post had also become a municipal burden.[4]   These
last obligations introduce us to the idea of the patrimonial
burdens, which existed wherever by law or custom expense was
incurred by the individual undertaking them.   There were few
in which such expenditure was not incurred, and the policy of
the dying Principate was to lay heavy imposts on capital, which
increased in proportion to the diminution in number of the
wealthier classes.   When exertion was met with this reward
it tended to relax, and a decaying agriculture and an enfeebled
commerce were the results of the oppression of the government.
Whatever the primary cause of these evils was, whether military,
social, or economic, they were doubtless aggravated by the
relentless system of imperial administration, which marshalled
citizens as though they were soldiers, treated all classes as the
fitting instruments of official life, and regarded the subject as
existing for the Empire rather than the Empire for the subject.

---

[1] *Dig.* 50, 2, 1.
[2] ib. 50, 4, 1, 3 "Illud tenendum est generaliter personale quidem munus
esse, quod corporibus labore cum sollicitudine animi ac vigilantia sollemniter
extitit, patrimonii vero, in quo sumptus maxime postulatur." But the two ideas
were often inseparable.   Hence the recognition of *mixta munera* by Arcadius
(50, 4, 18).   For a complete enumeration of *munera* see Kuhn *Verfassung* i. pp.
35 ff.
[3] *Dig.* 50, 4, 1, 2 ; 50, 4, 18, 8, 16 and 26.   [4] ib. 50, 4, 1, 1.

§ 3. *The Worship of the Emperor*

One result of the discipline which we have described was doubtless to create a strong, though not a warm, imperial sentiment. A gentler bond of union amongst the provinces and of attachment to the imperial house was to be found in the carefully cultivated world-religion which expressed itself in the form of Caesar-worship.

The cult of the Emperor, although stimulated and encouraged by the imperial government, was by no means a purely artificial product. Had it offended against Roman or Italian sentiment, it would have been strangled in its birth ; and had it met with no genuine response from the subject nations, coercion[1] and rewards would probably have given it merely a precarious and transitory existence. The worship assumed two forms, neither of which was a strain on the religious beliefs of the age. In its application to the living Emperor, it was merely a reverence permitted to his spiritual personality, that *numen* or *genius*, the abstract duplicate of man, the ever-present guardian-angel to whom, as realised in the self, the Roman had often drunk or prayed. If to the mind of the barbarian the genius and the self were still more truly one, the conception of the new worship was simpler but by no means less strong. The reverence paid to the dead Caesar was a still more natural effort of grateful piety, not unwelcome to a cultured society which accepted Euhemeristic explanations of the gods, and indigenous at least amongst the Greek-speaking and oriental portions of the Empire. In the provinces, too, all the sordid aspects of imperial humanity were removed ; to the provincial mind Caesar was a potent and unseen power, a distant incarnation of wisdom and order, a being whose sway was far wider than that of any local god, whose ordinances penetrated to the ends of the earth, and in whose hands the safety and happiness of the human race were set.[2] The idealism which to-day makes of a king something more than a man, had,

[1] That coercion was sometimes employed is shown by Tacitus *Ann.* iv. 36 "objecta publice Cyzicenis incuria caerimoniarum divi Augusti, additis violentiae criminibus adversum cives Romanos. Et amisere libertatem."

[2] Cf. Plin. *Paneg.* 80 "velocissimi sideris more omnia invisere, omnia audire, et undecumque invocatum statim, velut numen, adesse et adsistere. Talia esse crediderim quae ipse mundi parens temperat nutu . . . tantum caelo vacat, postquam te dedit, qui erga omne hominum genus vice sua fungereris." Boissier

in a less fastidious religious environment, made of the Roman
Emperor a god, and even in the more prosaic West, in countries
such as Gaul or Spain or Britain, where Caesar-worship required
a certain amount of cultivation, we must suppose an under-
current of genuine belief.

The first step taken in the inauguration of the new worship
was a happy one. It was a graceful act to honour a predecessor,
who had been the ruler of the Roman world, and might be
regarded as a martyr in its cause, and Octavian permitted the
consecration of a temple to *divus Julius*,[1] who was regarded, from
a sentimental if not from a legal point of view, as the founder
of the new dynasty. His own worship the Emperor prohibited
in Italy, and he declined an altar in the *curia*.[2] But in the year
20 B.C. a temple dedicated to him under the name of Augustus
rose at Panium in Palestine,[3] and in the next year the form of
dedication to "Roma and Augustus," which associated his *numen*
with that of the city, and whose modesty secured his consent,[4]
began to spread through the provinces. A temple with this rite
sprang up at Pergamum,[5] and in 12 B.C. a similar worship, which
replaced that of the native sun-god Lug, was established for the
Gallic nobles at Lugdunum.[6] An attempt was also made to
consolidate the infant organisation of the new province of
Germany by establishing an altar at the Oppidum Ubiorum
(Köln) as the centre of its religious life.[7] Rome itself could not
wholly be deprived of a cult that was becoming universal, and in
8 B.C. a recognition of the divinity of Augustus was permitted in
the only form which he would allow during his life-time. His
genius was associated with the household gods or *Lares* in the
worship of the *vici* of the capital.[8] The movement spread
through Italy. The old *magistri vicorum* become the *magistri
Larum*, and soon gain the title *magistri Augustales*. They are

(*La Religion Romaine* i. pp. 206, 207) quotes a very similar passage from Bossuet,
which concludes "qu'il faut obéir aux princes comme à la justice même ; ils sont
des dieux et participent en quelque façon à l'indépendance divine."

[1] Dio Cass. li. 22.   [2] ib. liv. 25.
[3] Joseph. *Antiq.* xv. 10, 3.
[4] Suet. *Aug.* 52 "templa, quamvis sciret etiam proconsulibus decerni solere,
in nulla tamen provincia nisi communi suo Romaeque nomine recepit."
[5] Eckhel *Doctrina Numorum* ii. 466.
[6] Dio Cass. liv. 32 ; Rhys *Hibbert Lectures* pp. 409, 421, 424.
[7] Tac. *Ann.* i. 57.
[8] Egger *Examen critique des historiens du règne d'Auguste* App. ii. pp. 360-
375.

found in every part of Italy, and beyond it in Sardinia, Narbonensis, Spain, Dacia, and even Egypt.[1]   On the death of the
first Princeps his complete deification was accorded by the
Senate,[2] and the recognition was followed by the permission to
erect temples in the provinces,[3] while private as well as public
initiative fostered the cult of *divus Augustus*.   The precedent set
in the cases of the first two emperors had firmly established the
practice of posthumous deification, and its denial to a Princeps was
almost equivalent to the condemnation of his reign.[4]   Although
the merits of Claudius as a divinity might be questioned, and
Vespasian, with sceptical tolerance, regarded his own deification as an inevitable consequence of his position,[5] yet by the
close of the second century the virtues of the Antonines had
made the worship of the deified Emperor a more genuine cult
than ever, and a man was regarded as impious who had not some
image of Marcus Aurelius in his house.[6]   This worship of the
Caesars had two lasting effects on the social and political life of
the Roman, Italian, and provincial worlds.

(1) It established a priestly aristocracy.   On the death and
deification of Augustus a college of *Sodales Augustales* was created
for Rome, consisting of twenty-one nobles, and containing in its
list members of the imperial house.[7]   *Flamines Augustales* held
the same dignified position in their provinces or in their native
towns, and were drawn from the aristocracies of the states.   The
Flamen of the worship of Roma and Augustus, that had its centre
at Narbo, wore the *praetexta*, was attended by a lictor, had a
front seat at games, and the right of taking part in the deliberations of the local Senate.   His wife, the *Flaminica*, was clothed
on festal days in white or purple, and, like the *Flaminica Dialis*
at Rome, might not be compelled to take an oath.[8]   The lower
and middle classes were not forgotten in the distribution of these
religious honours.   From the *magistri Augustales*, whom we have

---

[1] Mourlot *Histoire de l'Augustalité dans l'Empire Romain* pp. 29-33.
[2] Tac. *Ann.* i. 73.
[3] Thus in 15 A.D. a temple was erected at Tarraco (Tac. *Ann.* i. 78).
[4] p. 363.
[5] Suet. *Vesp.* 23 "Prima quoque morbi accessione, 'Vae,' inquit, 'puto,
Deus fio.'"
[6] *Vita Marci* 18.   [7] Tac. *Ann.* i. 54.
[8] See the inscription of Narbonne in Rushforth *Latin Historical Inscriptions*
n. 35.   In this case the *Flaminica* was the wife of the *Flamen*, as at Rome ; but
this was usually not the case in the municipal towns.   See Marquardt *Staatsverw.*
i. p. 174.

already mentioned, developed an *ordo Augustalium*, which existed before the death of Augustus both in Italy and the provinces, and the cult with which it was associated was partly of spontaneous origin, partly cultivated by the imperial government, and may in some cases have been founded by the municipal towns themselves.   The *Augustales* were not priests, like the *Flamines* and *Sacerdotes*, but merely an order with certain *insignia* —the *praetexta*, the *fasces*, the *tribunal*—which they displayed in the performance of their official duties, and they have been compared to magistrates without secular magisterial functions.[1]   The form which the organisation assumed was the appointment of *sexviri* or *seviri*, probably by the senate of the municipal town ; after the year of service they pass into the order of *Augustales*.[2] The order was composed mainly of freedmen—of a class, that is, whose birth excluded them from the public offices of their states, but who, forming as they did a large portion of the trading population, contributed, perhaps more than any other, to the economic vitality of the towns.   The worship of Augustus, by giving them *insignia* and certain proud moments in which they appeared to dazzling effect before the public eye, compensated to some extent for the loss of privileges which the law withheld.

(2) Caesar-worship was the only force that gave a kind of representative life to the provinces.   Great provincial diets (*concilia, communia, κοινά*) made their appearance both in the Eastern and Western world.   Asia had already dedicated temples to kings, proconsuls, and to the city of Rome ;[3] and in the Hellenic world the national assemblies which survived the Roman conquest may have suggested, or may even at times have been continued in, these new amphictyonic gatherings.   The favour shown by the imperial government to this proof of loyalty soon led the West to follow the example of the East, and the establishment of the worship of Roma and Augustus at Lugdunum, by creating a *concilium* for the three Gauls, was the prototype of a similar organisation in other European provinces.

---

[1] Mommsen *Staatsr.* iii. p. 455.

[2] This was the usual type, but there were local variations, and the relation of *sevir* to *Augustalis* was not always the same.   In Cisalpine Gaul we have *seviri et Augustales*, where the ex-sevir retains his title.   In southern Italy *Augustalis* is used for *sevir*.   See Mourlot *op. cit.* pp. 69-72 ; Rushforth *op. cit.* p. 64.

[3] For a "templum et monumentum" in honour of the governor see Cic. *ad Q. fr.* 1, 1, 9, 26.   A temple to Roma was erected by Smyrna as early as 195 B.C. (Tac. *Ann.* iv. 56).

Eventually every province of the Empire seems to have evolved a diet of some kind, and even Britain, the least organised of Roman dependencies, possessed at Colchester a temple to the deified Claudius.[1] The high-priests of the cult (*sacerdotes provinciae*, ἀρχιερεῖς) were chosen annually from the most distinguished families, and delegates (*legati*, σύνεδροι) from the various districts or states, which made up the province, were despatched to the yearly meetings (*concilia*, κοινά). These delegates elected the high-priests and voted the sums required for the purposes of the cult. But they felt themselves to be representatives of the province; they voiced its nationality and represented its collective interests as no other power did, and it would have been impossible except by force to limit their utterances to purely religious questions. This compulsion the government did not attempt. It permitted, perhaps encouraged, these delegates to make representations about the condition of the province,[2] and even to utter complaints about the conduct of Roman officials.[3] It is a pity that the imperial government did not do even more to preserve the fast-waning sense of nationality; but the value of what it did is proved by the fact that these assemblies and the dignified orders which they created survived into the Christian Empire. Titles such as Asiarch, Syriarch, Phoenicarch, derived from the high-priesthood of Caesar's cult, were respected by Constantine's legislation,[4] and survived like ghosts of the pagan past to haunt for a time the life of a new œcumenical church which, through a fuller faith and a higher allegiance, had effected its triumph over the old.

[1] Tac. *Ann.* xiv. 31 "templum divo Claudio constitutum quasi arx aeternae dominationis aspiciebatur."

[2] Imperial rescripts to *concilia* or κοινά are frequent. See *Dig.* 47, 14, 1 ; 49, 1, 1 ; 48, 6, 5, 1. Cf. 1, 16, 4, 5.

[3] Plin. *Ep.* iii. 4, 2. Where, as in this passage, the *legati* of a province are represented as making a complaint, they doubtless represent the *concilium*. In A.D. 62 a *senatus consultum* was passed "ne quis ad concilium sociorum referret agendas apud senatum pro praetoribus prove consulibus grates" (Tac. *Ann.* xv. 22).

[4] *Cod.* 5, 27, 1 (A.D. 336).

APPENDIX I

THE existence of a *comitia tributa populi*, as distinct from the *concilium plebis tributim*, was first demonstrated by Mommsen (*Römische Forschungen, Die patricisch-plebejischen Tributcomitien der Republik*). The chief lines of evidence on which the proof of the existence of this parliament rests are as follows :—

(i.) We have a series of passages which prove the continued distinction of the Populus and the Plebs and of patrician and plebeian magistrates, and which show that these magistrates could only summon the bodies of which they were respectively the representatives. These passages are :—

Festus p. 293 " Scita plebei appellantur ea, quae plebs suo suffragio sine patribus jussit, plebeio magistratu rogante."

ib. p. 330 " Scitum populi (est, quod eum magistra)tus patricius (rogavit populusque suis suf)fragis jussit. . . . Plebes autem est (populus universus) praeter patricios."

ib. p. 233 " cum plebes sine patri(bus a suo magistratu rogatur) quod plebes scivit, plebi(scitum est : plebs enim cum) appellatur, patrum com(munio excluditur)."

(ii.) There are abundant evidences of the early existence of a *comitia* of the tribes :—

(*a*) The law of the Twelve Tables (451 B.C.) ordained, with respect to jurisdiction, " de capite civis nisi per maximum comitiatum . . . ne ferunto " (Cic. *de Leg*. iii. 4, 11). The mention of the " greatest *comitia* " clearly implies the existence of a lesser one with judicial powers ; and as this is not likely to have been the *comitia curiata* of the period, it can hardly be any other assembly than the *comitia* of the tribes.

(*b*) The quaestors were first elected by the people in 447 B.C. (Tac. *Ann*. xi. 22), and in later times their appointment was made by a *comitia* of the tribes (Cic. *ad Fam*. vii. 30).

(*c*) The first legislative act of the people gathered *tributim* is attributed to the year 357 B.C. (Liv. vii. 16 (consul) "legem novo exemplo ad Sutrium in castris tributim de vicensima eorum, qui manu mitterentur, tulit ").

The *comitia tributa populi* was probably created between 471 B.C., the date at which the Plebs began to meet *tributim*, and 451, the date at which the existence of such an assembly is hinted at in the Twelve Tables.

(iii.) In the developed Republic we find an assembly meeting by tribes—

(*a*) which is presided over by magistrates of the people, e.g. by the consuls Manlius (Liv. vii. 16) and T. Quinctius Crispinus (Frontinus *de Aquaed.* 129), by the dictator Caesar (Cic. *ad Fam.* vii. 30), and by P. Clodius as curule aedile (Cic. *pro Sest.* 44, 95 ; *ad Q. fr.* 2, 3) ;

(*b*) which elects magistrates of the people, e.g. the quaestors (Cic. *ad Fam.* vii. 30 "comitiis quaestoriis institutis . . . ille (Caesar) . . . qui comitiis tributis esset auspicatus") and the curule aediles (Gell. vii. 9 "[Cn. Flavium] pro tribu aedilem curulem renuntiaverunt") ;

(*c*) which legislates. This legislative power is shown by the *lex Quinctia de aquaeductibus* of 9 B.C. (Frontinus *de Aquaed.* 129) ;

(*d*) and exercises judicial power. This judicial power is shown in the trial of Milo for *vis* in 56 B.C. (Cic. *pro Sest.* 44, 95 ; *ad Q. fr.* 2, 3). The prosecutor was a curule aedile, and the trial took place in the Forum (" ejectus de rostris Clodius," l.c. § 2).

Perhaps the most striking demonstration of the existence of this assembly is contained in the prescription to the *lex Quinctia de aquae-ductibus* (Frontinus l.c.), which runs as follows :—

" T. Quinctius Crispinus consul populum jure rogavit populusque jure scivit in foro pro rostris aedis divi Julii pr(idie) [k.] Julias. Tribus Sergia principium fuit, pro tribu Sex. . . . L. f. Virro [primus scivit]."

Here we find an assembly of the Populus, presided over by a magistrate of the people, meeting in the Forum and voting by tribes. It can, therefore, be none other than a *comitia tributa populi.*

Although the formal difference between this assembly and the *concilium plebis tributim* was great—the one being summoned by magistrates of the people, the other by plebeian magistrates ; the one electing to popular, the other to plebeian offices ; the one passing *leges*, the other *plebiscita*—the material difference between the two bodies was small. This consisted in the exclusion of Patricians from plebeian gatherings. When the consul or praetor summoned the tribes, the members of the few patrician families could attend ; when the tribune summoned the tribes, these members were bound to keep away.

APPENDIX II

A LIMITATION OF THE TRIBUNATE IN THE REIGN OF NERO

TACITUS in the *Annals* (xiii. 28, 2), in describing certain limitations on the powers of tribunes and aediles which were introduced in the year 56 A.D., mentions one respecting the tribunate, the nature of which has never yet been explained. He expresses it in the words "prohibiti tribuni jus praetorum et consulum praeripere, aut vocare ex Italia cum quibus lege agi posset"—"the tribunes were forbidden to usurp the authority of praetors and consuls, or to summon out of Italy persons liable to legal proceedings." It seems generally to be agreed that the *aut* here is conjunctive, not disjunctive, i.e. that there is the closest connexion between "jus praetorum et consulum praeripere" and "vocare ex Italia," and it seems that this must be the case; for Tacitus, vague as his references are in this chapter, could never have referred to anything so indeterminate as a "usurpation of the authority of praetors and consuls," without some specification of the sphere or extent of this usurpation. I shall, therefore, assume that the second clause is explanatory of the first, and that the "summons from Italy" in some way defines the "usurpation"—although, as will be seen, this assumption is by no means necessary to my main argument, which will centre round the expression "vocare ex Italia."

The remarks of commentators on this passage have been for the most part confined to expressions of bewilderment at the constitutional anomalies it displays. They make the inevitable comment that the tribune had properly no right of *vocatio*, although he sometimes exercised it (Varro ap. Gell. xiii. 12), and that, if even he possessed this right, it ought not to have been exercised outside the city walls. The only positive fact to be elicited from such statements is that the *vocatio* here referred to is some kind of personal summons; who is summoned or for what purpose are questions which they seem to regard as incapable of an answer. The opinion of an eminent writer on Roman Law, who attempts to push his analysis deeper than this, exhibits only the desperate nature of the means which have to be applied to elicit a meaning from the passage. Karlowa (*Röm. Rechts-gesch.* i. p. 530) suggests that the tribunes had allowed accused persons to escape summonses in criminal trials which were to take place before the Senate—the initiation of such trials belonging properly only to the consuls and praetors. He does not seem to feel the obstacles that beset the path to this conclusion. He has to take *lege agere* in the unusual sense of the legal fulfilment of a penal law; he does not show why Tacitus should have written "vocare ex Italia" in place of the more natural "vocare a senatu"; he fails to remember that the tribunician intercession in a criminal trial before the Senate was, even in the reign of Tiberius, becoming a power of pardon vested in the Princeps, and that its use by an ordinary tribune might bring death to the rash interceder (Tac. *Ann.* vi. 47; cf. xvi. 26).

To discover the true sense of the passage we must seek for some sphere in which the tribunician veto continued unimpaired during the Principate; but, before doing this, we must ask whether the words used by Tacitus offer any suggestions of such a sphere. It is possible to translate the words "vocare ex Italia" as meaning "to summon from any part of Italy," "to summon, i.e., from Rome and Italy"; but I venture to think that *ex Italia* excludes the idea of Rome, and that the meaning of the words is "to summon from a municipal town of Italy to Rome." On what grounds such a summons might be made is shown by the words "cum quibus lege agi posset." The sphere of the summons is civil jurisdiction in the *municipia* as divided between the Roman and the local authorities by statute on the settlement which gradually followed the close of the social war— a settlement known to us chiefly through the *lex Rubria*. The whole sentence, if literally though somewhat clumsily translated, would state that "the tribunes were prohibited from summoning litigants from an Italian town in cases where a civil action at law would have been possible in that town."

On this hypothesis, the sphere of the tribune's power referred to is the very familiar one of the veto on appeal in civil jurisdiction. How frequent the *appellatio* to the tribunes in matters of civil juris-diction was during the later Republic is shown by the fact that, out of the four private orations of Cicero, two—those for Quinctius and for Tullius—record the use of this appeal (Cic. *pro Quinct.* 7, 29; *pro Tullio* 16, 38, 39); and that this appellate cognisance continued during the Principate is shown by the obvious interpretation of the well-known lines of Juvenal (vii. 228)—

Rara tamen merces quae cognitione tribuni
Non egeat—

words which almost certainly mean "it is seldom that such *merces* does not lead to a court of appeal."

It may seem strange that the veto of these purely city magistrates should be thought of in connexion with municipal jurisdiction, until we remember the anomalous nature of the settlement made after the social war. By that settlement jurisdiction in Italy is a mere annexe to jurisdiction in Rome ; technically it *is* jurisdiction in Rome, as is shown by Gaius (iv. 103-105), who recognises no interval between the jurisdiction of law *intra primum miliarium* and the jurisdiction of the *imperium* in the provinces. The praetor's formula and the praetor's writ run through the whole of Italy, although the praetor himself cannot quit Rome for more than ten days during his year of office (Cic. *Phil.* ii. 13, 31) ; and, if the appellate power of the tribune was to be preserved, it had to be regarded as coextensive with the *imperium* of the magistrate whom he vetoed. The intercession of the tribune in municipal jurisdiction required no creation by law ; it was still the veto of one city magistrate by another within the walls of Rome. If even the tribune's ordinances and his *coercitio* were valid without the walls, it could be explained in accordance with the pre-vailing fiction ; but the supposition of such an extension is not absolutely necessary, as the following pictures of what probably took place in a conflict between the central and the local courts will show.

Suppose Aulus Agerius brings an action against Numerius Negidius in the town of Arpinum. The local magistrate decides to take the case. Numerius Negidius denies the competence of the court and appeals ; to whom ? In the first instance, probably to the colleague of the local magistrate, for the *lex Rubria* (c. xx.) forbids the inter-cession only in the case where the local court is admittedly competent. This colleague pronounces the veto, the *judicium* is quashed ; all that the local magistrate can now do is to compel the parties to enter into a *vadimonium* to appear before the praetor, and the case moves to Rome. But supposing, when it has got there, that the praetor decides that it was really within the competence of the municipal magistrate and issues an order that it shall go back ? Now Numerius appeals to the tribune. The veto is issued and, if the case is to be tried at all, the praetor is bound to take it.

We can also imagine a case with the same preliminaries in which Numerius appeals to the colleague of the local magistrate against the competence of the local court, but in which this colleague declines to interfere. Is Numerius left stranded ? Unquestionably there must have been in such a case a further appeal to Rome, whether to the praetor or perhaps, in this case, to his higher colleague the consul. But the praetor or consul now decides against Numerius. The appeal is made to the tribune, and the decree of the consul or praetor may be quashed. The case, if it is to be tried at all, must be tried at Rome.

2 G

In both these instances the tribune pronounces his veto within the city, and yet in both, if his decision is improper, his position is one of " vocare ex Italia cum quibus lege agi posset." In both cases it is not a true use of magisterial *vocatio*, and thus one of the difficulties discovered by commentators in this passage is removed ; it is simply an illustration of the positive effects of a negative power. Just as the tribune can by a persistent veto force the praetor to alter his formula (Cic. *Acad. Prior.* ii. 30, 97 ; *pro Tullio* 16, 38), so by a persistent denial of the praetor's orders to the local magistrate he can force the praetor to judge. We do not know the method by which the positive effect of the veto was in this case secured, but it is clear that some means must have been provided for having a municipal action tried at Rome when the municipal court had been declared incompetent.

But, apart from the procedure springing from these rigid rules of competence, there is some evidence of a discretionary power of what is called *Romam revocatio*, which was exercised and abused by magistrates towards the close of the Republic. The *Fragmentum Atestinum* (perhaps a part of the *lex Rubria*) enacts (l. 16 sq.) with reference to municipal jurisdiction—" ejus rei pequn[*iaeve*] quo magis privato Romae revocatio sit . . . *ex hac lege nihilum rogatur,*" i.e. this law does not permit (or imply) a *revocatio* to Rome in the specified cases. We do not know what magistrate effected this *revocatio*. With respect to criminal jurisdiction in the provinces, it was the duty of the consuls (Cic. *in Verr.* i. 33, 84) ; and, if they exercised this power in civil jurisdiction as well, the *jus consulum praeripere* of our passage may refer to tribunician interference with this consular prerogative. It may be worth noting that Plutarch (*Caes.* 4) associates the power with the tribunes ; his narrative of this trial of P. Antonius is almost unquestionably wrong, but it may be taken to show that in his belief (i.e. in a belief current during the Principate) the tribunes had something to do with summoning cases to Rome.

Hitherto we have been dealing with the praetor and the *judicia ordinaria*. Is it possible that the tribune also interfered with the extraordinary jurisdiction created during the Principate, and thus with the judicial powers of the consuls ? The consular jurisdiction in *fideicommissa* had been given to praetors by Claudius (*Dig.* 1, 2, 2, 32), but not the whole of it. Quintilian shows that in greater matters it still belonged to the former (*Inst. Or.* iii. 6, 70 " non debes apud praetorem petere fideicommissum sed apud consules, major enim praetoria cognitione summa est "). If the consuls tried the case when the *fideicommissum* was very large and the praetors when it was smaller, it is not altogether impossible that the municipal magistrates might have tried local cases when the sum, which was the subject of the trust, was insignificant. It is thus possible that questions of the competence of local and Roman magistrates may have cropped up in reference to this question; although I should prefer to explain the *jus consulum praeripere* of Tacitus on the already mentioned hypotheses of some consular right of *vocatio* or *revocatio* in matters of ordinary jurisdiction.

Much must remain obscure; we cannot get at the details of the procedure. All that we can do is to show that there is evidence for the tribune's interference with the rights of magistrates in matters of municipal jurisdiction, and to suggest methods of interference. Nor can we determine the precise limitations of his authority introduced by the change of A.D. 56. But it clearly took from the tribune the final decision as to when a civil case should be summoned from a municipal town to Rome. Either his *intercessio* in this matter of municipal jurisdiction was abolished, or his veto was made purely suspensory. In this very chapter of Tacitus we find that the enforcement of the tribunician *multa* is subjected to the decision of the consul. Similarly, with reference to the power which we have discussed, the urban praetor or the consul may have been declared absolutely competent to decide, after cognisance, when a case should be tried in the local courts and when it should be reserved for the tribunals at Rome.

INDEX OF SUBJECTS[1]

(The references are to the pages)

---

[1] References to subjects will also be found in the Index of Latin words.

Procurators, 414
Prohibition, magisterial right of, 119, 173-176
Property, tenure of, 5, 8, 35 ; Servian classification, 69 foll. ; registration by censor, 221-223 ; tenure by foreigners, 295
Provinces, 317 foll., 426 foll. ; jurisdiction, 155, 325 ; revenues, 231, 286, 417, 429 foll. ; formation, 284, 285 ; arrangements of Sulla, 201, 251, 322 ; of Gracchus, 180, 201, 322 ; of Pompeius, 323 ; of the Principate, 345, 401, 428
Public works, 209, 232, 413
Publilian law, 124, 125, 126, 216

Quaestors, delegates of king, 63 ; of consul for jurisdiction, 80, 161, 246 ; for finance, 81, 155, 178, 394, 432 ; in the field, 117, 141 ; functions, 212, 216 ; no vocatio or prensio, 181 ; appointment, 81, 102 ; qualifications, 184, 364, 373 ; under Principate, 369

Ramnes, 3, 40, 67, 73
Religious ideas, 36, 46, 51, 162, 440 ; their connexion with the clans, 16 ; international influence of, 56, 289, 291
Religious sanctions, 54, 99, 109
Representation, 312, 443
Rescission of sentences, 248
Responsibility of magistrates, 181, 217
Revenues, 229
Revolution, 332
Rights, 31, 33, 136, 138 foll., 240, 241 ; see Caput and Citizenship
Romanisation of provinces, 436
Rotation in tenure of power, 198, 199

Scourging, 168
Senate, 147, 151, 261, 262 ; relation to king, 58 foll. ; to consuls and other magistrates, 81 foll., 264, 267; to Princeps, 348, 359, 362, 376 ; powers, 59 foll., 83, 273, 276, 282 foll., 395, 397 ; control of legislation and elections, 125, 254, 273 foll., 377 ; procedure, 268 foll., 348 ; insignia, 265 ; revision, 219,

263, 347, 374 ; reform attempted by Sulla, 266, 335, 373 ; under the Principate, 373 ; conscripti, 82 ; senatorial order at Rome, 399, 411 ; in municipalities, 438.
Servian organisation, 65 foll., 138, 145
Servius Tullius, 58, 62, 138
Slavery, 24 foll., 105, 141 foll. ; see Manumission
Solon, 69, 127
Sulla, 146, 180, 183, 189, 197, 202, 204, 207, 213, 221, 234, 253, 254, 266

Taxation, Roman theory of, 319 ; direct, 320, 431 ; tithes, 321, 431 ; see Tribute
Testaments, 26 foll., 106, 135, 136, 144, 251, 295
Tities, 3, 40, 67 (priores, posteriores, 73)
Treaties, 56, 60, 139, 244, 283, 291, 345, 372, 376 ; commercial, 293
Tribes, original, 3, 40, 41, 66, 67 ; Servian, 66 foll. ; Republican, 101, 223, 252
Tribunate, consular, 112-114 ; military, 364, 373 ; of the Plebs, 93 foll., 108, 365 ; inviolability, 99, 345 ; power of prohibition, 119, 176 ; intercession, 178 foll., 346, 370 ; jurisdiction, 168, 169, 371 ; relation to the Senate, 161, 179, 371, 375 ; to the Plebs, 96, 124, 126, 346
Tribunician power possessed by Princeps, 338, 370
Tribute, from citizens, 41, 75, 137, 138, 222, 303 ; from subject states, 319 foll., 430
Triumph, 156-158
Triumvirate (43 B.C.), 338
Twelve Tables, 7, 16, 19, 26, 29, 87, 91, 92, 102, 104 foll., 111, 126, 161, 205, 241, 281

Valerio-Horatian laws, 108 foll., 124, 126, 236
Varian commission, 175, 248
Vestals, 52, 53
Voting: procedure, 258, 259 ; basis of division, 253 ; deprivation of right of, 241 ; freedmen's vote, 146 ; rights of new citizens, 312

INDEX OF LATIN WORDS

(The references are to the pages)

2 H

INDEX OF AUTHORS CITED

I. LATIN AUTHORS

II. GREEK AUTHORS

III. INSCRIPTIONS

THE END

Printed by R. & R. CLARK, LIMITED, *Edinburgh*

www.ingramcontent.com/pod-product-compliance
Lightning Source LLC
Chambersburg PA
CBHW020408100426
42812CB00001B/249